THE STUDY OF
THE BIBLE
IN THE
MIDDLE AGES

THE STUDY OF
THE BIBLE
IN THE
MIDDLE AGES

by

BERYL SMALLEY

Fellow of St. Hilda's College, Oxford

UNIVERSITY OF NOTRE DAME PRESS

To
A. M. L.

TABLE OF CONTENTS

220.7
Sm 63
c.2

59569

v

LIST OF PLATES

I. A copy of the *Gloss* on St. John's Gospel written in England in the later twelfth century, now MS. Bodl. Lyell I (f⁰ 4ʳ). Sixteen glosses are ascribed in contemporary hands in pencil and ink to 'Anselmus' (Anselm of Laon). The gloss ascribed to Anselm which is shown in the plate is taken from John the Scot's commentary on St. John (P.L. XXII, 286). Anselm made use of John the Scot for his own compilations. *facing p.* 56

II. MS. Lambeth 435 (f⁰ 21ʳ): a Hebrew Psalter with a gloss in Latin and Anglo-Norman. The gloss was written by an anonymous English scholar, about the middle of the thirteenth century. The plate shows, near the top of the left hand margin, his transcription of the Tetragrammaton as IAHAVE. *facing p.* 347

ABBREVIATIONS

PREFACE TO FIRST EDITION

A BOOK so ambitious in scope as this one could only be produced as a result of collaboration: I am very grateful to all who have helped. My especial debts are to Prof. F. M. Powicke, to the late Mgr. George Lacombe, to Dom André Wilmart and the Benedictines of Mont César, to Fr. Daniel Callus and Fr. Thomas Gilby, O.P., to Dr. Eleanor Rathbone, and to Dr. R. W. Hunt who contributed criticism and information to each section as it was written. The late Dr. H. Kantorowicz kindly wrote a note on legal and medical glosses, for purposes of comparison, which has been included in Chapter II. ii. For the Jewish sources of the Victorines I depended on the collaboration of the Rabbi Dr. L. Rabinowitz, for the Hebrew material in Chapter VI. iii on that of the late Mr. H. Loewe, who first realized the importance of the Lambeth Psalter and arranged for our work on it. Dr. N. Rubinstein has made the indexes.

The Jex-Blake research fellowship at Girton College enabled me to undertake the writing of the book, and the kindness of the Fellows in extending their hospitality for two years enabled me to finish. The Council of Trinity College, Cambridge, generously made me a year's grant from the Birkbeck lecture fund to work on the Hebrew-Latin Psalter in the College Library with Mr. Loewe. A grant from the Hort fund covered the expenses of photography.

The book is dedicated to Mrs. K. Leys of St. Hilda's College, who introduced me to historical research.

I have to thank Mr. J. P. R. Lyell for allowing me to photograph a manuscript of the *Gloss* on St. John in his collection for Plate I. This manuscript is important as it considerably strengthens the case for ascribing the compilation of the *Gloss* on St. John to Anselm of Laon. Unfortunately I did not see it in time to mention it in the text. Plate II is reproduced from my pamphlet on Hebrew-Latin Psalters, with acknowledgments to the publishers, Messrs. Shapiro, Vallentine & Co.

The war has prevented me from checking my references to many manuscripts. Two of my transcripts from MS. Pembroke College, Cambridge 45, are lost, and the volume is now inaccessible; so no Latin text can be given for the translations on pp. 110-11, 119-20. Since my translations are intentionally free I give the Latin text in full, either in a footnote or in the appendix, wherever I am quoting from an unpublished source. Much of the ground has been covered already in a series of very technical articles which I have written during the last ten years. I have not duplicated references or reproduced the Latin of passages quoted from manuscripts in my articles, in order to economize space. I have omitted to give a bibliography for the same reason. A full bibliography for so wide a subject would be a book in itself. A selective list of important and relevant works will be found in the footnotes. Similarly the indexes are intended as a working guide and do not aim at completeness.

B. S.

ST. HILDA'S COLLEGE,
OXFORD, 1940

PREFACE TO SECOND EDITION

THE aim of the present edition is to incorporate recent studies, including my own. I have filled out the introductory chapter on the Fathers in the light of the many new discoveries and appreciations which have appeared since 1940 and I have recast and expanded the chapter on the Friars. Chapters II to V and the appendix have been brought up to date, with the addition of a section to IV. A further ten years or so of work on a subject will naturally cause one to revise one's 'Conclusions': I have rewritten mine entirely. My College kindly allowed me to take a sabbatical term in order to prepare the new edition for press; but the material had to be collected during vacations.

The danger in revising a book is that the footnotes rise like a tide and threaten to swamp the text. I have tried to keep them within manageable limits, even at the cost of incompleteness. Only the most recent book or paper on a given subject has been quoted, provided that it has an adequate bibliography. The lifting of war-time restrictions makes it possible to have adequate indexes.

Since I wrote the first preface my debts of gratitude have increased. The medievalists who inhabit Bodley have a pooling system, centred in the Keeper's study. I am guiltily conscious of drawing more from the common stock than I ever put into it. The present Keeper, Dr. R. W. Hunt, and Dr. D. A. Callus of Blackfriars have shown me unwearied kindness. This book and the papers on which it is based could hardly have been written without their suggestions and criticisms. Mr. N. R. Ker has generously handed over to me discoveries that he has made in his researches into medieval libraries. Mr. A. Campbell and Dr. O. Pacht have helped me on technical points. It has been a pleasure to collaborate with Mr. Raphael Loewe, M.C., the son of the late Herbert Loewe, who contributed so much to my work in Cambridge. Mr. Raphael Loewe has helped me with the technicalities of Herbert of Bosham on the *Hebraica* in the St. Paul's manuscript discovered by Mr. Ker. He allows me to quote the conclusions of a paper which is to be published in *Biblica*, 1953, and I constantly apply to him to unravel references to the Hebrew text and rabbinics. Among the librarians who have helped me, too many to name individually, Mlle M.-Th. d'Alverny of the Bibliothèque nationale in particular has been my prop and stay. Fr. J. Perrier of Le Saulchoir has been kind enough to lend me his descriptive catalogue and notes on the biblical commentaries in the Bibliothèque nationale manuscript collections. I was deeply honoured as well as grateful for the encouragement and the detailed and constructive criticisms that His Eminence, Cardinal Mercati, the librarian of the Vatican, sent me after reading my first edition; I have used all his comments and emendations.

Perhaps my greatest debt of all is to those at home and in college who have stood between me and the cooking and cleaning that eats up the leisure of most women today.

B. S.

ST. HILDA'S COLLEGE, OXFORD
        JUNE 10, 1951

INTRODUCTION

THE Bible was the most studied book of the middle ages. Bible study represented the highest branch of learning. The Venerable Bede was better known for his commentaries on Scripture than for his *Ecclesiastical History of the English People*. When St. Boniface, apostle of Germany, 'famous keeper of the celestial library', called Bede the 'candle of the Church', he must have seen

> . . . bright candles
> over the holy white scriptures.[1]

Bede himself put his commentaries on Scripture first in the list of his works; and he was typical. Many of the men of letters whom we remember for other reasons, as Stephen Langton for *Magna Carta*, were also famous as biblical scholars. We must add the host of obscurer persons, the monks, canons, friars, and secular masters who expounded Scripture in the cloister or the school. Their biblical commentaries and aids to study account for a good proportion of the monastic or cathedral library.

Such knowledge was not confined to the specialist: both the language and the content of Scripture permeate medieval thought. To make an accurate translation of a literary text in medieval Latin the student needs a concordance to the Vulgate, and even that may prove insufficient; his author may be alluding to a patristic or scholastic comment on the verse he is quoting, as clear to the author and his readers as it is unintelligible to the translator. What promised to be simple translation involves researches into the medieval Vulgate, its text and its gloss. Epic and chronicle have biblical reminiscences.[2] The Frisians, comparing themselves to the chosen people, inverted the order of events in their history, so as to get a closer correspondence with the Old Testament.[3] This group of Frisian chronicles supplies an extreme example of the tendency to pour one's material into a traditional

---

[1] From a ninth-century Irish hermit poem, transl. K. Jackson, *Studies in Early Celtic Nature Poetry* (Cambridge, 1935), 5.
[2] J. Crosland, *The Old French Epic* (Oxford, 1951), 74.
[3] H. Reimers, 'Die lateinische Vorlage der "Gesta Frisiorum",' *De Vrije Fries*, xxxiv (1939), 96-151; J. Hoekstra, *Vier Friese Kronieken* (Zaltbommel, 1948).

mould. In the middle ages tradition began with the story of Creation as it is told in the book of Genesis.

Curiously enough, however, the historians of medieval culture have neglected a vital factor in the object of their studies. Historians have been reproached as a class for preferring quantity to quality in their choice of material.[1] In this case the reproach is unfounded, since not even the vast quantity of works on the Bible has succeeded in catching their attention. The bulk of medieval commentaries remains in manuscript. Of the tiny proportion which has been printed the editions, with very rare exceptions, are old and uncritical. Many have been ascribed to the wrong authors. Specialist articles and reference books have been accumulating in recent years; the student who goes patiently through all the relevant publications may find that some of his problems have been solved by modern scholarship. It is just as likely that he will have to resign himself to checking date, authorship and text without help from anyone.

Instead of working on single commentaries or groups of commentaries, the student may want to use a textbook, outlining the development and offering some judgment on the value of medieval Bible studies. Then he will find himself in an even worse quandary. Until a few years ago the standard books on the subject were the *Histoires critiques* of Richard Simon, published in 1678 and 1693. Scholars of the Enlightenment and their successors in the nineteenth century naturally allowed their prejudices to colour their estimate. They were just casting off the shackles in which medieval exegetes had laboured and their chief concern was to point out the contrast with themselves. Thus Farrar allotted a chapter to medieval exegesis in his *History of Interpretation* preached at Oxford as the Bampton lectures in 1888. He reminds us of his own classic, the school story, *Eric or Little by Little*, where the elder boy turns on his naughty junior 'a noble look of sorrow and scorn':

'We approach the subject of medieval exegesis with every desire to judge it in the kindliest spirit; but we are compelled to say that during the Dark Ages, from the seventh to the twelfth century, and during the scholastic epoch, from the twelfth to the sixteenth, there are but a few of the many who toiled in this field who added a single essential principle or furnished a single original contribution to the explanation of

[1] A. J. Toynbee, *A Study of History*, i (London, 1934), 6.

the Word of God. During these nine centuries we find very little except the "glimmerings and decays" of patristic exposition. . . . Not one writer in hundreds showed any true conception of what exegesis really implies. . . . They . . . give us folio volumes of dogma, morality, and system, which profess to be based on Scripture, but have for the most part no real connection with the passages to which they are attached.'[1]

'Mere glimmerings and decays' in 1888 expressed the general opinion of medieval culture as a whole. The middle ages were still 'barbarous'. In the same year Paulin Martin began to publish his papers on Roger Bacon and the Latin Vulgate and the Paris text of the Vulgate, where he compared Bacon to Richard Simon and pointed out the importance of Stephen Langton as an exegete. From his austere point of view of textual criticism, he was astonished to find such science as Bacon's 'dans un temps qu'on traite communément de barbare. De singuliers barbares en effet que ces grands hommes du treizième siècle!'

Denifle and Berger in the 'eighties and 'nineties followed up the researches of Martin. In the twentieth century two great Benedictine scholars, Morin and Wilmart, treated many problems of medieval exegesis as part of their work on patristic and medieval literature. Although far less attention has been concentrated on this than on other branches of medieval studies, still, enough has been done by these men and others to show that the middle ages was a period of creation. Very few persons nowadays would dismiss the twelfth and thirteenth centuries as a time of 'decadence' in economic activity, in the techniques of government or in science and art. Yet the word continues to be used in histories of exegesis,[2] for lack of any attempt on the part of specialists to popularize the results of nineteenth and twentieth-century scholarship. The lack has been especially regrettable in that medieval exegesis has a double interest for historians. On the one hand, the expert would like to know what his predecessors accomplished in the way of pure scholarship; on the other hand, the history of interpretation can be used as a mirror for social and cultural changes. A book as central to medieval thought as the Bible was, must necessarily have been read and interpreted rather differently by different genera-

[1] 245-6.
[2] See for instance, J. Coppens, L'histoire critique de l'Ancien Testament (Tournai, Paris, 1938), 6.

tions. There may be underlying continuity; there are bound to be changes in emphasis.

The gap was so obvious that two writers set out to fill it almost simultaneously. My own first edition appeared in 1941. Fr. Spicq published his *Esquisse d'une histoire de l'exégèse latine au Moyen Âge* in 1944. Neither of us could even know of the existence of the other's book until the war was over and normal communications re-established. Actually it seems that we supplement each other. Fr. Spicq is a professional theologian and an amateur historian, while I am a professional historian and no theologian at all. Moreover, his scope is both wider and narrower than mine. Fr. Spicq has carried his survey into the fourteenth century; mine stops about 1300. He has restricted himself to printed matter; I have explored manuscript material, though only a fraction of the total. The reader who is interested in our subject ought to read us both, since he will find two separate kinds of information and even more, two separate points of view.

Not everyone will have the courage to tackle two heavy volumes, and seeing that readers now have a choice, it is more than ever necessary to warn them what they may expect from me. The treatment of so huge a subject has to be highly selective.[1]

Teachers in the middle ages regarded the Bible as a school book *par excellence*. The little clerk learned his letters from the Psalter[2] and the Bible would be used in teaching him the liberal arts.[3] Hence Bible study is linked with the history of institutions from the very beginning. My method has been to trace its development in the framework of two characteristic institutions which the middle ages produced, the religious Orders and the schools, the latter concentrating themselves into universities in the course of the twelfth century. One must take into account both the spiritual moods of the cloister and the course of study prescribed by the academic syllabus.

---

[1] In revising my first edition I have profited from reviewers' criticism. M. W. L. Laistner, *Speculum*, xvii (1942), 146-8, and A. Souter, *Journal of Theological Studies*, xliii (1942), 99-102, have been particularly helpful. I am afraid, however, that if I were to use all the information which all my reviewers have so generously supplied, the book would become far too long for publication.

[2] F. Falk, *Bibelhandschriften und Bibeldrucke in Mainz von achten Jahrhundert bis zur Gegenwart* (Mainz, 1901), 28-9, gives examples of the use of the Psalter in primary education.

[2] A. Allgeier, 'Exegetische Beiträge zur Geschichte des Griechischen', *Biblica*, xxiv (1943), 265.

The Bible was the book of professed religious; *lectio divina* was a traditional part of the monastic routine. When a religious Order distrusted learning its reading was 'holy' without being 'serious' in a scientific sense; on the other hand, an Order friendly to learning produced biblical scholars: the ninth-century Benedictines, the Victorines, the friars. Therefore the history of biblical scholarship depended on that of religious organization and reform.

The Bible was prescribed as a 'set book' for theologians in the medieval schools. The student who wanted to become a master of theology had to attend lectures on the sacred page. This involves us in the history of teaching methods. We must follow the centralization of studies at Paris, the development of class-room equipment, the *Gloss* or standard commentary and its uses, also the development of academic functions supplementary to the lecture, the university sermon and the disputation. These exercises determined the form and so to some extent the content of medieval exegesis.

Sacra pagina marked the final stage of study; the scholar came to it fresh from the liberal arts. Developments in grammar, rhetoric, and dialectic always influenced Bible studies. They determined the technique of the teacher, his intellectual interests and his cast of mind. Still more did the prevalent philosophy affect him. The contrast between St. Augustine and the newly recovered Aristotle, which aroused his strongest passions, upset or modified his most cherished notions about the universe and its Creator, was bound to have a disturbing effect on his study of the Creator's special book. Aristotle caused him to see Scripture as freshly as he saw all creation.

But his study was not an end in itself or, as he considered, it would have degenerated into 'curiosity'. Science must lead the scholar to wisdom; nor is his academic circle shut off from the outside world. Hence *sacra pagina* included instruction in the student's private religious duties and prepared him for pastoral charge. Ecclesiastical as well as religious reform movements had their influence on *lectio divina*.

In so far as it was affected by external circumstances, Bible study might develop spasmodically and unexpectedly. It had also its own internal law of development. Its history, like that of most human activities, was a history of specialization. In the early part of our period sacred doctrine resembled secular government in being undifferentiated and unspecialized. Like the Norman and Angevin monarchs the 'queen of the sciences' held her 'royal court of all works', her officials being the monks and masters who expounded the sacred page. To study exegesis apart from other branches of theology is like studying, say, the judicial aspect of the Curia Regis as distinct from the fiscal and administrative. Gradually in the twelfth and thirteenth centuries exegesis as a separate subject emerges. It had its own technical aids to study, and its auxiliary sciences of textual criticism and biblical languages. Even though the personnel of its teachers was still undifferentiated, a scholar distinguished between his work as a theologian and his work as an exegete.

Changes in form and intellectual fashion take place against a background which has one unchanging element. A desire to study the text of the Old Testament would always lead scholars to compare the Latin with the Hebrew. The study of Hebrew would always lead to contact with Jews. The Christians lacked an unbroken tradition of skill in semitic languages which would have enabled them to dispense with Jewish help, had they wished to do so. In fact, far from avoiding the Jews, Latin scholars asked them for information on rabbinics as well as for guidance in the Hebrew tongue. The Jews of northern France and the Rhineland, from Rashi onward, supplemented their traditional lore by an original method of exegesis. Hence Christians of the twelfth and thirteenth centuries who consulted the rabbis would get two types of answer to their questions: they would collect old traditions and specimens of the traditional interpretation, and they would make the acquaintance of a living contemporary scholarship, which could influence their own approach. The Christian knowledge of rabbinics in the middle ages used to be underestimated. Rashi was thought to have made his first appearance in Latin commentaries with Nicholas of Lyre in the early fourteenth century. His influence on Lyre was classed not as typically medieval, as indeed it was, but as a factor in the Reformation:

> Si Lyra non lyrasset
> Lutherus non saltasset.

This *dicton absurde*, as a French scholar called it as long ago as 1893,[1] has been finally disproved. Or else we must put the beginning of the Reformation in the school of St. Victor

---

[1] J. Soury, reviewing *Quam notitiam* in *Bibl. de l'Ecole des Chartes*, liv (1893), 738.

and the circle of scholars surrounding St. Thomas of Canterbury.

A history of Bible studies must take account of institutions and movements; it must be written mainly as a history of scholars. Some periods seem to give more scope to personality than others and the twelfth century was one of them. We picture the conflict between cloister and school in terms of Bernard and Abailard, the conflict between Church and State in terms of Becket and Henry II, because these men strike us as both individual and typical. It was only fitting that the same century should have produced a correspondingly outstanding figure in the narrower sphere of biblical scholarship. Sure enough, when one looked for him he was there. Every signpost pointed to the Abbey of St. Victor at Paris. At St. Victor was Master Andrew, typical of all specialists and scholars, but sharing in the definite, daring quality which distinguished St. Bernard, Abailard, Henry II and St. Thomas Becket. Andrew applied his Hebrew studies to Scripture as Abailard applied logic to the principles of faith; and he had fewer predecessors than Abailard. Master Andrew of St. Victor is so forgotten and yet so important a figure, his influence so decisive in the history of biblical studies, that it is not disproportionate to allot him a whole chapter, a sixth of our total space.

The last ten years have brought further proof of his significance. It turned out, quite unexpectedly, that he had a pupil in Herbert of Bosham. Herbert was Becket's secretary and biographer; hence we have another link between St. Victor and the *eruditi Sancti Thomae*. Andrew has also found an editor for one of his works. Fr. Calandra of Palermo has published a critical text of the commentary on Ecclesiastes and his introduction has extracts from some of the others.[1] He has made a study of Andrew's linguistic knowledge and has added to my list of quotations from Andrew by later writers. Unfortunately the first commentary to go into print is one of the shortest and not the most interesting. It is to be hoped that some scholar will choose to edit Andrew on the Pentateuch and the Prophets.

The interplay of ideas, institutions and character forms

---

[1] I am most grateful to Fr. Calandra for sending me a copy of his edition, published at Palermo in 1948. He was not able to use my book, since no copy was obtainable. I have substituted his edition for my transcripts for quotations from Andrew on Ecclesiastes, with a few modifications.

the outline of my book. I have kept on the whole to chronological arrangement and have picked out for description
those teaching circles where biblical studies were most
flourishing at a given time.

Some defence is needed for choosing the conventional date
of 1300 as my boundary. In practice I have sometimes over-
stepped it, but the choice was dictated by a limitation in
my subject matter. I deal only with the Bible in Latin and
with its study by ecclesiastics. My scholars are men whose
calling obliged them to meditate and comment on the Bible.
The whole question of Scripture in the vernacular and of the
lay approach to it has been omitted. The reason is that we
must look to the clerks at this period for new and constructive
ideas in interpretation. From the eighth century onwards,
where my story opens (for the first chapter is merely introductory), the laity was handicapped by being illiterate. A
knight at the court of Charlemagne asks intelligent, though
rather naive questions about clerical exegesis.[1] A Count of
Guignes in Flanders of the late twelfth century, 'although
he was altogether lay and unlettered', would listen atten-
tively to the reading of Scripture and understood not only
the literal but even the mystical sense of the Prophets, the
historical books and the Gospels.[2] Both these men were
regarded by their contemporaries as exceptional. This is
not to accuse the laity of ignorance: visual aids and oral
teaching would combine to give even the medieval peasant
some sort of notion of the content of Old and New Testaments. It means, however, that the layman was getting his
ideas at second hand from the clerk:

> 'Now you talk to me again of Loth and his wife, whom I
> have never seen or known, nor their city, nor have we been at
> one time. But I have heard say that an angel commanded
> them to leave the city where they had dwelt and not to look
> back, and because she looked back the woman was changed
> into a statue of salt. But to me it was never commanded that
> I should not look back. . . .'

A lay baron is sending this letter to an ecclesiastic about
1143. He struggles to answer clerical arguments, recognizing
his disadvantage. He has 'heard say' while his correspondent

---

[1] *M.G.H., Epistolae*, iv, Ep. 136, 205-8.
[2] From the chronicle of the Counts of Guignes by Lambert of Ardres,
M.G.H., Scriptores, xxiv, 598.

has read the story which is quoted and can use it to point a moral.[1]

The balance begins to be redressed towards the end of the thirteenth century. Already in Italy where the tradition of a literate laity was stronger we hear of occasional preaching by a Podesta or a court official, tolerated by the ecclesiastical authorities. In the early fourteenth century a secular ruler, Robert the Wise of Naples, is composing and delivering sermons in abundance.[2] The same century saw the first reappearance of learned heresies involving the interpretation of Scripture. The orthodox teaching had not gone unchallenged, but the theories behind popular resistance to it almost escape the historian. The chronicle of Radulphus Glaber tells of a heretic who held that the Prophets were partly to be believed and partly not. He drew the simple and direct conclusion that the peasants need not pay their tithes.[3] That is all we know of him. There is more evidence for the evangelism of Valdès and his followers and for the various systems of the Cathari.[4] It is doubtful whether either the Poor Men of Lyons or the Cathari have any more place in a history of biblical scholarship than the leader of a peasant movement. The Valdensians differed from the Catholics only in points of emphasis until they were driven from the Church and thereby subjected to the influence of other sects. As for the Cathari: the Catholic exegetes of the middle ages have been frowned on because they made so much use of the allegorical or mystical interpretation; but they accepted the Scriptures as historical and only wanted to find a symbolic value in history. The Cathari would dispose of events in Scripture by moving them from the earth to a spirit world.[5] Interesting as he may be from other points of view,

[1] Brian Fitz-Count to Henry of Blois, Bishop of Winchester, printed by H. W. C. Davis, 'Henry of Blois and Brian Fitz-Count', *English Historical Review*, xxv (1910), 297-303. Brian had received a better education than most laymen, since he was brought up at the court of King Henry I.

Some recent studies on the Bible and vernacular culture are: H. Vollmer, 'Bibel und deutsche Kultur. Veröffentlichungen des deutschen Bibel-Archivs in Hamburg', *Materialen zur Bibelgeschichte und religiösen Volkskunde des Mittelalters*, Neue Folge v (Potsdam, 1931); G. Kisch, *Sachsenspiegel and Bible* (Notre Dame, Indiana, 1941); H. Rost, *Die Bibel im Mittelalter* (Augsburg, 1939).

[2] W. Goetz, *König Robert von Neapel (1309-1343)*, (Tübingen, 1910); see 29-30 for earlier instances of lay preaching.

[3] ed. M. Prou (Paris, 1886), 49-50.

[4] A. Dondaine, 'Aux origines du Valdéisme', *Archivum Fratrum Praedicatorum*, xvi (1946), 191-235; H. Söderberg, *La religion des Cathares* (Uppsala, 1949).

[5] A. Dondaine, *Un traité néo-manichéen du XIIIe siècle le Liber de duobus principiis* (Rome, 1939), 20-26.

the Neo-Manichee is a marginal figure to the historian of
Bible studies. In the fourteenth century Catholic scholars
had a new experience. They met with antagonists who could
argue on their own ground, men who had studied and taught
at universities and who used the same terminology and the
same apparatus. The Averroists in the thirteenth century
had also been on a level with the orthodox in this respect;
but their arguments had turned on philosophy rather than
theology. Marsilio of Padua and John Wyclif, on the
contrary, carried their attack into the field of exegesis.

Two reasons, therefore, make 1300 a convenient halting
place. It permits the exclusion of Bible study by laymen and
heretics in favour of concentration on the clergy. It marks
the end of a period when the Church had a safe monopoly
of learning. The restriction of letters to a narrow circle made
for tolerance within that circle. The Church showed a
liberal attitude to scholarship which tended to disappear
when the Vulgate came under criticism from humanists and
reformers.[1] If we are looking for a critical approach to
interpretation in the twelfth and thirteenth centuries, we
must go to the new religious Orders, Cistercians, Canons
Regular, Friars Preacher and Minor, all zealots for the faith
and the papacy. Their members held views which would
have charmed Erasmus and annoyed his opponents. We
shall find that our medieval scholars are inventive as well
as conservative; their most common fault is extravagance,
not obscurantism.

As a farmer, having enclosed his field, fences round the
dangerous pot-holes inside it, so having marked my boundary,
I ought to warn readers against the worst gaps in treatment.
In the first place, the medieval Vulgate has been accepted as
something given. I have adopted, in writing, all the assumptions held by medieval students about its date, authorship
and provenance. The composition and previous history of
Old and New Testaments interest me here only in so far as
they impinged on the consciousness of a medieval scholar.
Thus Philo Judaeus comes into the introductory chapter
because he was known in the middle ages, at least indirectly.
I have not attempted to write a history of the Vulgate text.
The interpretation of certain parts of the Bible has been

_____

[1] It did not disappear altogether; see M.-D. Chenu, 'L'humanisme et réforme au Collège Saint-Jacques de Paris', *Archives d'histoire dominicaine*, i (1946),
130-54.

treated much more fully than that of others. This has been partly due to chance: I have not happened to find commentaries on the Canonical Epistles and the Acts of the Apostles that struck me as worth studying. The Pauline Epistles and the Apocalypse have been set aside by design. St. Paul provided a focus for theological teaching. Hence medieval commentaries on his Epistles have attracted the historians of scholasticism. To include their researches would have meant enlarging my scope out of all proportion. The Apocalypse, too, would have intruded its own special problems; it has anyway been the subject of a monograph.[1]

My first edition enlarged on the twelfth to the neglect of the thirteenth century. I have spent the last few years in my spare time in reading lectures given in the friars' *studia* at Paris and Oxford. They fill out the picture for the thirteenth century; but they have diverted me from the gaps still open in my account of the Victorines. A group of scholars in France has meanwhile formed the project of editing or re-editing all the Victorine literature. So I leave to them the compilation of a list of manuscript copies of Hugh of St. Victor's notes on various books of the Old Testament. More serious is the absence of any proper investigation of the Jewish sources of Hugh, Andrew and Richard of St. Victor. My collaborator, Dr. L. Rabinowitz, began a comparison between the Victorines and the rabbis. I summarized his findings in my first edition and we drafted a joint paper, setting out the evidence. Then the war interrupted us and after his war service Dr. Rabinowitz removed to South Africa. The question remains where we left it in 1939.

Another neglected side of my subject is the disputations between Jews and Christians, the Christian missions and the schools for training missionaries in oriental languages.[2] The Bible in disputation and in mission work has an obvious connection with the Bible in the classroom; but this line of study would have drawn us beyond our geographical limits. We are mainly concerned with the schools and universities of north-western Europe. Disputations and missions, if

[1] W. Kamlah, 'Apokalypse und Geschichtstheologie', *Historische Studien,* cclxxxv (Berlin, 1935).
[2] See especially A. Berthier, 'Les écoles de langues orientales fondées au XIIIe siècle par les Dominicains en Espagne et en Afrique', *Revue africaine,* lxiii (1932), 84-103; P. Browe, *Die Judenmissionen im Mittelalter und die Päpste* (Rome, 1942).

fully described, would carry us into Spain and the Moslem countries bordering on the Mediterranean.

The experienced medievalist will find many more gaps in my argument. Two modern books on medieval exegesis have appeared and we are still only at the beginning. An adequate study would require a whole team of specialists. We would need experts in Greek and Hebrew, patristic and rabbinics, Byzantinists, scholars familiar with the contents of medieval libraries, historians of theology and of humanism. My book will have served its purpose if it brings this kind of collaboration any nearer.

CHAPTER I

THE FATHERS

I. THE LETTER AND THE SPIRIT

'I PUBLISHED three books [on Genesis] from the sayings of the holy Fathers concerning the letter and the spirit . . . For the Word came into the world by Mary, clad in flesh; and seeing was not understanding; all saw the flesh; knowledge of the divinity was given to a chosen few. So when the Word was shown to men through the lawgiver and the prophets, it was not shown them without suitable vesture. There it is covered by the veil of flesh, here of the letter. The letter appears as flesh; but the spiritual sense within is known as divinity. This is what we find in studying Leviticus . . . Blessed are the eyes which see divine spirit through the letter's veil.'[1]

Claudius of Turin sums up the patristic tradition as it had reached the scholars of Charlemagne's day. The Word is incarnate in Scripture,[2] which like man has a body and soul. The body is the words of the sacred text, the 'letter', and the literal meaning; the soul is the spiritual sense. To explain the literal sense is to expound *litteraliter vel carnaliter*; *littera* is almost interchangeable with *corpus*.[3] If, in rare moments of scepticism, a medieval scholar questioned the truth of Scripture, he never doubted that it had letter and spirit; he only feared that the spirit might be bad.[4] Naturally, then, he

[1] *In Libros Informationum Litterae et Spiritus super Leviticum Praefatio*, P.L. (1844 edition) civ. 615-17. From Origen, *Hom. in Lev.* i. 1.
[2] St. Jerome compares Scripture to the body of Christ in expressions which sound extravagant to modern readers. See G. Morin, *Etudes, textes, découvertes*, i (1913), 243-4.
[3] An anonymous fifth-century commentator on St. Mark writes on Mc. vi. 28-9, *P.L.* xxx. 608: 'Corpus Iohannis sepelitur, caput in disco collocatur: littera humo tegitur, spiritus in altari honoratur et sumitur.' The body of John is buried, his head is laid on a dish: the letter is covered with earth, the spirit is honoured and received at the altar. The commentator is comparing St. John the Baptist to the Saviour; the dish reminds him of the paten, the round, shallow vessel used at Mass. See G. Morin, 'Un commentaire romain sur S. Marc de la première moitié du Ve siècle', *Rev. Bén.* xxvii (1910), 358.
[4] Otloh of St. Emmeran (d. 1070) describes his doubts in his *Liber de Tentationibus*, *P.L.* cxlvi. 33: '. . . all the books of the divine law are written so as to give an outward show of religion and virtue; inwardly they call for another reason and interpretation.'

I

understood the relationship between letter and spirit in the
same way as he did the relationship between body and soul.
This depended on his philosophy of life and on his way of
living.

Turning to Claudius, we find an ascetic view, tinged with
Neoplatonism, just as we might expect from a monk whose
chief authority among the Fathers was St. Augustine. The
letter is a garment for the spirit, with a suggestion of cloak or
concealment, which the commentator must penetrate. It is
necessary to the spirit, as the body is necessary to the soul in
this mortal life. The spiritually minded commentator will
accept the letter, but treat it ascetically, as the good religious
treats his flesh, in order to devote himself to the spirit.

We then discover that what we should now call exegesis,
which is based on the study of the text and of biblical history,
in its widest sense, belongs to the 'literal exposition'. The
'spiritual exposition' generally consists of pious meditations
or religious teaching for which the text is used merely as a
convenient starting-point. It follows that so long as this
conception of Bible studies holds good, we shall have many
commentaries containing little exegesis.

> 'It is as though we were invited to focus our eyes not on the
> physical surface of the object, but on infinity as seen through
> the lattice . . .; the object . . . exists—as it were—merely to
> define and detach a certain portion of infinite space, and make
> it manageable and apprehensible.'[1]

This description of the 'pierced technique' in early northern
art is also an exact description of exegesis as understood by
Claudius, if we substitute 'text' for the 'physical surface' of
the artists' material, and 'truth' for 'infinite space'. We are
invited to look not at the text, but through it.

To understand the strength and solidity of the tradition
we must realize how far back into classical antiquity it goes
and what urgent purposes it served. The allegorical interpretation marks a stage in the history of any civilized people
whose sacred literature is 'primitive'. They dispose of what
conflicts with their present moral and intellectual standards
by reading their past as an allegory. It is only at a much
later stage that they come to see it as a process of historical
development. Greek commentators found allegories in
Homer, and the Hellenized Jew, Philo of Alexandria, found

[1] R. Hinks, *Carolingian Art* (London, 1935), 82-3.

them in the Septuagint. Philo Judaeus has been called 'the Cicero' of allegory; he did not invent but popularized, without always reconciling, a number of allegorical traditions.[1]

His purpose was to show that whatever the letter of the inspired text might say, its inner or spiritual meaning was in harmony with Platonism, the current philosophy of the Gentiles. Philo was a practising Jew; he represented his people on a delegation to the Roman emperor. Hence he could hardly have dismissed the letter altogether. Indeed, he disclaims any such intention:

> 'Why, we shall be ignoring the sanctity of the Temple and a thousand other things, if we are going to pay heed to nothing except what is shown us by the inner meaning of things.'[2]

The Law is an historical institution, literally binding on Jews, as well as having an inner meaning. Philo must have admitted the propriety of a study of the literal sense of the text, since he says that he will leave it to those who specialize in such matters.[3] His *Questions and Answers* even contain an occasional literal solution to the difficulties arising from Scripture.[4] But he brings out the overriding importance of the allegorical sense when he says of the prophet Samuel:

> 'Probably there was an actual man called Samuel; but we conceive of the Samuel of the scripture, not as a living compound of soul and body, but as a mind which rejoices in the service and worship of God and that only.'[5]

Allegory conferred a quality of universality on Jewish law and history. Philo expressed this view in a metaphor which gains in meaning if we think of its political background: the Romans had fused their conquests into a world empire. Those who interpret in the literal sense only are 'citizens of a petty state'; the allegorists are 'on the roll of citizens of a greater country, namely, this whole world'.[6]

---

[1] See E. Stein, 'Die allegorische Exegese des Philo aus Alexandria', *Zeitschr. f. d. alttestamentl. Wiss.*, Beiheft 51 (1929); also P. Heinisch, 'Der Einfluss Philos auf die älteste christliche Exegese', *Alttestament. Abhandl.* i. 1, 2 (Münster, 1908).

[2] *De Migratione Abrahae*, xvi, trans. F. H. Colson and G. H. Whitaker (Loeb Classical Library), iv. 186.

[3] H. A. Wolfson, *Philo* (Cambridge, Mass., 1947), i. 57-63.

[4] For the editions and translations of the *Questions and Answers* see H. L. Goodhart and E. R. Goodenough, *A General Bibliography of Philo* (New Haven, 1938), 133.

[5] *De Ebrietate*, xxxvi (Loeb Classical Library, op. cit.), iii. 395.

[6] H. A. Wolfson, op. cit. 61, quoting *De Somniis*, i. 7, 39.

The chief function of allegory was apologetic. It enabled him to read philosophy into the Scriptures and to exalt such details as might seem trivial or scandalous to a higher level. It also provided the right medium for the discussion of what interested him. Modern scholars differ in their interpretation of the content of his thought, as distinct from his method; but the main direction of his interests is clear. Philo conformed to the intellectual tendency of his day, which stressed the 'other worldly' and moral element in Platonism and sharpened the contrast between mind and matter. He dwelt on the choice, confronting a man of means and leisure, such as he was, between indulging the appetites and cultivating the spirit. Introspection was revealing a ghostly demesne of abstractions and experiences which could be expressed most naturally, in default of a scientific terminology, by personifications and symbols drawn from the outward events of life: marriage, travel, warfare. Scripture enabled Philo to make his conceptions more precise and intelligible. Further, it allowed him to develop a train of thought and yet dispensed him from the need to build up a system. He allegorized not only the text he had taken as his starting point, but other passages suggested by the first. Any attempt to classify or systematize his ideas involves the construction of a gigantic card index; the result may be something that Philo himself would hardly have recognized.[1] Just as the possibility of clothing his thought in metaphors suited his subject matter, so the free and flexible exegesis of revelation suited his mental attitude of compromise between creative thought on the one hand and acceptance of authority on the other.[2] Those of his readers today who prefer to do their thinking in the margin of a literary or historical text will sympathize with him. In any case, he had chosen a medium of expression which was to have a long and brilliant future. It will not be wholly superseded throughout the period covered by this book.

The procedure demanded a specialized technique and it is here that the modern student feels least at home. In the first place there seems to be no clear distinction between passages which Philo regarded as having a literal plus an allegorical meaning and those which, being superstitious or

---

[1] See the review by E. R. Goodenough of A. Wolfson's *Philo*, *Journal of Biblical Literature*, lxvii (1948), 87-109.
[2] E. Bréhier, *Les idées philosophiques et religieuses de Philon d'Alexandrie* (2nd edn., Paris, 1925), 312-13.

fabulous, like the anthropomorphisms in Genesis, must be interpreted as purely allegorical, that is, allegorical in their primary sense. Hence there is no rule for determining what would strike a modern commentator as most important. The rules for constructing allegories, on the other hand, bewilder by their number and their complexity. The line between reality and imagery seems to be melted. Reading Philo, one has the sensation of stepping 'through the looking glass'.

One finds, as did Alice, a country governed by queer laws which the inhabitants oddly regard as rational. In order to understand medieval Bible study one must live there long enough to slip into their ways and appreciate the logic of their strict, elaborately fantastic conventions. Philo admits that anything in Scripture may signify any other thing provided that it obeys the rules of an intricate pseudo-science, the allegorical interpretation. Allegory is 'a wise architect who directs the superstructure built upon a literal foundation'. Every syllable of the inspired text may serve in laying this basis. Hence the commentary takes the form of essays, each having its basis in a short passage of the text. It proceeds by digression.

The 'rules' for building derive mainly from number-symbolism and etymology. He comments on the six days of Creation:

> 'It was requisite that the world being most perfect of all things that have come into existence, should be constituted in accordance with a perfect number, namely six.'

Six is

> 'the first perfect number, being equal to the product of its factors (i.e. $1 \times 2 \times 3$), as well as made up of the sum of them (i.e. $1+2+3$) ... We may say that it is in its nature both male and female, and is a result of the distinctive power of either. For among things that are, it is the odd that is male and the even female. Now of odd numbers 3 is the starting-point, and of even numbers 2, and the product of these two is 6.'

The properties of the number seven are 'beyond all words'.[1]

Etymologies were more helpful even than numbers. The conception went back to primitive word-magic. Hence Philo believes that a biblical name is a perfect description of the thing:

[1] *De Opificio*, iii; xxx, op. cit. i. 13, 73.

'. . . with Moses the names assigned are manifest images of
the things, so that name and thing are inevitably the same from
the first and the name and that to which the name is given
differ not a whit.'[1]

It follows that the etymologist can give a true description of
persons and places. Certain etymologies were biblical; in
other cases an etymology might be invented. Philo, who
probably knew little, if any, Hebrew, could apply the principle also to Greek words, since he held the Septuagint to be
verbally inspired. It gave a rich scope to his fantasy: one
cannot always say where etymology ends and the play upon
words begins. Then, closely connected with its etymology,
is the description of the thing. Its special characteristics
determine what it signifies:

'The serpent is a fit symbol of pleasure, because in the first
place he is an animal without feet sunk prone upon his belly;
secondly because he takes clods of earth as food; thirdly because
he carries in his teeth the venom with which it is his nature to
destroy those whom he has bitten. The lover of pleasure is
exempt from none of these traits. . . .'[2]

Philo's activity falls into the first half of the first century
A.D. It was natural that towards the end of this century
and beginning of the next Alexandria should become a point
of fusion for Christian and Philonic exegesis. We can see the
process at work in Origen, who praised Philo, while regarding himself as a disciple and continuator of St. Paul; he com-
bated and borrowed from both Jewish rabbis and gnostic
heretics. Great efforts have been made recently to disentangle the various strands in Origen's commentaries.[3]
These give us our last chance to distinguish what would soon
be no longer various traditions juxtaposed, but one tradition
of interpretation. It would admit of different emphasis and
of development; it would not, throughout the middle ages,
admit of question in principle.

Origen inherited the Christian teaching that the Old
Testament prefigures or foreshadows the New: *omnia in
figura contingebant illis*. This conception of allegory differs

---

[1] *De Cherub.* xvii, op. cit. ii. 43.
[2] From *De Opificio*, lvi, op. cit., quoted by F. A. Wright, *A History of Later
Greek Literature* (London, 1932), 193.
[3] On Origen's exegesis see the studies and bibliographies in J. Daniélou,
Origène (Paris, 1948), 139-90; H. de Lubac, *Histoire et esprit: l'intelligence de
l'Écriture d'après Origène* (Paris, 1950).

from Philo's in that both the sign and the thing signified are conceived as historical and would have no significance if they were not.[1] Today it is sometimes distinguished from allegory and called 'typology'. Origen found four kinds of type in the Old Testament: prophecies of the coming of Christ, prophecies of the Church and her sacraments (the Red Sea, for instance, signifying baptism), prophecies of the Last Things and of the kingdom of heaven, finally, figures of the relationship between God and the individual soul as exemplified in the history of the chosen people: 'God's ways in the guidance of the soul are the same as those by which he guides his people and hence we have the right to draw spiritual teaching from Exodus and from the Canticle.'[2] The two last kinds of types, eschatological and mystical or moral, can be found in the New Testament also. Origen is drawing his material, so far, from the New Testament and early Christian writers. He only has to systematize their treatment of Scripture. He goes on to add the more comprehensive and cosmic sort of allegory which he found in Philo. This easily shaded into the Christian moral or mystical type, since Philo, too, had been interested in religious psychology and in the moral progress of the soul. For Origen, as for Philo, the whole of Scripture, not merely certain passages, has a deeper meaning to be explained by the commentator. Clement of Alexandria, who may have been Origen's teacher, had anticipated him here. Otherwise his predecessors seem to have thought rather in terms of finding types than of allegorizing meticulously every phrase of their Bible.

The various sects of gnostic heretics had used allegory in a more radical way. They took the Old Testament in its literal sense and rejected it as the work of a demi-god. The New Testament or selected parts of what became the New Testament were interpreted allegorically so as to represent their particular cosmic theories. Origen substituted his own more orthodox but still highly speculative opinions on the primeval causes of disorder in the universe and the process by which harmony was being re-established. The Bible in its literal sense told too much of men, too little of spirits and of cosmic

[1] See G. Wuttke, 'Melchisedech der Priesterkönig von Salem', *Zeitschr. f. d. neutestamentl. Wiss.*, Beiheft 5 (1927).
[2] J. Daniélou, 'Les sources bibliques de la mystique d'Origène', *Revue d'ascétique et de mystique*, xxiii (1947), 128.

forces to satisfy him; hence the Gospels concealed the eternal Christ in their record of his earthly life and ministry. In thus transposing his thought from the terrestrial to the super-terrestrial plane, Origen resembled most other intellectuals of his day, whether they were Catholic, heretic or pagan. To show that acceptance of Scripture was compatible with philosophy formed an important part of Christian apologetic. The thoroughgoing use of Philonic allegory implied an equally thorough borrowing of the Philonic rules for allegorical interpretation. Recent studies have traced the history of particular allegories and types in pre-Christian and patristic writers. We can watch the changes in meaning and see how the concepts and lore of antiquity were transmitted to the middle ages in the guise of symbolism.[1] A quotation from one of the pseudo-Clementine homilies illustrates the way in which Philo's belief in the mystical value of etymology was adopted. This statement, not known directly but handed down as part of the Alexandrian heritage, will become an underlying assumption of medieval exegesis:

'Pythagoras held that he who gave names to things must be reputed, not only as the wisest, but as the most ancient of sages. Hence we must carefully scrutinize the Scriptures, since it is agreed that they are written in parables. We must search in names for the meanings which the Holy Spirit intended to relate to realities *and which he teaches us by inscribing, so to speak, his thought in the words*, so that when we have studied them with care we may discover the sense of names which have multiple meanings, and that the meaning hidden in many of them may declare itself and shine forth, after being tested and studied.'[2]

Clement and Origen also inherited Philo's uncertainty as to the classification of biblical figures and metaphors. Origen justifies the 'spiritual interpretation' from the impossibility of understanding a precept like: *if thine eye offend thee pluck it out* according to the letter. Scripture for him was a mirror, which reflected the divinity now darkly, now brightly; it had body, soul, and spirit, a literal, moral, and allegorical sense,

[1] J. Daniélou, 'La typologie d'Isaac dans le christianisme primitif', *Biblica* xxviii (1947), 363-93; H. Rahner, 'Mysterium lunae', *Zeitschr. f. kath. Theol.* lxiii-lxiv (1939-40), 311-49; 61-80; 'Navicula Petri', ibid. xlix (1947), 1-35; L. Welsersheimb, 'Das Kirchenbild der griechischen Väterkommentare zum Hohenlied', ibid. lxx (1948), 393-449.

[2] *Eclogae propheticae*, ed. Stählen (Leipzig, 1909), 146-7, quoted by J. Lebreton, 'Le désaccord de la foi populaire et la théologie savante', *Revue d'histoire ecclésiastique*, xix (1923), 495, n. 2. The italics are mine.

the first two for 'simple believers' who were 'unable to understand profounder meanings', the third for the initiates, the Christian gnostics, who were able to investigate *the wisdom in a mystery, the hidden wisdom of God*.[1] The 'sense' of Scripture refers both to its content and to the method of the commentator in explaining it. 'Allegory' includes both teaching expressed by the sacred writer in figurative language and the commentator's allegorical explanation of an historical event or institution. Origen believed that the whole of Scripture had a spiritual but not the whole of it a bodily meaning, and this led him in some cases to interpret subjectively, according to his own ideas. He was too fascinated by the spirit, just as Philo had been, to define the letter clearly.[2]

It would be wrong, however, to think of allegory as merely a learned exercise. Origen used it in the service of the Christian people. It lay at the very core of the Christian life as lived in the liturgy. Origen preached daily on the lessons for the day. An allegorical interpretation enabled him to satisfy the needs of his hearers, while explaining a text which he had not chosen and which the liturgy imposed on him.[3] The development of public worship in the Church and the technique of preaching went together, two aspects of a single process. Apart from its liturgical function, allegory became a weapon in polemic with the antagonists of Christianity and in controversy among Christians at a time when the Church was still persecuted and her dogma still fluid. A newly discovered papyrus records a conference between Origen and certain bishops, held in Arabia or Palestine, perhaps about 245.[4] Origen had been called upon to answer various questions on doctrine, put to him before an assembly of Christians who did not merely listen, but took part as

---

[1] *De Principiis*, iv. 11, 18.
[2] To take one example, in his *Homilia in Numeros*, xvi. 9. Origen comments on the blessing of Balaam: *it shall not lie down till it devour the prey and drink the blood of the slain*: [xxiii. 24] 'Who will be so contentious an upholder of the historical sense, who so brutal, that he will not in horror take refuge of necessity in the sweetness of allegory?' He therefore interprets the prophetic metaphor as referring (in·its primary sense), not to the Israelites' entry into their promised land, but to the advent of Christ: 'the people of faithful Christians hear these words and embrace them, and follow him who says "except you eat the flesh of the Son of Man and drink his blood you shall not have life in you" ' (ed. Baehrens (*Die griechischen christlichen Schriftsteller*, vii, 1921), 151-2.
[3] H. de Lubac, op. cit. 131-5.
[4] 'Entretien d'Origène avec Héraclide et les évêques ses collègues sur le Père, le Fils, et l'Âme', ed. J. Scherer, *Publications de la Société Fouad I de Papyrologie: Textes et Documents*, ix (Cairo, 1949).

'witnesses'. The report, consisting in notes taken down on the spot, brings Origen to life before us and shows him using allegory to settle a difficulty, arising from a literal interpretation of Scripture, which troubled simple men, even leading them to doubt the immortality of the soul. Two texts of the Law (Lev. xvii. 11 and Deut. xii. 23) seem to imply that the soul is in the blood. The 'Arabian' heretics held that it was. How, then, can the soul survive the death of the body? Origen feels compelled to answer this question by propounding a mystery which ought not to be spoken before profane ears. He begs his hearers to purify their hearts in order that they may be fit to understand. The bodily man in Scripture is doubled by the interior, spiritual man. The sacred writers refer to the parts of this second man under sensible names: the eyes and ears signify the understanding; to raise the hands in sacrifice means to lift up the spirit to God. Origen collects many texts where the bodily members and the five senses are employed in a figurative sense. Sometimes, in explaining the figure, he finds a deeper meaning. Thus *the very hairs of your head are all numbered* was said to the disciples who were Nazarenes with shaven heads, and hence it must refer to spiritual protection.[1] It follows that the blood which is mentioned in these two texts of the Law must belong to the interior man, as we read in Genesis: *of the blood of your souls account will be asked* (ix. 5). So the prohibition to eat flesh which has the lifeblood in it does not refer to the blood of the body. It is another allusion to the spiritual as distinct from the carnal man. The difficulty has gone. The soul is not inherent in that physical blood which dries up in death and remains with the body in its tomb.

Origen then points to the consequences of restricting oneself to the literal sense of Scripture: it negates the hope of immortality. The soul does not remain with the body after death and before the resurrection. It is liberated and rests with Christ. That is why Christians dare to suffer for the sake of the truth. He ends with a passionate exhortation to martyrdom. Release from the body will bring, not death, but a better life:

' "Now am I ready to die for the truth. Now, faced by what is called death, I despise it. The beasts, the cross, the flames, the torments, let them come! I know that on the instant of

[1] ibid. 165.

expiring I shall leave my body and be at rest with Christ. For this we struggle, for this we fight. Let us mourn at being in the body, persuaded not of being soon in our bodies in our graves, but of being freed and exchanging our bodies for a more spiritual state. Destined to depart and to be with Christ, how we mourn, we who are in the body!"

Bishop Philip having entered, Demetrius, another bishop, said: "Here is our brother Origen teaching that the soul is immortal." '

And so the report ends.

The actuality of the scene forbids one to think of allegory as an artifice, imposed on Scripture by philosophers who were 'out of touch with the masses'.[1] Rather was it a necessary condition of the spread of Christianity among the people. By no other means, at that time, could the taboos of primitive tribes, as described in the Law, have been spiritualized for the benefit of men who were hardly less primitive.

The public worship of the early Christian includes hearing sermons on Scripture as read in the liturgy. His private life also should centre on the study of Scripture. Origen promises him that his understanding of its mysteries will develop as part of the growth of the 'interior man'. We must make our hearts into an ark or cupboard for the books of the Bible.[2] This would have seemed an apt metaphor at a period when the sacred books or scrolls were kept in cabinets or narrow cases of the type represented in the mosaic of St. Laurence in the mausoleum of Galla Placidia at Ravenna and in the picture of Esdras in the *Codex amiatinus*.[3] It lost its appositeness when books were spread out on library shelves; but the sense of intimacy and inwardness remained. Origen here foreshadows the *lectio divina* of early monasticism, which would identify asceticism and spirituality with the understanding of Scripture in its mystical sense. In speaking of the sacraments, he puts more emphasis on Scripture than on the

[1] J. Lebreton, 'Le désaccord de la foi populaire et la théologie savante', *Revue d'histoire ecclésiastique*, xix (1923), 481-506, xx (1924), 5-37, discusses this problem, though he does not consider the use of allegory for popular purposes.

[2] *Hom. in Gen.* ii. 6, quoted by H. de Lubac, op. cit. 347. Origen is commenting on the building of Noe's ark; we have come to associate an ark with a kind of houseboat; but the word used in the Septuagint and the Vulgate can also mean chest for books. Hence de Lubac is probably right in seeing an allusion to a chest when Origen puts the 'divina bibliotheca' into the ark of the heart.

[3] P. Courcelle, 'Le grille de S. Laurent au Mausolée de Galla Placidia', *Cahiers archéologiques*, iii (1948), 29-39.

Eucharist; the Logos was incarnate in the flesh of the holy text.[1]

A necessary part of his whole system, and also part of his inheritance from Christian tradition, was the view that the interpretation of Scripture was a grace or 'charisma'. Origen's pupil, St. Gregory Thaumaturgus, believed that his master shared the inspiration of the sacred writers themselves: the same Spirit which inspired the prophets inspired Origen to interpret their prophecies.[2] The claim will be made subsequently for other great masters of the mystical interpretation. The Holy Spirit speaks through the mouths of St. Gregory the Great and of St. Bernard of Clairvaux when they expound Scripture.[3] Just as the evangelists are represented in medieval iconography as writing at the dictation of angels, so St. Gregory, composing his commentaries, listens to a dove which perches on his shoulder with its bill to his ear.[4] All this goes back to Origen's teaching.

And yet the soberest scholarship of the middle ages derived its permit and its direction ultimately from Alexandria. Both Clement and Origen insisted on the value of profane science for Bible study; the idea went back to Philo. The cycle of liberal arts and sciences, later known as the *trivium* and *quadrivium*, leading up to philosophy, prepare the student to understand Scripture and to refute objectors.[5] Their programme might be called the *Magna Carta* of medieval scholars; it would be latinized by St. Jerome and schematized by St. Augustine. Much of the requisite secular learning would be focused on the allegorical and mystical sense; but Origen also founded the scientific study of the

---

[1] H. de Lubac, op. cit. 336-73; J. Daniélou, *Origène* (Paris, 1948), 74.

[2] *In Orig. orat. panegyrica*, c. 15, *P.G.* x. 1093-6, quoted by H. de Lubac, op. cit. 46.

[3] Anselm of Laon: '. . . videamus quid dicat S. Spiritus in *Moralibus* . . .' (G. Lefèvre, *Anselmi Laudunensis et Radulfi fratris eius Sententias excerptas edidit G. L.*, Evreux, 1985, 29), quoted with other examples by J. de Ghellinck, *Le mouvement théologique du XIIᵉ siècle* (2nd edn., Bruges, 1948), 476; John of Salisbury says of St. Bernard: '. . . scripsit . . . in illa subtilissima et utilissima expositione Canticorum, quam procul dubio per os eius dictavit Spiritus sanctus'; *Historia pontificalis*, ed. R. L. Poole (Oxford, 1927), c. 11, 26-7. On Joachim of Flora see below, p. 289.

[4] See Paul the Deacon, *S. Gregorii Magni vita*, *P.L.* lxxv. 58; C. Nordenfalk, 'An Early Mediaeval Shorthand Alphabet', *Speculum*, xiv (1939), 443-7. The picture reproduced here (plate I) shows Gregory working at his homilies on Ezechiel. A fresco at St. Benedict's, Subiaco, shows him writing the *Moralia in Iob*, with the dove at his ear and Job, naked and covered with sores, at his feet.

[5] P. Camelot, 'Clément d'Alexandrie et l'utilisation de la philosophie grecque', *Recherches de science religieuse*, xxi (1931), 38-60; J. Daniélou, op. cit. 31.

literal. He was such a giant that he could concentrate on allegory and yet leave vast monuments of literal exegesis. Sacred history, the geography of Palestine, and particularly textual criticism interested him.[1] He consulted contemporary Jews and occasionally takes over a rabbinic explanation (on the dimensions of the ark, for instance). He collected all the existing translations from Hebrew into Greek that he could find for comparison with the Septuagint and the Hebrew. He did not extend his work on the text to cover the New Testament, however.

We shall find that medieval scholarship will reflect Origen's method, attitude and limitations. The Jew will be consulted on linguistic and historical problems. Variant readings will be collected and compared. Where the version received by the Church, for Origen the Septuagint, conflicted with other versions, he would not reject the former but would set them side by side and would comment on both. The habit of making double commentaries on double texts without choosing between them will become ingrained. Whether it derives from Origen or from a natural hesitancy shared with him, the limitation of textual criticism to the Old Testament will continue. Indeed, this part of the Bible will get the lion's share of attention from scholars, though not of course from theologians and homilists. Here we have a parallel with Origen, if not a case of direct influence.

Alexandrian exegesis penetrated to the Latin middle ages, when knowledge of Greek had declined, by two main channels: indirectly through the Latin Fathers and directly through translations of Origen's works. Rufinus' translations of some of his homilies were used by the compilers of the *Glossa Ordinaria*. Hence the standard commentary of the middle ages familiarized generations of students with 'select extracts'. The homilies were widely diffused. They were still being copied in the twelfth century and recent research has shown that Bernard of Clairvaux drew on them freely. Medieval students realized that certain of Origen's views had been condemned as heretical; but this could be abstracted and did not prevent their learning from him.[2]

[1] ibid. 139-44, 176-9.
[2] See G. Hoquard reviewing a modern French translation of Origen's homilies on Genesis, *Revue du Moyen Âge latin*, i (1945), 192-3; G. Bardy, 'Saint Bernard et Origène', ibid. 420-1; J. Leclercq, 'S. Bernard et Origène d'après

To write a history of Origenist influence on the west would
be tantamount to writing a history of western exegesis.

It was otherwise with the Antiochenes. They exercised so
slight an influence on the west that the evidence may be
discussed here and now instead of *passim*. It is sometimes
just as important for an understanding of history to realize
what did not happen as to know what did. The failure of
Antiochene exegesis to penetrate the Latin has as much
significance in a negative way as the success of the Alexandrians.

The Antiochenes might have counteracted Alexandrian
influence, since they set out to correct the abuse of the
allegorical method. They did not stand for the crude
literalism of Origen's opponents, the Arabians, who identified
the soul with the blood, or the millenarists, who interpreted
the Apocalypse as giving an exact date for doomsday.
Their aim was to define the senses of Scripture more
precisely. The literal sense, according to them, covered
the whole meaning of the writer, including his metaphors
and figures. The spiritual teaching contained in a prophecy
and intended by the prophet was classified as *theoria*, to
distinguish it from the mere grammatical construction of
his words.[1] They accepted, in addition, a spiritual sense,
which transcended the literal, but they restricted themselves to typology and they limited the number of types
to be found in the Old Testament to a very few passages.
Both Antiochenes and Alexandrians saw the Old Testament as essentially a prophecy of the New and they
differed only in the kind of proofs they offered. To
the Alexandrians each word concealed a mystery. The
Antiochenes wanted to find really sure and watertight
arguments that a prophecy must be accepted as such. Their
criteria remained subjective;[2] but they succeeded in creating
a very different atmosphere in their works.

[1] A. Vaccari, 'La θεωρία nella scuola esegetica di Antiocha', *Biblica*,
i (1920), 3-36.
[2] J. Guillet, 'Les exégèses d'Alexandrie et d'Antioche: conflit ou malentendu?',
Recherches de science religieuse, xxxiv (1947), 257-302; F. Ogara, 'De typica apud
Chrysostomum prophetia', *Gregorianum*, xxiv (1943), 62-77.

un ms de Madrid', *Rev. Bén.* lix (1949), 183-95; cp. E. Gilson, *La théologie
mystique de Saint Bernard* (Paris, 1934), 27-8. Detailed study of the sources of
medieval writers, as it proceeds, is uncovering more borrowings; see J.-M.
Déchanet, 'Guillaume et Plotin', *Revue du Moyen Âge latin*, ii (1946), 258, on
quotations from Origen by William of St. Thierry, the friend and admirer of
Bernard.

The emphasis has shifted back to earth and to man on earth. Theodore of Mopsuestia expresses his attitude to man when he answers the question, in his commentary on Genesis: 'How is man, alone of all other creatures, made in God's image?' Not, as some of his contemporaries say, because man has the power to reason and command. This man shares with the angels. Man is godlike because he shares in the divine power to create by devising new combinations, as in constructing a ship, a house or a town.[1] Hence the personalities of biblical history play a greater part in Theodore's work than in Origen's.[2] In explaining the Psalms, for instance, Theodore keeps on the plane of Old Testament history, treating David as essentially a prophet of his own people and trying to enter into his thought as a ruler of Israel. Only four Psalms are accepted as messianic: ii, viii, xliv, cix. Similarly Theodore refuses to admit that the prophecy in the 'suffering servant' passage, *he shall be led as a sheep to the slaughter, etc.* (Is. liii. 7) was intended by the prophet to refer to the crucifixion. The fact that a New Testament writer quotes a passage from the Old Testament need not necessarily prove that it was originally intended in this sense: St. Paul and others would adapt their text to their argument, as all preachers do. Antiochene principles favoured the development of biblical scholarship. Theodore has been called 'the first and very likely the only commentator of antiquity to introduce literary criticism' into the study of his text. That they also gave scope to the preacher is proved by the homilies of St. John Chrysostom. He showed that the literal sense of Scripture could be used as a basis for moral exhortation, without recourse to allegory.

Theodore died in 428 and his works were condemned for christological heresies (unfairly we are now told) at the Council of Constantinople in 553. The ban had a much more serious effect on his memory and on the survival of his writings than a similar condemnation had on Origen's. Nevertheless, a few works written on Antiochene principles were translated or composed in Latin.[3] The Pelagian bishop, Julian of Aeclanum, took refuge with Theodore when he was driven from his see. Theodore received him kindly,

[1] R. Devresse, 'Essai sur Théodore de Mopsueste', *Studi e Testi*, cxli (1948), 13.
[2] See the study of Theodore's exegesis, ibid. 55-93.
[3] The evidence for the knowledge of Antiochene works in the West is reviewed by M. L. W. Laistner, 'Antiochene Exegesis in Western Europe', *Harvard Theological Review*, xl (1947), 19-32.

though without in any way committing himself to Pelagianism.[1] Julian's exile gave him an opportunity to study Antiochene exegesis. Its comparative naturalism and rationalism might well attract a man who combatted the doctrine of original sin and who was accused of saying: 'What reason urges, authority cannot arrogate.'[2] He wrote a commentary in Latin, probably soon after his flight from Italy in 420, on three of the Minor Prophets: Osee, Joel, Amos.[3] Here he criticizes Origen and Jerome for their use of allegory and neglect of the context, keeps to the literal sense and 'theoria',[4] and restricts the messianic interpretation of the prophecies. Commenting on Joel ii. 28-31, he says, provocatively and with obvious enjoyment, that St. Peter was preaching the gospel, not expounding the prophecy when he quoted this passage (Acts ii. 17); hence the Apostle's speech does not exhaust its meaning.[5] This commentary had an interesting history. Only two copies are known to have survived into modern times; one has now disappeared, the other is a tenth-century manuscript originally from Corbie. The presumption is that it was very little known, and no one as yet has found any quotation from it in the middle ages. The writer's heresy does not account for its neglect;[6] traces of Pelagian doctrine in it are hardly obvious; the authorship was so far forgotten that bibliographers came to ascribe it to Rufinus, the great admirer of Origen! One might allege the difficulty of Julian's Latin; but language was no deterrent to a medieval scholar who really wanted to master the contents; witness the study of verbal translations from Greek and Arabic. Julian also wrote a commentary on the books of Solomon; this has been lost except for a quotation from the section on the Canticle by Bede, who must have had access to a copy.

---

[1] R. Devresse, op. cit. 3-4, 161-5. Pelagius himself does not seem to have accepted Antiochene principles of interpretation. He held that whatever in the Old Testament conflicted with his sense of equity and justice should be interpreted symbolically; see G. de Plinval, *Pélage, ses écrits, sa vie et sa réforme* (Lausanne, 1943), 210.

[2] Augustine, *Contra Iulianum*, i. 29: '. . . quod ratio arguit non potest auctoritas vindicare'.

[3] *P.L.* xxi. 959-1104; see G. Morin, 'Un ouvrage restitué à Julien d'Eclane: le commentaire du Pseudo-Rufin sur les prophètes Osee, Joël et Amos', *Rev. Bén.* xxx (1913), 1-24, for bibliography and notice on Julian's life and works.

[4] 'Theoria' is defined *P.L.* xxi. 971.   [5] ibid. 1049.

[6] Julian went down to history in a double capacity: as a heretic and opponent of St. Augustine and as a local saint, venerated for his generosity to the poor of his diocese in time of famine; see G. Morin, op. cit. 21.

Then there was a commentary on the Psalter of Antiochene origin which survives in incomplete form in two manuscripts both of the early middle ages, at the Ambrosian Library, Milan, and at Turin.[1] A quotation from the comment on Ps. lxxxii has come to light recently in an unexpected place, a commentary on the Psalter by Remigius of Auxerre (c. 900).[2] The rest of Remigius' exposition, with only one exception, which is not a verbal quotation from the Antiochene commentary,[3] as the first is, keeps to the Latin patristic tradition of explaining the Psalms as prophecies of Christ. The Antiochene fragment, having got so far, had now reached a *cul-de-sac*. Remigius had a wide circulation and his commentary was used by the compilers of the *Glossa Ordinaria*: they did not include either of the passages where he interprets the Psalm as referring to Old Testament history. The same thing happened to a remark by St. Jerome, with 'an Antiochene ring', in his prologue to Ecclesiastes; he says that Pss. lxiv and lxxi refer to Solomon according to the historical sense.[4] It did not catch the attention of medieval scholars, although it must have been read frequently.

Theodore's commentary on the Pauline Epistles was translated into Latin and had a great success because it was mistakenly ascribed to St. Ambrose. Under cover of this irreproachable name it survived in the form of extracts in many compilations. But the fact has more significance in

[1] Edited with its glosses in Old Irish in the Ambrosian MS. by G. I. Ascoli, 'Il codice Irlandese dell'Ambrosiana', *Archivio Glottologico Italiano*, v (1887). The authorship is composite; see A. Vaccari, 'In margine al commento di T. Mopsuesteno ai Salmi', Miscellanea G. Mercati, i, *Studi e Testi*, cxxi (1946), 173-98; M. L. W. Laistner, op. cit. (p. 15, n. 3).

[2] A. Vaccari, 'Il genuino commento ai Salmi di Remigio di Auxerre', *Biblica*, xxvi (1945), 98. The commentary exists in two recensions. Vaccari suggests that the passage in question may have been added to Remigius' original draft as it is only found in one of them. If so, it must have been an early interpolation; one of the MSS. listed by Vaccari is tenth-century. I looked up the passage in MS. Paris, Bibl. nat. lat. 546, fol. 126ᵛ.

[3] On Ps. lxxviii: 'Totus hic psalmus ad litteram intelligendus est nec eget allegoriarum mysteriis. Tantum enim fletus sanctorum historialiter commemorat, quibus temporibus Iude et fratrum eius deflebant eorum miserias et calamitates, qui ad sacrificia cum amara necessitate cogebantur. Potest etiam ex persona ecclesiastice congregationis accipi, deflentes miserias et mortes quas persecutores sanctis martyribus infligebant' (ibid., fo. 121ʳ⁻ᵛ). Remigius therefore is suggesting a double exposition, one for Old Testament history and one for Christian times. He goes on to explain the text of the Psalm in both senses. Ps. lxxxii, on the contrary, is only explained in the former sense.

[4] A. Vaccari, op. cit. (above, n. 1), 176-8.

the history of theology than in that of exegetical method. The Epistles did not lend themselves to an allegorical interpretation in any case; the most Alexandrian-minded of commentators would busy himself with the straightforward theological teaching contained in his text when he expounded St. Paul. So Theodore, disguised as Ambrose, could do nothing to alter the Latin approach to those books where allegorical interpretation was customary. The homilies of St. John Chrysostom in translation were also read and appreciated. He was by far the best-known representative of Antiochene principles in the west and, at the same time, the author who could teach his readers least about Antiochene exegesis. The great orator, as Julian of Aeclanum complained, proceeded 'rather by exhortation than by exposition'.[1]

Lastly, Junilius Africanus composed a little manual in Latin, soon after 551, translated from the teaching of a master at Nisibis, Paul the Persian: *Instituta regularia divinae legis*.[2] He gave a simple definition of the relations between the senses with rules for the interpretation of prophecy and metaphor. The chief modern authority on Theodore of Mopsuestia finds little of Theodore in the *Instituta regularia*, 'apart from a very slight section on the messianic Psalms'. The school of Nisibis derived from, but was not identical with, that of Antioch, and Junilius probably represented only one trend of its teaching.[3] However, the messianic Psalms presented one of the most important problems that confronted medieval Latin scholars; Theodore's doctrine on the subject could have given a decisive twist to their study of the Psalter. The *Instituta regularia* had a wider circulation than other works of Antiochene origin. Twenty-three manuscripts are known to survive. But their dates are significant: only one is claimed as twelfth-century and one other as fifteenth; the vast majority of copies are early. Records of the book in medieval library catalogues give the same impression; so do quotations in medieval writers.[4] Cassiodorus knew it; but he only quoted from it once in his commentary on the Psalter, so far as I can see. The passage is a definition of prophecy of an obvious and harmless kind.[5] It got into the

---

[1] *P.L.* xxi, 960.   [2] Ed. H. Kihn (Freiburg im Br.), 1880.
[3] R. Devresse, op. cit. 273-5. The correct form of the name is 'Junilus'; but it seems admissible to keep the traditional spelling here.
[4] M. L. W. Laistner, op. cit., 27-32.
[5] Junilius: 'Quid est prophetia? Rerum latentium praeteritarum aut

prologue to the Psalter in the *Glossa Ordinaria,* where it merges easily into the Latin tradition.[1] Aldhelm, the Anglo-Saxon scholar, knew the *Instituta regularia;*[2] but Bede did not use it. 'In the theological writers of the ninth century and after there are very few discernible traces of Junilius.'[3]

The evidence fits into an intelligible pattern. Much of the Antiochene material was irretrievably lost to the medieval Latin student. He never at any time had an opportunity to soak himself in the works of Theodore. On the other hand, enough material existed in the early middle ages to enable a Latin reader to learn at least the principles of Antiochene exegesis and to experiment with them for himself, if he wished. We shall see that some of the early Irish scholars availed themselves of the opportunity. But they were alone in doing so. The Antiochenes in fact were generally neglected.

The reason must be that our Latin student preferred the Alexandrian method to the Antiochene. The former satisfied a paramount emotional need and corresponded to a world outlook while the latter struck him as cold and irrelevant. The Antiochenes did not disappear from the patristic inheritance immediately, since they benefited from an overall veneration for the Fathers. Then came the whole-sale destruction of libraries, followed by a process of discrimination and sifting. Knowledge of the Fathers shrank within narrower limits and the Antiochenes tended to be left outside. When biblical scholarship revived in the twelfth century, exegetes would have been thrilled to learn of the Antiochene approach to the problems which were perplexing them. It would have offered them a Christian alternative in the conflict between Latin patristic and Jewish interpretations of the biblical prophecies. Later on, in the thirteenth century, the friars under the influence of Aristotle began to rediscover the spiritual value of 'the letter'. They

---

[1] Laistner finds 'a seeming reminiscence of Junilius in John of Salisbury' (*Policraticus,* i. 12, ed. C. C. Webb, i. 51). John is almost certainly quoting, not Junilius, but Cassiodorus in the *Glossa Ordinaria.*

[2] M. R. James, 'Two Ancient English Scholars', *Glasgow University Publications,* xxii (1931), 13.

[3] Laistner, op. cit. 31.

---

praesentium aut futurarum ex divina inspiratione manifestatio' (ed. Kihn, 473).

Cassiodorus: 'Sciendum est sane quod omnis propheta aut de praeteritis aut de praesenti aut de futuro tempore loquatur . . .' (*P.L.* lxx. 12).

could not guess that the Antiochenes had been before them.

Antiochene exegesis as a distinct method had been for-gotten by the time it would have been useful, forgotten beyond hope of recovery. It was missing from the vast amount of material to be 'received' in the twelfth and thirteenth centuries from Greek originals. We may therefore concentrate on the Alexandrians and on the Fathers of the Latin Church.

The allegorical method captivated the Latin world, and could be used more freely since it had ceased to be dangerous. Neither St. Hilary nor St. Ambrose regarded it as an in-strument of speculation as Origen had done. The Latin Fathers made their allegories conform to orthodox theology, which was more clearly defined than it had been in Origen's time. The educated Roman convert was a rhetor rather than a philosopher. The contrast between Christianity and pagan philosophy troubled him much less than the 'rustic simplicity' of the Scriptures, and their 'artless' style; he missed the conventions and carefully prepared flourishes that he was accustomed to. The allegorical exposition satisfied some of his longing for complexity and ingenuity. 'I don't know why', St. Augustine says, referring to the text of the Canticle: *thy teeth are like a flock of sheep* [iv. 2], 'I feel greater pleasure in contemplating holy men when I view them as the "teeth" of the Church, tearing men away from their errors and bringing them into the Church's body with all their harshness softened down, just as if they had been torn off and masticated by the teeth.'[1] He tells us how the allegorical interpretation in St. Ambrose's preaching drew him nearer to the Church.[2]

St. Ambrose made Philo Judaeus the basis of his com-mentary on Genesis, his only criticism being that Philo as a Jew could only understand the moral and not the allegorical sense; a Christian exegete must supplement him by finding types of Christ and his Church.[3] On the Hexaemeron he took the literal exposition from St. Basil, who represented the Cappodician school which stood midway between Alexandria and Antioch; but he added allegories and he used Origen for his commentary on St. Luke.[4] His inspiration and much of his material came directly from Alexandria.

St. Jerome passed on a more complicated tradition. He

---

[1] *De Doctrina Christiana*, ii. 6, trans. M. Dods.   [2] *Confessions*, v. 14; vi. 4
[3] *De Cain et Abel*, i. 4-5.   [4] See the edition of C. Schenkl, *C.S.E.L.* xxxii

drew material from many different sources; his interests changed and developed; he was too hurried to be consistent or systematic. At first the Alexandrian method attracted him, especially the translation of Hebrew names as a basis for the spiritual interpretation. Then the Origenist controversy warned him off an exaggerated use of allegory, though it did not prevent his continuing to quote Origen.[1] His own studies in Hebrew increased his interest in the letter. His last commentary, on Jeremias, is mainly literal.

Hence he uses 'every possible permutation' in his definition of letter and spirit and of the various senses.[2] The traces of the Antiochene distinction between allegory and *theoria* which have been found in his commentaries are confused and occasional.[3] In the same commentary he says in one passage that the spiritual sense is *founded* on the literal, and in another that we must *substitute* a spiritual sense when the literal is unedifying; the story of Judas and Tamar, therefore, is not literal truth but an allegory. In the same way he held that the Sunamite woman, who was brought to David in his old age, was a mere 'figure' of wisdom.[4]

But St. Jerome was more than a channel for Greek learning. He followed Origen's example in studying Hebrew and consulting Jews: in fact, he sometimes quotes the rabbinic traditions in his source without acknowledgment.[5] He went further, however, and herein lies the originality of his contribution to medieval culture. As a Hebrew scholar and humanist he brought the Bible closer to the Latin-speaking world. The Old Latin was an unliterary translation from the Septuagint; the Vulgate was based on the 'Hebrew Truth' as St. Jerome lovingly calls it. The language, 'where the rustic Latin of the first Christian centuries mingles with the Hebraising Latinity of St. Jerome',[6] was the beginning of a new era, when eastern poetry penetrated into the speech

---

[1] P. Courcelle, *Les Lettres grecques en Occident de Macrobe à Cassiodore*, 2nd edn. (Paris, 1938), has made a detailed study of Jerome's Greek culture and Greek sources, 37-115. His conclusions emphasize the extent of the debt to Origen, 88-101.

[2] L. Schade, 'Die Inspirationslehre des heiligen Hieronymus', *Biblische Studien*, xv (1910), 110.

[3] See A. Vaccari, op. cit. (p. 14, n. 2).

[4] *P.L.* xxv (1845), 1003; xxii. 527-8.

[5] G. Bardy, 'Les traditions juives dans l'œuvre d'Origène', *Rev. Bibl.* xxxiv (1925), 217-52.

[6] S. Berger, *Histoire de la Vulgate pendant les premiers siècles du Moyen Âge* (Nancy, Paris, Strasbourg, 1893), vii. See also F. Stummer, *Einführung in die lateinische Bibel* (Paderborn, 1928), 4-124.

of the western peoples. The prefaces to the translations, and some of the commentaries, bring the sacred writers to life. St. Jerome's scholarship gave him insight into their characteristics. There had been a tendency, which culminated in the Montanist heresy, to think of the biblical writings as dictated, in their every syllable, by God, the writers being mere passive instruments. St. Jerome, on the contrary, upheld a human element in inspiration; God speaks 'not in the ears of the prophet, but in his heart'; though God supplies the content, the language and the choice of metaphor depend on the writer's environment and education. He discusses the style of the Pauline Epistles: the Apostle was not, as many suppose, speaking from modesty when he declared himself to be 'unskilled in speech'; a Hebrew of the Hebrews and a Pharisee, he could not explain the depths of his meaning in Greek, and could barely find the words for what he thought. Neverthless his style was wonderfully effective; 'as often as I read him, I seem to hear, not words, but thunder'. He points out the idiosyncrasies of the Prophets: Isaias writes 'as a man well born, of urban speech, with no taint of rusticity'.[1]

St. Jerome left a tradition on one hand of fanciful spiritual, on the other of scholarly literal interpretation. Medieval students could take their choice. They could use his commentaries as a model for the invention of allegories or revere him in his other capacity: 'modernus ille synagoge alumpnus, totius litterature fundamentum, pater Ieronymus'.[2]

A further influence in favour of the letter was the work of 'Ambrosiaster' or 'Pseudo Ambrose', the 'great unknown' commentator, writing between 366 and 384, whose identity has remained a puzzle. He used Latin authors rather than Greek and his approach to Scripture was independent and matter of fact. Interested in the Jews, he had 'a real idea of historical method and development'. Allegory had little attraction for him.[3]

St. Augustine welded together these different elements into a philosophy of Bible study.[4] The *De Doctrina Christiana*

---

[1] L. Schade, op. cit. (p. 21, n. 2), 27 ff.; *P.L.* xxvi. 558; xxii. 502; xxviii. 771; Jerome develops Origen in his treatment of the Epistles; his treatment of the Prophets is original. See Schade, 17-21.
[2] See below, p. 187.
[3] See A. Souter, *The Earliest Latin Commentaries on St. Paul* (Oxford, 1927).
[4] P. Courcelle, op. cit. 185-93, has shown that Augustine knew and used some of the works of Origen in translation, as well as other Greek Fathers.

contains a summary of his whole position, considered in relation to exegesis. St. Jerome gave the medieval scholar his text and his learned apparatus; St. Augustine told him what his aim should be.

In so far as he was a Neoplatonist, St. Augustine put the spiritual sense above the literal. His world was 'a clear mirror where our thought sees in all things the reflection of God'.[1] The words of Scripture reflect their divine author, just as creation reflects its Creator. His world was a graded hierarchy where 'all beings are necessarily superior or inferior one to another by the mere fact of their being different';[2] so with the senses of Scripture. He defines man as 'a rational soul which uses a body', with the accent on the transcendence of the soul; so the spirit transcends the letter; their connection is tenuous and artificial, depending on the mechanical rules of allegory. As an original Christian thinker he gave the 'letter' a concrete chronological reality which it had never had before. The narrative of Scripture is fitted into a philosophy of history based on the Incarnation. St. Augustine accepted the historical truth of the letter more wholeheartedly than St. Jerome. We must believe in the fact; then and then only may we seek its spiritual meaning.

The only case where the fact, as related by the sacred writer, may be doubted is when it does not conduce to charity. St. Augustine stressed charity where the Alexandrians had stressed wisdom. The whole end of Bible study is to increase our love for God and our neighbour: 'We must meditate on what we read till an interpretation be found that tends to establish the reign of charity.'[3] Since charity implies purity and faith, 'whatever there is in the word of God that cannot when taken literally be referred either to purity of life or soundness of doctrine you may set down as figurative'.[4]

In his exegesis St. Augustine tries to steer a middle course between literal and allegorical exposition. He gives the literal sense a wide meaning, taking it to include metaphor.

[1] E. Gilson, *Introduction à l'étude de St Augustin* (Paris, 1931), 27.
[2] ibid. 74.   [3] *De Doctrina Christiana*, III. xv (23).   [4] ibid. x (14).

His theology was independent, however, and not tied to his sources, 193-4. The extent of Augustine's knowledge of the Greek language and researches into the Greek text is still a subject of controversy. See Courcelle, ibid. 137-53 and the review of his first edition by G. Bardy, *Revue du Moyen Âge latin*, i (1945), 312-18.

He prefers to give both a literal and a spiritual interpretation to the same text, the one signifying or prefiguring the other. He very seldom sacrifices the literal sense to a subjective spiritual interpretation. His feeling for history and his common sense suggest explanations conducive to charity, even where the narrative seems at first sight to be unedifying. Certain customs described in the Old Testament, such as polygamy, were permissible to primitive people; the sins of righteous men, such as David's adultery, are recorded in order to warn us against pride. There are exceptions, as when he explains that Jacob set up the rods before the flocks as a prophecy of Christ, not with the purpose of cheating his father-in-law,[1] which denies the story its historical significance. He gave his authority to the rules of Tyconius the Donatist for explaining contradictions and finding prophecies in Scripture in various fanciful and violent ways.[2] But on the whole St. Augustine made sacred history more alive and immediate, as St. Jerome had made the sacred writers.

In this way the medieval scholar's view of Scripture was determined. Sacred history unrolled itself before him, neatly divided into 'ages of man', beginning on the spring day of the Creation. He had a vivid perception of the story: the *Rule* of St. Benedict forbids that the books of Kings and the Heptateuch should be read in the evening, in case they might over-excite the hearers. The Old Testament characters were living and near to him. St. Gregory felt that his own anxieties, fevers and indigestion had specially equipped him to expound the sufferings of Job: 'Perchance it was this that Divine Providence designed, that I, a stricken one, should set forth Job stricken, and that by these scourges I should enter more perfectly into the feelings of one that was scourged.'[3] But this familiar procession of patriarchs and prophets, the Saviour and his Apostles, was the literal historical sense, which the scholar shared with the laity. Another procession walked beside it, more sharply outlined, darker or brighter. Here were the types of the spiritual interpretation, the Church and the Synagogue, virtues and

---

[1] *Quaestiones in Heptateuchum*, i. 93. A speech, a law, and a benediction are also interpreted as having no literal meaning, i.e. no relation to their historical context but only to Christianity, ibid. i. 123; ii. 90; v. 56.

[2] Tyconius was known to medieval students mainly through the *De Doctrina Christiana*. See F. C. Burkitt, 'The Book of Rules of Tyconius', *Texts and Studies* (ed. J. A. Robinson), i (1894), xxiv.

[3] *Moralia; Praef. in Iob* (Library of the Fathers), i. 10.

vices, the Old Testament's foreshadowings of the New. The layman was just able to perceive them. He saw them in windows and on the walls of churches; he heard hints of them in sermons. To move in their mysterious company was the special duty and privilege of the clerk. A twelfth-century poet defines theologians as those

> 'who compared the rod of Jesse
> to the virgin birth,
> or the bush of Moses' vision,
> or the fleece of Gedeon,
> wet with glassy dew.'[1]

We begin to realize the complexity of their study when we hear of simple people's mistakes. According to the spiritual sense, the raising of Lazarus prefigures the sacrament of penance; Lazarus signifies a man in mortal sin, who repents, confesses and receives absolution; this is a commonplace:

> 'After the raising of Lazarus it was said to the disciples: *Loose him*. By this it is clearly shown that God quickens a repenting sinner but he is never loosed save by the ministers of the Church.'[2]

An ignorant monk at St. Edmundsbury so confused the literal and spiritual senses as to teach in a sermon that *Lazarus died in mortal sin* and for that reason stank after three days![3]

We realize too from this example how deeply the spiritual interpretation will penetrate language, thought, politics, and finally everyday life. The types are so real and so familiar that they may be used as arguments from authority, as well as for illustration. Their influence may be beneficent or sinister. The Synagogue is always opposed to the Church in the allegorical interpretation as darkness to light, and gradually this type becomes identified with the living Jew, increas-

---

[1] K. Strecker, *Moralisch-satirische Gedichte Walters von Chatillon* (Heidelberg, 1929), Gedict. i. 9:

> qui aptabant virgam Jesse
> partui virgineo,
> seu rubum visionis,
> sive vellus Gedeonis
> sparsum rore vitreo.

[2] F. Bliemetzrieder, 'Trente pièces inédites d'Anselme de Laon', *Rech. Théol. anc. méd.* ii (1930), 70; derived from Pseudo-Augustine, *De Vera et Falsa Poenitentia, P.L.* xl. 1122.

[3] 'Electio Hugonis', *Memorials of St. Edmundsbury*, ed. T. Arnold (Rolls Series), ii. 60. It is a tract describing a disputed election, 1213-15.

ing, perhaps helping to create, his unpopularity.[1] Philo's 'wise architect' had built a prison for the Jewish people.

II. LECTIO DIVINA

The book of mysteries was also an encyclopaedia which contained all knowledge useful to man, both sacred and profane. St. Augustine accepted this Alexandrian concept and worked out its consequences for Christian education. Bible study is the highest kind of Christian learning. Since the content of Scripture is encyclopaedic, it calls for encyclopaedic knowledge in the student; hence all the resources of late-antique culture are brought to bear upon Bible reading.

From the point of view of scholarship it was a decadent culture. Fourth-century men of letters were concentrating on the reading and interpretation of classical literature; yet they were literal rather than literary in their approach to it. Professors expounded the poems of Virgil not as a whole, but, after a short introduction, piecemeal, line by line, or even word by word. They dwelt particularly on grammar, which was always their main preoccupation, then commented on the historical, mythological, or topographical details mentioned in the passage under review. Their comments reflected the contemporary state of science. Erudition, the accumulation of curious and marvellous facts, had become more interesting than the investigation of natural laws. These same tendencies reappear inevitably in patristic, and through them in medieval, commentaries on Scripture. The pagan learning which St. Augustine recommended could not include scientific method; he could only insist on the best training that the schools of rhetoric could supply: Scripture requires the same erudite treatment as the pagans give to Virgil.[2]

The sciences and liberal arts are necessary in so far as they contribute to an understanding of Scripture. The student needs language, grammar and history in order to understand the literal sense, dialectic to distinguish true doctrine from false, arithmetic for number symbolism, natural history for the symbolism of beasts and birds; rhetoric, the crown of the higher education, is necessary not only for his

[1] J. Parkes, *The Conflict of the Church and the Synagogue* (London, 1934).
[2] See on this subject H. Marrou, *St Augustin et la fin de la culture antique* (Bibl. des Ecoles d'Athènes et de Rome, cxlv, 1938).

own studies, but to enable him to teach and preach what he has learnt. The fourth book of the *De Doctrina Christiana* is a guide to preaching. *Lectio* and *praedicatio*, reading, teaching and preaching, are different aspects of the same process. We learn by sharing our learning.

Bible study includes the study of Catholic tradition which St. Augustine does not distinguish from Scripture. It is part of theology, and theology is Bible study; so is philosophy, since their purpose is the same. Scripture is the starting-point and the way to blessedness, which is the goal of Christian philosophy and is reached through love.

The various forms which patristic exegesis had taken showed how this programme might be realized. The four main categories go back to Origen. Textual criticism is represented by the *Hexapla*, and St. Jerome distinguished three kinds of exposition: the homily which was often preached, the tome or commentary, where Origen 'spread the sails of his genius to the wind and made for the open sea', and the *scholia*, short notes on isolated passages which presented special difficulty. The series of 'questions and answers', which the Fathers found in secular and Philonic literature and adapted, belong to much the same class as *scholia*.[1] The commentary was flexible enough to contain the three others within itself; and St. Augustine's four separate commentaries on the opening of Genesis showed how the same text could be used as a framework for different kinds of material. The *De Genesi contra Manichaeos* and the *De Genesi Opus Imperfectum* are mainly apologetic. The *De Genesi ad Litteram* is theological, philosophic, and speculative; it discusses the problems of Creation, and the last book is a treatise on vision, suggested by the 'deep sleep' cast upon Adam. The commentary on Genesis which closes the *Confessions* shows how exegesis might also be an act of prayer: 'the exercise of that joyful charity which comes of at last finding God and seeks to find him again in his works'. *Lectio* began and ended in *oratio*.

This was the foundation of the contemplative life, as it was lived by the Fathers of the desert and described to the West by St. John Cassian. His *Conlationes* supplement the *De Doctrina Christiana*; they are a monastic guide to Bible

---

[1] See G. Bardy, 'La littérature patristique des *Quaestiones et Responsiones* sur l'Écriture sainte', *Revue Biblique*, xli (1932), 210-36, 341-69, 515-37; xlii (1933), 14-30, 211-229, 328-352.

D

study. Cassian claims to record the sayings of simple, un-
learned men; but a certain literary artifice enters into his
presentation. He quotes Origen and has absorbed the teaching of a keen Origenist, who retired to the desert, Evagrius
of Pontus. His hermits are a mouthpiece for Alexandrian
mysticism,[1] with its stress on the Bible. 'The instancy of
reading' equals fasts and vigils as a weapon in the monastic
combat. As a beginner the monk can only drive out the
worldly memories that invade his head by meditation on
Scripture, prolonged and stable. Then, as he progresses in
the contemplative life, an understanding of Scripture will
be his reward.

The 'science of religious men' consists in two parts. The
first, practical, is purification and amendment of life, which
prepare the mind for Bible study better than any academic
learning; the second, theoretical, is the interpretation of
Scripture. Cassian distinguished four scriptural senses, one
literal or historical and three spiritual; he gave an example
which caught the fancy of the middle ages and became
classical: Jerusalem, according to history, is a city of the
Jews; according to allegory it is the Church of Christ;
according to anagoge it is that heavenly city of God *which is
the mother of us all* (Gal. iv. 26); according to tropology it is
the soul of man, 'which under this name the Lord often
threatens or praises'.[2]

As he grows in purity of heart, so the monk increases his
perception of the spiritual senses. It is a logical consequence.
Spiritually interpreted, Scripture mirrors the monastic
combat, with its satisfactions and its temptations. The 'eight
principal vices' that beset the monk are the seven nations,
which the children of Israel were commanded to destroy,
and the land of Egypt, which they were commanded to
leave. Egypt signifies the first vice, gluttony. The other
seven can be destroyed radically; as the seven nations might
be destroyed and their land possessed by Israel; but gluttony
never; it can only be abandoned; even the monk is obliged
to eat![3] Naturally the most experienced monks would be
the most expert in finding these spiritual meanings.

Following Cassian the founders of western monasticism
incorporated *lectio divina* or *lectio sacra* into their rules. St.

---

[1] P. Courcelle, op. cit. (p. 21, n. 1), 214-16; O. Chadwick, *John Cassian:
a Study in Primitive Monasticism* (Cambridge, 1950), c. i, v and *passim*.
[2] *Conlationes*, xiv. 8.   [3] ibid. v. 16-19.

Benedict allotted two hours on weekdays, three in Lent, to private reading; on Sundays it replaced manual work. The books of the Bible were to be distributed to the brothers for reading during Lent.[1] In his rule for nuns St. Caesarius of Arles ordered two hours of private reading a day, and reading aloud during spinning. Even when about their other work, the nuns were 'always to ruminate something from Holy Scripture'.[2] In addition to reading at meal times the religious would hear the lessons read out in church; and at the eight daily offices prescribed by St. Benedict they recited the whole Psalter each week.

From the fifth to the ninth century, roughly speaking, the conditions necessary for study in western Europe could only be found in a monastery. The scheme prescribed by St. Augustine would have to be realized, if at all, in the practice of *lectio divina* in the monastic routine. The two things were quite compatible. St. Augustine himself had drawn up a rule, and lived in common with his clergy. St. Jerome had been typically monastic in his devotion to *lectio divina*.[3] He and the group of women under his direction differed from the religious of the *Conlationes* only in that their Bible studies included scholarship, and that for St. Jerome 'to read without also writing' was 'to sleep'.[4] The *lectio divina* of western monasticism drew its inspiration from St. Augustine and St. Jerome as well as from Cassian. It meant something widely different from the pious exercise which is now known as 'spiritual reading'.

We can watch the fusion between the two traditions. St. Eucher of Lyons contrives to harmonize Cassian with St. Jerome by a clever manipulation of words; he slips *disputatio* into Cassian's definition of theoretical or contemplative science, so as to connect it with a comparison between the 'celestial philosophy' of Scripture and the physics, ethics and logic of secular learning which he found in St. Jerome.[5]

[1] A. Mundó, ' "Bibliotheca", Bible et lecture du Carême d'après S. Benoît', *Rev. Bén.* lx (1950), 65-94.
[2] *Statuta Sanctarum Virginum*, xviii, xix, xx. The reading centred in Scripture. A curious letter of the sixth century in Gaul, professedly written from one nun to another, is evidence of the zeal with which *lectio divina* and the spiritual interpretation were practised in convents. It is composed almost entirely of moralized quotations. *M.G.H., Ep.* iii. 716-18.
[3] See D. Gorce, *Lectio Divina* (Paris, 1925).
[4] St. Jerome writes to Pope Damasus: 'In your eyes to read without also writing is to sleep.' *Ep.* xxxvi.
[5] *Formulae Spiritalis Intelligentiae, Praef.*, ed. K. Wotke, *C.S.E.L.* xxxi. 3-6.

Cassiodorus shows his courtier's tact in reconciling Cassian with St. Augustine. The prologue of the *De Doctrina Christiana* defends the use of secular learning in Bible study against those who think they can understand Scripture by divine illumination, without any help from man; and this was not unlike the claim of the desert Fathers who instructed Cassian. Cassiodorus admits that God has sometimes granted understanding to simple people in answer to their prayers; but we must not tempt him by asking for miracles: 'let us pray that what is hidden may be revealed to us, and let us by no means desist from our studies'.

Cassiodorus had hoped to found a secular school for sacred studies. Since this proved to be impracticable he built a monastery, provided a library, and wrote the two books of the *Institutiones* to explain its uses. His magnificent and carefully planned collection included 'a whole armoury of translations from Origen', as well some of Clement of Alexandria. Although Vivarium disappeared and its library was dispersed or destroyed after his death, Cassiodorus' work for scholarship was by no means wasted. Apart from his own writings, some of the translation that he had made, the *Antiquities* of Josephus, for example, would be used for biblical studies all through the middle ages. Some of the actual manuscripts survived. They were taken to the papal library at the Lateran and thence to other places; some even reached Northumbria, where they were used by Bede.[1] To Cassiodorus the writings of the Fathers were rungs in the ladder which led up to *lectio divina* and heavenly contemplation.[2] He advised which commentaries should be read on which books, and gave a list of introductions to Bible study: Tyconius, Augustine, Hadrian, Eucher, Junilius. The second book of the *Institutiones* passes from theology to the seven liberal arts which were its necessary preparation. Cassiodorus provided a summary, of the kind that St. Augustine had recommended, to save the student from wasting time and enable him to embark on the higher wisdom as soon as possible.

[1] P. Courcelles, op. cit. 336-82.
[2] *Lib. i, Praef.*, ed. R. A. B. Mynors, *Cassiodori Senatoris Institutiones* (Oxford, 1937), 4.

Neither St. Jerome nor Cassian is mentioned by name but St. Eucher was comparing *Epp.* xxx, cxx with *Conlationes*, xiv. 1-4 and 8. St. Augustine describes the desert Fathers as 'viventes in orationibus, in lectionibus, in disputationibus'. *De Moribus Ecclesiae*, i. 69, *P.L.* xxxii. 1338. This may also have influenced St. Eucher.

His commentary on the Psalter represents a wonderfully conscientious, academic attempt to put his preaching into practice and to use the secular sciences as an aid to Bible study. He clarifies the literal sense by definitions of loving precision; the *cathedra* of Ps. i. 1 seems to have roused his memories of the Ostrogothic court:

> 'A *chair* is a form composed of matter, suitable for seating, which receives our curves softly from behind, and like a cunning receptacle enfolds us, bent into its lap.'[1]

He struggles to find the arts which, according to the Alexandrian tradition, pagan authors had originally learnt from Scripture. 'Schemes and tropes' in the Psalter are not obvious; but 'delicious fish are drawn from deep water and before they were caught no human eye had seen them'.[2] Cassiodorus was a patient fisherman:

> 'Ps. lxi. 1 is an *epitrochasmos* (and we had never noticed it though we say it so often!); Ps. xli. 17 is a *quinquepartite* syllogism, elaborately worked out; xliii. 15 is an *anaphora* or *relatio* . . . and so forth, on every page of the commentary: we are accustomed to hypallage, pleonasmos, synecdoche, climax, but epembasis, ethopoeia, auxesis, ennoematice, . . . are less familiar, with many others.'

He ends triumphantly:

> 'Lo we have shown that the series of Psalms is filled full with grammar and etymologies, with schemata, with the art of rhetoric, with topica, with the art of dialectics, with music, with geometry, with astronomy, and with the expressions peculiar to the divine law.'[3]

Cassiodorus expounding the 'letter' reminds one of a small child, importantly filling his bucket with water and pouring it out. He shows how barren a study it could be if it were undertaken without any more scientific equipment than the late-antique tradition could provide. St. Augustine, without knowing Hebrew, had dwelt on 'the expressions peculiar to the divine law'. He realized that the Old Testament had a beauty of its own, if it were judged independently of rhetorical standards; and he stressed the need for linguistic studies. But in the sixth century, *triste siècle*, all that a scholar could do was struggle to preserve his own Latin culture, and the

---

[1] *Com. in. Ps., P.L.* lxx. 28. [2] ibid. 20-1.
[3] J. Chapman, *St. Benedict and the Sixth Century* (London, 1929), 89, n. 2.

elementary things in patristic thought. The spiritual exposition, which takes up the greater part of Cassiodorus' commentary, gave more opportunity for this than the literal. After reading Cassiodorus it is no surprise to pass on to St. Gregory, the master of 'spiritual' exegesis, in whose words 'the keys to this art may best be found'.[1] They represent another attempt, by a greater man than Cassiodorus, to realize St. Augustine's teaching in the practice of *lectio divina*.

The *Moralia in Iob* originated in the monastic *collatio*, the daily conference[2] where the abbot preached and the monks were allowed to ask questions suggested to them by their reading. The *Homilies* on the Gospels and Ezechiel were preached to the clergy and people of Rome while St. Gregory was pope. In each case the exegesis depended on the audience:

'I know that very often I understand many things in the sacred writings when I am with my brethren, which, when alone, I could not understand . . . Clearly, as this understanding is given me in their presence, it must be given me for their sakes. Hence God grants that understanding increases and pride decreases, while I learn, on your behalf, that which I teach you. For, really, very often I hear what I am saying for the first time, just as you do.'[3]

Thinking of his audience, St. Gregory construes St. Augustine's teaching, that all knowledge useful to man is contained in Scripture, to mean that each text contains, or points him towards, what is useful to any particular man at any particular moment. Scripture resembles the wheels of the beasts in the vision of Ezechiel: *When those went these went, and when those stood these stood, and when those were lifted up from the earth the wheels were also lifted up together and followed them: for the spirit of life was in the wheels* (Ezech. i. 21): just so with *lectio divina*; it corresponds with the state of the student; it goes, stands, is lifted up with him, like the wheels, according as he is striving after the active life, after stability and constancy of spirit, or after the flights of contemplation.[4]

---

[1] Guibert of Nogent, *De Vita Sua*, ed. G. Bourgin (Paris, 1907), 66: '. . . Gregoriana dicta, in quibus artis huius potissimum reperiuntur claves . . .'
[2] St. Gregory gave the *Moralia* in their first form as lectures to the monks who had accompanied him on his mission to Constantinople, and who took refuge with him 'from the waves of earthly occupation' in the study and discussion of Scripture, enjoined by the *Rule* of St. Benedict. *Praef. in Iob*.
[3] *Hom. in Ezech*. II. ii, *P.L.* lxxvi. 949.
[4] ibid. I. vii, *P.L.* lxxvi. 847-8.

Thus the expositor, knowing the needs of his audience, is bound to make suitable provision, no matter what text he happens to have reached. St. Gregory sees that the solution lies in constant digression. Very good: to meander like a river is the ideal:

'. . . he that treats of sacred writ should follow the way of a river, for if a river, as it flows along its channel, meets with open valleys on its side, into these it immediately turns the course of its current, and when they are copiously supplied, presently it pours itself back into its bed. Thus unquestionably, thus should it be with everyone that treats of the Divine Word, that if, in discussing any subject, he chance to find at hand any occasion of seasonable edification, he should, as it were, force the streams of discourse towards the adjacent valley, and when he has poured forth enough upon its level of instruction, fall back into the channel of discourse which he had prepared for himself.'[1]

St. Gregory was preaching at a moment when civilization seemed to be condemned. He finished his homilies on Ezechiel with a barbarian army at the gates of Rome, when men returning with their hands chopped off told him that some were prisoners, others dead.[2] Spiritual instruction was what his audience needed, simple for the clergy and people, more advanced for the religious. The problems of biblical scholarship did not concern them. It was 'very superfluous' to inquire into the authorship of the book of Job; enough to know that the Holy Spirit was its real author; 'if we were reading the words of some great man with his epistle in our hand, yet were to inquire by what pen they were written, it would be an absurdity'.[3] St. Gregory reduces the literal exposition to a bare minimum. It consists mainly in doctrinal discussion: how to excuse the curses uttered by the holy man Job, or on the nature of prophecy. His originality lies in his adaptation and extension of the spiritual senses.

Their functions are described in a metaphor which medieval scholars accepted as definitive:

'First we lay the historical foundations; next by pursuing the typical sense we erect a fabric of the mind to be a stronghold of faith; and moreover as the last step, by the grace of moral instruction, we, as it were, clothe the edifice with an overcast of colouring.'[4]

[1] *Praef. in Iob* (op. cit., p. 18), i. 6-7.
[2] *Hom. in Ezech.* ii. x, *P.L.* lxxvi. 1072.   [3] *Praef. in Iob*, 15.   [4] ibid.

The 'typical' sense included Cassian's allegorical and anagogical sense, that is, the finding of types of the Church past and present, and of the Last Things. The finding of types was well designed to educate St. Gregory's hearers. It enabled him to connect a résumé of some doctrinal point to each passage, and to refute heresies — a traditional function of exegesis. The text Job xxviii. 19, *the topaz of Ethiopia shall not be equal to it* (to wisdom), means that 'the virtues of the Gentiles *shall not be equal to* the holiness of the Son of God'. It is an occasion for Gregory to explain the Catholic doctrine of the Incarnation and to warn his audience against heresies which deny our Lord's divinity.[1] The moral sections, on the other hand, contain his teaching on the religious life and on ethics. Here he finds what he requires in each text by his use of 'testimonies'. The brothers for whom Gregory wrote the *Moralia* had asked for an allegorical and moral interpretation, 'with the addition of somewhat yet harder, that I would crown the several meanings with testimonies, and that the testimonies, which I brought forward, should they chance to appear involved, should be disentangled by the aid of additional explanation'.[2] A 'testimony' is a 'parallel passage', which he adduces in accordance with the old rule that one passage in Scripture must be interpreted by comparison with others. The spiritual interpretation of his text suggests another text containing a word which has the same spiritual meaning as the first. This second text is then interpreted according to its spiritual meaning; this suggests another; and so on, until the commentator 'falls back into the channel of discourse which he had prepared for himself'. The 'testimonies' might be called the soft soil through which the discourse forces its way towards the valleys of seasonable edification.

To us, this is a most annoying system. Everything in St. Gregory's teaching is attached, however loosely, to the thread of the text, which precludes any attempt at coherence or logical arrangement. But if we take a series of two or three homilies, or one of the thirty-five books of the *Moralia*, we can see how suitable it was for educational purposes. In two or three addresses, or hours of study, St. Gregory's hearers or readers would get a series of lessons on doctrine, prayer and ethics, in a well arranged and carefully varied time-table.

[1] *Mor.* xviii. lii, *P.L.* lxxvi. 88-90.   [2] *Praef. in Iob*, op. cit. i. 5.

St. Gregory was following St. Augustine's instructions in putting whatever learning he possessed at the service of Scripture: rhetoric in the balanced rhythm of his sentences, which never failed in the gravest political crisis; study of the Fathers, religious experience, a deep knowledge of psychology, which he expressed in scriptural language by the medium of the three senses. This became so natural to him that even when he wrote a non-exegetical treatise, the *Liber Regulae Pastoralis*, on the duties of prelates, he conveyed his meaning by quoting and moralizing biblical texts. Exegesis is teaching and preaching. Teaching and preaching is exegesis. This was the strongest impression left by St. Gregory on medieval Bible study.

The spirit of intellectual curiosity which we miss in Gregory revived again both in the Spanish encyclopedist, St. Isidore of Seville, and in the Irish scholars of the seventh century. The effort of the Irish in particular to collect and understand the patristic writings led them to go behind the classic Latin sources. They knew and diffused the translation of the commentary on the Psalter deriving from Theodore of Mopsuestia of the Antiochene school; and the literal, rationalistic tendency of the Antiochenes shows itself strongly in the Pseudo-Augustine's *De Mirabilibus Sacrae Scripturae*,[1] written in the mid-seventh century. The author limits himself to the historical sense of scriptural miracles, since, as he says, to treat of their spiritual sense would demand 'many more books and longer toil'. He argues that God's work of creation was completed on the seventh day; since then God has governed his creation without making anything new; miracles, which are extraordinary acts of governance, can therefore be explained as 'the calling forth of some new principle which normally lies hidden in the depths of nature'.[2] He therefore tries to find the natural basis of the preternatural: the plague of Egypt which turned water into blood was a hastening of the slow process by which water becomes the blood or sap of a living organism, and similarly with the miracles of Christ.

The patristic tradition ends with the Venerable Bede, the last writer whom Roger Bacon was prepared to accept as an 'authority'. His predecessors had saved as much as they

---

[1] *P.L.* xxxv. 2146-2200.
[2] J. F. Kenney, *The Sources for the Early History of Ireland*, i (New York, 1929), 277.

could of the Fathers' teaching. Bede presented it to the
barbarians 'in simple language but with subtle sense'.[1] His
importance lies in his faithful presentation of the tradition
in its many aspects. His commentaries on the books of
Samuel and Proverbs are in the narrow, moralizing manner
of St. Gregory and Cassian:

> 'If we seek to follow the letter of Scripture only, in the Jewish
> way, what shall we find to correct our sins, to console or
> instruct us, when we open the book of the blessed Samuel and
> read that Elcana had two wives, we especially, who are celibate
> ecclesiastics, if we do not know how to draw out the allegorical
> meaning of sayings like these, which revives us inwardly, cor-
> recting, teaching, consoling?'[2]

Significantly, this class of Bede's exegesis proved especially
useful to St. Boniface in his missionary work.[3] Other commentaries are in the tradition of scholarship handed down by
St. Jerome and revived by the Irish. It is true that Bede was
a compiler, as indeed in many passages St. Jerome had been,
that like his Irish contemporaries he knew almost no Hebrew,
and less Greek and secular Latin literature than has been
ascribed to him.[4] But research is increasing our admiration
for his Christian Latin learning and his judicious handling of
his sources. Bede affected medieval scholarship in two ways;
he made a wide range of authors readily accessible and he
set an example of eager curiosity in their use. He had
St. Jerome's ardour for *lectio divina*, disciplined by the
Benedictine Rule.

---

[1] Alcuin, *Ep.* clxi.

[2] *Samuelis Prophetae Allegorica Expositio, Prol., P.L.* xci. 499-500.

[3] St. Boniface sends to England for 'what seems most useful as a manual and
as a help to our preaching, his [Bede's] works on the lessons for the year and
the Proverbs of Solomon'. *M.G.H., Ep.* iii. 398.

[4] E. F. Sutcliffe, 'The Venerable Bede's knowledge of Hebrew', *Biblica*, xvi
(1935), 300-6; M. L. W. Laistner, 'The Library of the Venerable Bede' in
Bede: his Life, Times, and Writings, ed. A. Hamilton Thompson (Oxford, 1935),
237-66. For a bibliography of studies on Bede's exegesis and relevant material
see W. Levison, *England and the Continent in the Eighth Century* (Oxford, 1946),
132-4, 143, n. 1. M. L. W. Laistner has given us a critical edition of Bede's
Expositio Actuum Apostolorum (Cambridge, Mass., 1939). For the diffusion of
Bede's exegetical works, see Laistner and King, *A Handlist of Bede Manuscripts*
(Ithaca, 1943), with the review by N. R. Ker, *Medium Aevum*, xiii (1944), 36-40.
See also, A. Vaccari, 'Scripsitne Beda commentarium in Iob?', *Biblica*, v (1924),
197-201.

CHAPTER II

MONASTIC AND CATHEDRAL SCHOOLS

I. THE CAROLINGIAN REVIVAL

T H E programme of the Carolingian revival, as stated by Charlemagne, was that of the *De Doctrina Christiana*: learning as a preparation for Bible study. Bible study meant the study of the sacred text together with the Fathers; the two kinds of authority were inseparable. The obstacles which Charles and his assistants had to overcome were general ignorance, acute local book famines and the corruption of the central subject for study, the sacred text. These two needs explain both the organized revision of the Vulgate text, and the form taken by Carolingian exegesis. Alcuin thought his revision of the Bible a suitable present for Charlemagne on the occasion of his coronation as emperor on Christmas Day, 800. The problems raised by the state of the text and the various attempts at revision made in this period are too complex to be discussed here,[1] and only the main outlines of Carolingian exegesis can be sketched in. The first necessity was to make the patristic tradition available and intelligible. Scholars achieved this end by adopting the methods of Bede. They prepared handy text-books or chains of select extracts. 'Picking flowers in the garden of the Fathers' or 'wavelets from the ocean', which began as early as the fifth century, had never been done so systematically.

To study the commentaries of Alcuin, Claudius of Turin, Raban Maur and Walafrid Strabo his pupil, to mention

---

[1] The most recent study with bibliography is by F. L. Ganshof, 'La Révision de la Bible par Alcuin', *Bibliothèque de l'Humanisme et Renaissance: Travaux et Documents*, ix (1947), 1-20. On the correction of the text by private enterprise by Theodulf of Orleans, see S. Berger, op. cit. (p. 21, n. 6), 145-84. Scholars recognize three principal families of MSS. of the Bible of the Carolingian period: the 'conservative' Spanish MSS.; the MSS. deriving from Theodulf's correction; the MSS. deriving from Alcuin's correction. The third class is the most numerous. English and more particularly Northumbrian texts seem to predominate in Alcuin's version; but there were other influences, some going back behind the Vulgate of St. Jerome to the Old Latin. Irish texts from the fifth to the ninth century are difficult to distinguish from Northumbrian; see A. Cordoliani, 'Le texte de la Bible en Irlande du Ve au IXe siècle', *Revue Biblique*, lvii (1950), 5-41.

outstanding names, is simply to study their sources. The few scholars who have undertaken this complicated and ungrateful work have shown that the compilers of the Carolingian period were less scientific than Bede, their 'master'. They worked in a more mechanical, less critical way. Instead of taking their quotations from the original patristic writers, they were apt to enlarge existing sets of extracts, or their memories of oral teaching derived from the Fathers, or to employ pupils to collect extracts for them. Hence the *pauperculus lector*, for whom, they tell us in their prologues, their work was intended, was getting his Fathers at third or fourth hand. We hear of occasional attempts to label the excerpts, so that he might at least know which Father he was reading. The labels easily dropped off in transcription, and there was no obligation to acknowledge debts to contemporaries. The choice of authors was more restricted; one no longer catches glimpses, as one does in reading Bede and Cassiodorus, of libraries with vast resources and of rare works, now lost, at the compiler's disposal.[1]

These were minor defects in a general scheme which succeeded. By the end of the ninth century a beginner could read almost any one of the biblical books with the help of a commentary pieced together from one or more of the Fathers. If his library were rich and up to date he could choose between a number of 'expositors', as the commentaries were called, for those books which had especial importance in doctrine or the liturgy, as Genesis, the first Gospel, the Pauline Epistles, and the Psalter.

The labour of compilation led in itself to more independent work. It showed up the inconsistencies and gaps in the patristic tradition. Scholars could hardly avoid comparing and then discussing, and filling in by their own compositions. Paschasius Radbertus and John the Scot, the two most original of the ninth-century commentators, both use the permission to 'discuss' which St. Eucher had given when he inserted *disputatio* into his definition of *lectio divina*. Paschasius

---

[1] The fundamental studies of exegesis from Alcuin to Paschasius Radbertus are by A. E. Schönbach, 'Ueber einige Evangelienkommentare des Mittelalters', *Sitzungsber. Wiener Ak.* cxlvi (1903); 'Otfridstudien', *Zeitschr. f. deutsches Altertum*, xl. (1896). See also A. Wilmart, 'Deux expositions d'un évêque Fortunat sur l'Évangile', *Rev. Bén.* xxxii (1920), 160, 174; 'Smaragde et le Psautier', *Rev. Bibl.* xxxi (1922), 350-9; P. Lehmann, 'Fuldaer Studien', *Sitzungsberichte der Bayerischen Akademie der Wissenschaften, Philos.-philol. und hist. Klasse* (Munich, 1925), No. 3, 52-3; J. Winaudy, 'L'œuvre littéraire d'Ambroise Autpert', *Rev. Bén.* lx (1950), 93-119. A complete list lies outside the scope of this book.

meant his twelve books on St. Matthew[1] to be a synthesis of authorities; in practice he sometimes compares and criticizes them; he draws out the doctrinal content of his text as fully as possible and defends the views he had put forward in the Eucharistic controversy.

John the Scot[2] had prepared for himself an acute problem of conflicting authorities by his studies in Greek theology, which diverged on many points from the Latin; and the metaphysical content of Scripture interested him more than allegories and moralities, as he openly said. What was he to do when a fascinating Greek theologian conflicted with the universally received testimony of St. Augustine? One alternative was to give both explanations, leaving no doubt as to his real preference by a turn of phrase; another was to reconcile the two, showing that fundamentally there was no disagreement; the boldest course was to discuss and select, admitting that as human authorities the Fathers stood below the divine authority of Scripture. The surviving fragment of John's commentary on the Fourth Gospel teems with arguments and discussions, which begin with the prophetic *quaeritur*.

To pass from the brilliant John to his contemporary, Haimo, is an anticlimax, Haimo being an obscure person, about whom we know nothing, except that he was probably a monk at Auxerre.[3] His commentaries (written about 840-60) are important because they were widely read from the tenth to the twelfth century, and because they give substance to the Carolingian revival. In Haimo we have a commentator who lacks the originality of John the Scot or Paschasius, and who yet contrives, in his humble way, to work along the same lines as they do. 'The bonds of tradition

---

[1] *P.L.* cxx. 31-992.

[2] His two exegetical works are a homily on St. John i. 1-14, and a commentary on St. John which was probably complete but has only survived in fragments. *P.L.* cxxii. 283, 297. See M. Cappuyns, *Jean Scot Erigène: sa vie, son œuvre, sa pensée* (Louvain, Paris, 1933), 222-32.

[3] On the Haimo question see E. Riggenbach, 'Hist. Studien zum Hebräerbrief', *Forschung. z. Gesch. des neutest. Kanons*, ed. T. Zahn, viii (Leipzig, 1907), 41-201. The author shows that commentaries on the Pauline Epistles, Isaias, the Minor Prophets and the Apocalypse, and the Canticles are almost certainly to be attributed to Haimo of Auxerre, the master of Heiric of Auxerre, instead of to Remigius of Auxerre or to Haimo of Halberstadt as is usually done. These commentaries are printed in *P.L.* cxvi and cxvii. The commentary on the Psalter printed with them is spurious, also those on Joel and Amos. Haimo's genuine commentaries on Joel and Amos are printed under the name of Remigius (Max. Bibl. xvi). Fragments of a commentary on Genesis have been discovered in a Berlin MS. (Rose, ii. 3).

are not yet broken, but they begin to loosen, and to leave space for independent judgement and investigation.'[1] Haimo stands on the line that divides the compiler of select extracts from the author of a commentary. His method is to give a choice of explanations for each text, and occasionally to raise and answer questions. Significant extracts from his teaching were published by his pupil, Heiric of Auxerre. Their title in the manuscript is *Scolia Questionum*. Interspersed among single texts of which each has a short explanation, we find questions, and a rudimentary concordance of conflicting texts.[2] They revived a type of patristic exegesis which had many potentialities.

Haimo and Heiric, following on Paschasius and John the Scot, prove that theological discussion was becoming a normal part of exegesis. A study of the unpublished commentaries of Remigius, the pupil of Heiric, might show us the movement developed a stage farther.

Up to date we have only a paper on his exposition of the Psalter.[3] Remigius evidently aimed at being 'short and clear'; he does not digress into theological discussions. Some of his 'moralities' are interesting as anticipating later methods. References to contemporary groupings of society break into the traditional abstractions: bishops, monks, canons and laymen figure in his comment on the first Psalm.[4] But Remigius takes us to our next point: the development of biblical scholarship. He discusses variant readings, making an occasional comparison between the Gallican version, which he takes as his text, and 'the Hebrew', which seems to mean

---

[1] Riggenbach, 56.

[2] MS. Bibl. Nat. 8818 (11th cent.), ff. 29ᵛ-44ᵛ. See L. Traube, *Rheinisches Museum* (1892), xlvii. 559-61. Riggenbach, op. cit., pp. 187-97, prints a selection of passages from the *Scolia* beside parallel passages from the commentaries of Haimo. The resemblance is striking; but Heiric's extracts are not taken verbally from the commentaries; in some cases he might have been excerpting from either, or both, of two passages in Haimo, where the same matter is treated. It is also quite possible that the *Scolia* represents jottings from lectures, or excerpts from Heiric's notes of his master's lectures. In a poem prefixed to the extracts he tells us that they are taken from his master Haimo.

[3] A. Vaccari, 'Il genuino commento ai Salmi di Remigio di Auxerre', *Biblica*, xxvi (1945), 52-99. For his commentary on Genesis, see J. de Blic, 'Walafrid Strabon, etc.' *Rech. Théol. anc. méd.* xvi (1949), 19, n. 40.

[4] A. Vaccari, op. cit. 73: 'Unus ordo electorum erit qui non iudicabitur et salvabitur, quales sunt apostoli ac perfecti monarchi, necnon et illi qui sua pro Domino dimiserunt. Hi tales non iudicabuntur, sed cum Domino ceteros iudicabunt. Alius ordo electorum erit qui iudicabitur et salvabitur, quales sunt boni canonici et laici, qui de facultatibus suis egentibus tribuerunt . . .' For the meaning of 'canonici' in the early Middle Ages see J. C. Dickinson, *The Origins of the Austin Canons, etc.* (London, 1950), 12-25.

the Hebrew text rather than the *Hebraica* translation of St. Jerome. He knew enough Greek to write a few Greek words in Greek letters, independently of his sources.

The initial step in the progress of biblical science was to work out the patristic distinction between letter and spirit. The distinction itself was bound to relegate the 'letter' to an inferior place; but before it could be even cursorily expounded, commentators had to decide what the letter was. Biblical scholarship would have no future if metaphor, prophecy and parable were to be included in the subjective 'spiritual' exposition.

The patristic tradition had no agreement as to the meaning of 'literal' and 'historical'. St. Gregory said that history was the foundation of allegory, yet he sometimes denied the historical sense; St. Augustine admitted that in rare cases one might deny a literal meaning in favour of the allegorical. The Thomist solution of the difficulty, that the literal sense is the whole meaning of the inspired writer, and the spiritual the significance which God has given to sacred history, would hardly have occurred to ninth-century scholars; they generally thought of Scripture as a letter addressed to them by God;[1] the evangelists were commonly represented by artists as writing at the dictation of an angel or the Holy Spirit. In default of the Thomist, some other way of distinguishing the senses had to be found.

Angelom of Luxeuil discovered not only the usual three, but seven senses, in the books of Kings and 'many other books'.[2] This is not, as it is sometimes supposed to be, a comic piece of over-elaboration; it is a real attempt to face the difficulties. The first sense is historical, that is, plain straightforward teaching: for example, *Obedience is better than sacrifices* [I Reg. xv. 22]; the second sense is allegorical, having no literal sense, like the girl brought to David in his old age [III Reg. i. 1-4], who signifies wisdom; the third sense is a mixture of the first two; it is literally true and also has an allegorical meaning, like the story of David and Bethsabee. The last two categories have evidently been invented by Angelom in order to harmonize the different treatment which St. Jerome and St. Augustine had ac-

---

[1] See St. Gregory quoted above, p. 33, and Alcuin, *Ep.* xxi. Agobard of Lyons preferred St. Jerome's view (see p. 22), *Liber adversus Fredegisum*, *P.L.* civ. 165-7.

[2] *Com. in Reg., Praef., P.L.* cxv. 245-6.

corded to these two female characters; St. Jerome said that the girl was merely a symbol, St. Augustine that Bethsabee was an historical character. The fourth sense contains teaching concerning God; the fifth is parabolic, that is, a contradiction with a mystical meaning;[1] the sixth concerns the first and second coming of Christ, the seventh moral teaching. Angelom's purpose seems to be to avoid the 'allegory or history?' problem by means of subdivisions.

John the Scot achieved more lucidity by his twofold division: (i) mystery or allegory; that is, historical event or institution, like the old Law; (ii) symbol, which includes metaphor, parable, doctrinal teaching. The first has both a literal and a spiritual meaning, the one for the simple, the two for the wise; thus the old Law prefigures the new. The second must be understood in the same way by all Christians alike, and the simple must believe, even if they cannot fully grasp the meaning.[2] John had worked his way to a conception of parable and metaphor which was not unlike the Antiochene *theoria*. He saw, too, that the whole of Scripture had a primary sense, to be accepted by believers, which included both history and poetry or doctrinal teaching, and that sacred history had in addition an allegorical sense.

Paschasius tacitly accepts the principle that the primary sense includes prophecy and metaphor. He steers a triumphant course through the difficult book of Lamentations, first briefly explaining the literal sense, which includes an explanation of metaphor, then constructing allegories and moralities on the basis of the metaphorical letter. Hence metaphor and prophecy have both (i) a literal and historical sense, intended by the prophet, (ii) a spiritual sense, discovered by the commentator.[3] This solution of the difficulty was generally received.

---

[1] This was a traditional method of harmonizing discrepancies in Scripture. Angelom gives the example of the title of Ps. xxxiv which has *Abimelech*, whereas in I Reg. xxi. 12, the name is *Achis*. The mystical interpretation of the name explains why the Psalmist used it instead of Achis.

[2] *Com. in Evan. Iohan.*, P.L. cxxii. 341-8.

[3] To give one example: *Com. in Lam.*, P.L. cxx. 1079-80: *Sordes eius in pedibus eius*, i. 9.
   (i) 'non quod ad litteram solummodo eam [Ierusalem] lugeat tantus propheta, eo quod sordidos gesserit pedes, quod frivolum satis videri potest, sed quia secundum interiorem hominem pollutos habeat gressus . . . Habuit autem et Synagoga pedes suos . . . In quibus profecto quia sordes eius erant, scelera videlicet et delicta, non *est recordata finis sui*. . . .'
   (ii) 'Mystice autem, nostra Ierusalem sordes gestat in pedibus: quia in huius vitae solitudine, nemo sine squalore incedit vitiorum. . . .'

In spite of the general preference for allegorical and moral senses, there were some interesting essays in literal interpretation. Raban improved on Bede by finding a literal as well as a spiritual exposition for the books of Kings. He collected scattered references from the Fathers and from the Jewish historian Josephus, and used the works of a Jew of 'modern times' learned in the Law.[1] This last reference has been traced to the author of the anonymous *Quaestiones Hebraicae in libros Regum et Paralipomenon*,[2] written on the model of St. Jerome's *Quaestiones Hebraicae in Genesim*, which give Hebrew traditions and compare the Hebrew text with the Vulgate. The author seems to have been a Christian who consulted Jews; he also left anonymous glosses on various Old Testament books and a short commentary on the Canticle of Debbora.[3]

Christian of Stavelot wrote a commentary on St. Matthew which, he tells us, was intended to be mainly historical. This is an unambitious little work, addressed to beginners, but interesting on account of the author's careful explanation of the grammatical sense and his attempts to illustrate the text by topical allusions, drawn sometimes from the surrounding country-side.[4]

Linguistic studies developed. Already the manuscripts of the Bible corrected by Alcuin's contemporary, Theodulf, bishop of Orleans, show traces of comparison with the Hebrew text.[5] Remigius has shown us that such comparisons were not exceptional. There were many attempts by scholars to learn at least the Hebrew alphabet. An Irishman of the ninth century, perhaps Sedulius Scotus, wrote a treatise in the form of a letter on the translation of the Psalter from Greek into Latin and on its textual emendation. The writer had a good knowledge of Greek. The emended text of the Psalter, with his prefatory letter, survives in three carefully written copies of the ninth and tenth centuries. A Greco-Latin Psalter, showing the text in parallel columns, was written in 909 at the Abbey of St. Gall, in the abbacy of Solomon III. It has been suggested that St. Gall may have

[1] J. B. Hablitzel, 'Hrabanus Maurus', *Biblische Studien*, xi (1906), 14-15.

[2] *P.L.* xxiii. 1329.

[3] *Quam notitiam*, 1-4. L. Ginsberg, *Die Haggada bei den Kirchenvatern*, I: *Die Haggada in den ps.-hier. Quaestiones* (Amsterdam, 1899), v. 105; *passim*.

[4] M. L. W. Laistner, 'A Ninth-Century Commentator on the Gospel According to Matthew', *Harvard Theological Review*, xx (1927), 129-49.

[5] E. Power, 'The lost ninth-century Bible of Carcassone', *Biblica*, v (1924), 197-201.

E

had contacts with Greek-speaking monks from southern Italy, who were driven north by attacks from the Saracens, and who may have saved some of their manuscripts.[1] John the Scot compared the Greek with the Latin text of the Fourth Gospel and found the original 'more significant'.[2] Greek scholarship at this period probably reached a higher point, at least in relation to exegesis, than it would do until towards the end of the thirteenth century.

Nevertheless, one should not exaggerate. John the Scot's commentary on the *De coelesti hierarchia* of Pseudo-Dionysius reveals a lack of elementary library facilities which held up the would-be student of Greek. John has to expand a biblical allusion in his author by quoting from the Latin Vulgate instead of from his author's text: 'For we have no Septuagint at hand'.[3] If a hellenist as enthusiastic as John the Scot was unable to find a reference book so essential to his purpose, access to the Greek text of the Old Testament must have been rare indeed.

The scholars of the eighth and ninth centuries had laid down the two lines, 'questioning' patristic authorities, and studying Hebrew, on which medieval exegesis would develop. Then came a sudden interruption. After the death of Remigius of Auxerre, about 908, there is no important commentary, and a dearth even of compilations, for about a century and a quarter. Holy abbots, as their biographers tell us, were still devoted to *lectio divina*, and we have un-verifiable references to their study of Hebrew; they left very little written exegesis. The cathedral schools, which were improving their organization at this time, did as little for biblical studies as the monastic.

It is a dramatic pause in the history of Bible studies and we should miss its significance if we explained it away as the demoralizing effect of war and Viking invasion. They certainly made scholarship difficult; but the real reason was a shift of interest. The Cluniac and other tenth-century

---

[1] A. Allgeier, 'Exegetische Beiträge zur Geschicte des Griechischen', ibid. xxiv (1943), 261-88. Note also the use of Greek characters for Greek words taken from the commentary of St. Jerome in the gloss on Isaias written at St. Gall in the ninth or tenth century, now MS. St. Gall 41; a specimen has been printed by J. de Blic, 'Walafrid Stabon et la Glossa Ordinaria', *Rech Théol. anc. méd.* xvi (1949), 22-3.

[2] M. Cappuyns, op. cit. (p. 39, n. 2), 225.

[3] *P.L.* cxxii. 245: 'Breviter commemorat visionem prophetae, quae sic in hebraica veritate scripta est; Septuaginta enim prae manibus non habemus, quos sequitur Dionysius. . . .'

religious reformers emphasized the liturgy at the expense of study. As the offices multiplied, *lectio divina* moved out of the cloister into the choir. This is no mere metaphor: it could actually happen. We hear of a monk of exemplary piety who always carried a glossed Psalter, so as to study the glosses while chanting the Psalms. If he came to a phrase that he did not understand, his eyes would at once turn to the glosses.[1] Plainsong was slow enough at this period to allow of meditation on the words as they were chanted.[2] Creative energy went to the invention of liturgical poetry and drama, to chronicles and lives of saints of the Order. The Cluniac abbots in their sermons and meditations concentrate on the dramatic, emotional aspect of Scripture. Their method might be called 'exclamatory';[3] it recalls the pious ejaculations inserted into their liturgy. Meanwhile the masters, in the cathedral schools especially, were more interested in the arts and sciences than in theology. Remigius, who left glosses on at least three books of the Bible, as well as on the grammarians and poets, shows a balance which his successors lost. Williram, abbot of St. Ebersberg, writing about 1060, complains that men who have learnt grammar and dialectic think them sufficient and neglect the Scriptures; those who have mastered theology bury their talent; they mock at the others' mistakes in reading and singing, without doing anything to instruct them or to correct their faulty books.[4]

This does not mean that the programme of the *De Doctrina Christiana* was abandoned for ever. It was being carried out in the lives of several generations, rather than in the life of the individual scholar as St. Augustine and Charlemagne had intended. After the 'alogical' period of the seventh and eighth centuries, scholars had begun to rediscover dialectic. During the tenth and eleventh centuries they learnt to handle it and to realize what it meant. Rhetoric as understood by Cassiodorus could be used as an aid to Bible study without any danger to the student's faith; the only risk was frivolity. Dialectic could be turned against Christian doctrine; and grammar in the hands of a trained logician could

[1] Peter the Venerable, *De miraculis*, i. 20, *P.L.* clxxxix. 886, quoted by J. Leclercq, *Pierre le Vénérable* (Saint Wandrille, 1946), 109.
[2] S. A. Van Dijk, 'Historical Liturgy and Liturgical History', *Dominican Studies*, ii (1949), 180-1.
[3] See especially St. Odilo, *Sermones*, *P.L.* cxlii. 991-1036; William of St. Bénigne of Dijon, *Opera* (ed. Levis, 1797), 96-116.
[4] 'Prologus in Cantica', ed. J. Seemüller, *Quellen und Forschung. z. Sprach- und Culturgesch.* xxviii (1878), 1-2.

raise complicated problems. Otloh of St. Emmeran found 'dialecticians simple enough to hold that Scripture should be construed according to the authority of dialectic, and to believe in many passages in Boethius rather than Scripture. Following Boethius they reproach me for ascribing the name of "person" to anything but rational substance'.[1]

When original written exegesis began again towards the middle of the eleventh century, it had gained by the long preparation. Commentators brought to their studies a fresh awareness of difficulties, with a new and more forceful technique.

II. THE GLOSS

We do not know who began it. The writings of these pre-Parisian commentators were to the Paris masters of the later twelfth and the thirteenth centuries very much what his own undergraduate essays are to a don. They have served their purpose and either gone into the waste paper basket or been put away and forgotten. Eleventh- and early twelfth-century exegesis survives mainly in extracts and quotations. We have references to lost works by famous scholars on the one hand; on the other we have anonymous works which show the characteristics of the period. Our problem is how to co-ordinate them. We have to eke out our knowledge by guesswork, and at present it is in that precarious state when a fresh discovery may upset all our ideas.

The hopeful sign is that fresh discoveries are being made, which point to unsuspected activity. The gloomy Williram, who knew only the works of Lanfranc among contemporary exegetes, was behind his times; we must not allow him to mislead us. We are beginning to see a great movement. Though we cannot yet discern the detail, we can trace its outline, at least provisionally.

The first step is to reconstruct the succession of schools and the personnel of the masters. By the eleventh century the cathedral schools have become more important than the monastic, with the exception of Bec under Lanfranc and St. Anselm. The eleventh-century schools are apt to have less stability than those of the Carolingian period. So much depends on the individual teacher, who passes from one

[1] *Dialogus de Tribus Quaestionibus, Praef., P.L.* cxlvi. 60.

cathedral to another. The typical Carolingian scholar has left solid traces in the *Gesta Abbatum* of his monastery; he ends his career as a bishop whose doings are officially recorded. The master of this later period is elusive both in his movements and in his character.

In looking for the beginning, one naturally turns to the outstanding teacher of the early eleventh century, St. Fulbert of Chartres (d. 1028). We know that he expounded Scripture to his pupils. We know that concise and literal exposition of grammatical and logical text-books was a feature of his teaching, and of his school.[1] We cannot help suspecting that it may have influenced his exposition of the sacred text. Our suspicions are heightened by fragments of a gloss on the Pauline Epistles which have just come to light under the name of 'Berengar'.[2] This is almost certainly St. Fulbert's pupil, Berengar of Tours, who is well known for his controversy with Lanfranc on the Eucharist. Berengar is sometimes referred to as a 'heresiarch'; but this is seeing him out of perspective. The fragments of his work on the Epistles give us concrete evidence for the 'strenuous vigilance in understanding and expounding Scripture' which was praised by his friend, Drogo of Paris, after a visit to Berengar at Tours, about 1040.[3] They explain afresh the reputation for holiness and learning, which his heresy does not seem to have affected.

The Berengar fragments are contained in several large collections of glosses on the Pauline Epistles, which include glosses ascribed to 'Drogo' and 'Lanfranc'. All the other glosses in these collections are either ascribed to the Fathers or are anonymous. A comparison between the Berengar, Drogo, and Lanfranc glosses shows that the three scholars worked on much the same method. 'Drogo', perhaps, may have been Berengar's friend, Drogo of Paris, who was a person of standing in the learned world. With Lanfranc's glosses we reach terra firma; they can be identified with Archbishop Lanfranc's. He had come from Italy to France to study and he seems to have begun to learn theology under

---

[1] A. Clerval, *Les Ecoles de Chartres au Moyen Âge* (Paris, 1895), 94-103, 108-16. The sermon ascribed to Fulbert, *P.L.* cxli. 278-306, is spurious; see J. Chatillon, 'Le contenu, l'autenticité et la date du *Liber exceptionum*, etc.', *Revue du Moyen Âge latin*, iv (1948), 364. No authentic work by Fulbert on Scripture has been discovered.

[2] On Berengar, Drogo, and Lanfranc see B. Smalley, 'La Glossa Ordinaria', *Rech. Théol. anc. méd.* ix (1937), 372-99.

[3] A. J. Macdonald, *Berengar and the Reform of Sacramental Doctrine* (London, 1930), 32.

Berengar.[1] Here, then, we have a possible succession. It is very tempting to make Berengar the centre of a movement which derived from his master St. Fulbert of Chartres, and which his pupil Lanfranc continued at Bec and Caen (1043-5 to 1070).

Then we have St. Bruno of Chartreux teaching at Rheims before he withdrew from the world in 1086. His scholastic career has been little studied. He expounded the Psalter and the Pauline Epistles.[2] Two glosses on the Psalter, which depend directly on his, suggest that he may have had an important influence.[3]

Then we have the certainly important, but exasperatingly mysterious Master Manegold, teaching at Paris, *modernorum magister magistrorum*. He retired to the house of canons regular at Lautenbach and died about 1110. We know him well as a political theorist, supporting the Church in her struggle against the Imperialists; we know him, too, as a master of arts, whose works on grammar and rhetoric were formative. His exegesis is known only from an anonymous gloss (Pseudo-Bede) on the Psalter which has been plausibly ascribed to him,[4] and about two-thirds of a column in one manuscript headed *Manegaldus in glosis super apostolum*, evidently an extract from his lost gloss on the Pauline Epistles.[5] We have to treat him as the X of our equation until this gloss has been recovered.

Manegold's connection with the investiture contest points us down a tempting byeway. Scholars in Italy who rallied to the papal cause employed their commentaries as weapons in polemic. The court of Countess Matilda of Tuscany pro-

---

[1] R. W. Southern, 'Lanfranc of Bec and Berengar of Tours', *Studies in Medieval History presented to F. M. Powicke* (Oxford, 1948), 27-48, discusses the evidence for Lanfranc's early life and analyses the thought of the two scholars.

[2] *P.L.* clii, cliii.

[3] B. Smalley, 'Gilbertus Universalis Bishop of London and the Problem of the *Glossa Ordinaria*', *Rech. Théol. anc. méd.* viii (1936), 51-60; 'La Glossa Ordinaria', ix. 375, n. 30.

[4] G. Morin, 'Le Pseudo-Bède sur les Psaumes et l'opus super Psalterium de Maître Manegold de Lautenbach', *Rev. Bén.* xxviii (1911), 331-40; B. Smalley, 'Gilbertus Universalis', op. cit. viii. 52, n. 93; A. Wilmart, 'Un commentaire des Psaumes restitué à Anselme de Laon', *Rech. Théol. anc. méd.* viii (1936), 326.

[5] MS. Laud. Misc. 216, fo. 4ᵈ: Manegaldus in glosis. *Inc.* Filius diversus est in persona a patre et non est diversus in essentia. *Expl.* De huiusmodi dicitur quicquid in Deo est, Deus etc. See O. Lottin, 'Manegold de Lautenbach source d'Anselme de Laon', *Rech. Théol. anc. méd.* xiv (1947), 218-23. Dom Lottin points out that a copy of this lost work was entered in a catalogue from Cremona dated 1201. There was another at Bury St. Edmunds; M. R. James, 'On the Abbey of St. Edmund at Bury', *Cambridge Antiqu. Soc. 8°* xxviii (1895), 10.

vided shelter and patronage. The biblical studies of this *milieu* illustrate the way in which political controversy sharpened the wits and led to a closer scrutiny of the sacred writings. The use made by Gregory VII of proof texts, generally moralized, is well known to historians. It is just one manifestation of a movement to review the Bible in the light of contemporary politics for the defence of the Church. Devotion and zeal for learning entered into the movement too. But the Italians seem to have had no direct influence on the northern schools. The themes of sun and moon and of the two swords, brought forward to prove the superiority of Church to State, became commonplace in exegesis without needing to be lifted from any particular author. So we must not allow ourselves to be diverted to Rome or Tuscany.[1]

From Paris we pass straight to Laon, whose cathedral, perched high on its rock, rises with astonishing definiteness and abruptness from the surrounding plain. In the same way, the school of Master Anselm of Laon and Ralph his brother dominates the intellectual life of the early twelfth century. Their school was flourishing about 1100; Anselm died in 1117, Ralph in 1134 or 1136. We do not know where either of them had studied, though it now seems that Anselm borrowed from Manegold:[2] borrowing always makes one scent a master-pupil relationship. Their lectures were attended by almost every contemporary theologian of any standing, and Anselm at present is attracting more attention than any other 'master of the sacred page'. It is at Laon that we find the first concerted effort towards theological systematization. The *Summa Theologica* traces its formal pedigree back to Laon. Modern scholars are occupied in assembling the writings which derive from the school, in trying to distinguish their relationship and to separate Anselm's work from his pupils'. They have shown us how far-reaching his influence was, and have established a direct connection between Laon and the later schools of Paris. It begins to look like a circle: Paris (school of Manegold), Laon, Paris.

[1] In my first edition I refused even to glance in this direction; but the study by Dr. B. Bischoff on John of Mantua was exciting enough to deflect me: 'Der Canticumkommentar des Johannes von Mantua für die Markgräfin Mathilde', *Lebenskrafte in der abendlischen Geistesgeschichte. Dank- und-Erinnerungsgabe an Walter Goetz*, ed. W. Stammler (Marburg/Lahn, 1948), 24-48. See also B. Gigalski, *Bruno, Bischof von Segni, Abt von Monte Cassino: sein Leben und seine Schriften* (Münster i.W., 1898).

[2] O. Lottin, loc. cit.

'Much remains to be done before we can hope for an *Anselme de Laon: sa vie, son œuvre, sa pensée*': I wrote this some twelve years ago. It has become clear in the meantime that such a title would be impossible. The most we can hope for is a book about the school of Anselm. The Master was one of those scholars who sink their own personality in team-work. This power to co-operate seems to have been the dominant trait in his character, for we do get a positive picture emerging from the universal expressions of reverence and praise. Little as we know of him, it is more than we know of Bruno or Manegold; and it suggests a more sympathetic figure than the restless Berengar or the legally-minded Lanfranc.[1]

Anselm had the combination of strength of character, clear judgment and peaceful disposition which is too rare for the comfort of its possessor. Peter the Chanter, writing perhaps fifty years after his death, still laments that Master Anselm was not permitted to finish the great work of glossing the whole Bible which he had begun: 'the canons whose dean he was, and many others, used often to hinder him in his work, by drawing him into their lawsuits, making much of him in adulation, oppressing the poor whom he was obliged to protect, or badgering him to take part in the business of his chapter'.[2] This agrees so well with the account of Anselm's behaviour in feud-ridden Laon by the contemporary Guibert of Nogent[3] that one readily believes the Chanter. His other reminiscence — 'Master Anselm used to say, on the day of the Passion, that we ought not to weep for Jesus; the Israelites wept for Moses, but not for Josue who prefigured Jesus Christ'[4] — conveys the same impression of calm as Anselm's own *glosula* on the Psalms, where he 'keeps

---

[1] The most recent study of the life of Anselm (correctly Ansellus) is by A. Wilmart, 'Un commentaire des Psaumes', op. cit. (p. 48, n. 4). Many articles by different scholars have been published in the *Rech. Théol. anc. méd.*; and see F. Bliemetzrieder, 'Anselms von Laon systematische Sentenzen', *Beitr. z. Gesch. der Philosophie des Mittelalters*, xviii. 2/3 (Münster, 1919); H. Weisweiler, 'Das Schrifttum der Schule Anselms von Laon und Wilhelms von Champeaux in deutschen Bibliotheken', ibid. xxxiii. 1/2 (1936).

[2] From the Chanter's gloss on the Psalter MS. Bibl. Nat. Lat. 12011, fo. 173ᵇ; see B. Smalley, 'La Glossa Ordinaria', 400, n. 1; op. cit. (p. 48, n. 3) 139-44, 174-5, 207.

[3] Op. cit. (p. 32, n. 1).

[4] From the Chanter's gloss on Deut. xxxiv. 8; MS. Balliol 23, fo. 112ᵈ '*Fleveruntque eum . . . unde Iehu Nave sepultus legitur, nec defletus, quia Iesum verum Iosue, scil Iesum Christum prefiguravit. Unde Magister Anselmus die passionis Iesum dicebat non esse flendum.*'

his serenity from one end of his gloss to the other, patiently defining and explaining . . . in his tranquil way . . .'[1] Peter Abailard, who had a sharper mind and a very different temperament, found his master wordy and second rate;[2] he belonged to a younger generation of more thoroughgoing dialecticians.

From Laon we make a brief excursion northward to Utrecht, where a Master Lambert is teaching, to the warmly expressed satisfaction of his pupils. He must have been roughly contemporary with Anselm, since the extreme dates for his teaching are about 1080 to 1120 and he is mentioned in documents between 1108 and 1112.[3] Although Laon overshadowed the fame of his school, he just comes into our survey. Substantial extracts from his commentary on St. Paul circulated together with quotations from Anselm in a compilation by Robert of Bridlington, which had considerable popularity in the twelfth century.

Then we end our wandering at Paris. Here Gilbert de la Porrée, a pupil of Anselm, and Peter Lombard continue the Anselmian tradition in their work on Scripture.[4] These two masters represent the transition between the period of scattered cathedral schools and the centralization of studies in the university of Paris.

The achievement of all these eleventh- and early twelfth-century scholars, from Berengar to Peter Lombard, like that of their ninth-century predecessors, divides naturally into two: the production of text-books or aids to study in the form of 'select extracts'; and independent exegesis. But now the two activities proceed together. We do not find, as we did in the Carolingian period, an older generation devoting itself entirely to the task of compilation. The schools of Laon and Paris made a striking advance in both compilation and original work. It will be more convenient, however, to take the two activities separately, disposing of the 'select extracts' before we consider the more original contributions to Bible study.

The first activity may be called the 'text-book movement'.

[1] A. Wilmart, op. cit. 28.
[2] *Historia Calamitatum*, iii, *P.L.* clxxviii. 123-4.
[3] J. M. de Smet, 'L'exégète Lambert, écolâtre d'Utrecht', *Revue d'histoire ecclésiastique*, xlii (1947), 103-10. I must congratulate the author on making this identification and so plotting a fresh centre on the map of early twelfth-century studies.
[4] See especially F. Bliemetzrieder, 'Robert von Melun und die Schule Anselms von Laon', *Zeitschr. f. Kirchengesch.* liii (1934), 117-70.

In the middle ages both teaching and original thinking centred in texts which had been handed down from an earlier period, whether it were an inspired text, the Bible, or a *corpus iuris*, or a classical author. Hence it was essential for teaching purposes that the text should have some standard exposition accompanying it as a gloss, for use in lectures, which should be accessible to all scholars and students, and which everyone could refer to in the certainty of being understood. We find this development both in biblical study and in Roman and canon law. All three sciences produced a *Glossa Ordinaria*.

The history of the biblical *Glossa Ordinaria* is imperfectly known, and the few certain facts have been obscured by fantastic misconceptions. The *Glosses* of the civilians and the canonists, on the contrary, have been intensively studied; there is no mystery concerning their authorship or the process of their reception. It seems advisable, therefore, in dealing with the biblical *Glossa Ordinaria*, to proceed from the known to the unknown. If we have before us a clear picture of the achievement of the civilians and the canonists in preparing their standard works it will be much easier to reconstruct the biblical equivalent. We shall know what to expect, and we may find the comparisons suggestive. In the following note the late Dr. Kantorowicz gives a résumé of the development of legal glosses and the emergence in civil and canon law of a standard or 'ordinary' gloss with a precision which students of the biblical *Gloss* will envy. The comparison which follows his note was suggested by him and is the result of our discussion.

Note on the Development of the Gloss to the Justinian and the Canon Law

By HERMANN KANTOROWICZ (*Cambridge*)

I

THE body of the Roman law as codified by Justinian 533-56, the so-called *Corpus iuris civilis*, consisted in the Middle Ages of (*a*) the three *Digesta* (*Digestum Vetus, Infortiatum, Digestum Novum*), (*b*) the *Codex* (Code books I-IX), (*c*) the *Tres Libri* (Code books X-XII), (*d*) the *Instituta*, (*e*) the *Authenticum* (a collection of Justinian novels). The history of the glosses to these law-books (which were far from being the only books to be glossed) falls into three periods which are sharply divided and between which there was very little connection. (1) The glosses in the age of Justinian refer to his Institutes; they are partly juristic in character, but are very few and anonymous. (2) The glosses written from about 600 to 1070 are again anonymous, but more numerous; they cover the Institutes and the Code, but are purely grammatical (synonyms, etymologies, construction, etc.). (3) Glosses of a juristic nature and often of the highest scientific value were written by the school of the Bolognese glossators. This school was founded by a former grammarian, Guarnerius (or Irnerius) towards the end of the eleventh century; continued by his pupils Bulgarus (d. 1166), Martinus and many lesser men; by their pupils, Rogerius (who died about 1170), Placentinus (d. 1192), Johannes Bassianus, Vacarius (who died about 1200) and others; then chiefly by the pupils of Johannes, Azo (d. 1220) and Hugolinus, and brought to a conclusion by Accursius (d. 1263). Of these 'pre-Accursian' glosses several hundred thousands have been preserved, but nearly all are unprinted. They cover the whole *Corpus iuris civilis*, particularly its most difficult and valuable portion, the three parts of the Digest. Usually they are signed by their authors with their *siglum* (g. = Guarnerius, b. = Bulgarus, Ioh. = Johannes Bassianus, etc.). The oldest of them, however, are often anonymous; they consist chiefly of mere references to— never quotations of—parallel or conflicting passages in the sources (*similia* and *contraria*). These references and most of the glosses proper were written in the margin of the text, but some of the shorter glosses were written between the lines, simply to save space.

The function of the glosses was threefold: to serve as notes for the delivery of oral *lecturae*; as materials for the composition of systematic text-books (*summae*); as commentaries for the benefit of future readers of the text. They were not published by the master but often copied from his book by his pupils. The content is almost exclusively juristic; interpretation and harmonization (*solutiones contrarietatum*) of the text (*litera*), and illustration of it by *quaestiones, distinctiones, generalia, casus*, etc. The interpretation is more or less literal, sometimes very free, but scarcely ever moralizing or allegorical; historical, comparative, logical, grammatical observations and variants (introduced by 'alias') are not infrequent. The authorities quoted are almost invariably either the glossators themselves or a few ancient philosophers (Aristotle, Boethius), and the Bible; the Roman jurists are the subject-matter of the glossators, not their authorities.

The glossators soon began to combine the single glosses into *apparatus* which claims to give a complete and coherent interpretation of a whole title of a law-book or the whole law-book; they comment on one word or one passage after another without changing their textual order. They were partly compiled, partly newly written by the same man and then published by him. The oldest *apparatus* of a whole title is that of Bulgarus to the last title of the Digest, *De regulis iuris*, to which one of his pupils, Placentinus, wrote *additiones*; later on another of his pupils, Johannes, wrote a new *apparatus*, supplemented by additions of his pupil Azo. The oldest *apparatus* of a whole law-book seems to have been recently discovered in a series of glosses on the *Institutes* by Martinus which needs to be further studied. Towards the end of the twelfth and the beginning of the thirteenth centuries all the Justinian law-books were provided with *apparatus* at Bologna; those written at other places (e.g. those by Simon Vicentinus) passed almost unnoticed. Such *apparatus*, of a more or less compilatory character, were published by Azo in two editions (*a. minor* and *maior*) on the *Digestum vetus*, the *Digestum novum*, the Code, and perhaps also on the *Infortiatum*; by Hugolinus on the three Digests, the Code, the *Institutes*, and the *Tres Libri*; finally, by Accursius, on the *Authenticum*.

Accursius, the *Glossator* as he came to be called, compiled all the previous *apparatus*, a great mass of single glosses, and writings of other genres (*quaestiones*, etc.) which all had originally been glosses, into one vast collection of more than 96,000 glosses, some of which are complete treatises. This work was acknowledged at once as the *glossa ordinaria*, i.e. the *apparatus* recognized by the law schools. It was written in the margins of the text, whereas the earlier *apparatus* had usually been copied *per se*. It was protected by the constant supervision of official correctors, and made the subject-matter of lectures. The earlier *apparatus* ceased to be copied and booksellers no longer kept them as part of their ordinary stock-in-trade. Only a few learned jurists continued to quote them and they were still bought and used, as a makeshift, by those who could not afford the expensive brand-new copies of the *glossa ordinaria*.

The instantaneous success of the Accursian gloss, attested by innumerable manuscripts and printed editions (from 1468 to 1627, generally in five folios), was chiefly due to the fact that Accursius aimed at compiling all the interpretations that had hitherto been put forward or could be put forward, thus enabling parties and advocates to pick out the most favourable to their cause; he often refrained from revealing his own opinion but gave preference to the doctrines of the conservative wing, the *nostri doctores* (Irnerius, Bulgarus, Johannes, Azo). He published the first edition in 1228. In his later years he made revisions and amplifications, the extent of which has not yet been ascertained. The first critical edition of the Accursian gloss is being prepared in Italy.

Nearly all the minor jurists of the thirteenth century (his sons and other *Accursiani*) contributed *additiones* to the *glossa ordinaria*, which consisted partly of new arguments and further problems, partly of *reprobationes*.

II

The gloss to the sources of the canon law was bound to develop on rather different lines. The glossators did not inherit a self-contained *corpus* of canon law distinct from theological doctrines and ecclesiatical provisions; it was in an early period of the school of Bologna that canonistic science emancipated itself; the collections of papal decretals which formed the subject-matter of the new science received constant additions. Hence, during the middle ages canon law never attained the status of a *corpus iuris* in the sense of a comprehensive codification; no *glossa ordinaria* ever existed apart from the recognized *apparatus* to the successive private or official collections.

In the Carolingian period some anonymous glosses, a few of them of some legal value, were written in various redactions of the important Dyonisio-Hadriana collection of canons.

The first law-book to be glossed was the *Concordia discordantium canonum*, generally called the *Decreta* (or *Decretum*) *Gratiani*. This again was a Bolognese work, compiled about 1142. Most of the canonists of the second half of the twelfth and early thirteenth centuries wrote, and usually signed, single glosses to it.

The date of the first *apparatus* to the *Decretum* is still uncertain; but there are known examples from the beginning of the thirteenth century. Some were written by well-known *decretistae* such as Laurentius Hispanus (d. 1248): others were published anonymously like the French work *Ecce vicit Leo* and the Bolognese works *Ius naturale* and the *Apparatus Palatinus*. These *apparatus* were the basis of the *glossa ordinaria*, compiled at Bologna about 1216 by Johannes Teutonicus; it had a success similar to that of Accursius, particularly after its revision and modernization by Bartholomaeus Brixiensis soon after 1245.

Other canonical collections received their *apparatus* later, and in most cases one of these *apparatus* attained to the dignity of *glossa ordinaria*.[1]

H. K.

---

[1] There is a mass of modern literature on the various glossators and some of the *apparatus*, but no comprehensive history of the juristic gloss has been written. The preceding note can be supplemented from the following writings: v. Savigny, *Geschichte des römischen Rechts im Mittelalter*, 2nd ed., vol. iii (1834), ch. 24; vol. iv (1850); vol. v (1850), ch. 42; v. Schulte, *Die Glosse zum Decret Gratians von ihren Anfängen bis auf die jüngsten Ausgaben* (in *Wiener Sitzungsberichte*, xxi, and separately, 1872); Conrat (Cohn), *Geschichte der Quellen und literatur des römischen Rechts im früheren Mittelalter* (1891), chs. 12, 17, 25; Neumeyer, *Die*

The biblical *Glossa Ordinaria* is a tremendous work. Each book begins with the prologue, or prologues, of St. Jerome together with other prefatory matter. The text is glossed, with varying degrees of thickness, in the margin and between the lines. It has been printed many times from the fifteenth to the eighteenth centuries, generally with the *Postillae* of Nicholas of Lyre and the *Additiones* of Paul of Burgos. It runs to six folio volumes in this form. The title *Ordinaria* is late; the twelfth- and thirteenth-century masters call it simply *Glosa*. We will therefore refer to it as 'the *Gloss*', and to the extracts, marginal and interlinear, which compose it, as 'glosses'. It is impossible to find a more precise terminology, and unfortunately 'a gloss' can refer to almost any exposition.

The fifteenth-century editors regarded the *Glossa Ordinaria* as a work of composite and uncertain authorship: 'diverse doctors at diverse times' had 'ordered' its glosses; 'and although it is not known precisely who wrote which, yet all were and are of the greatest authority in the eyes of all'.[1] This vagueness was preferable to a bibliographical legend which ascribed the marginal glosses to Walafrid Strabo (d. 849), the interlinear to Anselm of Laon. The edition of Migne, which is the most recent, proceeds on this assumption. Anyone who has tried to use it knows how worthless it is. The attribution to Strabo has even led to a differentiation between the functions of the marginal and interlinear glosses; the first are said to explain whole passages, the second the single words of the text. In reality the *Gloss* on the Bible exactly resembles that on the *Corpus Iuris* in this matter; the shorter glosses were put between the lines for convenience and for no other reason. No manuscript containing the marginal without the interlinear or vice versa has ever been found.

[1] *Biblia cum glossis ordinariis* (Venice, 1495).

gemeinr. Entwicklung d. internat. Privat- und Strafrechts, ii (1916), 60, n. 1 (on Accursius); Juncker, 'Summen und Glossen', in *Z. d. Sav. Stift. f. Rechtsgesch*. xlv (1925), *Kan. Abt.*; Genzmer, 'Die Justinianische Kodification und die Glossatoren', in *Atti del Congr. Intern. di Dir. Rom.*, Bol. 1933, i (1934), 389-96; Meijers, 'Sommes, Lectures et Commentaires', ibid. 435 (on Martinus); van Hove, *Prolegomena (Commentarium Lovaniense in Codicem iuris canonici*, i. 1 [1928]); Kuttner, *Repertorium der Kanonistik*, i (Città del Vaticano, 1937), and the following writings of the author of this note: 'Das Principium decretalium des Johannes de Deo', in *Z. d. Sav. Stift. f. Rechtsgesch*. xliii (1922), *Kan. Abt.*; 'Accursio e la sua biblioteca', *Riv. d. stor. di Dir. ital*. ii (1929); *Studies in the Glossators of the Roman Law*, with the collaboration of W. W. Buckland (1938).

The medical glosses present special problems. Miss Susan Carrington will discuss them in a forthcoming paper in *Mediaeval and Renaissance Studies*.

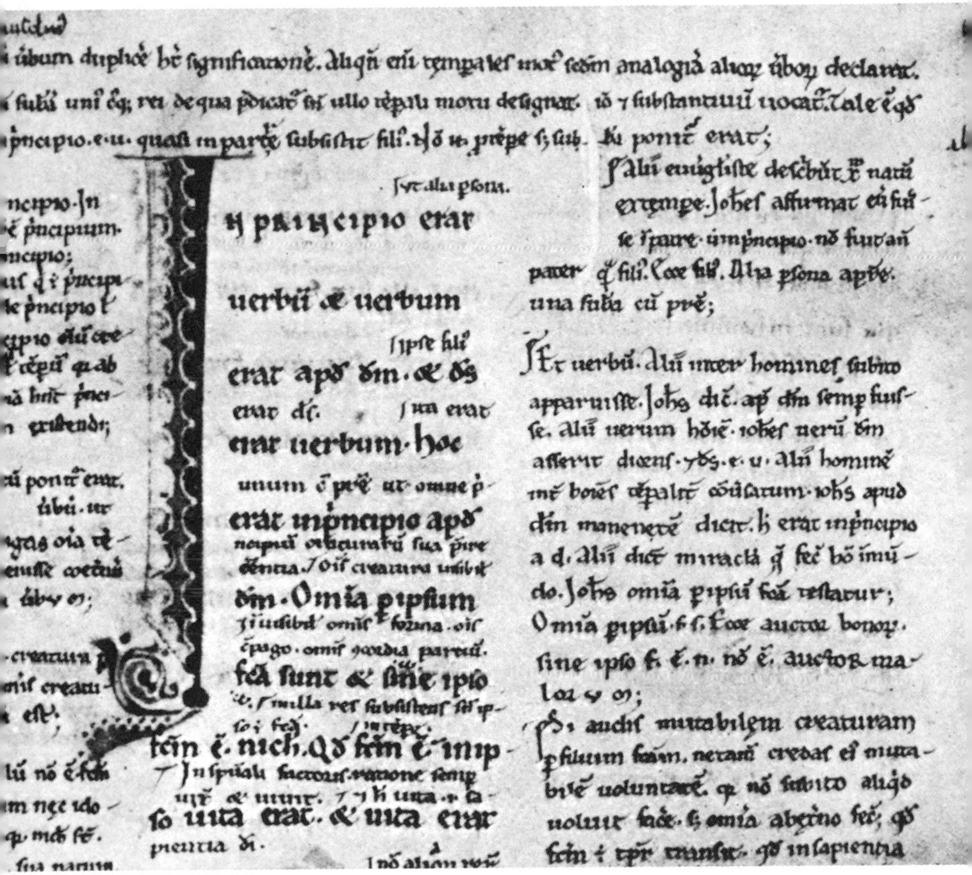

I. MS. Bodl. Lyell 1, fol. 4[r]. The *Gloss* on St. John

The myth of Walafrid Strabo's authorship dies hard, since it is preserved in bibliographies and library catalogues. It lives on even in the works of so great a scholar as J. de Ghellinck. He still believed that the *Gloss* most probably originated with Strabo, while admitting that it had been added to by others.[1] Quite recently, however, J. de Blic, in a posthumous article, has given the *coup de grâce* to the legend.[2] He started with the genuine works of Strabo, that is, with commentaries on the Psalms and the Canonical Epistles which are plausibly ascribed to him, also a marginal and interlinear gloss on certain of the Prophets, noted by S. Berger as coming from Strabo's circle; it is roughly contemporary and belonged to St. Gall, which had close relations with Strabo's abbey, Reichenau. Berger thought he had detected some resemblance between these works and the *Gloss*, hence that the nucleus of the *Gloss* on some books of the Bible derived from Strabo.[3] De Blic showed that the similarity was superficial. Both the early works and the *Gloss* depended on much the same patristic authorities, hence a deceptive likeness; but the choice of extracts and the modifications imposed on them were quite independent of one another.

The problem of the *Gloss* on the Pentateuch was more delicate. Some of the glosses in the *Gloss* on Genesis and Exodus are ascribed to 'Strabus', both in the printed editions and in manuscript, and a number of writers of the late eleventh and the twelfth century quote him on the same two books. Manegold of Lautenbach, for instance, quotes 'Walfredus Strabo in collectario suo'. Two explanations were possible: Strabo might have compiled the *Gloss* on the Pentateuch himself, adding comments of his own to his patristic extracts and marking them with his own signature; alternatively, a later scholar might have compiled the *Gloss*, making extracts from a commentary by Strabo to add to his other sources.

De Blic showed that the second hypothesis was correct. Strabo did in fact leave commentaries on the Pentateuch, his aim, as he says in his preface, being to abridge the much longer works of his master, Raban Maur. The glosses headed

[1] *Le mouvement théologique du XIIe siècle* (2nd ed., Bruges, etc., 1948), 104-12.
[2] 'L'œuvre exégétique de Walafrid Strabon et la Glossa ordinaria', *Rech. Théol. anc. méd.* xvi (1949), 5-28.
[3] S. Berger, *Histoire de la Vulgate, etc.* (Paris, 1893), 133-5.

'Strabus' in the *Gloss* are extracts from these commentaries. So his share in the *Gloss* boils down to 'a few dozen short quotations in the *Gloss* on Genesis and about as many on Exodus'. The rest of his work on the Pentateuch, and on the other books examined, the glossators ignored. Further, the genuine works ascribed to him are all written out continuously and not in the form of glosses; so it cannot even be held that he suggested, however indirectly, the lay-out of the *Gloss*. He simply had nothing to do with it.

The cream of the joke is that medieval scholars did not think very highly of Strabo. His dependence on Raban was too obvious. De Blic found two manuscripts of the ninth to tenth century (Rheims 130, Le Mans 213) in which Strabo's commentary on Exodus begins with the verse:

'Hunc librum exposuit Hrabanus iure sophista,
Strabus et imposuit frivolos hos titulos.'

The same collection in two rather later manuscripts, eleventh and twelfth century (Tours 69 and 70), has a note stating that the scribe had wished to copy only the commentaries of Raban, but as he was not able to find them all, he had used Strabo, 'Raban's abbreviator'. Had de Blic been able to visit Grenoble, he would have found two other manuscripts of the same type, which contain some even more telling comments on Strabo's reputation. Grenoble has a collection of early commentaries and glosses from the Grande Chartreuse and lesser Charterhouses which would repay a closer study than I was able to make on my short visit. MS. 267 is a compilation of the twelfth century,[1] originally from the Chartreuse of Ecouges, containing first Isidore, then Raban on Genesis, then Strabo on the remaining books of the Pentateuch, conflated with Isidore on Exodus and Leviticus. The heading to the commentary on Exodus brings out the derivative nature of Strabo's work:

'The annotation of Strabo, pupil of Raban, on Exodus, according to the opinions of his master, with the addition of almost all Isidore's exposition in place.'[2]

MS. Grenoble 266, twelfth-century, from the Grande Chartreuse, has the same collection, plus a long preface by the

---

[1] Not thirteenth as the catalogue states in an otherwise excellent description. On both manuscripts see *Cat. gén. des MSS. Dept.* vii (Paris, 1899), 101-3.

[2] fo. 129ᵛ: 'Adnotatio Strabi, discipuli Rabani, super Exodum secundum magistri nichilominus sententiam, adiuncta huic suis locis Isidori pene tota de eodem libro expositione.'

compiler. He must have been an abbot or at least in charge of education in a religious community, since he intends his compilation to be read *in conventu*. He explains that he has made it up from the works of Raban, Strabo and Isidore, sometimes providing a double exposition, so that the reader may choose. Then he continues:

'For Strabo of whom we speak was Raban's pupil and he annotates rather than expounds the four books, according to his master's opinions. But when we had finished Raban's fine exposition of Genesis, and we sought to continue it with an equally satisfactory exposition of the remaining books, two commentators only were to hand, giving us trouble enough: on the one hand Strabo, who went through the four books of the Law after a fashion, following his master; on the other hand Isidore, who has something worth saying on the several books of the Heptateuch.'

He has therefore combined Strabo and Isidore for Exodus and Leviticus. He goes on to Strabo on Numbers and Deuteronomy, with the warning that they are not to be read in community but only in private:

'Further, we sanction the separate reading of Strabo's annotation of Numbers and Deuteronomy by certain students, but not in community. Only Isidore's treatise on either book is to be read there. The exposition of Exodus and Leviticus which has a combination of Strabo and Isidore will of course necessarily be read aloud in community. For here Strabo expounds quite adequately, as if with a beginner's carefulness, and Isidore's opinions, joined to his, are by no means contemptible, indeed much better, had we perceived it in time.'[1]

Further investigation might well establish the relationship between these six manuscripts, all alike in essentials and yet with individual variants. It might even disclose the identity

[1] fo. 1ᵛ: 'Strabus enim iste, de quo sermo habetur, discipulus Rabani fuit et secundum magistri sententiam quatuor libros magis annotat quam pertractat. Sed cum perfecissemus super Genesim egregiam expositionem Rabani et quereremus prosequi de residuis libris expositionem eque acceptabilem, erant cure satagente(s) pre manibus duo, hinc Strabus, qui post magistrum suum quatuor libros legis utcumque exequitur, inde Isidorus, qui de singulis Heptatici libris aliquid honeste dicit. . . .
Proinde, si placet, adnotationem Strabi super Numeros et Deuteronimum seorsum quidem legi a quibusdam studiosis sancimus, in conventu vero non, sed et Isidorum cedimus de utroque tractatum. Illa nimirum expositio super Exodum vel Leviticum, que mixtim Strabum et Isidorum continet, necessario recitabitur in conventu. Ibi utique Strabus, utpote in prima studii vigilantia, admodum convenienter exponit, et Isidori non contempnende sunt admixte sententie, valde quidem melius, si perspexissemus ante tempus.'

of Strabo's critic. At least we have learnt from him that Strabo on the Pentateuch was regarded as a stop-gap to Raban, who seems to have been in short supply. Strabo had merely abridged his master and his work on the last two books of the Law was so slipshod as to be unsuitable for community reading; it was only allowed to selected students. So much for the putative author of the *Glossa Ordinaria*!

But these collections do not only explode a fallacy; they contribute some positive information on the pre-history of the *Gloss*. If our anonymous critic was expressing a common opinion, that Strabo's work deteriorated as it proceeded through the books of the Pentateuch, then we can understand why the glossators chose extracts from Strabo on Genesis and Exodus only. We can also see why they should choose him at all. Strabo was being copied in a number of miscellanies, sometimes separately and sometimes amalgamated with Isidore. Although these miscellanies are written as continuous commentaries and not as marginal and interlinear glosses, they had the same purpose as the *Gloss*: their compilers aimed at providing a running guide to the text by the selection and conflation of authors. The compilers may have played something of the same role in the antecedents of the *Gloss* on the Pentateuch as used to be attributed to Strabo.

Long before de Blic published his paper on Strabo and the *Gloss*, research on its origins had been proceeding from the other end. This had led a number of scholars, especially Wilmart, to deny Strabo's authorship and to suggest a twelfth- rather than a ninth-century setting for its preparation.

The known facts concerning the authorship of the *Gloss* are as follows. The central figure is Anselm of Laon. Peter the Chanter, as we have seen, tells us that Master Anselm began to gloss the whole of Scripture, but was not able to finish his work; and Peter's story corresponds to what we know from other sources. Anselm was certainly responsible for the *Gloss* on St. Paul and the Psalter, probably for that on the Fourth Gospel. His brother Ralph compiled the *Gloss* on St. Matthew; his pupil Gilbert the Universal compiled the *Gloss* on the Pentateuch and the Greater Prophets and Lamentations, some time before he became bishop of London in 1128. The evidence for the authorship of the *Gloss* on the Lesser Prophets is conflicting. The English writer,

Robert of Bridlington, working probably in the 1150s, quotes it as 'the glosses of Gilbert the Universal'. A twelfth-century copy of the *Gloss* on the Lesser Prophets from the Cistercian abbey of Dore in Herefordshire, now at the British Museum, MS. Harl. 4981,[1] has a note in a hand of the later twelfth century on the flyleaf:

'Hec glosatura est magistri Radulfi fratris magistri Anselmi. Alia est secundum magistrum Gilebertum universalem. Expositores huius libri: . . . (a list of patristic writers follows).'

I examined the copy of the *Gloss* very carefully to verify that it was the standard text. I also eliminated the possibility that the gloss of Ralph referred to in the note might be, not the main gloss in the volume, but a later one written in the margins in a hand very like or identical with the hand which wrote the note. But this second gloss uses expressions and chapter divisions which are not found as early as Ralph's and Gilbert's period. Therefore either Robert of Bridlington or the writer of the note must be mistaken. Robert is probably the earlier witness; on the other hand, no glosses in the *Gloss* on the Twelve Prophets are ascribed to Gilbert and we shall see that he did leave signed glosses in the *Gloss* on the Pentateuch, the Greater Prophets and Lamentations. The *Gloss* on the Twelve Prophets *may* be by Ralph, in which case we must add an unknown gloss on the same book to the writings of Gilbert the Universal. The interesting point is that twelfth-century writers themselves had conflicting ideas on the compilers of the different parts of the *Gloss*, only knowing that they were connected with Anselm. The evidence becomes slighter still for the *Gloss* on the Acts and the Apocalypse. A prologue ascribed to Gilbert de la Porrée prefaces the *Gloss* on the latter; another scribal note seems to connect a 'Master Alberic' with the *Gloss* on Acts. Master Alberic of Rheims was another pupil of Anselm and contemporary, perhaps friend, of Gilbert the Universal.[2] Many books of the Bible remain unaccounted for. Even if, merely on the grounds of probability, we ascribe a larger share of

[1] N. R. Ker, *Medieval Libraries of Great Britain* (London, 1941), 36. Mr. Ker very kindly pointed out the note to me.

[2] 'La Glossa Ordinaria', 366. Dr. R. W. Hunt found another interesting reference in a twelfth-century copy of the *Gloss* on the Apocalypse, MS. Bodl. Auct. D.IV. 12 (*Summary Catalogue* 2096). There is a note at the end of the prologue, fo. iv: 'Apocalipsi expositores sunt Beda, Haimo, Primasius, Ambrosius, Alber'.' Is this also Master Alberic?

the *Gloss* to Ralph and Anselm, we have a trustworthy statement by Peter Comestor that neither of them glossed the Gospel of St. Mark; so there must have been other collaborators whose names are unknown.[1]

These compilers were all referred to, like Accursius, as *glosatores*; they were spoken of as having 'ordered' (*ordinare*) the *Gloss*.

Theologians were more often content to be anonymous than legists; the canonists, who were generally also churchmen, come somewhere between. Master Gilbert the Universal was the only one of the biblical glossators who regularly signed his own glosses when he made his own comments or cross-references, and who proclaimed himself openly as compiler of the *Gloss* on a whole book: he ends the *Gloss* on Lamentations 'let this be sufficient for the exposition of the Lamentations of Jeremias, which *I, Gilbert deacon of Auxerre,* have drawn from the founts of the Fathers'. This versatile person, famous everywhere for knowing everything, 'universal' in his knowledge as in his friends, was a famous and, his enemies said, an unscrupulous lawyer, who practised at the Papal Curia; so it is probably thanks to his legal training that we have definite evidence for his share in the work.[2] Neither Anselm nor Ralph has left any sign as to which part of the *Gloss* he compiled, or which glosses, if any, were added to excerpts from the Fathers. The little we know about this has had to be gleaned from other sources.

We have no means of dating the various parts of the *Gloss*, except very roughly by the careers of the glossators. Even so, we notice that it appeared nearly a century before the two legal ones. There is an obvious reason. Irnerius stood in very much the same relation to Justinian as that in which Origen had stood to St. Paul; he had little but his actual text before him. The text had to be expounded before the expositions could be 'ordered'.

---

[1] From here to the end of the section see B. Smalley, 'Gilbertus Universalis', *Rech. Théol. anc. méd.* vii (1935), 235-62; viii (1936), 24-60; 'La Glossa Ordinaria', ibid. ix (1937), 365-400; 'A Collection of Paris Lectures of the Later Twelfth Century in the MS. *Pembroke College Cambridge 7*', *Cambridge Historical Journal*, vi (1938), 110-13. See Plate I.

O. Lottin has supplied further evidence for Anselm's authorship of the *Gloss* on St. Paul, 'Nouveaux fragments, etc.', *Rech. Théol. anc. méd.* xii (1940), 52.

[2] The same self-assertiveness has been noted as an unusual trait in the theological works of Simon of Tournai, who was also a canon lawyer. J. Warichez, 'Les *Disputationes* de Simon de Tournai', *Spic. Sac. Lov.* xii (1932), xviii-xix.

The legists necessarily began later than the theologians; but they worked more quickly; they produced their expositions, their first *apparatus*, and their standard *Gloss* in little more than a century. The theologians continued the same process over hundreds of years; Anselm of Laon and his assistants, working about 1100-30, were doing for the Fathers and their successors what Accursius did in the 'twenties of the thirteenth century for the twelfth-century Bolognese. Again, the reasons for the difference are obvious. The theologian's material was practically unlimited, since his text was a divine encyclopaedia with many senses. Equally important, the production of a *glossa ordinaria* demanded a certain degree of centralization in teaching; and that was not achieved, either in law or theology, until the twelfth century.

We notice the same comparative slowness on the part of the theologians if we take either the 'pre-history' of the biblical *Gloss*, that is, the preparation of the earlier *apparatus* which it superseded, or the history of its reception as *ordinaria*.

Ever since the reforms of Alcuin, and even earlier, the Vulgate had been accumulating both prefatory matter, centred in the prologues of St. Jerome, and explanatory matter in the form of glosses; all this material varied from copy to copy. In the eleventh and early twelfth centuries the commentator on Scripture normally used one of these *apparatus*, which he called an 'expositor'. As we saw, the eighth- and ninth-century scholars had been active in producing them. The eleventh-century scholars followed their example. We can sometimes watch the growth of an *apparatus*, and see how successive layers of glosses came to overlay the text. Lanfranc's glosses on the Pauline Epistles, 'excerpted from the sayings of the Fathers', received at separate times two additional sets of glosses, one ascribed to St. Augustine, the other to 'Ambrose'. A copy of Lanfranc's glosses, together with these two additions, served as 'expositor' to a certain anonymous scholar, who quotes it in his commentary as *glosa*, just as later masters referred to the *Gloss*. The same expositor was merged in two other big collections which also contained glosses ascribed to Berengar and Drogo, combined with individual material. MS. Grenoble 32, from the Chartreuse des Portes, is an excellent example of an expositor which at first sight looks just like an early copy of the *Gloss* and turns out on examination to be quite different. It contains a marginal and interlinear gloss on Proverbs, Ecclesiastes and Lamentations, written in the early to mid-twelfth century. It not only differs from the *Gloss*, but seems to have no common material, whereas there is at least something in common between the *Gloss* and the collections containing the Lanfranc, Berengar and Drogo glosses.

The *Gloss* of Anselm and his assistants took some years to oust these earlier *apparatus* from favour. We have fairly good evidence that the *Gloss* on certain books was copied at Paris before 1137; but it was not recognized at once, like that of Accursius, as the standard text. Scholars quoted it as 'the glosses of Gilbert the Universal' or 'Anselm', or anonymously. They seem to have regarded it as one *apparatus* among many of the same kind. Gilbert de la Porrée, Anselm's pupil, and Peter Lombard seem to have been responsible for instituting it as the standard. Gilbert de la Porrée made an expansion of the patristic glosses in Anselm's *Gloss* on St. Paul and the Psalter, which he read before his master at Laon, 'causa emendationis', and this expansion became known as the *Media Glosatura*. Peter Lombard also expanded the *Gloss* on these two books, religiously preserving the Anselmian text as a nucleus; and this *Maior* or *Magna Glosatura* (written between 1135-6 and 1142-3) is said to have 'displaced all other glosses' in the schools for the two biblical books which it covered.

The Lombard, as his pupil Herbert of Bosham tells us in the preface to a magnificent edition of the *Magna Glosatura*, intended to remedy the obscurity and brevity of the older glossator, Master Anselm; the idea that his expansion should be read publicly did not occur to him. But the Lombard's systematic exposition of theology, the *Sentences* (finished in 1152), became a text-book in the teaching of doctrine, and in the *Sentences* he used both his own *Magna Glosatura* and the *Gloss*. This must have given fresh authority to the work of Anselm and his collaborators. Twelfth- and thirteenth-century scribes and commentators connect both Gilbert de la Porrée and Peter Lombard with the *Gloss* in various other ways. Until research has made these allusions more intelligible we can only say that Gilbert and the Lombard must have made some use of the *Gloss*, probably in their oral teaching.

In the next generation lectures on Scripture began to take the form of glossing the *Gloss*, or, on St. Paul and the

Psalter, the *Magna Glosatura*. So far as we know, the earliest example of a gloss on the *Gloss* is a series of lectures on the Gospels by Peter Comestor, given probably before he became Chancellor in 1168. He refers to it simply as *Glosa*, and compares it to a *vetus glosa*, which must mean one of the earlier *apparatus*.[1] From about the middle of the twelfth century, a glossed Bible normally contains the same set of prefaces and glosses, that is to say, the *Gloss*. There are variations from copy to copy in detail, but no large-scale changes or additions are made; the early printed editions are not very different from the manuscripts. From Paris the *Gloss* was spread throughout Latin Christendom and accepted as the standard work.

If we compare it with the legal one, we realize that it grows and spreads itself in a more irregular and haphazard way. Its compilation and circulation were less centralized and organized. Typically, when we look for a biblical Accursius, we find, not one man, but a very nebulous band of collaborators, working in at least two different centres, Auxerre and Laon. This explains why the outstanding problem of its history is that of its sources. Owing to its composite authorship, there is a separate tradition of sources for each book. Here no comparison, but only years of detailed study will avail; no one has yet had the courage to trace and check the sources of the *Gloss* on any book. The material was too vast for the glossators to incorporate all the existing *apparatus* into one. They had to select, and our difficulty is to know on what principle: how far did they rely on extracts which their predecessors had collected?

We know that the *Gloss* on St. Paul was based on an earlier compilation, since it has many glosses in common with the expanded Lanfranc-Berengar-Drogo *apparatus*. The *Gloss* on the Pentateuch might prove to owe something to the collections which combined Isidore, Raban and Strabo. Traces of the *Gloss* on the Gospels have been discovered in eighth-century glosses.[2] Clearly, the glossators started from

---

[1] In his gloss on Mt. ii. 12 (quoted in 'La Glossa Ordinaria', 368) and in the *Historia scholastica, in Evan.* c. 70, additio i, *P.L.* cxcviii. 1573: 'Nota quod super hunc locum habetur in antiqua glossa: . . .' The passage quoted is not in the *Gloss*, ad loc.

[2] See the very detailed studies of the MSS. of the *Expositio* of the Gospels (printed from a bad text in *P.L.* cxiv among the works of Strabo as the *Marginal Gloss*) by B. Griesser, 'Beiträge z. Textgesch. der Expositio IV Evangeliorum', *Zeitschr. f. Kath. Theol.* liv (1930), 40-87; 'Die hss. Ueberlieferung der Expositio IV Evangeliorum des Ps. Hieronymus', *Rev. Bén.* xlix (1937), 279-321. He

earlier *apparatus* rather than from the original patristic sources.

A full investigation of the sources would throw a much needed light on Anselm's method in using these earlier compilations. Did he and his collaborators just take what they could get in the nearest libraries, or did they deliberately choose as their foundation some *apparatus* which was at that time the most widely known and approved? The second is the more attractive suggestion; it awaits proof.

For whatever reason they were chosen, the range of authors quoted in the *Gloss* is wide. The better known of the Latin Fathers down to Bede, Origen and Hesychius in translation, Raban, Strabo, Paschasius, John the Scot, Haimo, Lanfranc, Berengar have all been laid under contribution. One of the glossators at least, Gilbert the Universal, added his own comments, and others anonymously may have done the same. They compiled, in fact, a representative selection of extracts from Fathers and masters from the third century to the early twelfth.

We cannot usefully discuss the value of these extracts, as they are 'ordered' in the standard aid to study. The *Gloss* was a school book; the glossators were teachers; their practical needs and purpose are too remote for our judgment. The only opinions on the *Gloss* worth having come from their immediate successors, those masters of the later twelfth century who had to use it as a set text when they lectured to their pupils. In a later chapter we shall hear them speak.

III. THE QUAESTIO

Exegesis could take the form of 'continuous' as well as marginal and interlinear glossing, text and gloss being written out in the same column consecutively, the text being underlined or marked in some way. The *Media* and *Magna Glosaturae* took this form, though in some manuscripts the continuous gloss is written beside the text, which is thus copied twice, once by itself and once with the gloss. A certain monk sends the autograph of his commentary to a friend with the request that it shall be copied 'not in the

---

concludes that the *Expositio* took shape during the eighth century; its sources were extracts from Augustine and Gregory, together with material from eighth-century glosses.

margins, as it is here, but continuously in pages, as expositions are usually written'.[1] We sometimes find the same work, Lanfranc on St. Paul for instance, written continuously in one manuscript, as a marginal and interlinear gloss in another. We cannot distinguish very sharply between the two forms. But since the space between the margin and the text was limited, and did not easily allow of long elaborations, independent exegesis tended to appear as continuous glossing.

A scholar might write both a marginal and interlinear gloss and a *glosula*, or continuous exposition, on the same book. Lanfranc has left an exposition of the Pauline Epistles which is fuller and contains quite other material than his marginal and interlinear gloss. Anselm of Laon left a *glosula* as well as his *Gloss* on the Psalms.[2] Though in this case they are connected, they are not identical and the *glosula* is the more original of the two. Now it seems that Anselm did the same thing for the Pauline Epistles. A compilation which exists in two manuscripts of the first half of the twelfth century under the title *Sententie de Apostolo Excerpte* contains two extracts ascribed to him. One, which is headed *Anshelmus*, or *Magister A*, is short and perhaps rather characteristic:

'If a man does not bring his common sense to bear upon Scripture, the more subtle, the madder, he is.'

The compiler says expressly of the other extract:

'On this verse of the Apostle [Heb. ii. 10], Master Anselm expounding, we have gathered this sentence.' It is a long discussion in which Anselm 'proves that the redemption of

---

[1] Robert of Tombelaine (d. about 1090), 'Prologus in Cantica', ed. Mabillon, *Vetera Analecta* (1723), 128.

[2] *P.L.* cxvi. 193-714. See A. Wilmart, 'Un commentaire des Psaumes restitué à Anselme de Laon', *Rech Théol. anc. méd.* viii (1936), 325-44. Dr. A. Landgraf has questioned the attribution on the ground that the commentary contains none of the characteristic doctrines of the school of Laon; 'Die Zuweisung eines Psalmenkommentars an Anselm von Laon', *Biblica*, xxiii (1942), 170-4. Dom Lottin found a comment on a text of the Psalms ascribed to Anselm which corresponds neither with the *Gloss* nor with the *glosula* ascribed to him; 'Nouveaux fragments, etc.', *Rech. Théol. anc. méd.* xii (1940), 51, n. 8. Neither argument seems to me as convincing as those brought forward by Wilmart in favour of Anselm's authorship. Anselm may well have reserved his discussion of doctrine for his lectures on St. Paul and his comment on a verse of the Psalms need not necessarily belong to a commentary on the Psalter. It was quite usual to quote a text and explain it apropos of some other text.

the human race could only have been accomplished by God, not by a creature, angelic or human'.[1]

Neither of these two sentences occurs in the *Gloss*. They read like extracts from a long, discursive exposition. It was only natural to regard them as fragments of a lost commentary or *glosula* and to hope that they might lead to its recovery. The supposition has now been confirmed. A discussion of problems arising from the Eucharist, printed among the letters of St. Anselm,[2] has been restored to Anselm of Laon and has been shown to consist in an extract from a commentary on 1 Cor. x. 16-17.[3] But the commentary itself is still missing. Continuous expositions on the Canticle, St. Matthew, St. John and the Apocalypse are also ascribed to him. Up to date we have a critical study of that on the Canticle only.[4] It exists in three recensions. Two may represent the master's oral teaching or extracts from it; the third (the printed edition)[5] is a more finished, literary production and may represent a working over of Anselm's material by his brother. The attribution to Anselm rests on good external evidence. If, as seems very probable, we ought to accept it, the *glosula* on the Canticle makes an interesting parallel to that on the Psalter. It is by no means identical with the *Gloss*, has the same moral preoccupations as the *glosula* on the Psalter, and resembles the latter in avoiding theological digressions. Some fragments of exposition on various books of the Bible attributed to him have quite recently been discovered, which may help us in time to recover the whole *corpus* of his exegesis.

---

[1] O. Lottin reviewing R. M. Martin, 'Œuvres de Robert de Melun' in *Bulletin de Théol. anc. méd.* iii. 337*, suggests that Anselm may be the author of a commentary on the Pauline Epistles used by Robert of Melun, since the *Sententie de Apostolo Excerpte*, MS. Arundel 360, contain two sentences ascribed to Anselm (ff. 60-1). Miss Rathbone found the same extracts in the same work in MS. Heidelberg Salem 103, ff. 117ᵛ-18ᵛ. Dom Lottin has published the long sentence 'Nouveaux fragments théologiques de l'école d'Anselme de Laon', *Rech. Théol. anc. méd.* xi (1939), 254-5. The short one reads: 'Si quis sano sensu non contemperat scripturas, quanto subtilius intelligunt [*sic*], tanto amentior est.' In MS. Salem 103 this is followed by a fresh heading *Cur anime infantium damnentur*, which suggests that the ensuing discussion is not meant to be ascribed to Anselm.

[2] *P.L.* clix. 255-8.

[3] O. Lottin, 'Anselme de Laon, auteur de la "Lettre" de S. Anselme sur la Cène', *Rech. Théol. anc. méd.* xiii (1946), 222-5.

[4] J. Leclercq, 'Le commentaire du Cantique des cantiques attribué à Anselme de Laon', ibid. xvi (1949), 29-39.

[5] *P.L.* clxii, 1187-1228.

This curious double exposition, which seems so wasteful at first sight, is less surprising if we remember that in the later thirteenth century the *bachelarius biblicus* or pupil-teacher had the tas. of 'reading' and construing the text and its *Gloss* in lectures for beginners, while the master expounded their doctrinal content to his more advanced students. At this early stage, Lanfranc and Anselm had to compose and read aloud their own text-books, as well as give their magisterial exposition.

One very special form of teaching accounts for another type of exposition which is distinct from both the *glosula* and the gloss. It consisted in taking one's text as the basis of a grammar lesson, and must have corresponded to the practice of teaching children to read from the Psalter, at a more advanced stage. A fragment entitled *Dicta Lanfranci archiepiscopi in Iob* begins:

> '*Horonias Hyades Rinocerota* are Greek accusatives; the Latin are Horiones Hyades Rinocerotĕs.'[1]

It is a collection of miscellaneous notes on grammar, strung together on the thread of the text. We have to skip over a century to the *Corrogationes Promethei* of Alexander Nequam to find an equivalent;[2] but this is just the kind of elementary stuff which would be least likely to survive. It is doubtful whether the masters themselves would have classified it as the study of Scripture, or as preparatory training in the liberal arts.

This curious relic of Lanfranc's teaching is useful to us as an introduction to the content of eleventh- and early twelfth-century glosses. Grammar has left its mark everywhere. It has penetrated into the *Gloss* on Lamentations. We find Gilbert the Universal supplementing the Fathers by an appreciation of the literary qualities of his text. The discipline of a century's concentration on grammar and rhetoric shows itself; Gilbert is less fanciful and more sophisticated than Cassiodorus:

> 'My silence will not silence the careful reader, in admiring the splendour of the rhetorical colours, the weight of the

---

[1] MS. Tours 317, fo. 190ᵛ. Lanfranc seems to start from Job ix. 9 and looks forward to xxxix. 9.

[2] Described by P. Meyer, 'Notice sur les *Corrogationes Promethei* d'Alexandre Neckam', *Notices et extraits des MSS. de la Bibliothèque Nationale*, xxxv (1897), 14-15. Dr. R. W. Hunt tells me that Lanfranc's *Dicta* corresponds closely to the grammatical commentary in the *Corrogationes*, though he also knows of other parallels.

sentences, the flowers of speech. He will find for himself the number of heads of rhetoric, the choice dialectic, the subtle arguments. He will teach, untaught, the abjectness of the rhetorical "lamentation", the severity of the incitement to "indignation", and the combination of both. In order to satisfy beginners, however, I shall not disdain to set forth the correct definition of rhetorical "lamentation" and "indignation". "Lamentation", as Tully says, is speech provoking the pity of the hearers. Its first head is that by which we show what happiness we had once and what misery we are in now, for example: *How doth the city sit solitary that was full of people* [Lam. i. 1]. "Indignation" is speech by which is professed either hate of a person or displeasure at an event; the first head here is from authority, when it is said: "What concern is this to the immortal gods?" [1] Similarly here: *Her Nazarites were whiter than snow, &c.* [Lam. iv. 7].

'I therefore initiate the more careful, penetrating reader by denoting in the first alphabet a few heads of "lamentation" and "indignation".'[2]

Even where the commentator of this period does not speak as a professional grammarian, he transfers technical terms. *Continuatio*, meaning 'the sequence of thought', or *inculcatio*, *per exaggerationem*, and so on, are used to describe the method of the sacred writers.

As a logician, he seeks to clarify the argument, follow the windings, and supply every missing link in the chain of thought. He suggests the implications of his author: 'as if he said . . .'; 'and it is as if he said . . .'; or he imagines an opponent, whose views his author is refuting: 'someone might say . . .' A gloss by Drogo shows how the commentator reorganizes his text on logical lines:

'*But knowing that man is not justified by the works of the law, but by the faith of Jesus Christ*, &c. [Gal. ii. 16]. For if this were so, then justification would not be in Christ alone. But justification is in Christ alone. For if justification is not in Christ alone, then we sin in deserting the law and seeking to be justified in Christ alone. But this is not so. For if it were so, then *Christ* would be *the minister of sin*. But *God forbid!* Therefore if Christ is not *the minister of sin*, we do not sin in seeking to be justified in him alone. But if we do not sin in seeking to be justified in him alone, then justification is in Christ alone. If this is so, then *by the works of the law no flesh shall be justified*. For if I say

---

[1] References to *Ad C. Herennium*, ed. F. Marx (Leipzig, 1923), 91, 70, 67.
[2] 'Gilbertus Universalis', *Rech. Théol. anc. méd.* vii. 252.

this, *I make myself a prevaricator,* if I desert the law, which, as I concede, justifies.'[1]

The method had its advantages in explaining to students the close reasoning of the Pauline Epistles. It was less happily applied to the Psalms. A gloss on the Psalter of the early twelfth century, which is probably based on a lost work of Lanfranc[2] and shows the logical, legalistic tendency of his gloss on the Apostle, reduces it to an absurdity. The Psalmist, who, in the words of Cassiodorus commenting on the chief of the penitential Psalms, 'has so wrought that his tears of penitence, running down the cheeks of posterity, shall never by any lapse of time be dried',[3] here becomes a contrite but knowledgeable prisoner-at-the-bar. We are in the atmosphere of the law court:

'*Have mercy on me, O God, according to thy great mercy* [Ps. l. 1]. This is said as if by a man under arrest, who does not attempt to plead innocent, since his crime is already manifest to his judges, but strives by his entreaties to win pardon, showing his penitence, putting forward his former merits, promising that he will behave well in future. First he prays forgiveness for his sin, then he confesses his crime of his own accord. It is as though he said: "*O God*" that is, my Creator, from whom my great and manifold iniquity is not hid, "*have mercy upon me according to thy great mercy*". Great iniquity calls for *great mercy*; that is, according to the measure of thy *mercy*, which is *great*, forgive me my great sin. *And according to the multitude,* that is, in the measure *of thy mercies* which are multiple in their effects, *blot out my iniquity* which is manifold; that is, by display of mercy *blot out* my murder, fraud, and adultery. Here he [David] shows that his sin was great, for it was adultery and much else besides; murder and fraud and many other things may be indicated here.

'*Wash me yet more,* that is, more than I am able to ask, that you may forgive what conscience fears, and add what my prayer does not presume; *from my iniquity,* that is, from adultery, by the faith of baptism; *and cleanse me from my sin,* that is, from murder, giving increase of virtue, that no filth may remain in me. Or *yet more,* that is, not only from actual but also from original sin *wash me and cleanse me.* Or *wash me yet more,* that is, as the iniquity is great, so may the washing be great . . . *For I know my iniquity,* that is, since I grieve for my sin and make satisfaction, I know that thou wilt blot it out; for it is written:

[1] MS. Berne 334, fo. 120ᵛ; 'La Glossa Ordinaria', *Rech. Théol. anc. méd.* ix. 390.
[2] Ibid. 374, n. 29.　　　　　　　　　　[3] *P.L.* lxx. 358.

God will not judge twice for the same offence; and I do not grieve momentarily for my sin, but constantly. . . .

'*To thee only have I sinned*: and since thou alone art supremely good, who hast never done evil to me or another, I am more to blame in having sinned to thee, than if thou wert such a master as did evil to me or another; and this ought to have restrained me from sin. . . .

'. . . *That thou mayst be justified in thy words, and mayest overcome when thou art judged*; that is, *when thou art judged* by men, who compare thee to others, *thou mayst overcome*, that is, thou mayst appear incomparably more worthy in the judgment of all men, and better in the sight of all thy creatures. Or *when thou art judged*; that is, when men blame thee for hunger, or too much rain, or such like, *thou mayst overcome*; for if they give heed to thy judgments, that is, why thou dost so, thou shalt be found in no way to blame. . . .

'Or: *to thee only have I sinned*; it is for thee only to punish the sins of kings and prelates, who have no lord over them save God alone. If a man of the people sins, he sins to the king and God; but a king to God alone. . . .'[1]

Drogo, Lanfranc, and Berengar use dialectic in order to tunnel underneath their text; they attempt to reconstruct the logical process in the mind of their author. Dialectic could also be used for building up a new theological structure with the text as a base. The patristic tradition of 'questioning' and discussing problems, which had been continued by ninth-century scholars, never seems to have lapsed altogether. Gerard of Czanad (martyred in 1046), an early, isolated figure of the theological revival, speaks of himself as 'disputing according to his poor capacity' in a commentary on Hebrews which is now lost.[2]

Neither Berengar, Drogo, nor Lanfranc inserts long theological discussions into his glosses; but these reappear in the works of Manegold, Bruno, Anselm and Ralph of Laon. It now seems clear that the lost work of Manegold contained *quaestiones*.[3] Anselm of Laon certainly introduced them into

---

[1] MS. Royal 3.C.V., fo. 104; see 'La Glossa Ordinaria', *Rech. Théol. anc. méd.* ix. 376-7.

[2] 'Quondam vero ibi, ubi dicitur in Psalmo: *ipsi peribunt, tu autem permanebis*, disputans secundum mediocritatem meam, in primo capitulo epistolae Pauli ad Hebraeos quicquid invenire ex apotheca Sancti Spiritus supra hoc potui, stilo latissimo commendavi.' Quoted by G. Morin, 'Un théologien ignoré du xi⁰ siècle, l'évêque-martyr Gérard de Czanad, O.S.B.', *Rev. Bén.* xxvii (1910), 519.

[3] O. Lottin, 'Manegold de Lautenbach, etc.', *Rech. Théol. anc. méd.* xiv (1947), 222.

his lectures. Dom Lottin has recently put forward a persuasive hypothesis: all the teaching in theology at Laon consisted in lectures on *sacra pagina*. Discussion of questions concerning the Creation, angelology, the fall, would take place within the framework of lectures on the Hexaemeron, while most other doctrinal matters would arise naturally from the text of the Pauline Epistles. The sentence collections emanating from Laon represent a rearrangement and systematization of the masters' exegesis. It was the work of pupils and assistants, who collected, sorted, added and touched up.[1] Consequently, two, at least, of Anselm's commentaries must have been rich in theological teaching. His pupil, Gilbert the Universal, continued the practice of introducing *quaestiones* into his commentaries. In his *glosula* on the Psalter he takes St. Bruno's commentary as his 'expositor', expands St. Bruno's discussions and puts them definitely into '*quaestio*' form; thus Abailard's use of the '*quaestio*' in his commentaries was less original than has been thought. He was not the first to revive the tradition, if, indeed, revival was needed. In the second quarter of the century these *quaestiones* multiply in number, in relation to the size of the commentary, and the use of dialectic increases their length. Each pupil enlarges on his master.[2]

The result is a new type of exposition composed of two fairly distinct elements. The running explanation is broken into by theological questions which the text or its exposition has suggested. A well-known example is the *Magna Glosatura* of Peter the Lombard on the Pauline Epistles. This is stuffed full of *quaestiones* suggested by the *Gloss* of Anselm, which the Lombard's work incorporates.

The *quaestio* element in the commentary tended to grow at the expense of the simple exposition. Master Robert of Melun wrote a commentary on the Apostle (1145-55) in which *quaestiones* occupy a very much larger space than comment;[3] and this represented a clearly formulated policy on his part. Robert was a thorough, independent teacher, combining 'the wisely conservative tendencies of Laon' with

[1] O. Lottin, 'Nouveaux fragments théologiques de l'école d'Anselme de Laon. Conclusions et tables', ibid. 159-65.

[2] See for example the *Commentarius Cantabrigiensis in Epistolas Pauli e Schola Petri Abaelardi*, ed. A. Landgraf (Notre Dame, Indiana, 1937). The commentator is a disciple of Abailard to whom he refers as 'the philosopher'; he writes 'before or not long after 1141'.

[3] R. M. Martin, 'Œuvres de Robert de Melun, ii. *Questiones de Epistolis Pauli*' (*Spic. Sac. Lov.* xviii, 1938). See the introduction i-lviii.

'the progressive and constructive spirit of Abailard'. He had a great preference for the *quaestio* as an exegetical instrument to the straightforward comment. He thought that too much glossing was being done. He inveighed against the superficiality and pretentiousness of overlaying the text with unnecessary quotation and explanation, in this reacting against the school of Anselm.[1] It seems, indeed, that glossing had become second nature to Anselm's pupils, and that they glossed whatever literature came within their reach. A long-suffering correspondent of one of them complains of the return of his own letter, so thickly glossed as to be unintelligible.[2] Robert intended to prune this luxuriance by concentrating on the *quaestio*.

The next stage, logically, is a commentary composed altogether of *quaestiones*, with no explanatory notes at all. The *quaestiones* were excerpted from the commentary of Robert of Melun and circulated separately as *Quaestiones de Epistolis Pauli*; and another, anonymous, set of *Quaestiones* on the Apostle seems to have been collected on this model.[3] In a second work of Robert, the *Quaestiones de divina pagina*, the text which originally served as a basis has disappeared. The modern editor can only tell us that many of the *quaestiones* seem to have been excerpted from a commentary on St. Matthew.[4] Then we have many collections of miscellaneous *Quaestiones* on theological matters. If they originally

[1] F. Bliemetzrieder, 'Robert of Melun', &c., op. cit. (p. 51, n. 4). We now have the full text of Robert's preface to his *Sentences*, containing his attack on glosses, ed. R. M. Martin, *Œuvres de Robert de Melun*, iii (Louvain, 1947), 3-25. Previously it was only printed in extracts. I reserve a full discussion of it to chapter V, where the actual handling of the *Gloss* in lectures will be described. Robert's editor does not agree that the attack was necessarily directed against Anselm of Laon (4, n. to line 23). As the *Sentences* were composed 1152-60, and as Robert is writing of contemporaries, Anselm cannot have been directly *visé*. But Robert's strictures on those who use the *Gloss* and the *Magna glosatura* must surely include those who compiled them and put them into circulation, hence the whole Laon tradition is being blamed by him.

[2] Philip of Harvengt, *Ep.* vii *ad Ioannem*, *P.L.* cciii. 57. 'Meas mihi epistolas, quas vobis miseram, remisistis, sed eas primitus tam crebro glossis marginalibus respersistis, ut quasi transire in colorem alterum compellantur, et iam non esse quod fuerant videantur.' Philip says that in one of these glosses his correspondent indignantly protested against the assumption that he had learnt the Scriptures from childhood in the cloister; no, he was a pupil of Master Anselm: 'Super hunc versiculum vestra glossa: "In claustro, inquit, et alibi, in scholis scil., didici; nec iuxta quorumdam praesumptionem ipse me docui, *sed a magistro Ansello didici*, quod non dico ut me commendem, sed ut vos tangam" ' (ibid. 58).

[3] Printed in *P.L.* clxxv. 431-634 and wrongly ascribed to Hugh of St. Victor. R. M. Martin, op. cit., ii. xlvi-xlvii.

[4] ibid. i. xxxii.

belonged to commentaries from which they were excerpted, these are untraceable; their existence is a mere hypothesis. The *Quaestiones de divina pagina* thus form an interesting link between two types of *quaestio* collections, one which can be traced back to an exegetical framework with some probability, one which cannot.

Quaestiones were not only excerpted from their original commentary and issued separately; they were also transferred to a different kind of work. When the Lombard compiled his *Sentences*, he transferred to them a number of questions from his *Magna Glosatura*; he was able to remove these *quaestiones* from their context, and to rearrange them in the systematic doctrinal scheme of the *Sentences*, without making any important verbal alteration. Here again we have a parallel in civil law. The *summulae* of the glossators were transferred from their original places in the margin of the Code or Digest and written out separately, or incorporated in collections of *distinctiones*. The few words at the beginning, which referred to a specific passage of the text, were eventually dropped out; but they sometimes survive in early copies as a 'clear and tangible illustration of that process by which the various forms of legal literature severed the umbilical cord that linked them to the text'.[1]

Hence we are faced with the difficult problem of distinguishing between exegesis and systematic doctrinal teaching. We know that later in the twelfth century some systematic instruction on doctrine was given, apart from the study of *sacra pagina*. It took the form of lectures on the Lombard's *Sentences*. We do not know exactly what stages it passed through before the *Sentences* were written. What theological teaching, as distinct from the exposition of Scripture, was customary before 1152? What theological text-books, if any, did the *Sentences* displace?

There seem to be two possibilities. The masters in monastic and cathedral schools had been in the habit of glossing various texts, the Athanasian creed, certain books of the Fathers, in addition to Scripture, and these glosses were doctrinal in content;[2] they may well have originated in

---

[1] H. Kantorowicz, *Studies in the Glossators of the Roman Law* (Cambridge, 1938), 73-5, 87. Dr. R. W. Hunt has found evidence for the *disputatio* as a separate exercise in the teaching of grammar in the later twelfth century; 'Studies on Priscian in the Twelfth Century — II; the School of Ralph of Beauvais', *Mediaeval and Renaissance Studies*, ii (1950), 19.

[2] I am quoting information given me by Dr. B. Bischoff from his knowledge

lectures. We also have the sentence books of the school of Laon, where Christian doctrine is set forth systematically. Do these books represent actual teaching or merely private study? We know that both Abailard and Hugh of St. Victor delivered their systematic theological works in the form of lectures.[1] How far were they improving on ordinary academic procedure? A modern scholar, who devoted himself to the editing of Anselm, held that already, in Anselm's period, specialization was taking place, 'if not of masters at least of the subjects they taught'; after the preliminary *artes liberales*, came the three branches of sacred science: *divina pagina* (Bible studies), *fides catholica* (doctrine), *lex ecclesiastica* (canon law).[2]

Nevertheless in Anselm's period theology was still commonly referred to as though it were synonymous with *divina pagina*. One of his pupils writes: 'Deliberately I sought out Laon, where for some time I studied the Old and New Testaments under Master Anselm.'[3] Dom Lottin, as we have seen, gives the weight of his authority to the thesis that Anselm restricted his teaching entirely to Scripture and that the sentence collections were made outside his class room. But the thesis is tentatively put forward. Teaching methods developed between the death of Anselm and the advent of Peter the Lombard. We know too little of the organization of studies in cathedral schools to decide on the exact limits of exegesis at this period; we can only speculate on the proportion of material, transmitted to us in other forms, which originated in biblical glosses and ought to be counted as exegesis.

But however little we know of its details, the main tendency of the cathedral school is clear; it leads away from old-fashioned Bible studies. St. Gregory had identified theology with exegesis. The eleventh- and early twelfth-century

[1] G. Paré, A. Brunet, P. Tremblay, *La Renaissance du XIIe siècle* (Paris, Ottawa, 1933), 256-66.

[2] F. Bliemetzrieder, 'Autour de l'œuvre théologique d'Anselme de Laon', *Rech. Théol. anc. méd.* i (1929), 480. He quotes the Bohemian chronicle of Cosmas, 1068, describing the qualifications of Mark, chaplain to the bishop of Prague: 'Marcus . . . in omnibus liberalibus artibus valde fuit bonus scholasticus, . . . in divina vero pagina interpres mirificus, in fide catholica et in lege ecclesiastica doctor magnificus.' *Fontes Rer. Bohem.* ii. 100.

[3] Hugo Metellus, *Ep.* xxi, *M.G.H., Lib. de Lite*, iii. 354.

of early MSS. in Germany, and by Dr. K. Schleyer from his study of works on the Creed. Dr. Hunt tells me that Alexander Nequam refers to a marginal and interlinear gloss on the Creed.

masters were inclined to identify exegesis with theology. Their work appears to be brilliant but one-sided, if we remember the promise of the eighth and ninth centuries. We find the theological questioning but not the biblical scholarship. It is no accident that the two favourite books for commentators were the Psalter and the Pauline Epistles, their creative energy being centred in the latter; St. Paul provided the richest nourishment to the theologian and logician. Next came the Hexaemeron, because it provided an opportunity to discuss the questions of Creation and angelology. Original work on the Law, the historical books of the Old Testament, the Prophets, the Gospels, and the Acts is lacking. We get an interesting confirmation of this in Abailard's *Historia calamitatum*. When he was a pupil of Anselm at Laon, 1121-3, he wanted to show up the derivative character of his master's teaching by lecturing himself on a book of Scripture. The prophecy of Ezechiel was picked for the experiment as being 'inusitata', not customarily taught in the schools.[1] So we know that at least one of the Prophets was notoriously neglected.

This one-sided development was quite natural. The innumerable problems arising from the reception of Aristotelian logic and the study of canon and civil law, the new possibilities of reasoning, the urgent need for speculation and discussion, all these produced an atmosphere of haste and excitement which was unfavourable to biblical scholarship. The masters of the cathedral schools had neither the time nor the training to specialize in a very technical branch of Bible study. This applied to the philosophers and humanists of Chartres as much as to the theologians of Paris and Laon. Even Bec, the last of the great monastic schools, had been no exception. Lanfranc was a theologian and logician; the genius of his pupil, St. Anselm of Canterbury, took another direction. His philosophical works eclipsed his biblical, which seem to have been lost.[2]

And yet, looking closely, we can see all the ingredients of a revival of scholarship; they only lack someone to bring them together. There were friendly contacts between Christian and Jewish scholars, which offered the possibility of learning Hebrew. The *Disputatio Judaei cum Christiano* by

[1] *Hist. calam.* iii, *P.L.* clxxviii. 125.
[2] St. Anselm says: 'Tres tractatus pertinentes ad studium sacrae scripturae quondam feci . . .', *Dialogus de Veritate Prol., P.L.* clviii. 467.

Gilbert Crispin, abbot of Westminster, written soon before 1098,[1] and the *Dialogus* between a Christian, a philosopher, and a Jew, by Peter Abailard, show a tolerance and an appreciation of the Jewish point of view which contrast strikingly with the bitterness of later controversy. Gilbert Crispin implies that his work had a background of actual conversations with Jews; and we have references to discussions in academic circles; Peter the Chanter, for instance, says that Gilbert de la Porrée converted some Jews, evidently in the course of an argument.[2] Abailard tells Heloise that he once listened to a Jew commenting on a text of Kings.[3] It is interesting to find the ten commandments and certain prophecies quoted in Hebrew as well as Latin, in the *Ysagoge in Theologiam*, a short theological *summa*, written probably 1148-52, which has been classified as 'school of Abailard'.[4]

Another pupil of Abailard, commenting on a text of the Pauline Epistles, refers to his master's questioning the Jews.[5] He is interested himself in refuting Jewish arguments;[6] but in one unmistakably personal passage he contrasts the Jewish love of letters favourably with the Christian:

'If the Christians educate their sons, they do so not for God, but for gain, in order that the one brother, if he be a clerk, may help his father and mother and his other brothers. They say that a clerk will have no heir and whatever he has will be ours and the other brothers'. A black cloak and hood to go to church in, and his surplice, will be enough for *him*. But the Jews, out of zeal for God and love of the law, put as many sons as they have to letters, that each may understand God's law . . . A Jew, however poor, if he had ten sons would put them all to letters, not for gain, as the Christians do, but for the understanding of God's law, and not only his sons, but his daughters.'[7]

[1] J. A. Robinson, *Gilbert Crispin Abbot of Westminster* (Cambridge, 1911), 64.

[2] From the *Summa Abel*, MS. Bibl. Nat. Lat. 455, fo. 71[b]: 'Item nota quod magister Gilbertus sic convincit Iudeos, et conversi sunt, dicens: Que lex melior et potius observanda, an illa scil. que sine misericordia precipit hominem lapidari si colligat ligna in sabbato, an illa que habet misericordiam, et que dimittit non tantum septies sed etiam usque septuagies septies, et illud: Vade et amplius noli peccare?' It seems certain that Gilbert de la Porrée is meant; the Chanter refers to him recognizably in another context as 'Master Gilbert'.

[3] *Problemata Heloisae*, xxxvi, *P.L.* clxxviii. 718.

[4] A. Landgraf, 'Écrits théologiques de l'école d'Abélard', *Spic. Sac. Lov.* xiv (1934), xl-lv.

[5] *Commentarius Cantabrigiensis* (op. cit., p. 73, n. 2), i. 65; 'Judei vero a philosopho sepe requisiti nullatenus dicunt se istam benedictionem posse assignare in carnali Ysaac, per quem vel cuius semen gentes potius extirpate sunt quam benedictionem susceperint.' 'The philosopher' for him is his master, Abailard.

[6] ibid. ii. 259, 278-80.　　　　　[7] ibid. ii. 434.

Most significant of all is Abailard's own recommendation to Heloise and the sisters of the Paraclite, that they should learn Hebrew and Greek, in order to understand Scripture in the original. It may surprise us that so technical a study, which Abailard himself had scarcely attempted, should have struck him as a suitable occupation for nuns.[1] We must remember that Heloise and Abailard were Benedictines; *lectio divina* was prescribed by their Rule. When the teaching of Scripture in the secular schools came under the influence of the liberal arts, the monk, in reaction, withdrew into himself, and clung to the conception of *lectio divina* as a devotional rather than an intellectual exercise.[2] He concentrated on the spiritual exposition, which tended to be crowded out by other interests in the secular schools, though it was never rejected. Abailard was proposing that Heloise should return to the scholarly ideal of *lectio divina* as taught by St. Jerome, whom he quotes.

Certainly Abailard had a precedent. It was the monks, rather than the clerks, who had shown signs of reviving biblical scholarship. The Benedictine, Sigebert of Gembloux, teaching at Metz about 1070, 'was very dear to the Jews of the city because he was skilful in distinguishing the Hebrew truth from other editions; and he agreed with what they told him, if it were in accordance with the Hebrew truth'.[3] St. Stephen Harding, abbot of Cîteaux, corrected the text of the Old Testament with the help of Jews, whom he consulted in French, as he tells us. His second volume was finished in 1109.[4]

The Cistercians continued the work of correction, though sometimes with more zeal than method. Nicholas Manjacoria, the learned monk of Trois Fontaines, was horrified

---

[1] *Ep.* ix, *P.L.* clxxviii. 325. See J. G. Sikes, *Peter Abailard* (Cambridge, 1932), 29-30, 43, on Abailard's knowledge of Hebrew.

[2] We need a general study of twelfth-century monastic commentators; see especially A. Wilmart, 'Le Prologue d'Hervé de Bourgdieu, etc.', *Rev. Bén.* xxxv (1923), 256; A. Landgraf, 'Der Paulinenkommentar des Hervaeus von Bourg-Dieu', *Biblica*, xxvi (1945), 113-32; Hervé died about 1150; D. Van de Eynde, 'Les Magistri du Commentaire "Unum ex Quatuor" de Zacharias Chrysopolitanus', *Antonianum*, xxiii (1948), 1-32, 181-220; Zachary of Besançon was a Premonstratensian canon, whose commentary on a Gospel harmony was written soon after 1150-52. On Richard of Préaux (d. 1131/32) see B. Smalley, 'Sapiential Books I', ii. 318-20. On commentaries on the Canticle, especially by Cistercians, J. Leclercq, 'Le commentaire de Gilbert de Stanford sur le Cantique', *Studia Anselmiana*, xx (1948), *Analecta monastica*, no. 5, 205-25.

[3] Godescalc, *Gesta Abbatum Gemblacensis*, *P.L.* clx. 641.

[4] *Quam notitiam*, 9-11.

to discover, while visiting a house of his Order, a brother in
the scriptorium copying into a good, early text of the Bible
all the additions that he could find in other exemplars,
convinced that the fullest version must be the most accurate.
Nicholas gently expostulated with him and formed a project,
which he afterwards carried out, to lay down rules for the
right procedure in textual criticism. He had already, when
attached to a church in Rome, corrected the text of the
Bible, consulting a Jew and learning from him something of
the scholarship of Rashi, although Rashi's influence is still
indirect and he does not give the names of his informant or
of his sources.[1] Nicholas paid special attention to the text of
the Psalter and his attitude to it is both typical and significant
for medieval textual studies. The student had three translations to choose from: the Roman, the Gallican or Vulgate,
and the *Hebraica*, Jerome's translation from the Hebrew.
Nicholas prefers the third as being closest to the original:
'In comparison with this', he says, 'other books of the psalms
hardly merit the name of Psalter.' But although it is closer
than the Roman or Augustine's or any others that he has
seen, it differs considerably from the 'Hebrew truth'. So
Nicholas is already comparing the *Hebraica* both with other
Latin translations, some obtained from commentaries of
the Fathers, and with the Hebrew text, in so far as he could
ascertain it by his own studies and by the help of contemporary Jewish rabbis. He gives his vote unquestionably
to the last.[2]

Nicholas died about 1145. He wrote his *Libellus de corrup-
tione et correptione psalmorum* between this date and 1140; his
correction of the Bible was made some time before. In the

[1] H. Denifle, 'Die Handscriften der Bibelcorrectorien des 13 Jahrhunderts',
Archiv f. Lit. und Kirchengesch. des M. As, iv (1888), 270-7; 601; *Quam notitiam*,
12-15; A. Wilmart, 'Nicolas Manjacoria, Cistercien à Trois-Fontaines', *Rev.
Bén.* xxxiii (1921), 136-43.

[2] '... Cuius quidem comparatione alia psalmorum volumina VIX sunt
psalteria nominanda. Verumtamen hec translatio plus veritati propinqua est
quam romana, etsi et illa et quam edisserit Origenes et quam exponit Augustinus et de qua tractat Ambrosius, sed et alie quascumque vidisse me recolo
multum dissideant ab hebraica veritate.' Quoted by A. Wilmart, *loc. cit.*,
139 from MS. Montpellier (School of Medicine) 294, fo. 145v.
A reviewer objected that 'the Hebrew truth' of Sigebert of Gembloux must
mean the Latin Vulgate; hence that Sigebert simply accepted what the Jews
said if it corresponded to the Latin Vulgate, and was not in consequence
investigating the Hebrew text. But Nicholas Manjacoria in the passage just
quoted is definitely contrasting 'the Hebrew truth' to Jerome's *Hebraica* version
of the Psalter and there is no question here of 'the Hebrew truth' meaning
anything other than the Hebrew text. The term was used ambiguously.

years 1141-43, Peter the Venerable, abbot of Cluny, was organizing a team of scholars to translate the Koran and other Arabic texts concerning Mohammed into Latin, believing that the first step towards converting the infidel was an understanding of his doctrines.[1] We are in the early days of a great movement for the translation of philosophic and scientific texts from Greek and Arabic for the benefit of Latin scholarship. Stephen Harding, Abailard and Nicholas Manjacoria have to be seen against this background. The correctors of the Bible lived at a time when translation from semitic languages was 'in the air'. If scholars could go to Spain, Southern Italy and Sicily in search of Arabic learning, the student of Scripture might well consult the Jew on his doorstep.[2]

Turning from the text to its interpretation, we may notice a commentary which makes a refreshing contrast with those originating in well-known schools. Master Lambert of Utrecht, in his exposition of St. Paul, shows himself more of a biblical scholar and less of a logician than most of his contemporaries.[3] The simple questions and answers raised by his conflicting authorities are innocent of dialectic. His interests are historical rather than theological. Instead of exploring the doctrinal content of his text, he likes to fill out the references to Old Testament or even pagan history. He tells anecdotes, for instance, to illustrate the origin of idolatry among the Greeks and Egyptians. The solid, leisurely character of the work suggests a different, and from our point of view a more hopeful, background. Though not monastic, it was evidently more peaceful and conducive to historical studies than Paris or Chartres.

We may doubt whether Heloise and her nuns made much progress in Hebrew; but Abailard's letter opens new possibilities. Biblical studies belonged to the cloister; the intellectuals of the twelfth century were flocking to the schools. A religious order, devoted both to *lectio divina* and to

---

[1] M-Th. d'Alverny, 'Deux traductions latines du Coran au moyen âge', *Archives d'histoire doctrinale et littéraire du moyen âge* XVI (1948), 69-131.

[2] It is sometimes alleged that the Cistercians 'legislated against' the study of Hebrew. The evidence is a decree of the General Chapter in 1198 that a monk of Poblet (in Catalonia), who was said to have learnt Hebrew letters from a Jew, should be committed to the abbot of Clairvaux for inquiry and correction; J. Canivez, *Statuta Ordinis Cisterciensis*, i (Louvain, 1933), 227. It is not stated that the monk in question was aiming at Bible study. Hebrew letters could also be used for casting magic spells.

[3] 'La Glossa Ordinaria', op. cit. (p. 79, n. 1), 372-4.

learning, settled at Paris, where theologians were interested in the Jews, might succeed in attracting intellectuals. The result might well be biblical scholarship which, once established, might find its way into the curriculum of the university.

CHAPTER III

THE VICTORINES

I. HUGH OF ST. VICTOR

THE *vita regularis et canonica* is one of the most interesting, and perhaps the most elusive, of twelfth-century religious ideals. The black cloak which he wore over his white habit distinguished the canon regular from the black and the white monks. He was not a monk, though he was a cloistered religious. His Rule was based on that drawn up by St. Augustine for secular clergy, widely adopted in Italy, France, and the Rhineland by the end of the eleventh century and spreading to England early in the twelfth.[1]

The movement has no St. Bernard to interpret it to us, no great succession of saints. The canons who comment on their Rule are curiously reticent. We know that its immediate practical object was the reform of the cathedral clergy; but it went far beyond. The laity enthusiastically founded new houses and the movement had special attractions for learned clerks.[2] A gulf had opened between monks and scholars. Contemporaries constantly stress their difference in function: the scholar learns and teaches; the monk prays and 'mourns'. The canons regular courageously refused to admit the dilemma.

This was especially true of the Abbey of St. Victor at Paris, founded in 1110.[3] The original impulse came from Master William of Champeaux, Anselm's pupil and Abailard's opponent, who withdrew from the schools to a small chapel, in a meadow on the left bank of the Seine, intending to lead a life of prayer and solitude. His pupils followed him, and he continued to teach in his retirement; they formed the nucleus of this foundation. Until about 1140, at least, the

[1] See P. Mandonnet, *St Dominique: l'idée, l'homme et l'oeuvre*, ii (Paris, 1938); ch. ii, *L'ordre régulier et l'imitation des Apôtres*, 103-92. His view that the *vita regularis et canonica* of the twelfth century was an attempt to anticipate the Order of Friars Preacher, which failed owing to the influence of the older monasticism, though suggestive, seems to be over-simplified.
[2] See R. W. Hunt, 'English Learning in the Late Twelfth Century', *Transactions of the Royal Historical Society*, xix (1936), 34.
[3] Fourier Bonnard, *Histoire de l'Abbaye Royale de St Victor*, i (Paris). References, unless specially mentioned, will be found here.

Victorines seem to have kept an open school;[1] they were unique at Paris in being both *scholares* and *claustrales*. The abbey also served as a kind of chaplaincy to the Paris students. Naturally, then, it reflected the schools from which its personnel was largely recruited; among the canons were Frenchmen, Bretons, Normans, English, Scots, Norwegians, Germans, and Italians. Its position as a wealthy corporation, whose chief benefactors were the French royal family, brought the advantage of a magnificent library and of wide contacts, as well as distractions. St. Victor was drawn into the stormy politics of the reform movement; the prior was murdered in 1133 for supporting the bishop of Paris against royal servants; one of the popes visited the abbey during his exile from Rome. A former royal chancellor retired there after his disgrace at court, bringing with him his curiously humanist correspondence, to be copied into the abbey letter-book.[2] Daughter houses associated St. Victor with places as remote as Wigmore and Bristol. It had an important economic function as a repository for valuables; a number of letters in the Victorine collection are informal cheques, made out to the bearer and crossed by allusions intelligible only to the addressee, usually the prior or sub-prior: 'you remember what I said to you that day in the infirmary. . . .'[3]

We must set these activities against the orderly background of Victorine customs, which prescribe a routine, austere but temperate, in a well-regulated household, where dishes must be wiped before being laid upon the table-cloth. Only these activities and this background can explain the strange richness and diversity of the Victorine literature. We remember it best for the religious lyrics, which have all attached themselves to the Breton poet, Adam, and for the mystical theology of Hugh and Richard; it includes history, chronicles, geography, grammar, philosophy, psychology, education, together with the usual sermons, commentaries, and various kinds of manuals. Only these activities and this background can explain the unity of spirit which underlies

---

[1] B. Bischoff, 'Aus der Schule Hugos von St. Viktor', *Aus der Geisteswelt des Mittelalters*, ed. A. Lang, J. Lechner, M. Schmaus, *Beitr. z. Gesch. der Philosophie und Theologie des Mittelalters*, Suppl. Bd. iii, i (Münster, 1935), 247.

[2] Hugh of Champfleury, who died in 1175. See A. Wilmart, 'Un Billet littéraire sur le retour du printemps dans un manuscrit de St Victor', *Rev. Bén.* xlviii (1936), 349-54.

[3] A. Luchaire, 'Les Recueils épistolaires de l'Abbaye de St Victor', *Bibl. de la Faculté des Lettres*, viii (1899), 45-6; Duchesne, *Historia Francorum*, iv. 746, *Ep.* DXIX.

the diversity, the special qualities common to the greater Victorines: 'subtlety with clarity, daring scrutiny of the mysteries of human being, a typical Victorine mysticism; yet a style which is lively, ingenious, sometimes eloquent, incomparably more attractive than that of the scholastics who succeeded.'[1] These traits of Abbot Achard are characteristic of his school. They would also apply to Hugh of St. Victor; but he has in addition a personal impressiveness, which contemporaries recognized by calling him 'a second Augustine'.

It is typical of Hugh that we have a detailed record of how he died, 'gentle, pious, humble and good', whereas we know little of his life, apart from his writings. He came to St. Victor from Lorraine or the Low Countries about 1118, and taught from about 1125 until his death in 1141. He managed within this short space of time to leave works which fill over two volumes of Migne.[2]

Of all these works the most neglected by modern scholars are his *Notulae* on various passages of the Octateuch, printed in an uncritical edition, under the pompous modern title: *Adnotationes Elucidatoriae*.[3] 'Ces notes offrent peu d'intérêt' is Hauréau's comment; his only good mark has gone to the treatment of Creation; for Hugh, 'although the most credulous of the medieval mystics, was less rashly realist than Duns Scot'. The neglect is particularly striking in comparison with the multitude of modern studies of Hugh's doctrinal and mystical works, his philosophy of history, his educational programme and his influence on the rising generation. 'His thought is biblical', we are often told; but this has roused no interest in his biblical studies. Actually, the *Notulae* mark a revival of scholarship. They opened up a new period, which in due course realized the scientific study desired and attempted by Hugh.

[1] G. Morin, 'Un traité faussement attribué à Adam de St Victor', *Rev. Bén.* xvi (1899), 218-19.
[2] On the works of Hugh see B. Hauréau, *Les Œuvres de Hugues de St-Victor* (Paris, 1886); J. de Ghellinck, 'La table des matières de la première édition des œuvres de Hugues de St-Victor', *Recherches de Science Religieuse*, i (1910), 270-89. Much remains to be done on the question of authenticity and the original form in many cases. I have not attempted to add anything to these studies. On his letters see L. Ott, 'Untersuchungen zur theologischen Briefliteratur der Frühscholastik', *Beitr. z. Gesch. der Phil. und Theol. des MAs.* xxxiv (1937). On his life see F. Vernet, *Dict. de Théol. Cath.* vii. 240 ff., F. E. Croydon, 'Notes on the Life of Hugh of St. Victor', *Journal of Theological Studies*, xl (1939), 232-53.
[3] *P.L.* clxxv. 29-114.

Even had the *Notulae* been lost, his other work would have enabled one to deduce their character. Hugh resembles the first Augustine in the unity of his thought, the 'whole' being so rich and self-consistent that no part of it can be considered separately. And the 'whole' implies a new attitude towards the study of Scripture.

In the first place, Hugh was both a religious and a scholar. As a contemplative religious, his supreme object was union with God through prayer and meditation on God's works, especially the Scriptures. St. Gregory had shown him how to achieve this highest kind of wisdom through the mystical exposition. As a scholar, he appreciated the modern development of the liberal arts, with its stress on dialectic; he saw that the commentary on Scripture was turning into a collection of *Quaestiones* and had a rival in the sentence book, while the Fathers taught that all science ought to serve as an introduction and guide to Bible study. Hugh's problem, therefore, was to recall rebellious learning back to the scriptural framework of the *De Doctrina Christiana*, adapting the teaching of Rome and Carthage to the very different climate of twelfth-century Paris. He published a *refonte complète* of the *De Doctrina* in his *Didascalicon: de Studio Legendi*.[1]

He begins with a description and analysis of contemporary sciences. The student of Scripture must welcome them: 'learn everything; you will find nothing superfluous; a narrow education displeases'.[2] But learn at leisure: 'more haste less speed'; 'it does not matter if you have not read everything; the number of books is infinite; do not pursue infinity'.[3] Hugh is raising a warning finger against 'reading with glosses' in the feverish manner of the schools. To this hasty, superficial reading he opposes the traditional studies of the cloister, slow, wide, and deep.

How could one press these new sciences into the service of *lectio divina*? The problem admitted no radical solution for Hugh. A Victorine was firmly persuaded that 'all good things go in threes'.[4] He was obeying no mere convention

---

[1] My references are to *P.L.* clxxvi. 739-838, since the new edition by C. H. Buttimer (Washington, Catholic University of America, 1939) has not been accessible to me.

[2] vi. iii. 800-1.   [3] v. vii. 796.

[4] On the importance of three in Victorine philosophy see B. Geyer, *Die patristische und scholastische Philosophie* (Berlin, 1928), 267, 269. The treatise by Achard, *De discretione animae, spiritus et mentis*, is another example; see G. Morin, 'Un traité inédit d'Achard de St-Victor', *Aus der Geisteswelt des Mittelalters*, op. cit. (p. 84, n. 1), 251-62.

when he expounded according to the three senses, but moving in the very rhythm of the universe. Learning, then, must be fitted into the threefold exposition. This could only be accomplished by developing both the form and the matter of traditional exegesis.

His changes in the form of *lectio divina* consist in introducing a special course of studies as a preliminary to the investigation of each sense. When the student has a sufficient grounding in the arts and sciences to approach the Scriptures, he must begin with the literal historical sense. He should therefore read Genesis, Exodus, Josue, Judges, Kings, Chronicles, the Gospels, and Acts, memorizing carefully the events, the persons, their time and place:

'Do not despise these lesser things. They who despise the lesser things gradually fail. If you scorn to learn your alphabet, you will never even make your name as a grammarian. I know there are some who want to philosophise immediately and say that fairy tales should be left to the false apostles. Their learning is asinine. Do not imitate such men.'[1]

Historical and geographical aids to study will therefore be needed at this stage;[2] Hugh himself prepared two chronicles and a map of the world.

Then the student may pass to allegory. This time he should proceed in the reverse order, beginning with those books of the New Testament which are richest in doctrine: St. Matthew, St. John, the Epistles, especially the Pauline, and the Apocalypse. Then he may safely pass from the New Testament to its foreshadowing. He may read the Hexaemeron, the Law, Isaias, the beginning and end of Ezechiel, Job, the Canticle, and Psalms.[3]

Just as the student needs geography and history for the literal sense, so he needs doctrine for the allegorical. Hugh compares systematic doctrinal teaching to the 'second foundation' of polished stones, which rises above the first, subterranean foundation of history, to support the wall of allegory.[4] He wrote his *summa*, the *De Sacramentis Christianae Fidei*, for this purpose;[5] the early drafts of it were given at St. Victor in a lecture course.[6] For himself, Hugh avoided

---

[1] VI. iii. 799-802.　　　　　[2] Cf. *De Scripturis*, xviii, *P.L.* clxxv. 25-8.
[3] *Didascalicon*, VI. iv. vi, 805-6.　　　　[4] Ibid. iv. 802-5.
[5] *Prologus: quare lectionem mutaverit*, 183; G. Paré, A. Brunet, P. Tremblay, *La Renaissance*, etc., op. cit. (p. 76, n. 1).
[6] B. Bischoff, op. cit. (p. 84, n. 1).

dialectic; but by his skilful manœuvre he admitted the
growing science of theology, with all its discussions, into the
building of *lectio divina*. *Quaestiones* become polished stones in
the wall.

The third sense, the tropological, occasions an equally
brilliant feat of synthesis. So far, *lectio*, used in its non-
liturgical sense, has meant study or lecture; we 'divide' our
text, distinguishing what is confused and investigating what
is hidden.[1] The object of *lectio divina*, however, is twofold:
we seek knowledge and virtue. The first two senses pertain
to knowledge, the third to virtue.[2] Hence the *Didascalicon*,
which treats of knowledge, says little of the third sense.[3]
Certain parts of the Bible and the works of St. Gregory are
useful here.[4] But this kind of study will lead the student
away from books: 'By contemplating the works of God we
learn what ours should be. All nature speaks of God, all
nature teaches man.'[5] *Lectio* and doctrine are for beginners.
The religious aims at contemplation through study, meditation, prayer, and good works.[6] Hence *lectio divina* includes
two separate exercises: the scholastic *lectio* or lecture and the
meditative reading or collation of St. Gregory and Cassian.

The one flaw in the *Didascalicon* from the point of view of
exegesis is that Hugh still adheres to the confused Alexandrian terminology by which history, allegory, and
tropology refer both to the subject-matter of Scripture and to
the method of its exposition. 'Allegory', for instance, equals
'doctrine', whether it be the teaching of St. Paul in his
Epistles or the commentator's allegorical exposition of the
Law. It was a concession to tradition. Hugh himself, as he
shows when he discusses the literal sense, was quite clear as
to the difference between content and comment. He says
that 'history' means *either* historical events *or* the primary
meaning of the words.[7]

It is very interesting to find an anonymous letter, probably
written by a Victorine, which clarifies and simplifies the
scheme of the *Didascalicon*, so as to avoid this confusing
double meaning of allegory. The writer is advising a young
religious who comes to *lectio divina* without any scholastic
education how he should proceed.[8] After learning the

---

[1] *Didascalicon*, VI. xii. 809.   [2] V. vi. 794.   [3] VI. v. 805.   [4] V. vii. 794.
[5] VI. v. 805.   [6] V. viii. 796-7; VI. xiii. 809.   [7] VI. iii. 801.
[8] *Epistola anonymi ad Hugonem amicum*, ed. Martène et Durand, *Thesaurus
Novus Anecdotorum*, i. 487-8. The writer must have been either a Victorine or
much influenced by Victorine thought.

names and order of the biblical books, he should read the whole Bible three or four times for the historical sense, noting carefully those passages which are not to be taken literally. Let him read the Law, Josue, Judges, Kings, Chronicles, together with Josephus and Egesippus, and various aids to study, especially the *Quaestiones* of St. Augustine, memorizing all the main historical facts. Then he should read the Prophets, noting what has been, and what remains to be fulfilled *ad litteram*. Then he should read the remaining historical books of the Old Testament, with Proverbs, Wisdom, Ecclesiasticus, Ecclesiastes; lastly the Psalms, Job, and the Canticle: these last three books have no useful literal meaning and should be interpreted, forthwith, of Christ and the Church. Then he should pass to the New Testament, with the appropriate reference books and a Gospel harmony.

Then, as a preparation for the allegorical exposition, he should study the sacraments of the Church 'which may be found at length in the book of Master Hugh'. Then, for tropology, the nature of virtues and vices, which is described in many books. Then read a manual on the liturgy, then the *De Doctrina Christiana* and the *De Civitate Dei*. Now at last he may read, according to the three senses, in any order of books he may choose.

Hugh effected a differentiation between the three senses, which enormously increased the dignity of the historical sense. Instead of contrasting the lowly foundation of the 'letter' with the higher spiritual senses, he groups together the letter and allegory, which pertain to knowledge and contrasts them with tropology! The importance of the letter is constantly stressed.

Two sets of ideas were responsible for raising his opinion of the letter. First, his interest in history. Hugh constructed a Victorine version of the philosophy of history which he learnt from St. Augustine. He thought in terms of human religious history, the history of salvation:

'the Word Incarnate is our King, who came into the world to fight the devil; all the saints who were before his coming are as soldiers going before the royal presence; those who came after, and those to come, until the end of the world, are as soldiers following the King. And the King is in the midst of his army.'[1]

[1] *De Sacramentis, Prol.* ii, *P.L.* clxxvi. 183.

Unlike the normal twelfth-century *summa*, the *De Sacra-mentis* is planned on historical instead of theological lines: the work of Creation and the work of Restoration. Book I takes us from the Creation to the Incarnation, and includes the sacraments of the natural and the Mosaic Law; Book II takes us to the Last Things, and includes the sacraments of the Church. Thus the history of the Church coincides with world history, in time, if not in scope: 'Holy Church began to exist in her faithful at the beginning, and shall last to the end. We believe that, from the beginning to the end, no period lacks its faithful to Christ.'[1]

The inspired history of Scripture, therefore, is the primary source of world history for Hugh: 'The principles on which historical evolution works are, at the same time, our key to historical understanding.'[2] Hence the importance of in-vestigating and establishing every detail.

Secondly: the sacramental trend of his thought, which is closely linked to the historical. Man's history is a history of sacraments. God has ordered the 'work of Restoration' through a series of sacraments, the natural, the Mosaic, the Christian. The 'work of Creation' is sacramental too; it is both historical and symbolical. Hugh follows up the days of creation with chapters on their mystical sense: *Sacramentum divinorum operum*:

'I think that some great sacrament is recorded here; every soul is in darkness and disorder while it remains in sin ... It cannot be disposed in the order and form of righteousness, unless it is first enlightened, so that it can see its own peril, and divide the light from the darkness....'[3]

Hugh was living in a period which saw a great expansion of sacramental practice and definition. We hear of his own personal devotion to the sacrament of the altar from the brother who witnessed his death.[4] This gives us a clue to his special feeling for the letter of Scripture.

The Eucharistic controversy of the ninth century, which shaped the doctrine of transubstantiation, had inevitably suggested a comparison between Scripture and the sacra-ment. Scholars were too accustomed to compare Scripture

---

[1] *De Arca Noe Mystica*, iii, op. cit. 685.
[2] W. A. Schneider, 'Geschichte und Geschichtsphilosophie bei Hugo von St. Victor', *Münstersche Beitr. z. Gesch.-Forsch.* iii. ii (Münster, 1933), 27.
[3] *De Sacramentis*, i. i. xii, 195.
[4] *Osberti Epistola de Morte Hugonis*, *P.L.* clxxv, clxii.

to 'bread', or even to the 'body of Christ', to miss an analogy between the mystical exposition of Scripture and the consecration of the Host; in both cases the material is instrumental to the spiritual. The question at issue, *utrum in mysterio fiat an in veritate*, could be applied to passages of the Old Testament which had perplexed St. Augustine; are they literal or figurative? It was natural that opinions concerning one should react on the other.

Paschasius Radbertus comes close to the parallel between exposition and consecration in his *Liber de Corpore et Sanguine Domini*, where he defends transubstantiation against the 'spiritualist school', who hold that the Eucharist is a mere 'pledge', 'similitude', or 'sign'.[1] Paschasius maintains that the bread and wine are truly changed into the body and blood of Christ; at the same time, the action of the celebrant is outwardly symbolical or figurative, since he sacrifices daily at the altar in memory of one past event. What is a 'figure' then? No one, says Paschasius, who reads the Bible has any doubt that the figures of the Old Testament are mere foreshadowings of the New. How, then, can the Eucharist be at the same time a figure, or shadow of truth, and actually true? Are these two things compatible? He answers that a 'figure' need not necessarily stand for something shadowy and illusory. As children, he says, we first learn to read by letters or signs; then we arrive by gradual stages at an understanding of Scripture in its spiritual sense. The fact that the letters signify something other than themselves does not make them illusory, or anything other than that which they are.[2]

Paschasius goes on to the sacrifices of the Old Testament, which he contrasts with the Eucharist. They differed from the Christian sacrifices in that here the actions of the celebrant were merely symbolical or figurative. But he gives 'figurative' a wide and historical meaning: the patriarchs, longing for the grace of our faith, 'which was, as it were promised them by these means, partook of it inasmuch as they perceived the sacrament of truth by faith and in signs'.[3]

Now Paschasius, as an exegete, was quite exceptional in his grasp of the letter. None of his contemporaries, whose

---

[1] *P.L.* cxx. 1255-1350.　　　　　　　　[2] iv. 1277-9.

[3] v. 1280-1: '. . . et si qua in his virtus sacranda latuit, totum ex ista gratia fidei qua fruimur praefulsit: quam profecto illi per haec quasi promissam suspirantes participabantur tantumdem per fidem, et de figuris sacramentum veritatis intelligebant'.

H

work has come down to us, distinguished the literal sense so
clearly or applied himself so closely to the literal meaning
of biblical metaphor as Paschasius in his commentary on
Lamentations.[1] This can hardly be accidental. The metaphors of Lamentations were 'figures of truth' in their literal
sense, as the prophet intended them, and contained for
Paschasius the fuller truth of Christian doctrine, when he
expounded them afterwards allegorically.

Nor was it accidental that when the Eucharistic controversy revived in the eleventh century the contrary
happened; St. Gregory's neglect of the letter served as an
argument against transubstantiation. Berengar of Tours,
or more probably one of his disciples, brings forward St.
Gregory's preference for the spiritual sense of Scripture in
support of a purely spiritual presence in the Eucharist:[2]

> 'According to passages from the holy Fathers we should
> believe, it seems, that after consecration the bread on the altar
> is changed into the substance of Christ's body spiritually, from
> his human nature, truly understood in him; and that he is
> present there in this way, the best. Hence Ezechiel says of the
> spiritual cubit which, we find in Gregory, cannot be under-
> stood in a fleshly sense: *these are the measures of the altar by the
> truest cubit, which is a cubit and a handbreadth*' [Ezech. xliii. 13].

St. Gregory, commenting on the vision of Ezechiel, says that
the literal or fleshly sense would be absurd, the measurements of the building being physically inconceivable as the
doors were bigger than the walls. According to him the
survey in all its detail has no meaning except as a series of
phrases which can be explained allegorically and morally.
He does not ask how Ezechiel pictured the building, but goes
straight to the spiritual sense.[3]

[1] See above, p. 42.

[2] M. Matronola, *Un testo inedito di Berengario di Tours e il Concilio Romano del
1079* (Orbis Romanus Biblioteca di Testi Medievali, Milan, 1936), 116:
'Secundum capitula quidem sanctorum patrum credendum videtur. panem
sacerdotali benedictione facta in altari. verti in substantia corporis christi
spiritaliter. ex humana natura eius in eo vere intellecta. et secundum hunc
optimum modum vere esse ibi presentem. Unde de spiritali cubitu qui iuxta
gregorium repperitur. carnaliter non potest intelligi. Ezechiel ait. *Iste mensure
altaris in cubito verissimo. qui habebat cubitum et palmum.*' The ascription of this
little treatise to Berengar himself has been disputed. See the reviews: *Bulletin
de Théol. anc. méd.* iii (1938), 250*-2*, nos. 551-3.

[3] *Hom. in Ezech.* II. i, *P.L.* lxxvi. 936: 'Cuius videlicet civitatis aedificium
accipi iuxta litteram nullatenus potest. Nam paulo post subdit hoc ipsum
aedificium calamo sex cubitorum et palmo ... Quae cuncta stare iuxta litteram
nullatenus valent.' Dom Matronola refers only to the *Liber Curae Pastoralis*,
iii. 9; but this does not explain the 'spiritual cubit'.

Controversy seldom ruffles the courteous manner of Hugh, but he deals severely with two errors, both 'spiritualist'. One concerns transubstantiation:

> 'What! is the sacrament of the altar not truth, because it is a sign? Then neither is Christ's death, because that is a sign, nor his resurrection, because that too is a sign. The Apostle clearly states that Christ's death and resurrection is a sign, a similitude, a representation, a sacrament, an example: Christ died *for our sins and rose again for our justification* [Rom. iv. 25]. ... Was not this truth? Then Christ did not truly die and rise again ... which God forbid ... Cannot the sacrament of the altar be a similitude and also truth?'[1]

The second error concerns neglect of the literal meaning of Scripture, and is condemned in the *De Scripturis* and the *Didascalicon*. This is not so much 'perilous' as ridiculous. Hugh pokes quiet fun at those who hurry over the literal sense in their haste to reach the mystery:

> 'The mystical sense is only gathered from what the letter says, in the first place. I wonder how people have the face to boast themselves teachers of allegory, when they do not know the primary meaning of the letter. "We read the Scriptures", they say, "but we don't read the letter. The letter does not interest us. We teach allegory." How do you read Scripture then, if you don't read the letter? Subtract the letter and what is left? "We *read* the letter" they say, "but not according to the letter. We read allegory, and we expound the letter not literally but allegorically . . . ; as *lion*, according to the historical sense means a beast, but allegorically it means Christ. Therefore the word *lion* means Christ." '

Hugh patiently explains that the literal sense is not the *word*, but what it means; it may have a figurative meaning; and this belongs to the literal sense. To despise the literal sense is to despise the whole of sacred literature:

> 'If, as they say, we ought to leap straight from the letter to its spiritual meaning, then the metaphors and similes, which educate us spiritually, would have been included in the Scriptures by the Holy Spirit in vain. As the Apostle says: *That was first which is fleshly, afterwards that which is spiritual* [1 Cor. xv. 46]. Do not despise what is lowly in God's word, for by lowliness you will be enlightened to divinity. The outward form of God's word seems to you, perhaps, like dirt, so you trample it underfoot, like dirt, and despise what the

---

[1] *De Sacr.* i. 8, vi. 466.

letter tells you was done physically and visibly. But hear!
that dirt, which you trample, opened the eyes of the blind.
Read Scripture then, and first learn carefully what it tells you
was done in the flesh.'[1]

We must not make the text: '*the letter killeth* an excuse for
preferring our own ideas to the divine authors'.'[2] Exposition
includes three things: the letter, that is the actual words,
their construction and syntax, which sometimes leaves
nothing to be explained; the sense, which is what the divine
writer means: a mere grammatical explanation of the words
does not always suffice for this, since the writer may be
expressing himself in an unusual or allusive way; lastly, the
sentence, which is the deep meaning to be derived from the
letter or the sense.[3] Hugh illustrates the 'sense' significantly
by a biblical prophecy: *And in that day, seven women shall take
hold of one man, saying: We will eat our own bread, and wear our
own apparel: only let us be called by thy name. Take away our
reproach* [Isa. iv. 1]:

'The words are plain and clear enough. You understand
each separate clause: *seven women shall take hold of one man* and
so on. But perhaps you cannot understand what it means as a
whole. You do not know what the prophet wishes to say,
whether he is promising good or threatening disaster. And, so
it happens, you think that a passage whose literal meaning
you do not grasp should be understood only in a spiritual
sense. So you say that the *seven women* are the seven gifts of the
Holy Spirit, who *shall take hold of one man*, that is Christ . . . who
alone "takes away their reproach" that they may find in him
a refuge. . . .
'Lo! you have expounded spiritually and you do not understand what it means literally. But the prophet could mean
something literally too by these words.'

Hugh explains that this is a prophecy of war and depopula-
tion; in those days sterility was a woman's worst 'reproach'.
There are many such passages in Scripture, especially in the
Old Testament, which were quite intelligible to those who
knew the idiom but, unless we take trouble, seem nonsense
to us.[4]
When he passes to the sentence or deep meaning, Hugh
puts forward a remarkable plea:

[1] *De Scripturis*, v. 13-15.   [2] *Didascalicon*, vi. iv. 804.
[3] Ibid. viii-xi. 806-9.   [4] 807-8.

'When we read the holy books, let us rather choose, from the great multitude of patristic explanations, which are drawn from few words [of the text], and corroborated by the Catholic faith, that which appears to have been certainly intended by the author. If this is uncertain, let us choose at least that explanation which is admissible in the context, and is consonant with the faith. If the context does not help us, then we must choose only that prescribed by the faith. It is one thing not to discern what the writer intended, another to err against piety. *If both are avoided, the fruit of reading is perfect. . . .*'

We must not struggle to read our own 'sentence' into the Scriptures, but rather to make the 'sentence' of Scripture ours.[1]

Hugh is criticizing the Gregorian tradition with its sublime disregard for the letter of Scripture. Similar recommendations to consider the context and the writers' meaning are commonplace in theological and legal works, the *Sic et Non* for instance; but here the illustration from Isaias shows that Hugh thinks particularly of prophecy and history. He had read Paschasius on Lamentations.[2] He makes an open demand for the literal exegesis of which Paschasius had quietly set the example. Both men were objective.

Hugh also had a vivid visual imagination, in this being typical of his century. Symbolism demands a keen perception of the sign. The roles of text and picture, that we are accustomed to, seem to be reversed in much of the twelfth-century educational literature. You begin with your picture, to which the text is a commentary and illustration. The most abstract teaching must take its starting-point from some concrete shape which the pupil can have visibly depicted for him. Hugh makes use of this method in his two treatises on Noe's ark. The *De Arca Noe Morali* originated in collations to his fellow religious. As he sat one day among the brethren, answering their questions, they ended by all exclaiming at the restlessness of the human heart, begging him to tell the reason and the remedy. He therefore wrote down that part of his address which he knew to have specially pleased his audience.[3] His subject, therefore, is psychological and religious: how to prepare our hearts for the peace of the divine indwelling; but he proceeds in a pictorial way:

[1] 808-9. Cf. St. Aug. *De Gen. ad Lit.* i. xxi.
[2] See below, p. 102, n. 1.
[3] *De Arca Noe Morali*, Prol., P.L. clxxvi. 617-19.

'As an illustration of this spiritual building I shall give you Noe's ark, which your eye shall see outwardly that your soul may be fashioned to its likeness inwardly. You shall see colours, shapes and figures which please the eye; but know that they are set there to teach you wisdom, understanding and virtue, to adorn your soul. The ark signifies the Church, and the Church is Christ's body; so I have drawn the whole person of Christ, head and members, in visible shape, to picture it for you clearly, that when you see the whole you may better be able to follow what is said of the parts.'[1]

The treatise therefore began with two pictures: Christ in majesty and a Noe's ark. Hugh is in such sympathy with his audience that we share their gratitude when these tangible forms appear. He keeps referring to himself as the artist. After discussing various opinions concerning the proportions of the ark, he continues:

'We have drawn this particular figure rather than the others, because the height of the sides cannot easily be shown on a plane surface. In *this* figure the beams rising from either side converge gradually until they meet at the top at a measure of one cubit.'[2]

In the accompanying treatise, the *De Arca Noe Mystica*, he describes himself drawing:

'First I find the centre of the flat surface where I mean to draw the ark. There, having fixed the point, I draw round it a small square to the measure of that cubit, in which the ark was completed. Then I draw another rather larger square around the first, so that the space between may appear to be the border of the cubit. Then I draw a cross inside the inner square, so that the ends meet each of the sides; and I paint it gold. Then I paint in the spaces between the cross and the square, the upper ones flame colour, the lower sky blue. . . .'

He explains the complicated symbolism of the cubit and its colours and then draws a diagram, carefully explaining how it represents the ark.[3]

Oh yes! we think of the Kindergarten. We smile when Hugh, with the gravity of one in the forefront of a scientific movement, rejects Origen's figure of the ark as top-heavy, and when he proposes 'little compartments', round the outside, for the amphibious beasts.[4] Our smile is mistaken:

[1] *De Arca Noe Morali, Porl., P.L.* i. ii. 622.   [2] Ibid. i. iii. 629.
[3] *De Arca Noe Mystica*, i. 681-4.
[4] *De Arca Noe Morali*, i. iii. 626-8. The question of the provision for amphibious creatures during the flood is raised, but not solved, in the Pseudo-Augustinian treatise, *De Mirabilibus Sacrae Scripturae*, i. 5, *P.L.* xxxv. 2156 (see above, p. 35).

a scientific movement is really afoot. Hugh is doing, for biblical history, what St. Anselm of Bec and Master Anselm had done for theology in their different ways. He is making the letter a proper subject for study, as they had made the content of the Christian faith. He wants to understand the literal meaning of Scripture exactly, so as to visualize the scene. He had that curiosity which set explorers in quest of El Dorado and led to the discovery of a continent.

II. HUGH AS AN EXEGETE

Hugh's exegesis conforms to his ideas. He is original in the books he chooses. He left no written work on the Pauline Epistles[1] and only a few notes on isolated texts of the Psalms, although these were the favourite books of contemporary commentators. He left notes on the literal sense of the Octateuch, homilies on part of Ecclesiastes, a threefold exposition of Lamentations, Joel, Abdias and perhaps part of Nahum,[2] with an exposition of the *Magnificat*, which, as

[1] The *Notae* and the *Quaestiones in Epistolas Pauli* printed among his works are spurious. Hauréau, *Les Œuvres*, etc., op. cit. (p. 85, n. 2), 27; the author may be Walter of St. Victor. H. Denifle, *Die abendländischen Schriftausleger bis Luther über Justitia Dei* (Mainz, 1906), 66.

[2] A. Wilmart, 'Le Commentaire sur le prophète Nahum attribué à Julien de Tolède', *Bulletin de Littérature Ecclésiastique de Toulouse*, vii-viii (1922), 235-79. Wilmart shows that the unfinished commentary printed *P.L.* xcvi. 703-58 was written by a Victorine, and probably by Hugh; he maintains the authenticity of the commentaries on Joel and Abdias. G. Morin, 'Le Commentaire sur Nahum du Pseudo Julien, une œuvre de Richard de St Victor', *Rev. Bén.* xxxvii (1925), 404-5, argued that the commentaries on Joel and Nahum should both be ascribed to Richard of St. Victor, on the strength of Bale's *Index*, ed. Bates (Oxford, 1902), 362. Bale, however, is merely copying from Boston of Bury, and the evidence of Boston's *Registrum* is not clear. It will be discussed in the forthcoming edition by R. W. Hunt, R. A. B. Mynors, and W. A. Pantin. Ottaviano, 'Riccardo di S. Vittore', *Memorie della reale Accademia nazionale dei Lincei cl. di scienze morali*, etc., serie VI, vol. IV. v (1933), 428, argues against Richard on internal grounds.

The commentary on Nahum, wrongly entitled *Super Ionam Prophetam*, is ascribed to Richard of St. Victor in a thirteenth-century manuscript from the Sorbonne, recently acquired by E. P. Goldschmidt & Co., 45 Old Bond St., London (MS. no. 2 in list 30: *Mediaeval Literature and Education*, 1938, 3-5). Mr. Goldschmidt has identified it with a volume in the Sorbonne catalogue of 1338 published by L. Delisle, *Cabinet des mss.* ii. 107: *Summe morales et tractatus modernorum doctorum*; in this catalogue also the commentary is listed among the works of Richard: *Idem super Ionam*. He very kindly showed me the manuscript and I was able to identify the so-called treatise on Jonas with the commentary on Nahum.

The thirteenth-century ascription to Richard is not conclusive, particularly as the manuscript and the catalogue both ascribe to him the commentary on Abdias, which at one time formed part of the MS.: there is manuscript authority for attributing this to Hugh. I agree with Wilmart that the style and content suggest Hugh rather than Richard.

we might expect, is mainly devotional, like his notes on the Psalter.

The order and date of these writings have never been studied and their origin is various. We know that the homilies on Ecclesiastes originated in collations or conferences, preached to the brothers, like his two treatises on the ark.[1] The commentaries arc literary productions, which contain references to the 'reader'.[2] The original form of his *Notulae*[3] is puzzling. There is a double tradition in the manuscripts. According to one tradition, the *Notulae* pass straight from Leviticus to Judges, and go on to Kings. According to another, this first series is followed by a second, containing notes on the books omitted, Numbers and Deuteronomy, and a whole series of additional notes on the Pentateuch and Kings; some of these are comments on verses which have already been dealt with in the first series; others which the first tradition has in their logical place are omitted from the first series and given here.[4] The printed edition represents a compromise. The notes on Numbers and Deuteronomy are printed together with the first series; the additional notes to Genesis come at the end of the notes on this book. This arrangement does not seem to have any manuscript authority. Andrew of St. Victor, who incorporated many of his master's notes into his own, was copying from a manuscript which represented the first tradition. He does not use the notes on Numbers and Deuteronomy, or the additional notes on Genesis. This is not necessarily an argument against their authenticity; but it does suggest that the two series of notes originated separately. It also suggests that Hugh's pupils collected them. It is most unlikely that Hugh's own written work could have taken so incoherent a form. 'We have only the debris of his teaching.'[5] Peter Comestor in the *Histories* or *Historia Scholastica* brings this remark home to us by quoting an opinion of Hugh on

---

[1] *Praefatio in Ecclesiastes, P.L.* clxxv. 114: 'nuper coram vobis disserui.'

[2] *Com. in Ioel*, 350; *Com. in Abdiam*, 376.   [3] 32-114.

[4] MS. Trinity College B. I. 25 (23), 12th cent. from Christ Church, ff. 39ʳ-73ʳ.

[5] A. Wilmart, 'Le Commentaire', etc., op. cit. (p. 97, n. 2), 265-6: '. . . nous n'avons guère que les débris de cette œuvre; il paraît bien que le célèbre maître ait pris habituellement pour texte de ses leçons l'Écriture et que les grands recueils des *Excerptiones* ou *Allégories* et *Miscellanea* ne soient autre chose que le résidu de ces cours, pour ne rien dire des diverses *Adnotationes* conservées et des gloses perdues ou inédites.' The *Excerptiones* and *Allegoriae* have now been attributed to Richard of St. Victor (see below, p. 106, n. 1), but the remark holds good for the *Adnotationes*, etc.

Genesis which is not found in any of the notes, though it is discussed by Andrew; Langton repeats another: 'Magister Hugo de Sancto Victore *dicebat.* . . .'[1] We are therefore left guessing as to the form which his teaching took. These notes were either *scholia* on isolated passages, or they were extracted from the literal part of a literal, allegorical and moral commentary, or from an introductory literal historical course on the Octateuch. In the latter case they foreshadowed the lectures which in the second half of the century were given on the *Histories*. This is quite probable, since Hugh was inventive in developing new forms. He seems to have been the first to open his course on the Pentateuch by glossing the prologue of St. Jerome *Desiderii mei*, which later became part of the academic routine.[2] His notes on Leviticus begin with a near approximation to the legal summulae, 'short writings which summarize systematically the content of a whole title or parts of it'; the form was invented by Bulgarus, who taught *c.* 1115-65.[3] After a short prologue Hugh summarizes the various kinds of sacrifice prescribed in Leviticus, the persons who are to offer, the times and seasons. This is not quite equivalent to the usual prologue, known as *accessus* or *materia*, with its *causa scribendi, materia, intentio*, which was common to the grammarians, the theologians and the lawyers. Summaries of the separate biblical books are rather rare, perhaps because the *Histories* provided a convenient substitute. Here again, Hugh was foreshadowing the *Histories*.

Hauréau, from a rapid glance, concluded that the *Notulae* were mainly mystical. On the contrary, they aim at being purely literal, as their title *ad litteram* indicates. Hugh has set himself an austere task and he is surprisingly successful:

'*But Melchisedech the king of Salem, bringing forth bread and wine* [Gen. xiv. 18], which was a token of peace among the gentiles, as the olive branch used to be. Note the order: *bringing forth* these things, he *blessed; by the most high God*: blessing pertained

---

[1] *P.L.* cxcviii. 1138. See B. Smalley, 'The School of Andrew of St. Victor', *Rech. Théol. anc. méd.* xi (1939), 147-8, 157.

[2] *P.L.* clxx. 29-32; it generally precedes his *Notulae* in the manuscripts. It is interesting to notice that a commentary on St. Paul which uses the *Gloss* and derives from the school of Laon, perhaps from Ralph of Laon himself, does not include commentaries on the prologues of St. Jerome. MS. Trinity College Cambridge B. I. 29 (27), ff. 48ʳ-103ᵛ. See 'La Glossa Ordinaria', op. cit. (p. 62, n. 1), 367, n. 5.

[3] H. Kantorowicz, op. cit. (p. 75, n. 1), 69.

to him, *for he was the priest of the most high God.* Or understand it thus: *bringing forth bread and wine* which were not mere food but a sacrifice, *for he was the priest, etc.*'[1]

Which of Hugh's contemporaries could have commented on the Melchisedech episode without explaining it as a 'type' of the Eucharist?

His prologue to Ecclesiastes[2] is even more striking, since here he was writing down material which he had actually preached, and the preacher was free to choose any means of edification which his text could give him:

'All Scripture, if expounded according to its own proper meaning [the literal], will gain in clarity and present itself to the reader's intelligence more easily. Many exegetes, who do not understand this virtue of Scripture, cloud over its seemly beauty by irrelevant comments. When they ought to disclose what is hidden, they obscure even that which is plain. I personally blame those who strive superstitiously to find a mystical sense and a deep allegory where none is, as much as those who obstinately deny it, when it is there.

'And so, in this work, I do not think that one should toil much after tropologies or mystical allegorical senses through the whole course of the argument, especially as the author himself aims less at improving, or at relating mysteries, than at moving the human heart to scorn wordly things by obviously true reasons and plain persuasion. I do not deny that many mysteries are included in the argument, especially in the latter part. As he proceeds, the author always, with increase of contemplation, rises above the visible ever more and more. But it is one thing to consider the writer's intention and his argument as a whole, another to think that certain of his *obiter dicta*, which have a mystical sense and must be understood spiritually, should not be passed over.

'So now we have undertaken to explain the superficial [literal] sense of his argument, so persuasive and beautiful that you may rejoice in understanding what has been written for you, this modest little discourse opening the way to intelligence.'

Hugh accordingly devotes himself to the Preacher's argument and its application. He resembles St. John Chrysostom in his capacity to draw a moral from the literal sense. His notes on the Psalter fall into the same category. Lacking the

---

[1] 51. The printed edition has: 'quod signum *est* pacis inter gentiles'. I prefer *erat* as Andrew has it.
[2] 113-15.

material for a literal, historical explanation, he dwells on
the mood of the Psalmist and draws out the full implication
of his words.

The commentaries on Lamentations, Joel, and Abdias
show us the logical working out of his method, since here
the exposition is threefold. He distinguishes with unusual
care between the senses and carries out his own teaching on
metaphor and prophetic idiom in his treatment of the literal
sense. Nor is he afraid to broach the difficult problem which
arises from it: How shall we explain a prophecy which may
refer either to a near or a distant event, to Old Testament
history or to the coming of Christ?

> 'That which is said: *The word of the Lord that came to Joel*:
> signifies in its spiritual sense that the fulfilment of the prophecy
> which follows belongs chiefly to the Incarnation of the Word
> [on account of the mystical meaning of *Joel* and *Phatuel*]. It
> can be understood *more correctly*, however, as referring to the
> siege and depopulation of the city and territory of Joel, when
> the town was besieged by the Assyrians under Senacherib, the
> land laid waste, the aspect of people and country, by the
> magnitude of disaster wholly changed.'[1]

Hugh consistently refers the prophecy to Old Testament
history, in its literal sense, until he comes to the text Joel
ii. 28, which is quoted in Acts:

> '*And it shall come to pass after this, that I will pour out my spirit
> upon all flesh.* This text is properly to be understood as referring
> to the advent of Christ. The prophetic riddle is solved with
> certainty, if we understand it to refer to the sending of the
> Paraclete.'

He defends this, against the Jews, as the primary, literal
meaning of the prophecy.[2]

Living over a century before St. Thomas, Hugh seems to
have grasped the Thomist principle that the clue to prophecy
and metaphor is the writer's intention; the literal sense
includes everything which the sacred writer meant to say.
But he has occasional lapses from his own standard. In one
passage he prefers the less probable alternative in explaining
the letter, because it makes a better foundation for the
allegory. *All they that passed by have clapped their hands at thee*:

---

[1] From the prologue to Joel, which is not included with the commentary in
P.L. lxxv. 321; it is edited by A. Wilmart, 'Le Commentaire', etc., op. cit.
(p. 97, n. 2), 266-8.
[2] 353-4.

they have hissed and wagged their heads at the daughter of Jerusalem
[Lam. ii. 15]. The literal sense is obviously that hostile
neighbours derided the afflictions of the Jews. Hugh maintains, without much conviction, that clapping and hissing
need not necessarily denote hostility; the 'wayfarers' were
compassionate friends: 'we may take clapping to denote
wonder, hissing despair, wagging the head sympathy',
although in the next verse they proceed from the opposite
emotion of contempt and ridicule. He explains that this
little manipulation will provide a better spiritual exposition.
The 'wayfarers' signify allegorically the Fathers, tropologically the saints of the Church, deploring the heresies or the
sins of their fellow Christians![1]

Hugh's philosophy teaches him to value the letter. It
does not teach him to regard the letter as a good in itself.
His great service to exegesis was to lay more stress on the
literal interpretation *relatively* to the spiritual, and to develop
the sources for it. He is comparatively independent in his
attitude to those sources which were already known and
used. On Lamentations, where the standard work was
Paschasius, Hugh explains the letter independently, though
on the same lines. Similarly on Joel and Abdias he does not
resort to verbal copying of the standard source, St. Jerome,
except occasionally where the matter is highly technical.
On the Octateuch he discusses the same kind of problems
as had interested St. Augustine, but by no means always
the identical ones.

He went beyond the customary sources, however. He
followed the advice of St. Jerome and St. Augustine to study
Scripture in the original, as far as he could. Andrew tells
us that his master 'learnt the literal sense of the Pentateuch
from the Jews', and this is confirmed by the *Notulae*. In
many places and particularly for difficult and uncertain
readings, he compares the Vulgate with a literal Latin
translation of the Hebrew, noting the variations and additions. He sometimes prefers the Hebrew to the Vulgate; it is
expressius, or *evidentius* to him, just as the original Greek of
the Gospel had been to John the Scot. He continues this
process in the *Notulae* on Judges and Kings.

---

[1] 296-7: '. . . Quia tamen secundum spiritualem intelligentiam convenientius
haec ad compassionem referuntur, dicere convenienter possumus quod per
plausum non insultatio, sed simpliciter manuum collisio exprimatur. . . .'—
Hugh has taken over the whole discussion from Paschasius (*P.L.* cxx. 1132)
and enlarged upon it.

In this, Hugh was only following the example of St. Stephen Harding; but he went further. Instead of depending entirely on French conversation with his Jewish teachers, he made some effort to learn Hebrew himself and transliterated certain words of the Hebrew text into Latin.[1]

He consulted the Jews on their exegetical traditions, as well as their text. Here he was following the example of Sigebert of Gembloux, and, unlike Sigebert, he has recorded them. On Joel i. 15: *Ah Ah Ah for the day* he says that he will not pass by in silence what he has heard from 'a certain Jew, fluent and expert in the fables of Gamaliel': the prophet seeks to avert God's wrath by recalling the three tribulations of his people, saying: *Ah* for the Egyptians, *Ah* for the Assyrians, *Ah* for the Babylonians.[2] This is a perplexing passage. The Hebrew text, which Hugh does not use for the Prophets as he did for the Octateuch, has only *'Ahāh*. Yet the explanation is typically Midrashic and does not seem to be quoted from any known Christian source. Is it possible that the 'fluent and expert Jew' invented an *ad hoc* explanation for the version quoted by his questioner?

Hugh also cites the Jewish opinion on the messianic prophecy Joel ii. 32, and this again cannot be traced to his principal Christian source, St. Jerome:

'Everything which we have expounded of Christ's coming, and the sending of the Paraclete, the Jews refer to their Messias, in whom, they say, the worship of the Law is to be fully restored. The Jewish people alone will receive him. They alone will call on him, and he will hear.'[3]

The references to Jews in the *Notulae* are more frequent and interesting. He was in closer contact with them at this stage. The two opinions quoted on Joel might have come from hearsay or from some unknown work in Latin. Those quoted in the *Notulae* prove that Hugh's teachers belonged to the contemporary North French school of rationalist exegetes founded by Rashi (d. 1105).[4] He gives at least one explanation which can be found in Rashi,[5] one which is

---

[1] The Hebrew characters in the printed edition of the *Notulae* were added by his pious editors; the manuscripts, however, show that the Latin transliterations in the printed edition are genuine.

[2] 333. [3] 358. [4] See below, pp. 149-55.

[5] On Gen. xlix. 12; 59. Dr. H. Hailperin has transcribed and explained this passage with reference to Rashi and made other helpful comments on Hugh's quotations from Jewish sources in his review of my first edition, *Historia Judaica*, iv (1942), 167-8.

explicitly ascribed by a later Jewish commentator to Joseph Kara,[1] Hugh's exact contemporary, and three, all on Exodus, which can be found in Rashi's grandson Rashbam, another of his contemporaries and leader of the rationalist school.[2] The idea of conversations at St. Victor between the Christian mystic and the grandson of Rashi has in it an element of the fabulous, though it differs from many famous 'meetings' in being historically possible. Hugh refers to his teachers as *Hebraei*; perhaps he only meant that one particular Jew was giving him various opinions, traditional in some cases, taught by contemporary scholars in others: 'my people say...' The identity and number of his *Hebraei* must remain obscure.

He notes their opinions with learned interest and detachment. On the blessing of Juda and Joseph [Gen. xlix. 10, 26] for instance he says:[3]

'*The sceptre shall not be taken away from Juda*; that is, a certain overlordship [*dominium*] which Juda had, as that he entered first into the Red Sea, or that he made the first oblation in the tabernacle which was built in the desert, or minor precedence of this sort. *Till he come that is to be sent*: the Hebrew reads: "till he come to Silo"; that is where Samuel anointed Saul as king; and the sense is "up to Saul and after him Juda shall have the leadership" because he delivered Joseph from his brethren. As for what follows: *and he shall be the expectation of nations*, the Jews refer it all to Juda,[4] because the Lord answered of his tribe: "Juda shall go up before you to war" [Jud. i. 1-2]; *nations* is what he calls the various tribes. ...

'*The blessings of thy father are strengthened with the blessings of his fathers: until the desire of the everlasting hills should come*; that is until the desired of all nations should come, who is Christ. Or "until the everlasting hills should be joined to the sky", as the Hebrew has it, that is: "blessed be Joseph everywhere"; as the saying goes: "where earth and sky meet", that is: "the whole world over".'

---

[1] On Gen. iv. 23; 44. The *opinio antiqua* comes from Rashi, the *quidam* corresponds to Joseph Kara. The former is the story that Lamech was blind and killed Cain accidentally while hunting. It is also found in the *Gloss* in loc., ascribed to Raban, but the ascription seems to be incorrect and I have not been able to find the source. A comparison between the story as told by Hugh and the passage in the *Gloss* shows that Hugh's wording is quite different and that he gives details not to be found in the *Gloss*. It seems probable, therefore, that he got it from a Jewish source independently.

[2] On Exod. i. 15; 61. On Exod. iii. 22; 62. On Exod. iv. 10; 62.

[3] 59-60.

[4] The printed edition omits *Judam*: 'Hebraei hoc totum ad ipsum referunt, de qua Dominus respondit: ...' The manuscripts generally have it and also Andrew.

Hugh has merely contrasted the Jewish and Christian explanations without discussion. On the spoiling of the Egyptians he prefers the Christian opinion, apparently because it strikes him as intrinsically more probable. Rashbam, wishing to defend the Jews against the charge of borrowing without giving back, says that the Israelites received silver from the Egyptians as 'a complete and unconditioned gift, since [as the previous verse says]: *I will give this people favour in the sight of the Egyptians*. This is its real meaning and a refutation of sectarians [Christians].' Hugh quotes this opinion and adds: 'But our commentators say with more probability that they borrowed.'[1] This is typical of his cautious attitude to the new sources he is opening up.

Hebrew studies represent a small fraction of Hugh's manifold activities. They are more important as promise than performance. They stimulated two of his pupils, Richard and Andrew, possibly others whose names are forgotten, to continue the work. We can study his principles of exegesis more fully in their writings than in the few notes which have come down to us from his teaching.

This, in fact, is the real significance of the Victorine programme. We know that it was destined to failure, taken as a whole. In his attempt to include the whole of sacred science in *sacra pagina* Hugh was struggling with forces stronger than himself. He was stretching the scriptural framework of learning beyond its endurance. The arts and sciences were to serve as an introduction to Bible study, theology or doctrine as an introduction to the allegorical exposition. The fruits of these studies would appear in the scholastic *lectio* which in turn was a preliminary to monastic contemplation. To all this he added new ideals of biblical scholarship.

The programme was both too conservative and too modern. It would have made any kind of academic specialization quite impossible and yet specialization was just what it demanded. Moreover it implied too high a tension between the academic and the religious life. Hugh's ideal exegete was a combination of Paris master and contemplative religious which only exceptional circumstances could produce. We know that by the end of the century the mystical anti-scholastic current at St. Victor had conquered the more intellectual current which Hugh represented, while in the

[1] 62.

schools theology was breaking away from exegesis. Hugh
had been pouring new wine into old bottles. Thanks to his
pupils, some of the wine was saved when the bottles burst.

III. RICHARD OF ST. VICTOR

The two disciples concentrated each on one aspect of their
master's exegesis: Richard on the spiritual, Andrew on the
literal; Richard being primarily a mystic, Andrew wholly a
biblical scholar. Since Hugh had taught them to regard the
letter as necessary, however, Richard made some contribution to scholarship, although it was not his main interest.
He planned a vast encyclopaedia on the lines indicated in the
Didascalicon as a help to students of Scripture. It was to
include a section on the liberal arts, a section on geography
and another on world history, with sermons, allegories and
moralities. The material has got scattered; some is still unprinted; some is printed under wrong names. Fr. Chatillon,
in an ingenious and convincing study, has recovered the
original plan and has pieced the fragments together. He
points out that the fragments do not quite correspond to the
plan; but Richard may have changed his mind or the
manuscript transmission may misrepresent him. In any case
it is an impressive witness to his belief in Hugh's programme
and to his own versatility. The compilation belongs to his
teaching period, probably 1153-60.[1] He also left notes on
certain parts of the Psalter, a commentary on the Canticle, a
treatise on the dream interpreted by Daniel, and the
Benjamin Minor and *Benjamin Major*, where the family of
Jacob and the tabernacle serve as a framework for his
teaching on contemplation; all these are spiritual. His
commentary on the Apocalypse and his explanation of
certain texts of the Apostle[2] are mainly doctrinal. But his
treatise on the Emanuel prophecy contains both literal and
spiritual exposition. His tracts on the tabernacle (intended

---

[1] J. Chatillon, 'Le contenu, l'autenticité et la date du *Liber exceptionum* et
des *Sermones centum* de Richard de Saint-Victor', *Revue du Moyen Âge latin*, iv
(1948), 23-51, 342-64. Richard's authorship of the *Allegoriae super Vetus et
Novum Testamentum*, *P.L.* clxxv, 638-828, had already been established by
P. S. Moore, 'The authorship of the *Allegoriae*, etc.', *The New Scholasticism*,
ix (1935), 209-25. See also *Richard de Saint-Victor, Sermons et opuscules
spirituels inédits. i. L'Edit d'Alexandre etc.*, ed. J. Chatillon and W-J.
Tulloch (Bibliothèque de spiritualité médiévale, Paris, 1951).

[2] On Richard's theological exegesis see L. Ott, op. cit. (p. 85, n. 2).

as a basis for the *Benjamin Major*) and the temple, on the visions of Ezechiel, and his chronology of the kings of Israel and Juda, are purely literal.[1] These last two groups are interesting for the light they throw on Hugh's teaching, and for comparison with Andrew, who interpreted the master in a different way.

Richard was a Scot. He came to St. Victor during the abbacy of Gilduin (1113-55) and died there in 1173. It is not certain that Hugh ever held an administrative office;[2] Andrew was far from successful in the office he held; Richard, on the other hand, was made sub-prior about 1159 and prior in 1162. The abbey letter-books show us how constantly people turned to him for help in their affairs. He must have possessed the practical common sense and organizing capacity which have so often distinguished the mystics. He was less scholarly than Andrew and less intellectual than Hugh. What attracted him in the letter of Scripture was not the movement of human history but the jewels, the songs, and the flowers. The sound of the luxurious oriental metaphors in the Canticle enchanted him, though the literal meaning struck him as so much nonsense. The spiritualists, reproved by Hugh, regarded the 'fleshly sense' 'as 'dirt'; Richard found it desirable. Puritans held that if closely studied it might rouse the passions which lead to sin; Richard accepted its pleasures with gratitude. Scripture provides for man's double nature; it raises the spirit by pleasing the sense.[3]

We must add to his sensitiveness to beauty a strong interest in architecture and then we shall understand his very individual type of exegesis. It is almost a parody of Hugh on the Noe's ark. Richard made long, minute descriptions of the tabernacle and Solomon's temple, where he managed to find 'delightful droll carvings'.[4] He depicted the beasts of Ezechiel's vision so graphically that one sees them, the eagle, 'having a longer neck than the others', dominating the group. He worked out a scheme of Ezechiel's building, by elaborate formulae, diagrams and sketches, showing all the features of late romanesque.

[1] All these are printed in *P.L.* cxcvi.
[2] He perhaps became prior in 1133; J. de Ghellinck, *Le Mouvement théologique du XII siècle* (Bruges, 1948), 187, n. 2.
[3] *Benjamin Minor*, xv, xxiv, 10, 11, 17.
[4] *De Templo Salomonis*, 236: 'delectabiles quasdam et jocosas caelaturas habebat.'

I

In expounding the visions of Ezechiel, Richard was under-taking what St. Gregory had refused to do on the score that they had no literal meaning. He was applying his master's criticism of Gregorian methods in a typical case. He there-fore justifies himself for contradicting St. Gregory in a very interesting prologue:[1] times have changed; our attitude to the letter nowadays is different:

'Many take much more pleasure in holy Scripture when they can perceive some suitable literal meaning. The building of the spiritual interpretation is more firmly established, so they think, when aptly grounded in the solid historical sense. Who can lay or firmly establish a solid foundation in a formless void? The mystical senses are extracted and formed from fitting comparisons of the things contained in the letter. How then, they ask, can the letter lead us to a spiritual meaning in those places where it contradicts itself, or is merely ridiculous? Persons of this kind are often scandalized rather than edified when they come to such passages of Scripture.

'The ancient Fathers, on the contrary, were glad to find passages which according to the letter could not stand. These "absurdities" of the letter enabled them to force certain per-sons, who accepted holy Scripture but mocked at allegorical interpretations, to resort to a spiritual meaning, since they dared not deny that the Holy Spirit had written nothing irrelevant, however foolish the letter might sound. This is the reason, in my opinion, why the ancient Fathers passed over in silence the literal exposition in certain more difficult passages, or treated it rather carelessly, when by perseverance they could doubtless have found a much more satisfying explanation than any of the moderns.

'But here I must say that certain persons, as though from reverence for the Fathers, will not attempt to fill their omissions, lest they should seem to presume. Having this excuse for lazi-ness, they idle at leisure; they mock, deride, ridicule other people's efforts to seek and find the truth . . . For our part, however, let us take with all greediness what the Fathers have discussed; let us investigate eagerly what they have left un-touched; let us offer with all generosity the fruits of our research, that we may fulfil that which is written: *Many shall pass over, and knowledge shall be manifold* [Dan. xii. 4].

'Lo! blessed Gregory expounds the wonderful vision of celestial creatures, seen by the prophet Ezechiel, according to the mystical sense. But what it means literally he does not say. Of the second vision he says that it cannot mean anything according to the letter. This is true, but only according to the

---

[1] *Prologus in visionem Ezechielis*, 527-8.

way he takes it here. If we decide to consider the same passage in a different way, perhaps we may be able to extract some suitable literal meaning. . . .'

When he approaches the second vision Richard excuses himself again:[1]

'I know that the Fathers passed carelessly over certain passages of Scripture, which they could easily have grasped. They wanted to find, and rejoiced in, passages which according to the letter could not stand; their intention was at least by these means to persuade men that allegory ought to be accepted, which very few were willing to admit in those days. Let no one take scandal if I say something other, or otherwise, than he finds in his glosses. Let no one scorn me for desiring to glean. Let it not surprise him that something has escaped the Fathers, or rather that they, who received the divine commandment and the divine boon to fill so many volumes with corn from the harvest of Scripture, have left something intentionally to the poor.

'Do you wish to honour and defend the authority of the Fathers? We cannot honour the lovers of truth more truly than by seeking, finding, teaching, defending and loving the truth. Do not ask whether what I say is new, but whether it is true.'

St. Gregory took certain measurements to refer to the whole building of Ezechiel's vision; hence he concluded that the door was bigger than the wall; hence that the letter was nonsense. Richard argues that the measurement refers not to the whole but only to one part,[2] which could be fitted into the rest of the vision. The very minuteness of the description teaches us how actual the building was to the mind of Ezechiel, and how carefully we ought to reconstruct its details.[3]

Lest we should feel impatient at his lengthy protestations, we have a series of homilies on the spiritual sense of Ezechiel by Richard's contemporary Robert of Cricklade, who was strongly in favour of the Gregorian view:

'Here notice and watch carefully to see how the prophet called the building sometimes temple, sometimes tabernacle, sometimes house, often sanctuary, here city. Hence is openly confuted the foolish raving of those who think that the building can be pieced together, or depicted physically, when it is not only a building, but also a city.'[4]

---

[1] 562.   [2] 540-1.   [3] 539.
[4] MS. Pembroke College Cambridge 30, fo. 145[a]: 'Hic notandum et sollerter intuendum quoniam edificium aliquando vocabat templum, quandoque taber-

The Victorines' campaign for careful consideration of the letter evidently met with opposition from commentators who preferred the old style.

Richard also followed his master's example in consulting Jews. He made inquiries from them before drawing up his chronological tables, and conflated their opinion with the Christian.[1] This is significant in view of his controversy with Andrew, whom he rebukes for judaizing. He did not disapprove of Andrew's sources, but thought they were used in an uncritical way. His discussions on chronological problems convinced him that the Jews were no wiser than himself on many points.[2] In his tract on the tabernacle he protests against certain persons (Andrew) who accept Josephus as authoritative, just because he was a Jew.[3]

'They think that he (as a Jew) saw the tabernacle, and wrote what was known to himself as true. It seems clear to me, from the witness of Scripture that he never saw it . . . Let Josephus be gladly admitted in those things which he knew from experience, or took from authoritative Scripture. Where he judges otherwise, I confidently prefer Exodus, or whatever other books I find in the canon, to him.'

Richard composed a long refutation, in two books, of Andrew's judaizing interpretation of the Emanuel prophecy [Isa. vii. 14];[4] Andrew gave the explanation told him by the Jews as the literal sense of the prophecy. Richard showed more understanding than Andrew of their master's teaching on prophecy in his defence of the Christian interpretation as literal. It is not Andrew's consultation with Jews that shocks him, but the acceptance of their view when it undermines the whole Christian interpretation of the Old Testament and endangers the faith of simple folk. If Andrew failed to understand the prophecy, he should at least have refrained from raising doubts in the minds of others. Here

---

[1] *De Concordia Temporum*, 241: 'Unde et antequam de his juxta petitionem tuam aliquid scriberem, per Iudaeos Iudaeorum scripta consului, et tam eorum scripta quam nostra in unam sententiam concurrere didici.'
[2] Ibid.: '. . . quamvis et ipsis hucusque veritas ipsa latuerit.'
[3] *De Tabernaculo*, 214.   [4] *De Emanuele*, 601-66.

naculum, interdum domum, plerumque sanctuarium, nunc civitatem nominat. Hinc stultitia delirantium aperte deprehenditur qui edificium illud putant materialiter posse componi sive depingi, quod non solum edificium est, sed etiam civitas.' Gerald of Wales says that Robert of Cricklade knew Hebrew: *De Principis Inst.*, ed. Brewer (Rolls Series), viii. 65. There is no trace of it in these homilies.

again, Richard maintains the tradition of Hugh of St. Victor, who would certainly have reproved Andrew for exaggerating.

But we miss something of Hugh in Richard's exegesis. The enterprise has gone. He is not deeply interested in scholarship. He does not refer to the Hebrew text. If his literal works were the only fruits of Hugh's teaching, the Victorine movement would hardly be worth investigating. It would amount to an attempt at clear sentence construction, accurate chronology and accurate description of certain objects or appearances of sacred history. It would force one to the depressing conclusion that, if this was what they meant by literal exegesis, commentators might as well have kept to their allegories and tropes.

Hugh's promise is fulfilled in Andrew, who, being merely a scholar, is unknown to text-books and almost unknown to modern works of reference.

CHAPTER IV

ANDREW OF ST. VICTOR

1. ANDREW'S LIFE AND CHARACTER[1]

WE happen to have more records of Andrew's life than we have of Hugh's or of Richard's. They are precious for the help they give us in dating his commentaries and also for the light they throw on his character. We need all the details we can get, since Andrew was an unusual person. He could only have flourished in the Victorine circle; even here it is a little difficult to believe in him.

A Victorine chronicle, composed soon after 1190, lists Master Andrew among members of the house who rose to distinguished positions outside it (the abbacy of Wigmore in his case) and who were pupils of Abbot Gilduin.[2] As Gilduin's abbacy stretched from 1113 to 1155, the chronicle does not help us to date Andrew's entry into the Order with any exactness. We know that he had produced his commentary on the Octateuch by about 1147. Hence it seems certain that he would have begun by studying under Hugh. Later scholars connected them: Stephen Langton quotes 'Andrew of St. Victor, following Master Hugh'.[3]

Then the canons of a daughter house of St. Victor in Herefordshire elected him as their first abbot. The *History of the Foundation of Wigmore* tells us how the canons 'heard talk of Master Andrew, who was then prior of St. Victor at Paris, master of divinity, serious and of many noble virtues. They

---

[1] The material for this chapter, unless specially mentioned, is taken from B. Smalley, 'Andrew of St. Victor, Abbot of Wigmore: a twelfth-century Hebraist', *Rech. Théol. anc. méd.* x (1938), 358-73. The main source is the Anglo-Norman *History of the Foundation of Wigmore* printed by Dugdale, *Mon. Ang.* vi. 444-8, and T. Wright, *History of Ludlow* (Ludlow, 1852), 102-32. Their original, which I have seen in photographs, is now MS. 224 of the University Library, Chicago, ff. 1-5. This is a fourteenth-century copy. The *History* was written by a canon of Wigmore at some time in the thirteenth century; he collected his material from men who had seen the original foundation of the house in Stephen's reign.

[2] ... et magister Andreas in ecclesia sancti Jacobi de Guiguemora, ... hii omnes canonici sancti Victoris Parisius et discipuli domini Gilduini abbatis ... Printed by J. C. Dickinson, *The Origins of the Austin Canons* (London, 1950), 284-5, from MS. Paris, Bibl. Nat. Lat. 15, 009, fo. 77ʳ, ᵛ.

[3] B. Smalley, 'The School of Andrew of St. Victor', *Rech. Théol. anc. méd.* xi (1939), 157.

sent to him, begging that he would consent to come to them, accept the office of abbot, and be their governor and prelate in the ordering of their affairs.' The historians of St. Victor have not listed him among the priors of the abbey, but there is one other possible reference to him as prior to reinforce the testimony of the Wigmore document. A treatise on Dictamen, now at the University Library of Graz, MS. 1515, has among its model salutations for the opening of formal letters, one addressed to 'A., Prior of St Victor' (fo. 57ᵛ).[1] The compiler of the treatise has included a salutation by Pope Lucius to the Emperor Conrad, which dates it 1144-45. At least some of the initials of the other dignitaries mentioned refer to real persons; some, on the contrary, seem to be make-believe: no bishop of Paris or archbishop of Mainz contemporary with Pope Lucius II had a name which could conceivably have been supposed to start with A. The salutation that interests us is addressed alternatively to 'P., Abbot of Cluny'. The solid reality of Peter the Venerable, Abbot of Cluny 1122-56, gives substance to the 'A., Prior of St Victor'. It may be, therefore, that the canons of Wigmore were justified in claiming the office of prior for their abbot elect. In that case Andrew would have to be fitted in between Prior Odo, whose date is given as 1130-48, and Prior Nanterus, 1148-52. His election to Wigmore was in or after 1147. The canons received him 'with great honour' and he was installed by the bishop of Hereford.

This distant colony of St. Victor was a baronial foundation which had been in existence for some years. The troubled state of the Welsh Marches in Stephen's reign, and the capriciousness of their patron, Hugh de Mortimer, who kept moving them from place to place, had involved the canons in constant difficulty and prevented their settling down under an abbot. Soon after Andrew's arrival they were moved again to a site near Wigmore, which they found so inconvenient that they asked leave to choose another. Permission was granted; so now they had the responsible task of deciding on a permanent home for the community.

[1] The treatise is described and dated by C. H. Haskins, 'An Italian Master Bernard', *Essays Presented to R. L. Poole* (Oxford, 1927), 215-16. He gives a list of the salutations. I am most grateful to the Director of the University Library, Graz, for sending me photographs. The words of the manuscript are: 'A., Dei gratia Parisiensis episcopus, licet indignus, reverendo in Christo, plurimum dilecto fratri A., sancti Victoris priori, vel P., Cluniacensi abbati, salutem', etc. Unfortunately only the salutation and no letter is given in the treatise. The hand is twelfth century.

At this point a 'distance' arose between Andrew and the canons. He 'left them to their own devices and returned to his house of St. Victor'. The cause is not stated in the Wigmore *History*, but we can read between the lines: the canons replaced him by Roger, who was 'only a novice in the Order but prudent in managing the temporalities'.

Andrew took up his work again at St. Victor, after what evidently seemed to him a long time: 'sicut *olim* . . . ita et nunc . . .' he says referring to his first exposition.[1] He had been away for a few years, at most, between 1147 and 1154-55. He expounded the Prophets and then, 'compelled by the many urgent requests of his friends', he started on the books of Solomon and finished Proverbs and Ecclesiastes.

Perhaps at some time while this work was in progress, he visited Rome, and was much impressed by the antiquities. This seems to be the most likely explanation of the curious fact that the only topographical references in his works occur in the exposition of Daniel, and both are to Rome. He compares the *tribes* [Dan. iii. 7] to the families of ancient Rome and to those of 'to-day', the Pierleoni and Frangipani;[2] on *the gate of Ulai* [Dan. viii. 2] he says: 'so at Rome there is a gate called the Tiburtine'.[3] The traditional interpretation of the ten horns in Daniel's vision as 'ten kings' who would divide the Roman Empire between them before their final destruction by anti-Christ rouses him to violent protest; he maintains that Rome will never be divided.[4] Then, in his exposition of Ecclesiastes, he seizes on the opportunity given him by the word *pomaria* [ii. 5] to explain that though here it means 'orchards', the Roman *pomerium* was the ancient boundary of the city.[5]

Meanwhile the canons of Wigmore had chosen a magnificent site, which their patron had granted, and the capable Roger had died, leaving the house in a much stronger position than he found it. Following the known tendency of institutions to alternate between an administrator and a scholar, they decided that they would like to recall Andrew.

---

[1] See below, p. 123.
[2] MS. Pembroke College Cambridge 45, fo. 117^d: see 'Andrew cf St. Victor'.
[3] ibid., fo. 125^a: 'Sicut Rome quedam porta est que dicitur Tibertina.'
[4] See below, pp. 128-9.
[5] Calandra, 16: 'pomerium locus erat Rome intra agrum, p.(er) R(ome) totius urbis circuitum, pone muros regionibus certis determina(tu)s, qui faciebat finem urbani auspicii. Hoc autem in loco pomeria vocat ubi pomifere arbores cuncti generis erant consite.' From A. Gellius, *Noctes Acticae*, lib. 13, c. 14.

The bishop of Hereford wrote a tactful, deprecating letter on their behalf to the abbot of St. Victor: the canons of Wigmore, having lost their shepherd, wished to return to the pasture whence had come their first shepherd, and to be under the yoke of obedience. They also sent 'the three most prudent of the brethren' to St. Victor to beg Master Andrew to come and be their abbot as before. They persuaded him 'with great difficulty'. 'He came with them, was received with great joy, and remained as their abbot, just as he had been.' This happened between the springs of the years 1161 and 1163, or very soon after.

This time Andrew stayed on at Wigmore and seems to have lost touch with the schools. Richard of St. Victor, who died in 1173, words his undated attack on Andrew's exposition of Isaias as though Andrew had long been lost sight of. He argues, not with 'Master Andrew', but with the disciples who 'still exist' and uphold their master's teaching. Their master was still living at that time. He died on October 19th, 1175, about three years after the foundation of his new abbey church. The canons buried him 'with great honour'.

The canon who wrote the Wigmore *History* has managed to draw, in a few lines, a character which Andrew himself confirms. He is not expansive as a writer, being too fascinated by the meaning of his text to make it into a peg for moral reflections. For that reason one listens intently when he speaks. Three of his texts induce him to break his silence and allow us to hear for a moment the Victorine, 'mestre de divinite, et de nobles vertues et plusurs, et sobre', whose reputation had travelled to the Welsh March.

On 1 Kings i. 3, *to adore and to offer sacrifice*, he suddenly gives a little exhortation on prayer:

> 'A good order! We should first *adore* God, and afterwards *sacrifice* to him. Adore him, not only with bowed head and bended knee, but in true humbleness of heart and complete submission of mind, as well as of bodily frame. He has no regard for your gift if you withdraw from him your heart. Beseech God first with pious, devout prayers. Afterwards you shall please him with sacrifices and gifts.'[1]

---

[1] MS. C.C.C. 30, fo. 51^c: 'Bonus ordo! Primum est Deum adorandum, deinde illi sacrificandum. Adora eum non sola incurvatione capitis et poplitis curvatione sed vera cordis humiliatione et omnimoda tam corporis quam mentis subiectione. Non respicit ad munus tuum si subtraxeris illi cor tuum. Roga Deum prius piis et devotis precibus, postea placabis eum hostiis et muneribus.'

With the same unexpectedness he bursts out on Dan. vii. 16:
*I went near to one of them that stood by and asked the truth of him
concerning all these things*:

> 'Of Daniel it is said: art thou even wiser than Daniel? Yet
> Daniel asks what he knows not from one who knows. Then
> why do *you*, surely less than Daniel, prefer to remain in shame-
> faced ignorance, rather than ask what you do not know from
> the learned and wise?
> 'Notice carefully that he "asks the truth" from "those that
> stand by", not from those who "minister" and hurry about.
> Wisdom is learnt from the leisured, in time of leisure, not from
> the hurried in time of disturbance.'[1]

Prov. xxxi. 3: *Give not . . . thy riches to destroy kings* draws
from him the exclamation:

> 'Professed religious should be ashamed to ask for so many
> and such unnecessary things; yes, and extort them from their
> dispensers!'[2]

Perhaps these last two comments were inspired by the
'distance' between Andrew and the canons of Wigmore;
perhaps they show the wistful impatience of a bystander
obliged to hurry and minister. The search for truth in study
was Andrew's ruling passion and he must have hated to be
disturbed. His last work, on Ecclesiastes, has a passage
which becomes very personal if we put it into its background.
Hanc occupationem pessimam dedit Deus filiis hominum [Eccles. i.
13] served as a text for many sermons against vain curiosity
and superfluous questions. Andrew had only to turn to the
homilies of his master Hugh. But he cannot bear to read the
text in this way. He makes the Preacher justify inquisitive-
ness instead of condemning it:

> 'He calls enquiry and research "this worst occupation" be-
> cause much labour brings little progress therein. He says that
> God hath given it *to the children of men, to be exercised therein*,
> because of God's gift, the soul, whose natural instinct is to *seek*

---

[1] MS. Pembroke 45, fo. 124ᵈ: '*et accessi ad unum de assistentibus et veritatem
querebam ab eo.* Si Daniel, de quo dictum est: "numquid (MS. unquam) tu
Daniele sapientior es?", a sciente querit quod ignorat, cur tu nescire pudens
potius (MS. prave) quam querere malens, illo satis inferior, a doctis et sapien-
tibus viris querere (MS. querente re) quod ignoras pigritaris? Diligenter
adverte quod ab assistentibus et non administrantibus et discurrentibus veritatem querit. Ab otiosis enim et in tempore otii et non a discurrentibus et
perturbationis tempore sapientia discitur.'
[2] MS. C.C.C. 30, fo. 106ᵃ: '. . . pudeat ergo religionem professos tot et tanta
superflua querentes, immo a dispensatoribus suis extorquentes.'

and search out concerning all things, that she may as it were pursue
and capture the hidden fugitive, truth, with what speed she
can; for all truth is hidden.'[1]

His feelings on having his natural instincts diverted from
'this worst occupation', and being sent to the wild Welsh
border, are perhaps expressed in the one letter of the
Victorine collection which is probably by him. It reads as
the literary exercise of a scholar, and alludes to some turn of
fortune which is never specified. Our only clue to its date
is that he calls himself not Abbot Andrew but Brother.

'To his beloved brother Thomas, his brother Andrew, most
forsaken, most wretched of all men, greeting, and the good
wishes he has for himself.

Dearest Brother,
Fortune's wheel for me is spinning swiftly, changeful as the
gusts of spring. She raised me lately to a better state, only to
thrust me down to the bottommost depths of adversity. She
smiled on me a little while ago with cheerful countenance; now
turning on me with a frown she takes away even my wish to
live. Woe! woe! to this brute who is allowed such boisterous
rule, such power to rage against us! Indeed I would rather my
last hour had come than that she had so overwhelmed me.'[2]

We can now ask the question which usually comes at the
beginning of a biographical notice. It has been left to the end
because we have no direct evidence for its solution. Was
Andrew an Englishman, as the bibliographers tell us? The
statement goes back to John Bale, who says that Andrew of
St. Victor was 'Anglus natione'. Bale took all the rest of the
notice from Boston of Bury; he cannot have been deducing

---

[1] Calandra, 12: 'Inquisitionem et investigationem de omnibus, *pessimam*
appellat *occupationem*, quia multum in ea laboratur et parum proficitur.
Dedit Deus filiis hominum. Divinitus data hominibus hec occupatio esse
dicitur *ut occupentur in ea* propter animam a Deo datam, cui insitum et naturale
est inquirere et investigare de omnibus, ut quasi fugientem et latentem veritatem—latet enim omne verum—quibus potest pedibus consequatur et com-
prehendat.'

[2] MS. Vat Regin. Lat. 179, fo. 203: 'Fratri suo dilectissimo Tome frater
suus desolatissimus et hominum quorumvis miserrimus Andreas salutem, et
quicquid sibi prosperitatis optat accidere.

'Frater Karissime michi valde volubilis omnique incertior verni flamine
facta est rota fortune que me nunc ad statum meliorem eductum in infimas
summe calamitatis partes detrusit. Hec paulo ante michi facie arridebat
seriori, nunc vultu lugubri in me invecta etiam spem vivendi michi subtraxit.
Vh'e vh'e huiusmodi belue cui tam violentum dominium, cui tanta in nos
seviendi facultas permittitur! Mallem quidem michi supremos dies imminere
quam hanc tam graviter in me corruisse.'
I owe this transcript to the kindness of the late Dom Wilmart.

from Andrew's abbacy at Wigmore, since this was unknown
to him. Therefore Bale had some source of information
which is now lost, or he was guessing. When we find that
Pits, in copying from Bale, has emphasized 'Anglus natione'
to 'in Anglia parentibus Anglis natus', and suggested that
Richard's attack on Andrew was due to the prejudice of a
Scot against an Englishman, we realize how a bibliographical
legend will grow like a snowball.

The *History of the Foundation of Wigmore* seems about to be
helpful, and then disappoints us. It tells us that the first
canons who came to the March from St. Victor found their
neighbours so rude and hostile that they asked for other Victorines, who knew the language and manners of the natives,
to replace them; so three canons, 'born and bred in England',
were sent to be the nucleus of the new house. We may suppose that they followed up their 'native' policy by electing an
Englishman as their first abbot; but the *History* says nothing
of this.

Then we have the evidence of Andrew's attitude towards
the French language, which again is negative. It must have
been common for Englishmen in the twelfth century to be
tri-lingual, speaking English, French, and Latin; and he was
living in Paris. We can deduce nothing definite from the
fact that he introduces French words into his glosses by the
expressions: 'Romana locutione dicere *solemus*'; 'in *vulgari* usu
loquendi . . .', or 'quam *vulgo* dicunt . . .', showing that he
regarded French as the current speech both for scholars and
for the common people. His more usual expression, however,
is 'in lingua Francorum' or 'quod Franci vocant . . .'; here
it is tempting, but rather fanciful, to see a slight distinction
in his mind between himself and the native Frenchman. We
have nothing so conclusive as Stephen Langton's report of
an Englishman who thought the English cry 'Wassail' a
hundred times more cheerful than 'esto hilaris!'[1]

We must either leave the question undecided, or we must
argue from the dangerous premiss of national characteristics.
But these are more respectable evidence now than they would
have been a few years ago. Professor Powicke has dwelt
convincingly on the essential Englishness of Stephen Langton.[2] Miss West has come to a definite conclusion in her
careful study of *Courtoisie* in Anglo-Norman Literature:

[1] 'Studies on the Commentaries', 7, n. 2.
[2] *Christian Life in the Middle Ages and Other Essays* (Oxford, 1935), 130-46.

'the modified form in which courtoisie presents itself would seem to point to the fact that already in the England of the twelfth and thirteenth centuries, with its curiously mixed population, there was beginning to show itself that sense of concrete reality apparently so typical of the Englishman of modern times'.[1]

The Anglo-Saxon on the eve of the Conquest may have been a good artist and poet; he was not intellectual.[2] The great English saint, Wulfstan of Worcester, won his village sports in boyhood and enjoyed being read to because it sent him to sleep.[3] The Anglo-Norman had more intellectual energy; but he generally preferred historical writing or biblical commentaries to abstract speculation, research and observation to reasoning. Typically, Peter of Blois disagrees with an opinion, universally received in the schools, that 'he who has one virtue has all', and the subtle distinction which was used to support it, because in common experience he found it untrue.[4]

It is difficult not to apply these recent studies to Andrew. Here we have a scholar at Paris who shows, not even that disapproval which betrays attraction, but a total lack of interest in the work of theological speculation and synthesis which goes on around him. He is independent enough to devote himself, in this unpropitious milieu, to an obscure and neglected branch of study which, we may note, was not his own original idea but his master's. He is pious, in a reserved way, without being mystical. He is a humanist, with a taste for antiquities. He revels in detail and shows confusion of thought when faced with the need for distinction and definition. He admits, with cheerful indifference, that he cannot hold his own against the Jews in argument.

My own impression is that Pits was quite right, however unscientific in his method, and that Andrew was English or Anglo-Norman. It grew on me slowly from a study of his writings, which shall be allowed to speak for themselves.

[1] C. B. West, *Courtoisie in Anglo-Norman Literature* (Oxford, 1938), 168.
[2] See the account of English culture on the eve of the Conquest by R. W. Chambers, who takes a favourable view of it, *The Continuity of English Prose* (London, 1932).
[3] The *Vita Wulfstani of William of Malmesbury*, ed. R. R. Darlington (Camden Soc., London, 1928), 6; 49.
[4] R. W. Southern, 'Some New Letters of Peter of Blois', *English Historical Review*, liv (1937), 416-19.

II. ANDREW AS AN EXEGETE

We must begin by asking, from Andrew himself if possible, what exactly he sets out to do. An important clue to the aim of his work will be its form. Roughly speaking, a twelfth-century exegete had three possibilities. He could comment on or gloss his text consecutively. According to William of Conches,[1] the comentator expounds the sense; the glossator expounds both words and sense. Glosses differ from commentaries in that they are usually meant to give students an adequate knowledge of their set text and the standard works on it. A commentary is a product of the cloister or the study, a gloss of the class-room; it often comes down to us as a *reportatio*, the notes taken by a student from his master's lectures. A third possibility was to expound, not the whole text but select passages, to pick out only those which presented special interest or difficulty. The last was a well-established tradition, going back to the patristic *scholia*.

Andrew has chosen this third category. In the manuscripts his works are called *notule, compilationes, expositio historica*. Only one copy has been labelled, and that by a later hand, as *glose*. Andrew himself speaks of his *expositiuncula, explanatiuncula*, or his *libri explanationum*. His exposition of the Octateuch is a development of Hugh's *Notulae*. Though he treats the Prophets and Proverbs more fully, and provides them with prologues, even here he makes no attempt to expound every passage. William of Conches would say that he 'glosses' some of his texts, where the words are obscure, and 'comments' on others. He is not giving a course of lectures, which would oblige him to cover a certain ground; he writes 'for himself', as he tells us, and is free to concentrate on what interests him. On the other hand, his 'little explanations' are more modest in their scope than 'commentaries', a word which Andrew applies to the vast works of St. Jerome. He has, in fact, taken the *scholia* form of exposition and expanded it to suit his purpose.

It is a specialist's purpose. Andrew claims to be expounding the historical sense. He excludes the spiritual exposition

---

[1] Dr. R. Klibansky kindly allows me to quote from his forthcoming book: 'in his (William's) recently discovered commentary on Macrobius, both "commentum" and "glosa" are concerned with the meaning and thought of the author, but "glosa", in addition, follows the text, closely explaining its structure and phrasing. In other words, the "glosa", by giving the *continuatio litterae*, expounds both the words and the sense; the "commentum" the sense only.'

on the one hand and theological questions on the other. He
has no time for homiletics or for doctrinal discussion. The
angelology, which tradition had attached to the first verse of
Scripture, is swept aside. Moses, intentionally as Andrew
believes, has 'passed by altogether the creation of the angels,
and their confirmation or fall'; he will do likewise:

> 'We too, of set purpose, shall omit what others think should
> be said about the angels on this passage, even should we have
> views.'[1]

He refers elsewhere to his views on the nature of angels and
dismisses them, promptly, if with a certain regret: *non est huius
temporis nec negotii.*[2] He will consider only what he thinks
necessary for an understanding of the letter.

Into this severely limited objective he puts 'all his energy',
and he approaches it in the spirit of a pioneer. He is going
to add something to the explanations of the Fathers. Like
Richard of St. Victor, Andrew has to justify himself for his
originality. Being more original than Richard, he is at once
more defiant and more deprecating, more adventurous and
more apologetic. In his prologues to the Prophets he lets
himself go. A cataract of eloquence, which can scarcely be
reproduced in modern English, tells of his hopes and fears
before the task that he sets himself; its difficulties appal and
yet enchant him:[3]

> '*Dark waters in the clouds of the air*' [Ps. xvii. 12]:

Andrew's readers would at once supply the *Gloss*: 'hidden
teaching is in the prophets'; for he continues:

> 'Our mental powers are so restrained and clouded that we
> may not perceive the fruitful showers of wholesome wisdom
> through the darkness of the prophets' words. But God com-
> manded *light to shine out of the darkness* [2 Cor. iv. 6]. Strong is
> his hand. By instruments of his choice and at his pleasure he
> can pierce with some light even our mental darkness, illumine
> with the ray of understanding, restore to sight the blindness of

---

[1] MS. Bibl. Nat. Lat. 356, fo. 1ᵈ: 'Sed quoniam creationem angelorum con-
sulto eum pretermisisse et his solis que ad hominum utilitatem spectant inten-
disse diximus, nos quoque quid alii in hac operis parte de angelis dicendum esse
senserint, quid etiam ipsi nos, si quid inde sentiamus, ex industria pretermisi-
mus.' Fo. 21ᵇ 'Sed ut iam diximus de angelis et de hoc eorum celo sive sit, sive
non sit, penitus omittimus.' And see below, p. 388.

[2] MS. Pembroke 45, fo. 129ᶜ.

[3] The Latin text of the longer passages quoted in this chapter is given in
the appendix.

the heart. Mighty, yet most munificent is God, in virtue of his unbegotten kindness. Whosoever asks and would receive, he will pour, abundantly as ocean water, the bright wisdom of their desire.

'Wisdom, too, offers herself to her lovers and goes to meet her studious ones. More: she faithfully promises the reward of blessedness to those who knock early at the gate of her hostel, joy of life everlasting to those who proclaim her. With joy she allures and gently draws us by the hope of her promises. For even should all others be excluded, righteousness is its own reward, and what more righteous for a rational creature than to investigate the truth? We think so. We have given ourselves over wholly to this, the toilsome search for wisdom, toilsome but pleasant, wholesome, fructifying; to this, I say, this pleasant toil, this toilsome pleasure.

'Since our poverty does not permit us to reach that studiousness which proclaims wisdom, which brings heavenly glory to its adepts, and is of service to posterity, let us at least with our every endeavour strive after a humbler kind, which *uttereth* not *her voice in the streets* nor *crieth out at the head of multitudes* [Prov. i. 20-21], distrusting her strength:

"Some point of moral progress each may gain,
        Though to aspire beyond it should prove vain."[1]

Fool! You cannot do what you will, if you will not do what you can. He is not altogether useless who is useful to himself.

'But suppose that, relying not on our own strength, which is slight, almost nothing, presuming on divine mercy's help, we should attempt that first studiousness we mentioned, that which overtops and excels: let no one conclude us to be so besotted with vanity as to set ourselves up as an author or as a teacher. God forbid that we should be so foolish as to stretch out self-confidently for what we cannot reach, exceeding our measure. It is better to stay safely on one's own level than to rise vainly above it. Enough for us, and those like us, if we thoroughly take in what we are taught.

'Are you fearful and chary of danger? Do not presume to teach; learning is safer. Are you soft and supine, impatient of toil? Lay aside the tablets and the pen: be content to read. But know that a strenuous knight must not shun every danger, nor a brave man fear toil. He who withdraws his body and his brain from toil must go without its profits. Worth, honour, glory, training, proof, patience, countless such things are the profits of toil, and he who refuses it will rightly be deprived of all these. Fear does not deter us from toil that brings profit. Would that our lack of skill and diffidence did not so either! 'I have decided to concoct some little explanation of the

---

[1] Horace, *Ep.* v. 1-32, trans. J. Conington (London, 1880), 98.

obscure prophetic writings, relying on divine help rather than on my own strength, as I did in time past, for the Pentateuch, Josue, Judges, Malachim. Their abysmal depth, perplexing intricacy, the startling diversity of people and things, have turned me in some measure from my purpose, fearing to begin the work.

' "What!" you say, "don't you expect and dread murmurs, backbiting, poisonous hisses, sniffs, frowns of displeasure, curling of the lip?"

'Yes indeed. Envy I should expect and dread, were I doing ought to arouse it. Were I writing anything new, important and enviable I should have reason, in these bad days, to fear what you have said. But I do not strive to din my work in fastidious ears, deaf to almost everything save the past.

"No one is obliged to take my gift."[1]

I keep watch for myself; I work for myself. Consulting my poverty, which cannot always have commentaries and glossed books to hand, I have collected together what is scattered and diffused through them, pertaining to the historical sense, and have concentrated it, as it were into one *corpus*. Lastly, if I could discover anything on the Prophets, whom I decided to study with especial care because of their obscurity, or on other books of the Old Testament, as the Jews or certain others, and my own study, showed it to me, or as God revealed it (for he sometimes grants even this to his servants), I thought good to insert it, lest what had been usefully learnt should be forgotten.'

We must strip this apology of its conventional modesty and its catch phrases. Andrew realizes that he is doing something new; so he tries to disarm criticism by protesting that he does it purely for his own satisfaction. His writings are an aid to memory for his own use. He works because he likes it.

Having let off steam in his general prologue, he approaches the prophecy of Isaias more calmly. His defence is more rational and more thorough-going. Here he pleads, not the insufficiency of his library, but that of his sources. The Fathers have not explained everything. Andrew becomes interesting. He does not, like Richard, attribute their silence to lack of opportunity or suggest that, given time, they would have done better than the moderns. Nor does he repeat the 'progress theory', the 'dwarfs on the shoulders of giants', which we connect with Bernard of Chartres.[2] It is

---

[1] Ovid, *ex P.* iii. 6. 58.
[2] See R. Klibansky, 'Standing on the shoulders of giants', *Isis*, xxvi (1936) 147-9.

K

true that Andrew quotes the famous phrase from Priscian; but he puts it as 'a question expecting the answer no': *are we, because younger, more far sighted than our elders?* Andrew prefers to justify himself by the very nature of truth. She is unfathomable. There is always something fresh to discover. He takes the example of St. Jerome, who, despite his admiration for the Greek exegetes, above all for Origen, thought it not superfluous to expound the Prophets. St. Jerome's forerunners had not exhausted their subject; nor does the Latin Father, 'as though he swore by their words', keep always closely to their footprints:

> 'He did not judge it idle, rash, or presumptuous, to apply himself to the same quest as the Fathers, who laboured before him to explain the Scriptures, or never would he, that wise, good, industrious man, who minded the proverb: "be sparing of time" have toiled so hard and made it his life work.
>
> 'Ah yes! he knew, the learned man, he knew, full well he knew, how hidden is truth, how deep she dwells, how far she screens herself from mortal sight, how few she receives, how laboriously they seek her, how few (they are almost none) may reach her, how partially and piecemeal they drag her forth. She hides, yet so as never wholly to be hidden. Careful seekers find her, that, carefully sought, she may again be found. None may draw her forth in her completeness, but by degrees. The fathers and forefathers have found her; something is left for the sons and descendants to find. So always: she is sought; something is still to seek; found, and there is something still to find.'

As St. Jerome had followed the Greeks, so Andrew will follow St. Jerome:

> 'It is not disrespectful, nor presumptuous, nor redundant, nor unnecessary, nor idle, for us lesser men to labour in the exposition of Scripture, because our elders have done so before us. So we follow the venerable Jerome in the same quest for truth as his, though with unequal step, rightly setting his explanation before ours, and leaving to the reader's judgement, whether, where we have put forth all our strength, we have not, by our labour, something progressed.'

This prologue is Andrew's *tour de force*, which he never surpasses. But his prologue to Ezechiel yields a good metaphor. If we compare it with Richard's, on the same prophet, we get some notion of the difference between them. Richard sees himself as a gleaner in the harvest field of the Fathers. Andrew sees himself as an explorer:

'With God as leader, who makes ways in the sea, paths in the stormy water, we take our way unfearing, through unknown, pathless places, no end in sight.'[1]

Here, perhaps, Andrew may remind us of the early twelfth-century exegete, Rupert of Deutz, who had God alone for his master. Andrew is considerably more modest than Rupert, however; divine revelation merely supplements his studies; he takes some equipment into the wilderness. Hugh of St. Victor advised his pupils to 'learn everything', and where grammar and rhetoric are concerned, Andrew has tried to follow the advice. Quotations or allusions from Cicero, Seneca, Sallust, Vegetius, lines from Virgil, Ovid, Horace, Juvenal, Lucan come appropriately to his pen. The question whether he was drawing on the originals as distinct from *florilegia* would require a long study, which would have to include the resources of the Victorine library; but his apt quotations at least compare favourably with the obvious tags used by masters of the later twelfth century for the enlivenment of their lectures. He is interested in grammar and notes the incorrectness of the Vulgate, when judged by the rules of the classical grammarians.[2] His own style is deliberate, forceful and varied, with a fondness for parenthesis which recalls that of Richard. He keeps the 'florid, elevated and figurative way' for his prologues and certain purple patches, writing his ordinary comments in simpler Latin. He generally follows the rules of Dictamen for rhythmical clausulae in the sentence endings of his more ambitious passages. Each sentence in his prologue to Genesis has one of the approved endings:[3] *incutiatur*; *conferénda promíttit*; *obsecutúris prescríbit*; *diligénter proséquitur*; *pénitus prétermíttit*; *maniféste inséruit*; *insinuáre curávit*. He is apt to forget them, however, in moments of excitement.

Natural science, on the other hand, has no interest for him. Neither has doctrinal theology; hence his quotations from the Fathers almost always derive from their commentaries on Scripture.

---

[1] The whole prologue is printed in the appendix.

[2] MS. C.C.C. 30, fo. 89ᶜ on Parab. i. 22: '*Odibunt* secundum novos translator posuit grammaticos cum secundum artem "oderint" posuisse debuisset.' Dr. Hunt tells me that he has not found any support for *odibunt* in the 'new', i.e. medieval, grammarians.

[3] See N. Denholm-Young, 'The Cursus in England', *Oxford Essays in Medieval History Presented to H. E. Salter* (Oxford, 1934), 70-2, for the rules of Dictamen.

His exegetical sources have been roughly classified by Andrew himself in his prologue to the Prophets. He has used 'commentaries and glossed books'; he has been instructed by 'Jews and certain others'. The Jewish sources will be discussed in the next chapter. Here it is enough to say that Andrew also claims to have been instructed on the literal sense of the Pentateuch by the Jews. The earliest manuscript of Andrew on the Heptateuch that we possess, probably from the abbey of Beaupré near Beauvais, written soon after the middle of the twelfth century, has the explicit:

> 'Liber sancte Marie de Prato extractus ex libris sancti Augustini sanctique Iheronimi, Iosephi, atque Origenis, aliorumque plurimorum, traditionibusque Hebreorum.'

He certainly makes constant use of Josephus, whom he quotes by name, and his pages are studded with expressions such as *asserit Hebreus, Hebreus meus dicit, tradunt Hebrei, apud Hebreos, Hebrei dicunt, si Iudeis de se credimus*. He learnt the explanation of Dan. ix. 24, *ab eruditissimis Hebreorum*. Some passages of his work on the Prophets definitely record a series of discussions, where questions are asked and answered, or not answered, by both sides. As well as repeating Jewish 'traditions', Andrew collates the Vulgate with the Hebrew text.

The 'commentaries and glossed books' mean patristic commentaries and the *Gloss*. Their scope varied on different books of the Bible; so it is better to take them in groups; Andrew had a wider range of authorities for the Octateuch than for the Prophets and 'Solomon'. The *Gloss* on the Octateuch accounts for his occasional quotations from Origen. He has used it for Augustine and Jerome; but he also knows St. Jerome's *Quaestiones in Genesim*, the ninth-century *Quaestiones in Regum et Paralipomenon* falsely ascribed to him, St. Augustine's *Quaestiones in Pentateuchum* and Raban Maur's commentary on Kings, in the originals. On the Tabernacle he transcribes from Bede, in the original too.

His principal stand-by is his master Hugh of St. Victor, as one would expect. Recent studies on the glosses, sentence books, and summas of the twelfth century are showing us how systematically the works of the masters were copied and developed by their pupils. Knowing that Andrew was supposed by tradition to be Hugh's pupil, one guessed that Hugh's *Notulae* would lie behind Andrew on the Pentateuch.

In fact, he has incorporated them, almost word for word, into his exposition of Genesis and Exodus. On Leviticus he acknowledges his debt explicitly. The *Notulae* here take the form of a little treatise on sacrifices, instead of notes on separate texts. So Andrew copies it out in full:

'We have set forth above the explanation of this book [Leviticus], as far as the gist is concerned, for the greater part without any alteration, according to others, who *like ourselves have been instructed on the literal sense of the Pentateuch by the Jews.* Now let us deal with the letter which they have left undiscussed.'[1]

Then he adds his own exposition.

For Numbers, Deuteronomy, and Josue we have no authentic *Notulae*. The few paragraphs printed by the seventeenth-century editors do not appear in Andrew's work, which is another argument against them. He does use those on Judges and Kings, in the form in which we have them.

Naturally he has studied his master's great work, the *De Sacramentis*. He refers to it expressly, though not by name, in the section on the Creation. It seems to be responsible for the few vague theological ideas that come into his exegesis.[2]

The Prophets and Solomon gave less opportunity for borrowing. Andrew does not use Hugh's published works on the Prophets or Ecclesiastes; but we cannot rule out the possibility of oral teaching. When he says 'the Jews and certain others' he may well be referring to Hugh. In discussing a text of Jeremias he says: 'certain persons, applying themselves rather to the literal sense, as their habit is, think that the letter should be explained in this way . . .';[3] he approves of their view. It might be taken from his master.

Otherwise Andrew had little but St. Jerome. No other Father, accessible to him, had expounded the literal sense of the Prophets; Andrew realized that he was taking up the work of scholarship where St. Jerome had left it. Hence he used St. Jerome on the Prophets as he had used Hugh on the Octateuch. His own exposition is supplementary; sometimes he contents himself with transcribing the commentary

---

[1] MS. C.C.C. 30, fo. 37ᵃ: 'Et quoniam magna ex parte huius libri explanationem, quantum ad sententiarum summam spectat, secundum alios qui ab Hebreis sicut et nos litteralem sensum pentateuci edocti sunt nullis penitus mutatis supra posuimus, nunc littere quam illi indiscussam reliquerunt insistamus.'

[2] For his view of original sin see below, p. 148.   [3] See below, p. 142.

of St. Jerome. His Minor Prophets are practically an abridgement of St. Jerome's. On these books, too, he used the meagre literal exposition contained in the *Gloss*.

Given his list of authorities, one must ask what value he ascribes to them; how far he respects them. The law and theology of the twelfth century were built up on the concordance and interpretation of authority. All the 'questioning' which went on around him in the Paris schools had authority as its basis. Obviously Andrew's own questioning had a special character. Old Testament history differed from theology in that a scholar could select and reject his sources at pleasure without involving himself in heresy. But the habit of respect for authority was very strong even here. Since there was no urgent need in matters of historical fact, as there was in matters of faith, to decide between the 'Yes and No', exegetes had evolved a system of 'Either, Or'. They would string together a list of alternative explanations connected by *vel* or *aliter*. In this way they satisfied curiosity and shifted the responsibility of choice to the reader. The reader would remember St. Augustine's teaching, that variant opinions about the literal sense of a text might be regarded as true, provided that they were not unedifying; and he would be in no hurry to decide either. If an exegete actually disagreed with a patristic interpretation, he expressed himself with great tact.

Not so Andrew. 'I wonder how Jerome can say . . . !' 'Blessed Augustine seems to hold, but . . .' 'We follow the Jews and Josephus rather than Bede.' 'Men of great authority give this opinion . . . they are misled.' 'I do not remember to have found an adequate explanation of this passage.' Andrew has no false modesty. He prides himself on his critical faculty:

> 'The whole context must be carefully considered and expounded, lest we who rebut the errors of others, if it be done more carelessly, be ourselves rebutted.'[1]

On the dream of Daniel (vii. 7-8) he has a long argument with an imaginary opponent. They differ about the meaning of the ten horns of the beast. Do the ten horns signify that ten kings shall divide the 'kingdom of the Romans' between

---

[1] MS. C.C.C. 30, fo. 61ᵇ: 'Diligenter attendenda et exponenda [est] totius littere series ne et nos qui aliorum errores redarguimus si negligentius actum fuerit merito redarguamur.'

them? This is the opponent's view. Andrew, stirred perhaps by his memories of Rome, holds that the horns appeared to Daniel not all together but successively; they represent ten successive kings of the Romans. He will not have it that Rome shall ever be divided. The opponent puts up a good fight and they abuse each other in the best traditions of humanistic scholarship:

> *The Opponent*: 'Now think you to escape, but bowing down your wretched head a tenth (and largest) wave shall overwhelm you . . . [his argument follows]. Now if some chance has snatched you from your peril, if you are still not totally demolished, if you have an argument left, produce it.'
>
> *Andrew*: 'I am snatched from no peril. I never incurred one. The dart which that strong right hand of yours thought to have hurled at me has neither pricked me nor pierced me. That you may know it, please listen patiently, while I clearly explain my views on this matter . . . There! You have my opinion such as it is. If perhaps you should think it ridiculous, you who are ready to refute it, I beg you, show forbearance.'

But here his opponent gives in:

> 'Remember that the victory in this contest rests with the future. That glory or shame it will bring us cannot be known, until the future shall declare it. Please proceed. Allow us to abound in our own sense, unless the sequel, or some passage of canonical Scripture forbid.'

Andrew, flushed with victory, can be generous:

> 'I had taken arms for close contest which the prayers of your supplication have dashed from my hands. It is no victory to vanquish you by force, that you by your humility may vanquish us. So let us proceed, as you wish.'

The baffled opponent is St. Jerome, and St. Jerome relying on Catholic tradition:

> 'We say what all the ecclesiastical writers have handed down: at the end of the world, when the kingdom of the Romans is destroyed, ten kings shall divide the Roman world between them. . . .'

Andrew has thinly disguised him as *aliquis*, and presented him with arguments, the better to attack him. In spite of his veneration for St. Jerome, he feels that they are both scholars together; there is no harm in a friendly disagreement.

His master receives the same critical treatment as authority. Although as a rule Andrew copies down the *Notulae*, he does not always accept them. Sometimes he will omit, or add an alternative explanation. In three places he rejects them openly, once with impatience:

'Certain persons expound the text in this way, if anything so frivolous can be called exposition . . . Then he [*sic*] makes another attempt which is just as futile.'[1]

After this we expect Andrew to justify his detachment. One need only hear the beginning of his work on the Pentateuch to feel sure that he will. It is very rare in reading through medieval commentaries to come across a striking phrase, an *incipit* that carries one with it. One must know the patient compilers of the ninth century, who boast in their prologues that they add nothing to the Fathers, and the quietly competent, long-winded Paschasius, in order to appreciate the vivid fragment of John the Scot on the fourth Gospel:

'Vox spiritalis aquilae pulsat aurem ecclesiae.'

In the twelfth century prologues become stereotyped. The glossator begins with a text; then he shows its application to the work in hand, and at the same time his ingenuity in finding connections between unrelated things. Here is a typical prologue, ascribed to the great Peter Lombard:

'He made also bars of settim wood: five to hold together the boards of one side of the tabernacle: and five other bars at the west side . . . And the board works themselves he overlaid with gold . . . [Exod. xxxvi. 31-4]. The five bars which hold together the boards of one side of the tabernacle are the five books of the Law, which uphold the Church against every shock; she is rightly called *the tabernacle* while toiling and militant in her pilgrimage on earth. The *five other bars at the west side* are the five prophetical books: Isaias, Jeremias, Ezechiel, Daniel and the book of the Twelve Prophets. They join together the boards on the other side of the tabernacle; for they firmly establish the doctrine of the Church's preachers, and overlay them with the gold of heavenly wisdom. . . .'[2]

[1] MS. C.C.C. 30, fo. 14a-b: 'Quidam hanc litteram sic exponunt, si tamen exponere est risu digna dicere . . . Item aliter exponere temptans non minus desipit . . .' He is criticizing the explanation given by Hugh of Gen. xx. 16, in the *Notulae*. P.L. clxxv. 52.
[2] B. Smalley and G. Lacombe, 'The Lombard's Commentary on Isaias and Other Fragments', *The New Scholasticism*, v (1931), 124, 137, 156.

The glossator goes on relentlessly through the *sockets of silver*, the *rings* and *plates of gold*. He needs this preliminary caper to settle him down to the second part of his prologue, where he deals with the matter and purpose of his author. But Andrew gets off straight from the starting-post:

'Difficile quod durum quod grave quod asperum est observatur, si nullum custodiendi premium proponatur, aut negligenti nullus pene timor incutiatur. Quod bene intelligens Moyses. . . .'

This *incipit* stands out from contemporary ones rather as John the Scot's from his. The author of the Pentateuch and his purpose claim us instantly. There is no playing on the number five because the matter in itself supplies the unity.

Even more surprisingly, it is the author's immediate purpose. Andrew concentrates on Moses and his Jewish audience. The story of the Creation is meant as a lesson to an ignorant people; the Trinity and the angels are passed over as liable to distract and mislead them into polytheism. Andrew could have taken his main idea from St. Augustine; and Bede is distrustful of the interpretation *in Filio* for *in principio*. The emphasis is new, however, and we go on to what seems to be a wholly original thought. The Hexaemeron was always treated as a form of prophecy. Andrew read in his *Gloss*:

'Just as Paul learnt the Gospel by revelation, so Moses was taught by the Holy Spirit about the Creation.'

Tentatively, Andrew proposes to substitute research for revelation. He suspects that some earlier source lies behind the Mosaic account.

'Harsh, heavy, hard commandments are difficult to keep, if no reward is promised the obedient and no fear of punishment held over the negligent, as Moses well understood. Before he gives the hard and heavy precepts of the Law, God's harsh and scarcely tolerable judgments, to an untutored people, lax from the soft living and many pleasures of Egypt, he relates God's blessings and manifold graces to them and their fathers; he promises that more good shall be granted them; he recalls the evils that God has brought, and foretells what he will bring on the disobedient. His purpose is to educate his hearers to a more careful observance of the Law he gives them, by counting the many great riches of heavenly favour. So carefully, in order, from the beginning, he tells of the blessings which God has bestowed on the whole human race, but more especially on this people and their fathers.

'To one of these blessings he gives, as it were, pride of place: that God has deigned to create these heavens, the earth, the other elements, and their adornment, for man, and for man's use and service. Since he means to stress what was done for man and for man's use, therefore, in describing the world's creation, he has altogether passed over the creation of the angels, their confirmation and fall. Nor, lest he occasion backsliding to an untutored people, prone to the worship of many gods which they had learnt in Egypt, has he made open mention of the Trinity. Yet he was careful to suggest the operation of Three Persons in all God's works: power in creating things from nothing, wisdom in disposing and guiding them, goodness in sustaining and cherishing.

'It is usual to ask how Moses, so long afterwards, could have known how the world began. No wonder if the grace of the Holy Sprit, which could reveal to him even the future, could also reveal the past; for nothing is so apt to our knowledge as what is past. Nevertheless, we may believe without absurdity that the holy fathers of old, Adam and his descendants, would commit the Creation carefully to memory, by frequent recital, or even in writing; for this especially causes us to praise God and love him. So it might come to the knowledge of Moses, who sought it by careful research.'

By concentrating on Moses and his purpose, Andrew cut the Gordian knot which had puzzled exegetes from St. Augustine onwards, the two accounts of Creation in Genesis i and ii. How reconcile the six days of Genesis i with the 'day' of Genesis ii. 4, and with the text of Ecclesiasticus: *He that liveth for ever created all things* TOGETHER [xviii. 1]? St. Augustine declared for the Creation *simul*, and worked out a complicated theory to explain it. According to him the 'six days' are allegorical and do not refer to a time sequence. Bede preferred to understand the six days literally. He says that the 'day' of Genesis ii refers in this, as in some other passages of Scripture, not to twenty-four hours but to the whole period of time mentioned in Genesis i. In Genesis ii the sacred author is going over his story again and filling in the gaps. Since Bede was immensely popular, exegetes could choose, if they had the courage, between his opinion and St. Augustine's. Arguments for and against the Creation *simul* are a normal part of the twelfth-century sentence book. Andrew found it fully discussed in the *De Sacramentis*, where his master had arrived at a typical compromise: God created all things at once and together in matter; he afterwards, during the six days, distinguished them in form. The conflicting views of his predecessors are treated with a characteristic blend of tact and frankness. Hugh begins by summarizing the arguments of the Fathers for the Creation *simul* in matter and form. To work in stages of time would be unworthy of an omnipotent Creator and suggestive of human weakness. This view is supported by Ecclesiasticus; Genesis itself, whence we derive our first knowledge of the Creation, speaks of the six days so ambiguously as rather, in some places, to prove them one. So the Fathers say that the distinction into six days is mystical; in literal truth each creature came into being in the form it now has.

Hugh believes, on the contrary, that to work by stages in no way derogates from the Creator's omnipotence. Undoubtedly God could have worked differently. But he made all things for the benefit of rational beings; so even the making was meant to set them an example. Man learns, from the six days, that his own moral perfection must come by stages. To be, and to be good, are separate in time, like the world's creation and adornment. If it be objected that nobody was there to profit from the lesson, Hugh replies that the angels, created on the first day, were there, and that man throughout the ages would have the written account before him.

Then he states and answers the philosophical objection to the Creation *simul* in matter only. Matter cannot exist apart from form; therefore we cannot speak of creation in formless matter, which was subsequently 'distinguished'. Hugh admits the first point; the world, he agrees, was never formless in the sense of wholly lacking form. But 'formless' in this context means rather: 'confused and lacking orderly disposition'. He adds that *simul* refers also to the creation of the angels: it means that the visible and invisible worlds were created together in the same instant.

Andrew had studied these chapters of the *De Sacramentis*. He disagrees with his master's conclusion. Not only that. The whole argument strikes him as profoundly irrelevant. Scrapping every *pro* and *contra* he seizes on one suggestion which Hugh had thrown out merely in parenthesis, and which in his opinion provides the whole clue: 'Genesis whence we derive our first knowledge' of the Creation. Genesis is our primary source. Does Genesis say that the world was created in six days? That is the problem. Why consider a later authority? Whether from forgetfulness, or deliberately, Andrew confuses the two 'sapiential books' and ascribes the *simul* text to Wisdom instead of Ecclesiasticus. According to St. Jerome, Wisdom was written by Philo Judaeus, and Philo perhaps was easier to discredit as an authority for the Creation than the anonymous author of Ecclesiasticus. But even as a trick it would be significant; it would show a feeling for the relative value of sources.

In the same way his harmonizing of the two accounts of Creation in Genesis i and ii, which is expanded from Bede's, may strike us as naïve. But what matters is the approach. His contemporaries try to solve the problem subjectively by moral and philosophical arguments; Andrew solves it objectively from the text. Fastening on this, he treats it as a unity and tries to deduce the meaning of the author. One remembers his suggestion that Moses drew on earlier sources . . . We are far away from the *De Sacramentis*; this is biblical science *in potentia*.

'*And every plant of the field before it sprang up in the earth.* According to the true Hebrew version this verse is separate from the one before, and begins a fresh section. He [Moses] has just recapitulated what he said above; now, from this verse upwards, he explains more amply and clearly what before he has run through briefly, in order to show what was done on which day. He dwells, with especial care, on the things which concern the common use of man, and which the untaught, less gifted mind can understand. Thus, in describing the work of the third day, he told us that God said: *Let the earth bring forth the green herb, and such as may seed, and the fruit tree,* and so on [Gen. i. 11], adding: *and it was so done,* without showing how it was done. So here, lest it should be conceived as done in the accustomed way, as it is now, he shows how it was done, saying: *Every plant of the field,* etc. This is the negative sense: No *plant of the field* had as yet sprung up *in the earth;* no *herb of the ground* as yet had grown, that is, in the way it did afterwards, but by divine operation, as he shows in the sequel. There are two ways, nowadays, in which plants spring up, and herbs grow, that is by nature and by human labour. He shows that in the beginning it happened in neither of these two ways. First, he eliminates the working of nature, saying: *For the Lord God had not rained upon the earth;* then human labour: *there was not a man to till the earth.*

'Read in this order: the plant of the field did not spring up, nor the herb give seed, that is, in the usual way; because as yet there was no rain and no human labour, the two things which are wont to make plants and herbs grow.

'Subtract something from the text, and you get a contrary: "take away the parts and you take away the whole". There are some who, misled by the translation, read this verse: *Every plant of the field*, etc. up to: *for the Lord God had not rained*, as the end of the verse above, in which we get the recapitulation. Hence whatever they have ravelled in six days, they are compelled, in one instant, to unravel; and what they have gathered from many verses they must scatter, with the tail end of one little verse. They rely on the witness of that apocryphal tract, the Wisdom of Solomon, against the first book of Scripture, which says that God worked, and finished his work in six days, and rested on the seventh. Hence they try to maintain that God made all things at once.

'This position involves them in many difficulties. That God created all things together, and yet did different things on the six days, may stand [they say] for this reason: he created all things "together" in formless matter; afterwards, in six successive days, he reduced each thing to its own form. Indeed, men of great authority give this opinion.

'Neglect of the right translation has unfortunately misled them, and the authority of the aforesaid tract. Granted that Philo, its author, thought so, nowhere do we find that Moses the author of our book [Genesis] thought like him. Moses afterwards recapitulates, not what another thinks, but what he thinks himself and has previously said. To *recapitulate* is to repeat shortly what you have said above, from the beginning. In a recapitulation something is often added, but not so as to destroy what goes before. It has been said above that God made all things on six different days. Therefore, to say in a recapitulation that he made all things together, this is not to add something to what is said above, but wholly to destroy it. Finally, if Moses is trying to express this in his recapitulation, why does he add the work of the third day only to that of the first? Why does he not add the work of all the other days, and say: "*these are the generations of the heaven and the earth, when they were created, in the day that the Lord God made the heaven and the earth* and the light and the firmament and all the rest in order"?'

Andrew shows this same historical sense in his approach to the Prophets. His prologues to Isaias and Daniel each contain a character study and life, which, as he says, are of great importance in commending their work to us. They are stylized portraits, like figures in a row of twelfth-century sculptures. Each is a little encomium of the prophet's virtues, drawn from Scripture and St. Jerome. But they have vitality. The few details at Andrew's disposal have been 'written up' with feeling.

'Seven things especially ennoble [Isaias] the author of this work: his noble race, his polished eloquence, his dignified office, his relationship with a royal house, his worth of character, his firm, enduring constancy, lastly his admirable holiness of life.

'That he was noble and of royal blood, is clearly proved, if Jewish tradition is true, by the marriage between his daughter and Manasses, the son of Ezechias king of Juda. His dignity of office lies in the fact of his being a prophet; and his father also was a prophet, as appears from his name at the beginning of the prophecy itself. How he was related to a royal house by affinity has been told above, where we showed that his daughter married a king. Plain proof of his worth and holiness is that he merited to see the Lord, as he writes himself; that his lips were cleansed by a live coal, brought from the altar by a seraph's hand; and chiefly that God testifies to Isaias being his servant, of whom he says: *as my servant hath walked, naked and barefoot* [Isa. xx. 3].

'His firm, enduring constancy, his intention to declare the truth, his courage in foretelling disaster to princes and peoples, kings and priests, lands and nations, towns, villages, cities and camps, these shine out clearly in the prophet's death, and the torments worse than death that he underwent. For wicked Manasses, it is told, who filled Jerusalem with the blood of prophets from gate to gate, sundered him with a wooden saw, because he confidently foretold the evils to come upon Juda which he had learnt by divine revelation. He suffered unto death, according to the sage's precept, for justice' sake, and manfully strove against wickedness unto blood. He was willing rather to lose his life, with honour, by exquisite torture, a way of death unheard of, than, shamefully forbearing, cede to falsehood, lay down his God-given office, suppress the truth for fear of fleeting death.'

Daniel, on the contrary, managed to turn his gift to good account. Andrew celebrates the wisdom of a captive who could rise to greatness in the land of his captivity:

'Ponder his prudence in all these matters, and in much else that we pass by for brevity's sake. You will marvel; I say too little, will gape with wonder. These gifts and many others which distinguished him, the divine mercy ever going before, won him, in the land of his homeless captivity, riches, power, wealth, possessions, purple raiment, a golden chain, the friendship of kings, the highest honours, a rank of dignity, immortal glory, lastly honour and security.'

In the same spirit Andrew points out the significance of the opening words in Ecclesiastes. It is an aristocratic book:

'This also commends the whole work to us, that its author is called *the son of David* the wise and good. Sons of great men seem to inherit their fathers' wisdom, just as sons of the simple and lowly are wont to be foolish and, not to say stupid, at least simple and less gifted. Hence we read in the Gospel that our Saviour astonished, by his wisdom in question and answer, those who considered only his humble birth. They asked in wonder: Is not this the carpenter's son? Is not his mother called Mary, and his brothers James and Joseph and Simon and Jude? Are not his brothers and sisters here with us? *And they were scandalised in regard of him* [Mk. vi. 3]; as though it were against reason and somehow unnatural, that such wisdom and prudence should be found in one of such simple, uneducated parents, whose "brothers and sisters", that is whose relatives, were simple and foolish as the people are. So to commend his work, as we have said, the author is careful to add that he is David's son, having wisdom and prudence as his inheritance. It often happens that a wise man has wise and prudent sons; their studies aid nature; nature their studies.'

He goes on to explain the importance of the title *King of Jerusalem* in commending the glory and authority of the author from the position of his city as a capital and religious centre. And just as Ecclesiastes is an aristocratic, so it is a sophisticated book, directed not to simple countrymen, but to the citizens of so great a city, advanced in wisdom, though not yet perfect.[1]

We can hardly expect that the special characteristics of each author, as described in the prologue, should be de-

---

[1] Calandra, 5-6: 'Et licet totius terre XII tribuum rex esset Salomon, specialiter tamen rex Ierusalem esse dicitur, cum propter ipsius civitatis dignitatem, que regia sedes et caput regni erat, tum propter templi prerogativam, et sacerdotum mansionem, et creberrimam divine legis in auribus populi recitationem in ea, et divini cultus in sacrificiis et ceremoniis et solemnitatibus et ceteris multiplicibus religionis ritibus multam frequentationem, et lectionis legis et prophetarum exercitationem.

Vel ideo hec verba regis Ierusalem esse dicit, ut quod ea que in his verbis traditur doctrina non rura et pagos incolentibus et qui in urbem pergere nesciunt, sed tante civitatis civibus, proficientibus scilicet et perfectioribus, etsi non perfectissimis, conveniat vel sic insinuet.'

I have amended 'spiritualiter' to 'specialiter', as it is clearly demanded by the sense.

The reference to the 'proficientes' and 'perfectissimi' springs from the traditional view that Proverbs was written for beginners, Ecclesiastes for the advanced, the Canticle for the perfect. It is interesting to see how Andrew has adapted this to his literal interpretation. According to him, Ecclesiastes' congregation was to be not only advanced in wisdom, but 'civilized'.

veloped in the exposition itself. This would be asking too
much of Andrew. He has voluntarily restricted himself to
writing notes rather than a full commentary. He fails to
carry out the theme of his opening to Genesis: the education
of a primitive people. On the Prophets, in spite of his wish
to follow St. Jerome, he has neither the learning nor the
genius of his great predecessor; he cannot explain how they
differ from one another; he comes no closer to the personalities behind his text.

What distinguishes him from contemporaries is his awareness that some personality is there. He does not lose sight of
the prophet in the prophecy. The promise: *there shall come
forth a rod out of the root of Jesse* [Isa. xi. 1] which sent other
commentators instantly to the Gospel, makes Andrew think
first of the prophet's reassurance to Juda and Israel. Isaias
is consoling the Two Tribes and the Ten alike:

> 'He has cheered with good hope the fallen spirits of the Two
> Tribes, and roused them from the heavy slumber of despair,
> promising escape from the danger, and defeat of the enemy
> that threaten them. Now, in this passage, he brings no little
> comfort to the Ten, of whose restoration as yet he has said
> nothing. He promises the Ten as well as the Two, that as rod
> and flower come forth from the root, so from the stem of Jesse
> a son shall come forth, who, filled with the sevenfold spirit,
> shall judge and reprove his servants in justice and equity. . . .
> 'Let us consider the letter: *And there shall come forth a rod.* The
> Lord shall do as is said above to free the Two Tribes from
> danger and care. To restore to their land, to reconcile and
> reduce to one people both Ten and Two, *there shall come forth a
> rod out of the root of Jesse and the spirit of the Lord shall rest upon him.*'

What is more remarkable, in explaining the vision, he
remembers the seer. When Richard expounds the vision of
Ezechiel, his one anxiety is to know what it looked like. He
wants to make an accurate description of the four creatures,
something that he can draw, as he drew the temple. Stephen
Langton and Hugh of St. Cher talk at length about pictures
of cherubim that they have seen, and compare them with
the vision. Andrew wants principally to know what the
appearance signified to Ezechiel: what was it intended to
teach the people for whom he wrote it down? Andrew
supposes that *the likeness of a man* in the 'living creatures' was
meant to draw people's attention and show the relevance of
the vision to their affairs:

'The prophet had called the creatures of the vision "beasts"; so they might be conceived merely as wild animals and hence as having little concern for man; then the men for whom this vision was written would heed it little, since it would have nothing in it that related to them. Therefore the prophet had added that: *this was their appearance. There was the likeness of a man in them* [Ezech. i. 5].'[1]

His commentary on Ecclesiastes is unusual for its reticence. Andrew is the only medieval commentator known to me who fears to add anything to his author. The others, convinced that their text hides a plenitude of meaning, hardly distinguish between exposition and amplification. Compare Andrew's candid comment on Eccles. i. 7: *All the rivers run into the sea, and the sea doth not overflow*:

'That which he says, *the sea doth not overflow*, has nothing to do with the present matter, but in speaking of the sea he did not like to pass over this characteristic in silence.'[2]

On Eccles. iii. 1-8, the passage beginning *Everything has its season*, he instances the occasions which make the various occupations seasonable. There is a time for war 'when reason and a just cause demand it', and so on. Then he warns us that all this is his own embroidery:

'Although we have assigned a season, that is to say, a seasonable opportunity to each one of the things aforesaid, yet the author, it seems, wants to indicate nothing else but that each several thing for which he said there was a season, has its own season, that is to say, its time and span, its changes and its passage.'[3]

Whereas other commentators think they ought to palliate Ecclesiastes' scepticism and pessimism,[4] Andrew allows the full force of his words.

[1] MS. Bodl. e Mus. 62, fo. 113ᵃ: 'Quia bestias nominaverat, ne bruta et inmitia tantum putarentur animantia et ita ad homines minus pertinere, minusque homines quibus hec visio scribebatur attenderent, cum nichil in ea contineretur quod ad eos spectaret, annectit quod talis erat aspectus eorum.'
[2] Calandra, 10: 'Quod vero ait "mare non redundat" ad presens negotium nil pertinet, sed de mari loquens, hanc eius proprietatem tacitus preterire noluit.'
[3] Ibid. 25: 'Quamquam uniuscuiusque eorum que premissa sunt tempus i.e. temporis opportunitatem assignaverimus, auctor tamen nihil aliud significare velle videtur, nisi quod singulum eorum quorum tempus esse dixit, suum tempus i.e. suam moram et spatium et mutabilitatem et transitum habeat.'
[4] B. Smalley, 'The Sapiential Books I', *passim*.

L

It would take too long to illustrate Andrew's interest in the chronology and geography of the Old Testament. He is a scholar with a scholar's joy in detail and a scholar's impatience with popular misconceptions. He persists in calling Ezechiel 'Iezechiel',[1] and it distresses him that the canticle of Sidrach, Misach and Abdenago should be known as the 'Hymn of the Three Children'. He calculates that the 'children' were close on forty years old when they were cast into the furnace; perhaps this erroneous idea has arisen from the text: *not a hair of their head had been singed* [Dan. iii. 94] which does not mention their having beards; Andrew recalls the text Dan. i. 3 which (as against the *Gloss*) he construes to mean that they were eunuchs, and therefore beardless.[2]

Perhaps the most characteristic trait of his exposition is his handling of the *quaestio*. Although he refuses to be led into irrelevant discussions, he cannot pass over a glaring contradiction on the literal meaning. We have watched him solving the *simul* problem by the simple process of deciding for the earlier authority. Some difficulties presented no such loophole. In two passages Andrew takes up the challenge and embarks on a real question. In each case the method is comparative; he 'distinguishes' by examining the context and the precise meaning it gives to a doubtful expression. And in each case the solution shows that naturalistic streak in Andrew that we have noticed before.

The first difficulty arises from St. Jerome on Jerem. i. 5: *Before I formed thee in the bowels of thy mother, I knew thee: and before thou camest forth out of the womb, I sanctified thee and made thee a prophet unto the nations.* St. Jerome is refuting a gnostic heresy, that Jeremias was a spirit who existed before his bodily conception. He says that the first half of the text refers to the foreknowledge of God: the second must be

---

[1] MS. Bodl. e Mus. 62, fo. 111ᶜ: 'Quod iccirco dicimus quia quidam tam in scriptura quam in pronuntiatione huius nominis errant.' Andrew has probably taken the correct spelling from Jerome.

[2] MS. Pembroke 45, fo. 118ᵃ: 'Quidam nostrorum istos qui in fornacem missi fuerunt pueros et ymnum quidem eorum ymnum trium puerorum appellant. Canonica autem hec scriptura, postquam de sompnio regis agere cepit, ubique viros et nusquam pueros illos vocat. Sive cum Ioachim filio Iosie sive cum Ieconia filio eius capti ductique sunt in Babilonia, quomodo post secundum vel in ipso secundo Egyptie captivitatis anno pueri erant? . . .' Fo. 118ᵈ: 'Hinc forsitan originem illa traxit opinio quia de barbe pilis nichil dictum est cum de capillis premissum sit, quod si viri fuissent scriptura nequaquam tacuisset. Hoc opinantes parum videntur attendere quod illi in domum principis eunochorum introducti spadones fuerunt et quod illi qui in pueritia castratur barba crescere non potest.'

'understood according to the Apostle: *When it pleased him who separated me from my mother's womb and called me by his grace to reveal his Son in me, that I might preach him among the Gentiles* [Gal. i. 15-16]. John the Baptist, also, was sanctified in the womb, received the Holy Sprit and prophesied through his mother's mouth.'

To a twelfth-century theologian the text suggested quite another problem: Were Jeremias and St. John the Baptist cleansed from original sin?

Andrew limits himself to the case of Jeremias. He begins by disposing of St. Jerome, whose comment he feels to be rather a red herring. If, as St. Jerome says, *before I formed thee in the bowels of thy mother I knew thee* means simply that God foreknew the prophet's existence, what is the point? God foreknows the existence of all men, good and bad alike. Why is it said specially to Jeremias? And what bearing has the case of St. Paul on the 'sanctification from the womb'? The Apostle speaks of his separation, not his sanctification; and on this latter word 'the whole question turns'; unless we were to read 'separated' as 'sanctified' — a violent distortion as all must agree.

'I ·never remember to have read that the Apostle was "sanctified" from the womb. He testifies of himself: *we also* . . . *were by nature children of wrath, even as the rest* [Eph. ii. 3].'

The case of the Baptist is altogether different:

'We believe that he was sanctified from the womb, as the archangel promised, for that full of the Holy Sprit, he leapt for joy in his mother's womb, at the coming of the parent of his Lord, and prophesied through his mother's mouth. But we read nothing of the sort concerning holy Jeremias, either before or at his birth.'

Having stated the problem, Andrew gives a current solution, which he then proceeds to criticize:

'Some admit that both St. John the Baptist and Jeremias were cleansed of original sin, from the womb, or within it. They say that what the sacraments of baptism or circumcision gave to others, these two received by divine grace while still in the womb. According to this opinion the text is clear: *Before thou camest forth out of the womb, I knew thee, I sanctified thee,* that is: "I cleansed thee from the stain of original sin". But then the knot of our first question still remains to be untied. How did God "know" the prophet before forming him *in the bowels* of his *mother*, unless it be said that before forming him *in the bowels* of the Synagogue in the manner of others, i.e. by circumcision, God *knew* him as her son by the aforesaid sanctification?'

This solution supposes an allegorical interpretation; *in the bowels of thy mother* must be read as: *in the Synagogue.* Andrew prefers to read it literally:

'Some according to their custom apply themselves rather to the literal sense and they think that the text should be explained in this way: while the prophet was still a child, God instituted him prophet, to prophesy to savage nations and be given unto the people. Hence God affords him faith and surety. The blessings already mercifully granted are a pledge for all future time; as though he said: "Fear not, Jeremias, that I should ever fail you now. Even before your birth I favoured you, blessing you with sanctity, deigning to recognize what was yet to come." Jeremias relies on God's promise. When, as we read in the sequel, he is given as prophet unto the nations, he excuses himself for his lack of eloquence solely on the ground of being a child.'

This solution is justified by a distinction: to *know* has several meanings:

'God is said to know things in two ways; either he has it in his knowledge, or he approves, loves, holds it dear. According to the first meaning it is said: *he knoweth both the deceiver and the deceived* [Job xii. 16]. According to the second meaning God says to Moses: *I know thee by name* [Exod. xxxiii. 12] and to the foolish virgins: *I know you not* [Matt. xxv. 12] that is, I do not approve, nor love, nor hold you dear. We too, when angry with people that we despise, or do not approve of, are wont to say: "Whence, or who are you?"'

'The text reads thus: *Before I formed thee in the bowels of thy mother I knew thee*: I, the Lord, who formed you, before I gave you human shape in the womb, *knew*, that is approved, and loved you as one known and dear, and already existing, for me, to whom the future is as the past; and this before your birth or your conception. Similarly the Apostle: *for when they were not yet born, nor had done any good or evil . . . Jacob I have loved: but Esau I have hated* [Rom. ix. 11, 13].

'*And before thou camest forth out of the womb, I sanctified thee*: in token of my love and approval, even when you were still in your mother's womb, I granted you such sanctity, that nothing but the holy and pure could please you after your passing to birth. Through the sanctity vouchsafed him, Jeremias is believed to have kept a perpetual virginity. *And made thee a prophet unto the nations.* Freely, without your deserving it, I inspired you with the grace of prophecy, and sent you to prophesy to the nations of my choice.'

Andrew has declared for the literal sense; he has interpreted 'sanctification' as 'preparation and pledge'. He refuses to allow that a miraculous element comes into it.

The second difficulty arises from a contradiction in the *Gloss* on Ezech. i. 1: *The heavens were opened and I saw the visions of God.* The marginal gloss reads: 'Not by the division of the firmament, but by the faith of the believer, to whom celestial secrets are revealed', the interlinear gloss: 'According to Origen [he saw] with his fleshly sight.'

Hence Andrew has to consider the nature of Ezechiel's vision: in what sense were 'the heavens opened'? We can guess that he will prefer the marginal gloss as more rational. He begins, however, by stating the problem in a provocative way:

'It follows that a man to whom the heavens are opened should see *the visions of God* which are above the heavens. Although all things are visible to divine majesty, and nothing is hidden from all-seeing God, he is said to see especially what is above the heavens, just as he is said to *be* especially in heaven, although in fact he is everywhere. So the prophet says that *the heavens were opened* and he *saw the visions of God*, because he saw what are beyond the heavens, the angelic beings, in whose own form and nature it is God's not man's to see.'

In what manner did the prophet see them? Andrew quotes from St. Augustine to prove that visions are not physical but spiritual, that is, intellectual, seen in the mind's eye. He adapts the quotations to the vision in question. Ezechiel says that *the heavens were opened* meaning that heaven had condescended to him. By heavenly favour celestial forms had been impressed on his mind. The concreteness of his phrase is a concession to our feeble understanding.

'The sacred writers often describe what is above, in terms of what is within, man's ken. We cannot see past a solid body unless it is first dissolved or removed; so the prophet is careful to tell us that *the heavens were opened.* Isaias also well knew that God could come to earth and leave the heavens unbroken, yet he condescends to human reason and custom, when longing for God's advent he says: *O that thou wouldst rend the heavens and wouldst come down* [Isa. lxiv. 1]. Moses writes that God said:

"The cry of Sodom is come to me; *I will go down and see it*".
[Gen. xviii. 21] ... Many expressions of this kind are conceded
to us by Scripture.'

Another rational explanation is that *visions* refer not only
to the vision described in the first chapter but to the prophecy
contained in the whole book. This would agree, he says,
with the Hebrew text which reads: *I have seen a vision from
God*:

> 'The sense is: the fact of my having *seen a vision*, and under-
> stood what will come upon you, upon the rest [of the people],
> and upon the City, is not from me but *from God*. In these
> words the prophet both shows his humility, and plainly teaches
> his readers that they must assent to what he will say as divinely
> inspired. According to this opinion what else does the "opening
> of the heavens" mean, but that a heavenly gift is vouchsafed
> him?
>
> 'If anyone would like to argue that *the heavens were opened* for
> the prophet's gaze to pass through them, that he might see God
> and the things above, we in no way hinder him; let him abound
> in his own sense. But let him ask whether reason or the nature
> of things allow what he wishes to argue. If he resort to the
> argument that divine omnipotence can do what nature cannot,
> enable a man to direct his gaze through the heavens and beyond
> them, we know that with God nothing is impossible and in no
> wise gainsay it. But he should realise this: in expounding
> Scripture, when the event described admits of no natural
> explanation, then and then only should we have recourse to
> miracles.'[1]

If only we had some record of Abailard's lecture on
Ezechiel, given at Laon in defiance of his master! All we
know about it is what Abailard himself tells us: like all his
doings it created a great stir. It would be interesting to
compare him with Andrew on the most obscure of the
Prophets. One suspects that Andrew would prove to be the
more original here, as he certainly is on the Hexaemeron.

If we call Abailard a 'rationalist' we must give the word
its twelfth-century connotation: we mean simply that he
desired to use his reason for the defence and understanding
of his faith; and by 'reason' his mastery of logic is meant.

---

[1] Andrew could have found this general principle in St. Augustine, see
P. de Vooght, 'La notion philosophique du miracle chez St Augustin. Dans
le "De Trinitate" et le "De Genesi ad litteram" ', *Rech. Théol. anc. méd.* x (1938),
317-43. But his bald and provocative statement is surprising, given his place
and date.

We cannot call Andrew a rationalist in this sense. He is not sufficiently interested in either logic or theology to apply one to the other. For instance, the problem of the beatific vision — whether man can attain to direct vision of the divine essence, had been table talk in the ninth century;[1] interest was reviving in the twelfth,[2] and the starting-point, St. Augustine's *De Videndo Deo*, lay ready to hand. It would have been very relevant indeed to Andrew's discussion of Ezechiel's vision; but he ignores it. 'Rationalist' as a description of Andrew takes on a different and almost eighteenth-century flavour. It applies less to his method than to his conclusions. It expresses a cult of 'common sense' and a definite preference for natural to supernatural explanations. This 'naturalism' was much rarer in the twelfth century than was the rationalism of Abailard.

We know that Abailard owed part of his reputation to his genius as a teacher. He evidently excited his pupils as much by the way he said things as by what he said. Andrew portrays himself as a lonely and rather morose scholar. He works for his own satisfaction; he has no wish to set up as a master of others. All the same, we know that Andrew too had devoted disciples, and one wonders whether in practice he shared Abailard's gift for teaching. His writings suggest that he did. We have seen how he stimulates and provokes by his readiness to argue. He also has the good teacher's desire to clarify. He can explain as well as discover. He has an aptitude for finding parallels which bring the familiar to the rescue of the unfamiliar. He watches for social and legal customs in modern times or antiquity which bear on those of the Old Testament. He observes for instance that *thou . . . advancest and camest to woman's ornament* [Ezech. xvi. 7] refers to young ladies' 'coming out':

> 'It was a custom of antiquity, indeed still is, among certain races, that before they were marriageable the girls even of noble families should go plainly dressed, but that when they "advanced" they should receive "woman's ornament", so as to please their future husbands.'[3]

[1] M. Cappuyns, 'Note sur le problème de la vision béatifique au ixe siècle', *Rech. Théol. anc. méd.* i (1928), 100.

[2] See *De Sacramentis*, ii. xiii, c. 18; *P.L.* clxxvi. 616.

[3] MS. Bibl. Nat. Lat. 14432, fo. 51: 'Mos erat antiquitus, sed adhuc quibusdam gentibus est, ut ante nubiles annos puelle etiam nobiles incultius incederent, illis vero adventantibus mundum muliebrem quo melius futuris placerent maritis acciperent.'

He explains the phrase *priests . . . whose hands were filled and consecrated* [Num. iii. 3] as a reference to investiture and seisin:

'It was a custom of antiquity that when a man entered upon an office, the enjoined office was conferred on him as a gift, by a piece of wood or a stone or something of that kind. It was what is popularly called the seisin or investiture of the office enjoined on him.'[1]

The problem of lay investiture, involving the right of a secular ruler to invest bishops with the ring and staff, would make the allusion very topical for Andrew's readers. A text of Isaias, *Lord, I suffer violence, answer thou for me* [xxxviii. 14] suggests to him the 'guaranty clause', which in the mid-twelfth century was becoming part of the formula in a deed of gift.[2] Andrew is commenting on his Hebrew version: *Lord, vindicate me.* He first explains the claim to prior possession, which brings the guaranty clause into operation; secondly, the guaranty clause itself; lastly he shows how they illustrate his text:

'*Lord vindicate me*, protect me. These Hebrew terms will be understood more clearly when their meaning is given in the tongue of the Franks: "Lord, reclaim me, warant me." When our belongings have been stolen or lost in any way, and we find others in possession, we "vindicate" them for ourselves, and so to speak "reclaim" them. But if those from whom we reclaim our belongings have bought them, or acquired them in any way from others, the latter must stand for the former, and "warant" [make good the loss of] what they have sold or granted.
'Lord, "vindicate" now for thyself and "reclaim" me thy servant, from sickness and death which have almost taken me to themselves. Guard and protect me as thine own possession.'[3]

---

[1] MS. C.C.C. 30, fo. 39d: 'Mos erat antiquitus, cum in aliquod ministerium aliquis assumebatur, iniunctum ministerium per lignum vel lapidem vel aliquid huiusmodi in manus illi tradebatur, et erat ut vulgariter loquitur saisina quedam et investitura iniuncti officii.'

[2] F. M. Stenton, *Transcripts of Charters Relating to Gilbertine Houses* (Publications of Lincoln Record Soc. 18, 1922), xxviii-xxix.

[3] MS. Pembroke 45, fo. 62b: ' "Domine vindica me;" protege me. Hebraicarum dictionum que hoc in loco ponuntur apertioris intelligentie causa secundum vulgatam acceptionem in lingua Francorum significatio est ponenda: "Domine calumpniare me, garantiza me." Res nostras furto ablatas, vel quomodocumque perditas, cum ab aliis eas possideri invenimus, nobis eas vindicamus et ut ita loquitur calumpniamur. Si vero illi quibus nos res nostras calumpniamur ab aliis illas emerint, vel quolibet modo acceperint, debent illi pro illis stare et que vendiderunt, vel aliquo modo contulerunt, garantizare. Domine iam me servum tuum quem morbus et mors iam sibi pene rapuit tibi vindica et calumpniare et quasi tuum protege et tuere.'

Andrew is doing much what Aelfric had done in the vernacular homilies, and Christian of Stavelot in his commentary on St. Matthew; he is explaining Scripture in terms of everyday life. But Aelfric had written for the parish priest and the laity, Christian for the 'simple-minded' brothers of his monastery. Andrew is writing for intellectuals; this is the novelty. Reversing the usual process, he adapts the methods of elementary education to the scholar. He substitutes straightforward comparisons for the subtle and ingenious ones which were considered proper for a clerkly audience. Not that topical and classical allusions in learned works had been infrequent; but they had been used mainly for polemics, or for ornament, or for light relief; sometimes they had been thrown out casually in passing. Andrew uses them with a difference. He intends that, instead of diverting or distracting the reader, they shall fix his attention more closely on the text. They shall really help him to grasp its meaning.

The exposition of Isa. i. 16-18 is the happiest example of his method that one could choose and will make a good conclusion. He explains the text with the aid of both pagan custom and Jewish law and tradition:

> *Wash yourselves: be clean. Take away the evil of your devices from my eyes. Cease to do perversely.*

Andrew contrasts this moral cleansing with the ritual purification prescribed by the Law, and with the pagan rites, of which he read in Ovid:

> 'Our sires believed that every sin and every cause of ill could be wiped out by rites of purgation . . . Fond fools alack! to fancy murder's gruesome stain by river water could be washed away.' [*F.* ii. 35-6, 45-6.]
> '*Take away the evil of your devices.* The prophet has commanded them to "wash themselves". Someone might mistake this cleansing for washing in water, and the various purifications by water [*baptismátibus*] which were used among both Jews and Gentiles, as Peleus says to Acastus:
> "O rid me of my sin," and the other did rid him of his sin. [*F.* 43-4.][1]
> 'So to specify the manner of washing, he adds: *Take away the evil.* They must *take away the evil* from their thoughts, because

[1] J. G. Frazer, *The Fasti of Ovid,* i (London, 1929), 55. Andrew has telescoped the passage; he runs together the references to Peleus and Alcmaeon.

even thoughts cannot be hidden from the eyes of God's majesty. *Cease to do perversely.* It is fittingly ordered that when evil thoughts are "taken away", they should "cease from perversity" in deed. Thoughts come first; deeds follow. . . .

'*If your sins be as scarlet*: the sense is: however loathsome in your foulness and sin you may have been, clean yourselves wholly. Above he said *wash yourselves*, which refers to stains and dirt; so now he expresses the filth of sin by scarlet and crimson, purity by snow and wool. Nothing looks filthier on vessel or vesture than the red stain of blood; it shows up more than any other; and we know when a thing is cleaned by its turning white.

'The soul as God creates her is innocent and clean. She is like a spotless white garment. But dwelling in a corruptible body, tempted by her invisible foe, the Devil, and her visible [man], her own will perverted, she is smirched by the filth of sin as though dyed in stains. When grievous sins deform the soul, red blood-stains discolour the whiteness of her garment to scarlet and crimson. The Law plainly teaches how hard it is to wash away such blood-stains from the soul's garment; it commands that the stained part of a garment be torn off and burnt [Lev. xiii. 56]; again: *every . . . garment mingled with blood shall be burnt* [Isa. ix. 5]. Yet they who do what the prophet has said will be wholly cleansed from these stains. He has chosen to compare the redness of blood to *scarlet* and *crimson* because they express redness with such intensity.

'Another explanation: according to a Jewish tradition, the sins of all men are preserved in writing on a shining white substance, that they may appear more readily to the Judge's eye. Hence, *the books were opened* and read before the Ancient of days, seated on his throne [Dan. vii. 9-10]; and the sin of Juda, so we read, is written on iron with an adamantine nail. Grievous sins are written in red and the other colours which adhere more faithfully to the parchment and strike the reader's eye more readily. So in these words the Lord promises to erase their sins, even though they were great enough to be written in vermilion or crimson. Nothing shall be left, where their sins were written, but the shining white substance that had their imprint. And so their sins, which before were red as crimson, shall be white as snow.

'Wool, thread, cloth, and soft stuffs of this kind, are dyed *scarlet*. Parchment, wood, stone, and hard ware generally, is painted *crimson*.'

Later he adds:

'When sins are said to be written in books, what else does it mean but that God remembers as though they were written?'

The Jewish tradition, which Andrew cites in explanation of his text, has brought us to his chief importance as a commentator. Had Andrew relied simply on his own mother wit and his knowledge of antiquity, he would be an arresting, but not a very significant, figure. For his purpose, these were not enough. The 'literal exposition' as he conceived it was a real science. A scientific work is bound to date quickly. It ceases to be valuable in itself; it is remembered for having opened up fresh lines of inquiry and fresh sources which later scholars have followed up. Probably the more successful it is, the sooner it will be old-fashioned. So the literal exposition to which Andrew devotes himself demands research work and would be pointless without it. He would be like a person rattling energetically at a locked door.

In fact, he had a key provided for him by his masters, St. Jerome and Hugh of St. Victor; and he had the courage to turn it. He went into the vast uncatalogued store-room of Hebrew learning, whose contents had been barely fingered, gingerly and at rare intervals, for the past seven hundred years.

The metaphor gives a poor idea of his adventure. His archives were living scholars. The learning that he asked from them was no dead tradition but something growing. A movement was in process in the Jewish schools as in the Christian. The Jews were developing new ideas and a new technique for the study of their sacred books; they combined conservatism and originality in much the same way as the Christians. Andrew had to take his Hebrew lore as it was presented to him by contemporary French rabbis. He could hardly collect his material without making some kind of intellectual contact.

III. THE JEWISH SOURCES[1]

The Jews of northern France in the twelfth century lived on generally friendly terms with their Christian neighbours. They were neither shut into ghettoes nor restricted to shop-keeping and money-lending, but scattered among the towns and villages in small communities, engaging sometimes in such 'country' pursuits as vine-growing and horse-coping.

[1] The material for this section was given to me by Dr. L. Rabinowitz. Lack of space prevents me from doing more than summarize his description of Jewish biblical exegesis, and from giving his bibliography.

The works of the north French rabbis show us a typically French, prosperous, middle-class people, who keep a rich table, set prudent limits to their families, in spite of the fertility rites of their weddings, lead respectable lives and practise their religion, are not intolerant and seldom saintly.[1] The school of exegetes deriving from Rashi seems to reflect both the typically French qualities of common sense and clarity and the prosperity and freedom from persecution of the north French Jews, which made it possible for them to criticize their own institutions and traditions in a scientific way.

Before the time of Rashi (1040-1105), two systems of biblical exegesis had been used in the Jewish schools: the *halachic* and the *aggadic*. *Halachic* exegesis consisted in the authoritative exposition of the Old Testament in order to deduce the rule (*halacha*) of life. With the close of the Talmud, about A.D. 500, all creative activity in this branch of exegesis came to an end. No one had authority to deduce a new *halacha* or to question the correctness of the rules obtained by the principles of halachic interpretation. The *aggadic*, midrashic, or homiletic method allowed more play to the imagination, since it regarded the biblical text rather as a peg upon which to hang moral doctrine and edifying tales. Daring imagery, allegory, moral stories, crude history, ingenious speculation, here and there a stray piece of literal interpretation, are all to be found in the Midrash; and since Midrash was not authoritative theology or doctrine, there was a continuous midrashic exposition up to the period of Rashi.

Rashi added a third method of exposition: the literal or rational. Stimulated by two important works, a grammar and a dictionary, by Spanish Jews, which were written in Hebrew and therefore accessible to him, he applied himself to the literal exposition of the whole Old Testament. Much of his commentary is strictly scientific and rational and in accordance with the spirit of the Hebrew language to which he was finely sensitive. He pays due attention to grammar and syntax, and shows an attractive, if rudimentary, appreciation of the principles of comparative philology. Biblical chronology and geography have an absorbing interest for

---

[1] The most recent study is by L. Rabinowitz, *The Social Life of the Jews of Northern France in the XII-XIV Centuries as Reflected in the Rabbinical Literature of the Period* (London, 1938).

him. Not·that Rashi breaks with tradition. His literal exposition may be in conflict with the *halachic*, but never excludes it. He also makes use of the *aggadic* method; his originality lies only in his preference for the literal as an alternative; he compares literal exposition and *aggada* to the two sparks of interpretation, which fly in different directions, and each is as important as the other.

The school of Rashi was more revolutionary. Joseph Kara (*d.* 1130-40) shows a definite antagonism to midrashic exegesis.

> '. . . whosoever is ignorant of the literal meaning of Scripture and inclines after the Midrash of the verse is like a drowning man who clutches at a straw to save himself. Were he to set his mind to the word of the Lord, he would search out the true meaning of the verse and its literal purpose. . . .
>
> 'I know that all the masters of *Aggada* and Talmud who do not budge from the interpretations of our rabbis will mock at me; but the enlightened will consider the path of Scripture in order to establish the truth of the matter.'

In spite of this confession of faith, Joseph Kara's commentary abounds in midrashic interpretations. The credit for having introduced a purely literal interpretation belongs to three contemporaries: Samuel ben Meir or Rashbam, the eldest, a grandson of Rashi, and two of Rashbam's colleague-disciples, Eliezer of Beaugency and Joseph Bekhor Shor of Orleans. Their dates are uncertain; Joseph, the youngest, was living about 1160. Rashbam reverses the method of Joseph Kara; he is reverent to authority in theory, independent in practice. In a well-known passage he reports a conversation with Rashi:

> 'And also Rabbi Solomon, my maternal grandfather, the enlightener of the eyes of the Exile, who commented on the Pentateuch, Prophets, and Hagiographa, set himself to expound the literal meaning of Scripture. And even I, Samuel son of Meir his son-in-law argued with him and before him, and he confessed to me that had he had the opportunity, he would have found it necessary to write other commentaries, more in accordance with the literal expositions, of which new examples come up every day.'

The last words reflect a feverish activity in literal exegesis, of which the works of these three scholars are the most important extant examples. With few exceptions they discard the two older methods of exegesis and aim at a purely rational exposition, even when it is in direct opposition to the *Halacha*. For this reason, the movement came to an end in the later twelfth century, in favour of strict orthodoxy. Their most interesting characteristics are, first of all, a fondness for explaining Scripture by reference to the customs of the country in which they lived. Rashbam even explains the meal which Jacob gave to Esau on the sale of his birthright, not as the price of the birthright, but as the *beveria* with which it was the custom in northern France to seal and celebrate a bargain. Joseph Bekhor Shor mentions this explanation of his master and calls it 'nonsense'. This illustrates the second characteristic of the school: their freedom and frankness in criticizing and disagreeing with their predecessors and contemporaries. Rashbam calls an explanation of Rashi 'vanity', though like the Christians they coat the pill by referring to their opponents anonymously. Another distinguishing trait is their use of the vernacular in explanation of words and sentences. Rashi confined himself to single words, but Joseph Bekhor Shor will sometimes render whole sentences into French.

Most important, perhaps, from our present point of view, is their rationalism, or naturalism. Whenever possible they will reduce biblical miracles to normal natural phenomena and they show critical insight which anticipates the scholarship of a later time. Joseph Bekhor Shor suggests the possibility of a double narrative in Genesis. His use of the words 'the writer of the book' in Genesis makes one wonder whether he is also suggesting a non-Mosaic authorship for the pre-Mosaic narrative. The author of a commentary on Ecclesiastes belonging to this school states categorically that the first two verses of Ecclesiastes are the addition of a later editor.

Joseph Bekhor Shor in particular consciously strains after originality in exposition; he loves 'debunking'. The following examples will show how he sets out to explain or, when this is impossible, to minimize biblical miracles:[1]

> Gen. xix. 26, the changing of Lot's wife into a pillar of salt; 'She tarried and was overtaken by the flow of lava; but the general opinion is that she was changed into salt.'
> Exod. vii. 20: '*The Lord met him and sought to kill him*; he was taken seriously ill; *so he let him go*; he recovered from his illness.'

[1] Joseph's commentaries on Genesis and Exodus have been edited by A. Jellinck (Leipzig, 1856).

Exod. vii. 20: '*And all the waters that were in the river were turned into blood*; only for a moment, during which the fish died; then it immediately reverted to water.'

Exod. ix. 8, the plague of boils: Joseph explains that in its essence the miracle was a natural thing, since hot ashes falling upon the skin produce blisters; the only supernatural element in it was that it affected everybody. 'God does not alter the laws of nature and therefore effected the miracle partly according to natural laws. For this reason he commanded Moses to cast the ashes. And so you will find with the majority of miracles that God does not alter natural laws.'

Exod. xv. 25: the sweetening of the waters was accomplished in a natural manner, as one sweetens a bitter food by putting spices into it.

Exod. xx. 12: '*in order that your days may be long*; if you honour your parents your children will honour you, support you in your old age so that you will not die prematurely.'

Exod. xxiii. 19: *Thou shalt not seethe a kid in its mother's milk.* The *halachic* interpretation of this verse was: thou shalt not boil any meat with any milk; the threefold repetition of the verse in Pentateuch instituted a threefold prohibition, one against boiling (without subsequent eating), one against eating, one against deriving any benefit of any kind from the forbidden article. Thus a binding law made a rigid separation between dishes which had meat as one of the ingredients, and dishes which had milk. Joseph, however, renders the Hebrew word for *seethe* as *cause to grow* or *ripen*, as in Gen. xl. 10, and so renders the whole verse as follows: 'The first of the firstfruits of thy land thou shalt bring into the house of the Lord: thou shalt not let the kid grow in its mother's milk, but after seven days offer it to God' in accordance with Lev. xxii. 27. This rendering cuts the ground from under the authority for the dietary laws prescribing the separation of meat and milk.

Joseph even denies the least supernatural element to the dreams of Pharaoh and his butler and baker, and of Joseph the patriarch. He says that Joseph dreamt of future greatness because such thoughts were in his mind during the day; he needed no divine insight for their interpretation. Any clever man could have interpreted them aright; Pharaoh himself ought to have understood them. On the giving of the Law he says that we are told how the writing penetrated through the tablets of stone only to explain the ease with which they were afterwards broken when Moses let them fall; in other words, the verse Exod. xxxii. 15 means just that the tablets were fragile.

All this goes with a firm belief in demons, witchcraft, and the evil eye. But it shows us a fresh and little-known side of twelfth-century culture.

This, then, was the background of the anonymous *Hebraei* whom Andrew consulted. We should gather from his own words that the consultation was oral; he says: *dicunt*; *tradunt*; *asserit*. He was interested, too, in modern Jewish practices, which he both compares and contrasts with those of the Old Testament. He comments on 1 Kings ix. 13: . . . *the people will not eat till he come: because he blesseth the victim*:

'The custom of the Jews is to say certain praises to God before they take food.'[1]

The contemporary Jewish habit of circumlocution, with examples from current speech, is brought forward to explain the threat implied in 1 Kings iii. 17: *May God do so and so to thee, and add so and so . . .*

'The Jews dread and carefully avoid words of blasphemy and grave adversity. Not only do they not pronounce such words themselves, but do not even report them as spoken by others. Hence they often change a word into its opposite, as here: "He hath blessed God and the king" [3 Kings, xxi. 10]. And in the usage of common speech, dreading to name fever or leprosy, they call them by their description or their opposite, saying *putmal* for fever, *grosmal* for leprosy, and *bon* for another disease.'[2]

He notes how strictly they still observe the dietary precept against boiling in milk;[3] but says that 'they still wear' the fringes prescribed by the Law '*in their synagogues*'.[4] Here he gives interesting confirmation from the Christian side of evidence in contemporary rabbinic sources that the wearing of fringes was being neglected.[5] Andrew and the rabbis, taken

---

[1] MS. C.C.C. 30, fo. 58b: 'Consuetudo Hebreorum est antequam cibum sumant laudes quasdam Deo dicere.'

[2] MS. Trinity College Cambridge, B.I. 29, fo. 107v: 'Abhorrent et diligenter cavent Hebrei blasfemie vel gravis adversitatis verba, non solum a se proferre, sed etaim ab aliis prolata representare. Unde etiam sepe in contrarium commutant verba, sicut ibi: Benedixit Deo et regi. In vulgari quoque usu loquendi febrem vel lepram abhorrentes nominare per descriptiones vel per contrarium verbum eas proferunt, febrem *putmal*, lepram *grosmal*, et quandam aliam infirmitatem *bon* appellantes.' *Put* means 'sale, infect, mauvais, méchant'; F. Godefroy, *Dict. de l'ancienne langue française*, fasc. lvi (Paris, 1889), 471.

[3] See below, p. 304.

[4] MS. C.C.C. 30, fo. 41b: '. . . usque hodie in synagogis suis habent Iudei fimbrias hyacinthinas ob recordationem legis celitus date. . . .'

[5] L. Rabinowitz, op. cit. (p. 150, n. 1), 177.

together, suggest that Jews in northern France were tending to wear fringes only on religious occasions, which marked a surprising slackening of their observance. Andrew knew more about the Jews, therefore, than he could have learnt from their books. Linguistic reasons also suggest that the contact must have been oral. It seems that he knew the Hebrew alphabet and a little grammar and syntax; but even a Christian who could spell his way through biblical Hebrew would have been quite incapable of reading the rabbinic Hebrew in which the Jewish scholars of northern France wrote their commentaries. We cannot expect to find any exact verbal parallels between the rabbis and Hugh's and Andrew's quotations. Neither side could speak the learned language of the other. They talked in the vernacular. Hugh and Andrew were translating into Latin what their Jews translated for them from Hebrew into French. Since we possess only fragmentary records of Jewish medieval exegesis, and at present are restricted to such fragments as are available in print, the problem of tracing the Victorine sources has been a very simple one. We can only ask ourselves: What *type* of information did the rabbis consulted by Hugh and Andrew give them, when they were asked what 'the Jews said' on a given text? We have worked on the rough-and-ready method of collating the *Hebraei* quotations in Hugh's *Notulae* on the Pentateuch and selected passages from Andrew, which could not be traced to any known Christian source, with the few Jewish sources at our disposal.[1]

The answer, for what it is worth, can be summarized as follows. In the majority of passages investigated the Jews give the old, traditional talmudic interpretation. In a few passages the interpretation, although it sounds typically midrashic, cannot be found in the obvious sources, and so presumably comes from Jewish oral tradition. Andrew's *Hebraei*, like Hugh's, quoted extensively from the teaching of Rashi. It was interesting to find that, whereas Hugh has parallels with Joseph Kara and Rashbam, Andrew has some strikingly close parallels with the younger scholar, his own contemporary, Joseph Bekhor Shor.[2] It was interesting, too, from the Jewish side, to find that Joseph Kara, Rashbam and

---

[1] Even here we have been obliged to neglect a very possible source, Ibn Ezra, for lack of time.

[2] See for example his comment on the precept against boiling, below, p. 304, n. 1; the last sentence refers to the view held by Joseph, above, p. 153. He contrasts this view with the *halachic*.

Joseph Bekhor Shor showed an increasing knowledge of Christian exegesis and an increasing desire to refute it. Eliezer of Beaugency, on the contrary, has no parallels with Hugh or Andrew, and does not refer to Christian interpretation. This makes us wonder whether it may not be possible to trace some connection between the Victorines and the schools of Joseph Kara, Rashbam and Joseph Bekhor Shor.

The actual extent and quality of Jewish influence on Andrew still remains incalculable, and probably must always remain so. It could not be estimated by tracing his *Hebraei* quotations. None of his parallels with Joseph Bekhor Shor reflect the particularly rationalistic quality of Joseph's thought, or his references to contemporary custom. Andrew's most interesting and original contributions to exegesis, quoted in the last section, are not ascribed to his *Hebraei* and seem to be of his own invention. How far does his very originality, his combativeness, his fondness for literal interpretation, for parallels from contemporary life, for inserting French words into his comments (this became very common in the later part of the twelfth century, but seems to have been rare among Christian commentators when Andrew was writing), his touches of rationalism, derive from his conversations with rabbis? Though we can explain them in part by the teaching of his master and by his study of St. Jerome, he certainly becomes a much less surprising and isolated phenomenon if we set him against the contemporary Jewish background. Fortunately he has left enough material in his writings to enable one at least to study the question: What did he think of the Jews and of their various methods of exegesis?

IV. ANDREW AND THE JEWS

By going to school with the Jews, Andrew set himself a difficult problem. He is proud of the learning they give him, and wants as much of it as possible; he plies them with questions. At the same time, he cannot accept their interpretation of important passages without abjuring his own faith. His Jews do not only 'state'; they 'fable', or even 'twist with their wonted shamelessness'. The Jews, on their side, were generous in giving information and able in defending it. Some of their arguments so impressed him that Richard accuses him of judaizing:

'. . . I have found many things stated rashly, and discussed in an uncatholic sense. In many places the Jewish opinion is given as though it were not so much the Jews' as his own, and as though it were true. On that passage: *Behold a virgin shall conceive and bear a son* he gives the Jewish objections or questions without answering them; he seems to award the prize to them, since he leaves them as though they were unanswerable.'

Andrew's interviews with his rabbis must have been a lively mixture of the tutorial and the *disputatio*.

We must try to disentangle these various elements, because Andrew is admitting us to a function which the historian has very seldom been allowed to attend. The public disputation between Jews and Christians is a kind of theological battle by single combat, where we watch the exchange of blows. This is something more informal and intimate. It tells us a little of the impression that one side makes on the other. The Jewish convert to Christianity, Herman of Cologne, has described vividly his first impressions of Christian preaching, how he listened fascinated to the allegorical interpretation of the prophecies, how he fell into an agony of doubt, and felt himself for some time to be neither Jew nor Christian.[1] We know that there was a reverse side: Christians occasionally went over to Judaism and learnt Jewish exegesis;[2] but in the nature of things we hear about these sympathies mainly from the prohibitions or proceedings against them. Andrew is probably unique in that he shows us the attraction at work.

The first point to strike one on reading through his commentaries is that Andrew brings his critical faculty to bear on the Jewish sources as he does on the Christian. He approves and disapproves. He criticizes from the point of view of reason as well as of faith, and more sharply from the former.

He will discriminate between the talmudic legends that are told him:

'The Jews hand down that when they were held captive in some foreign land, and God willed their return to their own, a voice was heard, its owner unseen, which warned them of their return; and that they might know with certainty that it came from God, not man, it sounded light and womanly in woodland

---

[1] *De sua Conversione Opusculum, P.L.* clxx. 808, 825.

[2] Conversions on both sides may often have had personal or economic motives; but cases of Christians becoming learned in the Jewish Law are known. See L. Rabinowitz, op. cit., 108-9.

groves, places which women do not usually frequent, loud and masculine in city streets where male voices made themselves less heard.'[1]

Probably this picturesque story would strike nobody as far-fetched in crusading Europe, accustomed to all kinds of portents. Andrew repeats it without any comment. But he is sceptical about the Jewish interpretation of Ezechiel's cherubim [Ezech. i. 5]:

'Below the fire would appear the aspect, as it were, of a certain celestial creature which they call *hasmal*. When they are asked what is the use of this creature in heavenly things, or its shape or colour, whether reason grants that it can live there, whether it has been seen anywhere on earth, they don't know quite what to answer.'[2]

Superstitions about the angels come in for scathing criticism:

'*A swift stream of fire issued forth from before him* [Dan. vii. 10]. The Jews fable that this stream is in heaven in the presence of God, for that many thousands of angels who neglect their allotted tasks are drowned there each day, and fresh ones are created daily in place of those which perish. Heaven forbid that anything of the sort should be believed of the holy angels, living ever in perpetual blessedness with God! Perish the ravings that assign torments to holy and blessed spirits! What else does the *stream of fire* issuing from the Lord, which was shown to the prophet, signify, than the enduring pain of hell that he has prepared for the aforesaid kingdoms?'[3]

He is shocked by the views of certain Jews on Ezech. ix. 6, the command to the angel: *Utterly destroy old and young . . . but*

---

[1] MS. Pembroke 45, fo. 63ª: 'Tradunt Hebrei, cum captivi tenerentur in aliqua terra et voluntas Domini erat ut in suam redirent, vox quedam audiebatur nec cuius esset videbatur que de reditu illos admonebat; et ut certissime Domini illam et non hominis vocem esse pateret, in saltibus et lucis que loca femine frequentare non solent gracilis et quasi feminea, in vicis vero et in urbibus ubi viri minus audiri solebant grossior et virilis ea vox audiebatur.'

[2] MS. Bodl. e Mus. 62, fo. 113ª: 'Infra ignem celestis cuiusdam animalis quod "hasmal" appellant quasi species apparebat. Huius animalis usum in celestibus vel formam vel colorem, vel si ratio admittit ut ibi subsistat, vel sicubi in terris sit vel visum fuerit cum ab illis queritur, non satis quid respondeant inveniunt.'

[3] MS. Pembroke 45, fo. 124ª: 'Hic in celis in conspectu Dei fabulantur esse Iudei in eo quod multa milia angelorum in ministeriis sibi deputatis negligentium agentium singulis diebus demergi, in quo loco pereuntium novos cotidie angelos creari. Absit ut quicquam tale de sanctis angelis in perfecta beatitudine cum Deo semper viventibus credatur. Pereant deliramenta que sanctis et beatis spiritibus etiam assignant tormenta.' See L. Ginsberg, *Legends of the Jews*, v (Philadelphia, 1925), 21.

upon whomsoever you shall see thau, kill him not. And begin ye at my sanctuary. . . .[1]

'Here certain of the Jews raise a question, which they try to solve, if solving is binding more tightly, and complicating further! They say it is the nature of certain heavenly spirits ever to rejoice in strict justice and to wish that God should always and in everything act according to the strictness of a just judgement, having no regard for mercy. Other spirits on the contrary are by nature softer and more prone to goodness and mercy. To satisfy their wish, that the whole people should not perish utterly as they deserved, the Lord commanded [the angel] to spare at least those who mourned for the sins of others [verse 4]. When the first spirits reminded him that it would be inequitable to spare these people, who had not tried to convert the others from evil, he commanded [the angel] to *begin* with those, who, according to what he had previously decided, were to have been spared.'

This is how the Jews explain: *Begin ye at my sanctuary.*

'See how rashly changing error and foolish wickedness pass judgement on changeless truth and wise, element equity!'

Andrew counters this opinion with two lines of argument. On one apparently the Jews hold their own:

'When it is objected that they make the divine will mutable, and the divine memory in need of jogging, they seem to answer something.'

But he silences them on the context. He points out that if their story were true, then no exception would have been made, none would have been signed with the *thau,* and we know that they were; otherwise *the man that was clothed with linen, that had the inkhorn at his back* would not have said: *I have done as thou hast commanded me*; for this command alone had been enjoined on him. At this, the Jews

'shameless though they are keep silence. What need is there, especially in Holy Scripture, to heed such frivolous despicable trifles and bring fables into the solution of prophetic riddles?'

Advanced Jewish commentators themselves would have agreed with Andrew in rejecting these 'fables', as he probably knew. When he has to deal with exegesis which does not strike him as legendary or fabulous, his attitude is quite different. He notes it down without stricture. On the

[1] See appendix for this passage.

question of the Fall, for instance, he mentions none of the Christian views about the state of innocence, but he does report his Jew:

'The Jew says that men would have been ruder and more like animals, but simpler and more innocent, had they not tasted of this tree; it was called the tree of knowledge of good and evil, because they who tasted it were to become sharper at knowing what was good, but astuter at devising evil . . . The Jew asserts that like children they did not notice their nakedness and therefore were not ashamed.'[1]

Again, when he comes to the prophecy of Balaam: *A star shall rise out of Jacob* [Num. xxiv. 17] he merely says:

'The Jews expound this of their Messias who is to do, as they think, the marvels which follow.'[2]

The Jewish explanation is sometimes preferred to the Christian as more rational; Andrew's common sense approves it. On the question of the animals taken into the ark, the *Gloss* says that *seven and seven, the male and the female* [Gen. vii. 2] means 'only seven of each kind' not fourteen or seven pairs. This has a mystical significance. The *clean beasts* were taken in an uneven number, the unclean beasts in an even (two of each kind), because the uneven number signifies 'the beauty of virtue', the even 'weakness'. More of the clean than the unclean were taken so that Noe might have wherewithal to sacrifice when he left the ark. The main point: 'seven only of each kind, not fourteen' was accepted by Hugh of St. Victor. Andrew prefers 'fourteen':

'But we, who try to expound the letter, not twist or destroy it, expound the text thus: *Of all clean beasts take seven and seven, the male and the female*, that is, *take seven* males *and* take *seven* females . . . The Jews too say that *of all clean beasts* fourteen were brought into the ark.'[3]

[1] MS. Laud Lat. 105, fo. 94ᶜ: 'Hebreus dicit quamvis rudiores et brutiores, simpliciores tamen et innocentiores homines esse futuros, si de hoc ligno non gustassent; ideoque lignum scientie boni et mali appellatum, quod qui illud gustassent ad cognoscendum quidem quid bonum esset futuri essent acutiores, sed ad machinandum malum astutiores.' Fo. 95ᵃ: 'Asserit eos Hebreus instar puerorum nuditatem suam non advertisse et ideo non erubuisse.'

[2] MS. C.C.C. 30, fo. 42ᵇ: 'Hebrei exponunt hoc de messia suo qui facturus est, ut arbitrantur, magnalia que sequuntur.'

[3] MS. Laud Lat. 105, fo. 96ᵈ: 'Nos vero qui litteram exponere non distorquere vel destruere studemus, hanc litteram sic exponimus: *ex omnibus animantibus mundis tolles VII et VII masculos et feminas*; i.e. tolles VII masculos et tolles VII feminas . . . Sed et Hebrei dicunt de omnibus mundis animantibus XIV in archam introducta fuisse.'

On the whole, in his exposition of the Octateuch, Andrew's attitude towards his Jewish sources is one of detached interest and curiosity. In this early work his material is still undigested. He does not, even mentally, put the Jewish and Christian sources into parallel columns for purposes of comparison. He is making a big scrap-book, into which he pastes indiscriminately any information he can come by. As to its value he reserves judgment. Here and there his critical faculty is roused. He feels sure that he understands the text and he brushes away the Jew or Christian who disagrees with him, sometimes both: 'I do not remember to have found an adequate explanation of this passage . . .' But this concerns a small point of no theological interest. It was easy for him to avoid committing himself on the law and history which make up the greater part of the Octateuch. It would scarcely be possible when he attempted the 'prophetic riddles'. No wonder that Andrew 'feared to undertake the task'. He must have seen those parallel columns imposing themselves: *Iudaei et Nostri*. By this time he was thoroughly 'bitten'. His Hebrew studies had gone a little to his head. Just as John the Scot, with his newly won knowledge, preferred the Greek to the Latin Fathers, so Andrew was fascinated by his Jewish teachers.

He does not tell us what his programme is going to be. There is no discussion of the nature of prophecy, only the Jewish definition of prophetic inspiration. He says on a text of Ezechiel: *the hand of the Lord was there upon him* [i. 3]:

'If we believe the Jews, this means that the power of divine inspiration, pouring itself into the human mind, displaces the man, and so takes possession of his breast, that even if he wishes he cannot retain in silence what he has secretly learnt by inspiration.'[1]

But we soon grasp his method. He has decided that controversial passages require a twofold exegesis. He will give:

(*a*) The Vulgate and its Christian explanation.
(*b*) The Hebrew text and its Jewish explanation.

Since the Christian is well known to his readers he will give it a brief mention and take especial pains to present the Jewish.

[1] MS. Bodl. e Mus. 62, fo. 112a: 'Si credimus Hebreis hoc significatur: quod divine vis inspirationis humane sese ingerens menti sic homine toto discedere iusso totum sibi pectus vindicat, ut etiam si velit omne quod ex inspiratione secretum hausit silentio supprimere non possit.'

His comment on Isaias ii. 22 sets the rule for what follows. It is highly significant of Andrew's attitude because here at least he had a clear lead from St. Jerome. The Vulgate reads: *Cease ye therefore from the man, whose breath is in his nostrils, for he is reputed high.* Andrew first gives the traditional Christian interpretation, which he abridges from St. Jerome:

> *'Cease ye therefore from the Man* that is, desist from persecuting the Man; *cease,* I say, *for he is reputed high* by God who sent him, and by those who believe in him. Before telling the cause why they should *cease from* him, the prophet proves that he is the true man, having *breath in his nostrils.* This is a manifest prophecy of Christ.'

Jerome explains that in Hebrew the same word stands for 'high' and for 'in what'? The Jews read it here as 'in what', so that the prophecy may not refer to Christ. 'For in what is he reputed?' that is: 'For he is reputed as nothing.' St. Jerome claims that this reduces the whole passage to nonsense; it destroys the causality: *Cease ye therefore from the man ... for he is reputed as nothing.* Only the Christian reading, *high,* will make sense.[1] Andrew, however, thought he could supply a perfectly good alternative. The prophet is referring to the political situation:

> 'But according to the Jews, who for *high* read *in what?* (for the Hebrew word means either *high* or *in what?*) it can be read thus: Ye who in the day of the vengeance of the Lord, when Nabuchodonosor king of Babylon shall fight against us, shall put your trust in king Pharaoh, and your fleshly arm, that is Egypt, who is man, not God, *cease from* him, that is: cease from your vain hopes in him, *for in what is he reputed,* either by God or men? As though to say: "he is nothing and of no import, sufficing not even to himself. Pharaoh is a broken reed to all who put their hopes in him".'[2]

---

[1] *P.L.* xxiv. 56.

[2] MS. Pembroke 45, fo. 7b: *'Cessate ab homine* i.e. desistite persequi hominem; ideo, inquam, *cessate* quia ipse reputatus est a Deo qui misit illum et a credentibus in eum *excelsus.* Ante suppositionem vero cause quare debeant ab eo cessare probat quod verus homo sit, halitum in naribus habens. Aperta est de Christo prophetia. Potest etiam secundum Hebreos qui pro excelso "in quo" legunt (verbum enim Hebraicum equivoce et excelsum et in quo significat) sic legi: Vos qui in die ultionis Domini preliante contra nos rege Babylonis Nabugodonosor fiduciam in Pharaonem regem et brachium vestram carnalem i.e. Egyptum qui est homo non Deus posituri estis, quiescite ab illo i.e. cessate frustra spem in illo ponere, quia in quo reputatus est ipse vel a Deo vel ab hominibus? Quasi diceret: nichil est et nullius momenti, etiam se ipsi adesse insufficiens. Baculus enim arundineus est Pharao omnibus in ipsum sperantibus.'

The comment on Isa. vii. 14-16, *Behold a virgin shall conceive*, etc., struck Richard of St. Victor as especially scandalous; but it is on just the same lines. Andrew had an argument with the rabbis who instructed him:

'When we expound this manifest prophecy of the conception and birth of our Saviour, and of the perfect virginity of his Mother, ever a virgin, concerning the same, as is right, the Jews, foes of the truth, rise against us and strive with their battering ram of mockery to break down the stronghold of our faith.'

They gave him Rashi's interpretation; the prophecy refers not to the distant but the immediate future: briefly, the bride of Isaias shall conceive a son and this shall be a sign of the deliverance of Israel from *the fury of Rasin king of Syria and of the son of Romelia*. To the Christian interpretation they objected that if the prophecy referred to the birth of Christ, then the sign would have come *after* its fulfilment, the deliverance of Israel from the two kings, instead of before, as logically it should. If Andrew is reporting them verbatim they were very eloquent. Is it possible to answer them? Andrew hesitates; honestly he does not think so:

'These are the darts which the Jews hurl against us, calling us perverters and violent distorters of Holy Writ. There is no need for us to answer them, since others have done so before us; but whether their answer is sufficient, let those who have answered judge. Nor would it be useful [for us to answer]. Were we to enter the lists with strength unequal to the doubtful contest, we might perhaps yield. Then the Jews, victorious, would insult not only us, but those whose sharp and lively skill would have vanquished them easily, had they competed. We have put forth all our strength; so now we leave deeds of bravery to braver men. Let us continue the explanation of the literal sense which we have begun.'[1]

For Andrew the 'literal sense' is the Jewish explanation.

Similarly the rod out of the root of Jesse [Isa. xi. 1] is expounded both of Christ and of the Jewish Messias, 'whom they are still awaiting'. Andrew repeats one of the messianic legends: the Messias was born on the day that Nabuzardan burnt the temple, and remains in the place which God has allotted him until the day of mercy. Andrew is able to use the same exposition for both his Jewish and his Christian sources:

[1] See *P.L.* cxcv. 601. Richard's text corresponds very closely to that of MS. Pembroke 45.

'Why does the prophet now speak of the Messias as *the root of Jesse* [xi. 10], when above he has said that the Messias shall come forth *out of the root of Jesse* as rod and a flower? If this does not refer to the Messias, or rather our Lord Jesus Christ, of whom else does the prophet speak? It cannot be said that this refers to Jesse, the father of David, already dead . . . The [Jewish] Messias, or our Christ, is called *the root of Jesse* because. . . .'

He goes on to give various reasons for the change of expression.

My just one is near at hand [li. 5] is expounded as:

'Understand either Cyrus, or according to us our Lord and Saviour, or according to the Jews their Messias.'

But when he comes to *the man of sorrows*, Andrew's imagination is so fired by the Jewish exegesis that he does not even mention the Christian. *The man of sorrows* refers collectively to the Jews of the captivity, who expiate by their sufferings the sins of their whole race. Or, according to another Jewish view, he is the prophet Isaias himself, who personifies his people and sacrifices himself for them. Perhaps the conception had some special appeal for Andrew. Perhaps he felt happy with an explanation that kept him within his familiar and chosen field of Old Testament history, and which did not look forward to the New. He enters into the spirit of it so eagerly that he is ready to manipulate the words of the text in its favour:

'The prophet', he says, 'is reverting to the time when this same people was grievously oppressed in the Babylonian captivity, when indeed there was *no beauty nor comeliness* in it. *And we have seen him*, I and the other prophets, or the prophet speaks of himself in the plural . . . *And we were desirous of him, despised and the most abject of men*: we sighed and mourned that he should be *despised and most abject of men*. Since desire calls forth sighing, *we were desirous* may also be read, without absurdity, as *we sighed*.'

When Andrew says 'without absurdity' it is a sign that he realizes himself to be on dangerous ground. One copy has a disapproving note in the margin:

'You punish your text with sufficient violence, while you strive too much to judaise!'[1]

---

[1] MS. Bibl. Nat. Lat. 574, fo. 70ᵛ: 'Satis violenter hunc textum exsequeris dum nimis iudaizare tu niteris.'

He continues:

> '*A man of sorrows*: The prophet is speaking of the people as though of one man, whom he calls *a man of sorrows* . . . *His look was* so *hidden and despised* that we even ourselves almost despaired of him; and *we esteemed him not* to be of the number of men; that is the people was so abject that it scarcely esteemed itself as of the number of men. *Surely he hath borne our infirmities*: by these words the prophet means that the people who were to suffer in the Babylonian captivity were to expiate not only their own sins, but also the sins of the unrighteous: "Surely that *man of sorrows* will carry our infirmities and sorrows, which we, for our sins, ought to bear." *And we have thought of him as it were a leper.* Here the prophet is numbering himself among those who supposed that the people of the captivity was to be taken captive for its own sins, and that its own sins required it to be separated as a leper from God's people, struck and humbled by God. "So we supposed" [says the prophet] "but this very people *was wounded for our iniquities* and *bruised for our sins*; it was scourged and bruised that we might have peace and be healed." Here the prophet numbers himself among posterity, for whom the chastisement of this people have brought peace . . . At last, by God's mercy it will be taken away *from distress* . . . *and judgement*, that is punishment, under Cyrus . . . *And he shall give the ungodly for his burial and the rich for his death*; the stricken people shall not perish, but *the ungodly and the rich*, that is the men of Babylon, unbelieving, absorbed by riches, shall be given to *burial* and *death* in its stead . . . *Because he hath done no iniquity*; this refers to the righteous; these things can apply only to the elect, and are said to them . . . [*Because his soul hath laboured*] *he shall see*: understand: what he has desired to *see*. We can say that, being led forth from the darkness of prison and tribulation, *he shall see* and understand; he shall be endowed with the gift of understanding . . . *Because he hath delivered his soul*: this can refer only to those who went into exile willingly, by the counsel of the prophets, as Jechonias and those who submitted to the Babylonians. *Unto death*: to be afflicted with afflictions as grievous as death . . . *He hath prayed for the transgressors*: the more chosen prayed to God simply for those of their people who were transgressing his law, that they might be changed for the better.
> 'But some of the Jews interpret this whole passage as referring to Isaias.'

Reading Andrew, one sometimes has to rub one's eyes! It is extraordinary to think that this was written at St. Victor, by a pupil of Hugh, that he was begged to continue his work, begged to resume his abbacy, and finally buried 'with great honour'. The twelfth century is full of surprises.

Most interesting and startling of all is his treatment of Daniel's prophecy [Dan. ix. 24-7]. On this passage in the last of the Prophets, Andrew makes his supreme effort. He tries to find a sort of *via media* between Christian and Jewish exegesis. The question is whether the 'seventy times seven' years 'shortened upon thy people' may be referred to the period between Daniel's prophecy and the coming of Christ. The Jews say that it means the period between the Babylonian captivity and the building of the second temple. Both these interpretations have their difficulties. It is a complicated chronological argument, which takes up three closely written folios; so we will not attempt to follow its ramifications. Andrew begins by giving the Hebrew version of the text instead of the Vulgate, and the Jewish interpretation:

> 'Since we have decided to give, in this part of our work, the exposition which we have received from the most learned of the Jews, it seemed right to give also the text which they say they have here.'

There is one point about their explanation which he cannot bring himself to follow:

> 'Even should we, although unwilling, approve everything else in the Jewish exposition of this deep passage of Scripture, to explain which our scholars have spent no little toil, I do not see how we can manage to approve *this*. . . .'

Typically 'this' is an historical point. The Jewish reckoning will not allow for the thirty years which 'historians and philosophers' allot to Cyrus of Persia after the overthrow of Babylon, nor for the ten years which the Christian reckoning allots to his two successors, Cambyses and Evilmerodoch.

A Christian apologist, the *aliquis* who always gets the worst of the argument, now bustles on to the scene:

> ' "The authority of canonical Scripture, which the Jews cannot and ought not to dispute, compels them to admit that Cyrus had other successors . . ." ' No, replies Andrew, defending the Jews: this cannot be proved from Scripture, and we cannot expect them to accept writings which they have never seen; especially as the biblical writings were contemporary with their narrative. (Evidently he found that, with the Jews, discussion must be limited to proofs from Scripture:)
> 'We do not ask them to contradict their own canonical Scrip-

tures in particular, which we too wish in no wise to contradict, or to remember writers whom they have never read, but let us ask that, saving authority if possible, they should not nullify our traditions by theirs. Let us so contest in this doubtful contest that tradition may not prejudice tradition, and we may seem to contend, not for the sake of victory, but in order to establish the truth. Since the canonical Scriptures stand for both sides, let us see whether they give reasonable support to one view rather than the other. And first let us treat of the seventy years of the desolation of Jerusalem [Dan. ix. 2] since the root of the question lies here.'

At length he decides for the Christian view of these 'seventy years of desolation'. He believes that the biblical writers, Daniel and Esdras, corroborate it.

'We say the same [as Daniel and Esdras do]. If this is turning from the right path, it is erring in company with great authorities. I know not whether it is not wiser and safer to err, as the Jews call it, with Daniel and Esdras, and with our elders, men of great diligence and skill, who follow them, than to walk with the Jews of to-day, what, if we believe them, is the right path. For the Jews of to-day care much more for money-making than for careful exegesis.'

This is the only time that Andrew forgets his manners; he sounds injured. The 'most learned of the Jews' must have escaped from an interminable argument by pleading urgent business elsewhere.

The discussion closes with Andrew's own view of the 'seventy times seven' years. It is based on the Jewish text, but differs from both the Christian and the Jewish interpretation. Andrew has selected and has evolved a reckoning of his own; but he does not allow it to be a prophecy of Christianity. He ends triumphantly:

'Having run briefly through these matters relating to the seventy weeks of years, we will proceed. The seventy times seven years of our translation have been expounded and assigned with sufficient care by our scholars; so we leave them untouched, according to the translation which our people use. We have expounded them to the best of our ability as they are read among the Jews. Let no one be surprised if we have counted to certain years now more, now less, giving various opinions, and in certain places following the Jews.'

For the text 'as read among the Jews', Andrew has an admiring affection. His constant refrain, on comparing it

with the Vulgate, is 'more clearly in the Hebrew'. He has a
simpliste attitude towards problems of textual criticism, which
is delightfully expressed in his comment on the Vulgate
version of Num. xxiv. 15: *Balaam the son of Beor, hath said:
The man whose eye is stopped up hath said. . . .*

> 'The Hebrew, and Origen's translation has: *whose eye is
> opened*. This reading fits into the context, whereas the transla-
> tion which we use is quite contrary to this same context. But
> to struggle with a false reading is not only idle; it is madness.
> Since all the rest of Balaam's speech is in praise of himself, why
> should he blame himself in this alone? Moreover when im-
> mediately afterwards he says that his eyes are *opened* [verse 16],
> why should he say here that they are *stopped up*, which is such
> a contradiction?'[1]

Andrew demands that his text should make plain sense and
he seems to find that the Hebrew fulfils this requirement
better than the Vulgate. Actually the problem was more
complicated than he thought. The Hebrew manuscripts
varied. Rashi's version of the text has: *whose eye is stopped up*,
as the Vulgate, and Rashi can only explain the contradiction by holding that Balaam was blind in one eye. Andrew
sometimes exposes mistakes in the Vulgate manuscripts. So
great is his reverence for the Hebrew that it does not strike
him to ask whether variations may not be found here too.

What are we to conclude about Andrew's attitude towards
the Jews and Judaism? Readers who have had patience
with him so far will have classified him, I am sure, as 'superficial'. He refuses to make decisions. As soon as he reaches
any fundamental point of doctrine his pursuit of 'the fugitive
truth' comes to a sudden halt. Is it a sceptical shrug on the
edge of the precipice? Does he believe that truth has taken
refuge on the Jewish side, among the rationalistic Jewish
exegetes who so impressed him? Or has he perhaps despaired
of finding her on either side? Is he doubtful and tormented,
like Otloh of St. Emeran, or happily eclectic, like a humanist
scholar?

Andrew never loses, even in his most vigorous moments,

---

[1] MS. C.C.C. 30, fo. 42[b]: 'In Hebreo et in translatione Origenis habet:
cuius revelatus est oculus, que littera convenientiam habet cum circumstantia,
cum nostra translatio qua utimur multum adversari eidem circumstantie
inveniatur; sed in exponenda falsa littera laborare non modo est otiosi sed
etiam furiosi. Cum cetera omnia in commendatione sui dicat quomodo in hoc
solo se culparet? Preterea cum statim post dicat quod apertos habet oculos
quomodo hic dicit se habere obscuratos cum hec tam contraria sint?'

the sober serenity of the Victorine. His disarming frankness, and his desire that the Jewish arguments should have fair play, are proof of it. His commentaries on 'Solomon', where debatable points do not crop up, show no sign of any reaction. He believes in his researches as firmly as ever. We can only understand his attitude towards his Jewish teachers if we consider his whole view of exegesis. The two things in his mind are inseparable. He thinks of them together: 'the Jews and the Letter'.

'Superficial' is what Andrew sets out to be. He undertakes to expound *iuxta superficiem littere*, 'according to the surface of the letter'. His use of this catch-phrase is significant. That he chooses to concentrate on the 'letter' does not mean that he rejects the 'spiritual exposition' in principle. On the contrary. He takes it for granted. On the famous text of Solomon [Prov. xxii. 20] he says:

> '*Behold I have described it to thee three manner of ways*: historically, tropologically, anagogically.'[1]

He has no idea of laying down new principles. He would shun such a thing; for Andrew, clear and intelligent about details, is a positive addle-pate about theories. Yet the task he set himself demanded a clear head indeed. No western commentator before him had set out to give a purely literal interpretation of the Old Testament, though many had attempted a purely spiritual one. There was general uncertainty as to the content of the letter. There were no rules for defining it, just as there were no rules for establishing one's text. Andrew would have to define how much the literal interpretation included for himself. It was a harsh problem for one who shrank from definitions.

Such guidance as he could get came from St. Jerome and Hugh of St. Victor. Hugh regarded the literal sense as important because it was the foundation of the spiritual; it was the wax of the honeycomb. He associated the literal sense with grammar and history, the allegorical with theology, the tropological with preaching. Conversely, his pupils would tend to dissociate theology and preaching from the literal sense. Then Andrew would have to collate his master's teaching on 'letter and spirit' with his other distinction; Hugh spoke also of 'letter', 'sense' and 'sentence' or opinion. The first two, letter and sense, mean the construing of one's

[1] MS. C.C.C. 30, fo. 102ᶜ.

text, and the explanation of its simple surface meaning, which includes metaphor and simile. Obviously both of these come under the literal sense, and so are Andrew's province. What of the 'sentence', the deep meaning or conclusion to be drawn from 'letter and sense'? This need not be an allegory or trope. It may be a theological or moral deduction; and there is a world of difference; allegory merely illustrates theology; a 'sentence' defines and establishes doctrine itself. Should 'sentences' be included in the historical exposition? Andrew decided not. Or perhaps he so identified allegory and theology that the dilemma never occurred to him.

This is the key to his treatment of the prophecies. A manifest prophecy of Christ is a 'sentence'. As such it may be mentioned, and then safely left to the theologians. Let the cobbler stick to his last. Andrew undertakes to explain the literal sense; he need not concern himself with mysteries. The Jewish explanation strikes him as plainer, simpler, more intelligible than the Christian, just what the literal sense was always said to be in comparison with the spiritual. If it was unedifying to Christians, the literal sense was admitted to be often unedifying. Edification and theological truth must be supplied by those who would build allegories and moralities on Andrew's 'literal foundation'.

Moreover St. Jerome had taught him to associate the literal sense with the Jews. There were two St. Jeromes: one who was fascinated by Alexandrian allegory and spoke slightingly of the literal or 'fleshly' sense; the other a scholar and humanist fascinated by the letter. This second was the 'venerable Jerome' whom Andrew intended to 'follow with unequal step'. But his own merits and defects were too like St. Jerome's for him to be able to distinguish them. Neither Andrew nor St. Jerome had a head for distinctions.

The saint taught him that Jews expounded in a literal or carnal, Christians in a spiritual sense. This was still regarded as the main difference between them. Andrew's contemporary, Bartholomew, bishop of Exeter (*d.* 1184), writes in his *Dialogue against the Jews*:

> 'The chief cause of disagreement between ourselves and the Jews seems to me to be this: they take all the Old Testament literally, wherever they can find a literal sense, unless it gives manifest witness to Christ. Then they repudiate it, saying that it is not in the Hebrew Truth, that is in their books, or they refer it to some fable, as that they are still awaiting its fulfil-

ment, or they escape by some other serpentine wile, when they feel themselves hard pressed. They will never accept allegory, except when they have no other way out. *We* interpret not only the words of Scripture, but the things done, and the deeds themselves, in a mystical sense, yet in such a way that the freedom of allegory may in no wise nullify, either history in the events, or proper understanding of the words, of Scripture.'[1]

Bartholomew's last clause points to the difficulty: history must not be replaced by allegory. Andrew learnt from St. Augustine that each text had a literal meaning. He deduces, incorrectly but excusably, that the literal meaning of a text must necessarily be what the Jews say about it. If you want to know the literal sense, go to the Jews.

Andrew went. It was the only form of biblical research open to him; and he gathered from the second, the scholarly Jerome, that, for the Old Testament at least, the Jews had a living tradition and were a useful source of information. Had he gone a hundred years earlier, he would have found no connection between 'literalism' and Jewish exegesis. He would have found that the Jews were just as devoted to allegory and fancy as the Christians were. Then perhaps he might have realized that there was a mistake somewhere. He might have been forced to reconsider his premises and analyse that misleading word 'literal'. But Rashi had directed Jewish exegesis into new channels; he had made it 'literal' in the sense that it kept closely to the text and preferred rational to allegorical explanations. Among the Jews, too, the relations between literal and allegorical senses were conceived rather differently; it was rather a question of choosing between them, than the Christian method of superimposing one upon the other. So Andrew's tendency to think that 'literal' meant the same thing as 'non-mystical' or 'rational' must have been confirmed by his Jewish teachers.

If the literal sense is defined simply as the whole meaning intended by the sacred writer, then there is no real connection between the letter and rationalism. The miraculous and symbolic element in Scripture may perfectly well be emphasized by an exponent of the literal sense. But commentators had not begun to think in these terms. They still thought of letter and spirit, in antithesis, as they thought of body and soul. We can easily understand how Andrew

---

[1] MS. Bodl. 482, fo. 1ᵈ. The treatise was written in Bartholomew's old age. See A. Morey, *Bartholomew of Exeter* (Cambridge, 1937), 109, 164.

N

would fuse together Letter, Jews, and Reason in his eagerness to investigate the literal meaning. The more modern of the Jewish exegetes must have given him just the rational and literal outlook that he needed.

He does not feel their exegesis to be dangerous. He conceives his own task too modestly for that. His chosen field is the letter. Not for him the mysteries of theology and apologetics. One would like to know how he retorted, when it was pointed out to him that his position 'scandalized the proficient and brought the less proficient into ill repute'. One would give much for his reply to the *De Emmanuele*. But when that was written he was back at Wigmore, preoccupied with Hugh de Mortimer and building the abbey church.

We are left with what looks like a contradiction. Andrew had accepted the current view of the literal exposition with all its restrictions; that is, he condemned himself, wittingly, to spend his life in grubbing among the 'literal foundations' while others did the building. This was his idea of the quest for truth! He must have seemed a rather harmful eccentric to some of his contemporaries. The qualified, relative enthusiasm of Hugh for the letter had become a devouring passion in his pupil. And the pupil brought such freshness and energy, such keenness of judgment and independence, that he triumphed in his task, in spite of the antiquated conceptions that he could not shake off; he succeeded in renewing biblical scholarship.

Probably Andrew could not have explained himself. He was an instinctive, unreasoning rationalist. The lyrical impulse of the twelfth century was taking a peculiar form in him. Theologians were building the complicated structure of their disputations on the basis of the Pauline Epistles. Mystics, like Richard, were soaring upward, on the wings of the spiritual exposition. Andrew was burrowing, pressing down closer to his text and its meaning:

> alta petunt levia
> centrum tenent gravia
> renovantur omnia.

It was the spring that Adam of St. Victor celebrated.

V. ANDREW'S INFLUENCE

Andrew gives content to an exclamation of St. Bernard which otherwise we might have passed over as one of the prophet's *beaux cris*.[1] St. Bernard is writing to Master Henry Murdac, urging him to leave his studies and enter the 'school of piety' at Clairvaux. Master Henry is reading the Prophets: why seek the Word in books when he has come to us in the flesh? He has long left the obscurities of the Prophets to reveal himself to sinners: he has come down from the cloudy heights of the Law to the plain of the Gospels:

'O had you once tasted a little of the fat of corn that filleth Jerusalem, how gladly would you leave their crusts to be gnawed by the lettered Jews!'[2]

This was probably written some time before Andrew expounded the Prophets. St. Bernard had his way and Henry Murdac entered Clairvaux before 1135.[3] He came from Yorkshire; we do not know where he earned the title of 'master' that St. Bernard gives him; we have no evidence to connect him with the Victorines. But he must have been doing something of the same kind as Andrew. The letter expresses in a striking manner what St. Bernard would have thought of Andrew's studies. He was reading the Prophets instead of the Gospels. He was gnawing the dry outer crust of Scripture, in the company of 'lettered' (i.e. literally-minded) Jews; the monks of Clairvaux were filled with the fat of its inner spiritual meaning as they listened to their abbot preaching.[4] Andrew's activities would have struck him as hardly less dangerous than the irreverent questioning and 'mapping out the Trinity' that he condemned in Abailard. We may wonder how many religious shared his opinion. The literal sense was well known to be misleading. Now Andrew's passionate embrace of the letter had produced a crop of judaizing commentaries, just as might have been expected. It was enough, one would think, to cause a

---

[1] I take the description from Dom Wilmart, '. . . Prophète inspiré qui jette de beaux cris', *Auteurs Spirituels et Textes Dévots du Moyen Âge Latin* (Paris, 1932), 252.

[2] *Ep.* cvi.

[3] *Dict. Nat. Biogr.* xxxix. 321-3. Henry Murdac died as archbishop of York in 1153.

[4] Bread signifies Scripture, the crust the letter, the 'crumb' the spiritual meaning. This allusion gives the key to St. Bernard's letter. *Lectio divina* in the Cistercian sense, i.e. the Scriptures lived and experienced as well as read, is contrasted with the intellectual study of Scripture in the schools.

strong reaction against biblical scholarship and the school of St. Victor.

In fact, we find the contrary. Biblical studies were continued, in a more orthodox spirit, by Andrew's successors, just as theological speculation continued after the condemnation of Abailard. The Cistercians themselves must have read Andrew; four of their libraries are known to have possessed copies of his works. In order to gauge the extent of his influence we may follow three different lines of evidence. They supplement one another and each one points to much the same conclusion.

First, we have the evidence of Andrew himself, of Richard of St. Victor, and of Roger Bacon. Andrew says that he undertook his last work, on Solomon, 'compelled by the many urgent requests of his friends'. The conventional phrase may have some meaning, since it does not occur in his earlier works. In the first book of the *De Emmanuele* Richard tells us that Andrew had disciples who upheld his view of the prophecy of Isaias: Richard will refute it, for the benefit of those who have already been, and may in future, be led astray.[1] Then, in the prologue to his second book, he says that the first book of his refutation has offended a certain disciple of Andrew's, who is still involved in error. The second book, therefore, consists in an argument between Richard and Andrew's disciple.[2] The latter shows a touching loyalty to his master. When Richard has brought him to reject the Jewish interpretation, he tries to deny that Andrew had taken any responsibility for it:

'Do not call it my master's opinion, but the Jews'; for of course he put it forward not as his own but as theirs.'

Richard is able to show that Andrew had given it as the literal sense of the passage. This was unfortunate, as the disciple has to confess. He tries to explain it away on the grounds of Andrew's general attitude; Andrew, he says, has warned his readers that in many places he is expounding not his own but the Jewish view. 'He ought to have made clear that very thing: whether he is giving his own, true, opinion, or the false Jewish one' is Richard's relentless answer. As a last resort the disciple tries the argument that Andrew was speaking 'in irony'.[3] Although he ends as a docile questioner, he never repudiates his master in so many words.

[1] *P.L.* cxcvi. 601.   [2] 633.   [3] 638-41.

Roger Bacon was writing about a hundred years later, 1271 or 1272. In the *Compendium Studii Philosophiae* he complains that many exegetes are giving 'authority' to 'a certain Andrew who expounds the Bible *ad litteram*'. Authority[1] ought to be reserved for the Fathers. It is significant that elsewhere Bacon makes the same complaint about the contemporary attitude to St. Albert the Great. Although he thinks that Andrew was 'a learned man and probably knew Hebrew', Bacon finds his exegesis open to criticism. Nevertheless he ends on a rare note of approval. To Andrew belongs the credit of sending exegetes to their original sources:

'In this, however, he is very praiseworthy: he stirs us up about the doubtful passages of our translation, in many cases, though not always, and sends us to the Hebrew, that we may seek our explanations more surely at the root. *Few would take thought for the true explanation of this passage and of many others, unless they had seen how Andrew treats it.*'[2]

Secondly, we have the manuscripts of Andrew's commentaries; and these confirm Roger Bacon's statement. Fifteen are known to survive; others may be hidden in the great mass of inadequately catalogued commentaries in our libraries. Fifteen seems a respectable total if one realizes that Andrew's public must have been austere and restricted; it corresponded to that which now takes the *Journal of Theological Studies* and the *Revue Biblique*.

The earliest manuscript is a beautiful copy of his work on the Heptateuch, written soon after the middle of the twelfth century, from Beaupré (MS. Bibl. Nat. Lat. 356). It has the *explicit* already quoted, proudly calling itself a book of extracts from the Fathers, Josephus, and the 'traditions of the Jews'. Then we have three Victorine manuscripts at Paris, written towards the end of the twelfth century: Andrew on the Heptateuch (MS. Lat. 14798); on Isaias, with the general prologue to the Prophets (MS. Mazarine 175); on Ezechiel (MS. Lat. 14432). The last two are so alike in size and script that one supposes that they originally went together; probably they formed part of a complete set of Andrew on the Prophets; both were bound up with miscellaneous material in the fifteenth century. A thirteenth-

---

[1] The meaning of this expression has been worked out by M. D. Chenu, ' "Authentica" et "Magistralia" ', *Divus Thomas* (Placentia, 1925), xxviii. 3-31. It is used for the Scriptures and the Fathers as opposed to the 'moderns'.
[2] *Compendium*, viii, ed. Brewer (Rolls Series), 482-3.

century Victorine manuscript (Bibl. Nat. Lat. 14803) has Andrew on Kings and Chronicles. The Vatican Library possesses an early thirteenth-century copy of his work on the Heptateuch, called 'Compilationes Andree super vetus testamentum', following a copy of Prepositinus on the Psalter, in MS. Barberini lat. 693, of unknown provenance. The *corpus* of Andrew's works was probably still available at Paris towards the end of the thirteenth century. MS. Vat. Lat. 1053 contains the whole set, except for his exposition of Jeremias, written in a Paris hand of the later thirteenth or early fourteenth century, bound up with other literal expositions of Scripture. It belonged to Cardinal John de Murro, who died in 1313, and was acquired from him by the Franciscans of Fabriano in Ancona. The Friars Preacher of the convent of Minerva at Rome had 'postills said to be Andrew's', some incomplete, on the Prophets, Kings, Proverbs and Ecclesiastes.[1] Andrew's works also spread to the Rhineland and Austria. The Cistercians of Eberbach had Andrew on the Octateuch, Chronicles, and the Minor Prophets, written in a hand of the mid-thirteenth century, now MS. Bodl. Laud Lat. 105. The Benedictines of Melk had 'Master Andrew's prologue in explanation of Isaias' as we see from their fifteenth-century catalogue.

Another important group comes from English monastic libraries. These are mainly *éditions de luxe*, larger, more decorated, and better written than the continental manuscripts, with the exception of the early one from Beaupré. The earliest English manuscript is an anonymous copy of Andrew on Kings, in a hand of the late twelfth century, from the Cistercian abbey of Buildwas in Shropshire, now MS. Trinity College Cambridge B.I. 29(27). The finest, now MS. Corpus Christi College Cambridge 30, contains 'Abbot Andrew' on the Octateuch, Chronicles, the Minor Prophets, Proverbs, and Ecclesiastes. M. R. James thought that the red initials of the title-page suggested the Cistercian abbey of Coggeshall in Essex;[2] but Boston of Bury saw a manuscript with exactly the same selection of Andrew's works at Guisborough Priory in Yorkshire. Wherever it came from, Andrew had found an appreciative reader, who noted

[1] G. Meersseman, 'La bibliothèque des Frères Prêcheurs de la Minerve à la fin du XVe siècle', *Mélanges Auguste Pelzer* (Louvain, 1947), 611.
[2] N. R. Ker thinks there is no evidence for the suggestion, *Medieval Libraries of Great Britain* (London, 1941), 128.

the important points in the margin and wrote: 'bona est expositio et utilis valde' beside the opening of Ecclesiastes. The monks of Worcester had Andrew on the Octateuch and Chronicles (the same College, MS. 217). Boston saw Andrew on Isaias, Jeremias, and Daniel at St. Edmundsbury, which is the present MS. Pembroke College Cambridge 45; one is grateful for this manuscript as it contains the only copy of Andrew on Jeremias that we possess. The Cistercians of Kingswood had Andrew on the two visions of Ezechiel, excerpted from his commentary on this prophet (MS. Bodl. e Mus. 62). The Kingswood treatise is interesting, since the taking of excerpts is a good test of the popularity of a medieval writer. These four latter manuscripts are in hands of the second, third, or fourth decades of the thirteenth century. Boston also saw copies of Andrew on Exodus, Leviticus, and Numbers at Newminster in Northumberland, on Exodus to Chronicles at St. Peter's, Gloucester.

The English manuscript tradition preserved the memory of Andrew's identity more faithfully than the continental. Whereas on the continent his works are either anonymous or ascribed simply to 'Andreas', in England we have the title 'Postille Andree canonici S. Victoris' written in a fifteenth-century hand on the flyleaf of MS. Pembroke College 45, 'Andreas abbas' in the contemporary title of MS. Corpus Christi College 30, and best of all 'Andreas de Wiggemor' in MS. Bodl. e Mus. 62.

A manuscript of a different type, now Corpus Christi College Cambridge 315, belonged to the Franciscans of Oxford; it contains Andrew on Kings and Chronicles, in a small unpretentious little book, meant only for use. Some friar has been reading him in the critical spirit recommended by Bacon. Andrew's comment on 1 Kings i. 28: '*ego commodavi eum Domino . . .* ideo non accepi eum tanquam mihi reservaturum et apud me retenturum . . .' has provoked a note:

> 'Andrew here uses false Latin; hence you may believe that he often speaks false Hebrew; for he says *reservaturum* and *retenturum* for *reservandum* and *retinendum.*'

On ii. 1: *dilatatum est os meum super inimicos meos, quia laetata sum.* etc., Andrew says that *quia* is not to be found in the Hebrew. The same thirteenth-century hand has written: 'falsum est!'

Latest of all, and for that reason perhaps the most significant, is a manuscript which belonged to the Dominicans of Venice, now MS. Bibl. Nat. Lat. 574. It is written in two Italian hands of the fifteenth century and dated Innocents' Day, 1461. Here we have Andrew on Isaias and Daniel, bound up in a collection which reflects the varied interests of fifteenth-century Italy. First comes a treatise by Constant of Capri on the martyrdom of Brother Anthony de Ripoli, O.P. in 1460 at the hands of the Moors;[1] then a series of rhyming epitaphs of Roman emperors and generals; then notes for preachers; then Andrew on Isaias, followed by the *Scrutinium Scripturarum* of Paul of Burgos, 'which he composed after his additions to the *Postillae* of Nicolas of Lyre, A.D. 1434, in his eighty-first year'; last comes Andrew on Daniel. The juxtaposition of Andrew, a 'judaizing' Christian and Paul of Burgos, a Jewish convert to Christianity, was not accidental; marginal notes show an interest in this aspect of Andrew's work. The scribe draws attention to the 'judaizing' distortion of *desideravimus* (Isa. lii. 2). A different hand has added a note, entitled 'Hebreorum fatuitates', at the end of the commentary.[2]

Andrew's exposition of the *Ecce virgo concipiet* had a history of its own, distinct from that of his commentary on Isaias, since it is quoted in the *De Emmanuele*. This treatise was one of the most popular of Richard's works and survives in many manuscripts. The first book circulated separately, without its prologue, under the title: 'The objections of Andrew, according to which the Jews oppose us on our Emmanuel.' In his anxiety to refute Andrew's exegesis, Richard introduced it to a much wider circle than it would otherwise have reached; he aroused interest in the Jewish arguments that Andrew brought forward.

Our third and surest type of evidence is the quotations of Andrew by later writers. The obvious place for our search to begin is the *Historia Scholastica*, the great summary of biblical history by Peter Comestor, the Paris master who became Chancellor in 1169 and died about ten years later. Peter had written one of the most popular books of the middle ages. It became a 'set book' in the schools and

---

[1] Described in Quétif Echard, *Script. Ord. Praed.* (1719), i. 907.

[2] *Guf* means *corpus* and is a place where all souls, according to the Jewish heresy, were stored from the beginning of the world, and thence they are taken when they are infused into bodies; hence it says in many places in the Talmud that the Messias shall not come until all the souls in this place are used up; the corollary follows that the Messias will not come so long as there is a pregnant woman among them (fo. 711).

formed the subject of lecture courses, just as did the *Gloss*;
hence it got its name, the *Historica Scholastica*; but the twelfth-
century masters knew it simply as the *Histories*. They call the
Comestor 'the Master of the *Histories*', as they call the Lombard 'the Master of the *Sentences*'. Outside the schools it
became a classic with both clergy and laity. It was translated into the vernaculars and versified;[1] it often figures in
medieval wills. The reverence and admiration inspired by
the author are expressed in his nickname 'Comestor' or
'Manducator', the Eater. He had eaten and digested the
Scriptures.

The Comestor says in his prologue that the cause of his
work was the pleading of his colleagues. They needed a
compendium of what was scattered and diffused in the Bible
and its glosses.[2] The *Histories*, it has been pointed out, were
really fulfilling the programme of the *Didascalicon*. Here
Hugh of St. Victor had taught that theology must begin
with a thorough grounding in biblical history. Peter was
providing just such a groundwork. He had written a text-
book for the students and an invaluable work of reference
for their teachers.

We know that the Comestor had personal relations with
St. Victor. He is said to have resigned his chancellorship
and retired there for his last years. If it is natural to find the
inspiration of the *Histories* in Hugh of St. Victor, it is also
natural to guess that they owe something to Andrew. The
Comestor's seventeenth-century editors noticed, with some
scandal, that he made use of Jewish and other unauthorita-
tive sources. They excuse him on the grounds that he is
merely reporting, without committing himself; he says
tradunt, narrant Hebraei, alii dicunt.[3] It was not surprising,
though of course delightful, to find that very often the
Hebraei and *alii* of the *Histories* mean Andrew.[4] They introduce passages which have been 'lifted' straight from his
commentary. Peter Comestor has used Andrew on the
Octateuch as a principal source for the *Histories*. The fact
has hitherto been overlooked because he does not refer to
Andrew by name. Peter follows the medieval custom of

[1] R. Martin, 'Notes sur l'œuvre littéraire de Pierre le Mangeur', *Rech. Théol.
anc. méd.* iii (1931), 54-5.
[2] *P.L.* cxcviii. 1053.   [3] Ibid. 1052.
[4] From here to the end of the chapter I am summarizing my article 'The
School of Andrew of St. Victor', in *Rech. Théol. anc. méd.* xi (1939), 145-67,
with a few additions. Those references which are not given will be found there.

borrowing from contemporaries without acknowledgment, and referring to them, when this is necessary, as *quidam* or *alii*. He must have been writing in Andrew's lifetime, since Archbishop William of Sens (1169-75) to whom the *Histories* were dedicated, died in the same year as Andrew. Hugh of St. Victor, on the other hand, had been dead long enough to be quoted by name. Peter refers to an opinion of 'Master Hugh of St. Victor', which he takes from Andrew's exposition; Andrew, writing in his master's lifetime or soon after his death, had referred to him as *quidam*. Great as Hugh's authority was, Peter agrees with Andrew in rejecting his opinion in this case, and he prefers Andrew's.

Another likely hunting-ground for quotations is a series of glosses on the Old Testament by another Peter, called the Chanter because he held this office at Notre-Dame; he died in 1197. We know him best for his great 'moralistic summa', the *Verbum Abbreviatum*, the only one of his works that has been printed; but he is also important as an exegete. So far as we know, the Chanter was the first of the Paris masters to lecture on the literal and spiritual sense of the greater part of Scripture. I have noticed a definite connection between these glosses and the *Histories*.

Like the Comestor, the Chanter must have been writing either while Andrew was still alive, or soon after his death, and Andrew's name is never mentioned in the glosses. But they contain even more quotations from Andrew than the *Histories* do. The Chanter sets the tone of his work by quoting Andrew's prologue to Genesis almost *in toto* in his exposition of Gen. i. 1. Then he goes through the Octateuch, using Andrew as his principal source, after the *Gloss*, for the literal exposition.

The first person, to my knowledge, to quote Andrew by name was far from the schools both in body and in spirit. He was 'Master Adam', canon of the Premonstratensian abbey of Dryburgh in Berwickshire; he was abbot from *c.* 1184 to 1188, then entered the Charterhouse at Witham and died there about 1212. 'Of medium height, rather fat, cheerful, bald, reverend in character as in years', Adam was a true contemplative, learned in a solid, old-fashioned way.[1] His

---

[1] On Adam see A. Wilmart, 'Magister Adam Cartusiensis', *Mélanges Mandonnet*, ii (Paris, 1930), 145-61; 'Maitre Adam chanoine prémontré devenu chartreux à Witham', *Analecta Praemonstratensia*, ix (1933), 207-32; F. Petit, *Ad Viros Religiosos, Quatorze Sermons d'Adam Scot* (Tongerloo, 1934).

treatise on the threefold sense of the tabernacle, written at Dryburgh in 1179 or 1180, is a typical product of the 'holy reading', which he gave himself to with 'inexhaustible zeal and incredible fervour'. He allots a whole book to the appearance of the Tabernacle and its ornaments, in order to collect as many and as certain details as possible for use afterwards in the spiritual exposition. For establishing these details he has consulted the work of Andrew as well as the *Historia Scholastica*; and 'Master Andrew' comes second only to St. Augustine and the Venerable Bede. Adam quotes him by name in the first chapter,[1] later on as 'a certain master more expert than others', 'that eloquent man', 'a certain man as eloquent as religious'.

It would be interesting to know how Adam's copy of Andrew came to Dryburgh. Since Adam had studied arts, not theology, before he entered religion,[2] he is unlikely to have brought it with him. It seems that copies of Andrew's works had begun to go round the English monastic libraries at least by 1180.

The next set of quotations takes us back to Paris. Stephen Langton, the greatest biblical scholar of the later twelfth century, uses him when glossing the Octateuch. Fortunately we know that Langton had reached the first book of Kings at the end of 1187 or very soon afterwards; hence Andrew must have been dead for about ten years when Langton began to gloss the book of Genesis. It was now decent to quote Andrew by name, and he is mentioned specifically seventeen times in Langton's work on the Octateuch. Apart from the *Gloss* and the 'Master of the Histories' no other name appears so often. Even Hugh of St. Victor appears only in four places, and in two of these he is connected with his pupil: 'Master Hugh of St. Victor used to say . . . and Andrew, who expounds the Pentateuch literally, holds to it'; 'Andrew of St. Victor says, following Master Hugh . . .' As one comes to expect in medieval exegesis, acknowledged borrowings are a signpost to others. Langton's glosses contain many unacknowledged quotations from Andrew. Collation shows that some of them have been taken directly from the original, not from the *Histories* or the Chanter's glosses.

---

[1] *De Tripartito Tabernaculo, P.L.* cxcviii. 635.

[2] This can be gathered from the extract of the Witham chronicle published by Wilmart, 'Maître Adam,' etc., 7.

Langton and the Chanter read their glosses as lectures in the schools at Paris and circulated them afterwards. The Chanter's were appreciated; Langton's could be described as medieval 'best sellers'. His celebrity as archbishop and champion of ecclesiastical liberties against a tyrant king came to swell his reputation as a scholar. Even had Andrew himself been forgotten, something of his work must have survived. It had gone to the making of the *Histories*; it had been impressed on the prodigious medieval memories of those students who came to the Chanter's and Langton's lectures; it had been circulated in their glosses. Hugh of St. Cher, the Dominican exegete, quotes Andrew via the *Histories*, the Chanter, and Langton. But his use by these three important scholars seems to have awakened the interest of readers and sent them to 'Andrew in the original'. We find this expression in a very popular aid to study, the *Vocabularium Bibliae*, or dictionary of biblical terms by William Brito, written after 1248 and before 1285. He quotes Andrew on *Mello* and *Ramathaim*: 'Andreas vero quidam expositor . . .' and 'dicit Andreas *in originali* super i Regum . . .'. *In originali* is usually applied to a patristic author; it means his original work as distinct from a collection of extracts like the *Gloss*, or quotations in later writers.[1] It is impressive to find Andrew referred to as though he were an 'authority'. It strengthens our belief in Roger Bacon's complaint about the 'authority' ascribed to him.

Far from being forgotten, he was even better known in the thirteenth century than in the twelfth. Neither the Comestor, the Chanter, nor Langton shows any knowledge of Andrew on the Prophets or Solomon. The Chanter and Langton seem to know the extract published by Richard in the *De Emmanuele*; otherwise they limit themselves to his work on the Octateuch. The anonymous author of a thirteenth-century *correctorium*, a list of amendments to the biblical text, quotes a passage from Andrew on Proverbs with warm approval: 'Andrew, that eminent exponent of the literal sense . . .' As the *correctoria* represent textual criticism of the most scientific kind known to the thirteenth century, it is significant that Andrew should be 'frequently quoted' there.[2] Another corrector mentions him also on Genesis and

---

[1] On the term *originalia* see G. Paré, &c., op. cit. (p. 76, n. 1), 151-2.

[2] H. Denifle, 'Die Handschr. der Bibelcorrectorien des 13. Jahrh.', in *Archiv f. Lit.- und Kirchengesch. des M.As.* iv (1888), 565 and n. 1.

Isaias.[1] Hugh of St. Cher quotes him both by name and anonymously on the Prophets and on Proverbs.[2] Guerric of St. Quentin O.P. quotes him frequently on Isaias, both via Hugh of St. Cher and independently.[3] A series of Paris commentators, including Nicholas Gorran towards the end of the thirteenth century, quotes him on Proverbs. William of Middleton O.F.M. quotes him in a commentary on the Pentateuch which had considerable popularity. Gorran quotes him in an even more popular commentary on the same book.[4] The Franciscan Spiritual, Peter John Olivi, quotes him on Kings, Isaias, Ezechiel and Ecclesiastes.[5] Olivi's use of Andrew on Ecclesiastes is particularly interesting, since other thirteenth-century commentators, even though they use Andrew on Proverbs, do not seem to know that he expounded the second of the books of Solomon. That they would have used his exposition, had it been available, appears from a quotation taken from Andrew on Proverbs discussing a passage in Ecclesiastes, which has been copied into a thirteenth-century commentary on this second book.[6] Olivi died in 1298. The commentators who quote Andrew on Proverbs, but not on Ecclesiastes, fall within the period 1230-75; most of them are working before 1260.[7] It seems that Olivi, the last in chronological order, had access to a book which his predecessors had wanted.

As well as appearing in formal quotations in continental sources, Andrew also keeps cropping up in marginal notes and glosses to thirteenth-century English manuscripts. A copy of Langton on the Pentateuch, Corpus Christi College Cambridge 55, has 'Andreas contra' written beside the gloss on Gen. i. 2, where Langton differs from Andrew. There are two extracts from his work on Genesis in an early thirteenth-century gloss to the *Histories*, from Christ Church Canterbury, now MS. Trinity College Cambridge 342 (B. 15. 5). Another copy of the *Histories*, which belonged to the convent of the Friars Preachers at Beverley (founded

---

[1] Calandra has found these corrections from Andrew in *Correctorium M*, MS. Ottob. Vat. lat. 293, of the Vatican Library; see Calandra, lxxxvi.

[2] Calandra, lxxxiii-v; 'Sapiential Books I', ii. 341-2.

[3] B. Smalley, 'A commentary on Isaias by Guerric of St. Quentin O.P.', *Studi e Testi*, cxxii (1946), 383-97.

[4] 'Sapiential Books I', iii. 59-60, 75, 247-8; 'Sapiential Books II'.

[5] Calandra, lxxviii-lxxxii.

[6] 'Sapiential Books I', iii. 245.

[7] Nicholas Gorran left no surviving work on Ecclesiastes.

before 1240[1]) and is now MS. University College Oxford Auct. II (190), has its margins covered thickly with notes and glosses in various thirteenth-century hands. For the section on the Octateuch hardly a folio is without some extracts from Andrew, taken verbally from his writings; and one of the hands has carefully marked those passages of the *Histories* where the Comestor has used Andrew as his source. Andrew's exposition of Isaias is twice referred to; even the section on the Gospels, *De ortu salvatoris*, has a reference to Andrew on Exodus. The Beverley Dominicans, if it was they who wrote the notes in their manuscript, must have made an intensive study of Andrew both on the Octateuch and on the Prophets. He is quoted nine times in an anonymous gloss on Exodus, copied in a hand of the later thirteenth century in the margin of the *Gloss*, in the MS. Kk. IV. 10, University Library Cambridge, fo. 126[r]. The original seems to have been written soon after 1226.[2] The author does not merely transcribe mechanically; he will sometimes comment: 'an argument for what Andrew says on a later text. . . .'[3]

These last few notes are not the result of long, systematic searches on my part, but of chance and guesswork. It seems that quotations from Andrew are typical in a certain class of manuscript. One begins to understand why all the English copies of Andrew's works which survive (with one exception) belong to about the second quarter of the thirteenth century; that is about a hundred years after the originals were written. It seems that at first he was known to a comparatively small circle and was appreciated more widely as time passed. The serious study of his works in England, to which the manuscripts and Roger Bacon witness, forms a background for the biblical scholarship of Robert Grosseteste and the Friars.

If we put all the evidence together, English and continental, we get a rising curve for 'influxus Andreae in posteros' to the end of the thirteenth century. Andrew on the Octateuch was used immediately and continuously; Andrew on the Prophets and Proverbs was not used, so far as we know, until after 1230; then commentators made up for their

---

[1] The first mention of Beverley Priory is in this year when a chapter was held there. *Calendar of Liberate Rolls, 1226-40*, 369. I owe this reference to Fr. Aquinas Hinnebusch.

[2] See below, p. 278.

[3] Fo. 152[v] on Exod. xii. 41: '*eadem die egressus:* "argumentum pro Andrea qui dicit quod de die exierunt de Egipto, ad illud Num: *profecti de Ramesse*"' [Num. xxxiii. 3]. The reference can be verified from Andrew on the same text.

neglect; lastly, Andrew on Ecclesiastes was quoted towards the end of the century. All the writers who quote him show esteem for his learning. They may disagree with his interpretation of certain prophecies or differ on points of detail; they seem to find him invaluable for reference. The later middle ages is largely unexplored territory from the point of view of Bible studies. Our evidence for Andrew's influence is slight, but so is our evidence against it. The Dominican scholar, Nicholas Trevet, and the Franciscan, Nicholas of Lyre, are quoting him on the Pentateuch and Octateuch respectively in the early fourteenth century.[1] The Venice manuscript shows that he was still being read in the later fifteenth. Even the post-Tridentine scholars have sometimes appreciated him. His 'portrait' with those of other distinguished Victorians hung in his abbey library in the seventeenth century.[2] Eighteenth-century bibliographers noted his freedom from the common faults of medieval exegesis. 'This is a polished, weighty writer who smacks in nothing of the childish and obscure' is Oudin's comment.[3] He impressed Dom Brial as outstanding in his period:

'Il en est effectivement peu qui réunissent comme lui la clarté et la précision, qui s'écartent plus rarement de leur objet, et sachent placer plus à propos l'érudition. Il avait la connaissance des langues grecque [?] et hébraïque, avantage peu commun dans son siècle.'[4]

Within the limits of his chosen subject Andrew's influence corresponded to his master's on theology as a whole. Hugh of St. Victor seemed to his contemporaries like a 'second Augustine'; Andrew was their second Jerome. He played a vital part in forming the Victorine tradition. Historians have missed its full richness by leaving Andrew out of account.

[1] Calandra, lxxxiii-v, has collected all the references to Andrew to be found in Lyre's postills.
[2] A. Franklin, *Histoire de la bibliothèque de St Victor* (Paris, 1865), 50.
[3] *Com. de Scrip. Eccles.* ii (Leipzig, 1722), 1268.
[4] *Histoire littéraire de la France*, xiii (1814), 409.

VI. A PUPIL: HERBERT OF BOSHAM

Herbert's commentary on the Psalter is a new discovery.[1] Mr. N. R. Ker found a copy during his investigation of medieval book collections in the cathedral library of St. Paul's in London. The manuscript had been hiding under the description 'Psalterium, xiv cent.' in an inventory drawn up in the nineteenth century. The true date is early thirteenth or even late twelfth century. The donor was Master Henry of Cornhill, who died as dean of St. Paul's after many years of service in the chapter in 1254. The contents of the manuscript were not only unknown, but wholly unsuspected. Herbert of Bosham appears in the bibliographies as secretary and biographer of his patron, Archbishop Becket, and as editor of the *Magna Glosatura* of his master, Peter Lombard.[2] He had never been credited with an independent work on Scripture, much less with advanced Hebrew scholarship. His exposition of Jerome's *Hebraica* in the St. Paul's manuscript was the kind of find that a medievalist dreams of and seldom gets.

Herbert deserves an important place in my study, but he is difficult to fit into an existing arrangement. He will not go into the chapter on monastic and cathedral schools. Although a pupil of the Lombard at Paris, he is not known to have taught there: his professorship was in Becket's household. Neither was he a monk. He tells us in his dedicatory letter, which prefaces the commentary, that he wrote it in retirement at the Cistercian abbey of Ourscamp. Bishop Peter of Arras (1184-1203), a former Cistercian abbot,[3] whom Herbert regarded as his spiritual director and to whom he dedicates his work, had given him the choice between entering the Order or teaching or writing. He decided on the third alternative. Herbert, therefore, was still a secular clerk or priest. He had spent most of his life at court, first in the service of Becket and then with some other prince or prelate. He finally retired to a monastery to live there as a boarder. 'The burden of the monastic life,' he felt, was beyond his endurance.

---

[1] This section summarizes my paper 'A commentary on the *Hebraica* by Herbert of Bosham', *Rech. Théol. anc. méd.* xviii (1951), 29-65. The Latin text of all my quotations will be found there, also a transcript of the dedicatory letter.

[2] See above, p. 64.

[3] J. Lestocquoy, *Les évêques d'Arras* (Arras, 1942), 13.

To put him under the wing of a Victorine means enlarging an already swollen chapter; but it is where he belongs. Herbert was almost certainly a pupil of Andrew. One cannot establish the relationship by the usual method of comparing texts, since Andrew left no written exposition of the Psalter for Herbert to quote from. However, Herbert has done his best to help, by making Andrew's general prologue to the Prophets the basis of his dedicatory letter to Peter of Arras. He quotes whole phrases from Andrew, in such a way as to suggest that he had the text before him or that he had made it his own by constant meditation. Further, he says that he has been studying the literal sense of the Psalter from his early youth and is writing down what he has learnt from 'masters of the Hebrews, Greeks and Latins'. The Latin masters are referred to as 'blessed ones'. Elsewhere Herbert calls Peter Lombard his 'chief teacher' of Scripture, thus implying that he had others besides Peter. On the face of things, Herbert could hardly have derived his interest in biblical scholarship from a master who was mainly a theologian and compiler of glosses.

His attitude to his text and to his authorities recalls Andrew's. He has the same feeling of adventure. Andrew was the first after Jerome to expound the literal sense of the Prophets; Herbert claims to be the first to expound the *Hebraica*. Both revere Jerome as their predecessor. To Herbert he is 'that modern pupil of the Synagogue, the base of all learning, Father Jerome'. Both men think of the Hebrew text and Jewish tradition and custom as their prime sources of knowledge. Although Herbert shows more interest in Greek than Andrew had done, both here and in his prefaces to the *Magna Glosatura*, his Greek teachers had not gone very far in their instruction; the emphasis is all on Hebrew. There is a close parallel in their conception of the literal sense of Scripture. Herbert accepted the spiritual exposition as unreservedly as Andrew. Hence one finds the same ambivalence in their approach to the letter. It is even more marked in Herbert. Whereas Andrew gives no special reason for concentrating on the literal sense, apart from a rather vague modesty, and leaves one to assume a scholarly inclination towards it, Herbert definitely puts forward his own unworthiness. He is not good enough to explain the mystical sense. In his dedicatory letter he uses the very metaphor of cleaving to the earth that occurred to one in speaking of Andrew:

o

'I am not striving after an understanding of the difficult spiritual senses, but with the animals that walk the earth, I cleave to earth, attending only to the lowest sense of the letter of the Psalter.'[1]

He regards the literal sense as compatible with moral instruction, but at the lowest level. This appears from the two places where he departs from a strictly grammatical and historical exegesis. Once it is to reprove persons who go to sermons for sheer pleasure in rhetoric; the other time he recommends a verse promising mercy as a comfort to the relapsed sinner. Both pieces are certainly addressed to beginners rather than to the advanced or proficient in the spiritual life. The second in particular has a personal ring, as though Herbert were speaking for himself as much as for others:

The words of this verse should be carefully heeded and memorized. If, when tempted, you have been in the habit of falling often into some great sin, resort, soon afterwards, to this verse and to the medicine of prayer which is taught therein. Know for sure that you will gain mercy before the hour of death and will be freed from bondage to that gulf of sin into which you fall so incessantly and on whose account you beseech and offer incessant prayers to the Lord. And if it should be delayed, do not mistrust him. Help will not be withheld, so efficacious is your constant prayer and so ready his mercy, as is taught in this verse.

There seems to be a real connection in Herbert's thought between his inaptitude, several times repeated, to understand the 'higher' senses of Scripture and the secular life he has been leading. One remembers the pen picture of him by his contemporary and colleague, William Fitz Stephen. The clerk is interviewing and defying King Henry II on behalf of his patron, the archbishop. Master Herbert of Bosham, tall and handsome in appearance, splendidly dressed in a mantle of green cloth of Auxerre, hanging down to his heels in the German fashion, answered the king with such spirit that one of the barons present said he would give half his land to have such a son as Herbert. The qualities that a baron would have wished to see in his son were hardly those of a clergyman. Hence Herbert, when he undertakes to

---

[1] '... non ad arduam spiritualem sensuum intelligentiam nitor, sed velud cum animalibus gressibilibus super terram, terre hereo, solum littere psalmorum sensum infimum prosequens' (fo. 1).

expound the letter of the Psalter, is showing, on an academic plane, the humility of the classic convert from worldliness; he performs the menial tasks of the community.

Yet Herbert flings himself into doing his 'chores' with a joy not usually evoked by the mere exercise of humility of heart. Practice belies theory. He loves the work for its own sake, just as Andrew had done. Nor does humility characterize his treatment of his authorities. He criticizes as ruthlessly as Andrew any opinion which clashes with the sense of the Hebrew text. On the other hand, he follows Andrew in criticizing also any Jewish legend for which he can find no scriptural warrant.

All these reasons justify the conclusion that Herbert was Andrew's pupil. Andrew may have been one of those 'blessed ones' who instructed him from his early youth. Chronologically his studies under Peter Lombard must have coincided with Andrew's stay at St. Victor: it is improbable that they never met, considering the smallness of the scholars' world at Paris. If they did not, then Andrew must have been his master in the wider sense that Herbert had read and pondered over Andrew's writings. Herbert's interest in biblical studies was of long standing when he expounded the *Hebraica*. A closer examination of his edition of the *Magna Glosatura* and of his published letters has shown that the interest went back at least to Becket's exile, 1164-70. Herbert spent this period in France. The Becket circle had close contacts with St. Victor. The Victorine chronicle records that Becket preached a sermon there in September, 1169.[1] By that time Andrew had returned to Wigmore; but Herbert could have heard talk of him and could have read his commentaries. The prologue to the Prophets, which underlies Herbert's dedicatory letter to Peter of Arras, is one of the least known of Andrew's writings. Herbert's use of it points to a familiarity with the whole *corpus*.

Herbert offers an example of Andrew's influence of a new and unlooked for type. He does not merely quote or read the master. He follows the master's example in undertaking independent work on the same lines. And he surpasses the master in scholarship, just as a good pupil should. Here we come to my second difficulty about Herbert. He is a little overwhelming. He explodes the conception that I had formed of a gentle progression in knowledge of Hebrew and

[1] J. C. Dickinson, op. cit. (p. 112, n. 2), 285.

rabbinics from Andrew and his predecessors down to Nicholas of Lyre. Mr. Raphael Loewe has made a study of Herbert's linguistic skill and Jewish sources, illustrated by an edition of his preface to the Psalter and exposition of two psalms. The study is being completed as I write;[1] but I may quote Mr. Loewe's conclusion:

> 'Herbert emerges as apparently capable of reading at least some rabbinic texts, possibly including Aramaic, on his own.
>
> 'My present impression is that in Herbert we have the most competent Hebraist whom the Western Church produced between Jerome himself and Pico della Mirandola and Reuchlin in the late fifteenth century, with the possible exception of Raymund Martini in the thirteenth century. Excluding, that is, Jewish converts to Christianity. . . .'

Herbert cannot possibly belong to the last category. His father was a priest (who took orders as a widower, he tells us) and all the evidence, both positive and negative, points to his being an Englishman, a native of Sussex.

The argument is too technical to be even summarized here; but one point leaps to the eye of anyone who turns the pages of the St. Paul's manuscript. We have seen that Nicholas Manjacoria and all three Victorines refer to their Hebrew sources anonymously. Nicholas of Lyre is supposed to have been the first Latin scholar to quote 'Rabbi Salomon' by name. In the first edition of my book I wrote at a venture: 'It would not be at all surprising to find references to "Rabbi Salomon" in some of the unexplored glosses of the late thirteenth century.' I was a century wrong. Herbert quotes a 'litterator hebreus', who is generally Rashi. A marginal note in the same hand as the text has, against two passages where Rashi is quoted: 'Salomon'. Against a third passage we have the name of the source quoted by Rashi: 'Dones filius Leward', meaning Dunash ibn Labrat; the 'w' is probably a corruption for 'bb'. The commentary shows that Herbert could distinguish and contrast Rashi, his modern Jewish source, and 'the ancient masters of the Synagogue'. He does not make Andrew's mistake of lumping them all together as 'the Jews'.

If Andrew used a Hebrew lexicon he does not say so. Herbert mentions one in giving the source for his comment on the last words of Ps. lxxxvi:

---

[1] It is to be published in *Biblica*, 1953.

'This is taken from a certain book of the Jews which they call *Maberez*, which means "addition", because it distinguishes the various significations of words, adding signification to signification.'

The 'Mahbereth' was a lexicon written in Hebrew by Menahem ibn Saruk in the tenth century and was one of the chief aids to study of contemporary Jewish scholars. Herbert's derivation of the name from 'addition' is described as 'quite legitimate' on linguistic grounds. He quotes it independently of Rashi. The consultation of a book written in Hebrew and intended for Jews would alone lift him out of the rank of mere beginner. He may also have made first-hand use of the *Targum*, 'an official translation, sometimes paraphrastic, of the Hagiographa, into Aramaic, traditionally ascribed to "Jonathan".' Herbert had acquired a considerable knowledge of and sensitivity to Hebrew grammar. His comments are dotted with transliterated Hebrew words. He does not use Hebrew letters; at least there are none in the St. Paul's copy. But then he was writing for readers and scribes who would not have understood them.

Material from Rashi's commentary appears on almost every page. In one place Herbert alters his text of the *Hebraica* in the light of Jewish exegesis. The parallels with Rashi are so close as to suggest he read him for himself. He claims in one passage to be giving the actual words of his *litterator*. The Jewish material which does not derive from Rashi is mainly traditional and may perhaps be explained by his having a fuller text than the present version of Rashi gives. No parallels have been found with Rashbam or Joseph Bekhor Shor; but there is evidence that he had some knowledge of the literature of Jewish Spain, possibly through an Arab-speaking informant. He had also seen a Jewish prayer-book or had questioned his teachers about their festivals.[1]

The Psalms presented as grave a problem as the prophecies to the commentator as who bold enough to determine their literal meaning. Herbert did not usually shirk difficulties. He liked to speculate. Discussing the text Ps. lxv. 18: *If I have looked at iniquity in my heart, the Lord will not hear me,* he raises the question of 'matter for confession'. The doctrine of penance was only just taking shape at this period; but confession of all mortal sins to a priest was coming to be

[1] These two paragraphs are taken from Mr. Loewe's forthcoming paper.

regarded as obligatory on the penitent.[1] Herbert thinks, on the contrary, supporting his view from the text, that sins of thought, as distinct from sins of deed, need not be confessed except to God. His *Life* of Becket describes the writer, when in the archbishop's household, indulging in obviously dangerous thoughts. He was wondering whether, if the Christian faith were unfounded, in that the Messias had not come, but must still be awaited, as the Jews say, God would impute a faith in Christ to righteousness. He decided that faith, even though not historically founded, was in itself a merit, and that the Christian sacrifice of the Mass, even if not miraculous, was at least purer and more natural (*sincerior*) than the bloody sacrifices of the Synagogue, which had spared neither the chaste turtle nor the innocent dove. He then had a dream, which Becket interpreted as referring to 'restless imaginings'. Herbert succeeded in putting them out of his mind.[2] Clearly his attack on the literal sense of the Davidic prophecies is going to be interesting.

Herbert has taken the problem a stage further than Andrew. Perhaps he has digested the lesson of the *De Emmanuele*. He brings forward the traditional, christological interpretation of each psalm, calling it *expositio ecclesiastica*. The expression probably means the *Magna glosatura* and it is also probable that he intended to compose a kind of 'literal' supplement to it. So he has committed himself to choosing. He will have to decide which of the psalms are messianic in their literal sense. Or one would think so: it is not always quite so simple. He may give first the Christian, then the Jewish interpretation, without deciding: 'But I shall not omit what the *litterator* thinks of this.' He may opt for the Christian and then proceed to set forth the Jewish on the pretext of showing how wrong it is. He may even, as on Ps. liv, contradict himself, saying first that according to the ecclesiastical exposition the psalm is a prophecy of the Passion and Resurrection; secondly that according to the literal sense it is a prayer of David against Achitophel and Doeg; thirdly, that 'whatever the *litterator* may pretend, the psalm manifestly prophesies our king and Messias and his betrayal by Judas'. In this case he is using 'the literal sense'

---

[1] See P. Anciaux, *La Théologie du Sacrement de Pénitence au XIIe siècle* (Louvain, 1949).
[2] *Materials for the History of Archbishop Becket* (ed. J. Robertson, Rolls Series), iii. 213-15.

ambiguously, contrasting it with what he takes to be the true sense. He cannot quite free himself from an inheritance of confused terminology. A coincidence between the Jewish and Christian interpretation always pleases him.

However, on certain texts he takes a stand against the Jews. His chief argument is the divergence between the traditional and the modern exegesis. The traditional Jewish interpretation had been messianic. Rashi often avoids the messianic interpretation and prefers to expound the text of David, 'in answer to the heretics, who err on this psalm', as he says explicitly in one passage. Herbert accuses him of changing his exegesis out of hatred of the Christians. In a lively piece of historical reconstruction, he argues that the Jewish people contemporary with Christ must have been accustomed to hear the psalms interpreted as messianic prophecies; otherwise, the Apostles would never have gained a hearing when they applied these prophecies to Christ in their preaching. Apart from the general principle, Herbert may engage in polemic on the grounds that the Christian interpretation agrees better with the context. Analysis of his commentary on the first twenty-five psalms (numbered according to the *Hebraica* version) shows that Herbert accepted the christological interpretation for ten of them, either in whole or in part: they are Ps. i-iv, vii-viii, xii-xiii, xvi, xxii. On Ps. ix and xxiv he is uncertain. The remainder he explains entirely in an Old Testament background. This represents a notable advance towards clarity.

Unfortunately, Herbert shares Andrew's indifference to method. He does not tell us what principle he follows in distinguishing between a messianic psalm and a psalm referring to David or Solomon. But he seems to be fumbling towards the Antiochene position that a quotation by a New Testament writer does not necessarily constitute proof of its being originally intended as a messianic prophecy. Ps. lxvii. 19: *Thou hast ascended on high; thou hast led captivity captive; thou hast received gifts in men,* is quoted in Eph. iv. 8 as: *Ascending on high, he led captivity captive: he gave gifts to men.* Herbert inclines to think that the psalmist is referring to Moses rather than to Christ, in spite of St. Paul's use of the passage. 'The Master', as he always calls St. Paul, has changed the words of the Hebrew, putting *gave* for *received,* by his apostolic authority, in order to prove his point. Herbert covers himself by a saving clause and by protesting that he is only repeating what he has learnt of the literal sense or what God has shown to him. His protests only underline his uneasiness at what is in fact a daring argument:

> 'According to the *litterator* the psalm speaks to Moses, as before it spoke to God concerning Moses, of whom it is plainly told that he ascended the mount to God, as it is written: "And Moses went up to God." What the psalm says next: *thou hast led captivity captive; thou hast received gifts etc*, is also to be understood of Moses, not that this was his own doing, but that God acted through him, as has been explained above.

> 'But it should by no means be passed over that this verse of the psalm is referred by Churchmen to the ascension of our king and Messias. Hence the Master adduces it thus: "Wherefore he saith: *Ascending on high, he led captivity captive: he gave gifts to men*." But the Master changes the words of the Hebrew, to prove what he intends, by apostolic authority, as aforesaid, especially in that he says *gave*, when according to the Hebrew truth *received* should be read, unless, as has been shown above, the import of either word may be the same.

> 'Let the Church's interpretation be preserved, here as elsewhere. What we have received from Jewish scholars and from others, blessed ones, and what the Lord has revealed to me from time to time, as I sit, concerning the literal sense of the Psalter, that I impart to others, without prejudice to the interpretation of the Church.'

Here, perhaps, we hear an echo of Andrew's oral teaching, invoked by Herbert in self protection at a critical point in his commentary. If so, it is precious as our only clue to Andrew's views on the New Testament. We see him comparing the Pauline Epistles with *Hebraica veritas*.

We shall end with a comment on Ps. xviii. 6, which owes nothing to the Jews, because it has a literary flavour recalling the Victorines. This will be our last sample of attempted fine writing. From now onward we shall hear nothing but colloquial Latin and the jargon of the classroom. The comment also points forward to the reception of the *Libri naturales*. We know from another of his works that Herbert had studied some of the new Aristotle. Here he brings old and new stuff together. While appreciating the poetry of the psalm, and noticing the Hebrew idiom, he says that David is speaking more as a natural philosopher than as a poet. The text is describing the course of the sun through the heavens: He *hath rejoiced as a giant to run the way. His going out is from the end of heaven, And his circuit even to the end thereof: and there is no one that can hide himself from his heat.*

'This is in the daily rising of the sun, when every morning renewed to us from heaven he comes forth clear and ruddy, and then runs nimbly and swiftly from east to west along paths well known to him; hence he *hath rejoiced etc.* Here we have a figure of speech customary among the Jews, in which the properties of animate things are ascribed to inanimate, as: "Hear, O ye heavens, and give ear, O earth," and: "I call this day heaven and earth to witness," "The ways of Sion mourn", and many expressions of the sort.

'He continues about the course of the sun, adding: *His going out is from the end of heaven etc*, as much as to say: if the sun did not run in the heights of the heavens, he would burn all men, and no one could hide himself from his heat. Or it may be read plainly and without implication, thus: *there is no one etc*: here he points out that all things are quickened by the sun's heat; and David here is rather a philosopher than a psalmist.'

And lastly a confession of ignorance about the fate of Herbert's commentary. I do not know whether it was quoted and studied. The evidence so far is all negative. Only the one copy seems to have survived. If there are any others they must be in uncatalogued collections; the dedicatory letter announces the authorship in the second line of the text so that even the least efficient cataloguer could hardly miss it. True, prologues were often omitted; but this would happen as a result of frequent copying. No quotations of Herbert by name have come to light, though it will be necessary to search for unacknowledged borrowing.

It would be tragic that so much learning should have been wasted. Andrew's public would have valued Herbert. We have seen that Andrew became more popular as the thirteenth century advanced. But this was only possible because he had been a well-known teacher, working at an established centre, where his commentaries would be preserved, perhaps catalogued, available to students and copyists when required. Herbert had no institution to back him and consequently no publicity. He was working in isolation in a Cistercian abbey. The very qualities that make him so engaging, his refusal to be pigeon-holed, his independence and many-sidedness, must have prejudiced his chances of ever becoming a classic. We must leave him in his backwater and return to the Paris schools.

CHAPTER V

MASTERS OF THE SACRED PAGE:
THE COMESTOR, THE CHANTER, STEPHEN LANGTON

I. LECTIO, DISPUTATIO, PRAEDICATIO

THE Victorines did not alter the monastic conception of *lectio divina*; they restated it, and in doing so they shifted the emphasis. The 'building' of exegesis had been growing top-heavy. Monks had concentrated on the 'upper story' and its 'painting'; scholars on theological questions. The Victorines saved the whole structure by strengthening its basis. Conservative, they went behind St. Gregory and Cassian to the historical tradition of St. Augustine and the learned tradition of St. Jerome. Belonging to their century, they had a strong sacramental sense, which gave them a new devotion to the 'letter' of Scripture. They still thought in metaphors which subordinated the literal sense to the spiritual; but they conceived it as something essentially laborious and creative; it was 'digging the foundation', not 'stripping off the veil' or 'breaking down the prison'. Andrew realized what a delightful occupation digging could be.

The Victorine programme, which Hugh set forth in his *Didascalicon*, and which Andrew and Richard tried to realize in their teaching, made *lectio divina* acceptable to the Paris scholar. The Victorines, being both *claustrales* and *scholares*, were able to transmit the old religious exercise from the cloister to the school. They managed to secure for biblical scholarship a share, even if it were a minor share, in the inquisitive energy which abounded at Paris. This is the subject of the present chapter. We have to follow the Victorine tradition in the hands of the Paris masters, to see how *lectio divina* changes into the academic lecture course.

The masters who made themselves responsible for continuing the Victorine tradition are the trio we met in the last chapter: Peter Comestor, Peter the Chanter, Stephen Langton. Mgr. Grabmann has grouped them together as the 'biblical moral school';[1] they have a common interest in biblical studies and in practical moral questions, which distinguishes them from those who were primarily theologians and dialecticians: Peter Lombard, Peter of Poitiers, Adam of the Petit Pont.

The word 'school' brings us on to dangerous ground. Our three masters represent three overlapping generations: the Comestor died about 1169, the Chanter in 1197; Langton, who died in 1228, became a cardinal and left the schools for good in 1206. It would be pleasant to arrange them neatly in order as masters and pupils; but this is not possible. On the latest evidence it seems that Langton may have heard the Comestor, but not the Chanter.[2] The Comestor himself seems to have been a pupil of Peter Lombard.[3] The Chanter's academic formation is unknown. If, on the other hand, we take 'school' to mean merely a common interest, we are confronted with the difficult border-line case of Peter of Poitiers. He was a pupil of the Lombard, a very subtle dialectician, and yet he made highly important additions to the *Historia Scholastica*. We need a critical edition of the *Historia Scholastica*, a thorough examination of the Comestor's Gospel glosses, and, even more urgently, a study of the central figure, Peter the Chanter, before we can say anything definite about their personal relations to one another, or to other teachers.

The solid reality behind the term 'biblical moral school' seems to me to be this: whereas other Paris masters left glosses on the Psalms and the Pauline Epistles, these three made original contributions to the study of Scripture as a whole, the Comestor in his *Histories* and Gospel glosses, the Chanter and Langton in a vast series of glosses, covering the Old and New Testaments.[4] Perhaps the work of other

[1] *Die Gesch. der scholastischen Methode*, ii (Freiburg i. Br., 1911), 467 ff.

[2] 'Studies on the Commentaries', 8.

[3] R. M. Martin, 'Pierre le Mangeur *De Sacramentis*', in *Spic. Sac. Lov.* xvii (1937), xxv-xxvi.*

[4] No comprehensive study of the manuscripts of the Comestor's and the Chanter's glosses exists. F. S. Gutjahr, *Petrus Cantor, sein Leben und seine Schriften* (Graz, 1899), 54, gives a list of the *initia* of the Chanter's glosses without referring to manuscripts. I have therefore used manuscripts of the Comestor and the Chanter noted by B. Hauréau in his *Notices et extraits de quelques mss. de la Bibliothèque Nationale* (Paris, 1890-3), i-vi *passim*.

The Langton manuscripts have been listed in 'Studies on the Commentaries'. I have made most use of MSS. Peterhouse Cambridge 112, containing Langton on the Octateuch and historical books of the Old Testament, and Trinity College Cambridge B. II. 26 containing Langton on the Twelve Prophets, which will be referred to as P. and T.; the librarians of these two colleges kindly

masters in this field remains to be discovered; at least these three were the most widely read and copied. And their inspiration came from the same source, St. Victor. It is often said that the *Historia Scholastica* of Peter Comestor fulfils an express wish of the *Didascalicon* and shows Victorine influence. This also applies to the less well-known glosses of Peter the Chanter and Langton. Langton actually glossed the Bible according to the order of books which Hugh had recommended to students. Hugh taught that the student should begin by acquiring an historical background; fairly early in his teaching career Langton glossed the *Historia Scholastica*. Hugh advised students to read the Gospels and Epistles, where the faith was revealed plainly, in order to learn the allegorical exposition; then they would know how to discern the figures of the Old Testament; Langton glossed the Gospels before he glossed the historical books of the Old Testament and the Prophets. He also extended Hugh's teaching on the order of books to be read by the student of allegory to tropology; he says that the moral teaching of the books of Solomon is plain and easily grasped, but that the Prophets require multiple exposition before they will yield it;[1] accordingly Langton glossed the Canticle, the Psalter, Wisdom, Ecclesiasticus, probably Proverbs and Ecclesiastes, before he glossed the Prophets. It looks like a carefully thought-out programme, based on a study of the *Didascalicon*. Langton first prepares himself by lecturing on the *Historia Scholastica*, the Gospels, the sapiential books; then he is ready to undertake the literal and spiritual exposition of the historical books; then he glosses the Epistles, and lastly, again in a literal and spiritual sense, the Prophets.[2] It is

---

[1] T. fo. 192b (on Zach. ix. 17): '*Frumentum* antequam ex eo panis fiat, teritur per quod sacre scripture difficultas significatur, cuiusmodi est in prophetis quos multiplici expositione frangi opportet antequam panis tropologie inde conficitur. Unde huiusmodi *frumentum electorum* dicitur esse, quia paucissimi sunt et electi qui per intelligentiam huius frumenti pane vescantur. *Et vinum*; quod delectabiliter bibitur et facile, unde significat sacram scripturam ubi facilis est, scil. ubi tropologia facile legentibus se offert, ut in libris Salomonis.'

[2] See above, pp. 87-9. Langton knew the *Didascalicon*. He quotes Hugh of St. Victor on Osee ii. 16 (which seems to derive from the *Didascalicon*, v. iii),

---

allowed me the use of P. and T. while I was collecting material for my doctoral thesis on Langton's glosses. In choosing copies of the works of all three scholars, as with Andrew of St. Victor, one has to be guided chiefly by convenience; it is not yet possible to pick out the better texts.

For Langton's life and writings see F. M. Powicke, 'Bibliographical Note on Recent Work upon Stephen Langton', *English Historical Review*, xlviii (1933), 554-7.

possible, of course, that this order had already been worked out by Peter the Chanter. His gloss on Judges certainly refers back to his gloss on the Psalter.[1]

Then we have the interest in practical moral problems, and the practical moral purpose, which manifests itself not only in their strictly theological works, but in their use of the spiritual interpretation for the *lectio*. The glosses of the Chanter and Langton bear more resemblance to the works of Hugh and Richard, so it seems to me, than the glosses of other twelfth-century masters do.

Not only the rules and the inspiration, but much of the material comes from St. Victor. All three of our masters quote from Andrew on the Heptateuch. He is at the core of their literal exposition. Moreover the Chanter also uses the *Histories*; Langton uses both the *Histories* and the Chanter's glosses.[2] In content, at least, the three are linked both to Andrew and to one another.

Lastly one cannot help remarking on their likeness in character. Langton has a quality of greatness which is lacking in the others; but all three are sensible, practical, with a strong sense of humour. The mere fact that one is able to speak of their 'characters' in itself differentiates them from most of the Paris masters, who are much more elusive.

[1] MS. Balliol 23, fo. 140[b] (on Iud. xiii. 18): '*Cur quaeris nomen meum, quod est mirabile?*; . . . solet queri super Psalmos quare ineffabile dicatur nomen tetragramaton cuius IV littere interpretantur principium vite passionis iste, i.e. hic quem representat legalis sacerdos habens laminam auream in fronte in qua scribitur nomen tetragramaton est principium vite adquisite morte passionis. Solutio est in glosis Psalterii.'

[2] He quotes the Chanter by name in his gloss on Ecclus. vii. 20: '*Noli praevaricari in amicum pecuniam differentem.*' His text differs from the Vulgate; he has *pro pecunia differenti.* MS. Balliol 20, fo. 9[b]: 'Cantor sic exponit: *pro pecunia differenti* i.e. *pro pecunia* que facit magnam differentiam inter personas scil. pauperis et divitis . . . nos autem sic exponimus . . .' See the Chanter's gloss, MS. Bibl. Nat. Lat. 15565, fo. 101[a]: '. . . faciente differentiam inter pauperem et divitem etiam in amicitia.' Probably Langton quotes the Chanter by name in this passage because he differs from him. In his gloss in Isaias he refers several times to *magistri*, and in one case he seems to be quoting from the Chanter: MS. Bibl. Nat. Lat. 14417, fo. 185[b] (on Isa. ix. 1: *Galilaeae gentium*): i.e. *Galilee* populose. 'Sic magistri exponunt, ut dicatur Galilea *gentium* pro numerositate habitatorum.' See the Chanter MS. Maz. 178, fo. 60[d]: 'populose *Galilee* que propter numerositatem habitantium dicitur *gentium*.' Normally Langton does not refer to the Chanter at all but simply reproduces him: for an example of this, see p. 236, n. 4.

as though he were quoting from memory in his own words: T. fo. 14[c]: 'Dicit magister Hugo sancti Victoris: Tanta est sublimitas sacre pagine super alias disciplinas quod significata aliarum sunt significantia in theologia. Illa enim que sunt res nominum et verborum in aliis facultatibus sunt nomina in theologia.'

The personal note in Langton's glosses and *Quaestiones* has impressed modern scholars. One finds something very similar in the works of the Comestor and the Chanter. Only Langton would think of explaining the text: *Fornication, wine and drunkenness take away the heart* [Osee iv. 11] by a snatch of song, where the world complains that love has stolen her heart:

> Unde et mundus in cantilena vulgari:
> Domine Deus! quis meum cor furatus est?[1]

Only the Comestor would compare the silence of the Church during the reading of the Gospel, where promises are fulfilled, to the silence of children clutching their promised apples.[2] The Chanter's glosses are often as amusing as his better known *Verbum Abbreviatum*. It may be that their interest in concrete things, in history, the liturgy, their fellow creatures, makes them more living to us than those whose preoccupations were mainly abstract. However we may explain it, they have in common a humanism that recalls the Victorines.

It is a humanism of thought, not of style. We have lost that sense of leisure which pleases us in the Victorine writings. The works of the Paris masters are meant not for quiet study in the cloister, but to prepare students for the examination which begins to loom on their horizon like a Judgement Day. On the one hand we have business-like text-books and aids to study; the *Historia Scholastica* takes its place as a 'set book' beside the *Gloss* and the *Sentences*; the Chanter published a Gospel harmony, the *Unum ex Quattuor*; a list of spiritual interpretations, the *Summa Abel*; and the *De Difficultatibus Sacre Scripture*, or *De Tropis Loquendi*, a technical study dealing mainly with language and grammar, for instance the various uses of the conjunctive *et*. On the other hand we have their glosses, which have come down to us in the most unliterary form conceivable, their students' lecture notes. We must say something of this *reportatio* system, since we depend on it entirely for our knowledge of their exegesis.

The medieval *reportatio* is distinct from the ancient stenography and shorthand which was used in the dictation of many patristic works. This method is said to have lapsed by the eleventh century when the Latin, on which the abbrevia-

---

[1] T. fo. 23ª.   [2] See below, p. 240.

tions were based, had ceased to be spoken outside learned circles.[1] It is also distinct from the practice of taking notes at lectures, which must be almost as old as the lecture itself. St. Gregory's *Moralia* were partly taken down from his lectures, partly dictated, when he had more time at his disposal. He was careful to revise the former portions so that the style should be uniform[2]. His pupil, Claudius, undertook the task of writing up his notes of some other homilies during Gregory's illness. He called his first edition of St. Gregory on the Canticles: *Expositio in Canticis Canticorum a capité de exceda relevata Domni Gregorii Papae Urbis Romae*, which has been translated 'commentaire complètement rétabli d'après les notes', the *scheda* being the leaf on which the notes were written. He, too, was careful to reproduce his master's literary style.[3] This system proved to be unsatisfactory, since too much scope was given to the pupil; St. Gregory recalled these particular homilies from circulation as doctrinally incorrect. Angelom of Luxueil in the mid-ninth century seems to be doing much the same as Claudius, but under proper supervision. He tells us that his commentary on Genesis began from his notes of his master's teaching, which his master helped him to expand and afterwards approved.[4]

Whether the commentary is dictated to a stenographer or written up from lecture notes, in each case the finished work is a literary production. The *reportatio* on the contrary has no pretensions to be literature. It is a product of the classroom, arising directly from the needs of the student, and is a cross between the two earlier methods, dictation and writing up notes. The 'reporter' is not a professional stenographer but a pupil, who instead of merely taking notes, tries to get down a full, consecutive account of the lecture. His report will be copied without re-composition, though it may need correction and the filling in of references.

We do not know whether reporting began, or was continued, at the school of Laon. We only hear that Master Anselm's disciples 'collected sentences' from his oral teaching,[5] which suggests something haphazard and unstereo-

---

[1] L. P. Guénin, *Histoire de la sténographie dans l'antiquité et au moyen âge* (Paris, 1908).
[2] *P.L.* lxxv. 512-13.
[3] Ibid. lxxvii. 1234. See B. Capelle, 'Les Homélies de St Grégoire sur le Cantique', *Rev. Bén.* xli (1929), 204-17.
[4] *P.L.* cxv. 108-10.   [5] See above, p. 67.

typed. Abailard tells us that those who had not at first attended his unauthorized lectures on Ezechiel began to come, and transcribed the glosses for the part of the course they had missed.[1] It is not clear whether they copied the master's own notes or *reportationes*. On the other hand, Dom Leclercq has pointed to what may well be two *reportationes* of the commentary on the Canticle ascribed to Anselm; these would put the *reportatio* system back into the heyday of his teaching.[2] Still, it may have been unusual and peculiar to Laon. Our first detailed description of a *reportatio* comes from St. Victor; and one's impression is that Hugh's pupils thought they were inventing a new and time-saving device. A student called Laurence published a treatise which seems to be an earlier version of Hugh's *De Sacramentis*, with a prefatory letter to his friend Maurice, explaining how his companions asked him to 'commend' Hugh's teaching 'to writing and memory, for the common use of myself and others'; once a week he brought his tablets for correction to Master Hugh. Laurence does not profess to be the 'author' of the work; but in some sense he has 'contrived' it.[3]

Then we find the *reportatio* as an established university practice as it remains in some places today: 'the lectures or their *reportationes* for which the master's clerk or later his bachelor may have been especially responsible, were copied and distributed'.[4] University statutes oblige the master to correct the report personally before it is published.[5] We still know only the outlines of the process; was there a

[1] *Hist. Calam.* iii, *P.L.* clxxviii, 125: '. . . ii qui non interfuerant coeperunt ad secundam et tertiam lectionem certatim accedere, et omnes pariter de transcribendis glossis, quas prima die incoeperam, in ipso eorum initio plurimum solliciti esse.'

[2] 'Le commentaire du Cantique etc', *Rech. Théol. anc. méd.* xvi (1949), 39.

[3] Ed. B. Bischoff, op. cit. (p. 58, n. 5), 250: '. . . rogatus sum a plerisque sociorum . . . quatenus ad communem tam mei quam aliorum utilitatem easdem sententias scripto et memorie commendarem . . . Semel in septimana ad magistrum Hugonem tabellas reportabam . . . Non enim me huius operis auctorem sed quodammodo artificem profiteor.' On the identity of Laurence and Maurice, see F. E. Croydon, 'Abbot Laurence of Westminster and Hugh of St. Victor', *Mediaeval and Renaissance Studies*, ii (1950), 169-71.

[4] Rashdall's *Medieval Universities*, ed. Powicke and Emden, i (Oxford, 1936), 490. A. G. Little and F. Pelster, *Oxford Theology and Theologians* (Oxford, 1934), *passim*.

[5] See the most recent discussion of reports in the law schools by H. Kantorowicz, 'The *Quaestiones Disputatae* of the Glossators', *Revue d'Histoire du Droit*, xvi (1939), 32-51. He gives a bibliography of the literature on both legal and theological reports. R. W. Hunt gives some interesting specimens of reporting in the arts course, 'Studies on Priscian in the Twelfth Century II', *Mediaeval and Renaissance Studies*, ii (1950), 3-6.

system of shorthand, which enabled the reporter to take down the whole lecture, or did he or the master fill in the quotations later from references? It is difficult to explain the relative accuracy of quotations from Andrew, for instance, by the Chanter and Langton. It has been suggested that the blank spaces in another twelfth-century gloss represent gaps in the report; the hurried reporter had intended to fill in his omissions afterwards and never did.[1] A copy of the report of a thirteenth-century Oxford *quaestio disputata* regularly leaves a blank for the references to the works of Aristotle which are quoted. Probably when the fair copy of the report was made the scribe had instructions to omit the references until they had been verified.[2] A thirteenth-century copy of a commentary on St. Matthew which belonged to the Dominicans of Bâle (now MS. B.III.18 of Bâle University Library) originated in a report so defective that the leaves look like pieces of cloth full of moth holes. Here not only the references, but much of the comment has had to be omitted.

From its very nature the report can have no pretensions to literary quality. One distinguishes it by its ragged, colloquial style and by its allusions to the master in the third person. Sometimes, too, the reporter intrudes himself, to comment, disagree, or complain (but this is in the law schools) that the rowdiness of his fellow students prevents him from reporting properly. Reporting was skilled work. We know that St. Thomas Aquinas found it hard to replace Friar Reginald of Piperno, who was a particularly reliable reporter, when his services were no longer available. It has been suggested that the regular alternation between personal redactions and *reportationes* in St. Thomas's lectures on Scripture was due to the need to economize his reporters' strength.[3]

The other students did not always rely on their one official reporter, but sometimes took notes themselves. We get a hint of a number of private *reportationes* of the same lecture course in a request of some students to the Oxford friar, Richard of Cornwall; they beg that: 'the writings, which in the zealous charge of brother Richard they have taken down from him with their own hands, may be granted them sever-

---

[1] A. Landgraf, Écrits théologiques de l'école d'Abélard', op. cit. (p. 78, n. 4), xxxvi.

[2] In MS. Bâle B. VII. 9. I am very much obliged to Dr. Daniel Callus for showing me his photographs of this *reportatio*.

[3] P. Mandonnet, 'La Chronologie des écrits scripturaires de St Thomas d'Aquin', *Revue Thomiste*, N.S. xi (1928), 42.

P

ally for their own use, for the private as well as the greater common good'.[1]

Hence, in rare cases, the same work has come down to us in several *reportationes*. Alongside the official *reportatio*, corrected and approved by the master, we have a private one, with a smaller circulation, which may be characterized by the university authorities as defective or bad; this has happened to certain *Quaestiones* of Duns Scot.[2] There are also two distinct *reportationes* of the university sermons preached by St. Bonaventure at Paris between Easter and Whitsuntide in 1273. One of them is fuller and survives in more manuscripts than the other; this second, shorter *reportatio* ends with an interesting statement by the reporter telling us how he worked. He took down the sermons in his notebook, just as he could snatch them from the speaker's mouth. Two colleagues were taking notes with him, but theirs were so confused and illegible as to be useless to anyone but themselves. *His* exemplar was corrected, since it was legible, by some of the audience; St. Bonaventure himself and many others are indebted to him for the copies they took of it. Then, after many days, when his superior gave him time and opportunity, he revised his hasty notes, and tried to put them in order, calling memories of the speaker's voice and gestures to his aid. He added nothing to what St. Bonaventure had said, except to amplify his quotations from the logical works of Aristotle and references to other authorities.

It seems probable that this shorter *reportatio* was a private one, and that the two other reporters whom it mentions prepared the official version between them, perhaps consulting their colleague's notes.[3] If the two *reportationes* are

---

[1] *Adae de Marisco, Ep.* cxcii, ed. J. S. Brewer, *Mon. Franc.* (Rolls Series), i. 349: 'Plures, ut audio, reperientur opportuni ad nunc dictum fratris obsequium, si scripturae quas ex studiosa praefati fratris R. vigilantia manibus suis conscripserint, singulis suae concedantur in usus utilitatis privatae, tam ad communitatis profectum ampliorem.' A. G. Little kindly gave me this reference.

[2] A. Pelzer, 'Le premier livre de *reportata Parisiensia* de Duns Scotus', *Annales de l'Institut Supérieur de Philosophie*, v (Louvain, 1924), 454. I have taken Mgr. Pelzer's definition of a *reportatio* and applied it to the Langton glosses.

[3] 'S. Bonaventurae Collationes in Hexaëmeron,' ed. F. Delorme, *Bibliotheca Franciscana*, vii (Quaracchi, 1934), 275.

'Haec autem, quae de quatuor visionibus notavi, talia sunt qualia de ore loquentis rapere potui in quaternum. Alii quidam duo socii mecum notabant, sed eorum notulae prae nimia confusione et illegibilitate nulli fuerunt utiles nisi forte sibi. Correcto autem exemplari meo quod legi poterat ab auditorum aliquibus, ipse doctor operis de ipso meo exemplari et quamplures alii rescripserunt, qui pro eo mihi debent grates.

'Elapsis autem diebus multis, concedente mihi copiam temporis et libri

collated, allowing for the reporters' additions, they give exactly the impression that one would expect from two sets of notes of the same lecture; they express the same idea in different words, and that which is normally shorter will occasionally be fuller than the longer one. We have a parallel from the English common law, in the various reports of the same case in the earlier Year Books.[1]

Reportationes of the thirteenth century help us to identify those of the lesser known twelfth. The glosses of the Comestor and the Chanter that I have examined are easily recognizable as *reportationes*. They contain expressions such as *inquit*,[2] *dicit magister*,[3] *his addit magister*,[4] *magister his non acquiescit*,[5] where 'master' cannot refer to anyone but the lecturer. Sometimes he is referred to in the first person, and sometimes in the same sentence we have a combination of first and third: 'I don't remember, he says, to have read this anywhere but in the *Gloss* on this text.'[6]

So far, only one *reportatio* for each gloss by the Comestor and the Chanter is known, though a thorough search might produce others. It is different with Langton. When we began to sort out the vast collection of Langton manuscripts, we found that each gloss existed in two, or more often three versions.[7] These were so unlike one another that the most

[1] G. J. Turner, Introd. to *Year Book 4 Ed. II, Selden Soc.* xix (London, 1914), xvii.

[2] The Comestor, MS. Laud Misc. 291, fo. 3ᶜ. The Chanter, MS. Brussels 252, ff. 36ᵛ, 70ᵛ; MS. Bibl. Nat. Lat. 15565, ff. 126ᶜ, 107ᵃ.

[3] The Chanter, MS. Balliol 23, fo. 89ᵇ.   [4] ibid., fo. 139ᶜ.

[5] The Chanter, MS. Bibl. Nat. Lat. 15565, fo. 34ᵇ.

[6] Ibid., MS. Brussels 252, fo. 70ᵛ: 'quod non memini, inquit, me legisse nisi in glosis hic.' We find the same combination of first and third person in the report of the disputations of Simon of Tournai, who taught at Paris in the last third of the twelfth century: J. Warichez, op. cit. (p. 62, n. 2), xiii, xlvi. The reporters of the *lectiones* are naturally more self-effacing than the reporters of *disputationes*. They do not intrude themselves, or comment on the master's views.

[7] 'Studies on the Commentaries', 166-82. In this paper I was only able to classify the versions of Langton's glosses on the historical books of the Old Testament. My classification of his glosses on other books of the Old Testament, which has not been printed, shows that the same problem exists for them too.

---

reverendo patre fratre Ch[unrado], ministro Alamaniae Superioris, rursum respexi quae scripseram veloci manu et nisus sum recolligere ordinate, co-operante mihi memoriae quo loquentis vocem audieram auditu et visu quo recordabar gestuum loquentis.

'. . . Nec tamen apposui quidquam quod ipse non dixerat, nisi ubi distinctionem librorum Aristotelis logicalium amplius quam ipse dixerat, distinxi. Alia autem non apposui, nisi quod etiam loca auctoritatum aliquarum signavi.'

See Fr. Delorme's comments, x-xvi. The longer and probably official *reportatio* is published in *S. Bonaventurae Opera Omnia*, v (Quaracchi), 329-454.

careless copying could not explain their divergences. It was impossible that they could have come from one original. When we put the variant versions in parallel columns we found just the same relationship which has since been shown to exist between the two *reportationes* of St. Bonaventure. We found that each version made the same points, and contained the same quotations; but they used slightly different words; one would merely allude to a point which was developed in the others; a version which in most places was briefer, would be more expansive than the others in a few places. In fact, they produced the effect of three *reportationes* of the same lecture. It seemed that only by collating them could one get the gist of what the lecturer had originally said.

In each group, one version exists in a greater number of copies than the others. The most popular of Langton's glosses, on the Twelve Prophets, has three versions: A, B, C; we have found twenty-four copies of A, as against only six of B and three of C. Rubrics in manuscripts containing the A version prove that the gloss was originally read in the schools; we have 'Expositio Magistri Stephani de longa tona super XII Prophetas sicut ipse legit Parisius'; 'Glose Magistri Stephani . . . in scolis ab eo lecte'; 'Tropologia super Duodecim Prophetas collecta ad lectiones Magistri Stephani de Langeton'.[1] All three versions have the unfinished, informal wording of reports; and the C version contains a reference to the master in the third person, clearly meaning Langton.[2]

[1] MS. Troyes 1004, fo. 119ʳ; MS. Bibl. Nat. Lat. 505, fo. 1ʳ; MS. Oriel Coll. Oxford 53, fo. 88ʳ; T. fo. 1ʳ.

[2] It occurs in the commentary on Zach. xii. 2: '*Behold I will make Jerusalem a lintel of surfeiting to all the people round about: and Juda also shall be in the siege against Jerusalem.*' St. Jerome explains this passage as a threat to the enemies of the Church. They shall be surfeited with the divine wrath. '*Juda*' represents those Christians who turned against the Church during the time of her persecution. Langton adapts St. Jerome's allegory to his own day. By '*Juda*' he understands wicked clerks. The three versions run as follows:

A (T. fo. 197ᵇ): '*Ecce ego ponam Ierusalem* id est ecclesiam *superliminare crapule* active in tantum ut qui persecuntur illam inebrientur calice ire Dei. Unde dicitur in Trenis: "*Gaude et letare filia Edom . . .*" [Lament. iv. 20] quasi diceret: Inebriaberis calice pene gehennalis et nudaberis quia peccata tua humano generi detegentur. Et hoc fiet in *omnibus populis in circuitu,* qui ecclesiam circumeuntes hostiliter eam persecuntur. *Sed et Iuda* scil. clerici, erit *in obsidionem contra Ierusalem*; quod hodie fit manifeste quia clerici magis quam laici ecclesiam persecuntur. . . .'

B (Bibl. Nat. 17281, fo. 79ᵃ): '*Ecce ego ponam . . . crapule.* Qui tangunt Ierusalem inebriabuntur ira Domini in inferno. Unde Ieremias in Trenis: "*Letare filia Edom . . .*" *Sed et Iuda . . . Ierusalem.* Hoc potest dici de clericis qui opprimunt alios et iudicant contra ecclesiam. . . .'

C (Troyes 1004, fo. 209ᵃ; Durham A. i. 7, fo. 203ᵈ): '*Ecce ego ponam* etc. Magister [Durham has an ñ here, possibly for *noster*] istud intelligit

The A version seems to be the fullest and most carefully prepared of the three. The glosses on the Twelve Prophets are typical of the other groups.

The most natural explanation of these variations is that in each group of glosses the more widely diffused version originated in an official report, approved by Langton, while the versions which survive in only a few copies originated as private, unauthorized reports with a restricted circulation.

However we may explain them, the variant versions are a chastening reminder of how little we really know. When we put several versions together and see what different shades of meaning they give us, we begin to realize the inadequacy of a *reportatio*, at least at this early stage of its development. It always leaves one with a sense of something missing, and sometimes with a feeling of suspicion. None of our three masters' reporters has obtruded himself at all obviously; and yet, without a very minute scrutiny, it would be unsafe to say that they have added nothing of their own.

But the *reportatio* has a special kind of attractiveness. It takes us straight into the Paris class-room where it was made. The very walls and benches rise before us when Langton explains how Samuel went to Bethlehem to anoint David on the pretext that his purpose was to *sacrifice to the Lord* [1 Kings xvi. 2] by comparing Samuel to his students:

'This was not Samuel's primary object in coming; it is an unusual way of speaking. Your reply to the question: "why do you come to the schools?" would not be: "I come to sit down and look at the walls"; and yet that is what you do.'

It is an intimate gathering. The master has 'a moral disciplinary authority of a paternal character' over his pupils. He should pray for them, Langton says, and ask for their prayers in return.[1] Langton stresses the association between them in his first lecture on the Twelve Prophets. His opening

[1] See 'Studies on the Commentaries', 165, for both references.

moraliter ad voluntatem suam. Unde iuxta glosam dicit quod comminatur hostibus ecclesie quod si [qui semper] perseveraverint in persecutione ecclesie, ruent in infernum, ibique habundantia pene inebriabuntur et opprimentur. Unde Ieremias: "*gaude et letare . . .*" *Et Iuda etc.* hoc adimpletur quando clerici impugnant ecclesiam. . . .'
We must understand *magister* to mean Langton; if any other authority were meant, at least one of the other versions would be likely to have a reference to him. We may translate: 'Our master gives a free interpretation of the passage. In accordance with the *Gloss* he says it is a threat to the enemies of the Church . . .' The sequel shows that Langton keeps to the *Gloss* for the first part and gives an independent explanation of the second part of the sentence.

text has been: *May the bones of the twelve prophets spring up out of their place* [Ecclus. xlix. 12]; so he continues:

'Desiring then, that these bones should spring up in my tongue, in my mind and in your minds, in my works and in your works, I have taken up the book of the Twelve Prophets to lecture on.'[1]

The difference in intellectual development between master and pupils was less marked than we are accustomed to, especially among the theologians, since the students had already spent years over the arts course and had perhaps taught as masters of arts before becoming students of theology. We must realize, too, the sense of election which united the small group of *litterati*, who had devoted themselves to the 'queen of sciences', as they gathered round the sacred page where all the secrets of this science were concealed. We must add the sense of responsibility which lay on the future prelates of Europe; for the schools were a path to preferment. We shall find Langton trying to sharpen their sense of responsibility, and warning them against pride.

It follows that the students were less passive listeners and reporters than those who attend modern university courses. Peter the Chanter, in his famous description of the lecture, connects it with two active exercises, disputation and preaching:

'The practice of Bible study consists in three things: reading (*lectione*), disputation, preaching . . . Reading is, as it were, the foundation and basement for what follows, for through it the rest is achieved. Disputation is the wall in this building of study, for nothing is fully understood or faithfully preached, if it is not first chewed by the tooth of disputation. Preaching, which is supported by the former, is the roof, sheltering the faithful from the heat and wind of temptation. We should preach after, not before, the reading of Holy Scripture and the investigation of doubtful matters by disputation.'[2]

Here we have the three academic functions: lecture, disputation, university sermon. The Chanter seems to treat them as distinct and separate. This certainly held good of the university sermon,[3] and 'the origin of the fully developed

[1] MS. Rawl. C. 427, fo. 69ᵃ: 'Volens igitur predicta ossa pullulare in lingua mea et vestra, in mente mea et vestra, in opere meo et vestro, librum XII prophetarum legendum assumpsi.'
[2] *Verbum Abbreviatum, P.L.* ccv. 25.
[3] See M. M. Davy, *Les Sermons Universitaires Parisiens de 1230-31* (Paris, 1931).

disputation can be traced back at least to the end of the twelfth century'.[1] But if we look through twelfth-century glosses we shall find it very difficult to distinguish between the *lectio* and the other two exercises. It has been stated that the *Summa super Psalterium* by Prepositinus of Cremona was 'preached, or at least written in order to be preached', and that the same applies to two other *Distinctiones super Psalterium*, by the Chanter and Peter of Poitiers.[2] The latter work contains a solitary 'dearly beloved!' which suggests an address to a congregation.[3] The Chanter's work on the Psalter, however, strikes me as similar in kind to his other glosses, which were normal lectures. In any case, the parts devoted to spiritual exposition in the glosses of our three masters resemble homilies; and we now have proof that the famous English preacher, Odo of Cheriton, drew largely on Langton's glosses for his material.[4] The line between *lectio* and *praedicatio* is thinly drawn.

Even more difficult to disentangle is the relationship between *lectio* and *disputatio*. Whole sections of Langton's glosses on the Pauline Epistles reappear in his collected theological *Quaestiones*, which presumably represent his disputations.[5] We are told that the disputation actually grew up within the framework of the lecture: the text and its glosses presented difficulties which master and pupils discussed at length; later, when lectures were given on the *Sentences*, the disputation was organized separately in connection with this book; then the lecturer on Scripture was relieved of his burden; theological questions were no longer his subject; he was able to go straight through his text without digressing. After this change in the syllabus, questions

---

[1] Little and Pelster, op. cit. (p. 202, n 4.), 29: 'the disputation as practised in the thirteenth century is a discussion of a scientific question between two or more disputants, of whom one undertakes the role of defender of a particular opinion, while the other or others raise objections and difficulties against this opinion . . . While in the case of the questions about the middle of the twelfth century it cannot be definitely decided whether they are disputations in the strict sense, we possess from the time about the turn of the century a goodly number of questions of Prepositinus, Stephen Langton, and Simon of Tournai' which can be described as disputations.

[2] G. Lacombe, 'La Vie et les Œuvres de Prévostin' (*Bibliothèque Thomiste*, xi, Le Saulchoir, 1927), 120-1.

[3] P. S. Moore, *The Works of Peter of Poitiers* (Catholic University of America, 1936), 82, n. 12.

[4] This has been established by Dr. A. Friend in his unpublished thesis on Odo of Cheriton.

[5] G. Lacombe and A. Landgraf, 'The *Questiones* of Cardinal Stephen Langton, no. III', *New Scholasticism*, iv (1930), 159 ff.

in the lecture are short and arise directly from the text.[1] Probably this is not a complete description of the origin and development of the disputation, which may well have been more complex.[2] Moreover it leaves unsettled the question: at what stage did the medieval scholars acquire a dialectical technique which would permit them to hold oral disputations, with respondent and opponent? Setting aside the big, public debates between Christian scholars or between Christians and Jews, when did the formal disputation as an academic exercise become technically possible? This question must be left to the experts. In the present discussion we are concerned with the *quaestiones* occuring in *lectiones* on Scripture, irrespective of the doubt whether they were dictated by the master or held with the students' co-operation. Our glosses do seem to illustrate successive stages in the 'splitting off' of the disputation from the parent *lectio*.

The process was certainly almost complete by Langton's time. That it was not quite complete is shown by the inclusion of questions from his glosses on the Apostle in his *Quaestiones*, which suggests that the *disputatio* took place at the end of the *lectio*, and dealt with problems arising from it. But all our efforts to find identical passages in the *Quaestiones* and Langton's glosses on other books have failed. In his other glosses the questions, though not always 'brief', almost always arise directly from the text and the *Gloss*; they are discussed as problems of exegesis, not as general problems. For instance, in expounding Jonas, he deals with the classic question whether the prophet 'lied' in foretelling the destruction of Nineve, which did not take place. Here he considers the problem in connection with the *Gloss*. In his *Quaestiones* he deals with the question of prophecy in general, the case of Jonas being discussed from a different point of view. In his glosses on Wisdom and Ecclesiasticus, which we know came early in his teaching career, he will sometimes touch on theological questions and suddenly break off:

'This, and this kind of thing, I leave to [the?] disputation.'
'Of this in [the?] disputation.'

---

[1] P. Mandonnet, *S. Thomae Aquinatis Quaestiones disputatae*, i (Paris, 1925), 1-12. R. M. Martin, 'Œuvres de Robert de Melun', op. cit. (p. 73, n. 3), I, xxxiv-xlvi.

[2] A. Landgraf, 'Quelques collections de "Quaestiones" de la seconde moitié du xiie siècle', *Rech. de Théol. anc. méd.* vii (1935), 122-6, shows that: 'la *quaestio* ne naissait donc pas exclusivement en union avec la *lectio*.'

'Concerning this: question.'

'But these expressions belong to the disputation rather than the lecture.'[1]

We find the equivalent to these expressions frequently in the biblical commentaries of Langton's contemporary, Alexander Nequam, and once in an anonymous Priscian gloss of the later twelfth century, when the master raises a theological point:

'But let these things be discussed in disputation.'[2]

So also Hugh of St. Cher:

'But these things are discussed better in disputation';

and we find almost the same words in the exposition of Isaias by Friar Thomas Docking, a pupil of Roger Bacon:

'. . . there are other reasons . . ., which we pass by for the present, *lest we should seem to dispute rather than lecture.*'[3]

At Paris in the mid-thirteenth, and at Oxford in the second half of the thirteenth century, we know that the disputation was separate from the lecture; so it seems only reasonable to give the same meaning to the expression when it is used by Langton or Nequam.

In the gloss on Tobias, which belongs to a later group than that on the sapiential books, Langton refers definitely to the disputation as a separate exercise. The *Gloss* on Tob. ii. 14 raises the controversial topic of 'servile fear'; Langton quotes it and brings out its implication: according to the *Gloss* it is mercenary and wicked to refrain from sin for the sake of reward; it follows then that servile fear, by which a man refrains from sin through fear of punishment, is paralleled by servile *love*, by which he refrains from sin through hope of reward: 'as this place has it and is very noteworthy in disputation concerning servile fear'.[4] Langton seems to be

---

[1] MS. Arsenal 64, fo. 140ᵇ: 'hoc et huiusmodi disputationi relinquo'; fo. 155ᵃ: 'de hoc in disputatione'; fo. 155ᵇ: 'de hoc questio.' MS. Bibl. Nat. Lat. 384, fo. 180ᶜ: 'Ista tamen verba potius sunt disputationis quam lectionis.'

[2] I have to thank Dr. R. W. Hunt for these two references.

[3] MS. Balliol 29, fo. 179ᵛ: '. . . sunt et alie rationes . . . quibus ad presens ne magis disputare videamur quam legere, supersedemus . . .' Quoted by A. G. Little, *Franciscan Papers, Lists and Documents* (Manchester, 1943), 112.

[4] P., fo. 156ᵃ: 'Nota glosam marginalem: mali non nisi servili timore Deo serviunt; mercenarii mercedem querunt; ideo beatitudinem que ipse est Deus nunquam recipiunt. Secundum hanc glosam mali sunt mercenarii si abstinent a peccato amore premii; ergo sicut timor quidam est servilis quo cessatur a malo timore pene, sic est quidam amor servilis [quo cessatur] a peccato amore

drawing his pupils' attention to a point which will be useful to them in disputation. It does not concern him any further as a lecturer, and he promptly passes on.

Then, in his gloss on the Minor Prophets, which belongs to about 1200, he distinguishes between the two exercises as sharply as possible by saying that a certain point is not to be conceded in lectures though it may be in disputation,[1] a contrast often noted by masters later in the century.

The Comestor and the Chanter represent an earlier, less differentiated state of *lectio* and *disputatio*. They do not limit themselves to questions relevant to the text and the *Gloss*, as Langton does, but discuss much more general topics, suggested by the *Gloss*, but going far beyond it. One illustration from the Chanter will show how he gets drawn away from his text on to the kind of topical problem that specially attracts him. He starts from Josue's command to *lay an ambush* (Jos. viii. 4) and the gloss quoted from St. Augustine. Here it is asked whether deceit in warfare is legitimate; St. Augustine replies that if the war itself be a just one, the use of ambushes does not make it less so; a war is just when the belligerent acts as an instrument of God's justice, not as himself the author of the war. The Chanter inquires what this means in practice. He decides that a people can only make a war without incurring guilt if they first have recourse to arbitration and get a decision in their favour; then the judge is the author of the war. The Chanter is thinking of the obligation of vassals to seek justice in the court of their feudal superior. But suppose that the belligerents are equals, having no superior, like the king of France and the emperor; then they incur war guilt. They ought to have submitted their claims to the papacy as the greater power. As a good Frenchman, the Chanter will not allow the feudal superiority

---

[1] MS. Maz. 177, fo. 92[d] (on Osee ii. 16): 'Glosa: Etsi recte posset dici quod propter similitudinem nominis ydoli debet vitari. Hinc est quod quidam in nullo sensu hoc concedunt: Pater et Filius et Spiritus Sanctus sunt tres omnipotentes. Ad hoc etiam inducunt illam partem glose Ieronimi. Ex hoc habemus ex solis vocibus inordinate prolatis heresim posse incurri. Dicimus quod hoc intelligitur de vocibus prophane novitatis, nec est concedendum in lectionibus sunt tres omnipotentes, sed in disputatione potest concedi ut omnipotens teneatur adiective.'

---

mercedis eterne, et hoc locus habet valde notabile [est] ubi disputatur de timore servili.' [Collated with MS. C.C.C. Cambridge 55, fo. 209[v].] Unfortunately Langton's collected *Quaestiones* contain no question on servile fear, the nearest approach to it being *de timore initali*; so we do not know whether he was in the habit of using the *Gloss* on this text in his own disputations.

of the Holy Roman Emperor; evidently there was no German in the class to contradict him.[1]

This example shows a simple form of question. The question is asked, solved by authority, and an application is drawn. Sometimes the argument is much more involved, and use is made of dialectic. It is difficult to know whether these questions can be called 'disputations'; we do not know if the students took part, whether they were encouraged to ask questions or to raise objections to the master's solution. A careful study of the Chanter's glosses would be informing on this point. Langton's glosses give me the impression that the talking was almost all done by Langton; though I like to think that a student is asking: 'What is the moon made of?' and getting: 'Holy writ does not say: neither do we', as his reply.[2]

Some account of the form taken by *lectio* has been essential, if we are to compare the exegesis of the 'biblical moral school' with that of Andrew. We have to make allowance for the all-embracing character of *lectio*. The master is lecturing on the text and its *Gloss*; but this leads to questions which may be only slenderly connected with either. He is also giving his pupils a moral training, and preparing them for the task of preaching to clergy and people. He is fitting them both for their academic career and for the ecclesiastical dignities which may be in store when their studies are over:

'. . . l'étude de la théologie se faisait en vue de la profession ecclésiastique et devait se conformer aux exigences de cette profession.'[3]

The glosses bear out this observation. They show how the master divides his attention equally between his text and his pupils; he has to think of them and their needs. He cannot concentrate as fiercely as Andrew. We must see how the Victorine tradition fares within this new academic framework.

---

[1] MS. Balliol 23, fo. 119[d]: 'Iusta bella diffiniri solent que ulciscuntur iniurias, si gens vel civitas que bello petenda est vel vindicare neglexerit quod a suis iniuste factum est, vel reddere quod per iniurias ablatum est. Sed hoc genus belli iustum est quod Deus imperat, apud quem non est iniquitas, in quo bello ductor exercitus vel populus non tam auctor belli quam minister iudicandus est. Inde est, ut dicit magister, quod ubi iudice auctore fit bellum, non est periculum. Sed si pares non habentes superiores, ut rex Francorum et imperator bellent, periculum est. Ad papam enim recurrendum esset, ut ad maiorem.'

[2] P., fo. 3[c]: 'Item queritur qua materia facta est luna. Non dicitur in sacra pagina, nec nos dicimus.'

[3] S. d'Irsay, *Histoire des universités françaises et étrangères des origines à nos jours*, i (Paris, 1933), 70.

II. THE LITERAL EXPOSITION

The greatest triumph for the Victorine tradition was the success of the *Histories*. Langton puts their author on the same level as the author of the theological classic, the *Sentences*; both are of the fellowship of Wisdom, Langton says:

'Blessed is the man . . . that lodgeth near her house and fasteneth a pin in her walls [Ecclus. xiv. 22-5] as they do who hand down some writing on Scripture, the Manducator who compiled the *Histories*, the Lombard who established [*statuit*] the *Sentences*.'[1]

The *Histories* received some useful additions. Peter of Poitiers, probably, completed the Comestor's text, which ended with the Gospels, by a compendium of Acts.[2] It was certainly Peter who wrote the *Compendium Historiae in Genealogia Christi*, 'the *Genealogy*' as Langton calls it,[3] which in many manuscripts is prefixed to the *Histories*. This is

'an abridgement of biblical history, given in the form of a genealogical tree of Christ. Beginning with Adam, the persons who formed the line of succession are enumerated in order. To each person is allotted a short biographical notice in the text, while in the margin are found their names enclosed in double circles. Sometimes crude drawings replace the names. Names and drawings are arranged in such a way that the line of succession from one person to another is shown. The work contains also biographical notices on some biblical persons who did not enter into the genealogy of Christ, and also accounts of kings and events of nations which surrounded the Hebrew people.'

Peter says in his prologue that his tables are intended to enable students to 'get up' their Scripture history, in spite of its prolixity, and their own poverty, which prevents their owning books. The tables, which have cost him great toil, will help them to retain in memory, 'as in a bag', the essential names and dates from Adam down to Christ.

Both the *Genealogy* and the *Histories* were interpolated and expanded in course of time. The best way to get an insight into the historical study of the Bible at about the year 1200 would be to examine glosses on the *Histories* and the notes

---

[1] P., fo. 17ᵃ.   [2] P. S. Moore, op. cit. (p. 209, n. 3), 118-22.
[3] P., fo. 74ᵃ. Langton quotes: 'sicut evidenter patet in Genealogia magistri Petri Pictaviensis.' On the whole subject of the *Genealogia* see P. S. Moore, 96-117; I quote his description of it.

written in the margins of early copies. Here we must be content with the fact that the *Histories* became a set book and that students were compelled to attend lectures on it. William of Auvergne, writing soon before 1223, complains that

'some are satisfied to have heard the preliminaries to Holy Scripture, such as the *Histories* or some other works. The rest they neglect.'[1]

Perhaps the 'other works' means the *Genealogy*. William is clearly referring to lectures. In the thirteenth century these lectures were given by the young *bachelarii biblici* who were not yet qualified to lecture on Scripture. The practice in Langton's day is not certain. Two glosses on the *Histories*, both of them *reportationes*, have been ascribed to him; they give a running exposition of the Comestor's text, brief and literal, but not excluding theological questions.[2]

During lectures on Scripture the *Genealogy*, inscribed on a skin, was hung up on the wall of the class-room.[3] Perhaps the fact that his pupils could see it explains why Langton refers to the *Genealogy* once only, while he quotes the *Histories* as regularly as he does his standard authority, the *Gloss*.

Thanks to these arrangements, the master could assume a general historical background on the part of his students. We shall follow him now as, word by word, he guides them along the sacred page, embedded in its prologues and its glosses.

So far, we have accepted the *Gloss* as a *fait accompli*, but this is to show less critical sense than one at least of our master's seniors, Robert of Melun. Robert was more radical in his attitude even than the Chanter. Whereas Peter the Chanter disapproved of a 'superfluity of glosses', Robert saw no use in the practice of reading with glosses at all. If he had had his way, medieval exegesis would have taken quite a different course. We ought to bear his criticism in mind as we follow our master through his lectures and try to see whether it is justified.

Robert felt that reading with glosses was putting the cart before the horse. Masters were reading the text for the sake of the *Gloss* instead of vice versa. Their defence of the practice was so aggressive that they might have bound themselves to

---

[1] 'Sapiential Books I', ii. 329.
[2] See the discussion in 'Studies on the Commentaries', 18-51, where extracts from the two glosses are transcribed.
[3] P. S. Moore, 108, n. 20.

it by oath and were ready to shed blood on its behalf. All glosses were regarded as holy, but those on the Psalter and Apostle (the *Magna Glosatura*) as the holy of holies. Now what, Robert asks, is the function of glosses? If the gloss says the same as the text, then it is just redundant; if it says something different, it can only be harmful. To the masters' defence of their glosses as having authority, Robert's reply is 'Nonsense!' In so far as the glosses are excerpts from the patristic authorities, the manner of excerpting has been such as to distort their true meaning. So the glosses merely waste time and distract the student from a serious study of the Bible and the Fathers.[1] We shall watch our master's procedure and judge how far Robert of Melun is exaggerating.

First we must outline the programme that our master has in mind when he proposes to expound the letter of Scripture. The literal exposition comprises the study of the text and its variants; the study of the literal sense, which is obtained by a process of historical and grammatical explanation; and finally any comments on this sense which suggest themselves to the master. His textual criticism, his explanation and comment will be conditioned by the particular copy of Scripture which lies before him and by the authorities which he has used in preparing his lecture. Since his text is the glossed text, both his exposition and his authorities for it will depend primarily on the *Gloss*. We shall be obliged to make several pauses, before we come to the literal exposition, in order to describe the text and glosses which are being expounded and the master's technique in treating them. Then, since the literal is a preliminary to the spiritual exposition, we shall have to pause again, in order to see how he distinguishes the first sense from the second. Then, at last, we shall arrive at the literal exposition itself.

The commentator begins his explanation of each book by a prologue, where he explains its authorship, its date (so far as these are known to him), the causes of its composition, its matter and purpose. He takes his schemata and definitions from the introductions to the *artes* which were being elaborated in the twelfth century on the basis of classical and late antique models.[2] To give one of the simpler examples, the

---

[1] *Sententie*, ed. R. M. Martin, *Œuvres de Robert de Melun*, iii (Louvain, 1947)' 4-25.

[2] R. W. Hunt, 'The Introductions to the "Artes" in the Twelfth Century', *Studia Mediaevalia in Honorem R. J. Martin* (Louvain, s.a.), 85-112.

'heads' used by Robert of Melun in his prologue to St. Paul are: *materia, intentio, ordo, modus*. A term was apt to 'stray from its original meaning' when transplanted from its place in the introduction to some grammatical, logical or rhetorical text to the prologue to a book of the Bible. The artists had used the distinction *extrinsecus, intrinsecus* to express the difference between 'the things it is necessary to know before beginning the practice of an art', i.e. what the art itself is, and 'the body of rules and precepts which we learn in order to practise the art'. Langton uses it to mean 'literal' and 'spiritual', so that 'extrinsically' the book is about the history of the Jews and so on, 'intrinsically' it is about the Christian Church or the faithful soul. The schemata naturally become more complex towards the end of the century and, as Dr. Hunt has pointed out, their meaning 'would be hardly intelligible to us if we did not know of the prototypes in the *artes*'. The whole subject is a striking illustration of the theologian's debt to his preliminary training in the *trivium*.

Each prologue begins with a text of Scripture which either literally or spiritually applies 'to the book which we have in hand'. If the master's invention gave out when he was preparing the course he could consult one of the many collections of anonymous prologues compiled for this emergency; prologues seem to have been regarded as common property and were borrowed without scruple.[1] Then he runs through the text of the prologues of St. Jerome on the book he is expounding and the other prefatory matter which had become part of the *Gloss*.[2] It seems that this explanation of the prologues occupied a whole lecture, probably the second in the series, the first having been devoted to the master's own. The Comestor says that a second prologue was added to the first in the *Gloss* on St. Matthew, in order to provide sufficient material for one lecture, since the original prologue had not sufficed.[3]

Then the master reads out the text and its glosses. His students, judging by the custom of a later date, were supposed to bring Bibles to class with them, and possibly these would be glossed. Nevertheless, text and glosses seem to have been read aloud. Our *reportationes* use the imperative:

---

[1] B. Smalley and G. Lacombe, 'The Lombard's Commentary on Isaias and Other Fragments', *The New Scholasticism*, v (1931), 124 ff.

[2] S. Berger, 'Les Préfaces jointes aux livres de la Bible', *Mémoires présentés à l'Académie des inscriptions et belles-lettres*, XI. ii (Paris, 1904).

[3] B. Smalley, 'La Glossa Ordinaria' (op. cit., p. 62, n. 1), 369.

'First note what is said in the gloss which begins thus . . . Then note the other gloss which begins thus . . . Then note this gloss . . . and go through it to the end.'[1]

Or they use the passive:

'Text and glosses having been read through as far as this place: *And she conceived again* [Osee i. 6], go back to the beginning, expounding allegorically.'[2]

An anonymous gloss of the early thirteenth century, written in the margins of a copy of the *Gloss* on Genesis, perhaps from Osney Abbey, Oxfordshire,[3] gives precise directions for reading the various glosses contained in the *Gloss*:

'Augustine and Bede are outstanding: therefore always read their glosses first.'

The writer then gives instructions on how to distinguish the glosses belonging to the prologue (*de introitu*) from those on the text (*de littera*). He indicates which are to be read severally (*incisive*), as opposed to consecutively:

'This is read as a series of glosses, attaching each to its place.'[4]

It is not certain whether the master treated the *Gloss* as a supplement to his text or expounded it like his text. The text alone is underlined in the majority of Langton's glosses. He says in one passage of his lectures on the Minor Prophets that a certain gloss is exceptionally difficult; he will therefore put it as a text. Each clause of this gloss is then copied out, underlined, and expounded as though it were a text of Scripture.[5] In the glosses of the Comestor and the Chanter,

---

[1] The opening of Langton's gloss on Genesis: P., fo. 2b: 'Primo nota quod dicitur in glosa que sic incipit: Sicut Paulus . . . Item nota aliam glosam que sic incipit: Cum in divina scriptura . . . Item nota illam glosam: Divina scriptura aliquando loquitur de eternis, et eam prosequere usque ad finem.'

[2] The opening of his gloss on the Minor Prophets: T., fo. 1c: 'Perlecta littera cum glosis usque ad hunc locum: *et concepit adhuc*, redi ad principium exponendo allegorice.'

[3] MS. Oxford, Magdalen College 121. See N. R. Ker, *Medieval Libraries of Great Britain* (Oxford, 1941), 78.

[4] Fo. 2r: 'Hec (glosa) legitur incisive, singula suis locis adaptando.'

[5] T., fo. 84b: 'Et nota hic misticam glosam Ieronimi que non parvam continet difficultatem, quam sicut textum hic ponemus, sic: *Unitas habet sacramentum unius Dei*; modo transi paulisper et dic: *quia unus et verus Deus est*; modo redi ad id quod dimisisti, sic: *et esse in hoc numero prima beatitudo*; quare dicatur *prima* dicemus iam. *Secunda in secundo* i.e. in decade. Istud, *secunda*, aut intelligitur ascendendo aut descendendo . . .' The *Gloss* on Amos v. 3 reads: 'Unitas habet sacramentum unius Dei et esse in hoc numero prima beatitudo est, quia unus et verus Deus est; secunda in secundo est. . . .'

however, and in one version of Langton's gloss on Isaias, the *Gloss* is always underlined just as is the text.

Perhaps there was no fixed procedure in reading and commenting on the *Gloss*. The masters, in any case, take care to attach each gloss to its proper context:

> 'Note carefully the order of the glosses. Take this to begin with . . . after that resume the little piece you left off in the middle of the gloss . . . and then go back to the remainder of the other gloss . . . ; now this gloss alone . . . and it can be read after all the aforesaid glosses or before them.'[1]

All this agrees exactly with the satirical description of contemporary procedure given by Robert of Melun:

> 'They dispute often and very sharply whether the gloss is construed in order, correctly divided, properly punctuated, fittingly attached (to the text). . . .
>
> 'Whoever knows how to read out the glosses, punctuate them and attach them to his text . . . gets the honour paid to a venerable doctor, as a marvel and object of special praise.'[2]

The text is divided into sections — as in the passage quoted above, where Langton takes Osee i. 1-6 as his first unit. Langton expounds each of these sections, which he seems to choose quite arbitrarily, first in the literal, then in the spiritual senses. The Comestor and the Chanter seem to follow the order of the *Gloss*; hence they sometimes put the spiritual exposition *before* the literal. The Chanter is true to his principles, in that his exposition is brief;[3] he does not give a full exposition of each passage as Langton does.

Before the text can be expounded, however, the master must decide what it is. In the thirteenth century a certain text was selected and received as a standard. But the master could choose from a variety of readings for almost every passage at this period. The same interest which Hugh and Andrew had shown in the emendation of the text is recognizable in the Comestor and the Chanter, while Langton amends systematically. He draws up lists of variant readings in doubtful cases; he collates them with the text as quoted by St. Jerome 'in the original' (St. Jerome's commentary as

---

[1] From Peter Comestor cited in 'La Glos: Ordinaria', 368-9. The glosses are denoted by their opening words. Simil examples could be quoted from the Chanter and Langton.

[2] op. cit., 11-12.

[3] In the *Verbum Abbreviatum* i, and also in his gloss on Isaias he inveighs against the 'superfluity of glosses'.

distinct from extracts in the *Gloss*); sometimes he compares the latter with the text as quoted by some other well-known commentator, Raban Maur for example; he compares two texts as quoted by St. Jerome and by Peter Lombard, referring probably to the glossed Bible which had belonged to the Lombard.[1] We know, from the notes of Herbert of Bosham to the *Magna Glosatura*, that the Lombard took an interest in textual variants.

Langton was famous for his emendations and is frequently cited in the thirteenth-century *correctoria*. It is related that when he was lecturing on the *Histories* he suggested an amendment of the text 1 Par. viii. 11 which was seized upon by his audience and immediately adopted. It appears in many *correctoria* and in Hugh of St. Cher, though not in the official Paris text. In this particular instance Langton's alteration deserved its success, for the words of the Vulgate, as they stand at present, make no sense. They run *Mehusim vero genuit Abitob*; Douay version *And Mehusim begot Abitob*. For *Mehusim* Langton proposed 'de Husim'. The context clearly shows that 'Saharim', understood from verse 8, is the subject of the sentence; Husim was his wife. The Authorized and Revised versions read 'And *of Huslim* he begat Abitub'. By changing a letter and substituting the two words for one, Langton was rendering a real service to the text and abolishing a purely illusory personage called 'Mehusim'.[2]

In making these suggestions, Langton does not presume to establish his text. The state of the Vulgate would have made this a remote ideal; in any case, as we gather from Andrew, and later from Bacon, the contemporary Hebrew had such a powerful attraction that it distracted scholars from the equally urgent task of purifying St. Jerome's translation. The 'either-or' system was distracting too. Langton delights in collecting alternatives. A reading which bears clear signs of corruption may be useful to him afterwards, for the spiritual exposition; Langton joyfully adds it to his list.

---

[1] 'The Lombard's Commentary on Isaias', op. cit. (p. 217, n. 1), 131-3; 'La Glossa Ordinaria', 370-1.

[2] J. P. P. Martin, 'Le texte parisien de la Vulgate latine', *Muséon*, vii (1888), 287 ff. Martin has verified the passage in Langton's gloss on the *Historia Scholastica*, Bibl. Nat. MS. 14417, fo. 89^c and 393, fo. 108^d. 'In Hebraeo vero *me* sonat *de*. Verum forte deberet ibi esse De Usim non *Meusim* et ita de Usi alia uxore genuit istos qui sequuntur etc.' The *correctorium* MS. 140 Bibl. S. Marco. Venice, fo. 126^c (time of Roger Bacon) reads 'Cantuariensis dicit quod Meusim duo sunt partes quia "*me*" idem est quod "*de*", hoc est "de-Usim". Quod verbum quidam rapuerunt de ore eius et in textu posuerunt "*De Usim*".'

Take, for instance, his treatment of the text Zach. i. 21 which describes the vision of the four horns which were to destroy Juda, and the four smiths who were to cast down the horns, 'to fray them' and to save Juda from her enemies. The Vulgate reads: '*Haec sunt cornua quae ventilaverunt Iudam ... et venerunt isti deterrere ea*'; Douay version: 'These are the horns that have scattered Juda ... And these are come to fray them.' Langton sets forth the above reading, and adds:

> 'That is the text given by Jerome and the Lombard, *but the other reading accords better with the tropology*—"deterere ea". The horns that scatter Juda are not only to be "frayed" or "broken", but "demolished", "ground away".'

They represent sin, and even the circumstances of sin must not be permitted to remain.[1]

His general attitude towards variations in the text seems to be that so long as the sense is more or less the same, the actual wording need not concern us overmuch. He contents himself with giving the two readings and suspending judgment. For Malachias iv. 1, for instance, he observes that Jerome, and also the Septuagint, have ... *et inflammabit eos dies veniens* ... Some books have *dies veniet*. The sense is more or less identical; but if we take the second reading we must put a stop after the words *et inflammabit eos* and take them with the preceding sentence.[2]

We begin to realize the difficulties under which masters and pupils were labouring before the adoption of a standard text and punctuation. But we also realize that instead of being appalled by these difficulties, Langton finds them rich in suggestions for his moral teaching.

Another problem was the lack of a standard chapter division in twelfth-century Bibles. One of the most usual medieval methods was to divide each book into large sections with a summary of contents at the head of each; these items were numbered and known as *tituli*. There were also various systems of capitulation, some giving fewer, others

---

[1] T., fo. 170ᶜ: '*Et venerunt isti* fabri *deterrere ea*, sicut enim dicit Ieronimus et Lumbardus; tamen alia littera que magis competit tropologie est *deterere ea*. Non solum enim predicta cornua sunt deterrenda vel confringenda, sed etiam deterenda, sive conterenda, ne alique reliquie Amalech in peccatorum circumstantiis supersint.'

[2] T., fo. 207ᶜ: '*Et inflammabit eos dies veniens*: hanc litteram ponit Ieronimus et etiam septuaginta. Quidam libri habent *dies veniet*; et est satis idem sensus. Sed secundum hoc clausula precedens terminatur hic *inflammabit eos*.'

many more chapters than our present system.[1] The official
text of Paris was divided into chapters, closely corresponding
to ours; they were gradually modified during the thirteenth
century until the correspondence was complete;[2] through
the Paris text this particular division became the standard
everywhere.

The custom of referring to chapters when quoting from
Scripture was either rare or unknown before the second half
of the twelfth century.[3] The development of the lecture and
reportatio system must have shown the convenience of such
references; the centralization of studies at Paris must have
shown the desirability of standardizing them. Hence we
find that our three masters mark three stages in the reception
and standardization of chapter division, previous to that of
the Paris text.

Peter Comestor simply tells us that chapters are used in
Gospel harmonies, but that he does not propose to mention
them; and he explains the difference between the *capitula* of
St. Jerome and those in current use. One example he gives
us proves that he is familiar with a system of division which
was afterwards superseded.[4] Peter the Chanter seems to
have been the first to refer constantly to chapter divisions in
his biblical quotations. He, too, is using one of the older
systems. The arrangement is still unstandardized. He will
sometimes compare two divisions of his text and prefer one
to another:

'*At the same time* [Jos. xxii. 1]. It is much better, (he says) to
begin the chapter *here*; others begin it above.'[5]

We turn from the Chanter to Langton with a feeling of
expectancy, since later chroniclers, Trevet and Knighton,

---

[1] O. Schmidt, *Ueber verschiedene Eintheilungen der heiligen Schrift* (Graz, 1892).
[2] Martin, op. cit. (p. 220, n. 2), viii. 457 ff.
[3] For this and the next two paragraphs my authority, unless specially mentioned, is A. Landgraf, 'Die Schriftzitate in der Scholastik um die Wende des
12. zum 13. Jahrh.', *Biblica*, xviii (1937), 74-94, where references to earlier
studies will be found; see also F. M. Powicke, *Stephen Langton*, 34; G. Lacombe,
'Studies on the Commentaries', 15.
[4] The following passages may be noted in addition to those quoted by Dr.
Landgraf: Comment on *spatiatim* in the *Gloss* prologue to St. Mark, MS.
Pembroke College, Cambridge, 7, fo. 229ᵃ: 'et noli intelligere capitula maiores
distinctiones que fiunt secundum ordinem tractatus, sed minores clausulas,
quandoque unius tantum, quandoque duarum linearum.' On Mc. viii. 36, ibid.,
fo. 246ᵃ: '*Quid enim proderit* . . . ad ingressum huius capituli lege glosam . . .'
[5] MS. Balliol 23, fo. 126ᶜ: '*Eodem tempore*, hic, inquit, magis et melius debet
incipere capitulum, alii supra.' From the context it seems that *supra* refers to
nullus hostium [xxi. 42].

have credited him with dividing the Bible into 'the chapters which the moderns use'; and lists of chapters, closely corresponding to that of the Paris Bible, are ascribed to him in various manuscripts.

A study of his glosses and *Quaestiones* shows that he often refers to chapters by numbers; and these numbers show two systems of divisions in use, one old and one new.[1] But the numbers as given by our manuscripts do not necessarily go back to the original *reportatio*. It is certain, in some cases, that they have been inserted later, either by Langton himself, or by scribes or pupils. They are interesting witness to the reigning confusion, but not to Langton's practice as a lecturer. When, on the other hand, we find him giving his references by words instead of numbers we feel more confident. It is easier to add numerals, in making a copy, than to revise the wording. We may accept these verbal references as genuine evidence for what was said in class.

We find that Langton refers either to the approximate place in the book from which he is quoting without giving the chapter: 'in Ecclesiasticus, *near the end*'; or to the chapter by its opening words: 'in that chapter of Ecclesiasticus: *The offering of him that sacrifices wrongfully* [xxxiv. 21], it is said: *He that sheddeth blood, etc.*'[2] The chapters thus quoted do not correspond with the modern system which has been ascribed to him. He is using one of the old systems. It would be interesting to see whether he had adopted the Chanter's; but at present there is insufficient evidence.

Hence, if the tradition which ascribes the present division to Langton is true, we must infer that he introduced it towards the end of his teaching period. This inference is borne out by a copy of his gloss on the Minor Prophets, MS. Troyes 1046, which is dated by the scribe as 1203. This is certainly not the original but a copy, since the text is already poor; it is poorer than in some later manuscripts. The colophon, however, is probably original to this manuscript; the appearance of the script corresponds to the date.

---

[1] Dr. Landgraf finds this double system in Langton's glosses on the Pauline Epistles and in his *Quaestiones*. I have found it myself in his Old Testament glosses.

[2] Lack of space prevents my giving more than two examples here; both are typical: T., fo. 206[c]: 'Item in illo capitulo Ecclesiastici: *immolantis ex iniquo* [xxxiv. 21] dicitur: *qui effundit sanguinem* [27].' P., fo. 11[b]: 'De prohibitione suffocati dicitur in Actibus Apostolorum [xv. 29] in illo capitulo: *Placuit Spiritui Sancto et nobis* [28].'

Unfortunately there are no marks of provenance. The gloss is divided into chapters, according to the biblical text, by numerals in red ink which have been inserted into spaces left for the purpose, and again by numerals in black ink in the margin; both red and black figures seem to have been written by the scribe of the text and colophon. They correspond to the modern chapter division, with nine exceptions, two of which, the omission of chapter iv in Jonas and Sophonias, might be due to carelessness; the remaining seven are slight divergences of one or two verses; for instance, Osee vi is marked at the present v. 14. Therefore, Langton's new division was known and was used in copying one of his glosses in 1203.

This copy of Langton on the Minor Prophets is significant, if compared with others of about the same or a little later date. These are either undivided, except by a later hand, or divided according to an older system. MS. Cambrai 333 (315) has the old-fashioned *tituli*; MS. Balliol 22 has forty-five chapters for Osee, eleven for Joel, thirty-three for Amos, and so on. A rather similar arrangement is found in a copy of the Chanter on the Minor Prophets, late twelfth or early thirteenth century, in MS. Bibl. Nat. Lat. 17988; here we have forty-six for Osee, eleven for Joel, forty-one for Amos.

MS. Troyes 1046 gives us valuable evidence for the fact that Langton was connected with the new division, and that this was known in France by 1203, although he did not use it in his lectures. That the chapter problem had been exercising him, comparatively early in his teaching career, is proved by a remark in his gloss on St. Jerome's prologue to Josue: *Monemusque lectorem ut . . . distinctiones per membra divisas diligens scriptor conservet*:

'By *portions*, that is by chapters, which are very necessary for finding what you want and for remembering. Here you have authority for chapter division.'[1]

Langton's improvement evidently came at the end of about thirty years of trial and error, in which the Chanter and other unknown masters had shared. It was the outcome of his teaching experience.

When we pass from the text and its division to the *Gloss*,

---

[1] P., fo. 107ᵃ: '*Per membra* id est per capitula . . . que valde necessaria sunt ad inveniendum quod volueris et ad tenendum memoriter. Hic habes auctoritatem distinguendi capitula.'

we find that the two elder masters seem to be on firmer ground. The Comestor and the Chanter both recognize some sort of official standard for the number of glosses to their text. They know which glosses are authorized and which ought to be inserted.

'... Now read the interlinear glosses; I want to note all that you ought to read here, for in certain books are many glosses in this place which ought to be added.'[1]

With Langton this vigilance over the glosses is relaxed. He takes for granted a certain diversity in the number of glosses. On Ag. ii. 6, for instance, he says:

'Note that Gregory expounds four clauses here in the *Moralia*; whence certain books have here a certain gloss, namely this: *He sows much* ... Certain books do not have this gloss and so we have put it here.'[2]

He also accepts a diversity of wording in the glosses; he compares his own copy of the *Gloss* with the Lombard's, just as he compares his own and the Lombard's text.[3] It seems that the text of the *Gloss* had got out of control in the years between its reception and Langton's lectures.

The Comestor and the Chanter also distinguish carefully between *expositor* and *glosator, ordinator glose*. The former is a patristic authority quoted in the *Gloss*, the latter one of those masters who was responsible for putting the *Gloss* together. The Comestor contrasts Raban Maur with 'the glossator';[4] the Chanter throws out warnings:

'And *this* gloss the compiler [*ordinator glose*] put in, not Jerome.'[5]

It is the same distinction as Herbert of Bosham observed in his edition of the Lombard's *Great Gloss*. Roger Bacon refers to it under a new name; he contrasts the *authentica* with the *magistralia*, and complains that the distinction was

---

[1] MS. Pembroke, 7, fo. 188ª: '... modo lege interlineares. Volo enim notare omnes quas debes hic legere quia in quibusdam sunt multe que appunctande sunt in hoc loco.'

[2] T., ff. 160ᵈ-161ª: 'Item nota quod Gregorius in *Moralibus* hic exponit quatuor clausulas. Unde quidam libri habent inde hic quandam glosam, scil. hanc: *Multum seminat* ... Quidam libri hanc glosam non habent, et ideo eam hic posuimus.'

[3] 'The Lombard's Commentary on Isaias', 132-3; 'La Glossa Ordinaria', 400.

[4] MS. Laud Misc. 291, fo. 6ᵈ.   [5] MS. Brussels 252, fo. 26ᵛ.

not being kept; the glosses of masters were treated as though they were 'authoritative', i.e. patristic.[1] Langton seems to mark a transition in terminology. He does not use the expressions *expositor* and *glosator*; he puts the distinction negatively in this way:

"part of this gloss is by Jerome, part is not. . . .'[2]

Then, in his later work, on Ezechiel, which must have appeared soon before 1206, I have found the expression *glosa magistralis*.[3] But the important point is the distinction, however it was expressed. None of our three masters deserves Bacon's reproach. They do not confuse their masters and Fathers. On the contrary they struggle to preserve the ascriptions of the glosses against the negligence of copyists who omit or misplace the names.

Apart from the problem of uniformity, the use of the *Gloss* involved grave disadvantages: no text-book can replace the study of original sources. The twelfth-century masters realized this keenly; they accepted the text-book system as a necessary evil, just as we do. Thus an English commentator, Ralph Niger, excuses himself for quoting the *Gloss*:

'We put the sacred expositions of the holy Fathers before our own researches, just as we heard them in the schools, but in brief, that those who read may understand, by reason of this very brevity, that one should go back to the originals for full knowledge of them.'[4]

To 'go back to the originals for full knowledge' is the aim of our three masters, especially Langton. His method is to make the *Gloss* his starting-point and to check the extracts by their originals. The *Gloss* on Genesis and Exodus, for instance, is chiefly composed of extracts from St. Augustine — *De Genesi ad Litteram* and *Quaestiones in Heptateuchum*: Langton refers to sections of these works which are not included in the

---

[1] See above, p. 175, n. 2.
[2] See below, p. 228, n. 2.
[3] MS. Corpus Christi College, Cambridge, 89, fo. 113b.
[4] The prologue to his commentary on Kings, MS. Lincoln Cathedral 25, fo. 6c: 'Sacras expositiones sanctorum patrum dumtaxat quas in scolis audivimus, nostris inquisitionibus superponimus, sub brevitate tamen, ut qui eas legerint ex ipsa brevitate intelligant ad originalia scripta fore recurrendum, ad plenam de eis notitiam habendam.' Though Ralph does not use the word *glosa*, collation shows that he was using the *Gloss*. His commentary was finished soon before Feb. 7, 1191. See the letters published by W. Holtzmann, *Papsturkunden*, ii (Göttingen, 1937), 453-4. Ralph had studied at Paris under Gerard La Pucelle.

Gloss;[1] but he does not find much use for the important work of Ambrose on the Hexaemeron, presumably because the glossator had not used it. Similarly with the *Gloss* on Judith, which is compiled from the commentary of Raban Maur: Langton makes Raban his chief authority, filling up gaps in the *Gloss* from Raban's original commentary. When he refers to 'Rabanus' instead of to *glosa* he is quoting from the latter work, not from the *Gloss*.[2]

The Minor Prophets give us some especially interesting examples of Langton's system. The *Gloss* on this book was composed almost exclusively of extracts from St. Jerome's commentary. Langton again uses the two sources, describing the latter as *Ieronimus in originali*, while the former is, as usual, *glosa*, or *glosa Ieronimi*. He does not only supplement one by the other, he actually compares the two. Commentators had some difficulty in explaining the meaning of the preposition in the phrase *Verbum Domini quod factum est ad Joel*. Langton explains the solution given by St. Jerome, as reproduced in the *Gloss*; then he goes on to say that Jerome's original text seems to contradict Jerome as quoted in the *Gloss*; so he gives what he supposes to be St. Jerome's meaning, and shows that in reality there is no contradiction in his thought.[3]

In another context, Langton corrects the *Gloss* by comparison with the original. Several lines of the original have been dropped out in the *Gloss*, to the great detriment of the sense. The *Gloss* comments as follows upon Nahum i. 2: *Ulciscens Dominus et habens furorem*, explaining that the divine wrath has a benevolent intent; it is an excerpt from St. Jerome:

---

[1] For example, P., fo. 19[b]. *Quaestio* on Gen. xxiv. 25: '. . . querit Augustinus quomodo potuerunt filii Rachel tantum malum perpetrare . . .' See Aug: *Quaestio CVIII in Genesim, P.L.* xxxv. 575.

[2] MS. Exeter College 23, fo. 12[d] (on Judith vi. 14): 'Unde nota quod dicit Rabanus quod magnum et precipuum in piis precibus sit adiutorium . . .' See Raban, *P.L.* cix. 555. Langton summarizes. I found only one case in the whole commentary on Judith where 'Rabanus' was traceable to the *Gloss*.

[3] T., fo. 61[c]: 'Unde glosa: "*ad Ioel* recte factum est verbum Dei, quod erat in principio apud Deum, porro *factum* non secundum se, sed secundum eum ad quem dicitur, fit. Unde 'factus est mihi in salutem'." Quasi sicut hec dictio *factus* nichil copulat Deo, cum dicitur "factus est mihi in salutem" . . . Sed huic expositioni contrarium videtur quod Ieronimus predicte glose continuat in originali, sic: "qui post me venit, ante me factus est, quia prior me erat". Sed istud intelligitur in evangelio de incarnatione, ergo et istud *factum* quod hic ponitur in textu de incarnatione, quod est contra predictam glosam. Dicimus [solution follows] . . . et ita planum est quod est in textu et in glosa.' See the *Gloss* in loc., and St. Jerome, *P.L.* xxv. 949.

'*Ulciscens Dominus* . . . Non quasi inimicus sed ut ligno, foeno stipulaque consumptis, purum aurum recipiat, et quidquid hostile et contrarium sibi invenerit, tollat, et in pristinum statum restituat et reducat.'

The sentence obviously means nothing; how can the dross be 'restored to its former condition' when it has already been purged away to leave only the gold? The key to the riddle is that only as far as *recipiat* is intended to apply to *ulciscens Dominus et habens furorem*. The next sentence, *Et quidquid hostile*, &c., is an extract from St. Jerome's comment on the sequel *ulciscens Dominus in hostes suos*, which introduces quite a new line of thought. Langton shows how this last passage has been taken from its context and joined to the former excerpt, the intervening words being omitted. 'With what effect', he adds, 'you may see for yourself.'[1]

In another passage he points out that a spurious addition has been made to the words of St. Jerome as they are reproduced in the *Gloss*. The first part only of the excerpt in the *Gloss* is genuine. Langton is right, as appears from a comparison of St. Jerome's commentary with the *Gloss*.[2]

Again the angry shade of Robert of Melun stands before us. Langton's efforts to control the glosses from their originals exactly confirm Robert's diagnosis of the whole problem of their relationship. Robert analyses the various ways in which an excerpt from authority can be made. You can abridge your original, retaining both the sense and the diction; you can retain the sense, while altering the diction; or you can alter both. The glosses, he complains, do often differ from their originals in sense, in diction and in sequence. Further, by removing a passage from its context you may alter its meaning, even if you keep the diction intact. And

---

[1] T., fo. 116d-117a: '. . . et post glosam ubi dicitur "non quasi inimicus etc." in originali sic: "non quod sit inimicus et ultor quod de diabolo dicitur, sed, quod amica sit eius ultio, et quasi ignis lignum, fenum, stipulum consumat, ut purum aurum remaneat et argentum" [this is quoted from St. Jerome, *P.L.* xxv. 1233]. Quod autem sequitur in glosa non continuatur precedenti in originali. Sequitur in originali: "Ulciscens Dominus in hostes suos . . ." Ieronimus: "secundum utramque intelligentiam corripit Dominus quem diligit et castigat omnem filium quem recipit. Ideo irascitur ut quod adversarium et inimicum sibi est, tollat ex hostibus et . . . in antiquum redeat statum" [St. Jerome, ibid.]. Nota hoc ultimum coniungitur cum precedentibus in illa glosa "Zelatus Dominus etc.", utrum autem bene, tu videris.'

[2] T., fo. 125b (on Nahum ii. 3): 'Nota glosam "*Clipeus* id est arma diaboli etc." Cuius pars est Ieronimi, pars non, ut patet per verba que posuimus in fine eius; dicitur quod mali quando ducentur in infernum indignabuntur "pro malis contra se que gesserunt et tamen contra Deum . . .".' Cf. St. Jerome, *P.L.* xxv. 1247.

you do violence to your author if you change his words, even if you retain the sense. To quote the emphatic conclusion: the glosses have no authority from the mere fact of being glosses:

'Hence we deny that a person expounding the sense of an author and changing his words is the spokesman of authority.'

Robert compels our sympathy. It is clear enough that the students are going to get a garbled version of authority from their glosses, unless the master is for ever checking them, in which case he might save himself trouble by dispensing with them altogether. Then, suddenly, we reach Robert's final proof in his indictment of glosses, and we are pulled up sharply. Behind all his seeming good sense on the subject of original sources lies a superstitious veneration for words. The conclusion of his argument warns us against taking his attack on excerpts as foreshadowing modern scholarship:

'If a person pronounces the words only of an author, even though he applies them in a sense other than that of the author, it is agreed beyond doubt that he should be granted to be the spokesman of authority. So we are bound by our own judgment to admit that authority resides in the words rather than in the opinion of the author. And so what we have said must necessarily be true: there is no authority in glosses which differ in their wording from the authorities whence they are believed to have been excerpted.'[1]

Robert, we now perceive, is not so much worried by the absence of any study of the Fathers as a whole, as by the alteration of their diction. He seems to think that an argument may be accepted as authoritative so long as it is in the form of a verbal quotation; the 'waxen nose' of authority may be twisted, provided that the words of authority be retained. His grievance against the *Gloss*, when we come down to bedrock, is that it violates the sanctity of the word. The fanatics of the *Gloss*, whom he attacks so bitterly, were in a sense more intelligent in their attitude to their authorities than he was.

[1] Op. cit. (p. 216, n. 1), 24: 'Unde aliquem sensum auctoris exponentem et verba mutantem, auctoritatis prolatorem esse negamus: cum solum verba auctoris pronuntiantem, etiam ea ad alium sensum applicantem quam ad illum in quo sunt ab auctore prolata, indubitanter constat esse concedendum auctoritatis fore relatorem; ex quo proprio convincimur iudicio, auctoritatem in verbis auctoris potius consistere quam in sententia. Et ideo verum esse quod diximus necesse est, scilicet, nullam earum glosarum auctoritatem esse que in verbis ab auctoritatibus sunt diverse ex quibus excerpte creduntur.'

They were ready to sacrifice the words in order to give their students some idea of the patristic opinions on Scripture.

And we may well ask whether Robert could offer any constructive alternative. In his survey of Scripture, introducing his *Sentences*, he insists, as his editor has pointed out, on the importance of the spiritual sense.[1] How was the student to discover the authoritative spiritual interpretation of a given passage within a reasonable space of time, without looking at the *Gloss*? If we try to look at the teacher's problem from a twelfth-century point of view, it seems that Robert's criticism of reading with glosses was unhelpful. True, our masters are obliged to spend valuable time in fussing over the punctuation, order, place, authorship and accuracy of their glosses. But Robert is wrong in accusing them of regarding the *Gloss* as an end in itself. It may have applied to some of his contemporaries; we must acquit our three masters of any such charge. They see the glosses rather as a pointer to their originals than as a substitute for them. As educators our masters are concerned to introduce their pupils to the right books in the best way. Nor do they merit the reproach of neglecting their text and of passing over questions. The length and thoroughness of their exposition will convince by wearying us.

Now at last, after diversities in the text and glosses have been dealt with, and the use of the *Gloss* vindicated, we may expect to have reached the commentary. Not yet, but we are getting near. We are preparing for the exposition of the letter. Hugh of St. Victor had taught exegetes to distinguish carefully between the literal and spiritual exposition, not to begin on the second until they had considered the first. Neither expositors nor glossators had been as alive to the distinction between letter and spirit as Hugh. Hence the masters who try to follow Hugh's teaching have the delicate business of sorting out the glosses and deciding which of them to expound in a literal sense and which in a spiritual:

'See that you do not confuse the glosses belonging to both expositions ... Here leave off the gloss, since what follows belongs to the other exposition.'[2]

[1] ibid., xvi.
[2] The Comestor on St. Matthew, MS. Laud Misc. 291, fo. 8a: 'Vide ergo ne commisceas glosas de utraque expositione ... Hic dimitte glosam, quia quod sequitur est de alia expositione.'

'[Here] you have no gloss for the letter except for this interlinear gloss.'
'This gloss can also be taken in a mystical sense.'[1]
'Up to here the gloss is metaphorical, from this place allegorical.'[2]

An anonymous gloss on the *Gloss* of Genesis takes the trouble to point out that certain passages in the *Gloss*, which really expound in a literal sense, are incorrectly headed 'mystical' or 'moral'.[3]

Peter Comestor feels that one can have too much of a good thing, even of the spiritual sense. He praises the compiler of the *Gloss* because, unlike another commentator, he has kept the spiritual exposition of the Gospel genealogy within bounds. It is a glorious burst of frankness:

'*Isaac begat Jacob*. In the glosses of Master Geoffrey Babion (he says) which are solemn and authoritative, you will find the whole genealogy expounded allegorically and tropologically. But he who compiled the glosses here has maintained so just a balance that he expounds what is said of these three patriarchs only morally, what follows of the others only allegorically. Then sufficient unto the day be the evil thereof; so let us add nothing here more than is needed.'[4]

The Chanter is puzzled by a difference between the *Gloss* and the liturgy. The words of Isaias *All they from Saba shall come bringing gold and frankincense* [lx. 6] are sung in the gradual of the Mass for Epiphany, as a *literal* prophecy of the Three

---

[1] The Chanter on Isaias, MS. Brussels 252, fo. 40ᵛ: 'Ad litteram non habes glosam nisi hanc interlinearem'; fo. 49ʳ: 'Potest etiam hec glosa esse de mystico sensu.'

[2] The Comestor on St. Mark, MS. Pembroke College, Cambridge, 7, fo. 231ᵇ: 'Hucusque est glosa metaphorica, ab hoc loco allegorica.'

[3] MS. Eton College 48, fo. 116ᵈ: 'hec autem glosa, licet mistica intituletur, toto litteralis'; fo. 117ᵃ: 'Nota quod hec glosa moralis intitulatur, quamvis ad litteram spectat.' On this MS. see 'Gilbertus Universalis', op. cit. (p. 62, n. 1), vii. 256. I think that the *Notulae super Genesim* are the work of a Paris master, possibly a *reportatio*, of the late twelfth or very early thirteenth century.

[4] MS. Laud Misc. 291, fo. 3ᶜ: '*Ysaac genuit Jacob*. In glosis, inquit, magistri Gau[fridi] Ba[bion] que solempnes sunt et auctentice, invenies totam genealogiam allegorice et tropologice expositam. Qui autem hic apposuit glosas ita temperate equilibravit ut quod dictum est de his tribus patribus tantum moraliter exponeret, quod autem sequitur de aliis tantum allegorice. Sufficiat ergo diei malitia sua, ut nihil preter quod opportet hic apponamus.' The description exactly fits the *Gloss* on this passage, and the excessively long exposition which Peter objects to is found in a commentary sometimes ascribed to Geoffrey Babion (printed *P.L.* clxii. 1230). See A. Wilmart, 'Un commentaire des Psaumes restitué à Anselme de Laon', op. cit. (p. 48, n. 4), 337, n. 45.

Kings. But the *Gloss* gives it a different, a mystical interpretation. Perhaps, he suggests, it was *after* St. Jerome's exposition of Isaias that the Church instituted the singing of this text in literal reference to the Three Kings.[1] In that case St. Jerome could not have been consciously opposing the liturgical use.

In their attitude to metaphor and prophecy we see the full result of Hugh's teaching. Andrew's hesitation before the Jewish arguments and the debate in the *De Emmanuele* counted for something too. Exegetes now had to decide definitely whether they would include metaphor in the historical sense, whether they would take a prophecy as referring literally to Christ, or whether this belonged only to the allegorical exposition. An anonymous gloss on the Psalter, of the later twelfth century, explains briefly that the prophecy *Behold a virgin shall conceive* is expounded 'literally of the Blessed Virgin, spiritually of the Church'.[2] Very significant is a parenthesis in the *Allegoriae super Tabernaculum* of Peter of Poitiers. It occurs in a part of his work where he has contented himself with merely transcribing his sources. Nevertheless, when he comes to Bede's definition of allegory, with Bede's example '*There shall come forth a rod out of the root of Jesse* etc., that is, the Virgin Mary shall be born of the stem of David and Christ of her', Peter feels compelled to add a qualification: 'but certain men say that this is history related metaphorically'.[3]

Bede was expounding the primary meaning of the prophecy; therefore, Peter thinks, he ought to have counted it as belonging to the historical sense. Peter cannot agree, even with Bede, his favourite authority, in classifying the primary historical sense as allegorical just because it contains a prophetic metaphor.

Peter the Chanter has broached the problem more explicitly in his comment on the prophecy of Balaam. Andrew, whose work lay before him when he prepared his lecture, said that the Jews expounded Balaam's prophecy *A star shall*

---

[1] MS. Brussels 252, fo. 171ᵛ: 'Hec tamen solent cantari in Epiphania ad litteram de tribus regibus . . . Non tamen exponitur hic sic. Forte post expositionem Ysaie ordinavit ecclesia ut hec cantaret die illo de tribus regibus ad litteram.'

[2] MS. Pembroke College, Cambridge, 7, fo. 1ᵈ: '*ecce virgo etc.* litteraliter de beata virgine, spiritualiter exponitur de ecclesia impleta.'

[3] Petri Pictaviensis, *Allegoriae super Tabernaculum Moysi*, ed. P. S. Moore and J. A. Corbett (Notre Dame, Indiana, 1938), 100-2: 'quidam tamen dicunt hoc esse historiam per metaphorice trans-sumpta verba narratam; . . .'

rise out of Jacob, and a sceptre shall spring up from Israel [Num. xxiv. 17] of their Messias. The Chanter justifies himself for accepting it in the Christian sense.

'Note that everything which is said of Christ up to *And when he saw* [verse 20] can be applied to David, except this *he shall waste all the children of Seth.*'

Since all save the descendants of Seth perished in the Flood, *the children of Seth* stand for all mankind.

'But David did not waste all mankind, nor the men of all nations, and this at least is true of Christ.'[1]

The clearest, firmest, and yet the subtlest treatment of the question appears in Langton, on the same text:

'This is a manifest prophecy of Christ. Hence no literal interpretation other than the prophecy ought to be understood. Thus should we expound the letter: *A star* Christ *shall rise* through incarnation *out of Jacob* the Jewish people . . . *And he shall possess Idumea*; all peoples shall be his, that is Christ's. Literally this was fulfilled under David; that [it might] mystically [signify that] Christ should strike the vices [i.e. *the chiefs of Moab*] and possess their lands, that is the men whom sin has in bondage.'[2]

Langton means that part of Balaam's prophecy had its literal fulfilment under David, and that this in its turn symbolized the coming of Christ. He counts it as part of the literal sense because he believes that it should all be included in the prophet's original meaning. He sees that metaphor, symbolism, and allegory can come into the literal exposition if they were present in the prophet's mind. We know that he kept the literal sense of the prophecy distinct, since the passage is given its 'spiritual exposition' later on; allegorically the *star* is the Blessed Virgin, the *sceptre* her Son; tropologically, the *star* is the 'light of good works', the *sceptre* 'chastisement of conscience'.

---

[1] MS. Balliol 23, for 42d: 'Et nota quod omnia que dicuntur de Chritso usque ad illum locum *cumque vidisset* possunt convenire David, preter illud: *vastavit omnes filios Seth.* Cum enim occisus esset Abel a Cain, non remanserunt nisi filii Cain. Sed *Adam iterum cognovit uxorem* et genuit Seth [Gen. iv. 25]. In diluvio autem perierunt omnes de genere Cain, et omnes de genere Seth preter Noe et eius filios. Constat ergo quod sunt *omnes filii Seth,* sed non omnes homines vastavit David nec omnium nationum homines, quod saltem de Christo verum est.' The same argument is more briefly put in the *Historia Scholastica, P.L.* cxcviii. 1239.

[2] 'Stephen Langton and the Four Senses', 65-6.

The idea has taken such firm root in him that he applies it to the moral teaching of the letter too. He distinguishes between the 'tropological sense' or moralization and the moral lesson which can be deduced from the straight-forward teaching of the text. The latter he calls *moralitas secundum litteram*. Commenting on the opening of Tobias, for instance, he says:

> 'See the morality according to the letter; take this: *in his captivity* [1, 2] Lo! he is praised for standing firm in adversity. . . .'[1]

We are not concerned with the treatment of prophecy or the reasoning, but with the distinction which is made between 'literal' and 'spiritual' exposition. A clear distinction was the condition of anything that we should call exegesis, as we shall see when we consider the nature of the spiritual senses. The twelfth-century masters were feeling dissatisfied. They do not question the system of the fourfold exposition; but they struggle to reduce it to order, to remove its ambiguities. They hint at earnest discussion behind the scenes.

The same applies to their comments on the 'letter', which at last we have reached. Our problem is to decide whether they continued in the spirit of the Victorine tradition. They show their appreciation of it by quoting Andrew; but do they follow his example of research and exploit the sources he had opened up for them? Only a thorough examination of their sources could answer this question. All one can say at present is: 'yes — to some extent'. The Comestor certainly quotes Jewish traditions which he does not take from the Fathers or Andrew. Both the Chanter and Langton, in glossing Isa. vii, show traces of fresh discussions with the Jews. The Chanter knows two Jewish explanations of the text; one might be derived from the *De Emmanuele*; that Emmanuel was the son of Isaias; the other was not mentioned by Andrew; that Emmanuel was Ezechias the son of Achaz. It seems that the Chanter had had personal contact with Jewish scholars, since he remarks that they have learnt dialectic. After quoting the Jewish view according to St. Jerome, he continues:

> 'The Jews of our time say otherwise, being versed in the sophism of composition. They say that it should be taken not as compounding but as dividing, thus: "she who is *a virgin shall conceive*, not however remaining virgin".'

---

[1] 'Stephen Langton and the Four Senses', 64.

Or, as a gloss which is based on the Chanter has it:
'The Jews of our time are *Parvipontani*', i.e. hair-splitting
logicians, after a characteristic of the school on the Petit
Pont.[1]

Langton, who knows the Chanter's gloss, has advanced
the argument a stage further. He repeats the Chanter's
objections to the Jewish view, with the comment:

'But this the Jews solve easily; for they read the text thus. . . .'

A fresh exchange of argument follows.[2]

By the turn of the century, when Langton was working,
Hebrew studies were becoming more common. Ralph
Niger and Alexander Nequam both knew some elementary
Hebrew and consulted Jews.[3] Paulin Martin points out that
Langton corrected the text from the original Hebrew. Of
the three examples quoted by Martin,[4] one has been taken
over by Langton from Andrew.[5] It is quite probable that
the other two were original to Langton; but one cannot be
sure that they represent a personal knowledge of Hebrew,
as distinct from an indirect knowledge, gained in talks with
Jews.

Langton certainly continues the practice of consultation.
On the *three crimes of Moab* [Amos ii. 1] the *Gloss* refers him
to 4 Kings iii. 26-7: *the king of Moab . . . took his eldest son . . .
and offered him for a burnt offering upon the wall.* The *reportatio*
of Langton's comment on this reads:

'Note that the *Gloss* and also the text of Kings seems to mean
that the king of Moab offered up his *own* son upon the wall.

---

[1] MS. Brussels 252, fo. 30ᵛ; see B. Smalley, 'A Collection of Paris Lectures',
op. cit. (p. 62, n. 1), 112-13. For 'predicationem' read 'divisionem'.

[2] MS. Bibl. Nat. Lat. 14417, fo. 181ᵇ. Neither the Chanter nor Langton,
however, approved of disputation with Jews. The Chanter recalls an occasion
when the Jews scored against the Christians; Langton says that a man should
not argue unless the Jews challenge him. MS. Bibl. Nat. Lat. 15565, fo. 101ᵈ
(on Ecclus. viii. 15: *Noli foenerari homini fortiori te, etc.*): '. . . ut in disputatione
Iudeorum et clericorum Remis, cum quidam opponeret quod solus Deus novit
cogitationem, respondit Iudeus multis exemplis hoc esse falsum.' MS. Rawl. C.
427, fo. 10ᵃ (on 1 Reg. xiv. 9: . . . *stemus in loco nostro, nec ascendamus ad eos*):
'argumentum est quod non est disputandum cum Iudeis nisi provocatus
fuerit quis.'

[3] See G. Flahiff, 'The Life and Writings of Ralph Niger', *Mediaeval Studies
of the Institute of Toronto*, ii (1940), 121-2. Dr. R. W. Hunt lent me his
transcript and notes of Alexander Nequam's commentary on Ecclesiastes.

[4] Op. cit. (p. 220, n. 2), 455.

[5] Langton's comment on 1 Kings v. 6 is taken from Andrew on the same verse.
MS. C.C.C. 30, fo. 56ᵇ⁻ᶜ.

But a certain very learned Jew told the Master that he offered not his own son, but the son of the king of Edom.'[1]

Langton's contemporary, David Kimhi, reports this opinion in the name of his father Joseph (1105-70).[2] On Ag. ii. 1, *In the four and twentieth day*, etc., the *reportatio* has:

'The Jews here have a big letter as at the beginning of a sentence, as a certain Jew told the Master, saying that it depended on the preceding chapter.'[3]

Perhaps the most interesting example that I have found is Langton's comment on the relative positions of Abarim, Phasga, and Mount Nebo, where Moses died [Deut. xxxiv. 1]. He gives the opinion of Andrew of St. Victor, 'who follows Master Hugh', and contrasts it with that of 'the modern Jews', who 'say otherwise'. This second opinion, I am told, is found in the compilation of Hazzekuni, who was Langton's contemporary. Langton is doing what Bacon recommended long afterwards, checking Andrew by his own knowledge of the Hebrew sources. Nevertheless, he goes on to prefer the Chanter's opinion; it 'seems truer' and 'the Master in the Histories' agrees with it.[4]

---

[1] MS. Maz. 177, fo. 95ᶜ: 'Nota quod predicta glosa et etiam textus Regum videtur velle quod rex Moab immolavit suum proprium filium super murum. Dixit tamen quidam Hebreus doctissimus magistro quod non immolavit proprium filium sed filium regis Idumee.'

[2] I have to thank Dr. Rabinowitz for this information.

[3] MS. Durham A.I. 7, fo. 198ᵛ: 'Apud Hebreos est hic magna littera quasi inchoativa sententie, ut dixit magistro quidam Hebreus, dicens eam pendere de precendenti capitulo.'

[4] I reproduce the whole passage, together with the sources, as an interesting example of the geographical *quaestio*. MS. Trinity College, Oxford, 65, fo. 291ᵇ:
Item supra in benedictionibus dicit: *Ascende in montem istum Abarim, in montem Nebo*. Item hic dicitur: *Ascendit ergo Moyses de campestribus Moab super montem Nebo, in verticem Phasga*. Quomodo est hoc intelligendum vel quomodo possunt simul stare hec? Respondit: Andreas sancti Victoris, magistrum Hugonem secutus, dicit quod Phasga provincia est, Abarim mons, Nebo oppidum quoddam, et quia dicitur *in montem Abarim*, hoc proprie dicitur, et est ibi intransitio; quod autem dicitur hic *super montem Nebo* improprie dicitur, et est ibi transitio, et est sensus, i.e. super Abarim, qui est iuxta Nebo oppidum. Hebrei moderni aliter dicunt: quod tam Abarim quam Nebo contra Phasga montes sunt, et quod Moyses in Nebo mortuus est. Verius videtur quod Abarim fuit mons quidam magnus per quem erat descensus in Nebo, cuius Nebo scil. vertex erat altissima, et dicebatur Phasga *cacumen* illius, et huic concordat magister in hystoriis.'
ll. 1-2. Deut. xxxii. 49.
l. 4. This opinion is not in the published works of Hugh.
ll. 5-6. Andrew on the same text, MS. C.C.C. 30, fo. 47ᵇ: 'Nabo oppidum est, mons eius est Abarim; *in verticem Phasga*; Phasga est provincia;

This is typical of Langton's attitude. He has a passion for reconciling his authorities (including the *Histories*) which turns his lectures into a kind of *concordantia discordantium glosarum*. Theologians were evolving a technique for interpreting their authorities with the aid of dialectic; so Langton instinctively applies the same method to geography. Where his sources differ about the place-names of Palestine, he has no hesitation in reconciling them by means of the 'distinction' and the 'equivocation', as though place-names were abstract terms.

Commenting on Amos i. 12: *I will send a fire into Themar, and it shall devour the houses of Bosra*, he devotes a good deal of space to the identification of *Bosra*.[1] The Bosra mentioned in this verse is the name of a city of Edom, derived from the Hebrew for 'fortified'. It is identical with the Bosra of Isa. lxiii. 1, and Jerem. xlix. 13 and 22, and to be distinguished from the town of Moab (Jerem. xlviii. 24) which is really the 'Bosor' of Ruben.[2] Langton was right, therefore, in distinguishing two separate Bosras, though he makes some mistakes in detail. He first marshals his authorities on the text in question. The *Interlinear Gloss* on Amos i. 12 says that Bosra is a city in Edom; St. Jerome says it is another name for the whole region of Edom: '*Bosrae* non sicut quidam putant alterius civitatis sed Idumaeae.' The *Gloss* on Isa. lxiii. 1, '*Who is this that cometh from Edom with dyed garments from Bosra?*' calls this Bosra a city of Moab, which is supported by Jerem. xlviii. 24, where Bosra is mentioned in the Burden of Moab: *Judgement is come upon . . . Bosra and upon all the cities of the land of Moab.* Yet in the Burden of Edom we have: *Bosra shall become a desolation and a reproach . . . and all her cities shall be everlasting wastes* [ibid. xlix. 13]. Therefore Bosra was identical with, or situated in, Edom. Considering the contradictions in his authorities, Langton proposes rather an ingenious solution: Bosra is the proper name of *a city in Moab*,

---

[1] The whole passage is too long to reproduce here. T., ff. 75d-76a: '. . . et ita secundum diversas significationes huius vocis *Bosra* locuntur hic glose. . . .'

[2] A. Legendre, art. 'Bosra', in *Dict. de la Bible*, ed. Vigouroux.

---

verticem Phasga montem Abarim appellat, replicans more scripture quod iam superius dixerat.'

ll. 10-12. The Chanter, MS. Balliol 23, fo. 111d: 'Nota quod Abbarim nomen est montis, Nebo nomen verticis eiusdem montis, cuius etiam montis nomen est Fasga, et inde potest videri terra promissionis.'

l. 12. Deut. iii. 27: 'Ascende cacumen Phasgae. . . .'

Historia Scholastica, *P.L.* cxcviii. 1259-60.

and it is also an adjectival term for the *region of Edom* meaning 'fortified'; we know from Jerem. xlix. 16 that Edom was
a land fortified with hills and caverns, *Thou that dwellest in
the clefts of the rocks and endeavourest to lay hold of the height
of the hill.* The glosses do not contradict one another, he
maintains, because they relate to diverse meanings of the
same term.

Similarly, when 'the Master in the *Histories*' disagrees with
St. Jerome on a geographical problem, 'some say that the
Master lies; but that is foolish, *we* say that there is an
equivocation'.[1]

This misapplication of logic seems much more wrong-
headed, from the point of view of scholarship, than the
system of 'either, or'. A string of alternatives at least
recognizes that a problem exists and that the data to solve
it are lacking. Dialectic was proving to be as bad for
scholarship as for the humanities.

If we turn to a further question: how far have the three
masters been influenced by Andrew's own exegesis, by his
personal approach to his subject? again the answer must be
'to some extent'. We miss Andrew's adventurousness and
his independence; in their quotations he has been 'watered
down'. The most independent part of Andrew's commentary
on the Pentateuch, his exposition of the Hexaemeron, is
omitted altogether from the *Historia Scholastica*. Langton
refers to it once only: on the question of how Moses got his
knowledge of the Creation, he throws out a bald summary of
Andrew's careful reasoning:

'Or it may be said that he learnt much from his predecessors.'[2]

The Chanter quotes most of Andrew's introduction, with
a little adjustment which is even more significant than
omission. Where Andrew says that Moses 'altogether passes
over the creation of the angels', the Chanter adds:

[1] P., fo. 112ᵃ on Josue xv. 15: '*The name of Hebron before was called Cariath-
Arbe*'. 'Et nota quod magister in hystoriis dicit in glosula quadam quod
civitas illa Gebron [*sic*] dicitur "Cariatarim" et in Paralipomenon "Caria-
tharb". Et contra Ieronimus dicit quod Cariatarim fuit una de civitatibus
Gabraonitis, ergo non fuit illa, falsum est ergo quod dicitur in illa notula.
Responsio. Dicunt quidam quod magister mentitus est, sed hoc insipientis est
dicere. Unde dicimus equivocationem ibi fuisse, et hec alia est ab illa quam
magister ponit.' *Historia Scholastica, P.L.* cxcviii. 1270.
[2] P., fo. 2ᵈ: '. . . et prius nota quod dicitur in glosa que sic incipit: *sicut
Paulus etc.* Ita enim queritur quomodo Moyses scivit mundi exordium; per
revelationem Spiritus sancti. Vel potest dici quod multa didicit ab ante-
cessoribus suis.'

'. . . according to certain [commentators] who say that the world was created according to the distinction of twelve days, with whom Bede seems to agree, and many others; but Augustine says that things were created together, as we shall say.'[1]

Andrew's point had been that the creation of the angels was not explicitly mentioned at all; the Chanter manages to ignore this statement by confusing it with the *simul* question. Still he is more faithful to his original than Hugh of St. Cher, who, in quoting Andrew, changes 'altogether passes over' into *'treats of'*![2] Again, in the book of Numbers, where all three masters make constant use of Andrew, each one omits his statement that the Jews refer Balaam's prophecy to their Messias. On the reading Num. xxiv. 15 . . . *the man whose eye is stopped up hath said* . . ., Langton omits Andrew's rash suggestion: the Vulgate makes nonsense, let us prefer Origen and the Hebrew;[3] the Comestor and the Chanter manipulate him:

'The Hebrew and Origen's translation have: "whose eye is opened". But the sense is the same; for while he slept, he saw in dreams what he was saying; hence his bodily *eye* was *stopped up*, the *eye* of his mind was *opened*.'[4]

Yet the manipulation itself shows a critical spirit: while admiring Andrew, the three masters take him with a pinch of salt. We notice the critical sense of the Victorines again in the Comestor, when he warns his pupils against an apocryphal tradition.[5] We notice, too, that the Comestor's interest in the letter is drawing him towards new sources for

[1] MS. Chartres 229, fo. 4ᵇ: '. . . pretermittit, secundum quosdam qui dicunt mundum creatum secundum distinctionem VII dierum, quibus Beda consentire videtur, et alii multi. Augustinus tamen dicit simul creata ut dicemus.' See above, p. 132.

[2] Post. in Gen. i (Paris, 1530), fo. 6ᵛ: '. . . ideo de creatione angelorum, qui etiam hominibus serviunt, in principio agit.'

[3] See above, p. 168.

[4] *Hist. Schol.*, *P.L.* cxcviii. 1238; MS. Balliol 23, fo. 42ᶜ.

[5] On the gloss 'Dicitur quod Ioseph Mariam facie ad faciem videre non poterat . . . de quo hic non agitur' to Matt. i. 25, *Et non cognoscebat eam . . .'* MS. Laud Misc. 291, fo. 9ᵇ: 'Tradunt quidam, sed non est autenticum, quod de facie beate Virginis quamdiu pregnans erat egrediebantur radii splendoris, et adeo habebat igneam faciem ut in eam non posset Ioseph dirigere oculorum aciem, et ita *non cognoscebat eam* quia non potuit eam intueri. Satis potuit sic esse, ut dicit Ieronimus. Dicitur enim in hoc libro forte de infantia Salvatoris, in quo etsi multa vera tamen respuit eum ecclesia velut apocriphum; sed non est ad hoc referendum quod hic dicitur "non cognovit".' This particular legend, which is mentioned with less detail in the *Gloss*, is not in the *Liber de Infantia Salvatoris* and it is not clear to which passage of St. Jerome the Comestor refers.

the literal exposition. They are not scientific, but useful for teaching purposes.

It has been pointed out that both in his *Histories* and in his glosses on the Gospels, the Comestor 'lingers with predilection on what relates to biblical archaeology and liturgy'.[1] 'Biblical archaeology' is rather a grand name for the Comestor's interest in the basilicas of the Holy Land and in the holy relics. His interest in the liturgy goes deeper. The twelfth century saw the development of liturgical drama; it is very likely that the Comestor's students may have taken part in one of the scriptural plays which were produced within the framework of the holy day services; we know that one of these plays, the *Ludus Danielis*, was written (about 1140) by the students of the cathedral school at Beauvais.[2] The Comestor is appealing to his pupils' experience, and is entirely in the spirit of his century, when he dwells on the historical and dramatic character of the liturgy. It is a mirror to Scripture. He refers them from the sacred page to the Mass, the offices, the processions, where they can see the same events represented; he shows how Scripture is re-enacted in the liturgy. There is no need to give examples from the *Histories* as they are readily accessible; instead we will quote from his first lecture on St. Matthew, where he strikes the key-note; he illustrates the meaning of *evangelium*, 'good tidings', by the reading of the Gospel at Mass, and shows how the passage from the Old Testament to the New is expressed by the Church:

'To teach this threefold pre-eminence of the Gospel, the Church does three things when the Gospel is read. To mark the revelation of things prefigured, she hears the Gospel with head uplifted. To mark the fulfilment of promises, she hears the Gospel in silence, as though by that silence she said: "now I get what was promised"; just as children are silent once they hold their apples. To mark the sublimity of the promises, she finishes the Gospel, full of grace and profit, with voice uplifted, whereas lessons from the Old Testament are finished with voice lowered, as though it were said: "there earthly things are promised; here supernal".'[3]

[1] A. Landgraf, 'Recherches sur les écrits de Pierre le Mangeur', *Rech. Théol. anc. méd.* iii (1931), 369.

[2] K. Young, *The Drama of the Medieval Church*, ii (Oxford, 1933), 290, 395 ff.

[3] MS. Laud Misc. 291, fo. 1ª: 'Ad insinuandam hanc triplicem evangelii pre-eminentiam, tria facit ecclesia cum legitur evangelium. Ad ostendendum enim quod per evangelium facta est figurarum revelatio, audit evangelium capite relevato; ad ostendendum quod in evangelio facta est promissorum

The Chanter and Langton use the same method. They are fond of instancing the liturgical use peculiar to a certain church, Notre-Dame for example, and we get odd sidelights on ecclesiastical custom. When the Jews were endangered by Holofernes: *the altar of the Lord they covered with haircloth* [Judith iv. 8]; hence, Langton remarks, began a practice which the Church follows now when captivity threatens; she blocks up her doors with brambles and thorns.[1]

Another device which had its uses in the class-room was the 'concordance'. The Victorines quote parallel texts only when they think it indispensable to their exegesis. The habit of supporting every statement by authority was growing, and perhaps, before the days of proper Bible concordances, it was necessary to give the students a table of references. The system is highly evolved in Langton's glosses. He nearly always makes a list of texts suggested by the text he is expounding, or in support of his interpretation of it; these texts in turn suggest others. Sometimes the list is actually headed *concordantia*; his glosses would in effect provide a clumsy substitute for the alphabetical works which the thirteenth-century masters invented and on which we rely today.

The *concordantia* has been quoted as a final example of the cumbrous paraphernalia which the masters were saddled with. Langton takes a section, comprising, let us say, four verses; he gives a list of variant readings; he gives out the order of the glosses and perhaps variant readings of them too; he collects alternative explanations (I have known him suggest six for one text, three of which he prefers); he solves questions arising from the glosses and their 'originals', and perhaps from the *Histories*, as a rule by 'concording' them; he makes a table of related texts, a 'concordance'; after that he still has to plod through it, according to the spiritual senses, all over again. By the time he has finished, we have forgotten what he said about the section before. All continuity in the explanation of the sacred writer's meaning has disappeared.

Medieval readers of the Langton glosses seem to have been

---

[1] MS. Exeter College 23, fo. 10ᵃ: 'Ecce ex hoc sumpsit initium quod modo imminente captivitate geritur ab ecclesia, scil. portas ecclesie spinis et vepribus obstruere.'

impletio, audit evangelium cum silentio, ac si ipso silentio dicat: iam optineo promissa. Solent enim pueri silere postquam tenent poma. . . .'

as overwhelmed as we are, both by their length and by their miscellaneous character. They solved the problem by making various kinds of extracts, their most effective method being to separate the literal exposition from the spiritual. For almost every book of Langton's glosses, one of the *reportationes* has been found in three forms; we have (i) the complete form, the original, which contains both literal and spiritual expositions, and also (ii) the literal and (iii) the spiritual, disentangled and each copied out separately.[1] Hence, in a number of manuscripts, we can read through the literal exposition consecutively without being disturbed by the sudden switch-over to allegory and morality. What we should call the 'serious' exegesis has been detached from the homiletics.[2] This gives us a set of comments which may fairly be compared with Andrew's, since they deal only with the letter, just as his do.

The two scholars make a striking contrast, as we have been led to expect. Though Andrew, like Langton, treats his book as a series of isolated sentences, his singleness of aim and his rapidity make his comments hang together. He is brisk where Langton is tedious. Andrew's exposition moves easily, where Langton's is clogged and disconnected, his goodwill and interest failing to master his over-elaborate apparatus. Perhaps a subject is bound to lose some of its vitality when it gets inserted into a university curriculum. The Victorine tradition of scholarship had to pay a price for its transmission, and it could only live by passing into the schools.

III. THE SPIRITUAL EXPOSITION

'Holy Scripture is God's dining room, where the guests are made soberly drunk . . . History is the foundation . . . allegory the wall . . . tropology the roof . . .' (Prologue to the *Historia Scholastica*).[3]

'*Why do you spend money for that which is not bread?* [Isa. lv. 2]. You, that is, who follow the letter which killeth, not caring for the

---

[1] 'Studies on the Commentaries,' 152-60. Unfortunately we do not know when, where, or by whom these extracts were made. The same division is found amongst most of the other Langton glosses, which I have examined since the 'Studies' were published.

[2] The gloss on Ruth is printed *in extenso* in three columns, showing the three different forms, 'full', 'literal' and 'spiritual'. ibid., 86-126.

[3] *P.L.* cxcviii. 1053. The Comestor refers to the 'sober drunkenness' of the mystics.

spiritual sense, and its fair morality, but for a superfluity of gloss . . .' (The Chanter on Isaias).[1]

'*Thy silver is turned into dross* [Isa. i. 22]. . . . This is the silver of which it is said: *The words of the Lord are pure words: as silver tried by the fire* [Ps. xi. 7]. Scholars turn it *into dross* when they abandon tropological and moral questions and pursue curious ones.' (Langton on Isaias).[2]

Our three masters, faithful to the Victorine tradition, believe in the superiority of the spiritual sense. It is better than the literal, better than theological questioning. Their *lectio* is a near cousin to the monastic *collatio*.[3] The 'master of the sacred page' corresponds to the abbot and feels sure that his vocation is just as dignified. Robert Courson, the Chanter's pupil, argues in his *summa* that: 'he who lectures publicly on Holy Scripture has taken a way of greater perfection than a monk of Clairvaux'.[4] Like the abbot, the master will put his trust in the spiritual senses. After the literal and theological exposition of his text he will turn to the spiritual, which makes the sacred pages edifying.[5] But we shall find novelty and adaptation here too. The spiritual exposition changes during the twelfth century, and nowhere more than in the class-room.

Allegory is fulfilling a new function. It is ceasing to be the learned, intellectual pursuit that it had seemed to Hugh. The lively monastic commentator, Guibert of Nogent (1053-1124), had already suggested that the allegorical sense had served its purpose; tropology, he thought, was now the more useful of the two.

---

[1] MS. Brussels 252, fo. 156ᵛ: '. . . qui sequimini litteram occidentem, non intellectum curantes spiritualem nec pulcritudinem et moralitatem sed glose superfluitatem.'

[2] MS. Laud Misc. 149, fo. 4ᶜ: 'Argentum est illud de quo: *Eloquia Domini eloquia casta.* Hoc argentum scolares *in scoriam* vertunt, cum scil. tropologicas et morales questiones relinquunt et curiosas sequuntur.'

[3] On the *collatio* see above, p. 32.

[4] Quoted by M. and C. Dickson, 'Le Cardinal Robert de Courson, sa vie', *Archives d'histoire doctrinale et littéraire du moyen âge*, ix (1934), 73.

[5] The Abbot Philip of Harvengt (d. 1182-3) identifies the monastic conception of *lectio divina* with the academic *lectio* in his advice to young Paris students: 'volo te non tam litteraliter quam spiritualiter erudiri', 'sic Scripturas capere, ut internam illarum dulcedinem diligas experiri'; 'habes quod ad refocillandum animam expedire perhibetur, divinæ series lectionis;' 'schola claustrum alterum dici debet'. *P.L.* cciii. 31, 165; 1589. Dom Berlière thought that Philip's idea of the schools was old-fashioned: 'il reste fidèle aux traditions du passé, sans paraître se douter de la transformation que subit la société qui l'entoure.' 'Philippe de Harvengt Abbé de Bonne Espérance', *Rev. Bén.* ix (1892), 192. If Philip's correspondents were attending lectures by the Comestor or the Chanter, his remarks would be quite up-to-date.

'Allegory does little more than build up faith; now, by God's grace, the faith is known to all, and though we ought often to impress it and repeat it to our hearers, we ought no less, indeed much more often, to speak of what will improve their morals.'[1]

Guibert was a good prophet. The systematic teaching of theology made allegory less valuable as an educational method in the schools. The twelfth century, however, saw a great revival of popular preaching; allegory could be used for instructing the laity, for presenting to them the Church and her sacraments in a concrete and intelligible form. The old Alexandrian conception of allegory as a way of imparting secrets, unfit for the simple, was becoming antiquated.

We can trace the change in vernacular homilies. Aelfric, whose homilies (written 990-4) were intended for preaching,[2] keeps on the whole to the literal sense. He refuses to expound the Gospel genealogy on the feast of our Lady's Nativity because it would involve him in allegory:

'This day's gospel is also very difficult for laymen to understand; it is all chiefly occupied with names of holy men, and they require a very long exposition according to the ghostly sense; therefore we leave it unsaid.'[3]

The Augustinian canon, Orm, who wrote Gospel homilies in a dialect of the north-east midlands, probably in the first years of the thirteenth century, gave as his purpose 'that simple men might understand the doctrines of the Church'. He teaches them these doctrines by means of elaborate allegory and number symbolism.[4] Orm's idea of what was suitable for 'simple men' differed profoundly from Aelfric's.

Allegory, it was admitted, might be beyond the capacity of parish priests; they ought 'at least' to expound the literal sense to their flocks.[5] The manuals for preachers which were multiplied in the thirteenth and fourteenth centuries sought to remedy this deficiency; they class the four senses as one of a number of devices for sermon making.

Even in preaching or writing for clerks, allegory could

---

[1] *Liber quo ordine sermo fieri debet*, *P.L.* clvi. 26.

[2] K. Sisam, 'Aelfric's Catholic Homilies', *Review of English Studies*, vii (1931), 16; viii (1932), 58.

[3] Ed. Thorpe, ii. 466.

[4] The *Ormulum* survives in one manuscript, probably the author's. J. E. Wells, *A Manual of the Writings in Middle English 1050-1400* (London, Oxford, 1916), 282-3; *Supplement*, ii. 1058.

[5] 'Litteratura pollere debetis, ut saltem litteralem sensum gregi vobis subdito exponatis.' Dr. R. W. Hunt kindly gave me this reference from a sermon of Alexander Nequam.

still be used, not so much to instruct as to kindle devotion. It could express to perfection the brightly coloured religious sentiment of the twelfth century. Hence it shows a tendency to become less abstract, more personal and descriptive, which culminates in commentaries on the Canticle, written in honour of our Lord's humanity and of his Mother.[1] But as Guibert of Nogent predicted, tropology had the more brilliant future. This third sense was able to satisfy the consuming and universal passion of the twelfth century, its appetite for satire.

An age which is 'fundamentally sure of itself' loves to be satirized. Believing in the divinely established office of its rulers and pastors, it enjoys hearing about their short-comings. The same for each rank of the social ladder; every person has his recognized function and only needs rousing to fulfil it. So the preacher 'holds a mirror' to society; he shows people what they are, and what they ought to be; they for their part delight in a spectacle which is both funny and edifying.

Tropology was easily adaptable to satire. Like allegory, it became more concrete. Instead of dealing mainly with the virtues and vices at war in the individual soul, it described external things, such as the behaviour of groups, or types, and religious and social abuses.[2] It now drew its inspiration less from St. Gregory's *Moralia* and more from his *Rules of Pastoral Care*. Just as allegory demanded a warm imagination, so tropology called for humour and keen observation.

The fourth sense, the anagogical or mystical, was still recognized by the Paris masters. Peter Lombard substitutes it for the allegorical in his classification of the senses:

'The historical sense is easier, the moral sweeter, the mystical sharper; the historical is for beginners, the moral for the advanced, the mystical for the perfect.'[3]

---

[1] B. Gigalski, 'Bruno Bischof von Segni', *Kirchengesch. Stud.* (1898), III. iv. 210 ff.; J. A. Endres, *Honorius Augustodunensis* (Munich, 1906), 16 ff. Typical works of this kind are commentaries on the Canticle by Philip of Harvengt and Alan of Lisle. *P.L.* cciii. 181; ccx. 51.

[2] The desire of twelfth-century commentators to find in Scripture a reflection of society, *ecclesia in statu presente*, is stressed by W. Kamlah in his interesting study: 'Apokalypse und Geschichtstheologie', *Hist. Stud.* 285 (Berlin, 1935). Satire predominates over the eschatological significance of the Apocalypse. See especially 63-4: 'Nicht einmal die Frage, was zur Zeit des Johannes schon Vergangenheit und was noch Zukunft war findet Interesse. Man will eben nicht wissen, "wie es gewesen ist", und auch nicht, wie es im einzelnen sein wird, sondern wie es immer ist.'

[3] In a sermon edited by B. Hauréau, *Notices et Extraits*, xxxii *b* (1888), 122.

As this sense treats of the mystical union between God and the soul, it is used in the cloister rather than the class-room. The twelfth-century mystics expand its technique in order to describe their religious experiences.[1]

A language will develop when important new things are to be said. This alone will explain the exuberance of the queer language of the spiritual senses. Both *scholares* and *claustrales* were bursting with new ideas. They expressed themselves most naturally in concrete images; their imagination was 'visual'; and they prized the support of authority beyond everything. The language of the spiritual senses provided both the imagery and the authority. Hence they exploited its resources to the uttermost. They increased its range and made it more flexible; they compiled 'spiritual dictionaries'. The spiritual exposition had its 'aids to study', just as the literal exposition and theology had theirs.

The spiritual dictionary of the twelfth century still needs investigating.[2] Further research would give us a much clearer understanding of a characteristic development. At present we are hampered by anonymity and lack of dates; we cannot find the original impulse. The most highly evolved form of the spiritual dictionary is the *distinctio*; we must touch on this, since it is of great importance in a study of the twelfth-century class-room.

The *distinctio* has a long pedigree, going back on one hand to alternative interpretations of the same word in patristic commentaries, on the other to lists of biblical words with their meanings,[3] like the *Formulae Spiritalis Intelligentiae* of St. Eucher of Lyons,[4] and the *Clavis Scripturae* of the pseudo Melito.[5] As M. Gilson has pointed out, all these attempts at

---

[1] The mystical sense is closely connected with the allegorical, because meditations on allegory lead on to mystical contemplation. See F. Petit, *Ad viros religios: quatorze sermons d'Adam Scot* (Tongerloo, 1934), 28; 94. It is sharply distinguished from the moral sense by Gilbert of Holland. Continuing the sermons on the Canticle after St. Bernard's death, he confesses his inability to expound in the mystical sense; he will confine himself to the moral. *P.L.* clxxx. 22; see E. Gilson, *La Théologie mystique de St Bernard* (Paris, 1934), 85 n.

[2] See the suggestive remarks of A. Wilmart, 'Les Allégories attribuées à Raban Maur', *Rev. Bén.* (1920), 47-56. A selection of these works was published by J. B. Pitra, *Spicilegium Solesmense* (Paris, 1852-8), ii, iii.

[3] G. Lacombe, *La Vie et les œuvres de Prévostin*, op. cit. (p. 209, n. 2), 112 ff.; P. S. Moore, op. cit. (p. 209, n. 3), 78 ff. These two studies are the most recent discussions of the *distinctio*.

[4] See above, p. 29, n. 5.

[5] Compiled from the works of St. Augustine, St. Gregory, and other Latin

systematization fulfil an expressed wish of St. Augustine's *De Doctrina Christiana*.[1] The *distinctio* is new in that it schematizes. Someone had the brilliant idea of making a table of meanings for each word, according to three or four senses, and illustrating each meaning by a text. This has been described as 'the simplest form' of the *distinctio*. It may either be written out or arranged 'schematically', like the following example, a *distinctio* on the word bed:

There is a bed
{
of Scripture—*Our bed is flourishing* [Cant. i. 15].
of contemplation—*There shall be two men in one bed* [Lk. xvii. 34].
of the Church—*Three score valiant ones surrounded the bed of Solomon* [Cant. iii. 7].
of conscience—*Every night I will wash my bed* [Ps. vi. 7].
of carnal pleasure—*You that sleep upon beds of ivory* [Amos vi. 4].
of eternal punishment—*I have made my bed in darkness* [Job xvii. 13].
of eternal blessedness—*My children are with me in bed* [Lk. xi. 7].
}

Here *bed of Scripture* is the historical sense (the literal meaning of the Canticle being metaphorical); *bed of contemplation* and *bed of the Church* the allegorical senses; *bed of conscience* and *bed of pleasure* the moral senses; *bed of eternal punishment* or *eternal blessedness* the anagogical senses.[2] A medieval scholar would recognize allusions to well-known passages in the Fathers, where all these spiritual meanings were explained.

This 'skeleton' *distinctio* could be elaborated by listing the properties or qualities of the thing designated by the word, and the interpretations which they suggested. It was a convenient way of grouping together the lore of natural history and the legends of the bestiary: the raven is black, he feeds on carrion, he cries 'cras cras'; hence he signifies the wicked, blackened with sin, who feed on vanity, who procrastinate.[3] And so on.

Collections of *distinctiones* were made, sometimes arranged

[1] *Introduction à l'étude de St Augustin* (Paris, 1931), 152, n. 1.
[2] I borrow the *distinctio* and its explanation from P. S. Moore, 79-81.
[3] This particular *distinctio* is taken from Langton's gloss on Genesis viii. 6. P., fo. 11ᵃ.

Fathers, probably in the eighth century. Pitra found it in a Greek translation, and took it for a lost work of St. Melito of Sardis (Pitra, op. cit. ii. i-xc; O. Bardenhewer, *Gesch. der altkirchlichen Literatur*, i (Freiburg i. Br., 1913), 463.

alphabetically, like the Chanter's *Summa Abel*,[1] and the *Distinctiones Monasticae* (perhaps by the English Cistercian, Ralph of Coggeshall),[2] sometimes arranged as a commentary on the text of the Psalter, like the *Distinctiones super Psalterium* by Prepositinus and Peter of Poitiers. By the fourteenth century their abundance in sermons to clergy and people had made them seem 'as cheap as silver in the reign of King Solomon'.[3]

Our earliest collections seem to belong to the last quarter of the twelfth century and to be the work of Paris masters. They were hailed with joy, as supplying a long-felt need. We hear the delighted appreciation of Peter, Prior of Holy Trinity, Aldgate, when he learnt of the new method in a sermon preached by Gilbert Foliot at a synod; I reproduce it with the comments of Peter's editor:[4]

' "The whole sermon was varied by certain *distinctiones*, adorned with flowers of words and sentences and supported by a copious array of authorities. It ran backwards and forwards on its path from its starting-point back to the same starting-point." He then gives an example. When Gilbert spoke of Christ as a stone, he brought forward the stone which the builders rejected, which is become the head of the corner, he brought forward the stone which Jacob set up for a pillar and on top of which he poured oil, he brought forward the stone that was cut out of the mountain without hands. Peter was so much struck with this method that he determined to write a work in which the *lector studiosus* might find all such passages collected together and arranged. This is really important because it is an early example of the *distinctio* method . . . It is unusual to get such a close view of the way in which a typical medieval form was transmitted.'

We can sympathize with Peter's welcome to the *distinctio*; it was both suggestive and labour-saving. You simply chose a key word in the text to be expounded, and looked up its *distinctio* in your collection; whether you needed an idea, or an allegory or trope for an idea already present, something in the table would be sure to help you.

Comparing the spiritual exposition of the biblical moral school with Hugh of St. Victor's, we shall find the content

---

[1] Pitra, op. cit. ii. xxviii.
[2] ibid., iii. 452; G. Morin, 'Le Cistercien Ralph de Coggeshall et l'auteur des *Distinctiones Monasticae*', *Rev. Bén.* xlvii (1935), 348 ff.
[3] See *Histoire littéraire de la France*, xxxv (1921), 466.
[4] R. W. Hunt, 'English learning in the late twelfth century', op. cit. (p. 83, n. 2), 33-4.

more original and the technique more artificial. The first is due to a difference in aim; the masters are intending not to help the religious in his meditations, but to train the scholar for an active career. The difference in technique is due to the rapid technical development of the twelfth century, especially the rise of the *distinctio*. As we should expect, the contrast between St. Victor and the Paris class-room is most marked in Stephen Langton, both because he was a great statesman and man of action, and because he was the youngest of our three scholars, working at the end of the twelfth and beginning of the thirteenth centuries. We will therefore concentrate on the Langton glosses. They represent the supreme achievement of the moral sense in the Paris *lectio*, just as St. Bernard's *Sermones in Cantica* represent that of the mystical sense in the monastic *collatio*.

We realize at once that Langton's purpose is as vigorous and coherent as St. Bernard's. Sir Maurice Powicke has shown us the inner unity of Langton's career from his study of the *Quaestiones* and their milieu. Langton was working in the centre of the ecclesiastical reform movement; Innocent III was his colleague. He discussed, from the reformer's point of view, just such practical problems, the nature of kingship, the limits of obedience, as he met with later in his dealings with John and the English barons. The glosses bear out the *Quaestiones*. They show us how, week in and week out, Langton was impressing the reformer's point of view on his students; they were the prelates of the future; he was preparing them for their task.

This is the ideal that he sets before them. The monastic *lectio* leads up to contemplation, Langton's to action:

'The word of the Lord must be turned into deed, we must act upon what we have read or heard.'[1]

The Paris masters admitted in their discussions of the action versus contemplation question that contemplation was better than action 'in essence'; but many of them felt that the life of the prelate,. which combined action and contemplation, was the most excellent life of all. Robert Pullus,[2] perhaps Peter Comestor[3] and Gerald of Wales[4] held this opinion, and

[1] On Gen. iii. 19, MS. Lincoln College, Oxford, 15, fo. 109d: 'Per hoc innuit quod verbum Dei debet converti in opus ut quandoque operemur secundum quod audivimus et legimus.'

[2] *Sententiae*, VIII. cxxi-xxv. *P.L.* clxxxvi. 933.

[3] B. Hauréau, *Notices et Extraits*, op. cit. (p. 197, n. 4), iii. 26.

[4] Quoted by F. M. Powicke, *Stephen Langton*, 132-3.

Langton agrees. He compares the solitude of the cloister to Paradise before the creation of Eve:

> '*It is not good for man to be alone* [Gen. ii. 18]; man is "alone" when he is away from the turmoil of the world; thus monks and holy men build for themselves solitudes. *It is not good* says the Lord for such a *man*, a contemplative, *to be alone*, without a companion; it is best that he should become active. *Let us make him a help like unto himself*, that is a people subject to him, who will minister to his temporal as he to their spiritual needs.'[1]

This is Langton's way of telling his students that man was meant to express himself in the art of government.

He defends the *activi* against the attitude of certain contemplatives 'who think that they alone have, as it were, purchased God' by renouncing the world.[2] The seculars number many fervent lovers of God, good men who pursue worldly glory without harm to their souls. Dignity and wealth do not estrange them from God; and though they are occupied now with the things of this world, hereafter they shall enter heaven in the abundance of their good works.[3] When some attain to the honours of prelacy we must not impute it to ambition; their aim is to serve the Church, to root out vice and restore their erring subjects to the right way.[4] Langton even warns the future pastors among his students against neglecting their subjects for the sake of contemplation. The waters of Jordan stood still while the

---

[1] My translation is a conflation of two versions:
(*a*) P., fo. 7ᶜ: 'Nota homo *solus* est quando separatus est a strepitu mundi scil. quando edificat sibi solitudinem in claustro, et de claustrali quando est disertus et discretus sepe fit prelatus. Unde hic dicitur: *non est bonum hominem* claustralem *esse solum*, sed optimum est ut fiat activus; faciamus ei adiutorium plebem *simile sibi*.'
(*b*) MS. Lincoln College, Oxford, 15, fo. 105ᵃ: 'Vel homo *solus* est qui extra strepitum mundi est, unde claustrales et viri sancti edificant sibi solitudines. *Non est bonum* dicit Dominus *hominem* talem *esse* solum quasi sine comite; *faciamus ei adiutorium simile sibi* i.e. plebem subditam que adiuvet eum ministrando carnalia et adiuvetur ab eo recipiendo spiritualia.'
[2] T., fo. 88ᵈ: 'Hoc contra illos claustrales qui cum videant seculares clericos vel laicos bonis temporalibus affluentes et mollibus et pretiosis vestibus indutos, credunt se solos quasi Deum emisse, eo quod talibus sponte carent.'
[3] P., fo. 179ᵈ [on 1 Mach. xi. 51]: '. . . licet gloriam assequantur in mundo, per dignitatem, per opulentiam tamen, non alienant se a Deo. Licet quandoque que mundi sunt agant, tamen *ingrediuntur Ierusalem* in visionem vere pacis, *cum spoliis*, i.e. in plentitudine bonorum operum.'
The 'interpretation' of the name Jerusalem was 'vision of peace'.
[4] P., fo. 149ᵈ: '. . . ita cum aliqui ad dignitatem prelationis ascendunt, reputantur a pluribus hoc causa ambitionis fecisse, tamen hoc fecerunt ut ecclesie prodessent, ut vitia destruerent, et subditos oberrantes in viam rectam reducerent.'

priests who carried the ark remained in the river bed; when they were come up and began to tread on the dry ground the waters returned into the channel and ran as they were wont before [Jos. iii. 13—iv. 18].

> 'So when the priest is vigilant the people stand firm and persevere; if he neglect to act *even for the sake of contemplation*, they often return to their old course.'[1]

Their pastoral zeal, Langton warns his students, will be opposed by vested interests in Church and State. The reformers' programme was the regeneration of society by an independent, reorganized Church; the prelates who were to effect his reform must be theologians, trained for pastoral care. The secular rulers stood in the way; they bestowed high offices in the Church on civil servants, trained in the royal court, who would be politically reliable. These 'curial bishops', in the reformers' opinion, treated their office not as a duty but as a perquisite. The storm raised by his own appointment as archbishop, which brought England under the interdict, was due to a difference in outlook between secular powers and ecclesiastical reformers which Langton had often explained to his pupils.[2]

Scholars must reprove these vested interests. The duties of the Old Testament prophets are now theirs. God's command to Osee to rebuke Israel: *Judge her, judge your mother*, is addressed to them, Langton tells them:

> 'This is said to students, when they leave their studies and return to the people from which they were born; they must judge her, not as a stepmother or an enemy, but as their mother.'[3]

Like Amos, they must expect persecution when they do this.

[1] MS. Bibl. Nat. Lat. 355, fo. 182ᵃ: '. . . quando vero sacerdotes vigilanter agunt, tunc populus stat et perseverat, sed cum negligunt actionem, etiam propter contemplationem, sepe fluit populus.'

[2] In practice, the scholar-bishops of the thirteenth century do seem to have been more active as reformers than the *curiales* and the monks. Miss Gibbs, in her study of the personnel of the English episcopate under Henry III, contrasts the record of the various types of bishop and she concludes: '. . . on the whole the contribution of the *magistri* to the life of their time was more original and substantial and many-sided than that of the other groups; their influence was more penetrating and certainly their memories more deep-rooted in the sympathies of ordinary people'. M. Gibbs and J. Lang, *Bishops and Reform* (Oxford, 1934), 50.

[3] T., fo. 9ᶜ: 'Hoc studentibus dicitur, ut si quando a studio revertantur matrem suam, i.e. gentem de qua nati sunt, iudicent; sed non ut hostem vel ut novercam, sed ut matrem.'

s

Just as the high priest of Bethel accused Amos to Jeroboam [Amos vii. 10-13], so the curial bishop will ally himself with his patron against the reformer. The traitor within the hierarchy is the real villain of the piece.

> '*Amasius* is interpreted "robust and cold". He typifies a bad priest or any bad greedy prelate, robust in evil and cold in good, a stranger to the fire of charity. For a whore, or a little worldly gain, he is ready to go two leagues or more on a winter's night; to hear a poor man's last confession he will not leave his table even for a few minutes . . . When he sees someone rightly preaching the way of truth, which he fears will put a stop to his evil ways, he keeps quiet about his own grievance, though this is his chief concern, and accuses the preacher to his king or prince, that he may seem to grieve at the disrespect to the king and incite him to vengeance. But notice that Jeroboam dismissed the accusation as frivolous, which shows that prelates are far wickeder than secular princes. Although the prince scorns the bad priest's false accusations, he does not desist from evil. *And Amasius said to Amos: Thou seer* you prophet and learned doctor who threaten us so terribly in your preaching *go, flee away into the land of Juda*; leave my bishopric or my parish, go back to your studies at Paris; *eat bread there and prophesy there*; keep your teaching and preaching to Paris. *In Bethel*, that is in my bishopric, *prophesy not any more*, that is preach no more. Your rebukes offend the king; this place belongs to him; it is his to choose and dispose of the parsons of this church. Bad prelates are wont to say: "The emperor or king delegates to us; we do this by his authority and privilege".'[1]

The good prelate, on the contrary, follows the example of St. Thomas Becket;[2] his prototype is Jonathan in the book of Machabees:

> '. . . he does not cease through fear of death to rebuke princes who attack the Church; he fears not to throw himself into the breach to defend her freedom; on her behalf he demands of the prince that he may enjoy his rightful privilege.'[3]

---

[1] T., fo. 92 c-d. The Latin is given in 'Stephen Langton and the Four Senses', 73.

[2] P., fo. 170b on two texts, 2 Esdras vi. 3, 11, Langton compares Nehemias to St. Thomas Becket, quoting his letter to Foliot: 'clavum teneo et me ad sompnum vocas', and his refusal to bar the doors against his murderers. *Materials for the History of Thomas Becket*, ed. Robertson (Rolls Series), v. 515; iv. 75.

[3] P., fo. 178d on 1 Mach. xi. 2: 'Hic Jonathan est prelatus bonus; non cessat pro timore mortis principes degrassantes in ecclesiam corripere, nec formidat se discrimini obicere pro libertate ecclesie . . . In munitionem ecclesie postulat prelatus a principe ut possit debito privilegio gaudere.'

Ecclesiastical freedom, like the liberty that the Jews won from the Romans, should be *registered in tables of brass* [1 Mach. xiv. 26].[1]

Langton is using tropology in order to set his own *Weltanschauung* before his pupils; one can find a complete picture of society, seen through his eyes, if one studies his spiritual exposition in detail. At the same time, he instructs them in a special aspect of their future duties, the task of preaching. It is the master's duty, he tells them, to incite his promising pupils to preach. This is an interesting passage from the point of view of university customs; Langton moralizes the story of Ruth; she signifies the student; the harvest-field is *lectio sacra*, the reapers the masters. Ruth *desired leave* to glean [ii. 7], because prayer should always be the preamble to a lecture; *she stood in the field*, attended the lecture that she might carry away (or 'report'; the word is *reportet*) in her bosom the ears, that is the sentences of the lesson. Booz, who signifies God, charged her not *to glean in any other field*, [8] that is, not to change over from theology to any other faculty.[2] *Booz asked of the young man that was set over the reapers: Whose maid is this?* [5]. When a student industriously gathers up the sentences of Holy Scripture at his lectures, the Lord inquires his status from the reapers, that is the doctors, when they call upon him to preach.[3] This seems to be a reference to the final examination and the inaugural lecture at the new master's inception.

Langton impresses on his pupils that they must preach to the laity also, and not confine themselves to their own cultured circle. A popular sermon is often more repaying to the preacher. *Samgar . . . slew of the Philistines six hundred men with a ploughshare*, whereas Aod slew only one man with his sharp sword [Jud. iii]:

'See! This makes clear that a preacher should not always

---

[1] P., fo. 182d: 'Libertas excelsa viris ecclesiasticis tabulis ereis debet scribi, i.e. indelibiliter consummari, ut possint tranquillitatis gaudere privilegio.'

[2] The glosses abound in warnings to students not to desert theology for the lucrative sciences, civil and canon law. This is to starve the laity who are left without teachers. T., fo. 94c: '*Nobiles interierunt fame et multitudo siti exaruit* [Isa. v. 13]: *Nobiles* sunt litterati qui cum habeant perspicax ingenium, acutissimam rationem et memoriam tenacem, et ita bene possunt sacre scripture masticare solidum cibum, *intereunt fame* cum per leges et decreta et ceteras scientias lucrativas famem sedare laborant; et ex hoc provenit quod *multitudo* laicorum *siti exaruit*, et exarescit, non habens qui ei ministret vel propinet simplicis intelligentie sacre scripture potum.'

[3] The Latin is printed in 'Studies on the Commentaries', 100.

use polished, subtle preaching, like Aod's sword, but sometimes a ploughshare, that is, rude, rustic exhortation. Very often a popular story [*exemplum vulgare*] is more effective than a polished, subtle phrase. Aod killed one man only with a two-edged sword, Samgar six hundred with a ploughshare; so, whereas the laity are easily converted by rude, unpolished preaching, a sermon to clerks will draw scarcely one of them from his error.'[1]

The popular sermon and the sermon to clerks are like two kinds of grain, barley and wheat; wheat is the more precious, barley much the more fertile and useful.[2] The *breasts* of Osee's curse [ix. 14] signify the two Testaments which are *dry* in a man who does not draw from them the milk of simple doctrine, as in those who seldom or never preach to the people but only to religious or clerks.[3]

Langton, himself a famous preacher, gives his students practical directions; they must have 'reported' innumerable devices for sermon-making. The glosses are sprinkled over with notes, pointing out the suitability of certain themes for particular kinds of sermons.[4] The allegorical exposition suggests special feast days and seasons: *Sermo in Nativitate Domini, Sermo in festo Omnium Sanctorum, Sermo in Adventu.* These sections are mainly devotional. More than once Langton quotes from the sequence, *Salve mater Salvatoris* which he ascribes to 'Master Adam of St. Victor':

> Thou art the throne of Solomon,
>   throne without equal
>   in substance or art;
>   white ivory of chastity,
>   red gold of charity
>   foreshadow mysteries.[5]

[1] 'Studies on the Commentaries', 173.
[2] T., fo. 64b: 'Quid per frumentum nisi doctrina sive predicatio clericis proposita? Quid per ordeum nisi predicatio laicis proposita? Que quamvis grossior longe tamen fertilior et utilior quam predicatio clericis facta.'
[3] ibid., fo. 46a: '... sicut quidam faciunt qui vix aut nunquam faciunt sermonem ad populum, sed ad clericos vel ad claustrales.'
[4] Perhaps these notes were not in the original *reportationes* of Langton's lectures. They are sometimes in the margins, sometimes in the text; sometimes the same note will be in both. Some copies of the same gloss have more notes than others. But they certainly go back to an early tradition: MS. Troyes 1046, the copy of the gloss on the Minor Prophets dated 1203 (see above, p. 223), has several notes: *Sermo ad prelatos et principes; Thema ad claustrales*; which are in the text.
[5] MS. Bibl. Nat. Lat. 384, fo. 192a: 'Unde in illa sequentia magistri Ade sancti Victoris *Salve mater salvatoris*.' It is quoted again as *quedam sequentia* in MS. Exeter Coll. Oxford 23, fo. 19b. He also ascribes the Easter sequence

Langton's allegorical exposition consists, for the most part, in comparisons of this kind. In prose, and elaborately worked out, they lose the charm with which verses invest them and make one either yawn or shudder. Nevertheless, they are raw material for an *Histoire du Sentiment Religieux.*

In the moral sections the notes prescribe the 'morality' as suitable for some special audience: *Sermo ad claustrales*; *Sermo ad moniales*; *Sermo in synodo.* Or we have even more concrete suggestions. The gloss on the fall of Holofernes is noted as 'an excellent theme on the death of some powerful worldling by whose fate others may be instructed'.[1] On Isa. xi. 8: *the weaned child shall thrust his hand into the den of the basilisk*, Langton explains that the *basilisk* is the devil, *the weaned child* the religious, who is *weaned* from love of the world; he alone dares to *thrust his hand into the basilisk's den*, that is the cloister, that he may pluck the devil from his heart. Only the *weaned* can do so. It was customary, at the opening of a solemn sermon, for the preacher to protest his own unworthiness; so Langton continues:

'This may be said to religious, to excuse oneself at the beginning of the sermon.'[2]

One sees a slight flick of the eyelid, and one wonders whether many religious audiences were charmed to attention by this exordium.

The story of Sisara and Jahel, the wife of Haber the Cinite [Jud. iv. 17-18], suggests a theme for a popular sermon. Jahel, who came of hostile stock, and yet befriended Israel, signifies St. Mary Magdalen. Just as Sisara, a Gentile, took refuge in her tent and she received him, saying: *come in, fear not*, so the sinner feels more assurance in entering a church dedicated to the Magdalen or some other saint who was converted from sin. He feels that such a saint will sympathize with him and be the more easily moved to compassion. This is noted as 'Sermon on the feast of the Magdalen or Matthew or some saint who was a sinner'.[3]

[1] MS. Exeter Coll. Oxford 23, fo. 15d.
[2] MS. Laud Misc. 149, fo. 31d: '. . . hoc potest dici claustralibus in principio sermonis ad se excusandum.'
[3] MS. Bibl. Nat. Lat. 384, fo. 92b.

Zyma vetus expurgetur to Adam of St. Victor: MS. Rawl. C. 427, fo. 2d. This is attributed to Adam by Alan of Lisle. Cf. F. J. Raby, *A History of Christian Latin Poetry* (Oxford, 1927), 353, 367, where the authorship of these two sequences is examined.

If this theme were ever used, let us hope that the audience was too simple to remember how the story of Jahel ends. These moral sections often contain the elements of a popular sermon. They have all the humour and the devices for capturing attention, which make twelfth-century homilies such racy reading. Langton, as he tells us repeatedly, believes in mixing grave and gay, and he has succeeded. Both he and the Chanter use popular proverbs: 'We shall know in the judgement who is bald and who has kept his hair';[1] 'swimming is easy when somebody holds your chin up';[2] Langton moralizes this proverb, saying that the devil offers to hold up our chins, as we struggle in the sea of this world, and urges us to 'take it easily'. Our masters also like little jingles that impress some pious thought upon the memory, and they tell moral anecdotes or *exempla*.

The appearance of *exempla* in their glosses is highly significant. It emphasizes their intention. The *exemplum* had not been unknown in learned works before the twelfth century;[3] but the clergy had regarded it as a method especially designed for instructing the laity. Thus William of Malmesbury in his life of St. Wulfstan of Worcester describes a sermon preached at the dedication of a church:

> 'The bishop was addressing these things to the people; and so of necessity he introduced *exempla*; but I [the author] am addressing men of letters; what I say is too well known to need exemplifying.'[4]

Langton, too, contrasts the *exemplum vulgare* of the popular sermon with the 'polished phrase' of the sermon to clerks.[5]

Both the anonymous pupil of Abailard, commenting on St. Paul about 1141, and the Comestor, make some use of the *exemplum*.[6]

So far as I know the Chanter is the first master who introduces it systematically into his lectures on Scripture. This, I think, is definitely connected with the revival of

---

[1] The Chanter on Isaias, MS. Brussels 252, fo. 16ᵛ: 'Unde dicitur vulgo: Apparebit in iudicio quis calvus fuerit et quis capillatus.'
[2] MS. Rawl. C. 427, fo. 27ᵇ: 'Suaviter natat cui mentum tenetur.'   See S. Singer, *Sprichwörter des Mittelalters*, ii (Bern, 1946), 52, no. 114.
[3] J. Th. Welter, *L'Exemplum dans la littérature religieuse et didactique du moyen âge* (Paris, 1927), ch. i.
[4] *The Vita Wulfstani*, op. cit. (p. 119, n. 3), 38.
[5] Above, p. 254.
[6] See *Commentarius Cantabrigiensis*, ed. A. Landgraf, op. cit. (p. 73, n. 2), ii. 306, 316. For the Comestor, MS. Bibl. Nat. Lat. 446, fo. 52ᵇ.

popular preaching, in which the Paris masters had a great share. When the Chanter deliberately brings a method of elementary education into the class-room he must be thinking not only of his pupils but of the lay congregations they will preach to. We know that some of the *exempla* told by Langton and the Chanter found their way into thirteenth-century sermons and into the 'example books', compiled as aids to preachers.[1] They must have been either spread by students or copied directly from the written glosses. Certainly the Paris class-room shows us the *exemplum* at its best. The element of the superstitious, the marvellous, and miraculous has little appeal for these two masters. They prefer cleverly chosen illustrations and repartee.

To this class belong the Chanter's stories of two canons of his native town, Rheims; they 'exemplify' the texts Job xx. 20 and 22: *when he hath the things he coveted, he shall not be able to possess them.* One canon got rich, and having nowhere to deposit his riches, he used to bewail his wealthiness more than he had his former poverty. *When he shall be filled he shall be straitened*: another canon put his money in a chest; so while he assisted at matins he was gnawed with anxiety about thieves; on the morrow he got rid of his money and gave it to the poor, 'in order to buy himself peace'.[2] A good sample of the 'repartee' type of *exemplum* is Langton's on the text Hab. ii. 11-12: *For the stone shall cry out of the wall . . . Woe to him that buildeth a town with blood.*

> 'A cur of a courtier to a certain king had built himself a house, marvellous in design, on the proceeds of robbery and extortion. He asked a clerk to compose a "memorial inscription" for the entrance, and the clerk did so, saying:
> > A house built on wrong
> > Will not last for long.'[3]

Langton's pupils must have enjoyed this story; it is the eternal theme of the poor scholar versus the business man.

Exempla, proverbs, and other devices are, so to speak, the spices of the spiritual exegesis. The real subject of the lecture is the technique of the exegesis itself, how to 'grind the corn of Scripture into the bread of tropology'. Langton reminds

---

[1] B. Smalley, '*Exempla* in the Commentaries of Stephen Langton', *Bulletin of the John Rylands Library*, xviii (1933), 121-9. I have not been able to study the Chanter's *exempla* as systematically as Langton's; such a study would be of great use for the history of this very interesting literary form.

[2] MS. Bibl. Nat. Lat. 15565, fo. 29ᶜ.

[3] '*Exempla* in the Commentaries of Stephen **Langton**', 128.

one of a master craftsman, initiating his apprentices into the 'mystery' of their calling. We catch a note of professional pride in his voice. On Osee viii. 9: *Ephraim hath given gifts to her lovers* he explains that *Ephraim* signifies sinners:

'But how do sinners give gifts to their lovers? Wait and see!'[1]

The comparison is particularly subtle:

'Some prostitutes take hire, others offer themselves freely, and so it is with sinners. Some find the opportunity to sin ready waiting them and these *take* hire; others seek out the opportunity; these *give* hire and offer themselves.'

The spiritual exposition, he points out to his pupils, gives him more scope than the literal. History is something that happened once for all and cannot be altered; tropology [i.e. moralization] is 'free'. The spiritual exposition may give quite an opposite sense to the literal,[2] one containing a threat where the other contains a promise and so on.[3] Since 'spiritually' a word may be given many meanings in the same text, it is permissible in the spiritual sense to diverge from the *Gloss*. Langton will sometimes content himself with the spiritual meanings suggested by the *Gloss* on his text; sometimes he will say expressly that he is taking an independent line.[4] All this is subject to the 'rules' of spiritual exegesis — the same rules as had been respected in the first century by Philo Judaeus. The spiritual interpretation must be based on the properties of the thing it signifies. The exegete shows his science by knowing these properties, his skill by adapting them. If his knowledge gives out, he must confess himself beaten, as Langton does on a text of Numbers: *the manna was like coriander seed* [xi. 7]:

[1] T., fo. 41c: 'Sed quomodo peccatores dant *mercedem amatoribus?* Attende et videbis.'

[2] ibid., fo. 138a: 'Cernis . . . quomodo ea que secundum litteram super Caldeis interpretati sumus nunc iuxta tropologiam videa[n]tur sonare clementiam et libertatem eorum qui de Caldeorum manibus evaserunt. Historia facta est et evagandi non habet facultatem, tropologia libera.'

[3] ibid., fo. 74c: '. . . ad litteram est comminatio, moraliter vero est promissio.' The Comestor too comments on the superior 'freedom' of the spiritual exposition. MS. Laud Misc. 291, fo. 5d: 'Ecce hinc potest perpendi quam laxis habenis, quam liberis evagetur spatiis allegoria, cum in fine huius glose et in alia glosa per Uriam iustum diabolus significatur.' The expression derives from St. Jerome's commentary on Isaias 'liberis allegoriae spatiis evagatur', *Prol. in Lib. v, P.L.* xxiv. 154.

[4] T., fo. 159c: 'Licet Ieronimus istum . . . accipiatur [*sic*] in malo, nos tamen moraliter accipiemus in bono.'

'We could discourse lengthily on this', he says regretfully, 'if only the nature and quality of *coriander seed* were known to us.'[1]

He has to fall back on *manna*, which is 'white and shining'; hence it signifies Holy Scripture. Sometimes Langton will collect all the known properties of a word in order to make a *distinctio*; sometimes he proceeds more briefly, basing his exegesis on one consideration only. He shows the students how to make the best of their material. If the interpretation of a Hebrew name does not give him the meaning that he wants, he shifts it round, as on the text: *If Galaad be an idol . . .* [Osee xii. 1]:

'Morally *Galaad* is interpreted "pile of witness"; but my tropology will not be taken from the interpretation [of the place-name] but from its inhabitants, the Ten Tribes, which signify the laity.'[2]

This second interpretation is one of Langton's favourites; he points out its appropriateness to current events: the Ten Tribes of Israel signify either the laity or the lesser clergy, in contrast to the Two Tribes of Juda, which 'generally, in this book of the Twelve Prophets, signify prelates'.[3] Here Langton is giving his students a key to the topical moral interpretation of the book. He teaches them how to treasure every detail in the literal sense that may be useful. In expounding the letter, he notes that a certain point is important for the spiritual exposition: 'hoc valet ad mysterium'. Then, when he expounds the same text again in the spiritual sense, he takes this detail as his basis.

As an illustration of Langton's method we may take one trope in particular of which he never tires; it is a moralization of iv Kings i. 2: *Ochozias fell through the lattices of his upper chamber which he had in Samaria, and was sick.* The key-word here is *Samaria*, which is interpreted *custodia*, that is, 'charge'. A dweller in Samaria, it follows, must be a prelate, one who has 'charge' of others. The house built in Samaria signifies his pastoral office, high and dignified, since it has an upper story. The lattice windows, through which little light penetrates, denote 'obscurity'; we think of the dark garrets where Langton's pupils were lodged in medieval Paris; hence *lattices* signify the perplexities of pastoral charge.

---

[1] 'Stephen Langton and the Four Senses', 71.
[2] ibid. 72.　　　　　　　　　　[3] ibid. 71.

Ochozias is a prelate, a curial bishop, who enters hastily and unprepared upon his office; its perplexities baffle him and bring him to grief; he 'falls through the lattices', and hurts himself; he sins grievously.[1]

Here we have all the ingredients of a successful trope: the smattering of erudition, the ingenuity, the wit, and the observation. The reformer's teaching is expressed concisely, and yet so aptly as to be unforgettable. Tropology may be a pseudo-science; it is at least alive. Conventions which were venerable to Philo seem to have renewed themselves in the Paris schools. The symbolism of the later middle ages has rightly been called decadent:

> 'Symbolism was in fact played out. Finding symbols and allegories had become a meaningless intellectual pastime, shallow fancifulness resting on a single analogy.'[2]

The symbol tyrannized, burying things under a weight of associations, which prevented freshness of perception. But in the twelfth century this is not yet true. With Langton, the thought is still mistress of the language; symbolism is her tool which she chooses and sharpens.

When this has been recognized, the corollary would seem to be that Langton has perfected the art of making the Scriptures say exactly what he pleases. We enjoy his trope because it is 'pure Langton'. It has purpose and meaning. It is not exegesis. We are face to face now with the question which has lain in wait for us since the beginning of the chapter.

We have seen that Langton gives his pupils certain rules for the technique of the spiritual exposition. Does he give any guidance as to its content? This seems to us to be wholly subjective. How far would Langton agree with us? Suppose that a pupil were to object that Ochozias ought to represent not a curial, but a scholar bishop, betrayed by his lack of political experience; how would Langton answer him? Does he, in fact, take the spiritual exposition quite seriously?

It is rather like asking what a medieval writer felt about

---

[1] T., ff. 33ᵃ, 89ᵇ, 208ᵃ.

[2] J. Huizinga, *The Waning of the Middle Ages* (London, 1927), 189. Prof. G. Owst in his study of medieval preaching, *Preaching in Medieval England* (Cambridge, 1926), *Pulpit & Literature in Medieval England* (Cambridge, 1933), seems to me to miss the distinction between the sermons of the twelfth century, which are fresh, and later ones which are often stale and second-hand.

plagiarism or forgery; but we must attempt an answer; and we must begin by distinguishing between the allegorical and the moral sense.

Langton actually tells us of a man who raised our own objection to the allegorical interpretation. On hearing that the red colour of the cow, which the Law commanded as a sacrifice, prefigured the blood of the Passion, this heretic said mockingly: 'It would be all the same if the cow had been black; the allegory is worthless; whatever the colour of the cow, some sort of allegory could be found for it.'[1] Langton mentions this only as an example of horrid impiety, needing no refutation. He has a test for the content of allegory. It must conform to the Christian faith. He takes care to scrutinize the allegories of Origen which he finds in the *Gloss* and explains in what sense these are orthodox.[2]

Hence allegory is regarded as illustrating and confirming established theological truth. It does not constitute proof in itself; Langton does not normally use allegorical arguments in his *Quaestiones*, where theological truth is under discussion. Having this criterion, he sees no objection to allegorical subtleties in his glosses. The same would apply to tropology, in so far as it could be judged by Christian morals. Many of Langton's remarks about prelates could have been justified by St. Gregory's *Rules of Pastoral Care*. But morals touch on politics. There was not so well-defined a body of political as there was of theological truth. It may happen that Langton will have no standard of truth which he can recognize.

One text leads him on to this dangerous ground. *The sun shall be turned into darkness and the moon into blood* [Joel ii. 13] naturally suggests to him the argument which high churchmen used in order to justify their policy against the secular power. The greater light, which rules the day, signifies the Church, the lesser light the State; as the moon receives her light from the sun, so the State receives her power from the Church, as a delegation. Closely connected with this is the argument of the two swords [Lk. xxii. 38].

Langton, as an Englishman, was a subject of the strongest monarchy in twelfth-century Europe. He also had a very

---

[1] T., fo. 37ᶜ. 'Stephen Langton and the Four Senses', 76.

[2] Origen, for instance, says that the diversity of sacrifices commanded by the Law signifies the diversity of human virtues; some men have a few virtues, others all. This conflicts with the received opinion that 'he who has one virtue has all', in habit, if not in use. Origen's allegory, therefore, refers to the *use* not the actual possession of virtue. 'Stephen Langton and the Four Senses', 74-5.

English dislike of extremes. Having stated the argument, he adds: 'But that is questionable.' We hold our breath. Langton is questioning a 'morality' which was commonly used as a political argument by the popes. If he rejects it, as offensive to his common sense, then what standard does he propose to judge by? Surely he must see that he is casting doubt on the whole method; that a trope has no value in argument; that it is purely subjective.

No such idea occurs to him. He returns to his text and finds a solution which gives him complete satisfaction. Properly interpreted, he thinks, the text expresses, not the extreme papalist point of view, but an English compromise, which pays due regard to the facts. It is idle to say that one power dominates over the other when both are liable to eclipse:

'It may be said that the moon receives from the sun the light of doctrine and the splendour of faith; but the sun often suffers eclipse from the action of the moon; the moon suffers eclipse from the shadow of the earth, and from the splendour of the sun, which blots her out. And now we are come to such a pass that *the sun is turned into darkness* of sin *and the moon into blood* of spoil.'[1]

We may think this a wretched evasion. It is no good our being impatient. Langton cannot criticize a method which is bound up with his whole conception of God and the universe. He is still living in an Augustinian world of mirrors and reflections. Scripture, like the visible world, is a great mirror, reflecting God, and therefore all and every kind of truth. Scripture, like man, has a soul, how much more important than the body or letter!

While this is assumed, not all the common sense of Langton can detect the flaw in the spiritual exposition; not all the scholarship of Andrew can switch people's attention on to the

---

[1] T., fo. 70ᶜ: 'Sol et luna sunt duo magna luminaria, quorum unum scil. sol preest diei, et alterum scil. luna nocti, et luna non habet lumen nisi a sole. Sol est ecclesie principatus, qui preest diei, i.e. spiritualibus; luna vero est principatus secularis qui preest nocti i.e. terrenis; et sicut luna lumen recipit a sole, sic principatus secularis est a principatu ecclesie. Unde in passione duo gladii Domino sunt allati. Istud tamen questionis est. Unde potest dici quod luna ista accipit lumen doctrine a sole et fidei splendorem, sed sol iste sepe sit passus eclipsim per lune interpositionem, et luna sit passa eclipsim per umbram terre obnubilantem et solis splendorem lune auferentem. Modo ad hoc devenit res, quod *sol conversus est in tenebras* peccatorum *et luna in sanguinem rapine.*'

letter. It is significant that the 'spiritual' excerpts from Langton's glosses were much more popular than the literal. The change could only come about by scholars starting from a fresh assumption. A revolution was needed. It happened in the thirteenth century, when the Dominicans and Dante did what the Victorines and their school had failed to do.

CHAPTER VI

THE FRIARS

I. POSTILLS AND POSTILLATORS

T H E *Patrologia latina* has acted as a path through the marsh. It has provided a modicum of printed matter, however shaky the editing and attributions may be. It comes to an end with Innocent III and the student has to find his own way. There is far more material, since more lectures are given as the schools develop; fewer have been printed. Hugh of St. Cher, St. Albert and St. Thomas make patches of terra firma, but they are far apart. And exploration must now extend to Oxford. Fortunately we have a good map to Paris in the *Répertoire* of Fr. Glorieux. It has called forth a series of corrections and additions, as all pioneer works do.[1] A. G. Little and Dr. D. A. Callus have plotted out the succession of masters at Oxford.[2] Using these guides the student may set out on his journey of discovery without being guilty of suicidal rashness. Even so, this part of my book consists of travellers' tales. They will give my own impressions of what the thirteenth century was like: a traveller tends to find what he is looking for.

I begin by listing the Paris masters who strike me as most influential, in the sense that they were quoted by their successors. There are insufficient data as yet to attempt the same thing for Oxford. Then I discuss new developments in the form and content of thirteenth-century commentaries.

We start from an almost uncharted piece of territory. Langton left the schools in 1206. The Friars Preacher opened

---

[1] See the review by V. Doucet, *Archivum franciscanum historicum*, xxvii (1934), 531-64; 'Fr Matthaei ab Aquasparta Quaestiones disputatae de gratia', *Bibl. franc. schol. med. aevi*, xi (Quaracchi, 1935), lxvi-lxvii; F.-M. Henquinet, 'Les écrits du Frère Guerric de Saint-Quentin', *Rech. Théol. anc. méd.* vi (1934), 188-93; 'Notes additionelles sur les écrits de Guerric de Saint-Quentin', ibid. viii (1936), 369-88; Spicq, 318-30; M. Grabmann, 'Ungredruckte exegetische Schrifte von Dominikanertheologen des 13. Jahrhunderts', *Angelicum*, xx (1943). My references, unless otherwise stated, are taken from the number of the theologian in the *Répertoire* or from one of these supplementary notices.

[2] A. G. Little, 'The Franciscan School at Oxford in the Thirteenth Century', *Archivum franciscanum historicum*, xix (1926), 803-74; *Franciscan Papers, Lists and Documents* (Manchester, 1943); A. G. Little and F. Pelster, *Oxford Theology and Theologians c. 1282-1302* (Oxford Historical Society, xcvi. 1934); D. A. Callus, 'The "Tabulae super Originalia Patrum" of Robert Kilwardby', *Studia Mediaevalia* (op. cit., p. 216, n. 2), 249-52.

their *studium generale* at St. Jacques, Paris, in 1229, the Friars Minor theirs in 1231. The intervening period is supposed to have seen a decline in biblical studies, which were revived by the friars. This seems to be an over-simplification, since it misses the tendencies at work in early thirteenth-century Paris.[1] What actually happened?

Common sense tells us that lectures on the Bible cannot have stopped, seeing that they were still prescribed by the syllabus. And there is positive evidence to the contrary. The early teaching at Oxford, as far as it has been investigated, springs from that of Paris at the turn of the century. In one instance we can trace the connection. John of Abbeville, a secular master at Paris, left moralities on the Psalter. They were probably excerpted from his full commentaries, just as Langton's moralities were excerpted, although in this case the full version has disappeared; nor do we find a separate set of literal excerpts to match the moralities.[2] John may have been a contemporary of Langton in the schools and he resembled Langton in ending his career as archbishop and cardinal. He represents a link between the era of the ' biblical moral school' and the second decade of the thirteenth century, continuing to teach after Langton's departure, until 1216 or even later. John's work on the Psalter circulated in a bewildering number of *reportationes*. One of them served as a basic source for the Dominican, Robert Bacon, when he lectured on the Psalter at Oxford about 1230-48. The most likely explanation of the relationship would be that Robert Bacon had been a pupil of John of Abbeville at Paris. Thus the first Oxford Preacher about whom we have any certain knowledge links up with a Paris master of the Langtonian type, in favour with the papal Curia and famed especially for his preaching: 'ad predicandum optimus theologus'.[3]

[1] See M-D. Chenu, *Introduction à l'étude de S. Thomas d'Aquin* (Montreal, Paris, 1950), ch. i.

[2] B. Smalley, 'Robert Bacon and the Early Dominican School at Oxford', *Transactions of the Royal Historical Society*, xxx (1948), 1-19. Other commentaries are ascribed to John of Abbeville. I have looked at his commentary on the Octateuch, which seems to survive in one copy only, MS. Rome, Angelica 509 (D.8.13). It resembles his commentary on the Psalter in consisting of moralities; but whereas one can only guess that the former originated in a full commentary, here there is clear evidence in the shape of allusions to the literal sense which have been left in when the moralities were excerpted: for example on Num. i. 1: 'Nota in primis sed quantum ad litteram differentiam inter tribum sive generationem et cognationem et familiam' (fo. 63ᵛ).

[3] See the chronicle of Alberic of Trois Fontaines for 1225, *M.G.H. Script.* xxiii, 916.

Robert Grosseteste must have used material of the same kind, almost certainly brought from Paris, when he lectured to the Oxford Franciscans, 1229/30-35. Eccleston tells us that Brother Agnellus 'persuaded Master Robert Grosseteste of holy memory to read lectures there to the brothers. Under him, within a very short time, they made incalculable progress in questions and in subtle moralities suitable to preaching'.[1] The tradition of Grosseteste's exegesis is being painfully and ingeniously pieced together and a general impression is emerging. Everything points to his loyalty to the methods used at Paris in the late twelfth and early thirteenth centuries.[2] A search for the sources of his moralities on the Gospels, which correspond well enough to Eccleston's account of his teaching, might reveal the name of his master. If it can be done for Robert Bacon, why not for Grosseteste? The results of such a search would tell us something of Paris at a little known period, as well as fixing the affiliations of the early Oxford masters.

Returning to Paris, we find Philip the Chancellor teaching between about 1206 and 1218, when he became chancellor of Notre-Dame. The large number of surviving manuscripts of his moralities on the Psalter proves their popularity and they were borrowed almost entire by a later secular master, Odo of Chateauroux.[3] Philip shows that the study of theology proper did not necessarily interfere with the teaching of Scripture. The same applies to an even more outstanding philosopher and theologian, William of Auvergne, teaching from some time before 1223 until his promotion to the bishopric of Paris in 1228. He left commentaries, probably delivered as lectures, on Proverbs, Ecclesiastes and the Canticle. Although he gives most of his space to the spiritual interpretation, William brings his knowledge of secular philosophy to bear on the literal sense in so new a way that it seems safe to call him original. Hugh of St. Cher quoted him extensively on Ecclesiastes.[4]

Other commentaries by secular masters are recorded for

---

[1] *De adventu fratrum Minorum in Angliam*, c. xi, ed. A. G. Little (Paris, 1909), 60-1.

[2] D. A. Callus, 'The Oxford Career of Robert Grosseteste', *Oxoniensia*, x (1945), 42-72; 'The *Summa Theologiae* of Robert Grosseteste', *Studies in Medieval History* presented to F. M. Powicke (Oxford, 1948), 180-208.

[3] This was the conclusion I came to on comparing Odo on the Psalter in MS. Oxford, Balliol College 37 with Philip in MS. Oxford, Bodl. 745 (2764).

[4] B. Smalley, 'Sapiential Books I', 326-37, 333-4.

this period and some of the many anonymous works of the thirteenth century perhaps ought to be added.[1] Nevertheless, it remains true that between Langton and Hugh of St. Cher no master left a long, consecutive series of glosses on Scripture.[2]

The evidence seems to warrant a reconstruction of the main outline of development at Paris in the twenty years or so between Langton's departure and the foundation of the *studium* at St. Jacques. Langton had pursued his exegetical teaching along three lines. He had perfected the technique of moralizing Scripture as an aid to preaching; he had inquired into doctrine; he had also shown his students how to manipulate and harmonize the complicated apparatus of glosses, distinguishing the literal from the moral, comparing the variant readings in glosses and text, quoting from and adding to those of his sources which explained the meaning of the letter. His successors followed up the first and second lines of study, to the neglect of the third. We have plenty of moralities on single books and plenty of theological *quaestiones*. The same scholar may be prolific in both, as was Philip the Chancellor. Philip composed the most popular moralities and most popular theological *summa* of his period. But owing to the process of specialization in teaching methods, the two are kept separate. Consequently, the relics of lectures on Scripture from this period consist almost wholly of moralities. We may of course credit their authors with lectures of the Langtonian type, which have disappeared, leaving only the moral excerpts. The point is that the rest

[1] A commentary on St. Luke in MS. Vat. Rossiani 107, fo. 1-136, in a hand of early to middle thirteenth century, may belong to this period. The style and method suggest it. The only modern quoted, apart from St. Bernard, seems to be Peter Comestor: the author refers to 'Manducator' in a *quaestio* on fraternal correction (fo. 46r), as well as to the *Histories* (fo. 15r, 27r). He gives a list of the orders in the Church: prelates, priests, Templars and Hospitallers, *contemplativi* (fo. 43r); the absence of the friars from his list suggests that he was working before the Mendicant Orders were well established. On the other hand, he uses the division *causa efficiens, materialis, formalis* which was not used by theologians in the twelfth century, in addition to the traditional *auctor, materia, intentio, modus agendi* (see below, p. 297). This struck me as lively and interesting stuff which ought to be studied. I have not found the incipits in any collection. They are: *Beatus homo quem tu erudieris* . . . Quia qui legit unum evangelium legit omnes . . . His visis accedamus ad prologum Ieronimi et postea ponemus alium introitum specialem in ipsum librum. *Lucas syrus natione etc.* Prologus iste dividitur . . . *Salutat vos Lucas medicus*, Col. iv. In hac auctoritate possunt satis convenienter notari . . . *Quoniam quidem multi etc.* Etiam hoc prohemio ostendit . . .

[2] Odo of Châteauroux left prologues to most books of the Bible, but no glosses except on the Psalter (*Rép.* no. 137).

T

of the lecture course was not considered to be worth preserving. Meanwhile, a flood of new and exciting material,
the Aristotelian and Arabic learning, was pouring into
Paris, giving rise to speculation, heresy and condemnations.
William of Auvergne begins to put the new Aristotle to the
service of exegesis. His postills, as we have them, are devoted
mainly to moralities; but there seems to be a slight attempt
to follow up Langton's third line of approach, stimulated by
the new philosophic movement of the time.

The work of the friars was to re-integrate all these different
strands of teaching, rather as the Victorines had done in
the early twelfth century. In fact the Dominicans in particular aimed at reviving and combining the tradition of the
Victorines, since they were religious, and of the biblical
moral school, since they were also active teachers and evangelists. Life at St. Jacques and indeed in all convents of the
Order centred on a modernized version of *lectio divina*. It
was to include scholarship, according to its interpretation by
St. Jerome and the long line of his successors. It was to include disputation and preaching. Perhaps we should begin
at the other end in assessing the aims of St. Dominic; but the
last activity implied the first: an order of preachers was
necessarily also an order of doctors.[1] Recent discussion has
underlined the part played by study in the routine of
Dominican convents from the very beginning.[2] More flexible rules and freedom from the administration of real property put the Preachers in a better position to pursue
learning than the older monastic Orders, including the
Canons Regular. It is interesting to find a learned canon,
Alexander Nequam, abbot of Cirencester, who died in 1217,
complaining that religion is becoming incompatible with
study. The cloister should be the perfect place for it; but
'the golden mean of regular discipline has departed and
there is too much stress on rules and regulations'.[3] The
Dominicans succeeded in combining the work of studious
contemplatives with the secular masters' zeal for popular
preaching and reform. The Franciscans followed their
example. It is true that the *ethos* of the two Orders is different:
St. Bonaventure expressed it by saying that the Preachers

[1] P. Mandonnet, op. cit. (p. 83, n. 1), 65-7.
[2] H.-M. Féret, 'Vie intellectuelle et vie scolaire dans l'Ordre des Frères
Prêcheurs', *Archives d'histoire dominicaine*, i (1946), 5-37.
[3] Dr. R. W. Hunt kindly gave me this reference from his unpublished thesis
on Nequam.

put learning before holiness, the Minors holiness before learning.[1] But in spite of their variance a member of one Order had no nice feelings about borrowing from another when he wanted help with his lectures. A few retouches sufficed to conceal any difference in doctrine. A student of biblical commentaries has to deal with the products of both Orders and cannot always distinguish them apart. The fruit of the new institutions is seen at once in the pages of the *Répertoire*. From Hugh of St. Cher onwards we have evidence for continuous lecturing on Scripture which differs markedly from that of the secular masters. In the first place, the custom of expounding the whole Bible or substantial parts of it is re-established. Secondly, the tilt away from Scripture and towards speculative theology is redressed. The friars seem to have been conscious that they were innovating or rather creating a new balance in returning to Scripture and they had to meet criticism from the seculars. An elusive but intriguing moralization of the story of the disciples plucking the ears of corn on the Sabbath (Mk. ii. 23-4) opposes all the friar students to their critics. It comes into the Gospel commentary of the Dominican, Hugh of St. Cher, written towards 1235.[2] The field of corn signifies the Scriptures; the disciples, plucking the ears, are the 'fratres studentes', who are 'very intent on the study of Scripture'; the Pharisees, who reproached the disciples, are the 'reprehensores', the critics of the friars and so, presumably, the secular masters of theology. The critics fall into two sub-sections, the 'morales' and the 'questioniste':

'The moralists say: "It is not good to include so many questions in theology." The questioners say: "It is not good to invent so many moralities." And each one criticizes that of which he is ignorant.'

So two groups of specialists are attacking the friars. One concentrates on moralities, another on *quaestiones*. Neither

[1] In Hexaëmeron, Coll. xxii (ed. Quaracchi, in *S. Bonaventurae Op. Omn.* v, 440): '. . . Hi sunt Praedicatores et Minores. Alii principaliter intendunt speculationi . . . et postea unctioni. Alii principaliter unctioni et postea speculationi.' I owe this reference to Dr. D. A. Callus.

[2] *Post. in Bibl.* (Paris, 1530-45), vi, fo. 86: 'Hi sunt reprehensores fratrum studentium qui nimis sunt intenti circa studium scripturarum. Dicunt morales: non est bonum in theologia tot questiones implicare. Dicunt questioniste: non est bonum tot moralitates fingere: et quilibet reprehendit quod nescit.'
See below for the chronology of Hugh's works, p. 272. If he went through the books of the Bible in order, as seems probable, he would have reached the Gospels towards the end of his professorship, which was in 1235.

can appreciate the value of the other's subject. The friars think that both kinds of activity are equally important and pursue them both. Hugh does not mean that the *quaestiones* ought to be included within the framework of lectures on Scripture. He is merely saying that theology in the general sense must cover Bible study as well as speculation and that the friars are refusing to neglect the one discipline for the sake of the other.

The third difference between the friars and the seculars appears in the character of their commentaries. No longer do moralities predominate. The Langtonian and Victorine technique is adopted and carried further. We can see this most clearly from the products of the school of St. Jacques, where the whole apparatus of Bible study is improved and overhauled. The Friars Preacher are famous for their great co-operative works on Scripture, the concordances and *correctoria* (lists of variant readings and amendments to the text). Hugh of St. Cher led and organized the movement. He held one of the two chairs of theology at St. Jacques, 1230-35, and continued to direct and supervise after leaving the schools, first as provincial of the Order, then as cardinal. His postills cover the whole Bible. They were to be found on the shelves of any self-respecting library in the later middle ages and were printed many times from the late fifteenth to the seventeenth century.[1]

Before considering their character, we must pause at the unfamiliar name. *Postilla* perhaps derives from 'post illa verba'.[2] It may perhaps refer to the fact that the comment was written out as a continuous gloss, interposed between the *loci* of the text. From about the time that Hugh's postills were circulated, the word came to designate all commentaries of this kind. The word *glosa* or *glosula* is no longer applied to continuous, but is restricted to marginal and interlinear glosses. An abridgment of the *Gloss* is called a *glosarium*.[3] The words *expositio* and *lectura* are also used; but the precise shade of difference between these two terms and *postilla* has not yet been satisfactorily worked out; so it will be simpler to adopt the name 'postill' for commentaries emanating from the schools.

[1] See the list of editions given by Spicq, 324.
[2] Du Cange, *Glossarium med. et inf. lat.* vi (1886), 434.
[3] B. Smalley, 'Some more exegetical works of Simon of Hinton', *Rech. Théol. anc. méd.* xv (1948), 104-5.

The history of the expression has still to be studied. Meanwhile various reasons suggest themselves to account for its substitution for *glosa*. This word was acquiring a pejorative meaning. It implied 'glossing over' instead of stating frankly what the writer intended. Already St. Francis had asked that no gloss should be put upon his rule.[1] The word had proceeded far along its downward path by the fifteenth century: Gascoigne objected that *glosa* could mean *falsitas* and wanted to save the reputation of the *Gloss* by re-naming it *expositio communis*.[2] Possibly this may have led to the more restricted use of the term. Possibly also 'postill' was felt to be a more precise expression. Its coming into fashion makes the interpretation of a medieval library catalogue much easier. A 'glossed' text in a catalogue of the twelfth century or later will normally indicate the *Gloss*, whereas 'glosses' may stand for a commentary of the Langtonian type or for sparse marginalia. *Postilla* can mean one thing only.

Another change in terminology was taking place about the same time. *Sacra pagina* was still being used for the Bible in the thirteenth century; but it tended to be replaced by *Biblia* or *Scriptura*, while a 'master of the sacred page' might be called a master or doctor of theology or divinity instead.[3] The preference for the latter terms reflects the increasing importance of speculative theology and doctrine and their separation from lectures on Scripture. Perhaps the gradual eclipse of *sacra pagina* and the narrower meaning given to *glosa* may have reacted on each other: they were intimately associated. One might gloss or lecture on the *Gloss* on the sacred page; one postillated (the verb is also used), not a page, but some book of Scripture. A subtle change in attitude seems to be discernible. We shall see that the content of a postill will come to differ from that of a gloss in many particulars.

Our great desideratum at present is a critical study of the manuscript tradition and of the sources of Hugh's postills.

---

[1] *Testamentum* in *Opuscula S. Francisci*, ed. L. Lemmens (Quaracchi, 1904), 79.

[2] Gascoigne prefers the term *expositio communis* to *glosa* and gives as his reason: 'Glosa enim si dicatur in vulgo aliquo putatur falsitas. Dicunt enim diversi heretici quod doctores sancti putative glosant evangelium secundum voluntatem suam propriam, quamvis verum est quod Dominus verba eorum confirmavit sequentibus signis, id est miraculis' (MS. Lincoln College, Oxford, 118, fo. 111ᵇ). I am very grateful to Dr. Callus for pointing out this passage and for giving me a transcript from the MS. The printed text is unreliable; *Loci e Libro Veritatis*, ed. J. E. Thorold Rogers (Oxford, 18881), 142-3.

[3] J. de Ghellinck, ' "Sacra Pagina",' *Stud. Med.*, op. cit. (p. 216, n. 2), 56-9.

The subject has been chosen for a thesis; so it is to be hoped that in a few years time the gap will be filled. Meanwhile it is possible at least to form a general picture of their scope and composition.[1] It seems that Hugh accomplished this enormous work, comparable to the *Gloss* in volume, during his five years of teaching and that he plodded through the books of the Bible consecutively from beginning to end. Hugh intended his postills as a supplement to the *Gloss*. They were to introduce the student to the achievements of biblical scholarship, in both literal interpretation and moralities, between the compilation of the *Gloss* and his own professorship. The need for such a work will occur to anyone who has experience of university teaching. The beginner can hardly be expected to find his way about the accumulation of modern writings without guidance. We have seen that the *Gloss* was supposed to introduce students to the *originalia*. Perhaps the postills had the same purpose; they certainly succeeded in sending readers to Andrew of St. Victor. Perhaps, on the contrary, Hugh thought that it would suffice to know the moderns in excerpts. He does not suppress the *Gloss* and the *originalia*; that would have entailed the inconvenience to students of using his postills and the *Gloss* simultaneously. He does add to his quotations of 'glosa' and of such-and-such a Father 'in originali' a wide range of extracts from twelfth- and early thirteenth-century commentators: the Victorines, the Chanter, the *Histories*, Langton, William of Auvergne. These quotations are difficult to spot because they are so often anonymous. My list results from a by no means exhaustive study of the postills on certain books of the Old Testament only.

For a single person to get through such a labour in five years' time, when he had other occupations besides lecturing on Scripture, is clearly inconceivable. The solution must be, given the character of the postills, that they resembled Anselm's *Gloss* and the later concordances and *correctoria* in being a co-operative enterprise. One can almost see the team of brothers in the cloister at St. Jacques copying select extracts at the master's direction. This is not to say that Hugh added nothing of his own. Certain pieces sound

---

[1] *Rép.* no. 2; H. F. Dondaine, 'Hugues de Saint Cher et la condamnation de 1241', *Revue de science philosophique et théologique*, xxxiii (1929), 170-4; B. Smalley, 'Sapiential Books I', ii. 338-47; 'The School of Andrew of St. Victor', op. cit. (p. 112, n. 3), 161-2.

original and do not seem to occur elsewhere; but until his sources have been pinned down it will be difficult to assess his contribution except as a compiler.

Hugh's postills became what he meant them to be: an indispensable supplement to the *Gloss*. Guerric of St. Quentin, whose professorship overlapped with Hugh's (1233-42), is already quoting 'Frater Hugo'.[1] Bonaventure, teaching 1253-57, used the postills so extensively as to suggest that he may have been Hugh's pupil before joining the rival Order.[2] St. Albert used them on the Gospels.[3] I have found no instance among the lesser men of their being ignored,[4] with one exception, and this obediently proves the rule. The Oxford Dominican, Simon of Hinton, teaching for a few years between 1248 and 1250,[5] does *not* quote Hugh's postills. Perhaps he did not know of them. We have seen that one of Simon's predecessors, Robert Bacon, may have brought his student notes from Paris for use at Oxford; but the latest work at Paris may have been inaccessible to an Oxford graduate. And the Oxonians at this period seem to have been rather independent.[6] They had had time to establish their own teaching tradition.

Hugh's postills served their purpose well until towards the end of the thirteenth century. Masters will criticize them sometimes, but make no attempt to replace them in a big way. Then two Dominicans, Nicholas Gorran and in the early fourteenth century Dominic Grima, working separately, propose to make new compilations of the same scope to incorporate recent scholarship. Gorran's purpose may be guessed at from the extent of his work, and from a cursory study of his sources. We do not need to guess at Grima's. He tells us in his preface that he planned to compose a *lectura* on the whole Bible and he dedicates the firstfruits, a *lectura* on the Pentateuch, to Pope John XXII.[7] He also states explicitly that he means to add references to

---

[1] B. Smalley, 'A commentary on Isaias', op. cit. (p. 183, n. 3), 386.

[2] C. Van Den Borne, 'De fontibus commentarii S. Bonaventurae in Ecclesiasten', *Archivum franciscanum historicum*, x (1917) 257-70; H. D. Simonin, 'Les écrits de Pierre de Tarentaise', *Beatus Innocentius PP. V: Studia et Documenta* (Rome, 1943), 180.

[3] See below p. 300.

[4] B. Smalley, 'William of Middleton and Guibert of Nogent', *Rech. Théol. anc. méd.* xvi (1949), 283-4; 'Sapiential Books I', ii. 338-9; iii. 49, 72-4, 243-7.

[5] See below p. 319.

[6] O. Lottin, *Psychologie et morale aux XIIᵉ et XIIIᵉ siècles*, i (Louvain, 1942), 112, 118, 190.

[7] MS. Paris, Bibl. Nat. Lat. 362, fo. 1ʳ-2ᵛ.

the works of St. Thomas Aquinas wherever they have any bearing on the text; and he has done so systematically. His project seems to have got as far as the Heptateuch and historical books of the Old Testament, but no further. The programmes of Gorran and Grima indicate that some scholars at least believed that the current biblical equipment needed modernizing.[1]

Neither of them succeeded in replacing Hugh. In the middle of the fifteenth century Thomas Gascoigne was still putting him next to St. Jerome as an exponent of the historical and moral sense; what Jerome had written in the classical, Hugh had written in a clearer and easier style in commenting on his text.[2] In so far as anyone superseded him, it was the Franciscan, Nicholas of Lyre; but Nicholas's purpose was rather different. He aimed at providing an up-to-date guide to the Hebrew text and to Jewish tradition, plus the usual moralities, whereas Hugh had turned rather to the Latins. There was room for both sets of postills.

The history of Hugh's compilation, therefore, throws light on the methods of the early thirteenth-century masters. They were more advanced planners than we might have supposed. The first thing the Paris Dominicans did was to provide the requisite library and class-room equipment for the study of Scripture. They could not buy it, since it did not exist. They had to make it for themselves. From the very beginning they engaged in team-work which must have called for both patience and organization on the part of the pupils and their master. The failure of later efforts to repeat their achievement surely illustrates the breakdown in co-operation that occurred in the later middle ages.

The *Postillae in totam Bibliam* needed supplementing by exposition of individual books. Bonaventure on Ecclesiastes illustrates how a single postill could become a classic. I have seen a large number of postills on Ecclesiastes of the later thirteenth and early fourteenth centuries: all quote Bonaventure and all quote him anonymously.[3] The diffusion of some of his gospel commentaries suggests that they may have been equally influential. Investigation might also show that the

---

[1] On Gorran see *Hist. lit.* xx (1842), 324-56; B. Smalley, 'Sapiential Books II'; L. Meier, 'Nicholas de Gorran, o.p., author of the Commentary on the Apocalypse erroneously attributed to John Duns Scotus', *Dominican Studies*, iii (1950), 359-62. On Grima, *Hist. lit.* xxxvi (1921), 254-65; Spicq, 344.

[2] W. Pronger, 'Thomas Gascoigne', *English Historical Review*, liii (1938), 620.

[3] B. Smalley, 'Sapiential Books I', iii. 41, 'II'.

English Franciscan, William of Middleton, who taught at Paris and Cambridge and died in 1257, ran Bonaventure close as a favourite.[1] They did not compete, since their postills cover different parts of Scripture. It is interesting to find that when a master produces a series of postills, a few only may become popular. The favoured few will circulate in expensive, well-written copies. The rest will remain in shabby little notebooks of the type written by a scholar rather than a professional scribe.[2] What determined the popularity of a postill may have been fullness of treatment or a happy choice of sources. The immediate influence of Albert and Thomas on biblical studies is still problematic. A comparison of the manuscript tradition for the various works of Albert has shown that his philosophical and scientific treatises were copied much more often than his theological. His postills on Scripture come very low on the list if popularity can be gauged from the number of surviving copies.[3] The biblical works of St. Thomas had more success judged by this standard; but we do not know how much they were quoted. William of Alton, who may have heard St. Thomas lecture on the First Gospel, does not seem to have used his exposition. Moreover William bases his postill on Isaias on Guerric's. According to the latest dating of St. Thomas's commentaries, the exposition of Isaias belongs to his last years at Naples; consequently William of Alton could not have heard it.[4] All the same, one cannot help remarking the complete absence of evidence for contact between William and Thomas. Perhaps, and it is only perhaps, both Albert and Thomas as commentators were too advanced for their contemporaries.

We must now consider the formal changes that come to differentiate a Paris postill from a twelfth-century gloss. Here we shall find a striking divergence between Paris and Oxford. At Paris the tendency is towards shortness and concision. The process of separating the theological *quaestiones* from the commentary that we watched in Langton

[1] B. Smalley, 'William of Middleton and Guibert of Nogent', op. cit. (p. 273, n. 4), 281-3; 'Sapiential Books I', iii. 53-9.

[2] ibid. iii. 77.

[3] B. Geyer, 'Die handschriftliche Verbreitung der Werke Alberts des Groszen als Maszstab seines Einflusses', *Studia Mediaevalia in honorem R. J. Martin* (Bruges, undated), 221-5.

[4] 'Sapiential Books I', iii. 62-8; P. Glorieux, 'Essai sur les Commentaires scripturaires de saint Thomas et leur chronologie', *Rech. Théol. anc. méd.* xvii (1950), 246-9, 251-3.

and his predecessors is completed. True, the *quaestio* form is retained. St. Bonaventure, in his postill on Ecclesiastes, disposes a row of *quaestiones* after each chapter or portion of a chapter. But these deal with points arising directly from the text. There is no need to assume an actual discussion behind them. The fact that his *quaestiones* reappear verbally or with slight modifications in almost all subsequent postills on the same book, proves that the *quaestio* here is a literary device, just as it is in a *summa*. Then the elementary work of reading and construing the text and its glosses devolved, in the course of the century, on the *bachelarius biblicus*, the commentary proper being reserved for the master.[1] Hence the magisterial lectures of the later thirteenth century are free of the innumerable quotations from the *Gloss* that encumber Langton's. This second change is common to Oxford and Paris.[2] The first is not. Quotations from the *Gloss* in an Oxford postill, however frequent, would be a mere drop in the bucket compared with all the other material contained there.

Our evidence about the Oxford practice is so contradictory that one can only interpret it as reflecting two currents of opinion. To start from what is quite certain: Robert Grosseteste more or less identified theology with Bible study. His letter to the regent masters in theology at Oxford, written as bishop of Lincoln and chancellor of the University, states his views clearly:

'He compares them to skilful master-builders who select with utmost care the stones destined for laying down the foundation . . . The foundation stones of the building, of which the masters in theology are the architects, are the prophetic and other books of the Old Testament, the writings of the Apostles and the gospels . . . The time best fitted for laying the foundation stones is the morning hour, that is, the time appointed for the *lectiones ordinariae*. All the lectures, especially at this time, should be, therefore, on the books of the New Testament or the Old. This is the traditional practice of our fathers and elders and the custom of the regent masters at Paris from which we must not recede. Finally, in order to show the extreme importance he attached to this vital point,

---

[1] The regent master would normally lecture on a book of the Old and a book of the New Testament concurrently; M.-D. Chenu, *Introduction etc*, op. cit. (p. 265, n. 1), 209.

[2] The only difference in this respect was that the Paris bachelor read the Scriptures before the *Sentences*, the Oxford bachelor reversed the order; Little and Pelster, op. cit. (p. 264, n. 2), 26, n. 3.

with renewed insistence he begs, warns and exhorts them to
dedicate their whole time in the *lectiones ordinariae* to the study
of the Bible.'[1]

Scholars are agreed that Grosseteste's own teaching must
have conformed to these principles. Dr. Callus suggests that
some of his surviving *quaestiones disputatae* originated in the
course of a *lectio*. 'A few traces of scholastic discussions' have
been found in his *Expositio super Epistolam ad Romanos*.[2]
Robert Bacon has several short *quaestiones* in his moralities
on the Psalter. He did not find them in his sources, as we
have them, and they have no parallel in any of the late twelfth-
and early thirteenth-century Paris moralities that I examined.
Then Simon of Hinton, teaching between 1248 and 1250,
produces the good, old-fashioned, diffuse type of commentary
that contains long *quaestiones*, some related, others only loosely
attached to his text. The sheer bulk of his exposition may be
judged from the fact that his postill on St. Matthew takes up
173 leaves of a volume $12\frac{5}{8} \times 9\frac{1}{4}$ in. in size, although the
postill is incomplete, lacking the prologues and the comment
on the first five chapters. Some of the *quaestiones* take up over
a page of the manuscript. Simon's reporter, moreover, has
given us positive proof that in some cases they represented a
class-room exercise. Difficulties arising from St. Jerome's
prologue to Jonas are being discussed. A series of objections
to a statement in it are brought forward. Then the reporter
writes:

'But the master vouchsafes to answer these objections. To
the first he says. . . .'

The replies follow in order.[3]

An anonymous postill copied into the margins of a copy
of the *Gloss* on Exodus in MS. University Library, Cambridge, Kk. iv. 10, in a hand of the later thirteenth century,
would fit nicely into the picture of Oxford at this period.[4]

[1] *Roberti Grosseteste Epistolae*, ed. H. R. Luard (Rolls Series, 1861), 346-7,
summarized by D. A. Callus, op. cit. (p. 266, n. 2), 56.

[2] ibid., 54, 64.

[3] 'Ad obiecta vero magister concedit respondere. Ad primum . . .' B.
Smalley, 'Two Biblical Commentaries of Simon of Hinton', *Rech. Théol. anc. méd.*,
xiii (1946), 62. Simon's collection of *Quaestiones* is a literary, not a class-room
work, perhaps part of an unfinished *summa*. He refers to them in his postill on
Matthew; B. Smalley, 'The *Quaestiones* of Simon of Hinton', *Studies in Medieval
History*, op. cit. (p. 266, n. 2), 211-14.

[4] The incipit is: *Fecit Belsebel in introitu tabernaculi tentorium*. I have not found
any other copy. Andrew is the only modern master mentioned by name; see
above, p. 184. The moralities are mainly on the subjects and prelates theme.

The text evokes a series of *quaestiones* on liturgical and practical points, which are not strictly exegetical in character: on the ordeal by water (apropos of Moses in the bulrushes); the reservation of the Host; whether a starving man is entitled to steal; whether a man is bound to enter religion at the bidding of his parents.[1] The argument is developed and supported by an array of authorities. The terms used, *concedimus; credo; expresse dico*, suggest some kind of disputation. The date would be right for the Oxford of Robert Bacon or Simon of Hinton: the postillator must have been working after 1226, since he refers to the Albigensian Crusade in the past tense. But its events and the problems left by it are still fresh in his mind. The lawfulness of slaying heretics and in what conditions occupies him more than any other question.[2] The position of the postill in a margin of a copy of the *Gloss* suggests Grosseteste himself.[3] At any rate, the *quaestiones* contained in it point to Oxford rather than Paris in the 1230s or '40s.

Thomas Docking, teaching between 1260 and 1265, seems to have beaten even the Oxford record for length. Little wrote of his commentary on the Pauline Epistles:

'When complete, the volume must have contained at least 1000 pages: each page measures nearly 18 by 12 inches, with double columns, and an average of about fifty-five lines to a column. One can only wonder that the scribe got three-quarters of the way through before ejaculating "Maria hilff!" '

Docking's postills contain many *quaestiones* as well as digressions which are not in *quaestio* form.[4]

Here, then, we have four witnesses, and even five if we include our anonymous work on Exodus, from about 1230 to 1265, including a secular, Grosseteste, two Dominicans and a Franciscan, to the practice of attaching theological teaching to the text of Scripture. It is done by holding discussions during the lecture course, in a manner which

---

[1] ff. 129r, 149v, 172v, 174v, 179v.

[2] fo. 146v:'. . . per hoc patet quod non peccabant in terra Albigensium qui simul Christianos cum Albigensibus occidebant, quod concedimus, cum iam esset eis signatum quod recederent ab eis ne invenirentur cum illis.' Fo. 174v (on Exod. xx. 13): 'Heretici dicunt quod non debemus eos occidere. . . . Habito quod liceat occidere hereticum queritur utrum quilibet sua auctoritate sine iudicio possit eum occidere. . . . Solutio: non occidetur nisi mediante iudicio. Si vero exierit lex dat propinquo potestatem occidendi.'

[3] D. A. Callus, 'The Oxford Career of Robert Grosseteste', op. cit. 60-6.

[4] A. G. Little, 'Thomas Docking', *Franciscan Papers, Lists and Documents* (Manchester, 1943), 98-121.

goes back to the Paris of Peter the Chanter. It represents a stage in teaching methods actually earlier than that of Langton. The only objection to a generalization based on this evidence would be that practice is not quite uniform. Both Simon of Hinton and Thomas Docking deviate from their own system, Simon in his postill on Job, Docking in his postill on Isaias. Neither of these contains *quaestiones*. Flat contradiction comes from Richard Fishacre, the Dominican master. In the prologue to his commentary on the *Sentences*, written about 1240-43,[1] Fishacre makes a sharp distinction between moral instruction, which is given in lectures on Scripture, and theological questions. The latter part, as being more difficult, is kept for disputation. Modern masters separate it from Scripture and teach it in lectures on the *Sentences*. Moral instruction must come first in order; otherwise the student will profit little or nothing from his course on doctrine. Fishacre is said to have composed 'beautiful moralities on the Psalter',[2] as well as his commentary on Peter Lombard's theological textbook. Perhaps he intended them as a guide to students reading their Part I, as it were. He says that his pupils will have taken Part I, when they start on his commentary on the *Sentences*, and are now embarking on Part II.[3] He agrees with Hugh of St. Cher in thinking that moralities and questions are equally important. He is here making the point that they ought to be studied separately. His statement conflicts with the practice of his successor, Simon of Hinton, who alternates moralities and questions in the same lecture course.

Then Roger Bacon, writing in 1266 and 1267, laments the passing of the custom observed by Robert Grosseteste, Adam Marsh and the wise men of old: they attached their

---

[1] D. A. Callus, 'Introduction of Aristotelian learning to Oxford', Offprint of *Proceedings of British Academy*, xxix (1943), 32.

[2] ibid.

[3] MS. Balliol College, Oxford, 57, fo. 4b-c: Verumtamen altera pars, scil. de moribus instruendis, a magistris modernis cum legentur scancti libri docetur; alia tanquam difficilior disputationi reservatur. Hec autem pars difficilior, de canone sanctarum scripturarum excerpta, in isto libro qui sententiarum dicitur ponitur. Unde non differt hec legere et disputare, et quia, ut dicitur Sap. i. (4): In malivolam animam non introibit sapientia, prius est ut affectus informetur moribus, quam aspectus desudet in questionibus circa fidem difficilibus, alioquin parum aut nichil proficiet. Unde Tim. 6, principio (1 Tim. vi. 4): Superbus est, nichil sciens, sed languens circa questiones et pugnas verborum. Quia ergo in precedentibus de moribus instruendis audistis, ratio ordinis et consummationis exigeret ut etiam secunda pars, que est de questionibus circa fidem difficilibus, nunc convenienter legeretur.

Dr. Callus was kind enough to point out to me this passage.

theological teaching to Scripture and did not use any other textbook.[1] Thomas Docking was a contemporary of Roger Bacon. Although he departed from Bacon's ideal by lecturing on the *Sentences*, he must have conformed to it in almost all other respects.[2] The early fourteenth century falls outside the scope of this book, but if anyone wishes to investigate its practice, he has only to take down the massive volume containing Robert Holcot on Wisdom.[3] It will be found in print on the shelves of most libraries that go back to the sixteenth or early seventeenth centuries. A glance at a few of Holcot's *lectiones* will convince him that the type of commentary favoured by Roger Bacon was still being written. The custom of lecturing on the *Sentences*, in fact, did not have the effect ascribed to it by Richard Fishacre of removing all difficult questions from lectures on the Bible and of confining these lectures to moral instruction. Neither does Roger Bacon's lamentation altogether correspond to contemporary practice.

There must have been a party at Oxford, whose views were expressed by Richard Fishacre, in favour of adopting the modern Paris method of specializing. Another party must have favoured the retention of the earlier Paris method, going back to the twelfth century, which was fostered at Oxford by Robert Grosseteste.[4] Roger Bacon was still advocating it in the 1260s. It looks as though the Oxford masters compromised. They adopted lectures on the *Sentences* but continued to introduce *quaestiones* of the old-fashioned type into their lectures on the Bible. It was not a very logical solution, perhaps; but each party kept something of its original programme. This is a reconstruction from scanty evidence. One hopes it may be tested by the discovery of more Oxford material.

We must now turn to changes in content in thirteenth-century postills. We have seen that the friars revived the traditions of the biblical moral school and of the Victorines. A revival implies changes and we shall find that these are

---

[1] *Opus minus* in the corrected text published by A. G. Little, *Archivum franciscanum historicum*, xix (1926), 809; *Opus tertium* (Rolls Series), 82.

[2] A. G. Little, 'Thomas Docking', op. cit. (p. 278, n. 4), 103, 118.

[3] Robert Holcot held the Dominican chair of theology at Oxford. His *Sermo finalis* was given soon after 1333; J. C. Wey, 'The *Sermo finalis* of Robert Holcot', *Mediaeval Studies* (Toronto, Canada), xi (1949), 219; B. Smalley, 'Sapiential Books II'.

[4] Dr. R. W. Hunt points out that Alexander Nequam's commentaries on the Psalms, which were given largely as Oxford lectures, are of the full, Langtonian type.

far-reaching. They go much further than the modifications
of Victorine teaching introduced by the Paris masters of the
twelfth century. In studying them we must reverse our
usual procedure and begin with the spiritual exposition
rather than the literal. In the spiritual we shall find decay,
in the literal originality and new developments.

II. THE SPIRITUAL EXPOSITION IN DECLINE

The spiritual exposition, however much it was practised in
the pulpit and in the schools, derived its vitality from religious experience in the cloister. It drew its sap through the
roots of *lectio divina* from the soil of the old monastic tradition,
the *Conlationes*, the *Moralia in Iob*, the *Sermones in Cantica* of
St. Bernard. The abbot of Clairvaux was truly the last of
the Fathers, unless we should include Richard of St. Victor
and a Victorine mystic of the early thirteenth century,
Thomas of Vercelli. Thomas influenced some of the first
Franciscan mystics and was friendly with Robert Grosseteste. He continued to use the spiritual exposition to express
himself. It seems, however, that after the first phase of
popularity Thomas suffered an eclipse until interest in his
writings revived in the fourteenth century.[1] This in itself
signifies a change of attitude. A new conception of the
spiritual life and of the place of *lectio divina* in that life was
leading to a decline in the spiritual exposition. Our surest
guidance in estimating the change will come from the
thirteenth-century mystics. We shall find them interpreting
lectio divina in ways that will make the spiritual interpretation
superfluous.

On the one hand, *lectio divina* becomes more intellectual.
Jordan of Saxony, writing the life of St. Dominic, says that
he spent four years in sacred studies during which time 'so
unceasingly, so greedily did he persist in drinking from the

---

[1] We are still waiting for a full study of the works and influence of Thomas of
Vercelli. See G. Théry, 'Thomas Gallus, aperçu biographique', *Archives
d'histoire doctrinale et littéraire du moyen âge*, xii (1939), 141-208; M. d'Alverny, 'Le
second commentaire de Thomas Gallus, Abbé de Verceil, sur le Cantique des
Cantiques', ibid. xvi-xvii (1940-42), 391-402, for bibliography and recent
work on his biblical commentaries; D. A. Callus, 'The Date of Grosseteste's
Translations and Commentaries on Pseudo-Dionysius, etc.', *Rech. Théol. anc.
méd.* xiv (1947), 186-210; 'An Unknown Commentary of Thomas Gallus on the
Pseudo-Dionysian Letters', *Dominican Studies*, i (1948), 58-73.

brooks of the Scriptures, that he passed, in tireless study, almost sleepless nights'. This might have come from the life of almost any clerical saint of an earlier period; but Jordan goes on:

'And so, since he embraced the commands of God with such eager love, hearing the voice of the Spouse with such good will and devoted joy, God added unto him the grace of science; he became not only apt for the milk of Scripture; with the understanding of a lowly heart *he probed the secrets of difficult questions, and swallowed the meat of enquiry with sufficient ease.*'[1]

The biographer of an earlier saint would have contrasted the milk of the literal sense with the meat of the spiritual. Here the milk is exegesis, or *lectio*, the meat is theological questions.

On the other hand, the technique of devotion is changing. It is systematized. The older tradition had not distinguished very sharply between *lectio* and *oratio*. For St. Jerome, *lectio* was the ascent of Mount Sinai;[2] for the twelfth-century author of the *Scala Claustralium*,[3] it is only the bottom rung of the ladder: *lectio, oratio, meditatio, contemplatio*. Contemplatives are advised not to linger on it. The Cistercian abbot, Gilbert of Holland, continuing St. Bernard's *Sermones in Cantica*, reproves the brothers who read more fervently than they pray:

'Reading ought to serve our prayer, prepare our mood [for contemplation], not encroach on our time and weaken our character.'[4]

The author of the *Meditationes Piissimae*, in the same tradition, accuses himself of being too fond of reading:

'But I, poor wretch that I am, run faster to reading than to my prayers; I read more gladly than I hear Mass. If someone is waiting to speak to me of his need, I take up a book that someone else wants; I read it, and reading lose the fruit of charity.'[5]

---

[1] *B. Jordanis de Saxonia Opera*, ed. J. J. Berthier (Friburgi Helvetiorum, 1891), 4.
[2] *Comm. in Is. Proph. praef. lib. ix, P.L.* xxiv. 314: 'sed jam proponamus Isaiae capitulum, et cum Moyse ingrediamur nubem et caliginem, ut clarificetur vultus noster'. Quoted by D. Gorce, op. cit. (p. 29, n. 3), 191. See also 182-91.
[3] *P.L.* clxxxiv. 475-84. Probably written some time before 1150 by Guy II of Chartreux, later prior. A. Wilmart, op. cit. (p. 173, n. 1), 230-40.
[4] *Sermo VII in Cant., P.L.* clxxxiv. 43.
[5] ibid. vii. 498. The Meditations have been wrongly ascribed to St. Bernard; Dom Wilmart told me that they are found in manuscripts of the early thirteenth century.

St. Francis shows the extreme of this tendency. He did not wish his friars to have the private use of books: 'When you have got a psalter then you'll want a breviary, and when you have got a breviary you'll sit in your chair like a great prelate and say to your brother: "fetch me my breviary" ':[1] his words to the novice are well known. When a friar, recalling his love for Scripture, wanted him to have something from the Prophets read to him in his illness, St. Francis answered that though it was good to seek God in Scripture, he had learnt enough for his meditations: 'I know Christ poor and crucified.'[2] We hear much of 'prayer and meditation' in the *Speculum Perfectionis*; the 'reading' which used to go with them has dropped out.

Nor is this only in Franciscan mysticism. It also applies to the 'devout female sex' of the Dominican Order, at least in the beginning. Jordan of Saxony, writing to Diana of Andalò, the nun entrusted to him by St. Dominic, tells the sisters to be 'instant in prayer, intent on meditation'. Although the convent had stated hours for reading, its omission here is significant. It does not appear at all in his letters. We expect to hear it mentioned when Jordan speaks of Diana's meditation book:

'What need have I, dear daughter, to write my little letters for your comfort, when you have far better, sweeter consolation, in taking and reading the book which is ever in your mind's eye, the book of life, the volume of law undefiled, converting the soul?'

But no, this book is not the Bible; it is the crucifix:

'This law undefiled, since it cleanses defilement, is charity, which you will find beautifully written, when you look on Jesus our Saviour, stretched out on the Cross as a parchment, written in purple, illuminated with his holy blood. Where, dearest, I ask you, can the lesson (*lectio*) of charity be so well learnt?'[3]

[1] 'Intentio Regulae', *Documenta Antiqua Franciscana*, ed. L. Lemmens (Quaracchi, 1901), 93.

[2] Thomas de Celano, 'Legenda Secunda', *S. Francisci . . . Vita et Miracula*, ed. E. Alenconiensis (Rome, 1906), lxxi. 249. The chapter is headed: 'Quid se scire cuidam fratri respondit cum hortaretur *ad studium lectionis*.'

[3] B. Altaner, 'Die Briefe Jordans von Sachsen', *Quellen u. Forsch. z. Gesch. des Dominikanerordens in Deutschland* (Leipzig, 1925), xx, Ep. xvi, xv. 18-20. Ep. xvi was probably written in 1230; Ep. xv in 1231, 1233, or 1235. See 115-16 and A. Walz, 'Intorno alle lettere del beato Giordano di Sassonia', *Angelicum*, xxvi (1949), 143-64, 218-32. The comparison between the body of our Lord on the Cross and a manuscript is commonplace, but significant in the context. On the increasing use of the crucifix see L. Gougaud, *Devotional and Ascetic Practices in the Middle Ages* (London, 1927), 75-9.

U

It has even become possible to compare the study of Scripture, to its disadvantage, with the way of the mystics. We find this startling development in the English *Mirror of Simple Souls*, which is probably a translation from a thirteenth-century French original, now disappeared. It is a little treatise on the way to perfection, written for contemplatives, and is generally considered to be daring, but not unorthodox. In one passage, where 'Holy-Church' and 'Love' are discussing the status of souls who attain to the mystical union, they contrast the works of Love with those of Reason, which are typified by glosses:

> ' "We will say", saith Holy-Church-the-less, "that these souls be in life above us, for Love dwelleth in them. And Reason dwelleth in us. Love leadeth them, and Reason leadeth us. But this is not against us," said Holy-Church-the-little, "but we praise them among the glosses of our scriptures." '

Later on, 'Love' is questioned by 'Holy-Church-the-little-with-all-his-rude-scripture',[1] as having a deeper knowledge of God. To appreciate these passages we must set them beside the *Ancren Riwle*, which goes back to the older monastic tradition:

> 'Often, dear Sisters, ye ought to pray less, that ye may read more. Reading is good prayer. In reading, when the heart feels delight, devotion ariseth, and that is worth many prayers. St. Jerome saith: . . . "Let holy reading be always in thy hand". . . .'[2]

How far from this we have travelled! In the older tradition, a contrast between contemplation and glosses is hardly thinkable: Scripture was the door to religious experience, because, mystically expounded, it contained all the secrets of the mystic life.

In the history of Bible studies, this dwindling of *lectio* has its positive side. The old allegories and moralities were fading before an intense realization of the literal meaning. The aim of St. Francis was to imitate Christ as 'literally' as possible. He told the novice who wanted a psalter that he too had been tempted to desire books; so he prayed to know God's will from the first text of Scripture that his eye should light on; it was: *to you it is given to know the mysteries of the kingdom of Heaven: but to them in parables* [Matt. xiii. 11, 13],

---

[1] Ed. C. Kirchberger (Orchard Books, London, 1927), 105, 115, 118.
[2] Ed. J. Morton (Camden Soc., 1853), iv. 287.

which he took as a command to poverty and simplicity.[1]
By a wonderful reversal, the *mystery* of the elect means to St.
Francis, not the mystical, but the strictest literal understanding of Scripture. Similarly, in their meditations, the
friars seek to share in the sufferings of Christ. The ideal is
not new, but it gains ground in the thirteenth century.
Reading is giving way to devotions, which signifies a more
historical approach to Scripture. What is evoked by the
crib, the rosary, the crucifix, is the Gospel in its literal
sense.

The spiritual exposition was doomed to artificiality as
soon as it ceased to give an outlet to religious feeling. Logically, its use should have been restricted; but the moralist
clung to his *distinctiones* even when the mystic abandoned
them. The trope was retained and enriched by all the new
facilities for satire that the friars had at their command.
They themselves were introducing new Orders into society,
whose customs could be praised or satirized.[2] Nevertheless,
we find signs of dissatisfaction with the spiritual exposition in
its traditional form. Some commentators show their distaste
for it by enlarging the literal exposition and pushing the
spiritual further into the margin. These are the saner, more
cautious spirits, whom we shall meet later. Other commentators try to revive and make it more immediate and
interesting. These are the extravagants, who must occupy us
for the moment.

One attempt at revival takes the form of a mild little essay
in conservatism, by the Franciscan, William of Middleton,
in his postill on the Lesser Prophets. Surprisingly enough,
he has drawn on the *Tropologies* on Osee by the Benedictine
abbot, Guibert of Nogent. They were written in the first
decade of the twelfth century. No other Paris or Oxford
commentator that I have read has quoted Guibert, nor does
he figure in the *Gloss* or other compilations that I have
noticed. He belongs to a generation that William of Middleton's teachers and contemporaries had practically forgotten. The masters of the later twelfth and thirteenth
centuries liked to quote mystical writers; but they had a
strong preference for the white monks. St. Bernard appears

[1] 'Intentio Regulae', op. cit.
[2] A. Dondaine, 'Un commentaire scripturaire de Roland de Crémone. "Le
livre de Job"', *Archivum Fratrum Praedicatorum* xi (1941), 115-16; A. G. Little,
Franciscan Papers, Lists and Documents (Manchester, 1943), 118.

frequently in their pages, another Cistercian abbot, Arnold of Bonneval, more occasionally.[1] A composite gloss on Scripture of the early thirteenth century gives a significant example of contemporary taste:[2] it has extracts from many Cistercians besides Bernard and from Hugh and Richard of St. Victor; the older Benedictine tradition is conspicuous by its absence. Now we see a thirteenth-century Franciscan returning to Benedictine spirituality.

Whether William had identified Guibert is uncertain. He calls him 'Gilbert' when quoting, and the presence of the *Tropologies* in a collection of works of Cistercian provenance may have misled him. At all events he must have approved of the character of Guibert's exposition. The *Tropologies* stand for a conscious effort to revive the tradition of St. Gregory and Cassian.[3] Guibert intends to investigate and exemplify the inner life of the contemplative religious by this means. He dedicates them to his friend St. Norbert for the very reason that Norbert was an acknowledged expert on religious psychology. Hence William, reading the *Tropologies*, would find there a more interior type of morality than he heard in the Paris class-room. He seems to have reacted against the external, satirical trope which was favoured by university lecturers and taken up a more religious attitude. He looked, perhaps, for a supplement to Hugh's postill on the Twelve Prophets; he rejected the Chanter and Langton as too superficial, and since none of the white monks had expounded this part of Scripture, he chose Guibert, as giving him just what he needed.[4]

This search for earlier sources is harmless, although depressing. William is reviving a revival. We have reached the dotage of the ancient Philo tradition. But instead of declining peacefully it has an attack of senile dementia.

Hitherto the spiritual exposition, at least in the West, had worked within recognized limits. It had been a way of finding in Scripture what one already believed, or what one observed in the life around one; anagogy showed what the Faith taught one concerning the end of that life. Scripture, spiritually expounded, reflected the past, the present, and

---

[1] B. Smalley, 'Two Biblical Commentaries of Simon of Hinton', *Rech. Théol. anc. méd.* xiii (1946), 69.
[2] 'Studies in the Commentaries', 133.
[3] Above, p. 244.
[4] B. Smalley, 'William of Middleton and Guibert of Nogent', op. cit. (p. 273, n. 4), 281-91.

the end of time. The span between present and Last Things was dark. Even those who had the spiritual sense divinely revealed to them, like Rupert of Deutz, had never pried into that patch of darkness. Even those who commented in the heat of political passion had never identified their enemies with anti-Christ. Exegetes had made no use of the popular speculations about his coming.[1] Some instinct of common sense must have restrained them; for if Scripture reflects all truth, and if God can reveal its sense to chosen students, why should this one particular patch of the mirror be blurred?

As the spiritual exposition became more systematic, there was less and less possibility of original interpretation. St. Gregory, St. Bernard and the Paris masters had left little for others to say. Religious fervour might find its outlet in some other direction; but a monk who clung to the traditional *lectio divina* and the spiritual senses would be drawn, irresistibly, to the only sphere that his predecessors had neglected. It is not surprising that a reformer of the Cistercian Order, the Calabrian abbot, Joachim of Flora, had a revelation one midnight in which a new kind of spiritual interpretation was shown to him.[2] Joachim had studied dialectic and he used it with remarkable effect in establishing his discovery. He had a reformer's loathing for the worldliness of the clergy; the use of the moral sense of Scripture to castigate abuses did not seem to be having much effect; he hoped that his new kind of exposition might 'stir up their sleepy hearts'. He came from a part of Italy where Byzantine influence was still strong; so it was natural for him to stress the Trinity, rather than the oneness of the Godhead, and this difference in conception gave him a new idea for the allegorical sense. Why should it express a simple relationship of promise and fulfilment between Old and New Testaments? Why should not Old and New Testaments prefigure some third period?

Joachim presented the arguments for his method in his *Harmony of the Old and New Testament* and worked out its

[1] W. Kamlah, op. cit. (p. 245, n. 2), 125-6, nn. 21, 23.
[2] Joachim died in 1204. I have used the account of his work and influence given by D. Douie, *The Nature and the Effect of the Heresy of the Fraticelli* (Manchester, 1932), 21-48. On his exegesis see H. Grundmann, 'Studien über Joachim von Floris', *Beiträge zur Kulturgesichte des Mittelalters und der Renaissance*, xxxii (Leipzig, 1927), chapter i; M. E. Reeves, 'The *Liber Figurarum* of Joachim of Fiore', *Mediaeval and Renaissance Studies*, ii (1950), 57-81.

implications in commentaries on the Gospels, the Apocalypse and Psalter.[1] They are a *reductio ad absurdum* of the spiritual exposition, so skilful and subtle that no summary can do justice to it. All the old conceptions are brought out and marvellously distorted. The *Harmony* begins soothingly, in the approved way, with a literal account of the divine judgments of the Old Testament. Then Joachim discusses their spiritual significance. He ascribes the Old Testament particularly to God the Father, the New to God the Son. The Jews understood the old Law literally or carnally, Christians understand the New Testament both literally or carnally and also spiritually; Joachim quotes the famous text of St. Paul on the need for both milk and meat [1 Cor. iii. 2]. Therefore, he reasons, we must expect a third age, belonging especially to the Holy Spirit, when the letter will be altogether cast aside and spiritual men will have perfect spiritual understanding of Scripture. As the Holy Spirit proceeds from the Father and the Son, so this spiritual understanding proceeds from both Old and New Testaments. The Old Testament period, beginning with Adam, corresponds to the order of wedlock, the New, beginning with Ozias king of Juda, to the order of clerks, the age of the Holy Spirit, which will begin with the new Elias, to the order of monks. As St. John the Baptist had prepared for the coming of the Son, so St. Benedict had prepared for this new age of the Spirit.

Two arguments are typical of Joachim's reasoning: if the Holy Spirit proceeded only from the Father, then the order of monks would have begun together with that of the clerks (and predictions would be impossible); but we believe the Holy Spirit to proceed from both; therefore the order of monks, which corresponds to the age of the Holy Spirit, must come in succession to the first two ages, proceeding from both of them. The second argument runs as follows: man was made in God's own image, that is, the image of the Trinity; he consists of a body, that is flesh and blood, and soul, that is *the breath of life*. Now *blood* is midway between body and soul: *For the life of all flesh is in the blood* [Lev. xvii. 14]. Just so, the order of clerks stands midway between the carnal order of wedlock and the spiritual order of monks.

---

[1] *Concordantia Novi et Veteris Testamenti* (Venice, 1519); *Expositio in Apocalypsim, Psalterium Decem Chordarum* (Venice, 1527); *Tractatus super Evangelia*, ed. E. Buonaiuti (Rome, 1930).

The life-giving *Rule* of St. Benedict pertains to the Holy Spirit, for what is contained there is spirit and life.[1]

This is the culmination of the patristic tradition which had identified the letter with flesh, and regarded the spiritual interpretation, the special prerogative of religious, as its antithesis.

Building on the principle that the events of Old and New Testaments together signify something in the age of the Spirit, and making a skilful use of instruments already available, the rules of Tyconius, the mystic meaning of numbers, the ages of the world as explained by St. Augustine, and genealogical tables, he was able to forecast the third age, which he believed to be imminent. It would begin with the coming of the first anti-Christ, and would be marked by a new contemplative order. The monks of the second age had not been perfect; even the Cistercians cared for multiplying flocks and herds: 'hence it is necessary that the true likeness of apostolic life should succeed them'.[2] He predicted the coming of twelve holy men, prefigured by the twelve patriarchs and the twelve Apostles.

Although Joachim was writing in the later twelfth century, 'Joachimitism' belongs to the second quarter of the thirteenth. Contemporaries seem to have found his ideas interesting and impressive without wanting or daring to borrow them. But the career of Frederick II and his persecution of the Church suggested the coming of anti-Christ, while the friars fulfilled Joachim's expectation of a new apostolic order. The seeming justification of his method caused intense excitement. Intelligent and sensible men thought there might be some truth in it. The Oxford friar, Adam Marsh, sending Joachim's works to Grosseteste for his opinion, refers to them as 'expositions' and 'interpretations' as if they were real exegesis.[3] Joachim was glossed. Spurious commentaries on Isaias and Jeremias were ascribed to him. He was fitted into the old Alexandrian conception of the 'pneumatic' interpreter of Scripture, the prophet who understands the Prophets by divine revelation. The Franciscan chronicler, Salimbene, brings it out clearly when he records a discussion, under the year 1248, between a Joachimite Minorite and a sceptical Preacher, of engaging common sense; this Preacher had as much use for Joachim's prophecies as

---

[1] *Concordantia*, ff. 9-10.   [2] *Concordantia*, fo. 59ᵛ.
[3] *Ep.* xliii, op. cit. (p. 204, n. 1), 146-7.

for the fifth wheel of a coach, remarking that Pope Gregory I had supposed the Lombard invasion to mean the end of the world and had been mistaken. The Franciscan begins by establishing, from Joachim's 'legend', with appropriate additions, that the abbot was a saint: 'You believe in the Prophets? Then why not in Joachim?' is the gist of his argument.[1]

Salimbene comments, in fairness to the abbot, that his disciples went too far. They came to grief by indulging in more precise calculations than he had intended.[2] The tendency reached its climax in the *Introduction to the Eternal Gospel*, published by a young Franciscan at Paris in 1254. This treated Joachim's works as the gospel of the third age which he had predicted, superseding the New Testament. The *Introduction* showed up the dangers of Joachimitism, and was condemned, with some of Joachim's doctrines, by a papal commission. His teaching became identified with heresy, and with the losing cause of the Spiritual Franciscans, who comforted themselves in their struggle for their primitive Rule by the thought that its author was Joachim's new Elias.

The Dominicans had taken less interest in his method from the beginning, but we hear of occasional dabbling even in their circles. Recently something resembling a 'sub-Joachimite' passage has come to light in a postill on Proverbs by an anonymous Preacher, who may have been John of Varzy, regent at Paris about 1270. I call him by this name in inverted commas to indicate the uncertainty of the identification. His comment is worth analysing, since it shows both Joachimite influence and originality on the part of the author.

'John' found in his sources an interpretation of Prov. xxx. 29-33 as a prophecy of the foundation of the Church and of the coming of anti-Christ. Men of unimpeachable orthodoxy, St. Gregory, Bede, Hugh of St. Cher, had interpreted the passage in this way. The lion stood for Christ, the cock for the order of apostles and preachers, the ram for the prelates of the Church, who withstand persecution; 'for there is no king who may resist him (the ram)'. Finally, he *that hath appeared a fool after he was lifted up on high* signified anti-Christ. 'John' converted these four orders in the Church into four ages in her history, though wisely refrain-

[1] *Cronica*, ed. O. Holder-Egger, *M.G.H., Scriptores*, XXXII (1905-8), 239-41.
[2] ibid., 239.

ing from predicting any date for the last age, when anti-Christ would appear. He makes each of the four ages represent one of the four cardinal virtues, symbolized by the three symbolic animals and the fool. The first virtue, fortitude, marks the age of the primitive Church, with the apostles and martyrs; it ended with the reign of Constantine. The second, temperance, marks the age of the patristic writers and desert fathers, when celibacy was accepted by the clergy of the western Church. St. Bernard was the last great figure of this second age. The third era, which to 'John' was 'modern times', was characterized by the virtue of justice, because the Church had power enough to subdue the world and to redress her wrongs. It had begun with the papacy of Innocent III. Previously the Church had to suffer persecution, either from tyrants or from pagan philosophers and heretics. Now 'there is no king who may resist' her. Innocent III deposed the emperor Otto IV, and Gregory IX deposed Frederick II. The last age will be marked by the prudence of those who see through the guile of anti-Christ. 'John's' periodization avoids the extremes of optimism and pessimism inherent in Joachimite prophecies. He is quite realistic. Prelates living in 'the age of justice' do not strike him as remarkable for virtue. They are, he believes, more powerful but also more negligent than their predecessors. Nevertheless, there are always some good prelates in the Church, except in the days of anti-Christ; then a prelate, if good, will be at once deposed.[1]

It sounds as though 'John' were trying to turn the Joachimite method against its exponents by putting it to a better purpose, as he thought. He would find in Scripture an accurate forecast of current events, instead of wild predictions of the future. 'We are not,' his argument seems to run, 'so far as we know, approaching either doomsday or the age of the Spirit; but we *are* living in the period of the victory of the papacy.' 'John' would agree with the editors of the *Cambridge Mediaeval History*, who give this title to the period of Innocent III and Innocent IV. He voices the thought of an Order which contributed much to the papal victory. Conflicts with the French monarchy lay in the future. For the present, the Hohenstaufen had been defeated and heresy brought under control.

Joachim warms the heart of the student of historiography.

[1] B. Smalley, 'Sapiential Books I', iii, 260-5.

He stimulated men to speculate on the course of history, to differentiate their own time from others. He provided a canvas on which each could paint his *Weltanschauung*, whether it were the rebellious, apocalyptic picture of the Spirituals or the more authoritarian scheme of a Preacher. But the place for his type of speculation is not exegesis. This discipline had to harbour strange visitors in the middle ages, as we have seen. In the thirteenth century it was slowly getting rid of them and becoming master of its own household. Joachim was the latest entrant and also the most dangerous to his host.

The method sank into contempt in the later part of the century without calling forth any elaborate refutation. St. Thomas considers it briefly in a question of the *Summa*: whether the new Law shall endure to the end of the world. He contents himself with showing that no third age of perfection on earth may be expected. Man approaches to perfection according to his carrying out the new Law, which will not be superseded in this life; we cannot expect the grace of the Holy Spirit in fuller measure than the Apostles had. The Holy Spirit taught them what was necessary to salvation, but not the details of future events, which it is not for men to know. The old Law cannot be ascribed solely to the Father, since it prefigures Christ; and the new Law belongs to the Holy Spirit, as well as to the Son. St. Thomas takes for granted the absurdity of forecasting the future by spiritual interpretation.[1]

This quiet dismissal bespeaks a change of attitude towards the whole question of the spiritual sense. The real exploder of Joachim's method was Aristotle. If Scripture ceases to be a mirror, or a flesh-imprisoned soul, or even an earth-rooted building, then the scope of its reflections, the degree of its refinement, the height of its pinnacles, all these will cease to matter. The exaggerations are not worth considering separately.

III. ARISTOTLE AND THE LETTER

The Aristotelian held that substance could only be known through its sensible manifestations. In adapting Aristotle to Christianity, St. Thomas united soul and body much more closely than the Augustinians had done. The soul is the form

---

[1] ia iiae, q. 106, a. 4.

of the body, present in all its parts, acquiring knowledge through the senses, not through innate ideas. Its dependence on body ceases to be a penance or hard necessity, and becomes 'proper' to it. Intelligence and physical sensitiveness go together: 'among men, those who have the best sense of touch have the best intelligence. A sign of which is that we observe *those who are refined in body are well endowed in mind*, as stated in *De anima*.'[1]

Transferring his view of body and soul to 'letter and spirit', the Aristotelian would perceive the 'spirit' of Scripture as something not hidden behind or added on to, but expressed by the text. We cannot disembody a man in order to investigate his soul; neither can we understand the Bible by distinguishing letter from spirit and making a separate study of each.

The Aristotelian thought in terms of causality rather than reflections. God, pure action, is the first mover, who moves the inferior causes from potentiality to act. Just as the body won a new dignity, so the inferior causes won a power of action which they had not possessed in the Augustinian tradition, and this also reacted on Bible study. As God is the 'first mover' of the universe, so he is the 'first author' of Scripture; the sacred writers are authors too, chosen by God as instruments of his revelation, and acting under his motion, but choosing their own words and their own material. Scripture began to seem less like a mirror of universal truth and more like a collection of works whose authors had intended to teach particular truths; so exegesis was bound to resolve itself into the scientific study of these authors. The exegete fastened his attention on the letter, which represented the words chosen by them or by their translators as the aptest to express their meaning.

Such a study became possible when Aristotle had broken down the identification of theology with exegesis. Under the influence of the Aristotelian concept of science, theologians brought themselves to admit in theory what they had long recognized in the practical organization of teaching. Theology is a 'speculative science'; it proceeds to new conclusions from the premises of revelation just as each of the inferior sciences starts from its own agreed assumptions. Its method is argumentative, not exegetical. At last theologians felt sufficiently sure of themselves to drop the fiction that all

[1] *Summa Theologica*, i, q. 76, a. 5, from *De anima*, ii, 9, 421a.

their work was a mere training for the allegorical interpretation. They formally freed theology from exegesis, and hence exegesis from theology.

It was natural that they should stress the first point rather than its converse. The difficulties raised by Aristotle, being metaphysical, had to be answered by reasoning and speculation; therefore the freeing of theology from exegesis stood for progress. The converse did not strike anyone, so far as we know, as a cause for rejoicing, and it raised a protest from Roger Bacon, who was old-fashioned in his attitude to Bible studies. He upheld the teaching of the *De Doctrina Christiana*, which made Scripture a divine encyclopaedia, written in cipher; he lamented that theological questions were no longer treated in lectures on Scripture. Nevertheless, though it might be ignored or even regretted, we can see that specialization was an achievement and had positive results.

Aristotle alone might have failed to make the revolution. It would have been difficult to apply his teaching to Scripture, difficult to break with the Philo tradition, if another Jewish philosopher had not shown how this could be done. Maimonides, like Philo, set out to harmonize the Old Testament with contemporary thought; but twelfth-century Arabic philosophy, with its strong mixture of Aristotle, called for a different method. The system of explaining by allegories would not have satisfied readers who wanted to know the mind of the author. Maimonides usually prefers metaphors or figures of speech to allegories. Instead of using 'rules' which are the same for every passage, he explains these 'figures' by a study of the context and the teaching of the prophet or lawgiver. In this he was influenced by a book which was inaccessible to the Latin middles ages, but well known to the Arab: Plato's *Laws*. The *Laws* gave Maimonides a clear picture of what the lawgiver and the prophets were like, and so a key to their meaning. '. . . Revelation, as understood by Jews and Muslims, had the form of Law. Revelation, thus understood, lent itself to being interpreted by loyal philosophers as a perfect, ideal law, as an ideal political order.' Hence 'they had to conceive, and they did conceive, of Moses or Mohammed as philosopher kings'.[1]

---

[1] L. Strauss, 'On Abravanel's Philosophical Tendency and Political Teaching', *Isaac Abravanel*, ed. J. B. Trend and H. M. J. Loewe (Cambridge, 1937), 97-8.

If we begin with the idea of a philosopher king whose aim is to teach and govern his people, we can find a reason behind every detail of his work.

'What edification for the mind, what progress in virtue, what joy could be derived simply from knowing who has been prince of a particular tribe?'[1] A twelfth-century scholar, perhaps Peter of Poitiers, had asked this question, and had found the answer in 'great and profound mysteries', that is, in the spiritual interpretation. Maimonides asks the same question; his reply is: not a mystery but a reason.

'Every narrative in the Law serves a certain purpose in connexion with religious teaching.'

Historical details make the narrative circumstantial and convincing, and may be an essential part of the story:

'The reader of the description believes that it contains superfluous matter, or useless repetition, but if he had witnessed the event of which he reads, he would see the necessity of every part of the description.'[2]

Christian commentators had despised the letter and dwelt on 'mysteries' because this was the only way they knew of rationalizing what seemed irrelevant and unedifying. Maimonides taught them to find reason and edification in the literal sense.

The *Guide to the Perplexed* was translated into Latin early in the thirteenth century. The history of its various translations and their penetration into the schools remains to be written, nor have we yet a perfect description of the translations of Aristotle. But if we compare the work of a series of postillators from Hugh of St. Cher to St. Albert and St. Thomas we shall get some idea of the change in exegesis.

Hugh of St. Cher, working 1230-35, is still fumbling in his attitude to the relation between literal and spiritual exposition. We have seen that his main purpose was to make a big compilation of twelfth- and early thirteenth-century sources. He remains in their atmosphere. He still, in his prologues, makes use of the twelfth-century method of division, which we find in Stephen Langton, stressing the importance of the inner, spiritual meaning: *materia (ex-*

---

[1] *Allegoriae super Numeros*, quoted by P. S. Moore, op. cit. (p. 209, n. 3), 77.
[2] *Guide for the Perplexed*, trans. M. Friedländer (London, 1904), 381-2.

trinsecus, intrinsecus); *intentio* (*litteralis, spiritualis*); *modus agendi*.[1]
He even seems to think that the literal sense may be 'what
the Jews say', just because the Jews expound according to the
literal sense: the same old muddle. Hugh, or whoever
assisted him, has transcribed many passages from Andrew's
'judaizing' interpretation of the prophecies of Isaias. They
are put forward as the literal sense, without any warning not
to believe them, and the Christian interpretation is left for
the section on the spiritual sense. The prophecy *Ecce virgo
concipiet*, it is true, is interpreted as referring to Christ in its
literal sense, but not the 'suffering servant' passage, nor, for
instance, the verse, *Send forth, O Lord, the lamb, the ruler of the
earth* (Isa. xvi). Some of my readers may like to imagine
Andrew as the Loisy of the twelfth century; but this will
not do for Hugh of St. Cher, professor in an Order founded
to combat heresy, and future cardinal. If Hugh gives the
Jewish interpretation of the prophecies as the literal sense,
it must surely be because he did not regard the literal sense
as having an edifying function, rather than from any serious
wish to modify the traditional Christian view of the Old
Testament. However, in other places, he does show new
influences and tries to clarify the relationship between the
senses, though not very happily. For instance, he expounds
Ezechiel's vision *litteraliter, imaginarie*, and *mystice*. In the
imaginarie section he describes the appearance of the vision,
in the 'literal' section what the appearance signified to the
prophet. Perhaps the *imaginarie* derives from Maimonides
on prophecy. If this is so, then Hugh has simply borrowed
an expression and rather clumsily adapted it. The influence
of Aristotle is important but formal on Hugh. He analyses
each book, and again each chapter, dividing and subdividing
according to the method of commenting on philosophical
texts. It is at least a step towards treating the book as a
whole and discussing the contents, instead of merely glossing
each paragraph.[2]

Guerric of St. Quentin, teaching at St. Jacques, 1233-42,
introduces us to a landscape of sharper, clearer outlines.
Not only does he follow Hugh in dividing and subdividing

---

[1] B. Smalley, 'A commentary on Isaias by Guerric', op. cit. (p. 183, n. 3),
passim.
[2] I. M. Vosté suggested that Hugh was the first theologian to try this method:
'ipse iam exhibet primum tentamen exegeseos per divisiones logicas, praecipue
in explicandis prophetis et epistolis paulinis.' *S. Albertus Magnus*, i, *In Novum
Testamentum* (Rome, 1932), 13.

his text; he goes further in adopting the Aristotelian scheme of the four causes in some at least of his prologues. According to this method the content of the book to be expounded was given under the headings *causa efficiens, materialis, formalis et finalis.*[1] The scheme had the advantage of focusing attention on the author of the book and on the reasons which impelled him to write. The book ceased to be a mosaic of mysteries and was seen as the product of a human, though divinely inspired, intelligence instead. The four causes were still an external pattern, which might be imposed on wholly unsuitable material, and they were still supported by a string of artificially selected texts; but they brought the commentator considerably closer to his authors. Guerric in fact takes more interest in the literal than in the spiritual exposition. His moralities tend to be mere abridgments of Hugh's; his remarks on the letter sound original. He attacks Hugh violently for his quotations from Andrew: not that he disapproved of using Andrew at all; he has drawn largely on Andrew, independently of Hugh. He objected to the judaizing interpretation of what he considered to be messianic prophecies in their literal sense. His reporter has written, after an account of the opinions of 'the Jews and Andrew', as adopted by Hugh:

'But Guerric calls this exposition a distortion of the text and a slander on the prophecy.'

Guerric felt strongly on the subject, it seems, just because he was giving his attention to the literal sense first and foremost. The first step in its exposition was to clear away the mists that surrounded the division between the senses, to establish that the literal sense was the full meaning of the author. Then and only then was it possible to appraise the content. Guerric was especially attracted by the metaphysical implications of his text. He draws it out, as he solves questions and difficulties, by a close verbal analysis. A problem that other commentators try to solve by all kinds of extraneous considerations, Guerric will settle without reference to anything else. He wanted to work out the author's meaning from what that author actually says. It was a rare virtue in him.

The pity is that Guerric's postills have come down largely

---

[1] R. W. Hunt, 'Introductions to the "Artes",' op. cit. (p. 216, n. 2), 107-9.
On Guerric see B. Smalley, 'A commentary on Isaias, etc.,' op. cit. (p. 183, n. 3, and 'The Sapiential Books I', ii. 338, 348-55.

in note form. Some of them read more like the headings that a lecturer takes to class to remind himself of what he is going to talk about, than a *reportatio* of the lecture. Hence one has to content oneself with a rough impression. But if favouritism were allowed to the historian, I would confess to a particular admiration for Guerric.

Bonaventure exploits to the full all those possibilities inherent in the literal sense that Guerric had just touched upon. His postill on Ecclesiastes, prepared 1253-57, contains some spiritual exposition; but here again the emphasis is on the literal. He recognizes the special character of the book, which according to tradition presented a discussion; the author, 'Solomon', puts forward diverse opinions and then sums up at the end. Bonaventure considers all the opinions and the problems arising from them, so that his postill is largely theological in character. His prologue goes straight to the central difficulty for a medieval reader of Ecclesiastes, who held, as Bonaventure held, that knowledge was a means towards sanctification: in what sense are we taught to despise all worldly things as vanity, when we know, at the same time, that the world reflects the goodness of its creator? The postill, prologue included, is a magnificent monument to the literal interpretation of a book having a specific aim and raising specific problems. Its popularity showed that Bonaventure's approach gave his readers what they wanted. So far, however, our masters have merely displayed an increasing interest in the literal sense and have given it a greater share of their attention. They have neither theorized about its relative importance nor criticized their predecessors for spending too much time on the spiritual.

With Albert the Great we pass to attack. Albert's postills probably belong to the end of his life, 1270-80.[1] They are later in their present form than those of Thomas, which have been dated at various intervals in his teaching career, 1256-73.[2] Albert may have been influenced by his pupil, but his postills were the fruit of a long life of teaching, at Paris 1242-48, Cologne 1248-54, '57-60. Hence we may take them as representing the generation between Hugh of St. Cher and Guerric on the one hand and St. Thomas on the other.

---

[1] I. M. Vosté, *S. Albertus Magnus*, i, *In Novum Testamentum* (Rome, 1932), 5-12; ii *in Vetus Testamentum* (Rome, 1932-33), 39-40, 53.

[2] P. Glorieux, 'Les commentaires scripturaires', op. cit. (p. 275, n. 4), 237-66.

St. Albert accepts the spiritual interpretation and uses it as subtly as any of his predecessors had done. His commentary on the Twelve Prophets opens with the same text as Stephen Langton's: *May the bones of the Twelve Prophets spring up out of their place* [Ecclus. xlix. 12]; but he gives its interpretation a twist which can only be intentional. Langton had compared the dry bones to the letter of Scripture, the marrow and fatness to the spiritual interpretation, difficult of extraction. St. Albert compares the bones to the literal sense, not because they are dry, but because they are solid, taking their solidity from 'the truth of things'.[1] With St. Albert the 'literal truth' takes on a new meaning. It is not an easy preliminary but a difficult goal.

A few illustrations will show how he concentrates on the literal sense. When he expounds the book of Lamentations he explains its fourfold division on the grounds of its historical subject-matter. It is a lament for the loss of prosperity, for the loss of glory, for present misery, for the contrast of the present with the happy past. Others (he means Paschasius and Gilbert the Universal in the *Gloss*) have given other explanations, as that man and the world consist of four elements, or that there are four seasons in the year:

'But *our* custom is not to concern ourselves with divisions which cannot be deduced from the letter.'

His commentaries on the Gospels, which are fuller than those on the Old Testament, show his purpose at its clearest. The story of St. Peter's denial had lent itself easily to moralization; St. Peter signified the sinner, the servants and bystanders three stages of sin: temptation, consent, misdoing. St. Albert remarks:

'All this can be expounded morally, but it does not seem profitable to me to distract my readers' minds from the piety of faith; so we pass over such expositions.'

In commenting on the temptation of our Lord in the wilderness to change stone into bread, he says: 'this is the literal truth', and goes on to reject the conventional comparisons between the hard stone and the Law, or the sinner's heart:

---

[1] 'Signant autem *ossa* Scripturae solidatem, in qua sicut dulcedo medullae latet spiritualis sensus . . . *Ossa* pluraliter, quia in singulis istorum, quattuor sunt sensus, historicus scil., solidatem habens ex rerum veritate . . .' Quoted by I. M. Vosté, ii. 6.

x

'I think it an absurd exposition, and *contrary to the mind of the author.*'[1]

When he tossed aside these fanciful explanations, St. Albert had his eye especially on Hugh of St. Cher, whose postills he was using.[2] He quite realized how new his method was.

St. Thomas defined the new position. His *Summa* opens with a statement of the whole problem of the literal and spiritual senses and their relationship. He takes the familiar distinction between words and things from the *De Doctrina Christiana*, and fits it into an Aristotelian framework. God is the principal author of Holy Scripture. Human writers express their meaning by words; but God can also express his meaning by 'things', that is by historical happenings. The literal sense of Scripture, therefore, is what the human author expressed by his words; the spiritual senses are what the divine author expressed by the events which the human author related. Since the Bible is the only book which has both a divine and a human authorship, only the Bible can have both a literal and a spiritual sense.

The problem of what ought to be included in the letter consequently solved itself. Commentators had groped their way to the position that figures and metaphors belonged to the literal interpretation without quite understanding why. But if the 'letter' is defined as the whole intention of the inspired writer, it makes no difference whether he expresses himself in plain language or symbolically or metaphorically. The literal sense, as St. Thomas explained, was not the figure of speech, but its content, that which it figured. The spiritual senses were not derived from the words of the writer, but from the sacred history in which he was taking part, and whose meaning at the time was known only to God, its author. It was equally clear that no arguments could be drawn from the spiritual senses, but only from the letter.[3]

---

[1] I have chosen these illustrations from those given by Vosté, i. 20-1; ii. 26.
[2] Vosté, i. 22; ii. 12-13.
[3] *Summa Theologica*, i, q. 1, a. 10, *Quodlibet*, viia. 14-16. P. Synave, 'La Doctrine de St Thomas d'Aquin sur le sens littéral des Écritures', *Revue Biblique*, xxxv (1926), 40 ff. The question whether St. Thomas followed St. Augustine in holding that a passage of Scripture might have more than one *literal* meaning has been much discussed: see in addition to Synave, F. O. P. Ceuppens, 'Quid S. Thomas de multipli sensu litterali S. Scripturae senserit'; S. M. Zarb, 'Utrum S. Thomas unitatem an vero pluralitatem sensus litteralis in Sacra Scriptura docuerit?', *Divus Thomas* (Placentia, 1930), xxxiii. 164-75, 337-59. The discussion shows either that St. Thomas followed St. Augustine, or that

St. Thomas drew the conclusions of this definition in his exegesis. He had ruled out the spiritual senses as an object of scientific study. 'In figuris presignatur' was the theme of his Eucharistic hymns, but rarely of his lectures on Scripture. Reading these against a background of modern exegesis, one naturally finds the medieval element in them startling; approaching them from the twelfth and thirteenth centuries, one is more startled by their modernity. Sometimes he will put fresh life into old conventions and sometimes ignore them. In his prologues, for instance, he may begin with a text in the conventional way, but then it becomes a means for probing into his subject. On the Psalter for instance:

> '*In all his works he gave thanks to the holy one and to the most High, with words of glory* [Ecclus. xlvii. 9]. This is said of David, in a literal sense, and may well be taken to show the cause of this work.'[1]

Sometimes he omits the introductory text altogether. His exposition of Job begins with the same forcefulness as surprises us in John the Scot and Andrew:

> 'As in things produced in the course of nature, gradually through the imperfect the perfect is reached, so it happens to man in his understanding of truth. . . .'[2]

This particular book will serve us as a measure for the distance between the Victorines, Hugh of St. Cher, St. Albert, and St. Thomas. The writer of the anonymous Victorine letter will allow *no* 'useful' literal significance to Job, let it be read forthwith of Christ and his Church.[3] Hugh of St. Cher will admit a certain literal intention: to show us the depths of human misery and to teach us patience. Still hypnotized by St. Gregory's *Moralia*, he says that the value of the book is practical rather than speculative.[4] Occasionally he abandons the literal sense and expounds

---

[1] *Expositio Aurea* (Paris, 1640), 259.
[2] *In Librum Iob Expositio* (Rome, 1562), 5.
[3] See above, p. 88.
[4] *Post. in Bibl.* (Cologne, 1621), iv, fo. 396ʳ: 'Theologie supponitur liber iste per omnes suas partes, magis tamen practico deservit intellectui. Unde infra, viia: *Militia est vita hominis super terram.*'

---

he did not make his meaning clear. In his exegesis he generally avoids long lists of alternative explanations, such as his predecessors were accustomed to give; and this suggests that he preferred only one literal meaning.

only in the spiritual.[1] St. Albert had learnt from Maimonides to read the book of Job as a philosophical discussion on providence and human suffering. He suggests this view in his prologue, together with the older one: the book shows us that the sufferings of the righteous will end in consolation, and are necessary to teach them wisdom in this life; it exhorts us to patience.[2] He honours the special character of the book by quoting from pagan poets and philosophers more frequently than in his other commentaries,[3] and he follows Maimonides in differentiating the arguments of the four friends. One has the impression of an experiment in exegesis, less attractive than it might have been because the argument between Job and his friends has been ruthlessly, tediously forced into the framework of a scholastic disputation, which God eventually 'determines' in favour of Job.

Unlike St. Albert, St. Thomas does not quote from the *Guide*; he has assimilated and made it his own, in principle though not always in detail. The aim of the book of Job, in his view, is to show 'by probable reasons that human affairs are governed by divine providence'. Patience is not even mentioned. The sufferings of a righteous man are a theme, chosen as the basis of discussion. Whether they are a true story or simply a parable does not affect the argument, although, St. Thomas adds, a text of Ezechiel [xiv. 14] seems to treat Job as an historical person. Surely, one asks, the traditional Gregorian view of the book must be recognized somewhere? Reading through the prologue one waits with some excitement to see what treatment it will get. St. Thomas leaves it to the last sentence: he proposes 'to expound this book compendiously according to the literal sense; for blessed Pope Gregory has opened its mysteries to us so subtly and discreetly, that it seems nothing more need be added'.

Thanks to his 'compendious' treatment, the 'purpose' never disappears behind the exposition of isolated texts. St. Thomas quotes less from the philosophers than St. Albert does, but he concentrates on the philosophy of the book. Taken with the last sentence of the prologue, the exposition illustrates for us the whole distance between St. Thomas and the Alexandrians.

---

[1] Fo. 432ᵛ on Job xxix; in other passages the literal sense is dismissed cursorily; fo. 434 on xxx: 'Litera plana est et aperta historia.'

[2] *Commentarii in Iob*, ed. M. Weiss (Freiburg i. Br., 1904), 1, 2.

[3] Vosté, i. 45-6.

The history of one particular text will illustrate this distance in greater detail. We may take a precept of the Law, *Thou shalt not boil a kid in the milk of his dam* [Exod. xxiii. 19], and see what it conveyed to various commentators from St. Augustine to St. Thomas. St. Augustine denied that the precept had any literal meaning. He felt that its absurdity would be inconsistent with the dignity of Scripture. Bringing all the resources of allegory into play, he interpreted it as a prophecy that Christ should not perish in the slaughter of the innocents.[1] Whether the lawgiver meant it for a prophecy; what it meant to the people for whom he legislated; whether, in practice, it was regarded as an actual law on the same footing as those which had a literal sense: none of these questions is answered or even asked.

They did occur to later commentators, who found the denial of the literal sense perplexing. John the Scot, in a valiant search for clarity, divided the content of Scripture into two heads, symbol and mystery. A mystery has an historical institution which has been recorded; examples are the Tabernacle and the Law in the Old Testament, Baptism and the Eucharist in the New. A symbol does not refer to any historical event; it is verbal; things are sometimes spoken of as though they had happened, when in fact it is understood that they have not. As examples of symbols John gives a poetic metaphor: *The mountains skipped like rams* [Ps. cxiii. 4]; the parable of Dives and Lazarus; doctrinal passages such as: *In the beginning was the Word* [John i. 1]; and, curiously out of place in this otherwise intelligible classification, the precept against boiling a kid in milk.[2] It was the only solution he could think of for St. Augustine's denial of the literal meaning, which forbade him to treat the precept as an ordinary part of the Law. The legal mind of Gratian, struggling with the same kind of problem, arrived at a different, but hardly more satisfying answer. Certain things were allowed on account of their value as 'the sacrament of things to come'.[3] He means, presumably, that such precepts were realities for the people who received them; but they could have no educative value, except to men endowed with the spirit of

[1] *Quaestiones in Heptateuchum*, ii. 90; *P.L.* xxxiv. 629.
[2] *Commentarius in Ioannem, P.L.* cxxii. 344-8.
[3] *Decretum*, cxxxi, q. i, c. 7, quoted by G. Le Bras, 'Les Écritures dans le Décret de Gratien', *Zeitschrift Savigny*, lvii (Kanon. Abt. xxvii, 1938), 63. Gratian instances the permission to the Jews to offer animal sacrifices and David's marriage to Bethsabee.

prophecy; they were intended for the instruction of Christians, reading the Old Testament. Gratian has done his best to adapt the Augustinian conception to a twelfth-century canon law book. By accepting precepts of the Old Law as historical, he has to make them out as irrational according to the historical sense; the allegorical sense must be added to save them from absurdity. We can watch our commentators reaching the same conclusion. Gratian's approach is preferred to John the Scot's.

Andrew found in his conversations with rabbis that the precept was still observed. He supposed, therefore, that it must have a literal sense, and that this was what the Jews believed and practised concerning it:

> 'The Hebrew word for which we have "lamb" or "kid" means rather "something separated"; the sense is: nothing which is separated from the flesh, that is, that which is conceived and brought forth by fleshly generation. The Jews think that this has to be prescribed on account of birds', which are allowed. 'To this day,' he continues, 'they do not cook the flesh of any "walking" animal in milk, or in any milk product, such as butter or cheese. They interpret the prohibition of any milk, and think that the mother's was specially mentioned because it was the most accessible.'[1]

He also gives a contemporary Jewish view.

When Stephen Langton had to face the contradiction between St. Augustine and Andrew, he inclined to Andrew:

> 'Augustine says he does not see how this can be understood literally, and that therefore we must have recourse to the spiritual meaning. But there may be a literal sense, i.e.: *Thou shalt not boil* it while it is still too young and tender. . . .'

[1] MS. C.C.C. 30, fo. 29b: 'Verbum Hebraicum pro quo nos hedum sive agnum habemus magis separatum significat, et est sensus: nichil quod separatum est a carne, i.e. quod per generationem carnalem conceptum et editum est, quod propter aves determinandum Iudei putant; nichil, inquam, tale in lacte coques. Observant usque hodie Iudei ut nullius gressibilis animalis carnes in lacte vel cum alio eorum que de lacte fiunt, scil. caseo vel butyro et huiusmodi coctas comedant. Non ideo putant in lacte matris sue agni scil. vel hedi vel separati dictum fuisse quod si in alterius pecoris lacte coquatur transgressio non sit, sed quia hoc lac paratius et magis presto quam aliud forsitan inveniri possit. Nec ideo nec de agno vel hedo hoc prohibitum quod de aliis animantibus fieri liceat, sed quod de hoc animali precipitur de omnibus potius, exceptis avibus que non de carne sed de ovis separantur, debere intellegi. Sunt tamen qui non de quolibet agno vel hedo hoc dictum putant, sed de his tantum que Domino offeruntur, de quibus Dominus in lege precipit dicens: *bos, ovis et capra cum generata fuerint vii diebus erunt sub ubere matris sue* . . . Hi hoc modo litteram exponunt: *Non coques hedum,* i.e. non offeres ad occidendum et coquendum dum est *in lacte matris sue,* i.e. dum recenter natus non herba pascitur, sed solo lacte matris sue alitur.' See above, pp. 153-4.

He then quotes from Andrew, and ends with allegorical and moral interpretations.[1] Hugh of St. Cher reproduces Langton.[2]

Andrew tacitly, Langton openly, have ventured to contradict St. Augustine by giving the passage a literal sense in spite of its 'absurdity'. They are curious to know what the prohibition actually covered. The idea that its literal sense might have any spiritual value does not occur to them. The spiritual value comes from the allegorical and moral sense.

The *Guide to the Perplexed* intends to show that the Law commanded nothing absurd. The prohibition is justified for hygienic reasons. 'Meat boiled in milk is undoubtedly gross food and makes overful'; moreover the purpose of the Law was to wean the Jews from idolatry; this kind of food had probably been used in offerings to idols.[3]

St. Thomas accepts the position of Stephen Langton: the precepts of the old Law had a literal, an allegorical, and a moral sense. He adds to this the teaching of the *Guide*; they had not only a literal sense but a literal reason:

'... The reason for whatever conduces to an end must be taken from that end. Now the end of the ceremonial precepts was twofold, for they were ordained to the divine worship, for that particular time, and to the foreshadowing of Christ ... Accordingly the reason for the ceremonial precepts of the Old Law can be taken in two ways. First in respect of the divine worship which was to be observed for that particular time: *and these reasons are literal.*'[4]

Just as the literal sense includes verbal metaphor, so it includes the religious significance of the ceremonial precepts. When he comes to the prohibition against boiling in milk, he states the objection that the literal sense is absurd, and gives an answer which has been partly suggested by Maimonides:

'Although the kid that is slain has no perception of the manner in which its flesh is cooked, yet it would savour of heartlessness if the dam's milk, which was intended for the nourishment of her offspring, were served up on the same dish.

[1] MS. Trinity College, Oxford, 65, fo. 133ª⁻ᵇ: 'Augustinus dicit se nescire quomodo hoc ad proprietatem littere possit intelligi; ideo recurrendum est ad intelligentiam spiritualem: et potest esse sensus ad litteram i.e. non coques eum dum adhuc nimis tener est et lacte matris nutritur ... Potest autem intelligi allegorice dupliciter: hedus est Christus ... Moraliter hedus est peccator. ...'
[2] Op. cit., i. 9ɪ.   [3] Op. cit., i. 371.   [4] iª iiªᵉ, q. 102, a. 2.

'. . . It might also be said that the Gentiles in celebrating the feasts of their idols, prepared the flesh of kids in this manner. . . .'

Prohibitions of this kind were not irrational at the time. The Law took man as he was, a compound of reason and feeling; it worked on his pity for animals in order to increase his kindness to his fellow-men.[1]

Modern study of primitive law has shown that the purpose of these precepts was more complicated than Maimonides and St. Thomas thought. But this is a very minor point. St. Thomas had brought Christian exegesis to a stage where the Old Testament precepts could be made a subject of scientific study. At the same time he was giving content to the teaching of the Fathers, that the Old Testament was a history of religious education.

We can see the effect of these changes in political science as well as in exegesis. When Dante, a pupil of the Dominicans, wanted to show the fallacy of the famous arguments from the sun and moon and the two swords, he was in a far stronger position than Stephen Langton. The question for him was not as it had been for Langton: Do the properties of the sun correspond perfectly with those of the Church? He considers, not the words in themselves, but the intention of the author: Did Moses intend the greater and lesser lights to signify the relations between Church and State? The sequence of his narrative of Creation makes this improbable. Rule is 'accidental' to man and a consequence of his fall. Why, then, should it be introduced before we are even told of man's creation? Similarly in the argument from the two swords, Dante sends us to the context. The words: *let him sell his coat and buy a sword* [Lk. xxii. 36] were addressed to the Twelve, and were a warning to prepare for persecution. *It is enough* meant not that two swords were the right number, but, 'since you have no more'. The character of St. Peter, as drawn by all four Evangelists, makes it most unlikely that he was using 'sword' in a different sense from his Master; his answers are always direct, hasty, unreflecting, corresponding to his sincerity and his 'natural purity and simplicity'. If, however, the words are to be understood *typice*, then they must refer to a parallel text: *I come not to send peace but a sword* [Mt. x. 34]. St. Peter was thinking of this spiritual warfare when he answered: *here are two swords*; he

[1] ibid., a. 6, ad 4.

meant that the Twelve were ready to fight by word and deed.[1]

This is not a concession to the 'spiritual interpretation'; it in no way resembles the solution contrived by Langton. Dante is still thinking of the intention of his author. *Typice* for him has the sense of 'metaphorically'. Hence it is part of the literal interpretation. He assumes all through the discussion that an argument, to be valid, must be based on this. If, conceding the utmost possible, the sun and moon and the two swords have a metaphorical meaning, then we must deduce it from a study of the context, and ask how Moses or the Evangelist intended it. Like St. Thomas, Dante uses the spiritual senses in poetry but not in argument.

These two express the change for us with the incisiveness of their genius. But we can see it in humbler people. The Franciscan, Thomas Docking, uninspired and conscientious, speaks in his lectures at Oxford of the 'subtle, noble, literal sense'.[2] An anonymous annotator of the *Gloss* on Isaias supplies the literal sense 'which is not given in the glosses'.[3] Friar Salimbene, who was a good gossip rather than a great doctor, refers to the sacred writers in the same familiar tones that he uses for popes, princes and beggars and all the men with whom he had contacts. This piece in his chronicle, where he describes the stylistic characteristics of the Evangelists and Prophets, could hardly have been written in any other century. Old and New Testament writers mix with the Fathers, ancient or medieval, and even with a pagan historian. All alike are artists whose style he can appreciate and who are intensely alive to him:

> 'Know that some writers or rhetors have been pleasant, smooth and honied, like Job and Isaias and Ecclesiasticus, John Chrysostome and blessed Gregory and blessed Bernard and many others . . . But others are very obscure in their diction, like Osee, Titus Livius, Orosius and blessed Ambrose,

---

[1] E. Moore and W. H. V. Reade, *Dante De Monarchia* (Oxford, 1916), iii. 8, 9; 369-70.

[2] A. G. Little, op. cit. (p. 278, n. 4), 112, n. 2.

[3] MS. Oxford, Bodl. Auct. D. 2. 10, fo. 86ᵛ: 'Sensus historie, de quo tacent glose . . .'
The gloss on the *Gloss* is written in a small, neat hand of about the third to fifth decade of the thirteenth century. The MS. is of unknown provenance. The author disputes with the Jews on the prophecies (fo. 19ʳ; 57ʳ), gives French equivalents for words in the *Gloss* and text (fo. 76ʳ; 86ʳ), and quotes 'Scotus in Gerarcria' on Isa. lxiii. 1 (fo. 102ʳ). I have not succeeded in tracing the quotation. I am grateful to Mr. N. R. Ker for pointing this manuscript out to me.

who in that story of a certain virgin at Antioch, speaks so obscurely, that he can hardly be understood. And be it noted that as Osee among the prophets and Mark among the evangelists and Ambrose among the doctors, so Orosius among the historians is held for weighty, difficult and obscure. Of Osee it is plain that scarcely one of his verses follows on from another ... Of Mark it is likewise plain that he followed in the footsteps of Matthew, for he repeats what Matthew has already said, without verbal adornment, for he had a rustic style and coarse, country grammar. But, because he was brief, he is highly praised by the saints and most of all by Bede, who expounded him ... Of Orosius it should be known that he was a Spaniard from a little town which is by the sea, whose name, though I knew it before, I don't remember now ... Let enough be said of this matter.'[1]

At some time in the thirteenth century commentators step back 'through the looking-glass', out of their world of reflections into everyday life. The first impulse seems to come from religious experience. We can see the Philo tradition losing its appeal, and collapsing into sheer fantasy, even before Maimonides and Aristotle supplant and discredit it. The scholars rationalize and hasten something which is already happening. The 'letter' of Scripture has captured not only their reason but their affection too.

IV. THE LIBRI NATURALES, ETHICS AND POLITICS

Aristotle did not only help his students towards a new theory of the letter; he supplied content for their exposition. The reception of the *corpus* of Aristotelian science presented scholars with the achievements of ancient civilization towards its zenith. Previously they had had little else but encyclopaedias compiled in the late Empire and early middle ages, when natural science had long been in decline, marvel, legend and symbol with a small admixture of fact. Their authors had not encouraged them to observe or experiment: Aristotle did. Scientific studies continued to be an affair of the library rather than the laboratory. To read and digest all the new books took time and energy. The testing of their truth would have to come later, and the

---

[1] *Cronica*, op. cit. 186-7. I have not attempted to render the technical meaning of *dictatores* and *dictamen*.

stimulus of research in applied science was lacking. Nevertheless, a beginning was made in the thirteenth century.
Setting aside the professional astrologers, alchemists and physicians and their contribution to astronomy, chemistry and medicine, we hear of *experimentatores*, observers and botanists among the artists. Roger Bacon was not the only one.[1] Postillators of Scripture would have studied Aristotle in the arts course; they would inevitably compare the *Libri naturales* with biblical science and cosmography. Moreover, a person accustomed to reading a scientific text, to reflecting on the mechanism of the universe and its component parts, will proceed to the study of any other text with new eyes. He will not be content to know that things happened but will ask how they happened. And he will fasten on to anything that adds to his stock of scientific knowledge.

Two possible misconceptions about the use of the *Libri naturales* may be cleared up at the outset. The series of papal prohibitions against the teaching of the new Aristotle at Paris is well known and its effects have been much discussed. It is now generally agreed that the prohibitions were addressed to the arts faculty only, and that in any case they had no lasting consequences. The theologians, though ordered by Gregory IX not to 'mingle the fictions of philosophers with the word of God', did not scruple to quote secular authors in their postills. The popes themselves set an example. Gregory himself, ironically enough, mingled Avicenna's *De anima* with the book of Genesis when urging the emperor to lead a crusade against the infidel.[2] Urban IV discussed such problems as the eternity of matter at his dinner table.[3] Secondly, there is still a widespread belief that the Friars Minor took more interest in natural science than did the Friars

[1] L. Thorndike, *History of Magic and Experimental Science*, ii (New York, 1923), 345, 378, 439, 546-8 and *passim*; A. C. Crombie, 'Robert Grosseteste and the Origins of English Empiricism', *The Cambridge Journal*, iii (1950), 356-67. Mr. Crombie's forthcoming book will deal more fully with the subject. For the reception of the *Libri naturales* and their introduction into the university curriculum, see M.-D. Chenu, op. cit. (p. 265, n. 1), 28-38, 63-4, 173-5. For the various translations and their dates and transmission see G. Lacombe, *Aristoteles Latinus* (Rome, 1939). The material for this section comes from my 'Sapiential Books I, II', unless otherwise stated.
[2] B. Smalley, 'Gregory IX and the Two Faces of the Soul', *Mediaeval and Renaissance Studies*, ii (1950), 179-82.
[3] According to a contemporary poet writing at his request; H. Grauert, 'Magister Heinrich der Poet in Würzburg und die römische Kurie', *Abhandlung der königl. bayerischen Akademie der Wissenschafts (philos.-philog. und hist. Klasse)*, 1912, 98.

Preacher. This is untrue. Contemporaries noticed in the early days of the Order of Preachers that recruits came in larger numbers from the artists than from the theologians. The student in arts brought his scientific interest with him when he entered the Order.[1] A hostile critic of the Preachers, a partisan of Frederick II, accuses them of teaching natural science to the people instead of preaching: they convert the pulpit into a master's chair.[2] The early Dominicans' interest in natural science formed a necessary background to the studies of St. Albert later in the century.

If there is a contrast in the attitudes to natural science to be found among thirteenth-century scholars, it is rather between Paris and Oxford. The English had a tradition of study, symbolized in such diverse spheres as travel to Spain in search of Arabic learning and the menagerie of beasts kept by Henry I in his park at Woodstock. This tradition is reflected in Oxford postills. They contain more quotations from the *Libri naturales* and apply them more intently to the text than was the custom at Paris. There must always be exceptions; but this seems to be the rule.

We may therefore take the two universities separately, beginning with Paris. Here all through the century we find a rising curve in the extent and accuracy of quotation. Two secular masters, Philip the Chancellor and William of Auvergne, are the first, to my knowledge, to quote the *Libri naturales* in exegesis. Philip, working before 1218, uses the *De animalibus* in his moralities on the Psalter. But he quotes them in a highly traditionalist way: Aristotle is supplementing the lore of the bestiary; he tells stories and makes lists of the properties of animals which can be moralized by the preacher. William of Auvergne, working before 1223, makes a more enterprising use of him. William's postill on Ecclesiastes (the only one that I have studied thoroughly) contains two traceable references to Aristotle. William puts the opening words of the *De anima* into his prologue and he turns to the *Meteorics* for confirmation of Ecclesiastes' account of the circular motion of water, i. 7: *All the rivers run into the sea, yet the sea does not overflow: unto the place from whence the rivers come*

[1] A. Dondaine, 'Un commentaire scripturaire, etc.', *Archivum Fratrum Praedicatorum*, xi (1941), 115-16; M. Grabmann, 'Die "Summa de astris" des Gerardo da Feltre O.P.', ibid., 51-82; R. Creytens, 'Hugues de Castello astronome dominicain du XIVᵉ siècle', ibid., 95-7.

[2] J. L. A. Huillard-Bréholles, *Vie et correspondance de Pierre de la Vigne* (Paris, 1865), 414.

they return, to flow again. Aristotelians will be surprised to hear that he found what he was looking for. In the *Meteorics* (ii. 2) Aristotle argues that rivers cannot flow both *in* and *out of* the sea or ocean. He attacks Plato's contrary opinion that rivers flow from a great central reservoir called Tartarus, and that 'all of them come round again in a circle to the original source of their flow'. Now the early translation of the *Meteorics*, which William had to use, omits Aristotle's own view and sets forth Plato's as though it were Aristotle's, without giving his refutation of it. Poor William, misled and delighted, says that Aristotle 'confirms the opinion' of Ecclesiastes. By another inaccuracy, for which he was more responsible, he refers to the *Meteorics* as the *De coelo et mundo*. That this interest in natural science was no mere flash in the pan he shows by also quoting a book on optics, ascribed to Ptolemy, which had been translated by the Sicilian emir, Eugenius of Palermo.

The first Dominican master at Paris, Roland of Cremona, had joined the Order from the arts faculty at Bologna. In his recently discovered commentary on Job the pagan philosophers burst forth exuberantly: almost the whole range of *Libri naturales*, including the Pseudo-Aristotelian *De vegetabilibus*, with Albumasar, Algazel, 'the Toledan astrologers', Avicenna, Galen, Ptolemy, the *Algorismus* and *Almagest* all appear in his pages. Roland defends the use of profane science in the study of Scripture. Not only quotations but observations are brought forward as arguments against the eternity of the world and other errors. There is talk of methods of measuring the earth's diameter and of the geological strata uncovered by excavation.[1]

One would not expect to find many quotations from the new Aristotle in the postills of Hugh of St. Cher. He and his assistants were compiling from earlier commentators who had not known the *Libri naturales*, apart from William of Auvergne. I have not found evidence of an independent use of them. Guerric of St. Quentin, on the other hand, who had studied medicine as well as arts before becoming a Preacher, refers to the *Meteorics* for a definition of rain on Job v. 10: *Who giveth rain upon the face of the earth*, and explains the physical origin of dreams from the *De somniis* on iv. 13: *In the horror of a vision by night, when deep sleep is wont to hold men.* The text Isa. i. 6, *wounds and bruises and swelling sores. They are*

---

[1] A. Dondaine, op. cit. (p. 285, n. 2), 109-37.

not bound up nor dressed with oils, roused his professional instincts and he gives a full account of the various kinds of injuries and their medical treatment.[1] Guerric's friend, the Minorite, William of Middleton, brings Aristotelian embryology to bear on the rise of the giants and on the purification after child-birth prescribed by the Law.[2] Anyone who wishes to study the range of quotation in the postills of Bonaventure can turn the pages of the Quaracchi edition, where all the references are annotated. To explain why river water is fresh, although rivers are said by Ecclesiastes to flow from the sea, he refers to an experiment, described by Aristotle, in filtering salt water to make it sweet. The text Eccles. i. 5-6, on the course of the sun, draws him into a long discussion on the motions of the heavenly bodies. Bonaventure set an example of the widest possible use of the *Libri naturales*. The practice was continued by his successors, though it becomes dangerous to assume that any quotation comes direct from the original after the publication of the great encyclopaedia of natural science by the Dominican, Vincent of Beauvais. The *Speculum naturale* circulated in a first edition, now lost, about 1244; in a later one, represented by the printed edition, about 1250.[3] Postillators found it useful.

Albertus Magnus resembles Roland of Cremona more than any other of his predecessors. He is like Roland in bringing his personal experience of persons and places as well as his scientific equipment to illustrate his exegesis. He makes a wide use of the *Libri naturales*, supplementing them with medical writers and philosophers, Greek, Latin, Arabic and Jewish. The mention of a stone, a plant or a living creature, a natural function such as sleep or pregnancy, or any kind of disease, will set him off on a disquisition based on some of his scientific sources.[4] Finally, one of the latest of our Preachers, Nicholas Gorran, adds two new works to the list. He quotes the Pseudo-Aristotelian *Problemata* (xxx. 14) to explain Prov. vi. 22: . . . *when thou sleepest, let them* (thy father's commandments) *keep thee*:

---

[1] B. Smalley, 'A commentary on Isaias, etc.', op. cit. (p. 183, n. 3), 385.
[2] On Gen. vi. 4 and Lev. xii. 1-7. MS. Paris, Bibl. Nat. Lat. 526, fo. 15, 138ᵛ. On this MS. see B. Smalley, 'Sapiential Books I', iii. 57-9.
[3] A. Dondaine, 'Jean de Mailly et la Légende Dorée', *Archives d'histoire dominicaine*, i (1946), 73.
[4] I. M. Vosté, op. cit. (p. 298, n. 1), i. 39-40, 43-7, 56-61; ii. 14-15, 24, 27. 31, 33, 35.

'The Philosopher in the book of problems says that we dream about what we are busied with or hope or wish.'

Prov. xv. 1, *A mild answer breaketh wrath*, agrees with Aristotle's remark in the *Rhetoric* (ii. 3), that dogs will not bite a person if he sits down.[1]

A study of thirteenth-century postills on the Hexaemeron should be of great interest for the history of the new science in exegesis. Such a study is promised for William of Middleton, but has not appeared at the time of writing.

The reading of Aristotle induced a naturalist outlook in students of arts and even in the theologians. Fresh illustrations are constantly put before us.[2] Do our postills provide any further examples? If so, we shall have proof that the new ideas are penetrating into the innermost preserve of theology, the study of Scripture. I can only give a tentative answer from the postills that I have seen. None of them is late enough to have been touched by Averroism, in any sense of that elastic term. And the postillators, when they touch on heresy, are always on the side of the angels. But they tell us something by their very insistence. Scepticism on the question of the immortality of the soul, the creation *ex nihilo*, the influence of the stars on human destiny, all these things are burning issues to thirteenth-century postillators, from William of Auvergne downward. William himself, Roland of Cremona, Bonaventure all assume that scepticism exists and must be refuted. They turn those scriptural texts which were employed by heretics against the heresies by long arguments. They show a much greater sense of urgency in defending the fundamental tenets of Christianity against attack than do the Comestor, the Chanter or Stephen Langton. These last three masters seem to be living in a less controversial atmosphere and strike one as almost complacent in comparison with their successors.

The *Libri naturales*, in any case, are on the fringe of the main questions that perplexed thirteenth-century schoolmen. The doubts raised by Aristotle took shape in controversy that was largely metaphysical and psychological in

[1] 'Sapiential Books II'. Neither occurs in Vosté's list of works quoted by Albert.
[2] G. Paré, *Le Roman de la Rose et la scolastique courtoise* (Paris/Ottawa, 1941); R.-A. Gautier, 'Trois commentaires "averroïstes" sur l'Ethique a Nicomaque', *Archives d'histoire doctrinale et littéraire du moyen âge*, xvi (1948), 187-336; O. Lottin, 'A propos de la date de certains commentaires sur l'Ethique', *Rech. Théol. anc. méd.* xvii (1950), 127-33.

content. The application of a scientific naturalism to particular miracles recorded in Scripture could play only a minor part in discussion, given the whole outlook of the combatants. Nevertheless, we do find indications that the miraculous element in Scripture was sometimes questioned. Boethius of Dacia held that dreams and visions had a physical origin.[1] Siger of Brabant suggested a tidal theory to account for the Deluge.[2] Neither Boethius nor Siger was a theologian. The nearest approach to this kind of controversy that I have found in a Paris postill is in John of La Rochelle on the book of Daniel. John entered the Franciscan Order about 1230 and succeeded Alexander of Hales as professor of theology at Paris in 1238; he died in 1246. As a contemporary of Guerric and of William of Middleton, he was teaching before the full implications of the new science could have been realized. His long years of teaching in the faculty of arts, before he joined the Friars Minor,[3] had given him an opportunity to study the *Libri naturales*. In his postill on Daniel we see him reflecting on their bearing on Scripture. In contrast to our other Paris commentators, who merely use them to illustrate their text, he tries to use them for explanation.

The discussion centres on the story of the miraculous fast sustained by the Hebrew children in the palace of the king of Babylon. After ten days on pulse and water, *their faces appeared fairer and fatter than all the children that ate of the king's meat* (Dan. i. 15). Some persons, John tells us, wish to find a natural reason for this miracle. To do so, they distinguish between two kinds of bodily sustenance: renewal of energy, which is obtained by taking physical food; conservation of energy, which may be obtained by a stimulus to psychological well-being, as happened to Moses and Elias. The passions of the soul, joy and sadness, naturally work for the retention or loss of physical strength, as it says in Proverbs: *A joyful mind maketh age flourishing: a sorrowful spirit drieth up the bones* (xvii. 22). Men of this opinion hold that a psychological cause, joy of the mind, enabled the Hebrew children to sustain their fast, and similarly with St. Mary

---

[1] In his *De somniis*, ed. M. Grabmann, 'Die Opuscula des Boetius von Dacien', *Archives d'histoire doctrinale et littéraire du moyen âge*, vi (1931), 287-317.
[2] In his *Quaestiones* on the *Meteorics*, ed. F. Van Steenberghen, *Siger de Brabant*, i (1931), 252; ii (1942), 669.
[3] D. H. Salman, 'Jean de la Rochelle et l'Averroïsme latin', *Archives d'histoire doctrinale et littéraire du moyen âge*, xvi (1948), 133-44.

Magdalen and other saints who fasted for long periods.[1]
But it is objected on philosophic grounds that natural heat,
so long as it is in the body, will always remain active, just as
fire cannot but act upon and consume what it touches.
Therefore loss of energy will always take place in the body
and constant renewal be necessary. So some, refining on the
point, used to put forward a twofold natural causation for
the renewal of lost energy: the multiplication of humours and
of spirits, of which each one suffices by itself. The multiplication of humours can only be effected by physical food, but
the multiplication of spirits can be effected by delectation of
the mind. They used to say, therefore (John has begun to use
the past tense), that both renewal and conservation were
effected by the multiplication of spirits. But against both
opinions, we read that Christ hungered when he fasted.
Hunger is nothing else but the desire for nourishment to
replace lost energy. But since spiritual delectation existed in
the soul of Christ to the highest degree, according to their
opinion there should have been no loss of energy in his body
and hence no hunger. To this they could reply, but without
prejudice to a better opinion, that Christ's hunger was real
but that it came of divine dispensation rather than of
necessity. For by dispensation of his assumed human weakness he hungered when it pleased him, not of necessity, nor
by reason of his humanity raised to the grace of union with
God, according to which the highest delectation existed in
the soul of Christ.[2]

[1] St. Mary Magdalen lived for thirty years in the wilderness, supported by
angels, according to her legend; James of Vitry, *Legenda aurea*, ed. T. Graesse
(Dresden and Leipzig, 1846), c. xcvi, 413.
[2] MS. Paris, Bibl. Nat. Lat. 15, 582, fo. 4b. I have tried to reconstruct the
argument rather than translate the passage exactly.
'*Apparuerunt crapulentiores.* Huius miraculi volunt quidam reddere rationem
naturalem, distinguentes duplicem sustentationem: quedam perditorum
restauratio et hec fit corporalibus cibis, quedam sumptorum conservatio et
hec potest fieri intensione dilectionis mentis et hec fuit in Moyse, Exod. xxxiv,
et in Helia, iii Reg. xix. Tantum enim in eis incendebatur spiritualis dilectio
ut nulla in eis fieret corporis deperditio. Passiones enim anime secundum de-
lectationem vel tristitiam naturaliter faciunt ad conservationem corporis vel
deperditionem, Prov. xvii: Spiritus tristis exsiccat ossa. Animus iocundus flori-
dam etatem facit, sicut dicunt accidisse in istis pueris et in Magdalena et aliis
sanctis.
Sed contra eos obicitur philosophice quod calor ipse naturalis dum est in
corpore semper agit et sicut ignis presens non posset non talem facere et
applicatus materie non consumere, sic nec calor naturalis. Semper ergo erit
in corpore consumptio et ideo necessaria erit continua reparatio. Ideo quidam
subtiliantes ponebant duplicem naturalem causam in reparationem deperdi-
torum: multiplicationem humorum et spirituum, quarum utraque sufficit per

Avicenna's account of the physical effects of the passions on health[1] has been applied in an unexpected way to the miraculous fasts described in the Bible and in legend. The result is even odder than the method by which it is reached. John's 'quidam' can only dispose of an Old Testament miracle by enhancing the miraculous element in the New. If psychological reasons will account for the health of the Hebrew children during their fast, then the hunger of Christ in the wilderness must be regarded as unnatural; otherwise it will not fit into the pattern. A strange outcome of naturalism! But what impresses us is the interest in physical processes and the search for rational explanations. Are John's 'quidam', who by the second paragraph are opining in the past tense, identical with John himself and his colleagues in the faculty of arts? I have only dipped into his postills here and there. A fuller study might disclose more examples of the same type of reasoning.

John's argument must have become familiar in the schools. St. Albert makes a brief reference to it when commenting on the same passage. He says, of the Hebrew children's proposal to fast: 'For the saints are refreshed even physically by spiritual delectation', instancing, as John had done, the fast of Moses in the wilderness.[2] When he comes to the account of the Hebrew children's ten days of low diet, he does not discuss the problem any further, but uses a characteristic terminology, saying of the sacred writer: 'Et subdit de experimento'!

Turning from Paris to Oxford, we notice first that the Oxonians had more elbow-room, since they preferred the

[1] See the penultimate chapter of the *VI Naturalium* of Avicenna, known as his *De anima*. Nicholas Gorran uses this passage explicitly to explain a text in Proverbs on the same subject as that quoted by John of La Rochelle: *Cor gaudens exhilarat faciem* (xv. 13); 'Sapiential Books II'.

[2] *Opera*, ed. A. Borgnet (1890-99), xviii. 463: 'Sancti enim delectatione virtutis etiam corporaliter reficiuntur.'

se. Multiplicatio vero humorum non potest fieri nisi ex cibis corporalibus, sed multiplicatio spirituum potest fieri ex ipsa intensionis iocunditate mentis. Ex multiplicatione ergo spirituum dicebant reparationem fieri et conservationem.

Sed contra ambos est de ipso Christo, qui legitur esurisse. Esuries enim nichil aliud est nisi appetitus nutrimenti in reparationem deperditi, sed cum in ipsa anima Christi fuerit summa dilectionis spiritualis intensio, nulla posset esse in corpore Christi deperdito et ita nec esuries. Ad quod ipsi possent dicere, sed sine preiudicio, quod esuries Christi vera erat, sed dispensanda, non necessaria. Ex dispensatione enim assumpte infirmitatis humane, cum sibi placebat, esuriebat, non de necessitate nature humane sublimate in gratiam divine unionis secundum quam erat in anima Christi summa delectatio.'

long, discursive type of postill. They also had ample opportunity to study the *Libri naturales*.[1] It is disappointing to find that neither of the two most famous masters, Robert Grosseteste and Roger Bacon, left an important legacy of exegesis. The latter was a master in arts, and so would have no occasion to lecture on Scripture; he only treated it incidentally.[2] The work of the former, as far as it can be judged from its fragmentary and inedited state, represents teaching at a rather low level, though it points to an interest in natural science. The words *rise from sleep* (Rom. xiii. 11), for instance, call forth a long discourse on sleep and dreams.[3] But both Grosseteste and Bacon must have given a stimulus to the use of the *Libri naturales* in Bible study. They had a strong belief in the importance of natural science for an understanding of Scripture and they both contributed to the study of the science itself. We cannot hold either of them responsible for the whole movement, since we find a knowledge of the new Aristotle from very early days. The first Dominican master, Robert Bacon, makes a number of allusions which are not found in his basic source, the lectures of the Paris master, John of Abbeville. Presumably Robert has added them.

Robert moralized data from the *De animalibus*, as Philip the Chancellor had done, quoted the *Ethica vetus*, possibly with one of its early glosses, and made one unflattering reference to the *De anima* (ii. 5). The last is particularly interesting as giving the spontaneous reaction of a pious soul to the new psychology. Aristotle's teaching on the sensual basis of knowledge clashed with the Augustinian. According to the traditional view, the human intellect could only function because it was illumined by God. Sense perception and human instruction were merely secondary aids to understanding: 'These things no learned man, but the Spirit gave him to know', says an early twelfth-century versifier writing of the school days of his hero.[4] A verse of the Psalm

---

[1] D. A. Callus, 'Introduction of Aristotelian Learning to Oxford', *Proceedings of the British Academy*, xxix (1944), 3-55.

[2] T. Crowley, *Roger Bacon: the Problem of the Soul in his Philosophical Commentaries* (Dublin, 1950), 17-80.

[3] D. A. Callus, 'The Oxford Career of Robert Grosseteste' op. cit. (p. 266, n. 2), 71.

[4] *S. Anselmi Lucensis Episcopi vita, a Rangerio successore, . . . scripta*, ed. V. de la Fuente (Madrid, 1870), 12:

Haec illi non doctus homo, sed spiritus ille
Scire dabat, . . .

seemed to express the accepted theory succinctly: *Thou hast taught me, O God, from my youth* (lxx. 17). Robert Bacon explains its meaning. God alone can truly be said to teach interiorly by his illumination of the understanding; human masters teach by merely external means. What then, he asks, shall we say to the Philosopher's statement that understanding is exercised by the soul, while sense perception comes from without; so that the exercise of the understanding is a voluntary, sense perception an involuntary process? Bacon's answer is to recall the boast which the Psalmist has put into the mouth of the proud: *Who have said: We will magnify our tongue; our lips are our own. Who is Lord over us?* (xi. 5). The verse had been traditionally referred to pagan philosophers. He has now disposed of Aristotle and goes on to quote Augustine on the subordinate role of the human teacher.[1]

We are told today, with many illustrations, that Latin scholars took a long time to grasp the incompatibility of Aristotle's theory of knowledge with the traditional Augustinian and that their first thought was to harmonize and to make a synthesis of contradictory elements.[2] Here is an Oxford master who sees at once that the two things will not go together. His uncompromising rejection of the doctrine of the *De anima* forecasts the later Oxford opposition to Thomism. His welcome to the *De animalibus* and the *Ethics*, on the other hand, shows that he did not disapprove of the new learning as such.

Robert Bacon's successor at several removes in the Oxford professorship, Simon of Hinton, followed his example in both respects. One of the texts adduced by Augustine in the passage quoted by Bacon is Mt. xxiii. 8: *But be not you called Rabbi. For one is your master: and all you are brethren.* When Simon comes to this text in his postill on St. Matthew he raises the question: 'whether one man can teach another?' He goes into it in more detail than Bacon had done and seems to accept unhesitatingly the doctrine, derived from one interpretation of Avicenna (and even of Averroes),[3] that the *intellectus agens* is to be identified with God. This doctrine safeguarded the divine action on the human intellect and so appealed to the Oxford men. Roger Bacon defended it

---

[1] *Libri retractationum duo*, i. 12. See B. Smalley, 'Robert Bacon, etc.', op. cit. (p. 265, n. 2), 14-17.

[2] F. Van Steenberberghen, op. cit. (p. 314, n. 2), ii. 357-497; D. H. Salman, op. cit. (p. 314, n. 3): T.Crowley, op. cit. (p. 317, n. 2), 200-7. Crowley, 163-7.

warmly in his Oxford period. It is interesting, therefore, to find Simon, too, taking it almost for granted.[1] As for the *Libri naturales*, Simon multiplies the elder Bacon's quotations a hundredfold.

Seven years ago, the only biblical work by Simon that was known was his *Moralia* on the Twelve Prophets. This has proved to resemble the hull of a sunken ship, sticking out of the water and indicating a vast mass underneath. Part of it has been salvaged. We now have his postills on the Twelve Prophets and on St. Matthew almost complete, his postill on Job and a section of his abridgement of the *Gloss*.[2] He refers his students to his own postills on the Fourth Gospel and on Romans; these have still to be discovered.

Simon commented on the literal and spiritual senses at about equal length. Either part, taken separately, surpasses the average Paris postill in bulk. Even so, he contrives to be one-sided in comparison with 'John of Varzy', for instance. Textual criticism and Jewish tradition do not interest him. He is no metaphysician. To make up for these deficiencies he illustrates in an impressive and often disarming way the impact of the new science. He also belongs to that group of commentators, far apart in time and space, but alike in spirit, Andrew of St. Victor, Stephen Langton, Roland of Cremona, who bring their text into relation with social life. The text, *I will break in pieces the bow of Israel* (Os. i. 5), suggests to him the long bow of the Welshman. He refers several times to the practice of mass knightings, which the English government was beginning to use as a device to make the duty of knighthood more popular, investing it with a kind of snob appeal.[3] He mentions the difference in accent of the 'northern' and 'southern nations' at Oxford to explain the words spoken to St. Peter in the High Priest's household: *Even thy speech doth discover thee* (Mt. xxvi. 73).[4]

[1] B. Smalley, 'Two Biblical Commentaries of Simon of Hinton', op. cit. (p. 277, n. 3), 76-7. Unless otherwise stated the material for Simon comes from here. On his philosophy of knowledge see also 'The *Quaestiones* of Simon of Hinton', *Studies in Medieval History*, op. cit. (p. 266, n. 2), 221-2.

[2] B. Smalley, 'Some More Exegetical Works, etc.', op. cit. (p. 270, n. 3). For a further proof of his authorship of the postill on Job, 'Sapiential Books I', ii. 338.

[3] N. Denholm-Young, *Collected Papers on Medieval Subjects* (Oxford, 1946), 65-6.

[4] This kind of topical illustration to the text must have been part of the school tradition. St. Thomas points to the various French dialects; see P. Glorieux, 'Les commentaires scripturaires de Saint Thomas', *Rech. Théol. anc. méd.* xvii (1950), 248.

He adduces the customs of the university and of noble households. His allusions to England, Englishmen and the English capital, London, are frequent enough to have inspired a marginal comment by a fifteenth-century hand which annotated his postills: 'videtur esse anglicus'.

No commentator has ever made a greater effort to envisage the objects mentioned in his text. The appearance of a noun, be it animal, vegetable or mineral, rouses in him a dogged determination to learn all about it. He must have worked surrounded by encyclopaedias and dictionaries. The old favourites, the *Etymologies* of St. Isidore, the *De natura rerum* of Rabanus and Papias' glossary are supplemented by the *Magnae derivationes* of Huguccio, the *Corrogationes Promethaei* of Alexander Nequam and the *Speculum naturale* of Vincent of Beauvais. Those who share his fondness for encyclopaedias will forgive his irrelevance. If you look up the word 'eye', for example, you may find a fascinating section on eye disease and its treatment and the temptation to insert it becomes irresistible. Simon's pupils would carry a lot of miscellaneous information away from his lectures. He wanted to know what things looked like. Even in his *Quaestiones* on the Decalogue, where he is supposed to be discussing problems of theology and casuistry, he spends a disproportionate amount of time on a biblical question, the disposition of the commandments on the tables of the Law. The difficulty was that if they were divided into five and five, the arrangement would have been asymetrical and contrary to the harmony and proportion observed by Providence in all his works. Perhaps the longer commandments were written on the tables without their gloss, to make them even. Here again, every possible authority has been consulted, including Josephus.[1]

The quotations from Aristotle come mainly from the *Libri naturales*. We find explicit or implicit references to the *Meteorics*, the *De animalibus*, the *De somno et vigilia*, the *De anima*, perhaps the *De respiratione*, the *Physics*. The medical works of Isaac Israeli, Dioscorides, Platearius, Avicenna are pressed into service. A reference to 'the Philosopher' on the nature of clouds, apropos of the text Job xx. 6, has hitherto defeated the experts:

'They are hollow like a sponge and receptive of the winds, as the Philosopher says.'

[1] B. Smalley, 'The *Quaestiones* of Simon of Hinton', op. cit. (p. 319, n. 1), 216.

No such statement could be found in the works of Aristotle. Eventually, Dr. Callus ran it to earth in a gloss on Bede's *De natura rerum*, where it is ascribed to 'philosophi'.[1] The gloss is printed with the text of Bede in the *Patrologia latina*, but its date is not given and we have no clue as to the author's or his philosopher's identity. Nor do we know whether Simon borrowed from it directly.

Simon will occasionally show a healthy scepticism about the information he found in his books, and even puts it to the test of experience. 'If this is true', he says, reporting the marvellous properties of precious stones from a lapidary quoted in the *Speculum naturale*. The goat has a nasty smell 'as Aristotle says and as experience teaches'. The word *zizania* in the parable of the wheat and the tares (Mt. xiii. 25) sends him botanizing. Simon collects four authorities on its meaning. Augustine and Jerome both make the point that the weed referred to must have been barely distinguishable from the young wheat. Jerome calls it *lolium*, Augustine *avena* or *lolium* or such-like. Rabanus in his encyclopaedia (quoting Isidore) adds a reference to the *Georgics* (I, 154):

'Avena, lolium, zizania, quam poetae semper infelix lolium dicunt.'

Isaac Israeli lists the medicinal properties of *zizania*. Simon compares his four authors and then proceeds to reject the Fathers' interpretation of *zizania* as *lolium*, 'cockle' in English. The cockle, he argues, is easily distinguishable from unripened wheat (the cockle, in fact, has a purple flower). The tares of the parable, therefore, must have been darnel or wild oat; he gives the names in English. They are grasses which might be mistaken for wheat. The cockle could not be, 'as is plain if one looks at it'.[2]

He shows the same anxiety as John of la Rochelle to understand the working of biblical miracles, but, unlike John, he does not screen himself behind 'quidam'. Previous commentators had been satisfied with Augustine's defence of the story of Jonas and the fish: Augustine had seen the skeleton of a fish big enough to hold a human being in its

[1] *P.L.* xc. 263: 'Philosophi quoque similiter opinantur aere denso terram sustentari, et esse in modum spongiae, atque in medio aeris mole sua immobilem pendere.'
Here the *earth* is likened to a sponge floating in the air; Simon seems to have adapted the comparison (with more aptitude than his source) to the clouds.
[2] 'Two Biblical Commentaries', 73-4.

belly. Simon wants to know how the prophet was able to withstand the fish's 'virtus digestiva' and how he managed to breathe, since even if there were space enough to hold air, would the air have been cool enough? Simon is thinking of the current theory that the function of respiration was to cool the heart. He decided that Jonas must have been granted 'impassibility' or that the fish's 'virtus digestiva' was restrained for the time being, while his heart temporarily lost its need of cooling or the air was specially conditioned for him.[1]

In his long string of questions on the Last Supper and the institution of the Eucharist, Simon is particularly interested in the problem whether the water poured into the chalice at Mass becomes wine, before transubstantiation. He thinks not, because 'experimentatores' say that wine and water can be artificially separated; wine tasters can distinguish well between a weak wine and a strong wine diluted; it would be contrary to Aristotle's teaching on the nature of physical change from one substance into another.[2] He discusses at length the manner of Christ's death on the Cross. St. Thomas has a *quaestio*: 'whether Christ was killed by another or by himself' (*Summa theologica*, iii, q. 47, a. 1). One of the arguments for the opinion to be rejected is the text Mt. xxvii. 50: *And Jesus again crying with a loud voice, yielded up the ghost.* Men weakened to the point of death lack the strength to give a loud cry. Therefore Christ died of his own volition. Simon asks the same question and he reaches the same conclusion as St. Thomas; that Christ was actually killed by his executioners. But whereas the arguments of St. Thomas are mainly logical and theological, Simon concentrates on refuting this one objection. It is a physiological treatment of the subject, softened by his pity for the suffering Saviour.[3]

Simon's postills were read on the Continent, though not as much as his little manual of theology. Of our five manuscripts, only two are in England. One, in an English hand, is now at Paris; one is in Rome and another at Bâle, from the library of the Bâle Dominicans. His abbreviation of the *Gloss* is only known from the catalogue and the remnants of the library

---

[1] 'Two Biblical Commentaries', 78-9.
[2] ibid. 85. The question arises from the validity of the sacrament if water has not been mixed with wine in the chalice.
[3] ibid. 79-80.

of the Dominicans of Bologna. It seems probable that Simon's works were publicized through the schools of his Order. Our next Oxford postillator, Thomas Docking, seems to have had an exclusively English public, but, though insular, it was bigger than Simon's. The manuscript evidence suggests that he was rediscovered by and appealed to the taste of fifteenth-century scholars; Thomas Gascoigne praised him. I know Docking only through A. G. Little's charming study.[1] This is admittedly incomplete and it raises questions which could be answered only from a reading of the manuscripts. Some years before his death, Dr. Little once told me 'not to forget Thomas Docking'. If I seem to have done so, it is because, in the first place, a writer as prolific as Docking would require a long period of research; in the second, because we already know some of the essential facts about him, thanks to Little, and the claims of the almost unknown seemed to be more urgent. It is unfortunate that his surviving postills are on different books from Simon's; so there is no ground for a detailed comparison.

Docking certainly accentuates the tendencies that we noticed in Simon of Hinton. He has an even larger range of quotations: Arab philosophers, Avicenna, Averroes, Algazel, are quoted by name; Maimonides appears frequently. A medical writer, unknown to Simon, Constantinus 'in Panthegni', takes his place beside Isaac Israeli. Ptolemy joins the writers on cosmology and natural science. Docking makes an even more thoroughgoing use of the *Libri naturales* in his exegesis. Some of his *quaestiones* might be lifted from a commentary on the *Meteorics* or the *De vegetabilibus*, rather than from the exposition of a biblical text. He is particularly interested in optics, the subject which loomed so large in both the philosophy and the experimental science of thirteenth-century Oxford. He applies a passage from Grosseteste's *De iride* to Moses' view of the promised land from the mountain. He goes considerably further than Simon in his observations on contemporary customs and superstitions, and on the habits of various types of humanity, youth and age for example. He must indeed have come near to realizing Roger Bacon's dream of the perfect commentator.

Readers of Little's paper will ask whether Docking knew Aristotle's *Politics*, a book which could not fail to have interested him. Apparently Little found no reference to

[1] Op. cit. (p. 278, n. 4).

it. As far as is known, the *Politics* is not quoted in biblical works until nearly the end of the thirteenth century.[1] The reason must be that the *Politics* came to the West later than the books on ethics and natural science. The Latin translation of the *Politics* began to circulate about 1260. A translation represented only a first stage in the reception of a book into the medieval schools: the translator kept to the letter of his text, throwing the onus of making it intelligible on to the commentator. The first commentators would restrict themselves to explaining what the author meant, without bothering about any further implications. The third stage would be discussion and criticism. It seems that St. Thomas and St. Albert performed this initial task of launching the *Politics* as a school book.[2] Hence it is not surprising that none of our postillators, even teaching after 1260, should have it at the tip of his tongue. One would expect the *Politics* to have a more far-reaching effect on exegesis than had the *Libri naturales*. The Bible is about man in society: after Genesis its references to nature, apart from man, are incidental. Hence the *Politics* could be applied more easily and relevantly. The interest of the thirteenth-century postills, from this point of view, is that they give us the background to its reception. They show an awareness of the problems of political institutions that only needed the *Politics* to provide a focus.

The most obvious symptom of this new awareness is the way postillators choose their material from books bearing on political and ethical questions. First, they go straight to the sapiential books of Scripture themselves. The patristic tradition on the 'three books of Solomon' was as follows: Proverbs and Ecclesiastes are preliminaries to the more advanced teaching contained in the Canticle. Ecclesiastes teaches us to despise the world and is meant for beginners in the spiritual life. Proverbs teaches us good behaviour and is meant for those progressing in virtue. The Canticle teaches initiates of the love of God. Twelfth-century commentators had tended to prefer the Canticle and had rather skimmed over the two preliminary books as less essential. The thirteenth century saw an increased output of commentaries on all the sapiential books, including Job, Ecclesiasticus

---

[1] See 'Sapiential Books II', for early fourteenth-century quotations.

[2] I am quoting the conclusions of the Rev. Dr. C. Martin in his thesis on commentaries on the *Politics* in the thirteenth and early fourteenth centuries, which is to be published by the Clarendon Press.

and Wisdom. Solomon could not displace the Psalmist and the Apostle as favourite authors in the schools; but he began to catch up with them. Not only is he the subject of commentaries, but quotations from him seem to multiply in other works.

The fashion in classical authors gives much the same impression. No author is quoted more often than Seneca in biblical commentaries of this period. His name appears occasionally in twelfth-century exegesis. The leaves of a thirteenth-century postill sometimes look as though the word 'Seneca' had been sprinkled over them with a pepper-pot. Robert Bacon even calls him 'the Philosopher', a title later reserved for Aristotle.[1] Then John of Salisbury's *Policraticus*, a survey of the courtly life of his times, with discussion of political problems, begins to penetrate into the class-room. The Franciscan master, John of Wales, popularized it in his *Breviloquium*. John of Wales was regent at Oxford probably before 1260 and at Paris 1281-83. It is significant that the Oxford Franciscan, Thomas Docking, and the Paris Dominican, Nicholas Gorran, the one teaching soon after John of Wales, the other writing perhaps simultaneously with him, should both quote the *Policraticus*. Gorran begins his exposition of the opening text of Proverbs, *The parables of Solomon . . . king of Israel*, with a quotation from John of Salisbury on the need for a king to be well educated.[2]

At the same time our postillators begin to let themselves be entangled in discussions on political questions. Earlier teachers had only touched on them in so far as they concerned the relations between Church and State. Our Paris masters and many another had defined this relationship, generally to the benefit of the Church, Stephen Langton being exceptionally cautious on the subject,[3] while commentators working during the Investiture Contest had engaged in violent polemic against the Empire.[4] In the thirteenth century one discerns a sincere though naïve interest in the problems of secular government. Hitherto, to judge from our commentators, the good ruler has been distinguishable by his docility to the clergy. Now something more is required of him. Hugh of St. Cher illustrates the text *A just king setteth*

---

[1] B. Smalley, 'Robert Bacon', op. cit. (p. 265, n. 2), 14. Seneca was considered to be a pagan, in spite of his spurious correspondence with St. Paul, until the fourteenth century; A. Momigliano, 'Note sulla leggenda del Cristianesimo di Seneca', *Rivista Storica Italiana*, lxii (1951), 325-44.
[2] 'Sapiential Books II'. [3] See above, p. 261. [4] See above, p. 48.

up the land (Prov. xxix. 4) by the example of Philip Augustus setting up the realm of France. Another text of Proverbs, *Playing in the world* (viii. 31), makes him think of changes in world dominion and draws from him a comment on the present situation. World dominion, he says, resembles a game of ball. The ball of empire is tossed from one power to another and 'sometimes it is divided, as it is today'. Presumably Hugh meant that power was divided between the various kingdoms of Europe and the Saracen states, whereas earlier on, as he explains, it had belonged to a succession of empires. He reminds one of Peter the Chanter in his contempt for the German claim to empire in Europe, though, significantly enough, the Chanter had given supreme jurisdiction to the papacy,[1] which Hugh does not mention in this context.[2]

Then for the first time we find short treatises on the duties of kingship inserted into commentaries. 'John of Varzy', the Dominican commentator on Proverbs, takes the opportunity offered him by his text to set forth the obligations of a good ruler to the commonwealth (*respublica*). The king has a right to suppress rebellion if his cause be just. 'John' passes some strictures on the habits of noblemen. They tend to make war for merely frivolous reasons. Having impoverished themselves by riotous living, they have to recoup themselves by robbery. The good king, on the contrary, fosters the resources of the commonwealth in real property and in chattels by refraining from taxing his subjects too heavily. He grants privileges so that he may find support from his people against a hostile invasion. He must regard himself as the steward, not the owner of his principality. Here 'John' or possibly an English interpolator into his postill cites the terms of the coronation oath, which are compared with those in the oath imposed on an ecclesiastical prelate when he takes office. Both secular and ecclesiastical rulers, we are told, swear to preserve the rights of their principality as far as they can, promising not to dilapidate its possessions and to recover what has been unjustly lost and dispersed.[3]

---

[1] See above, p. 212.   [2] 'Sapiential Books I', ii. 345-6.
[3] ibid. iii. 254-9. For a discussion of the terms of the English coronation oath at this period see H. G. Richardson, 'The English Coronation Oath', *Speculum*, xxiv (1949), 44-75. For a type of episcopal oath corresponding to that described in the postill see H. Bradshaw and C. Wordsworth, *Statutes of Lincoln Cathedral* (Cambridge, 1892-97), ii. 34. I have to thank Canon Srawley for kindly sending me this reference.

The significant point about 'John's' disquisition is not its originality, for it has many parallels, but its place in a postill on Proverbs. All these remarks on kingship have been suggested by Prov. xxi and xxix, 1-5. Another postillator on Proverbs, connected with 'John of Varzy', applies the teaching of Pseudo-Dionysius' *De coelesti hierarchia* to the text Prov. viii. 15-16: *By me kings reign, and lawgivers decree just things etc.* He adapts the concept of hierarchy, an essential ingredient of medieval thought, to the political order with unusual concreteness. The definition of hierarchy given by Pseudo-Dionysius is 'divine order, science and action' (*ordo divinus, scientia et actio*). Our postillator adds 'or executive power' (*sive executio*) to the last word of the definition. He glosses 'divine order' as 'power ordained' (*potestas ordinata*) and 'authority of power' (*potestatis auctoritas*). This brings it into line with Solomon's teaching on the divine sanction of political authority and simultaneously inserts the notion of hierarchy into Solomon's teaching. The Church is put above the State in this hierarchy; but both powers are ordained by God.[1]

Some of the English Franciscans held left wing doctrines in the 'time of disturbance' in England, 1258-67. The *Song of Lewes*, composed by a Friar Minor, makes propaganda for the cause of Simon de Montfort and his party.[2] Docking would have been teaching within this period. Little interprets one of his comments as an expression of approval for de Montfort's regime:

'It seems to me, but without prejudice to a more balanced judgement or opinion, that if some man who is prudent and well fitted for the business of rule, seeing God's people endangered by defect of government, should aspire to the dignity of ruling solely for the love of God and the benefit of the subjects, his aim is good and he desires to do a good work.'[3]

It certainly sounds like an apology for the Earl, and it is difficult to see how such a remark could be anything but topical.

Our commentators are increasingly interested in man as a political animal. They do not quote the *Politics*, but they would if they could. The desire to speculate on political questions, which led Thomas to write *On the governance of*

---

[1] The idea may have been suggested by Hugh of St. Victor's commentary on the *De coelesti hierarchia*, but the postillator works it out and applies it himself; 'Sapiential Books II',

[2] Ed. C. L. Kingsford (Oxford, 1890).   [3] Op. cit. (p. 278, n. 4), 108.

princes, is present in them to such an extent that it bursts out in their comments on Solomon.

St. Albert gets closest to the desideratum. He actually quotes 'Aristoteles in Politiis' in his postill on St. Matthew.[1] The quotation raises a number of technical points which cannot be discussed here. But this much is certain: the passage quoted comes from the *Ethics* rather than the *Politics*. The most likely explanation would seem to be that Albert wrote this part of his postill at least before he had read and commented on the *Politics*.[2] He must have known of it from hearsay and perhaps deduced its contents. Hence he represents an interim stage, when the *Politics* was known to exist and the commentator on Scripture was reaching out towards it without having it in his grasp.

His reference occurs in a treatise[3] of the type we found in 'John of Varzy' on Proverbs; but here the subject is much more developed. Indeed it deserves to be called a *De regimine principum* in miniature. Albert is defining the meaning of *regnum*. He discusses the various forms of government and outlines the duties of the ruler in justice, finance, law, defence and education, illustrating copiously from a wide variety of sources; hence his allusion to the *Politics*, obviously a prime authority on such topics. And to what text, the reader will ask, is this little treatise on politics attached? It prefaces a comment on the petition in the Lord's Prayer, *Thy kingdom come*. The earlier medieval commentators had felt that their only fatherland was the kingdom of heaven: *For we have not here a lasting city: but we seek one that is to come* (Hebr. xiii. 14). They remembered and often quoted this text whenever they came to the word *city* or *kingdom* in their explanation of Scripture. Albert has quite reversed the order. He begins his account of the kingdom of heaven by discoursing on earthly politics. We are entering a new world.

---

[1] *Opera*, ed. Borgnet, xx. 267: Dicit enim Aristoteles in Politiis quod 'ad rempublicam continendam non sufficit sermo instructivus, qui sufficit tamen ad ignorantium doctrinam: neque etiam sufficit sermo persuasivus, qui sufficit ad bonorum et studiosorum informationem: sed propter eos qui nolunt iustitiam colere, et pietatem amare, opportet esse sermonem coactivam'.

[2] *Eth. Nich.* x. 9, 1179b, 1-1180a,4. There is no such exact equivalent in the *Politics*. I am very grateful to Dr. Conor Martin for his help when I appealed to him to trace this quotation. He will deal with the problems arising from it in a forthcoming paper in *Mediaeval and Renaissance Studies*.

[3] 265-9.

V. HEBRAICA VERITAS

The first steps of commentators in their new Aristotelian universe, where things were themselves and not cryptograms, have been regarded with some prejudice. The scholastic method of exegesis has almost as poor a reputation as the allegorical. The great schoolmen were not primarily biblical scholars. St. Thomas and St. Bonaventure, it has been said, came to the Bible as theologians, St. Albert as a philosopher.[1] The very concentration on Aristotle, which enabled the Dominicans to effect a change in exegetical principles, tended to prevent their new principles bearing fruit.

Biblical scholarship demanded just that humanist culture which the twelfth century had developed and the thirteenth century neglected in favour of science and metaphysics. The *Histories* went out of fashion in the schools of the later thirteenth century and ceased to be a 'set book'.[2] Without an historical and literary background the master's division or subdivision of his text is no more relevant than the allegory and trope. It is still subjective, especially when he bases his division on the chapter system, which had been imposed on the text for simple convenience. His analysis, for a modern reader, is just as remote from reality, just as tedious, and considerably less amusing, than the *distinctio*.

Roger Bacon, the most popular of English thirteenth-century scholars, denounces the whole scholastic method in a well-known passage. He objects to the arbitrary analysis by chapters, to the arbitrary concordances and rhythms, imported from commentaries on the philosophers, the lawbooks and grammarians.[3] He accuses his contemporaries of

---

[1] I. M. Vosté, op. cit. (p. 298, n. 1), i. 35. Vosté has shown that St. Albert had a smattering of Greek and Hebrew but not enough to allow of his reading Scripture in the originals. He took his readings from the *correctoria*. St. Thomas also knew a little Greek; there is no evidence that he knew any Hebrew. See H. Pope, 'St. Thomas as an Interpreter of Holy Scripture' in *St. Thomas Aquinas* (Oxford, 1925), 118-21.

[2] See A. G. Little and F. Pelster, op. cit. (p. 264, n. 2), 25-6. They state that the *Histories* were replaced by postills which 'presumably changed according to time and place'.

[3] *Opus Minus*, ed. Brewer (Rolls Series), 323: 'Quae fiunt in textu principaliter legendo et praedicando, sunt tria scil. divisiones per membra varia, sicut artistae faciunt, concordantiae violentes, sicut legistae utuntur; et consonantiae rhythmicae, sicut grammatici. In istis tribus stat praecipuus modus artificum exponendi Scripturam. Et haec licet utilia sunt, tamen tracta sunt de philosophia.'

neglecting scientific Bible study. Their ignorance of the biblical languages vitiates their interpretation, and their principles of textual criticism are unsound. Bacon's abuse is so plausible, so carefully documented by his lists of their 'horrible' errors, his language so fresh and vigorous, that one tends to see thirteenth-century Bible study through his eyes. Therefore, before asking what technical progress was made by his contemporaries, one ought to ask whether Bacon is a reliable witness, and what his suggestions for reform were worth.

Bacon was a rebellious reactionary, or a reactionary rebel. He called upon men to think for themselves, instead of relying on authority. His own thinking, at least about the Bible, was extremely conservative.[1] He had no use for the new conception of the letter. He clung ferociously to the old Alexandrian view that the Scriptures contained all knowledge, philosophy having been divinely revealed to the patriarchs, and that the literal sense was important as a foundation for the spiritual: theology and philosophy were reducible to Bible study.[2] He believed in Hugh of St. Victor's method: language to establish the text, science to expound the literal sense, the better to work out the spiritual.[3] He approved the technique of Richard of St. Victor on the tabernacle and temple: geometry is necessary.

'in order that the Noe's ark, the tabernacle with all its furniture, the temple of Solomon and Ezechiel may be described physically . . . Otherwise it is not possible for the literal sense to be known, nor, in consequence, the spiritual. The holy and wise men of old strove after this. I have seen some of their work, and this is how Scripture represents things, that we may know old and new, and see with our eyes the cult of that people which prefigures the new.'[4]

The only difference between the educational schemes of Bacon and Hugh of St. Victor was that the field of knowledge had been enlarged in the meantime. Bacon required a much more extensive and intensive preparation for Bible study. Consequently his programme was even less practicable than the Victorine. Even Thomas Docking, who did his best t) achieve the type of all-embracing commentary that Baco

---

[1] See A. G. Little, 'Roger Bacon', op. cit. (p. 278, n. 4), 72-97.
[2] *Opus Tertium*, 79-83.   [3] *Opus Minus*, 349-59; *Opus Tertium*, 203.
[4] ibid. 226.

recommended, failed in one respect. His accomplishments did not extend to linguistics.[1] Simon of Hinton had the same gap in his knowledge. It would have been difficult for any one scholar to equip himself with all the sciences contained in the *Libri naturales* plus a thorough grounding in theology plus Greek and semitic languages.

The separate items in his programme, on the contrary, if isolated from their context, have a very modern sound. In repeating, Bacon has made his own the arguments of St. Jerome and St. Augustine for studying Scripture in the original. He explains how knowledge of Hebrew and Chaldean is indispensable to an understanding of the idiom and rhythm, and hence of the meaning of the Old Testament, and Greek to an understanding of the New.[2] He points out that Latin thought, like the Latin language, is derivative. Consequently we need not only the Greek text but the Greek Fathers.[3] We must go to the sources. *Veritas in radice*: this is Bacon's war-cry.[4]

His consistency appears all the more clearly when he turns from the original texts to their Latin translation. Although, as a scholar, his ideal was to study the sources, Bacon took for granted that the starting-point for students would be the text read at lectures, the Latin Vulgate. Therefore, it was necessary to get as close as possible to the original of that.[5] The Paris masters had proposed a particularly bad text as their standard. This was being circulated by the stationers and would soon spread over Christendom. This bad text was still further corrupted by irresponsible corrections. Quite alien readings were being inserted from biblical quotations in the commentaries of the Fathers, from the liturgy, and from the Hebrew.

Bacon held that correctors ought to concentrate their attention on restoring the original text of St. Jerome. He proved, step by step, that this was the version used by the Church (with the exception of the Psalter), not a mixed version as his contemporaries supposed. He begged the Pope to set up a commission for the revision of the Vulgate by competent scholars. They should work on manuscripts

---

[1] A. G. Little, op. cit. (p. 278, n. 4), 105.
[2] *Opus Maius*, ii, iii; *Opus Tertium*, 264-7; *Compendium Studii*, 438-9, 464-6.
[3] ibid. 474.   [4] *Opus Minus*, 332.
[5] ibid. 330-49. See P. Martin, 'La Vulgate latine au XIIIᵉ siècle', *Muséon*, vii (1888), 88, 169, 278, 381; 'Le Texte parisien de la Vulgate latine', ibid. viii (1889), 444; ix (1890), 55, 301.

older than the Paris text, collect the more common readings, and go to their translator's original when in doubt.

His attitude to the medieval accretions of the Vulgate followed logically from his attitude to the text. He disliked the anonymous prologues which had been added to the authentic ones of St. Jerome.[1] He disliked the non-patristic glosses.[2] He recognized that the Vulgate demanded a knowledge of St. Jerome's vocabulary and background which the glossators had not possessed. The *Gloss* on Ezech. xxiii. 41: *Sedisti in lecto pulcherrimo, et mensa ornata est ante te* expounds it as referring to fornication, quoting the line of Ovid [*Metam.* v. 603]:

Et quia nuda fui, sum visa paratior illi.

Bacon rightly denies that *lectus* in this context means 'bed'. The *Gloss* is mistaken. *Lectus* here is the couch, *triclinium*, on which the ancients reclined at their meals.[3] Actually he was being more classical than St. Jerome, who says in his commentary '. . . ut sederes in *lectulo* libidini praeparata'. The glossator, Gilbert, was merely illustrating St. Jerome by a tag supplied from his own 'universal knowledge'.[4] Bacon foreshadows the artists of the sixteenth century, who painted the Last Supper with Christ and the Apostles not sitting on benches but reclining on *triclinia*, according to the only antique setting they knew: 'a deliberate pursuit of archaeological accuracy'.[5]

Bacon's contribution to biblical scholarship was three-fold. He made some useful lists of current errors, false etymologies, and so on, taken from the standard aids to study (the list contained various mistakes of his own).[6] He laid down rules both for the study of the original and for the restoration of the Latin: 'on extrairait facilement de ses ouvrages un petit volume de grandes maximes, bonnes à

---

[1] *Opus Minus*, 337: 'Nam nec S. Hieronymus contra hoc in quibusdam prologis, qui male ponuntur in Biblia nostra, qui non sunt in sua, transfert male . . . ' On these prologues see above, p. 217, n. 2.

[2] *Compendium Studii*, 459; *Opus Minus*, 353; *Opus Tertium*, 211.

[3] *Opus Minus*, 355-6.

[4] The line quoted by Bacon is in the printed editions of the *Gloss* and can be verified in a twelfth-century manuscript, MS. Pembroke College, Cambridge, 61, in loc. As it is not in Raban's commentary on Ezechiel it was very probably added by Gilbert the Universal. Brewer has *mensa* for *visa*. Bacon may have taken this corrupt reading from later manuscripts of the *Gloss*.

[5] A. Blunt, 'The Triclinium in Religious Art', *Journal of the Warburg Insitute*, ii (1939), 271. Bacon could have found the idea in Jewish sources. See Kimḥi, in loc.

[6] For instance his explanation of Hexapla, *Opus Minus*, 337.

lire, et saines à méditer'.[1] Most important and valuable, he composed Greek and Hebrew grammars; fragments, probably of his rough drafts, have been discovered and published, which show that he had a good working knowledge of both languages;[2] and at least for the former, his project seems to have been original.[3] But just when he appears to be most scientific and progressive, he will produce one of those disconcerting ideas which made him suspect to his contemporaries. He guaranteed to teach enough Hebrew or Greek for reading purposes within three days by a certain method. This is mysteriously unspecified; but one can guess it. Probably he administered his grammar by magic arts.[4]

Bacon, then, was not strictly speaking a biblical scholar. No work of his directly on Scripture has been preserved. Nor did he resemble one in character. We must not take him as representative, any more than we must take St. Albert, St. Thomas or St. Bonaventure. The typical scholar, in the thirteenth century as now, was a more limited person than any of these four. He was working for a small circle, not writing, as Bacon was, at the special request of the pope. Bacon exaggerates both the neglect and the ignorance of his contemporaries. The *homo sapientissimus* whom he mentions, who had spent over thirty years on the correction of the text and the literal exposition,[5] was not so isolated as he makes out. While Bacon was saying, brilliantly, convincingly, and three times over, what ought to be done, others were quietly attempting it. They succeeded in some ways, in spite of the scholastic method and the decline of humanism.

Having broken, let us hope, the spell of Bacon, we may turn to these less spectacular men. Bacon does not mention their improved organization of teaching[6] and apparatus.

In the first place the chapter division was gradually standardized. Philip the Chancellor seems to have brought the method of referring systematically to chapters into common use about 1225.[7] Then various subdivisions of the chapters were tried, which led up to the present arrangement in verses. Hugh of St. Cher may have been the first to refer

---

[1] P. Martin, op. cit., vii. 384.

[2] J. L. Heiberg, 'Die griechische Grammatik Roger Bacons', *Byz. Zeitschr.* ix (1900), 479-91; E. Nolan and S. A. Hirsch, *The Greek Grammar of Roger Bacon and a Fragment of his Hebrew Grammar* (Cambridge, 1902).

[3] A. G. Little, 'Roger Bacon', op. cit.

[4] See a forthcoming article by E. Jaffé and B. Smalley, 'Roger Bacon and the *Ars Notoria*', *Journal of the Warburg Institute*.

[5] *Opus Tertium*, 89-94.   [6] See above, pp. 275ff.   [7] See above, p. 222, n. 3.

to these· subdivisions by letters of the alphabet. He also organized the drawing up of Bible concordances, the technique of which was altered and improved during the century.[1] This is only the best-known example of a great movement for tabulating references to the Scriptures and the Fathers, which is impressing students of medieval libraries.[2] Aids to study in the form of biblical dictionaries, William Brito's being the most popular, struck Bacon as unscientific; but they are a sign of the general activity. Scholars rarely praise popular text-books. Another sign is the publication of geographical descriptions of Palestine.[3]

Even the Paris text of the Vulgate, which Bacon denounces for its corruption, becomes intelligible if we understand what its function was. Bacon's remarks have been construed to mean that, about 1226, a committee of masters selected a particularly bad and late text as their standard for use in the schools and recommended it to the Paris stationers.[4] Some standardization was necessary, and the lecture system gave them little choice. The 'set book' for students was the Bible and its *Gloss*. Since the *Gloss* had been prepared in the twelfth century, they could not have chosen an earlier manuscript as their exemplar. Their standard text had to be the glossed text, and hence a late one. Scripture, as expounded at Paris, was the text in the light of both patristic and medieval tradition, indissolubly wedded to it in the *Gloss*.[5]

---

[1] E. Mangenot, art. 'Concordances' in *Dict. de la Bible*, op. cit.

[2] See for instance S. H. Thomson's 'Grosseteste's Topical Concordance of the Bible and the Fathers', *Speculum*, ix (1934), 139-44; Kleinhans, 'De Concordantiis Biblicis S. Antonio Patavino aliisque attributis', *Antonianum*, vi (1931), 273-326; D. A. Callus, 'The *Tabulae super Originalia Patrum* of Robert Kilwardby, o.p.', *Studia Mediaevalia* (op. cit. p. 216, n. 2), 243-70; 'New MSS of Kilwardby's *Tabulae*, etc', *Dominican Studies*, ii (1949), 38-45.

[3] See P. Mandonnet, art. 'Dominicains', in *Dict. de la Bible*.

[4] Bacon's actual words are: 'Nam circa quadraginta annos [sunt] multi theologi infiniti et stationarii Parisius parum videntes hoc proposuerunt exemplar': *Opus Minus*, 333 (written in 1267). The committee appointed to select and standardize a text is an ingenious suggestion of Martin. The textual variations noted by Langton show how necessary standardization must have seemed for class-room purposes. Martin also verified the false readings mentioned by Bacon in a number of Paris Bibles. Bacon's constant references to the *exemplar Parisiense* make it clear that a certain text was commonly used at Paris. How exactly it came to be accepted is a minor point. This is a matter for further inquiry, like the precise manner of the reception of the *Gloss*.

[5] See H. Glunz, *The Vulgate in England from Alcuin to Roger Bacon* (Cambridge, 1933), 259-65. I agree with Dr. Glunz that the Paris text must have been a glossed text. He goes further and holds that it was the glossed text which had belonged to Peter Lombard. Since Langton actually contrasts this *Liber Lombardi* with the glossed text which he (Langton) was lecturing on (see above, p. 225, n. 3), this conjecture seems highly improbable.

Thus the Friars Minor of Padua had given to them a glossed Bible, 'de littera et apparatu Parisiensi'.[1]

The Paris masters, from the early twelfth century onwards, had no illusions as to its quality. The *correctoria*,[2] or lists of corrections and alternative readings, which were first introduced by the Dominicans, represent a specialization and systematization of the textual criticism in Stephen Langton's lectures. Their continuity with earlier scholarship appears in the frequent quotations of Andrew and Langton by Hugh of St. Cher in his *correctorium* (1244-63).

Bacon held that the correction merely aggravated the evil; correctors did not restrict themselves to St. Jerome's translation, but collected readings from other versions, which then crept into the text. He was attacking especially the Dominican corrections. Investigation of Hugh of St. Cher's correction shows that Bacon was not altogether just. Hugh says in his introduction that his main sources are the glosses of the Fathers, the original Greek and Hebrew, and also — what Bacon approved of — ancient Latin Bibles, going back to Charlemagne. Moreover, like his predecessors, he collected many of his alternatives for interest, without committing himself either for or against them. They were liable to be inserted into the text by the fault of copyists, for which he was not responsible, as had happened to the *Hexapla* of Origen. Nevertheless, it seems that Hugh was confused as to his main purpose, as Bacon said. He did not distinguish the restoration of the Vulgate text from its comparison with the originals and with other versions. He was trying to combine two things which were both necessary but required to be kept separate. Other correctors shared his confusion. The aim becomes clearer in some later *correctoria* which were drawn up by the Franciscans. Bacon's friend, the English Franciscan, William de la Mare, who was teaching at Paris about 1274-5 and died probably in 1285, prepared the *Correctorium* D which impressed Denifle as the most learned and scientific of the century.[3] Both he and an anony-

---

[1] A. M. Iosa, *1 cod. MSS. d. bibl. Ant.* (Padua, 1886), 48-9. I have seen the collection. The gloss is the *Ordinaria*.

[2] On the *correctoria* see *Quam notitiam*, 26-36; H. Denifle, op. cit. (p. 80, n. 1); E. Mangenot, art. 'Hugues de St Cher', *Dict. de la Bible*, where full references are given.

[3] Denifle tentatively identified him with the *homo sapientissimus* referred to by Bacon, 298, 545. On William's life and works see E. Longpré in *Dict. Théol. Cath.* viii. 2467-70; *Rép.* no. 317.

mous contemporary corrector,[1] author of the *Correctorium* E, state explicitly that the Vulgate text is not to be altered wherever it diverges from the Hebrew. Both were competent Hebraists and assumed that scholars would also study the originals. It would be difficult to say, at present, whether they owed their ideas to Bacon, or vice versa. They were the second generation of correctors and could learn from the mistakes of the first.

That this learned apparatus was actually used appears from a reading of thirteenth-century postills. References to Scripture and to the Fathers alike become much more precise than formerly. For a book of the Bible the chapter and often its subdivision will be given, for a Father the title, book and chapter. I have found two commentators making systematic use of the Dominican *Correctorium* B on Proverbs, supplemented by other corrections. They are two Friars Preacher: 'John of Varzy' and Nicholas Gorran. It is significant that Gorran, working at the end of the thirteenth century, refers to it more constantly and cites it explicitly as 'the *correctorium*'.[2] St. Albert had something of the same kind on his work-table,[3] while Salimbene by a casual remark uncovers the activity that was going on. 'The provincial', he says under the year 1249, 'kept my mate at Bologna to correct his Bible for him.'[4]

Thanks to the work of Martin and Denifle, we know more of the *correctoria* than of any other side of thirteenth-century Bible study. Berger also showed the importance of the *De Hebraeis et Graecis vocabulis glossarum Bibliae* by William de la Mare and the *Liber Triglossos* of Brother Gerard of Huy (a Franciscan, probably belonging to William's school). Both give instruction on Greek and Hebrew grammar; William adds notes, mainly linguistic, on the text. He knew Rashi's exposition and refers to it as the *perus*.[5] All these aids to scientific study resemble the concordances in being only the more obvious symptoms of a great movement for approaching the original sources.

Bacon complained of slow progress in the study of Greek: there had been a revival under Grosseteste; since then the work of translation had lapsed. Bacon's praise of Grosseteste is fully borne out by recent study of his translations and of

---

[1] Denifle, 298-311. [2] 'Sapiential Books I', iii. 247-53, 'II'.
[3] I. M. Vosté, op. cit. (p. 298, n. 1), i. 18-19; ii. 11.
[4] Op. cit. (p. 290, n. 1), 333. [5] *Quam notitiam*, 36-48.

those of his circle.[1] Grosseteste's commentaries on the Hexaemeron and the Psalter show a deliberate cult of the Greek Fathers. When he could not get the original he used a catena.[2] It was no search for novelty as such. Grosseteste shows his earnestness by using the Latin translation of St. Basil on the Hexaemeron, which had been known to Bede, but had been little used in later centuries; the compilers of the *Gloss*, Andrew, the Chanter, and Langton all ignore it. He borrowed, and kept, a copy of St. Basil from the monks of St. Edmundsbury, leaving them a collection of twelfth-century glosses on the *Gloss* in pledge. The exchange was symbolic. Grosseteste preferred the original sources to lectures on 'select extracts'.[3]

The next generation of commentators continued to prize those works of the Greek Fathers which were available in translation. The book which St. Thomas Aquinas preferred to the whole town of Paris was St. John Chrysostom on St. Matthew (translated by Burgundio of Pisa in the later twelfth century). The story of the influence of Greek patristic in translation on Latin exegesis remains to be written; but we can be sure of its importance.[4]

The extent of Greek linguistic studies in connection with the text of Scripture forms another gap in our knowledge. Dr. Allgeier has listed thirty-two Greco-Latin Psalters, in hands ranging from the sixth century to the thirteenth, which were diffused over the whole of Western Europe.[5] He has also discovered two separate translations of the Psalter into Latin from the Septuagint in two manuscripts written in hands of the twelfth century (one perhaps a little earlier).[6] His researches have proved that at least some medieval scholars understood the value of Greek and applied it to the most widely read book of the Old Testament. The next step would be to try to relate all these manuscripts to

---

[1] See E. Franceschini, 'Grosseteste's Translation of Maximus', etc., *Journal of Theological Studies*, xxxiv (1933), 355-63; S. H. Thomson, 'A Note on Grosseteste's Work of Translation', ibid. 48-50, where references to other recent papers will be found. And see above, p. 266, n. 2.

[2] M. R. James, 'Robert Grosseteste on the Psalms', *Journal of Theological Studies*, xxiii (1921), 183-5.

[3] B. Smalley, 'A Collection of Paris Lectures', etc., op. cit. (p. 62, n. 1), 103-5.

[4] See the suggestive remarks of M.D. Chenu, *Introduction, etc.*, op. cit. (p. 265, no. 1), 127-9.

[5] 'Exegetische Beiträge zur Geschichte des Griechischen', *Biblica*, xxiv (1943), 261-5.

[6] 'Die mittelalterliche Überlieferung des Psalterium etc', *Oriens christianus*, iii-iv (1928/9), 200-31.

the centres of learning in which they were produced and to see whether they had any effect on local Bible studies, as Dr. Allgeier has done for Bamberg in the tenth, Bâle and Wurzburg in the ninth centuries. Of the thirteenth century it seems true to say that at least a superficial knowledge of Greek became more common than formerly; but only one of the correctors whose works have been studied, the Franciscan, Gerard of Huy, actually knew more Greek than Hebrew.

Hebrew, in fact, absorbed and must to some extent have distracted Bacon's contemporaries from the study of Greek. Here he does them less than justice. The thirteenth century marked a steady progress. Perhaps the peak of twelfth-century Hebrew scholarship was not surpassed: Herbert of Bosham may have reached greater proficiency than any of his successors. The increasing vogue of Andrew's commentaries[1] indicates both a growth of interest and a failure to replace them by something better. But knowledge of Hebrew became at least more widespread than formerly and a number of scholars made themselves into good Hebraists. In rare cases their names are known to us, as with Gerard of Huy and William de la Mare. Generally, however, the thirteenth-century Hebraist is anonymous. We are lucky if we know what part of Europe he came from. We must probably resign ourselves to continuing ignorance on this score, but systematic researches would eventually enable the sum total of Hebraism to be estimated. These would involve a search through manuscript collections for Hebrew-Latin texts of Scripture and for Hebrew texts with Latin glosses, and a study of contemporary postills. We would probably also learn, when the results of the inquiries were put together, how far thirteenth-century Hebrew studies were co-ordinated and how far they represented mere isolated efforts.

The notes which follow from here to the end of the chapter are intended to give some idea of the type of evidence which is accumulating at present and the type of conclusion to be drawn from it.

First of all there are some general considerations. Dr. Altaner has stressed the importance of Jewish converts as teachers of Hebrew, particularly in Dominican circles.[2]

---

[1] See above, p. 184.
[2] B. Altaner, 'Zur Kenntnis des Hebräischen im Mittelalter', *Biblische Zeitschr.* xxi (1933), 288-308.

Mandonnet thought that a school for Hebrew studies was actually established at Paris about 1236.[1] Next come individual manuscripts. There is a Christian introduction to the Talmud in a Paris manuscript of the mid-thirteenth century.[2] An Oxford manuscript, Bodl. Or. 135,[3] contains a Hebrew-French-Latin glossary, also thirteenth-century. A Christian, probably in the south of France, whose knowledge of Hebrew was defective, has written in Latin equivalents to the Hebrew. There are also Latin headings and transliterated Hebrew initials in another hand, of the late thirteenth century. The same manuscript has a collection of rabbinic saws annotated with references to the Vulgate, written in above the Hebrew (fo. 356[r] et seq.) It belonged to Grandison, Bishop of Exeter 1327-69, who gave it to Exeter College, Oxford. The cathedral library of Lichfield possessed a 'Hebrew lexicon'. Unfortunately it cannot be traced;[4] so we do not know whether it was the real thing or some 'interpretation of Hebrew names'. But all this together suggests an interest in the Hebrew language and in rabbinics which could serve as a background to serious Bible study.

Two Oxford manuscript copies of Peter Comestor's *Histories* show a knowledge of Hebrew on the part of their owners or their glossators. One copy, now MS. 190 of University College, belonged to the Friars Preacher of Beverley and has already been noticed as containing glosses with many references to Andrew.[5] It used to have in it a Hebrew text of the description of the porch of Solomon's temple, following on the Latin text: the leaves got separated and are now bound in the back of MS. 113 of the same College.[6] Another copy of the *Histories*, now MS. Bodl. Rawl. C.46, is probably from an English religious house. It is written in

[1] See P. Mandonnet, 'Dominicains', op. cit. (p. 334, n. 3), 1471-2, on the study of Hebrew in the Dominican Order. In *St Dominique*, op. cit. (p. 83, n. 1), i. 195, he states without giving references: 'vers ce temps (1236) une école d'hébreu semble avoir été établie à Paris'.
[2] E. Klibansky, 'Zur Talmudkenntnis etc.', *Bez. des christl. M. A.'s zum Judentum*, 458-62.
[3] Neubauer 1466, *Summary Catalogue* 3086, printed by Neubauer & Böhmer, 'Un vocabulaire hébraico-français', *Romanische Studien* i (1897), 163-96; see D. Blondheim, 'Le glossaire d'Oxford', *Revue des études juives*, lvii (1909), 1-18.
[4] N. R. Ker, 'Patrick Young's Catalogue of the Manuscripts of Lichfield Cathedral', *Mediaeval and Renaissance Studies*, ii (1950), 151-68. Young calls the volume 'Lexicon hebraicum una cum Isidori etymologiis rursus, fol.' ibid. 158.
[5] See above, p. 183.
[6] Coxe, *Cat. Cod. Coll. Oxon.* i. 34; R. W. Hunt, 'The MS. Collection of University College, Oxford', *Bodleian Library Record*, iii (1950), 31.

a hand of the thirteenth century which could be either English or French. It contains many glosses, among them a set in a fourteenth-century hand which gives a number of English words. The flyleaf has a note in an English-looking hand recording that 'Abbas Iohannes de Brach⁻' celebrated his first Mass on Sunday, May 8th, 1280. The abbreviated surname does not help to localize the book. Only a very fortunate chance would enable one to identify Abbot John. The thirteenth-century glosses which concern us here are mainly about grammar and etymology; but they also refer to Aristotle's logic and metaphysic,[1] to Origen's 'Peryarchon'[2] and to Maimonides, 'nobilis Iudeorum philosophus'; his explanation of the vision of Jacob's ladder 'agrees well with the saints' '.[3] A second reference to Maimonides is more interesting from a linguistic point of view. The glossator is annotating the chapter in the *Histories* on Noe's descent from the ark. He compares the Latin Vulgate version of Gen. viii. 21 with Maimonides' text of the verse as quoted in the *Guide* and with the text used by the Spanish convert from Judaism, Petrus Alphonsi, in his *Dialogi.*[4] Alphonsi's work, written 1106-10 (in Latin) to explain the reasons for his conversion, was quite popular in the middle ages; the monks of Bury St. Edmund's had a copy, for instance;[5] but I have never before found it used as a guide to the Hebrew text. The glossator knew enough of the language to attempt a comparison, transcribing the Hebrew in transliteration, though missing the finer points in his authors.[6] He also

---

[1] Fo. 6ᵛ, 95ʳ.

[2] Fo. 7ᵛ, against the chapter *De formatione mulieris*: 'Peri, id est, de Periarchon principatus. Peryarchon est liber in quo Origenes dicit Christum adhuc in aere pro demonibus pati debere, sicut in terra pro hominibus passus est. Quod falsum est.' It is an allusion to the *De princ.* iii. 5-6, which the glossator knew only at second hand.

[3] Fo. 26ʳ: 'Rabi Mosu, nobilis Iudeorum philosophus, hanc apparitionem erecte scale philosophice exponit, dicens scalam illam esse ordinatam cognitionem creature et creatoris, gradus autem scale dicit esse scientias (MS. scientia) sermonales et doctrinales et naturales et morales et (sic, ad?) Deum (sic).' The last part of the gloss seems to be incomplete, a word or two having dropped out after 'Deum'. It is an allusion to the *Guide*, i. 15; but Maimonides' point has been worked out and elaborated. The glossator adds an alternative allegorical interpretation, which is not in the *Guide*, and concludes: 'et bene concordat ista expositio sanctis.' The *ista* presumably refers to Maimonides, since the allegorical one is derived from the patristic and does not need to be harmonized.

[4] Fo. 14ᵛ. The references are to the *Guide*, iii. 22, ed. Friedländer (London/ New York, 1904), 298, and to the *Dialogi*, *P.L.* clvii, 645.

[5] M. R. James, 'The Abbey of St. Edmund at Bury', op. cit. (p. 48, n. 5), 15.

[6] As the questions raised in this passage are too technical to be treated here, Mr. Raphael Loewe will deal with them in a forthcoming paper.

tries to connect Jewish liturgical practice with Old Testament history. He says on the chapter in the *Histories* on the giving of the Law, apropos of Exod. xix. 18: *All the mount was terrible*:

'Thence it is that the Jews still quake at their prayers representing the quaking of the mount.'

There seems to be no Jewish tradition to this effect; but here again we find proof of interest, if not of knowledge.[1]

References to the Hebrew text and to rabbinic tradition are also found embedded in thirteenth-century postills. William of Middleton and William of Alton both supply examples.[2] The works of William of Middleton, particularly, would repay further study from this point of view. But these are the kind of *fiches* that one only collects when going through the material primarily for other purposes. The passages which do not derive from *correctoria* or earlier sources in the average Paris lecture are rare in my experience, hence all the more interesting when they do occur.

Another potential source of information is the text of thirteenth-century Bibles. Quite recently a new translation of the Psalter from the Hebrew came to light in a pocket Bible acquired by the British Museum, now MS. Egerton 2908. It was written in northern or central Italy in the thirteenth century. A Franciscan catalogue of saints follows the text and there is an erased note of ownership on the flyleaf: 'Ista biblia est fratris Iohannis . . .' (fo. 390[b]).[3] Unfortunately the writing is minute and so rubbed away as to be barely legible for most of the Psalms. On a few pages, however, it is still sharp enough to be read without too much eye-strain, especially in an enlarged photograph, and it is to be hoped that we shall one day have a more detailed study of the translator's competence and method. The discovery makes one wonder what surprises are in store for the librarian who goes systematically through the medieval

---

[1] Fo. 47[v]: 'Inde est quod Iudei adhuc in orationibus suis tremunt, representantes illum tremorem montis.' Mr. Loewe writes: 'I cannot find any Jewish connection of this phenomenon with Exod. xix. 18, where, it may be noted, the Septuagint and some Hebrew manuscripts have "the people" instead of "the mount", as in v. 16. Perhaps the glossator has just drawn a deduction from the analogy of expressions in vv. 16 and 18.'

[2] B. Smalley, 'Sapiential Books I', iii. 59-61, 76-7.

[3] *Catalogue of Additions to the British Museum, 1911-1915* (London, 1925), 423; A. Allgeier, 'Eine unbekannte mittelalterliche Psalmenübersetzung', *Römisch Quartelschrift*, xxxvii (1939), 437-9.

Bibles in his care. This Italian Franciscan copy is quite ordinary except for the Psalter; only its pretty illuminations mark it out as more interesting than many others of the same kind. There is no note or rubric to warn us that the Psalter is not the Roman, Gallican or *Hebraica*, but an independent version. Then we have the evidence of Hebrew texts possessed by Christian libraries. Of course they may have been acquired merely as show pieces or as curiosities and one must look for evidence that they were actually studied. The Hebrew Psalter, now MS. Laud. Or. 174, which belonged to Bury St. Edmund's, makes a good illustration. The Latin incipits of the Psalms have been noted in the margins in a scholar's hand of the later thirteenth century. Although there are no glosses, these titles would suggest that at least one of the monks took more than a casual interest in Hebrew.[1] Parallel texts giving both Hebrew and Latin versions are more significant, since they witness to a desire to compare and to learn. Some of these manuscripts, like the Hebrew-Latin Psalter at St. Victor, are known to us only from old library catalogues;[2] others survive, like the beautiful Hebrew-Latin Psalter at Westminster.

Berger pointed out that one group of Hebrew-Latin manuscripts, in English hands and all at present in English libraries, contained, in addition to the Hebrew and the Vulgate, a new Latin translation from the Hebrew.[3] The Hebrew and Vulgate are in parallel columns; the Psalters are exceptional in having a double Latin version, the Gallican or Vulgate, and the *Hebraica* of St. Jerome, which is next to the Hebrew. The new Latin translation is written as an interlinear gloss to the Hebrew, word for word. The translator's identity is unknown. He obviously intended his work for scholars wishing to compare the known Latin versions with the original. He took the wording of the Vulgate as the basis of his translation and adapted it, so as to give a more literal rendering where he found disagreement. Berger felt convinced that the same scholar was responsible for the

---

[1] Neubacher, 117. Described by M. R. James, 'The Abbey of St. Edmund at Bury', op. cit. (p. 48, n. 5), 87-8. A few details need correction. James post-dated the Latin titles and his transcript of the scribble on the flyleaf is inaccurate. As far as can be made out it reads: 'Fui Parisius mcclxx prix haut puto. Fui Andegavis . . . sponte relicta . . . nomina tallentium (?) . . . .'
[2] L. Delisle, *Le Cabinet des mss. de la Bibl. nat.* (1874), ii. 229.
[3] *Quam notitiam*, 49-53.

whole. His work survives in copies which give an almost complete translation of the Old Testament. None of them has any marks of provenance. His translation is not the same as that in MS. Egerton 2908, though a careful scrutiny might reveal some common elements.

A study of the three surviving manuscripts of the Psalter has cleared up a little of the mystery which surrounds him.[1] We know that his translation of the Psalter, at least, was ordered by Grosseteste. The bishop of Lincoln had it written over the Hebrew of his Psalter, 'where three or four Psalters' were 'contained together in one' (*simul coniunctim*). It is quoted by a later commentator as the *superscriptio Lincolniensis*.

The earliest existing copy is MS. Corpus Christi College, Oxford 10, written in hands of the second quarter of the thirteenth century. An anonymous prologue prefixed to the Psalters in this manuscript explains the aim of the new translation. I think that the author of the prologue was Grosseteste. He takes responsibility for publication and justifies himself for doing so; but he does not claim to be the translator. The freshly devotional tone of the prologue, the decision and the wide outlook, all remind one of Grosseteste, scholar, bishop and saint.

Contemplating the mysteries hidden in the Psalter, he approaches, with reverent humility, 'even the literal Hebrew veil or outer rind'. He excuses himself for the novelty of his undertaking. Many scholars have translated the Psalter without intending disrespect to one another; St. Jerome altered and corrected his own. His text is corrupt and needs correction. The Vulgate disagrees in many passages with the Hebrew. The writer gives examples, showing the discords between the Vulgate and 'the Hebrew', which he quotes in the new Latin translation. It is only right, he concludes, to know and concord both Scriptures of the Church, who is mother and mistress of all peoples alike:

'Therefore, in order to quiet this collision and conflict in their mother's womb, it may be thought not unprofitable to bring the peoples together into the unity of faith under the leadership of Christ, by reconciling such differences, through a

---

[1] B. Smalley, 'Hebrew Scholarship among Christians in Thirteenth-Century England, as illustrated by some Hebrew-Latin Psalters; a paper read to the Society for Old Testament Study', *Lectiones in Vetere Testamento et in Rebus Judaicis* (1939), no. 6. References unless specially mentioned will be found here. The pamphlet has photographs of the four Psalters described. It was prepared in collaboration with Mr. H. Loewe.

knowledge of both tongues and both Scriptures, and to put them side by side, lest, because they differ, they should always fight. 'This zeal of God's house incites me to publish the Scripture of the Hebrews, as confirmation for the faithful and as a call to the infidel; yet in such a way that if it be found superfluous, or lacking, or erroneous, let brotherly charity remove, or add, or correct. I refuse not the spur of reproof or correction but only that of enmity. For *let the just man reprove me in mercy: but let not the oil of the sinner fatten my head* [from Ps. cxl. 5].'[1]

The conventional invitation to 'alter and correct' was accepted. We have evidence that later scholars appreciated Grosseteste's guide to the Hebrew Psalter and studied it intensively. His original *superscriptio* is lost; but we know that at least four copies of it existed. We have two complete: the MS. Corpus 10, which contains the prologue, and a rather later copy, MS. Trinity R. 8. 6. The MS. Corpus Christi College, Oxford 11 contains many quotations from a third. A later writer, the Cambridge Franciscan, Henry Cossey (who died probably in 1336), quotes extensively from a fourth.[2] If all these are collated and compared with the quotations in the prologue, which presumably were taken from the original *superscriptio* belonging to Grosseteste, we find a number of differences. They cannot be explained by scribal carelessness, but are due to intelligent revision and comparison. Sometimes they derive from different shades of meaning in the Hebrew, sometimes from variants in the Hebrew text; one will follow the Ķere or read text, another the Ķetib or written text.

[1] Fo. 1d: '. . . Ideoque non estimo minus ecclesie que omnium nationum mater est et magistra utramque scripturam cognoscere, necnon et utramque concordare. Scio enim quod in utraque dissonantia sit, ut plerumque quod est in nostra desit in illa, et quod in illa est desit in nostra, necnon et in eodem loco dissimiliter habeamus et aliquando opposito modo . . . [examples follow].

'Unde propter huiusmodi collisionem in utero matris et pugnam mitigandam, non inutile credi potest dissonantias tales conciliando per diversarum linguarum notitiam et scripturarum, Christo duce, gentes in unitatem fidei congregare, et ne per dissonantiam scripturarum semper pugnent, scripturas pariter coaptare.

'Zelus igitur domus Dei me stimulat ut ad confirmationem fidelium et infidelium vocationem scripturam Ebreorum edisseram, ita tamen ut si superfluum inveniatur caritative tollatur, ac minus suppleatur, ac devium fraterne corrigatur. Non enim correptionis aut correctionis stimulum renuo, sed invidie; *iustus enim in misericordia increpet, oleum autem peccatoris*', etc.

The last clause is a rough quotation from Ps. cxl. 5. The 'increpet' is evidently taken from the *superscriptio* (in loc.), since the Vulgate has: 'increpabit', and the *Hebraica*: 'arguet'.

[2] In his commentary on the Psalter, MS. Christ's College, Cambridge 11. See 'Hebrew Scholarship', etc. On Cossey see A. G. Little, op. cit. (p. 278, n. 4), 139-41.

We also have the evidence of marginal glosses to the Psalters. MSS. Corpus 10 and Trinity R. 8. 6 both have a few linguistic glosses and transliterations of Hebrew words. Since there is no common material, here we have two unknown scholars working independently of each other. MS. Corpus 11, which contains a Hebrew-Latin Psalter (the *Hebraica* only) written in the late thirteenth century, has both a marginal gloss and a kind of *correctorium*. The *superscriptio Lincolniensis* is quoted as *Iudeus dicit* among the variant readings collected.[1] This Psalter too has its prologue, in which the anonymous glossator explains the purpose of the manuscript. It is an attempt to group all the known Latin versions together for comparison with the Hebrew.

The glossator begins by enumerating the 'six or seven' Latin translations of the Psalter which he has been able to find.[2] He has had the *Hebraica* written beside the Hebrew, in order that those skilled in both languages may see how far it differs or agrees. He has noted by signs in the margin the variant readings from these other versions, except those of 'the Vulgate, which is called Gallican', since almost everyone either possesses or knows it by heart. This is his conclusion:

'And so in this manuscript I have written all the aforesaid translations briefly beside the *Hebraica*, that having tested them all I may choose that which is better, and that one may bear witness to another in refutation of the worse. The extent of error in our Vulgate version appears in the Hebrew; and the other translations witness it too, now one, now another, now several together, almost at every verse, for it sometimes has more, sometimes less, sometimes other than the true one [i.e. the Hebrew]. The same, more or less, with all the translations, for that which is called St. Jerome's differs less from the Hebrew; but it does sometimes, owing to corruption introduced by others, or to his own carelessness or lack of skill, for "the good Homer sometimes nods". He does not claim to have set down the Hebrew truth altogether, but to have changed nothing wittingly. . . .

'But as he was instructed and helped by the earlier translations, so am I, both by his and the others (for that reason I

---

[1] Berger noticed that this Psalter had no interlinear translation, but did not see that extracts from the *superscriptio* were quoted among the *marginalia*.

[2] Prof. S. H. Thomson has now taken over responsibility for work on the *Superscriptio* and its connections. I hope that he will edit the two prologues and give us a fuller study of the medieval tradition regarding Psalter translations as part of his work on Grosseteste.

have noted them), and also by the Jews. I make bold to correct any one of them, by the witness of the others, following now one, now another, now none of them, but demonstrating from elsewhere. And this I do, not presumptuously nor rashly, but after very careful collation and examination of ours and inquiry into the Hebrew truth, and so with manifest condemnation of error and the witness of the Jews.'[1]

The difference in tone between this prologue and Grosseteste's is very striking. It signifies half a century's progress in Hebrew studies. The anonymous glossator of MS. Corpus 11 sees no need to justify himself as an innovator, no need to compare the Vulgate in detail with the Hebrew, no need to rely on any one translation. Being able to read the original, he can make his own choice. His naïve arrogance towards St. Jerome and the Fathers in general is one of the accepted signs of 'coming of age'. His glosses show an extensive knowledge of Hebrew and a smattering of Greek. He has questioned the Jews unweariedly as to their liturgical traditions and constantly quotes Maimonides. He has collated four copies of St. Jerome's *Hebraica*; he has noted the variants in Hebrew manuscripts as well as in Latin, and has consulted 'his Jew' as to the better text.

This enterprising scholar is connected in some way with the English Dominican, Nicholas Trevet, who left a commentary on the Psalter, dedicated to John of Bristol (his provincial, 1317-20). Trevet breaks with the custom of

---

[1] Fo. 110ᵛ (the note has been put at the end instead of the beginning: 'Hanc notulam debui posuisse in principio'):

'Itaque in hoc codice iuxta Hebraicam breviter conscripsi, quoad diversitatis notitiam, omnes pretactas translationes ut omnibus probatis tenerem quod melius est, et ut una alteri attetetur ad reprehensionem peioris. Quantum autem sit error in nostra usitata, patet in Hebreo, testibus quoque aliis translationibus, nunc quidem una, nunc alia, nunc simul pluribus pene per singulos versus, quia quandoque minus, quandoque plus, quandoque aliter habet a vero. Similiter et quelibet aliarum licet sit magis et minus; nam illa que dicitur Ieronimi minus discordat ab Hebreo, et tamen aliquando, sive per corruptionem ab aliis factam in translatione sua, sive per suam negligentiam aut imperitiam, quia quandoque bonus dormitat Homerus [Horace, *A.P.* 359]. Unde ipse non asserit se omnino veritatem Hebraicam posuisse, sed nihil de ea scienter mutasse. . . .

'Sed sicut ipse instructus et adiutus per precedentes translationes, ita ego tam per illam quam per ceteras, propter quod eas contuli, quam etiam per Hebreos, audeo quamlibet earum corrigere, et ceterarum attestatione, nunc unam nunc aliam nunc nullam earum sequens, sed aliunde convincens, et hoc, non quidem presumptuose aut precipitanter, sed diligentissima nostrum collatione et examinatione et Hebraice veritatis inquisitione, et sic manifestissima erroris reprobatione et Hebreorum attestatione.'

II. MS. Lambeth 435, fol. 21ʳ. Hebrew Psalter with Latin and Anglo-Norman gloss, written in England in the mid-thirteenth century

expounding the Gallican version and chooses the *Hebraica* of St. Jerome instead. He often refers to the Hebrew text, and his quotations correspond to the *superscripti Lincolniensis.* Collation with the gloss in MS. Corpus 11 shows that this was an important source for Trevet's commentary.[1] Sometimes there is verbal identity, sometimes expansion or compression. The fifteenth-century scholar, Thomas Gascoigne, who knew Trevet's commentary and quotes from it directly, notes that he saw a copy of Trevet on the Psalter at a London stationer's 'containing a translation from the Hebrew with a parallel Hebrew text'.[2] Gascoigne's description suggests the MS. Corpus 11 itself. Perhaps the MS. Corpus 11 was Trevet's own note-book, which he afterwards worked up into a commentary; we know that he did make preliminary drafts of his commentaries on other books. Or perhaps the anonymous glossator was his master. Further research on Trevet's exegesis must settle which.

In the meantime, it is pleasant to connect our earliest copy of the *superscriptio* with Grosseteste, our latest with Trevet, the Trinity Psalter filling up the gap between. Lastly we have Henry Cossey, whose three main sources are the *superscriptio Lincolniensis,* Nicholas Trevet, and Nicholas of Lyre.[3]

Another interesting group of Psalters contains the Hebrew text alone, with a Latin-French gloss. A Hebrew Psalter which came into the possession of Thomas Gascoigne and is now MS. Bodley Or. 621 has notes in a hand of the thirteenth century, probably English, giving transliterations and French or Latin equivalents to many of the Hebrew words. A manuscript of the Bibliothèque Nationale, Hébreu 113, noted by Berger, has the same type of gloss on the first ten psalms. MS. Lambeth 435 has a much fuller gloss.[4] Its margins have linguistic notes, comments on Old Testament history, on

---

[1] The MS. Bodley 738, which contains the full text of Trevet's commentary on the Psalter, has been used for collation. I am very grateful to Miss Ruth Dean for giving me a list of the manuscripts of Trevet on the Psalter and other information from her doctoral thesis on Nicholas Trevet.

[2] W. A. Pronger, 'Thomas Gascoigne', *English Historical Review*, liii (1938), 621; liv (1939), 20.

[3] Cossey quotes verbatim from Trevet's commentary.

[4] The late Herbert Loewe allowed me to use his paper on the Lambeth Psalter, read to the Society for Old Testament Study. A fuller account, with references and an illustration, will be found in 'Hebrew scholarship, &c.'. See Plate II.

anti-Jewish polemic, and interpretation; its interlinear gloss gives an almost complete translation of the Psalter from Hebrew into a quaint mixture of French, Latin and Latinized French; notes on Hebrew grammar and syntax cover the flyleaves. The hands of the glossators in both MSS. Hébr. 113 and Lambeth 435 are not long after the middle of the thirteenth century, whereas the glosses in MS. Bodl. Or. 621 might be rather earlier. The Lambeth glossator has marked English characteristics, and the names scribbled on one of the flyleaves struck M. R. James as possibly Norfolk. Otherwise not one of the manuscripts has any mark of provenance. All three glossators write in the hands of scholars rather than professionals.

None of the three shows any sign of acquaintance with the *superscriptio Lincolniensis*, nor, judging from a rapid survey, do they seem to depend one on another.[1] Here then we have three private note-books of scholars, all separately studying the Psalms in the original.

The Hebrew script in both the Hebrew and the Hebrew-Latin Psalters raises an important problem. The little MS. Bodley Or. 621 stands apart. It resembles the unglossed Hebrew Psalter which used to belong to the monks of Bury, now MS. Laud Or. 174,[2] in that both are professionally written and prettily illuminated and could easily have been acquired from Jews. This must have happened quite frequently: we know that Henry Cossey used a Hebrew Psalter belonging to a recent convert, 'Master I'. All the other Psalters, both the *superscriptio* group and MSS. Hébr. 113 and Lambeth 435, have their Hebrew text written by scribes who, although they wrote well, did not observe the technical rules of the highly specialized Jewish profession. The same kind of script is found in another thirteenth-century Hebrew-Latin Psalter, which lacks the interlinear translation and the *Hebraica* of St. Jerome, but otherwise resembles the *super-*

---

[1] For example, both MSS. Héb. 113 and Lambeth 435 have a note on *scelerum* Ps. v. 11, giving various Hebrew words for 'sin'; but they are not identical.
MS. Hébr. 113, fo. 3ʳ:
    Het. peccatum grande.
    Avon. peccatum parvum scil. fornicatione.
    Pesa. culpa.
MS. Lambeth 435, fo. 3ʳ:
    Pesa est culpa quam homo facit quasi in despectu domini sui. ⎫ ita
    Attaz est peccatum quod homo facit quasi ignoranter.   ⎬ differunt
    Avon est peccatum scienter et pro edia corporis sui. ⎭

[2] See M. R. James, *The Abbey of St. Edmund at Bury*, op. cit. (p. 48, n. 5), 3, 87.

scriptio group, MS. Westminster 2.[1] The scribes in each case have failed to keep the left-hand side of their column straight. They make many mistakes and omissions. Almost each folio has some correction. The scribe of the Lambeth Psalter does not scruple to erase the Tetragrammaton, when he has added it accidentally. As William de la Mare noted, a Jewish scribe would never erase the holy name; he encircled it to show that it had been written superfluously.[2] It seems unlikely that Christian scribes could ever have learnt to form such beautiful Hebrew characters. The glossators of MSS. Lambeth 435 and Corpus 11 frequently write Hebrew words in their linguistic comments; their clumsy script is very different from that of the Psalters. In some cases the mistakes in the Psalters are due to confusion with the Hebrew of another psalm, where the wording is similar but not identical. Only a man who knew the Hebrew Psalter thoroughly by heart would have been liable to make a mistake of this sort. The existence of six Hebrew Psalters, all written by amateurs, can hardly be a mere coincidence. It suggests that Jewish converts were regularly employed by Christian scholars to write Hebrew, or that there was some working system of enlisting non-professional Jewish services.

The value of the *superscriptio* and of the Latin-French gloss in the Lambeth Psalter, as translations, requires further study. Both are objective and even stimulating in their fresh literalness; they aim at keeping close to the Hebrew and a comparison of their ideas gives some interesting variants. The Lambeth glosses particularly contain some surprises, both linguistic and historical.

This glossator was able to write and understand Hebrew, though he knew less than the glossator of MS. Corpus 11, and he makes some mistakes. He had a Jew to instruct him: 'rabi dixit . . .' A grammatical note and a Midrash are ascribed to his rabbi. He also refers to an unfamiliar Hebrew spelling which he saw 'in my master's book', probably the rabbi's own Psalter.

[1] See J. A. Robinson and M. R. James, *The MSS. of Westminster Abbey* (Cambridge, 1909), 64. I did not mention this Psalter in 'Hebrew Scholarship' as it has no *superscriptio*. The initials rather resemble those of MS. Corpus 10; but the hand is different and the Hebrew has been written first as in MS. Trinity R. 8. 6, whereas in MS. Corpus 10 the Latin was written first. The hand appears to me to be second quarter of the thirteenth century. There is one linguistic note in the margin.

[2] *Quam notitiam*, 41.

Old Testament scholars will be astonished to hear that he used the more widely accepted modern transcription of the Tetragrammaton. He writes it as IAHAVE,[1] which comes very close to JAHWEH. How he arrived at it is a mystery and unfortunately he does not discuss it. The 'monstrous form' Jehoveh was already known to Christians in the later thirteenth century. Henry Cossey seems to compromise between Jehoveh and Jahweh by writing IEHAVE. The *superscriptio* merely translates: 'Deus'; the glossator of MS. Corpus 11 says that the Jews read it as 'Adonai', that is 'Dominus'.[2] The glossator of the Lambeth Psalter could hardly have derived his form from the Fathers. St. Jerome used IAHO; the IABE of the Greek Father, Theodoret, was probably unknown to him; nor was he likely to have been in contact with the Samaritans, who until quite recent times pronounced 'Jahweh'. His transcription seems to have been unknown to the Renaissance scholars. Only more detailed work on thirteenth-century glosses would show whether he were exceptional in his own period or not.

If we pass to his interpretation we find that his point of view is unusual in a Christian commentator. This is his gloss on Ps. cix. 1, the prophecy quoted in the Gospel and in Acts:[3] *The Lord said to my Lord: sit thou at my right hand: until I make my enemies thy footstool.* He expounds it, not of Christ, but of David and Saul or of David and Solomon; a play on the Hebrew word suggests David's persecution by Saul the Benjamite:

'David here calls Saul his *lord*; or David prophesied of Solomon his son.

'*Sit* or wait, as if to say: "suffer". Thus the Lord told David that he should suffer Saul, *until*, etc.

'*Iemini* [i.e. *at my right hand*] shall be called Benjamin and Saul came of Benjamin.'[4]

He expounds verses 6-7: . . . *he shall crush the heads in the land of many. He shall drink of the torrent in the way*, of Ezechias' victory over Sennacherib [*Isa.* xxxvi-xxxvii]. The names are carefully transliterated:

---

[1] Fo. 21ʳ. See 'Hebrew Scholarship, &c.'.
[2] Fo. 34ʳ.   [3] Matt. xxii. 44; Acts ii. 34-5.
[4] Fo. 101ʳ: 'David vocat hic Saulem dominum suum vel David prophetavit super Salomonem filium suum.
'*adsede* vel attende, quasi diceret: patere. Ita dixit Dominus ad David quod pateretur Saulem donec etc.
'Iemini vocabitur Beniamin et Saul venit de Beniamin.'

'Chaneherebbe was king of Nineve and Assyria which were great lands. Hizkiiia, who was of the stem of David, conquered him.'[1]

'This was Chaneherebbe who invested Jerusalem and returning crossed Jordan with all his men and boasted of himself; and the Lord sent angels from heaven and turned back his army and Hizkiiia conquered him; and of the latter Isaias prophesied and said: *Behold a virgin etc.*'[2]

His sources for this interpretation are the Midrash and Rashi.[3] Either he accepted them as giving the true literal meaning of the Psalm and denied it a messianic character, or he was merely jotting them in his note-book among the curious things which his rabbi told him. Perhaps he was a spiritual descendant of Andrew, who had read and admired Andrew's interpretation of Isaias.

When Cardinal Cajetan, the great Thomist of the early sixteenth century, undertook to expound the Psalter literally, he supposed himself to be one of the first to do so:

'Only that sense of the Psalter which they call literal is clear to none, but still obscure, since almost all who have published commentaries on it have propounded only the mystical senses. The Psalms are read and sung so often in church that their literal meaning ought to be plainer and clearer than that of other books.'[4]

Cajetan cannot have studied the English commentators of the thirteenth and early fourteenth centuries. The glosses in MSS. Lambeth 435 and Corpus 11 are exclusively literal; so are the commentaries of Nicholas Trevet and Henry Cossey, not to mention Herbert of Bosham's. The technical side of his subject had such interest for Trevet that he illustrated it by drawings of the Psalter as a musical instrument. Like Cajetan, he restricts the number of the messianic Psalms; and even in this residue he keeps the Jewish exposition as a con-

[1] ibid.: 'Chaneherebbe fuit rex de Nineve et Assur que erant magne terre. Hezkiiia qui fuit de prole David vicit illum.'
[2] Fo. 102ʳ: 'Hic fuit Chaneherebbe qui obsederat Ierusalem et convertendo obibat Iordanem tot quos habuit et iactavit se et misit Dominus angelos de celo et converserunt [*sic*] exercitum suum et Hezkiiia vicit illum et super istum prophetavit Isayas et dixit: *ecce virgo etc.*'
[3] For the interpretation of Iemini, *at my right hand,* as a reference to Saul the Benjamite see the utterance of R. Shalom the Levite in Midrash Ps. cx, section 5, ed. Buber, fo. 233ᵇ. The idea is to be found in the Targum. The source for his comment on 6-7 is Rashi, in loc.
[4] Quoted by A. Allgeier, 'Les Commentaires de Cajétan sur les Psaumes', *Revue Thomiste,* n.s. xvii (1934), special no. 41-5.

trast to the Christian. On Ps. xxi, for instance, he says that he shall give the literal meaning according to both interpretations, 'that truth may appear more clearly when set beside fiction',[1] thus betraying his interest in the Jewish view. Cajetan's title to his commentary, *Psalmi Davidici ad Hebraicam veritatem castigati et iuxta sensum quem literalem vocant enarrati*, would perfectly suit either Trevet's or Cossey's, while the Lambeth glossator goes further in excluding a christological interpretation than any of them.

It is perhaps even more surprising to find a literal interpretation of the Canticle. This book, according to western tradition, had always been expounded of Christ and the Church, Christ and the faithful soul, or, from the twelfth century, of the Blessed Virgin. The same MS. Vat. Lat. 1053, which contains an almost complete collection of Andrew, has an anonymous *Expositio Hystorica Cantici Canticorum secundum Salomonem*: ff. 105ᵃ-114ᵈ. It is written in the same Paris hand as the rest of the manuscript, about 1300;[2] and the one Hebrew word that occurs in it (fo. 107ᵇ) is in the ordinary Anglo-French script. The author consistently uses the modern chapter division; hence he must have been working after about 1230. He does not refer to verses, nor does he divide and subdivide, which suggests that he worked before the end of the thirteenth century. Unfortunately the scribe who produced this text, or his predecessors, did not understand the references to Hebrew and the text is sometimes unintelligible. No other copy is known. The association with Andrew, and the fact that the work is called by the same title as Andrew's, *expositio historica*, must mean either that the commentator took Andrew as his model, extending Andrew's method to the Canticle, or that a later student remarked the similarity and had them copied together into the same volume. In either case, a comparison with Andrew on the Prophets shows, very forcibly, what progress had been made in the period between the two.

---

[1] MS. Bodley 738, fo. 40ʳ⁻ᵛ: '. . . expressam valde continet prophetiam de passione Christi secundum litteram, quamvis Iudei dicant compositum de liberatione populi Israel per Hester a persecutione Aman. Ponemus autem expositionem litteralem utroque modo ut pateat magis veritas posita iuxta umbram.' On Ps. cix he discusses and disputes the Jewish interpretation of Saul or Solomon (fo. 198ʳ); his source here is MS. Corpus 11, fo. 92ʳ. On Trevet's exegesis see A. Kleinhans, 'Nicolaus Trivet O.P. Psalmorum Interpres', *Angelicum*, xx (1943), 219-36.

[2] See above, p. 176.

Like Andrew, this anonymous commentator refers to the Hebrew; but he could read it in the original and he understood some technical points of Hebrew grammar.[1] Like Andrew, he aims at giving a literal exposition; that is, he wants to explain the meaning and purpose of his author, in this case Solomon. Like Andrew, he has recourse to rabbinic tradition. His main sources are Rashi and the Midrash. The prologue is almost a verbal translation of Rashi, with the same scriptural quotations. In one place he even refers to the Pešiḳta, presumably because Rashi on the same text refers to it as his source.[2] He does not acknowledge Rashi; but he does give the names of the rabbis in two anecdotes which he takes from the Midrash.[3] He is much closer to his

[1] His translations from the Hebrew are literal:
Fo. 105ᶜ on Cant. i. 4: '. . . pelles Salomonis; in Hebreo habetur sicut cortine Salomonis.'
Fo. 106ᵇ on Cant. i. 15: 'lectulus noster floridus; Hebreus habet frondosus.'
Fo. 107ᵇ on Cant. ii. 13: 'Surge tibi.'
Fo. 114ᶜ he notes on viii. 12: 'Mille tui pacifici. Hebreus habet tibi Salomoni et ideo patet quod li tui et li pacifici sunt genitivi singulares.'

He may be transliterating Hebr. le by li, and his meaning seems to be that the preposition le in 'my vineyard which is mine' and again in 'to thee Solomon' can express a genitive, which is quite true. The same comment appears in the Postilla of Nicholas of Lyre, in loc.: 'Tui pacifici sunt genitivi casus singularis numeri.' But Father Daniel Callus suggests that li may also be the usual li or ly of the scholastics, which points out a special meaning of a word.

[2] Fo. 107ᵇ on ii. 13: '. . . in alio autem qui dicitur pēisqualsa [sic, for Pešiḳata, the old form] exponitur idem sic: Ficus protulit grossos suos quia in illo triduo quo fuerunt tenebre in terra Egypti, Exod. x, mortui sunt omnes peccatores magni Iudeorum qui non erant digni liberari de Egypto, et ideo tunc, quia noluit Dominus quod viderent Egyptii mortem Hebreorum et letarentur; et tunc vinee florentes dederunt odorem i.e. residui qui remanserunt egerunt penitentiam et placuit Deo.' The whole passage is in Rashi, ending: 'so this is explained in the Pešiḳta'. See Pešikta Rabathi, xv, ed. Freedman, fo. 75ᵃ.

[3] Fo. 105ᵃ (prologue): '. . . Unde dicit rabi Eliezer quod rex quidam tradidit sextarium frumenti pistori suo ut inde faceret ei panem; fecit ille ex illo frumento primo panem nigrum et grossum pro familia; alium fecit subtiliorem pro armigeris et militibus; tertium fecit de simila, quasi panem regium. Sic Salomon de sapientia sibi data fecit primo Proverbia pro insipientibus . . .' Fo. 108ᵇ on iii. 11: 'Quesivit rabi Hanina a rabi Symeon filio rabi Helyeser sapientissimi, utrum aliquando audivisset a patre suo exponi id quod dicitur: in dyademate quo coronavit eum mater sua. Respondit ille quod pater suus hoc exponens dicebat quod rex quidam habebat filiam unicam quam ex magna dilectione vocabat filiam suam; post, crescente amore, vocavit eam sororem suam; tandem ex amore excellenti vocavit eam matrem suam. Sic Deus populum Israeliticum gentem peculiarem vocabat filiam, Ps. [xliv. 11]: audi filia, et inde post sororem, idem v: aperi michi soror mea [2], tandem matrem, Ys. li: attendite ad me populus [sic] meus et tribus mea me audite [4] Hebreus habet: et mater mea me audite. Hec enim sunt nomina amoris: filia, soror et mater. Ideo dicit hic in dyademate quo coronavit eum mater sua. Audita tam eleganti responsione rabi Hanina osculatus est caput rabi Symeonis.' Both these anecdotes are in the Yalkut, a collection of extracts from the Midrash; but the second one follows the original Midrash more closely than the Yalkut.

written sources than Andrew; they are no longer simply
Hebraei. He probably relied on oral tradition also, since at
least one of his explanations is not in the obvious sources,
though it might well be a Midrash.[1]
The whole content of the work is rabbinic. The theme is
God's love for Israel, as the prologue explains:

'Solomon, foreseeing in the spirit that the people of Israel
would be taken captive, in manifold captivity, and being in
captivity would bewail God's former love and familiarity
towards her, when she was his peculiar people among all
nations, as she was called in Deut. vii: *The Lord thy God hath
chosen thee etc.*, and that she would say the same, Osee ii: *I will
go and return to my first husband*, and foreseeing what God has
promised to give her at the end of time, composed this book,
under the metaphor of a woman, who is left widowed by her
husband, still alive, and who desires and sighs to return to him,
and is joined to him in love, remembering the love of her youth.
And the bridegroom has compassion for her in her hardship,
recalling the kindness of her youth, her good works and
beauties, which joined him to her in strong love, that thus he
may convey to her that he has not humbled her willingly, nor
quite repudiated her, but rather that he is still her husband and
she still his wife. . . .'[2]

The Canticle is then expounded of the Exodus, the giving
of the Law and so on. There is not one christological allusion
from beginning to end of the 'historical' section. Nevertheless, if we consider his sources, we see that the author's
selection from the rabbis is a thoughtful and deliberate one.

[1] Fo. 107ᵃ on ii. 12: '*Tempus putationis advenit*; Hebreus habet tempus cantus
quasi diceret: tempus venit quando cantabitis canticum scil. in exitu maris
rubri, Exod xv; *vox turturis* que est avis casta et habet gemitum pro cantu et
significat Mariam sororem Moysi que castissima fuit et interpretatur amari-
tudo.' The crossing of the Red Sea is derived from his sources, but not the
reference to Miriam. He may have taken one of the Christian expositions of
the Blessed Virgin and adapted it to the Mary of the Old Testament; if so, it
would be a curious inversion of what was generally done.
[2] Fo. 105ᵃ: 'Salomon previdens in spiritu quod populus Israel captivandus
erat multiplici captivitate et in captivitate positus lamentaturus erat super
familiaritate et amore Dei quondam ad ipsum, quando erat ei populus pecu-
liaris de cunctis gentibus, ut dicitur Deut. vii: *te eligit Dominus Deus tuus* . . . et
dicturus erat idem, Osee ii *Vadam et revertar* . . ., et ea que ei promisit daturum
in fine dierum, composuit librum hunc sub metaphora mulieris que derelicta
est vidua a viro suo adhuc vivo et desiderat et suspirat reverti ad ipsum, et
unitur ei per amorem, recolens amorem adolescentie sue. Sponsus etiam ipse
compatitur ei in angustia ipsius, recordans misericordias adolescentie eius et
pulcritudines eius et rectitudines operum eius, quibus coniungebatur ei amore
forti, ut per hoc notificet ei quod non ex corde humiliavit eam, nec repudiavit
eam simpliciter, immo adhuc ipsa est uxor eius et ipse vir illius.'

Unlike Andrew, this commentator is far from supposing that the literal exposition is everything which 'the Jews say'. He has restricted himself to the Old Testament and rigidly excluded all the many messianic interpretations of the rabbis. If his Solomon does not prophesy the coming of Christ, neither does he refer to the Jewish Messias. The commentator shows his intention clearly in the last sentence, where he refers for the first time to the spiritual sense. Instead of giving one of the usual spiritual interpretations, he keeps the unity of his theme, the promise to Israel:

'And I say that all this is fulfilled spiritually, as regards the Jews converted to Christ, and further shall be fulfilled spiritually, as regards the Jews who are to be converted at the end of the world.'[1]

Nicholas of Lyre lies outside the scope of the present volume. Trevet and Cossey have inserted themselves into it through their connection with the *superscriptio Lincolniensis*. But already it is plain that Lyre represents the culmination of a movement for the study of Hebrew and rabbinics. He owed much to the past.[2] All the evidence that we have considered, aids to study, glosses and postills, library contents, translations from the Hebrew, acceptance of rabbinic tradition as an aid to the explanation of the literal sense, adds up to make an impressive total. Our thirteenth-century scholars carry on and enlarge the method of their twelfth-century predecessors. Many of the manuscripts are of unknown provenance and may therefore have been written or annotated by monks or seculars. Even if we subtract all the doubtful ones, the friars are still a long way ahead. In the application of linguistic knowledge, as of scientific and philosophical theory, to biblical studies, it has been the century of the friars.

---

[1] Fo. 114d: '. . . et ego dico quod hec omnia sunt impleta spiritualiter quantum ad Iudeos ad Christum conversos et adhuc spiritualiter complebuntur quantum ad Iudeos in fine mundi convertendos.'

[2] Spicq, 335-42. See also H. Hailperin, 'The Hebrew Heritage of Christian Biblical Scholarship', *Historia Judaica*, v (1943), 133-4.

CONCLUSIONS

IT is time to end a long story and to draw conclusions. Lastly, attempting an even more daring generalization, one may ask whether the history of Bible study throws any fresh light on medieval culture. One fact stands out clearly. It might have been deduced beforehand and it is proved by the evidence. But however obvious it is worth stressing: biblical scholarship in the strict sense has depended on institutions which imply a certain level of material prosperity and security. As Andrew of St. Victor put it, speaking for scholars of all periods:

'Ab otiosis et in tempore otii et non a discurrentibus et perturbationis tempore sapientia discitur.'[1]

The interpretation of an ancient text is bound to be subjective to some extent. It will derive from the interpreter's preconceptions and from the techniques which he has at his disposal. But in order to be a scholar at all he must wish to use and to improve upon existing techniques with the aim of entering into the mind of his author. It would be quite wrong to suggest that no individual will ever propose this aim to himself in unpropitious circumstances. Few scholars can have had a more stormy career than Julian of Aeclanum in the fourth century, driven from his bishopric and from successive places of refuge by barbarian invasion and doctrinal conflict within the Church. Nor have the most productive and influential scholars needed lives of seclusion and leisure. On the contrary, they generally had at least part of their time very heavily occupied with politics and administration. There are many examples of the scholar bishop, from Theodore of Mopsuestia to Robert Grosseteste of Lincoln. Even Andrew ended his life as an abbot in an unsettled border area. Those monastic commentators who explain in their prologues that they are writing in order to occupy their abundant leisure, contributed less to scholarship than those who had to snatch their time from other business. Yet an isolated scholar means a mere dead end. The research worker, to be productive, must have library facilities. To be influential, he needs copyists, readers and

[1] See above, p. 116.

356

pupils. Hence the significance of his work for the future depends upon his finding a response in the present. Otherwise he may be forgotten; and the danger of neglect may threaten not only an individual, but a whole generation. We have seen an entire school of exegesis fall into an oblivion so profound that its successors remind us of men building on the site of a buried city, unaware of the civilization lying beneath their feet.

Theodore of Mopsuestia and his pupils, including the Latin, Julian of Aeclanum, disappeared from the ken of western commentators. Some insignificant fragments survived; the method and the inspiration were lost. The Victorines had to start again from the beginning. This time the movement for deepening and improving the literal interpretation caught on. Some Paris masters, notably the Comestor, the Chanter and Stephen Langton, continued the Victorine tradition and they had brilliant successors among the friars. It all collapsed into oblivion again. We know too little of the biblical studies of the later middle ages to write them off as a period of decline; but certainly the masters of the fourteenth and fifteenth centuries allowed the memory of Andrew and his disciples to perish, otherwise Cajetan would not have thought himself so original in explaining the literal sense of the Psalter. He had much the same feeling of lonely adventure as Andrew and Herbert of Bosham had experienced.

Modern scholarship of the nineteenth and twentieth centuries has been necessary to uncover the achievements of the Antiochenes and of the Victorines. It has been a process of excavation and the finds lie in disconnected layers. There are two interruptions, one stretching from the fifth to the twelfth century, and if we include the scholars of the Renaissance, then there are two fresh starts. In each case, a few works of the preceding 'culture' survived and retained popularity: the textbook of Junilius Africanus from the first phase, the *Histories* of Peter Comestor and the postills of Hugh of St. Cher from the second, but they did not suffice to pass on either the method or the spirit of the movements producing them. The fresh starters experienced all the thrills and difficulties of pioneering. It is pathetic to see how each one sets off to make his way 'through unknown, pathless places', to borrow Andrew's vivid metaphor, in utter ignorance of his forerunners.

The conditions in which biblical scholarship in its various phases has developed, revived and flourished have some marked common features. The Alexandrians had founded it: both literal and spiritual exposition stemmed from Origen. The Christians of Alexandria had been subject to persecution by the imperial government. On the other hand, that government itself represented stability and order. The Antiochenes were better off. They had the protection of a Christian empire and they lived in a province that was still comparatively sheltered from the barbarians. Antioch in the lifetime of Theodore remained as it had been before the crisis, a city of tumults and novelties, but still prosperous.[1] The Antiochene experiment in exegesis broke down. That, no doubt, was due partly to Theodore's condemnation and the blackening of his memory by faction. More important, his scholarship ceased to be interesting. The Latin Fathers, followed by the assistants of Charlemagne, made Bible study serve their present needs. They retained both the literal sense and textual criticism, but only as a basis for the spiritual interpretation. First and foremost the Scriptures were a means to holiness. *Lectio divina* formed one side of the ascetic triangle: reading, prayer, contemplation. Equally vital was its role in upholding the faith. The long line of commentators who developed the spiritual senses were not only contemplatives but men of action. They built up the Church, defending her doctrines against pagans, Jews and heretics. They rallied her to the defence of the Christian State under Charlemagne. They supported the Gregorian reform against the secular power. They set forth the duties of clergy and laity.

They subordinated scholarship meanwhile to mysticism and to propaganda. It was natural in troubled times, when chroniclers were beginning their paragraphs not 'Eo tempore . . .', but 'Ea tempestate . . .' The decline of biblical scholarship is less surprising than its endurance. The wonder is that even in a minor degree it survived, as a thread, if a slender thread, in the skein that ran from the Alexandrians to the Victorines.

Hugh, Richard and Andrew were teaching in the period c. 1130-70. They had a background of hopefulness. We have heard cries and lamentations breaking into our com-

[1] R. Devresse, *Le patriarcat d'Antioche depuis la paix de l'Eglise jusqu'à la conquête arabe* (Paris, 1945), 111-14.

mentaries: the Lombards are marching on Rome; the Vikings have sacked Paris. Now Jerusalem is a Christian city again, in the hands of the Latins. Population is increasing, land being reclaimed and colonized, trade expanding. Newly-founded Orders are flourishing. The Church has won her battle for an independent place in feudal society. Conflicts with the State turn on marginal questions of privilege, which rouse tempers but do not threaten the existence of either party. The system of relationships which is classified as 'feudalism' seems to offer a guarantee of order. Not since the second century, perhaps, has the scholar been vouchsafed so strong a sense of security.

The end of the twelfth and the opening of the thirteenth century saw another crisis. But this time it was not universal: it mainly affected the Church. Heresy and anti-clericalism constituted a real danger. Again the crisis was reflected in biblical studies. The speculations of Joachim signified a new wave of mysticism. St. Bernard had presented an alternative rather than a threat to the scholars; they had to choose between the schools and the cloister, since the method of his *Sermons on the Canticle* could not be transplanted. Joachim's method could: indeed it had a strong appeal for intellectuals anywhere. However, the crisis passed over. Heresy and anti-clericalism were suppressed or mitigated, while the mendicant Orders recruited scholars in the service of the Church. Interest in Joachimism gradually receded, until, by the third quarter of the thirteenth century a Dominican commentator on Proverbs is turning the tables on him. The period beginning with Innocent III is no prelude to the reign of anti-Christ, but 'the age of justice'. The Church militant seems almost to be the Church triumphant. And this coincided with the hey-day of biblical scholarship, when the Victorine conquests were maintained and enlarged.

Perhaps the general crisis of the later middle ages, which has been analysed recently,[1] brought biblical scholarship into disfavour again, making it seem frivolous and irrelevant. Master Eckhart may have been the Joachim of the fourteenth century. But this falls outside our argument. What does concern it is the change which has taken place in the attitude of modern scholars to medieval exegesis within the last ten

[1] R. Hilton, 'Y eut-il une crise générale de la féodalité?' *Annales: économies — sociétés — civilisations* (1951), 23-30.

years. The spiritual exposition, predominant in patristic and medieval commentators, had few defenders ten years ago. There was a certain rather tepid admiration for St. Thomas for having defined its limits, but only blame for the extravagance and subjectivism of its exponents. Now the revived interest in mysticism has led certain students to reverse their judgment.[1] Even though the tendency is confined to a small circle, it provides a fascinating though alarming example of the way in which the history of exegesis prolongs itself in that of its historians. Revolution and uncertainty have discouraged biblical scholarship in the past and stimulated more subjective modes of interpretation. Conditions today are giving rise to a certain sympathy with the allegorists. We have a spate of studies on medieval 'spirituality'. The scholars who tried to counteract its effect on exegesis are still too little appreciated.

What did medieval scholarship achieve in its brief flowering? Julian of Aeclanum accused Jerome of combining the allegories of Origen with 'the fabulous traditions of the Jews'.[2] Our scholars looked to Jerome as their master. The judgments on their work passed by modern students follow closely that of Julian. Their 'passion' for Hebrew perplexed and rather distressed Paulin Martin; Samuel Berger thought they had taken the wrong path. They preferred Hebrew to Greek. Their rabbinic masters, instead of correcting, could only reinforce the allegorical method of the Fathers.

'Those very men whom we have found to be masters of Hebrew scarcely surpassed mere beginners in Greek; and this was indeed unfortunate. The study of Hebrew was almost wholly given over to tradition; in the Jewish schools that method of interpreting Holy Scripture always flourished which had been received from the Fathers, that is, allegorical, unduly remote from the literal sense. The true Greek tongue knows no gloss and serves no authorities and makes men free. This was the reason why not Bacon but Erasmus inaugurated the new times.'[3]

There are two counts in Berger's accusation: neglect of Greek and the bad effects of Hebrew. Probably the first charge has been exaggerated, but on the whole it must

---

[1] A.-M. Dubarle sums up and discusses this tendency, 'Le sens spirituel de l'Ecriture', *Revue de science philosophique et théologique*, xxxi (1947), 41-72.

[2] *P.L.* xxi. 962: '. . . vel per allegorias Origenis, vel per fabulosas Iudaeorum traditiones, tota eius defluxit oratio'.

[3] *Quam notitiam*, 58.

stand. The Carolingian revival included the study of the Greek language and its application to the text of the Bible. Even so, we have seen that John the Scot had to translate the Old Testament quotations of Pseudo-Dionysius without the aid of the Septuagint,[1] and this was to prove prophetic. Later scholars showed an impressive activity and determination in translating both Christian and pagan authors from Greek into Latin. They did not put the same amount of energy into working on either the Septuagint or the Greek New Testament.

The little that is known of Byzantine exegesis suggests a different emphasis and points to a close connection between the study of the Bible in Greek and the predominance of the New Testament in Bible studies. In the twelfth century the patriarchal school at Byzantium had three masters of theology: the professor of the Gospel, who was rector of the school, the professor of the Apostle, the professor of the Psalter.[2] The pre-eminence of the Pauline Epistles and of the Psalter in the teaching of Scripture is common to East and West alike; but whereas in the West the theologians were called indiscriminately 'magistri sacre pagine', at Byzantium the highest title was professor of the Gospel. A fourth master, with the title of 'rhetor interpreter of Scripture' is found in a list of the fifteenth century; it is supposed that he had the special function of teaching the Old Testament.[3] But it seems that in the twelfth century the Old Testament must have been left to the professors' assistants and that its exposition was regarded as less honourable than that of the Psalter, Apostle and Gospels. In the West the great revival of biblical studies in the twelfth century bore principally on the Prophets and historical books; in the thirteenth century the sapiential books came into special favour; the Canticle was always popular with commentators. The contrast between Paris and Byzantium serves to bring out the favour accorded to Hebrew and the Old Testament at Paris.

The roots of this preference for Hebrew lie deep in medieval Latin psychology. Something must be allowed for the actual physical obstacles that a westerner had to encounter if he wanted to become proficient in Greek. He would have to make the journey to Byzantium or to southern Italy or

[1] See above, p. 44.
[2] L. Bréhier, *La civilisation byzantine* (Paris, 1950), 494.   [3] ibid.

Sicily, while he could learn Hebrew from the Jew next door. But the translators of Aristotle from Greek managed to surmount the expense and inconvenience involved in their enterprise. So we need to look further. The preference was implicit in the Christian tradition as it was received by western scholars. It came to them via Jerome from Origen, who had consulted Jews and who had not dared to extend his researches on the text from the Old to the New Testament. Medieval scholars did not accept this tradition in any blind or unquestioning fashion. We have had many examples of their criticizing their sources, both patristic and Jewish, on points of detail. They accepted it in principle and they made it their own because it was not dead to them but living. Their authors' example corresponded with a view of the universe. The Hebrew language had a magic pre-eminence over others. Hebrew was the mother of tongues and would be the current speech in heaven, even though the blessed would be able to speak all languages.[1] Greek must have seemed to have little sanctity compared with the alpha and omega of speech. Joined to his realist conception of words, this veneration for the mystical properties of Hebrew persuaded the medieval Hebraist that his studies were taking him to the crux of the matter. He was penetrating the innermost spring of meaning in his text.

Another characteristic set of ideas led him to consult contemporary rabbis. The medieval scholar, it has been said, had 'no sense of perspective, but a strong sense of continuity.'[2] Thus the Rome of the papacy still symbolized imperial Rome and a student of the classics would feel separated rather by his inferior degree of wisdom than by time from his authors. Similarly the Jew appealed to him as a kind of telephone to the Old Testament. Here was a people which spoke the language of Moses and observed the Law and had a vast store of traditions about Bible history. Our scholar also possessed a marked capacity for abstraction. His reverence for the Rome of the Caesars never blinded him to the defects of contemporary Romans, the account of whose vices exhausted his vocabulary. So in his dealings with the Synagogue he abstracted his disapproval of its present-day representatives from his veneration for its past. The Jew,

---

[1] From a letter by a monk to an anchoress, describing the joys of heaven, about 1080; A. Wilmart, 'Eve et Goscelin', *Rev. Bén.* 1 (1938), 81.
[2] H. Waddell, *The Wandering Scholars* (London, 1927), ix.

however despised and persecuted, could put him in touch
with the patriarchs, the prophets and the psalmist.
No such obvious source for the study of the New Testament presented itself. There was certainly scope for criticism
of legend and superstition. We have heard Peter Comestor
warning his pupils against apocrypha. A succession of
scholars undertook to refute the persistent legend of the
triple marriage of St. Anne; we have at least two treatises on
the subject and Herbert of Bosham records a very Senior
Common Room type of conversation at St. Denis, enlivened
by the comments of the physician and future abbot, William
of le Mire. William had visited Syria and had studied the
dedications of churches there.[1] Peter Comestor also showed
a promising interest in biblical archaeology. But these
researches are rather a side-line. The Gospels were often
harmonized. Commentators tried to make the contents alive
and intelligible, as well as offering them for devotion; but
one misses any concerted effort to break new ground and to
open up new sources of information. Occasional critique of
superstition does not compensate for the lack of fresh material.
Moreover, a substantial section of the New Testament, the
Pauline Epistles, was resigned to the theologians. Dialectic,
not scholarship, was the chosen instrument for expounding
St. Paul.

Berger's charge, therefore, is proved on its negative side.
But it seems to be less a criticism of medieval scholarship
than a statement about medieval mentality. No accident,
not even reverence for the Fathers, caused the medieval
Latin scholar to concentrate his forces on the study of
Hebrew and of the Old Testament, leaving the New high
and dry. To imagine him doing otherwise would be sheer
anachronism. Hebrew appealed to his emotions, his philosophy and his sense of history.

If we pass over his limitations and turn to his positive
achievements within their limits, Berger's view becomes
much more questionable. The detailed study of the Hebrew
text and the new translations represent a great gain and a
real emancipation. 'The Hebrew Truth' has ceased to mean

---

[1] M. R. James, 'The Salomites', *Journal of Theological Studies*, xxxv (1934),
287-97; G. Albert, J.-M. Parent, A. Guillemette, 'La légende des trois mariages
de Sainte Anne. Un texte nouveaux', (*Etudes d'histoire littéraire et doctrinales du
XIIIe siècle*, Publ. de L'Institut d'Etudes Méd. de Montréale, i. 1932); B. Smalley,
'A commentary by Herbert of Bosham on the *Hebraica*', *Rech. Théol. anc. méd.*
xviii (1951), 37-9.

the Latin Vulgate and has come to mean the original. Was the rabbinic material accompanying it quite unhelpful? In the first place, the two things went together. The Hebrew text was no more separable from its traditional commentaries than the Vulgate was from its *Gloss*. Acquaintance with one necessarily involved the other. In the second place, there are three elements in the rabbinic material which have to be distinguished. Berger, doing pioneer work, was not in a position to differentiate. The traditional Midrash and legend gave him the impression that Latin scholars, when they turned from patristic to Hebrew commentators, were jumping out of the frying-pan into the fire. Reading through some of their quotations from the rabbis, one may well agree with him. But the Jewish sources included linguistic and grammatical comments which facilitated the study of the text and raised fresh problems. Lastly, there was the rationalist, literalist interpretation which developed in the school of Rashi. This could have only a transitory influence on the Christians, since the school had disappeared by the early thirteenth century. But Rashbam and Joseph Bekhor Shor do seem to have lent something to Hugh and Andrew of St. Victor. Their general influence on Andrew is imponderable; his whole attitude to his studies may have been affected by his contacts with contemporary rabbis. Maimonides, in the next century, also exercised a rationalizing influence, though of a more strictly philosophical kind. Altogether, the Christians made a sound bargain when they studied Hebrew, with Jewish thought and tradition. They got some good grain, even if it came to them mixed with a lot of chaff.

Moreover, they learnt by reaction, not only by reception. This is another aspect of the debt which was naturally hidden from Berger. The Jewish interpretation of the prophecies, especially the non-messianic interpretations of Rashi, acted as an electric shock. It was all the greater when Andrew accepted them as the literal sense of the Old Testament. His judaizing tendencies set Christian commentators a puzzle, and the various solutions put forward testify to hard thinking. Andrew's interpretation could be accepted more or less *en bloc*. So respected and respectable a teacher as Hugh of St. Cher seems to have taken this line, with only slight reservations. Herbert of Bosham compromised between the Fathers and Rashi on the messianic psalms, rejecting and selecting. The majority, especially Richard of St. Victor and Guerric of St. Quentin, strenuously resisted Andrew's concession. The dispute gave a powerful stimulus to the clarification of the relations between the literal and spiritual senses and the definition of the content of the letter. The weakest spot in Andrew's exegesis had been his failure to examine this theoretical problem. He seems to have relied on the spiritual exposition to make up for his judaizing exposition of the letter, without facing the consequences for Christian apologetic of transferring the christological interpretation of key passages from the literal sense to the spiritual. The commentaries of Paris masters contain many signs that the problem was exercising them. St. Thomas supplied a solution on the basis of his Aristotelian philosophy which has been justly admired. But it was the final stage in a long process of discussion and meditation by his predecessors. They owed much to Andrew and his Jewish teachers for posing the problem so urgently.

A survey of medieval scholarship must include a reassessment of Andrew. The last ten years have made it possible to see him in better perspective. A study of thirteenth-century postills has disclosed the extent of his influence and has shown how far he was imitated. My conclusion is that he was even more significant than I thought at first. Although I have done no further work directly on his commentaries, I have often had to refer to them to check quotations and make comparisons. Each time I fall under the spell of his pages. There is nothing quite like them. Herbert of Bosham has an improved theory and a better knowledge of Hebrew; but he is wordy where Andrew is terse and he is less absorbed in his author. The masters of the later twelfth and thirteenth centuries have such a multiplicity of interests that no one of them follows Andrew's example in devoting himself exclusively to the text and its literal interpretation. On the other hand, their use of his writings has proved to be much greater than one suspected. They display their debt by quotation, acknowledged and unacknowledged, by imitation and by criticism. Mr. Ker's discovery of Herbert on the *Hebraica* and Mr. Raphael Loewe's study of Herbert's sources, his quotation of 'Rabbi Salomon' by name, well over a century before Nicholas of Lyre, all this has changed the picture of the progress of biblical studies in the thirteenth century. It seems now that Andrew and Herbert mark a peak and the friars a plateau. In the thirteenth century knowledge of Hebrew becomes more widespread; Andrew himself is better known; the general level of technique rises; there are new translations, new researches into rabbinics, more borrowing from Rashi. But there is no second Andrew and no second Herbert.

Biblical scholarship in the narrow sense which we have been considering represents a mere fraction of medieval activity in handling the Scriptures. We shall be able to appreciate this activity if we define scholarship more widely. Suppose we think now of the Bible in its physical form, as a set of books for use in the study or class-room with its learned apparatus. We see instantly what an evolution the middle ages marked, more especially the twelfth and thirteenth centuries. By 1300 the Bible has been divided into its modern chapters, after various experiments. Sub-divisions of the chapters are being tried out, which will lead to the present system of numbered verses. Two major reforms of the text have been introduced: the first by Alcuin under Charlemagne, the second by the propagation of the Paris Bible with its gloss. Both reforms attained their object of imposing some degree of standardization. Alcuin purified the text as well as standardizing; the Paris masters, tied to their glossed text, supplemented it by drawing up *correctoria*. Concordances to the Vulgate and the Fathers date from the thirteenth century. By the end of the century one could look up one's text in a concordance, find a list of variant readings by consulting *correctoria*, and probably discover what Augustine had said about the points arising from it. Glossaries, dictionaries and other aids to study filled several shelves in any well-stocked library. A few, such as the interpretations of Hebrew names by St. Jerome, would date from the patristic period, but most of them would have been composed quite recently. Given all these aids to study, one was expected to quote one's references exactly, putting book, chapter and the equivalent of a verse for Scripture; author, title, book, chapter for patristic. The whole library technique, in fact, had approached the modern with surprising suddenness.

In the twelfth century also the text acquired its standard commentary, the *Glossa Ordinaria*. Anselm of Laon and his assistants compiled the *Gloss* from the writings of the Fathers, probably making use of existing *florilegia* as their starting-

point, from early medieval commentators, from their immediate predecessors, such as Lanfranc and Berengar, with
notes and cross-references of their own. The *Gloss*, enlarged
and expanded for the Psalter and the Apostle by Peter Lombard in his *Magna Glosatura*, with the *Histories* of Peter
Comestor and the *Genealogies* of Peter of Poitiers, formed an
indispensable minimum for the teaching of 'sacra pagina'.
In the thirteenth century the postills of Hugh of St. Cher
provided a modern supplement to the *Gloss*, which they
resembled in being the fruit of team-work. Students hence-
forward had a selection, not only of patristic and early
medieval, but of twelfth and early thirteenth-century masters
on their desks. We may think that the *Gloss* and the postills
were unnecessary adjuncts. If so, we shall be no more
severe on them than were Robert of Melun and Roger
Bacon respectively. Granted, however, that the Paris
masters regarded the *Gloss* at least as a pointer to the
original sources, we can hardly condemn a system which
persists to this day: we still put anthologies and select
extracts on the school syllabus, and we still use textbooks.

The glossators and postillators built for the future. Their
apparatus outlasted the middle ages. The postills remained
popular. The *Gloss* with its later additions was a standard
reference book for both Catholic and Anglican divines in the
early seventeenth century. An Oxford sermon, preached
about 1620, very probably by the President of Corpus Christi
College, Thomas Anyan, has on one page quotations from
'Lyranus', 'Gorrham', 'the Ordinary glosse', 'the Intersall
(interlinear) glosse', Pereira, Bucer and a choice of Greek
and Latin Fathers.[1] This preacher may have been exceptionally eclectic; but John Donne also seems to have used
the *Gloss* in its expanded form. He possessed a copy, and
many allusions in his *Divine Poems* can be traced to the excerpts contained there, without recourse to the *originalia*.[2]
The medieval Bible survived intact into the Counter-
Reformation period. Modern scholars, while shearing off
its accretions, have kept the chapter division as a permanent
memorial.

If we examine a Paris postill of the later thirteenth century

---

[1] MS. Bodl. Top. Oxon. f. 52, fo. 4ᵛ. See the notice in *Bodleian Library
Record*, ii (1949), 67.
[2] Miss H. L. Gardner kindly allows me to refer to her forthcoming book, *The
Divine Poems of John Donne*, to be published by the Clarendon Press.

we shall be equally impressed by what is *not* there. Masters have reduced both form and content of their lectures to something more closely resembling a modern university course. St. Thomas, perfecting the tentative efforts of his predecessors, has supplied a theory of the relations between the senses which lays the stress on the literal interpretation, now defined as the full meaning of the author. A process of specialization has separated doctrine from exegesis. We can estimate the change by comparing a lecture by Langton with one of some hundred years later. Langton's lecture is so diffuse and swollen as to remind us of some animal about to bear a litter, her young all formed and alive inside her. In the next century the young are born and go their separate ways. The theological disputation becomes a separate exercise; the concordance makes the long string of related texts redundant; the bachelor has taken the work of 'reading with glosses' off the master's shoulders. The art of preaching is not actually taught as a separate subject in the schools; but the production of the *ars praedicatoria* and the *exempla* collection has relieved him of the need to put so much instruction on preaching into his lectures. He is free to concentrate on the establishment, division and analysis and exposition of the content of the text itself. Of course there are exceptions. The older system has survived at Oxford, though some Oxford men disapprove of it. The Paris masters are not wholly consistent in avoiding irrelevance, as, heaven knows, would be true of lecturers in any period.

If we try to plot the geographical centres of development in Bible studies we shall find that our map has clear outlines. We begin in the Mediterranean area, pause at Rome and Byzantium to hear St. Gregory the Great, pass to Northumbria and Ireland, and back to the monastic schools of the Rhineland and southern Germany and the Frankish centres of the Carolingian Empire. Then, in the eleventh and early twelfth centuries, studies are decentralized in the schools of the Netherlands and of northern France, with outlying areas in Rome and other schools or courts of central and northern Italy and southern Germany. After that, the concentration at Paris absolves us from the need to move outside the city and its suburbs, except to visit thirteenth-century Oxford, and to glance at some of the friars' *studia*.

So far we have spoken of places rather than persons. The personnel of these schools is largely international. Nevertheless one cannot but be struck by the number of Englishmen among the biblical scholars working both in England and on the Continent. The list in my first edition can now be lengthened. To Bede, Alcuin, Robert of Melun, Stephen Langton, Alexander Nequam, Robert Grosseteste, Roger Bacon, William de la Mare, Thomas Docking, Nicholas Trevet, Henry Cossey, can be added a formidable recruit in Herbert of Bosham, with Simon of Hinton, William of Middleton and William of Alton. Andrew's country of origin remains unknown; but it seems highly likely, considering his election as abbot of Wigmore and considering the number of Englishmen who studied at St. Victor,[1] that he came from England. I have omitted a compiler of the type of Robert of Bridlington and a moralist like Robert Bacon, though the latter might qualify if we had his commentary on the Psalter in its original form.

The number goes beyond mere coincidence. Its implications I leave to others, remarking only that it is not proof of superior piety nor of any peculiar insular view on the place of Scripture in theology. There was a difference in emphasis between Paris and Oxford on the form that lectures on Scripture ought to take; Grosseteste and some other Oxford masters preferred to include theology in exegesis instead of separating the two disciplines. But William of Middleton and William of Alton, who taught at Paris according to the specialized Paris method, were as prolific, if not as discursive commentators as the Oxonians, Simon of Hinton and Thomas Docking. The special interest that Englishmen seem to have taken in biblical studies derives more probably from the interest in antiquities and in the writing of history which goes back to the Anglo-Saxons. Our biblical scholars fit into place beside the poet of *Exodus* and the piece on the ruins of Bath, the compilers of the Anglo-Saxon Chronicle, the twelfth-century historians and the thirteenth-century Matthew Paris.

'. . . dry are all the roads, grey are the highways; the sea swept aside, the ancient foundations, which never before have I heard of men faring over, shining fields, the buried sea-bottoms, which hitherto the waves have always covered. . . .'[2]

The description of the crossing of the Red Sea in *Exodus* betrays a romantic attitude to the uncovering of 'ancient

---

[1] F. E. Croydon, op. cit. (p. 202, n. 3).

[2] Trans. R. K. Gordon, *Anglo-Saxon Poetry* (Everyman), 128.

foundations'. It is shared by Andrew and perhaps by other commentators, in spite of their prosiness and lack of sentimentality.

Now we may look at the totality of medieval exegesis, including the meditation and instruction which play no part in scholarship in any modern sense. It is here, perhaps, that we see the greatest of all changes. The commentator of the early middle ages cut his text, as the mason might cut his stone, into a framework, enabling the reader to focus his mind on the eternal and infinite. By the end of our period he is treating it as a solid background to his series of pictures from biblical history, pictures which may also be genre scenes. A thirteenth-century postill resembles the row of panels round or across the doors of a Gothic cathedral. They are isolated, but vivid and human studies. The decoration that breaks up the series into squares or rectangles recalls the elaborate analysis by division and subdivision which the postillator imposes on his text at the beginning of the book and of each chapter.

The twelfth century marks an intermediate stage between the first and second treatment. It is the great period of sacramentalism and symbolism. Their inspiration is less exclusively Augustinian than formerly. Pseudo-Dionysius presents a sacramental universe in which material things have greater value, as channels, one might almost say flasks, for the transmission of divine reality.[1] The Victorines have a strong sense of natural beauty which expresses itself in their sudden pleasure in 'the letter'. Scripture in its literal sense possesses for them the two sensory qualities in beautiful objects especially noted by the moralists for condemnation: translucency and softness to touch.[2] It is *pulchre lucens*, transparent to the divine light, and *tactu placens*, to be expounded with artistic sensuousness. Richard of St. Victor, in particular, approaches the letter consciously as an artist.

Our Paris masters of the twelfth century regard their text in a less sensitive and more business-like way, as practical men who have to train their pupils for prelacy, with all its responsibilities and its temptations. But their outlook is

---

[1] M.-D. Chenu, 'Naturalisme et théologie au XIIe siècle', *Recherches de science religieuse*, xxxvii (1950), 16. I owe much to this stimulating synthesis.
[2] See W. S. Hecksher, 'Relics of Pagan Antiquity in Mediaeval Settings', *Journal of the Warburg and Courtauld Institutes*, i (1938), 212-13.

essentially the same as the Victorine. They press the names of things in Scripture into an educational role. The persons, the place-names, the flora and fauna, the landscape and commodities of Bible history interest them as the subject for moral lessons. Langton feels frustrated because he does not know the properties of manna and coriander seed. The description of the object need reach no meticulous standard of accuracy; legend will do, provided that it be authenticated by tradition. Always, however, the moralist must keep within sight of material reality. His lesson must start from the characteristics of the thing mentioned in Scripture, even though it ends a long way off.

This attitude remains undisturbed in the early thirteenth century. The change comes approximately with the reception of the *Libri naturales*, coinciding with the pre-eminence of the friars in theological teaching. The rediscovery of nature noted by historians of medieval art[1] forces itself on the attention of the student of postills. The postillators are getting interested in things in themselves. All creatures, whether works of nature or art, become worth examining. Salimbene was a trained theologian and preacher who knew all about allegories and moralities; but read his description of the 'crown of empire', captured by the men of Parma from Frederick II, 'as big as a stewpot', with its heavy ornaments.[2] He recalls it not at all as a symbol, even of the imperial dignity, but as an object, which he saw and handled, and which fascinated him. The things in Scripture make the same sort of appeal to the postillator. What he cannot touch and look at he can find described scientifically in the *Libri naturales*. He may even get help from nature itself. Simon of Hinton compared the tares in the parable of the sower with varieties of English weeds and wild flowers. Similarly the interest in the working of natural processes in man and the universe leads to inquiries into the physics of Bible narratives. These inquiries take a form which may strike us as gross or at best naïve: how did Jonas resist the *virtus digestiva* of the fish in its belly? Did the Hebrew children's morale enable them to flourish during their fast? Such questions bespeak a driving desire to understand exactly how things happened.

[1] L. White, 'Natural Science and Naturalistic Art in the Middle Ages', *Speculum*, lii (1947), 425-35.
[2] Op. cit. (p. 290, n. 1), 203.

The words and events of Scripture retain all their symbolic value. But the postillator has diverted his attention. He is treading on earth, with occasional upward glances, instead of floating above it, descending only now and then. The symbolizing process may even be stood on its head, as when St. Albert prefaces his comment on *Thy kingdom come* with a treatise on the governance of princes.

There are two aspects of this application of nature study to Bible study. One concerns the history of religious sentiment. The actual narrative of Scripture, the story of the nativity, infancy, ministry and passion is perceived more intensely. The scene itself becomes too absorbing in its human pathos to need the aid of symbol in transmuting it into something different. Rather, it acts as a focus for symbols of a new type. Incidents are painted over and filled in with details suggested by devotion. On the other hand, we are watching a stage in the secularization of medieval thought. Let us compare the digressions and extraneous matter in early medieval and in thirteenth-century commentaries; we can find plenty, even in the specialized, stream-lined type of postill which evolved at Paris. The purpose of digression had been pious, mystical or apologetic. With the Investiture Contest ecclesiastical politics began to infiltrate. Our Paris masters wanted to reform the Church by satirizing abuses, to defend her privileges by making the clergy respected. Our thirteenth-century postillators remain loyal churchmen, with the same aim in life. They have not as yet digested the *Politics*. But the problems of secular government are claiming more of their attention. The State is looming up before them as something important in itself, quite apart from its hostility or friendliness to the clergy. The anonymous Paris Preacher, who may have been John of Varzy, St. Albert and Thomas Docking all show an interest in secular politics; Simon of Hinton, while he avoids political discussions, thinks at once of the contemporary royal or noble household, kingdom or principality when he wants an illustration. We have evidence for the rise of this kind of naturalism in the thirteenth-century schools from many other sources; but its setting in postills on Scripture, the last place where one would expect to find it, makes it particularly significant. Early medieval and many twelfth-century commentators had digressed 'anagogically', in order to describe the bliss of heaven, tasted in the 'sudden ecstatic flights' of contemplation or to be attained hereafter. Now we find digressions about the best sort of earthly government and the ruler's duty to augment the value of his kingdom in real property and movables. A growing interest in classical antiquity accompanies the growing interest in things present. Classical tags and *exempla* had been common in the twelfth century. Now the volume increases. The *Libri naturales* and Greek and Arabic works on medicine and natural science predominate; but the *Policraticus* of John of Salisbury, with its store of ancient literary learning, is beginning to be used as a reference book, supplementing the encyclopaedists. Again we can watch an earlier process working in reverse. Langton had moralized Ovid; Gorran uses the *City of God* as a source of information on the views of pagan philosophers.

All these quotations and allusions form a small proportion of a thirteenth-century postill. They matter because they are new, not because they are plentiful. The men we have studied keep a balance between their duties as masters of theology and their secular interests. Bonaventure shared the Victorine belief in profane learning as a guide to Bible studies, even in its new Aristotelian dress. Thomas concentrated on defining and vindicating the value of the literal exposition. Albert was versatile and voluminous; there was room for many mansions in his long postills. The lesser folk conform to one or other of these three patterns.

But if we fix our eyes on what is coming to be, we may hazard a guess on the future of exegesis in the later middle ages. On the one hand secular interests and naturalism will increase; on the other there will be a corresponding reaction to mysticism.

APPENDIX TO CHAPTER IV, II AND IV

Passages from Andrew's Commentaries referred to or quoted in Translation and not given in the Footnotes.

Note. These passages are not edited but are transcribed in each case from a single MS., and only the more obvious sources have been noted. Some account of the MSS. used has been given above, pp. 175-8. The passages are placed in the order in which they have been quoted, with cross references.

P. 121: PROLOGUE TO THE PROPHETS

MS. *Maz. 175*

Tenebrosa aqua in nubibus aeris. Tenetur quodammodo mentis fo. 93ᵃ
acies et quasi quibusdam tenebris obducitur, ne fructiferas
sapientie salutaris irrigationes in obscuris prophetarum verbis
perspicere valeat. Verum eius, qui de tenebris lumen splendes-
cere dixit, non invalida manus est, quando et per quos placuerit, 5
his quoque nonnullam lucis portiunculam tenebris infundere
cecutientesque cordis oculos, immissis intelligentie radiis, illu-
stare et in perspicacitatem revocare. Potens est quidem, sed
nichilominus pro ingenita benignitate munificentissimus est
Dominus. Quicumque¹ sit qui postulet et accipere velit, desidera- 10
bilem sapientie fulgorem quasi aquas maris effundet.
     Ipsa quoque lux sapientie dilectoribus se suis offert et ultro sui
studiosis occurrit. Parum dixi; sed et beat[it]udinis premium iis
qui ad postes hostii sui mane pulsaverint, et eterne vite felicitatem
[iis] qui ipsam elucidaverint, fideliter pollicetur. Cuius spe 15
pollicitationis gratanter illecti et suaviter attracti, quodque verus
recte factorum, etiam si omnis aliorum spes premiorum exclusa
sit, fructus est recte fecisse, nichil rectius a rationali creatura
quam cognitione veritatis invigilare debere fieri, non mendaciter

¹ MS. qui t̄m.

l. 1. Ps. xvii. 11.   ll. 2-3. *Gloss* in loc.: i.e. obscura est doctrina in prophetis.
l. 4. 2 Cor. iv. 6.   l. 7. Cp. the first verse of the sequence 'Veni, Sancte
Spiritus', . . . Veni, lumen cordium.

arbitrantes, laborioso quidem sapientie studio, laborioso sed
iocundo, sed frugifero, sed salutifero, huic, inquam, huic et
iocundo labori et laboriose iocunditati nos totos mancipavimus.
Sane quoniam ad eam que in elucidatione sapientie consistit
5 diligentiam, arduam quidem et firmamenti splendorem cultoribus
suis conferentem, multorum quoque etiam posterorum usibus
servientem, nostre nos exilis vene tenuitas aspirare non permittit, vel eam vilioris vene secunde que neque foris et in plateis
vocem dare neque in capite turbarum clamitare, suis diffidens
10 viribus audet, totis nisibus apprehendere elaboremus. Est
quodam prodire tenus si non datur ultra. Insani capitis es quia
efficere non potes quod vis, si nolis quod possis. Non penitus
inutilis est qui vel sibi utilis est.
Si quando tamen non nostris freti viribus, que satis tenues,
15 immo que fere nulle sunt, sed de divine miserationis opitulatione
presumentes, illam, illam excellentem et supereminentem, quam
prefati sumus, diligentiam agressi fuerimus, nemo nos ea vanitate
captos existimet ut vel novorum auctores librorum vel aliorum
doctores haberi desideremus. Absit ut usque adeo desipuerimus
20 quatinus nosmetipsos non metientes[1] et ad que attingere non
possumus extendentes propriarum metas virium excedamus,
cum potius sit solide subsistere in se quam inaniter rapi supra se.
Bene nobiscum nostrique similibus agitur si quos legimus et
audimus totos in nos transfudimus.
25 Meticulosus es fugitansque periculi; docere ne presumas;
tutius enim audies. Mollior es et enervior impatiensque laborum;
positis pugillaribus et calamo, aliena legere contentus esto.
Noveris tamen neque strenui militis esse periculum omne
fugitare neque viri laborem formidare. Qui labori subeundo
30 cervicem et humeros avertit, consequenter et que ex eo commoda
fo. 93b se|quuntur non apprehendit. Dignitas, honor, gloria, exercitatio,
probatio, patientia et innumera huius generis laborem sequuntur,
quibus omnibus merito privatur quisquis laboribus adversatur.
Sicut a nullo fructuoso quidem opere laboris metus nos absterret,
35 sic utinam vel imperitia vel virium diffidentia non avocaret.
Proposui sicut olim super Pentateuchum et Iosue et Iudicum
et Malachim ita et nunc, magis ope divina quam viribus fretus,
aliquam explanatiunculam super obscura prophetarum scripta
cudere, sed alta illius abissi profunditas et intricata perplexitas et
40 subitanea tam personarum quam rerum varietas summam operi
manum imponere diffidentem paulominus a proposito revocarunt.
Quid, tu inquis, nichil mussitationes, nichil obliquos morsus,

[1] MS. mentientes. MS. Vat. Lat. 1053, fo. 151d metientes.

ll. 8-9. Prov. i. 20. ll. 10-11. Hor. *Ep.* i. 1, 32. l. 22. This seems to derive
from a saying which Hugh of St. Victor ascribes to Plato, *Hom. in Eccles.*, *P.L.*
clxxv. 122, but which is not in Plato's works.

nichil virosa livoris sibila, nichil bis quinos in displicientie signum
utramque faciem scalpentes articulos, nichil naris subsanna-
tiones, nichil oris perversiones vel attendis vel metuis? Attenderem, certe attenderem, et invidiam metuerem, si quid invidiosum
agerem. Si quid novum, si quid magnum, si quid invidia 5
dignum scriberem, non immerito que supradicta sunt in his
diebus malis formidarem. Non fastidiosis aliorum auribus et ad
omnia fere preter antiqua surdescentibus que respuant intrudere
laboro. Cogetur nemo munus habere meum. Michi ipsi vigilo,
michi ipsi laboro; mee paupertati, que non potest semper pre 10
manibus vel commentarios vel libros habere glosatos consulo,
que in predictis sparsim diffuseque dicta sunt libris, ad historicum
quidem spectantia sensum, summatim colligens et quasi in unum
corpus succinte compingens. Postremo si quid vel in prophetis
quibus precipuam ob nimiam eorum obscuritatem curam im- 15
pendere decrevi vel in ceteris veteris instrumenti libris, vel
Hebreis sive quibuslibet aliis pandentibus, et proprio labore vel
divina revelatione, quia etiam in huiusmodi desiderium sibi
servientium nonnunquam Dominus exaudit, investigare potui, ne
quod utiliter apprehendit dampnose mentem fugiat, interserere 20
visum fuit. Si eum quem prophete habuerunt in scribendo nos in exponendo ordinem servare vellemus, ab Osee incipiendum esset;
Principium enim loquendi Domino[1] fuit in Osee. Sed quoniam
ipse aliis XI minoribus prophetis in uno volumine coniunctus est, 25
simul cum illis exponetur. Ab Ysaia ergo, qui merito inter prophetas dignitatis et ordinis primatum obtinet, inchoantes et ab
illo ad Ezechielem et deinde ad Ieremiam transeuntes, tandem
Deo volente et vita comite, in XII exponendis summam operi
manum imponemus. 30

Pp. 124; 136; PROLOGUE TO ISAIAS

MS. *Maz. 175*

Introitus Andree in Ysaiam. fo. 40ᵃ
In explanando Ysaiam, omnium quorum apud nos existit
commendata scripto prophetia prophetarum nobilissimum, nisi
forte contra quod scriptum est proverbium, acta ne agas, agere
velimus, multum nobis temporis vigiliarum sollicitudinis atque 35
sudoris necesse est. Siquidem XVIII explanationum libris, vir
litteratissimus, et omnium contemporaneorum suorum doctissimus, sanctus presbyter Ieronimus, tanta illum diligentia involuta
queque et implicita patenter evolvens et explicans elucidavit, sic
studiosis et ingenii acumine pollentibus reddidit, ut, ne quid 40
aliud dicam, otiosi et acta agentis, vel temerarii potius et pre-

[1] MS. Dominum.

l 9. Ovid *Ex P.* iii. 6. 58.   l. 24. Osee i. 2.   l. 34. cf. Terence *Phormio* 419.

sumptuosi et vehementer arrogantis esse videatur illi quam diximus expositioni aliquid addere vel opus quod exponit, aliter exponere. Si ibi quelibet exponenda sufficienter exposita sunt, si quid addideris non inmerito in superfluis reputabitur. Dicere
5 aliquid minus ibi esse, vel aliter quam debuit, quid aliud est quam tanto talique viro liquido derogare? An forte nobis posterioribus aliquid revelatum est, quod non illi priori, ut nobis loquentibus taceat? Aut forte perspicacius et acutius, utpote iuniores qui sunt perspicaciores videntes mentis acie quo ille non
10 potuit, penetramus? Hec et huiusmodi de se supra id quod sentit in se arroganter existimare, quid aliud est quam ventos pascere et sibimet ipsi verba dare?

Que pauca ex pluribus prelibavimus, et cetera eiusdem generis, satis superque, ne quid post beatum Ieronimum quod ad exposi-
15 tionem Ysaie pertineret auderemus, perterrere nos poterant, nisi quia et ipse, post tantos et nostros et precipue Grecos viros, iudicio omnium eruditissimos, qui sicut ipse testatur in Ysaiam plurima conscripserunt, in eundem prophetam explanationis libros scribere incepit et perfecit. Miratur pre omnibus Origenem,
20 et magnis eum usque ad celum extollit preconiis, nec tamen post illius dubitat et suam in Ysaiam apponere explanationem, nec quicquam in ea re vel ipsi vel ceteris prophete eiusdem explana-toribus iniurie inferre se iudicat, nec ad aliorum minorationem spectare existimat si sacrorum reseratione eloquiorum depromit
25 quid sentiat. Sed nec acta agere, nec superfluo labore se sudare reputat si post maiores suos in Ysaiam commentariorum libros scriptitat, presertim cum nec ipsi quecumque dicenda essent in predicto propheta ad unguem usque persecuti sunt, nec ipse, tanquam in eorum verba iurasset, illorum penitus vestigiis in-
30 hereat. Si otiosum vel temerarium vel presumptuosum esse post patres, qui explicandis evigilaverunt scripturis, ei rei veritatis investigande gratia studium et operam adhibere iudicaret, nunquam vir sapiens, industrius, et bonus, et qui bene meminisset scriptum esse: tempori parce, tantam huic studio operam im-
fo. 40ᵇ 35 penderet, totamque in eo | etatem consumeret. Novit certe, novit vir eruditus, novit, inquam, et optime novit quam abstrusa sit veritas, quam alte subsederit, quam procul a mortalium oculis se in profundum demerserit, quam paucissimos admiserit, quanto labore ad eam penetratur, a quam paucis vel potius
40 nullis ad eam pervenitur, quam difficiliter et minutatim eruitur. Sic se tamen obstitit et occultavit ut non penitus lateat. Sic a diligenter querentibus invenitur, ut item si diligenter queᵣita fuerit inveniatur. Nemini tota contingit; particulatim, et ι.t ita dictum sit, frustratim eruitur. Sic eam invenerunt parenies et
45 avi, ut nepotibus et filiis superesset quod invenirent. Sic semper queritur, ut semper supersit quod queratur. Sic semper invenitur,

l. 8. Priscian, *Institutiones Grammaticae*, ed. Hertzius, i. 1.

ut semper supersit quod inveniatur. Non est ergo quippiam
derogare, non est presumere, non est perperam agere, non est
otiosum vel superfluitas, quia maiores nostri in sancti expositione
eloquii veritatis indagationi vacuaverunt, eiusdem investigationi
in scripturarum explanatione nos minores invigilare, venerabilem 5
itaque Ieronimum, licet impari pede sequentes, eiusdem explanationem nostre qualicumque non inmerito preponentes, in
veritatis inventione, cui et ipse, et ubi totis viribus elaborabimus,
lectoris arbitrio relinquentes utrum aliquid, vel non, laborando
profecerimus.   10
Hec hactenus: nunc ad rem redeamus. Ad commendationem
sequentis operis plurimum valet si precognita fuerit laudabilis
vita ipsius auctoris. Auctorem enim huius operis VII sunt que
precipue nobilitant: generis nobilitas, eloquentie urbanitas,
officii dignitas, regie domus affinitas, morum honestas, laudabilis 15
propositi constans et firma stabilitas, postremo commendabilis
vite sanctitas. Quod nobilis et de regia styrpe oriundus fuerit,
filia eius, si vera est Iudeorum traditio, regi Manasse filio Ezechie
regis Iude connubio iuncta, evidens est argumentum. Eloquentiam et eloquii urbanitatem ipse subsequens tractatus patenter 20
indicat. Officii dignitas in eo quod propheta est consistit, sed et
patrem eius prophetam fuisse, quod nomen eius in principio
prophetie ipsius ponitur manifeste declarat. Qualiter vero regie
domui per affinitatem coniunctus erat, ibi dictum est, ubi filiam
eius regi nupsisse monstravimus. Honestatis morum et sanctitatis 25
vite ipsius patens indicium est quod Dominum, sicut ipse scribit,
videre meruit, quod labia eius carbone de altari manu seraphim
allato purgata, ad summam, quod ipse servum illum esse suum
testatus est dicens: sicut ambulavit servus meus nudus et dis-
calciatus, etc. Quam constans et firmus et stabilis in proposito 30
veritatis manifestande, quam confidens in enuntiandis cladibus
futuris, tam principibus quam populis, tam regibus quam
sacerdotibus, tam terris et nationibus quam opidis et urbibus et
municipiis et viculis fuerit, | mors eius ipsa, et metuenda plus fo. 40ᶜ
morte tormenta, luce clarius edocuerunt. Traditur enim ab 35
impio Manasse, qui Ierusalem a porta usque ad portam sanguine
implevit prophetarum, serra sectus lignea, eo quod mala que
Iudee superventura, Domino revelante, didicerat, confidenter
enuntiaverat. Pro iustitia, iuxta viri sapientis preceptum, usque
ad mortem agonizans, et impietati usque ad sanguinem viriliter 40
resistens, voluit per exquisita supplicia et inaudito mortis genere,
loquendo veritatis gratia, laudabiliter vitam perdere, quam

l. 14. St. Jerome, *Prol. in Is.* (see *Gloss* in loc.): vir nobilis et urbanae eloquentiae.
ll. 18-19. Pseudo-Jerome, *Quaest. Hebr. in Par.*, *P.L.* xxiii. 1399: Tradunt
Hebraei eumdem Manassen filium fuisse filiae Isaiae. . . .
ll. 27-8. Is. vi. 6.   ll. 29-30. Is. xx. 3.   ll. 35-7. St. Jerome, *Com. in Is.*
xv. lvi, *P.L.* xxiv. 546, and in *Gloss* Is. lvii. 1.

falsitati cedens turpiter retinere et, omisso quod a Domino acceperat officio, transitorie metu mortis veritatem tacere.

P. 125: PROLOGUE TO EZECHIEL

MS. Bibl. Nat. Lat. 14432

fo. 37ᶜ   Nostris longe viribus impar, ut parcissime loquar, nimis audacter et presumptuose, ne dicam temerarie et impudenter, 5 opus agressi fuissemus, in Iezechielem libros explanationum scriptitare, si nostra et non illius qui infirmos fortes facit ope freti, tante difficultatis laborem, tamquam arduum et ineluctabilem summis etiam ingeniis, subiissemus. Illius inenarrabilis benignitas qui, despecta contumacium et elatorum arrogantia, dat 10 humilibus gratiam, qui rudibus et imperitis in se confidentibus affluenter aspirat sapientiam, nostre humilitati, ruditati et imperitie tanti conaminis prestat fiduciam. Hoc duce, ignote regionis et invie, cecam et occultam perventionis, tamen prope ducem qui dat in mari viam et in aquis torrentibus semitam, non 15 diffidentes viam carpimus. Sic ubi rectum explanationis iter incesserimus, ducis peritie, sic ubi erratum fuerit, nostre devianti ascribatur imperitie.

    Hystoricam egregii doctoris Ieronimi expositionem nostre qualicumque, sicut in ceteris operibus nostris premittentes, quod 20 Dominus inspirare voluerit, nostreque labor industrie vel a se vel aliunde mutuari potuerit, ad communem legentium utilitatem in unum, Domino iuvante, conferemus. Eadem causa utramque explanationem commiscuimus ut pro suo eligat arbitrio lector quod magis placuerit.

P. 129: COMMENT ON DAN. vii. 7-8: . . . et habebat cornua decem.

MS. Pembroke, Cambridge 45

25   Quod pro cornu accipi debeant reges in sequentibus, ipso fo. 125ᵃ dicente angelo, instruimur; quod X simul reges Romanorum regnaverint actenus visum non est. At dicat aliquis: Esto quod simul in eo nunquam tot reges fuerint; per successionem multo plures, de quorum numero X, qui forte inter ceteros eminuerunt, 30 illa X bestie cornua significant. At littera sequens nos ad hoc assimile confugere non permittit. Persequamur igitur sequentia, si quo tamen modo predicto tutari refugio valeamus pertemptantes.

l. 9-10. Iac. iv. 6; 1 Petr. v. 5.
l. 14. Is. xliii. 16.
l. 27. St. Jerome, Com. in Dan., P.L. xxv. 531: . . . Ergo dicamus quod omnes scriptores ecclesiastici tradiderunt: in consummatione mundi, quando regnum destruendum est Romanorum, decem futuros reges, qui orbem Romanorum inter se dividant, et undecimum surrecturum esse regem parvulum, qui tres reges de decem regibus superaturus sit. . . .

Considerabam cornua: decem cornua bestie attentius intuebar. *Et ecce cornu aliud parvulum ortum est de medio eorum.* Si parvulum istud cornu, aptum predictis, aliud fuit et de medio eorum ortum necesse, nec necesse est ut et illa iam fuerint, quando exortum est, et id XI^um bestie cornu sit. Quod id XI^um sit, inquies, negare, 5 cum a X predictis aliud sit, non possum; sed quod illa omnia, quando exortum est, fuerint, fateri non compellor. Potuit enim fieri ut post quorundam decessum, | quibusdam nondum exortis, fo. 125^b illud parvulum emerserit; ideoque dicam quod de medio cornu exortum sit, quia inter prima et ultima exurrexerit. 10

Iam nunc evasisse te credis, sed miserabile caput tuum decima nunc superinclinans obruet unda. *Et tria de cornibus primis evulsa sunt a facie eius.* Ecce tria cornua prima, et inter X maxima, a parvulo sunt evulsa. Erant, igitur, quando et illud erat. Necesse est itaque ut tu concedas, quandoquidem quod per successionem 15 sint stare potest, quod, diviso inter se regno, simul plures in Romano regnaturi sint. Si quis te casus discrimini eripuit, totusque nondum consumptus es, si quid forte habes, in medium licet ut proferas.

Nulli sum ereptus discrimini, qui nullum incidi, teloque tuo, 20 quod te tam valida in me contorsisse dextra putabas, nec punctus quidem sum, necdum confossus. Quod ut tibi melius appareat patienter queso ut audias, donec super hac re quid ego sentiam patenter aperiam. Decem reges in regno futuros Romano per X cornua significatos intelligo. *De medio eorum* i.e. in ipso tempore 25 regni eorum, et de inter ipsos, et in terra eorum, regem parvulum exorturum, et quoniam parvi vel nullius ponderis momenti in oculis illius de X, qui tunc regnum optinebit Romanorum, apparebit, contemptum iri, deinde, collectis in unum viribus, cum eo a quo contemptum est conflicturum, et contra eum 30 invaliturum, duosque alios, hoc interfecto, qui contra victorem creabuntur, invicem sibi succedentes ab eodem expugnandos et perimendos victoremque, tribus aliis regibus superatis, tot elatum et magnum victoriis effectum, totum eundem regnum occupaturum et optenturum, in Ierosolimis quoque cum Iudeis 35 templum reedificaturum et in eo, iuxta quod apostolus ait, tanquam ipse sit Deus, sessurum, et in diebus illius latam sanctorum et electorum persecutionem Dei et oppressionem, eo auctore, futuram, qualis non fuit ex quo | gentes esse ceperunt fo. 125^c usque ad illud tempus, ita ut in errorem inducantur etiam si fieri 40 potest electi, eumque tamdiu in regno floriturum quousque Dominus noster Iesu Christus oris sui spiritu impium interficiat.

En super hac re meam habes qualemcumque sententiam, que si tibi forsitan exsufflanda videatur, eam qui refellere paratus es, queso [ut] parcius agas. Facessant in me, facessant iniurie; sit 45

ll. 11-12. Ovid *M.* 11. 530: vastius insurgens decimae ruit impetus undae.
ll. 36-42. 2 Thess. ii. 4-8.

modus pene victo victum fuisse. Meminisse debes huius certaminis victoriam ex futuro pendere, nec satis posse constare quod ex eo gloria quod manat confusio, nisi cum rei adhuc future exitus declaraverit. Perge, igitur, si placet, et nisi sequentia vel
5 aliquis canonice locus scripture reclamaverit, nos in nostro sensu habundare patiaris. Iam arma cominus congressurus arripueram, que de manibus supplicationis tue preces excusserunt. Non enim tantum nobis est te viribus superare ut tu nos humilitate superes. Nunc igitur, quoniam sic tibi placet, ad reliqua per-
10 gamus.

P. 131: Prologue to the Pentateuch

MS. *Bibl. Nat. Lat. 356*

fo. 1ᵃ   Difficile quod durum, quod grave, quod asperum est observatur, si nullum custodiendi premium proponatur, aut negligenti nullus pene timor incutiatur. Quod bene intelligens Moyses, cum dura et gravia legis mandata, aspera et pene importabilia Dei iudicia, rudi populo et Egyptiaca mollitia et multis deliciis
15 fere effeminato traditurus esset, beneficia Dei et gratiam multiplicem, tam in ipsos quam in patres eorum, replicat, et plura adhuc eis bona in futurum conferenda promittit, malorum etiam que sibi non obsequentibus Deus intulit, recolit et que illaturus est non obsecuturis prescribit. Ut, igitur, multas et magnas divine
20 gratie divitias enumerando, ad diligentiorem legis, quam traditurus erat, observationem auditorum animos erigeret, seriatim ab ipso mundi exordio gratuita Dei beneficia, toti humano generi et precipue illi populo | et eorum patribus collata, diligenter
fo. 1ᵇ   prosequitur. Inter que Dei beneficia quasi precipuum obtinet
25 locum quod etiam celum hoc sidereum, et terram et cetera elementa eorumque ornatus, ad usum hominum et servitutem, divina gratia creare dignata est; et quoniam [ea] sola, que ad hominis usum et propter hominem facta sunt, prosequi intendit, ideo, de creatione mundi agens, angelorum creationem et eorum
30 vel confirmationem vel lapsum in operis exordio penitus pretermittit; et ne rudi populo et ad multorum culturam deorum quam¹ in Egypto didicerat prono ad errores declinandi aliquam occasionem daret nullam Trinitatis mentionem operi suo manifeste inseruit. Hanc eandem tamen personarum Trinitatem in
35 omnibus Dei operibus ipsius ostendendo, in rebus ex nichilo creandis potentiam, in disponendis et gubernandis sapientiam, in sustentandis et fovendis benevolentiam, insinuare curavit.

¹ MS. quod.

ll. 35-8. Perhaps a verbal reminiscence of the sermon *De operibus sex dierum* attributed to Hugh of St. Victor in some MSS. (see MS. Bibl. Nat. Lat. 13422, fo. 66ᵛ), *P.L.* clxxvii. 1087: Potentia creat, sapientia gubernat, benignitas conservat.

Solet queri: quomodo Moyses tanto tempore post conditi mundi scire potuit exordium? Non est mirum | si Spiritus fo. 1ᶜ Sancti gratia, que ei revelare potuit etiam futura, potuit revelare preterita, presertim cum nichil tam nostre subiacet cognitioni quemadmodum id quod preteritum est; quamquam non absurde 5 credi potest sanctos antiquos patres ipsumque Adam posterorum suorum memorie frequenti narratione, vel etiam scripto, cum hoc maxima divine laudis causa et nostri in ipsum amoris sit, mundi creationem mandare curasse, sic ad Moysi notitiam, qui eam diligenter investigare curavit, pervenire potuisset. 10

P. 134: COMMENT ON GEN. ii. 5-6

MS. *Bibl. Nat. Lat. 356*

Sequitur: *Omne virgultum agri necdum oriebatur in terra: omnisque* fo. 11ᵃ *herba regionis necdum germinabat.* Versus iste secundum veritatem Hebraicam a supradicto diversus est et capitalis sententie principium. Recapitulatis enim que superius dixerat, ab hoc loco que succincte superius transcurrit, ut quid quo die factum esset 15 ostenderet, diffusius et evidentius explicat. Ea tamen precipue diligenter exequitur que in communi hominum usu versantur, et a rudibus et minus capacibus animis percipi possunt. Quia, igitur, in opere tertie diei Deum dixisse dixerat: *germinet terra herbam virentem et afferentem semen et lignum pomiferum* etc., et 20 subiungit: *et factum est ita,* nec qualiter factum sit ostendit, ne putaretur usitato modo, quo nunc fit, fieri, qualiter hoc factum sit hoc in loco ostendit, dicens: *omne virgultum agri* etc.; et est sensus sic per negationem: nullum virgultum agri adhuc oriebatur in terra; nulla herba regionis adhuc germinabat, eo scil. | 25 fo. 11ᵇ modo quo postea factum est, sed divina operatione, quod in sequentibus ostendet. Duobus modis ista i.e. ortus virgultorum et germinatio herbarum nunc fiunt, natura viz. vel humana operatione. Neutro horum modorum hoc tunc factum fuisse demonstrat; et primum operationem nature removet dicens: *non* 30 *enim pluerat Dominus Deus super terram,* deinde operationem humanam: *homo non erat qui operaretur terram.* Continuatio: virgultum non oriebatur, herba non germinabat, usitato scil. modo, quia necdum pluvia erat nec humana operatio, quibus modis hoc fieri solet. Locus a partibus remotis: maxima pro- 35 positio, unde partes absunt et totum abesse.

ll. 1-4. *Gloss. Prol. in Gen.* Sicut Paulus per revelationem didicit Evangelium, ita Moyses, docente Spiritu Sancto, conditi mundi exordium. ll. 14-16. Bede, *Hexaemeron, P.L.* xci. 40: ... possumus intelligere quia nunc apertius Scriptura voluerit explicare quomodo supra dixerit. ll. 19-20. Gen. i. 11. ll. 25-8. Hugh of St. Victor, *Adnot. in Pent., P.L.* clxxv. 38: Quare nec opere naturae, sicut modo, nec opere artificis tunc provenirent incrementa rerum aperit dicens: *Non enim pluerat* . . . Bede, op. cit. ll. 35-6. Boethius, *De top. diff.* iii, *P.L.* lxiv. 1197a.

Qui vero hunc versum scil. *omne virgultum agri* usque *nondum enim* per finem precedentis, in qua recapitulatio fit, translatione decepti faciunt, quicquid sex diebus texuerant uno momento retexere et quicquid multis versibus collegerant unius versiculi
5 cauda dispergere compelluntur, et dum contra autentissimam scripture huius, que omnium divinarum prima est, auctoritatem,

fo. 11ᶜ ubi Deus omnia opera sua sex diebus fecisse et comple|visse narratur et in septimo requievisse, apocriphi illius libelli qui Sapientia Salomonis intitulatur freti testimonio, semel [*sic*]
10 Deum omnia fecisse asserere conantur, multis difficultatibus implicantur. Quod Deus omnia simul creaverit, et quod sex diebus diversa operatus sit, hac ratione stare potest, quia simul omnia creavit in informi materia, que postea succedenter sex dierum operatione in propriam cuique formam redegit. Revera magne
15 auctoritatis viri hanc opinionem ponunt. Nimirum non recte servata translationis veritas ad hoc sentiendum illos pertrahit et libelli quam supradiximus auctoritas. Esto quod Philo, auctor illius libelli, ita senserit, Moysen vero, huius operis auctorem, nusquam ita sensisse repperimus, nec secundum hoc quod alius
20 sensit, sed secundum quod ipse sensit et prius narravit, postea recapitulavit. Recapitulatio enim brevis supradictorum a capite est repetitio. In recapitulationibus tamen quedem frequenter adduntur, sed que supradicta non destruant. Cum supradictum sit Deum omnia in sex diebus diversis fecisse, in recapitulatione
25 dicere eum omnia simul fecisse, hoc non est supradictis aliquid

fo. 11ᵈ addere, sed omnia supradicta | penitus destruere. Denique si in recapitulatione hoc asseverare contendit, cur tertii diei opus tantum primi diei operationi adiungit, et non potius, adiunctis ceterorum dierum operationibus, dicit: *iste sunt generationes celi et*
30 *terre, quando create sunt in die quo fecit Dominus Deus celum et terram*, et lucem et firmamentum et cetera omnia per ordinem?

P. 136: FROM THE PROLOGUE TO DANIEL
MS. *Pembroke, Cambridge 45*

fo. 111ᵃ . . . In his omnibus et multis aliis, si diligenter attenderis, prudentiam eius vehementer admiraberis; parum dixi; obstupesces. Hec et multa alia, quibus preclare ornatus fuit, virtutum
35 et gratiarum bona, divina semper preeunte gratia, in terra captivitatis et peregrinationis sue opes, facultates, pecunias, possessiones, purpuram torquem, regum amicitias, summos honores, magne dignitatis gradus, et immortalem gloriam, postremo honorificentiam et securitatem, illi pepererunt. . . .

ll. 1-18. See St. Augustine, *De Gen. ad Lit.* IV. xxxiii; v. xxiii, *P.L.* xxxiv. 317-18; Hugh of St. Victor, *De Sacramentis*, I. ii-v, *P.L.* clxxvi. 187-190.
ll. 17-18. St. Jerome ascribes Wisdom to Philo Iudaeus, *Prol. in Lib. Sap.* See *Gloss* in loc.

P. 137: COMMENT ON ECCLES. i. 1: *filii David* . . .

Calandra, 4-5

Hoc ad totius commendationem operis spectat, quod filius David, viri scil. sapientis et boni, fuisse dicitur. Sapientium namque et magnorum filii virorum quasi hereditariam habere videntur sapientiam, sicut e contra simplicium et ignobilium filii idiote et, ne dicam insipientes, simplices et minus prudentes esse 5 solent. Hinc ergo est quod in evangelio solam in salvatore nostro carnis ignobilitatem attendentes, cum sapientiam et prudentiam illius in respondendo et interrogando obstupescerent, admirantes dicebant: Unde huic hec sapientia et prudentia? Nonne hic est fabri filius? Nonne mater eius dicitur Maria et fratres eius 10 Iacobus et Ioseph et Symon et Iudas? Nonne fratres eius et sorores omnes sunt apud nos? Unde ergo huic omnia ista? Et scandalizabantur in eo, tanquam adversum rationem et nature quodammodo repugnans videbatur, ut in homine de tam simplicibus et imperitis orto parentibus, et cuius fratres et sorores, i.e. 15 consanguinei et consanguinee, ut reliqui de plebe, simplices essent et idiote, tanta esset sapientia et prudentia.

Propter operis itaque commendationem, ut diximus, quod ipse esset filius David, quasi hereditariam habens sapientiam et prudentiam, ipse operis auctor annect[er]e curavit. Frequenter 20 enim evenire solet ut sapientis filii, iuvante naturam industrie at industrie natura suffragante, sapientes sunt et prudentes. . . .

P. 141: COMMENT ON JEREM. i. 4-5

MS. *Pembroke 45*

Hucusque prefatio: non est intelligendum quod ante con- fo. 76ᶜ
ceptionem, ut heretici quidam suspicati sunt, fuerit Ieremias, quia Dominus dicit: *priusquam te formarem in utero novi te,* sed quod 25 prescierit eum futurum Dominus, cui necdum facta iam facta sunt, et qui vocat ea que non sunt tanquam ea que sunt. Quod autem sanctificatur in utero iuxta illus apostoli debemus accipere: Postquam autem placuit ei qui me segregavit de utero matris mee et vocavit per gratiam suam ut revelaret evangelium suum 30 per me ut evangelizarem gentibus. Iohannes quoque Baptista sanctificatus in utero et Spiritum Sanctum accepit et movetur in vulva, et per os matris loquitur. Quod autem dixit: *et prophetam in gentibus dedi te* | illud vult intelligi quod in ipso propheta postea fo. 76ᵈ
lecturi sumus, quod non solum Ierusalem sed et multis in circuitu 35 nationibus prophetaret.

Si autem idcirco Dominus dicitur novisse Ieremiam, priusquam

ll. 9-13. Matt. xiii. 55-7. l. 6. Calandra has 'viro' for 'nostro'.
ll. 23-36. Verbal quotation from St. Jerome, *Com. in Jerem.* i. 1, *P.L.* xxiv. 682-3.
ll. 29-31. Gal. i. 15-16.

in utero formaret, quia prescierit eum futurum, cum indifferenter
tam bonos quam malos presciat futuros, quid est quod ad eum
specialiter dicitur quod ad omnes eque pertinere potest? Sancti-
ficatum esse in utero quomodo accipere possumus secundum
5 illud apostoli: placuit illi qui me segregavit de utero matris mee
etc. cum nequaquam apostolus dicat: qui me in utero sanctificavit, sed: qui me de utero matris mee segregavit, non video.
Apostolus dici[t]: postquam placuit ei, Deo scil. qui segregavit,
i.e. separavit, me de utero matris mee, i.e. de consortio synagoge,
10 secundum illud: Segregate mihi Paulum et Barnabam in opus
ad quod assumpsi eos, vel ad litteram de utero matris, postquam,
inquam,[1] placuit ei qui hoc michi fecit, et postquam vocavit me
per gratiam suam, ut revelaret filium suum in me, ut evangeli-
zarem eum in gentibus, continuo non adquievi carni et sanguini
15 etc. Hec littera, nichil in se dubitationis, nichil scrupulositatis
habens, satis planam et perspicuam se legentibus offert. Nichil
hic de sanctificatione ab utero dicitur, in quo verbo tota questio
versatur, nisi forte segregationis verbum quispiam ad sanctificationem significandum sibi distorquere conetur: segregavit i.e.
20 seorsum a grege aliorum hominum per sanctificationem constituit.
Quod violenter esse distortum, omnibus claret. Sed et hoc nusquam me legisse recolo quod apostolus ab utero sanctificatus est,
quin potius ipse de se testatur dicens: Eramus et nos sicut ceteri
ire filii natura. Beatum vero Domini Baptistam ab utero sancti-
25 ficatum, secundum quod archangelus promiserat, credimus, quia
Spiritu Sancto repletus in ventre matris in adventu Domini sui
genitricis in gaudio exultavit, et per os matris prophetavit. De
sancto autem Ieremia, nec ante ortum eius nec in ortu quicquam
tale factum fuisse legimus.
30   Quidam tam beati Iohannis quam Ieremie ab utero vel in
fo. 77ᵃ utero sanctificationem in originalis | peccati remissionem accipi-
unt, asserentes quod ceteris baptismi vel circumcisionis sacra-
mento, illis utero inclusis divina collatum gratia. Ecce secundum
istos planum est quod dicitur: antequam exires de utero *novi te*,
35 sanctificavi te, i.e. ab originalis peccati labe mundavi te, sed
adhuc questionis alterius nondum solutus nodus perdurat: quomodo scil., antequam in utero formasset, prophetam Dominus
novisset, nisi forte dicatur quod priusquam eum in utero synagoge
aliorum more formasset, iam illum per supradictam sanctifica-
40 tionem illius filium noverat. Quidam, litterali magis more suo

[1] MS. unquam.

ll. 9-11. Probably from the *Gloss* on Rom. i. 1. Act. xiii. 2. l. 14. Gal. i.
16. ll. 23-4. Eph. ii. 3.
ll. 32-3. This view was sometimes put forward. See *Sententie Anselmi* (ed.
Bliemetzrieder, Münster 1919), 89: Nam et Iheremiam in utero matris sue
nullis sacramentis intervenientibus sanctificavit. But see St. Augustine *Contra
Iul.* iv. cxxxiv, *P.L.* xlv. 1429: Quia et Ieremias et Iohannes quamvis sancti-
ficati in utero matrum, traxerunt tamen originale peccatum.

sensui se applicantes, sic hanc litteram potius exponendam esse
arbitrantur. In puerilibus adhuc annis constitutum, Dominus ad
prophetandum ferocissimis prophetam gentibus et in manibus
populi missurus, fiduciam et securitatem, ex collatis iam misericorditer beneficiis, ut in tempus omne futurum, prestat, quasi 5
diceret: Ne timeas, Ieremia, me tibi iam existenti aliquando ad
opem ferendam deesse, qui nondum nato in conferenda sanctitate,
nondum formato in cognitionis dignatione, propitius affui. Qua[1]
pollicitatione fretus, cum statim in sequentibus datus propheta
gentibus dicitur, solam que ex puerili etate inerat eloquentiam 10
excusat.

Nosse dicitur Deus aliquod duobus modis, vel in notitia habere,
vel approbare, diligere, familiare habere. Secundum primum
dicitur: Novit Dominus decipientem et eum qui decipitur.
Secundum alterum Moysi dicit Deus: Novi te ex nomine; et 15
fatuis exclusis virginibus: Non novi, i.e. non approbo, non diligo,
non familiares vos habeo. Nos quoque indignantes eis quos non
approbamus sive despicimus: Unde vel qui estis vos? dicere
solemus.

Littera sic legitur: *priusquam te formarem in utero novi te*, i.e. ego 20
Dominus, for |mator tuus, in utero priusquam tibi humane fo. 77[b]
figure formam conferrem, *novi* i.e. approbavi, et tamquam notum
et familiarem meum dilexi te apud me, cui futura facta, et iam
existentem, cum nondum natus, immo nec conceptus, eras.
Simile huic in apostolo legimus: cum nondum, inquit, nati 25
essent aut boni vel mali aliquid egissent, Iacob dilexi, Esau odio
habui. *Et antequam exires de vulva sanctificavi te*; et approbationis
mee et dilectionis dignatione, etiam cum adhuc intra materni
vulvam uteri detinereris, tantam tibi contuli sanctitatem ut et
nascentium portam egresso nichil nisi sanctum et mundum 30
placere potuisset. Ex hac sanctitatis collatione in perpetua
virginitate creditur permansisse; *et prophetam in gentibus dedi te*;
gratis et absque tuo merito prophetie gratiam inspirans, misi te
ad prophetandum gentibus electione comprehensis.

P. 143: COMMENT ON EZECH. i. 1

MS. *Bibl. Nat. Lat. 14432*

Aperti sunt celi et vidi visiones Dei. Consequens est ut cui aperiun- 35
tur celi visiones Dei, que supra celum sunt, videat; et licet divine fo. 37[c]
maiestatis cuncta subiecta sunt oculis et cuncta cernentem Deum
nichil latere possit, ea tamen precipue que supra celos sunt videre
dicitur, sicut, quamquam ubique sit, in celis specialiter esse com-
memoratur. Apertis itaque celis, Dei visiones se dicit vidisse 40

[1] MS. Quia.

l. 14. Job xii. 16. ll. 15-16. Exod. xxxiii. 12. l. 16. From Matt. xxv. 12.
ll. 25-7. From Rome ix. 11, 13.

quia ea vidit que supra celos sunt, angelicas viz. virtutes, quas Dei non hominis est in sua ipsorum forma et natura videre; quoniam ea vidit que nullius aciei perspicacitas penetrare valet, celorum interpositione a nullo terresti animante videri possunt, 5 celos asserit apertos fuisse. Cum spiritualia sunt que visa sunt, nec a corporis unquam luminibus videri possunt, totam illam visionem spiritualem fuisse perspicuum est. . . .

fo. 38ª Esse autem angelica et celestia spirituum administratoriorum corpora, licet eorum dimensiones, formas et qualitates nesciamus, 10 diversis sacre scripture testimoniis, nisi alterius hoc esset negotii, facile probaremus. Divinorum scriptores eloquiorum hominibus in suis operibus loquentes, multa de iis que supra homines sunt secundum ea loquuntur que apud homines fiunt. Dicturus propheta se visiones Dei que supra celum sunt vidisse, quoniam 15 apud nos [ea] que solidi cuiuspiam corporis interpositione a nobis disparantur, nisi reseratione vel ablatione, videre non possumus, apertos fuisse celos premittere curavit. Sic Isaias quoque, Domini celorum interpositione seclusi desiderans adventum, licet optime nosset eum ad terras integris posse descendere celis, 20 humane tamen rationi condescendens et consuetudini, utinam, inquit, dirumperes celos et descenderes. Moyses quoque Dominum dixisse scribit: clamor Sodomorum venit ad me, descendam et videbo utrum clamorem opere compleverint, tanquam sine descensione qui omnia etiam antequam fiant videt hoc videre non 25 potuisset. Multe sunt in scripturis huiusmodi locutionum urbanitates. Vel visiones Dei vocat futurorum revelationes, quas totum subsequens opus explicat, quas nisi divino munere et inspiratione vidisse non poterat. Huic sententie Hebraica veritas consonare videtur: Vidi visionem a Deo. Sensus est: quod vidi visionem, et 30 intellexi quid vobis et his qui in terra remanserunt et urbi superventurum est, non a me sed a Deo est. Quibus verbis et suam non ingrati humilitatem munus acceptum profitentis, et illos et iis que dicturus est tamquam divinitus inspiratis adquiescere debere patenter aperit. Secundum hanc sententiam apertio celorum 35 quid aliud innuit nisi quod hoc celitus munus illi collatum fuit?

Si quis contendere voluerit apertos fuisse celos, ut per eos radius oculorum prophete directus Deum et que in superioribus fiunt videret, nos nichil impedimus quin in suo sensu habundaret; ipse tamen viderit an ratio rerumque natura fieri sinat quod 40 asserere contendit. Sin autem ad hoc confugerit ut dicat non per naturam sed per divinam potentiam factum ut in terris homo positus ultra celos celorum aciem dirigat, scientes Deo nichil esse impossibile, nichil resistimus. Verumtamen in scripturarum

l. 7. Quotations from St. Augustine, De Gen. ad Lit. xii. xxiii-iv, which I have omitted. ll. 20-1. Is. lxiv. i. ll. 22-3. Gen. xviii. 21. ll. 36-8 Gloss on Ezech. i. 1: Non divisione firmamenti, sed fide credentis, cui revelata sunt secreta coelestia: Secundum Originem oculis carnis.

expositione cum secundum naturam res de qua agitur nullatenus fieri potest tunc demum ad miracula confugienda noverit.

P. 147: COMMENT ON Isa. i. 16-18

MS. *Pembroke* 45

Quia lavari eos preceperat, ne quis hoc de lavacro in aquis et fo. 5^b variis baptismatibus que tam apud Hebreos quam gentiles erant (quod Peleus, loquens Acasto, declarat, dicens: Solve nephas 5 dixit; solvit[1] et ille nephas), errore deceptus acciperet, lavandi modum subiungit, dicens: *Auferte malum etc.* Malum iubet auferri a cogitationibus, quia nec ipse divine maiestatis oculos latere possunt. *Quiescite agere perverse.* Ordo congruus ut ablatis cogitationibus malis cessetur ab actionibus perversis. Precedunt 10 enim cogitationes; sequuntur operationes. . . .

Si fuerint peccata vestra etc. Sensus: quantumcumque fedi et in fo. 5^c peccatis horrendi fueritis, ad plenum mundamini. Quia superius dixerat *lavamini*, quod ad sordes et maculas pertinet, nec fedior, sive in veste sive in vase, quam rubea cruroris macula, que plus 15 etiam ceteris apparere solet, inveniri potest, nec pollutorum mundatio melius apparet quam si in candorem versa fuerint, ad exprimendam peccati feditatem, coccinum et vermiculum, ad significandam candorem, nivem et lanam ponit. Anima qualis a Deo creata est innocens et munda nec ullo feditatis nevo detur- 20 pata; quasi candida quedam vestis est. Hec ex corruptibilis inhabitatione corporis et invisibili hostis, demonis, et visibili, hominis, suggestione et propria voluntatis perversitate multis et variis peccatorum sordibus, quasi quibusdam maculis infecta, polluitur. Quando gravioribus deformatur peccatis anima, alba 25 prius vestis in modum coccini vel vermiculi rubris et cruentibus decoloratur maculis. Quante sit difficultatis a veste anime lavare maculam sanguinis lex pa|tenter edocet, que hanc iubet a reliqua fo. 5^d veste abrumpi et igni consumi, et alibi: Vestimentum mixtum sanguine erit in combustionem et cibus ignis. Ab his tamen 30 maculis facientes que predicta sunt plene mundabuntur. Peccata coccino vermiculoque in ruboremque sanguini assimilari voluit, quia illa ruborem intensius exprimunt.

Vel sic: *Si fuerint peccata vestra ut coccinum etc.* Peccata omnium, si vera est Iudeorum traditio, in candidissima scripta servantur 35 materia, ut facile iudicis appareant oculis. Hinc est quod coram sedente vetusto dierum in throno libri leguntur aperti, peccatum quoque Iuda stilo scriptum esse ferreo in ungue adamantino

---

[1] MS. solum.

l. 3-4. Ovid. Fasti, ii. 44. See above, p. 147, n. 1.
l. 2-3. Lev. xiii. 56.
l. 3-4. Isa. ix. 5.
l. 13. Dan. vii. 9-10.

legitur. Gravia queque peccata minio ceterisque coloribus, qui subiectis membris fidelius adherent et legentium oculis facilius occurrunt, scribuntur. His verbis Dominus promittat quod peccata eorum, etsi tanta fuerant [non] nisi candidissima que subiecta
5 fuerat materia appareat, et ita peccata prius rubra ut vermiculum velut nix alba erunt. Lana, filum, vestes et huiusmodi molliora coccino inficiuntur; carte, ligna, lapides et duriora queque vermiculo pinguntur.

P. 159: COMMENT ON EZECH. ix. 2-11

MS. *Bibl. Nat. Lat. 14432*

fo. 46ᵇ   Hebreorum quorundam est hec questio, quam ipsi sic solvere
10 conantur, si tamen solvere est arctius stringere et amplius implicare. Celestium quorundam spirituum hanc esse dicunt naturam, ut iustitie semper gaudeant districtione, et voluntatem habeant ut Deus in omnibus secundum iusti districtionem iudicii semper agat, nullum ad misericordiam habens respectum.
15 Econtra sunt alii quibus natura mollior est animusque ad pietatem et misericordiam magis inclinatus. Quorum satisfaciens voluntati Dominus, ne totus omnino, sicut meruerat, deperiret populus, ut vel illis, qui super aliorum peccatis dolebant, parceret, precepit.
20 fo. 46ᶜ   Cumque ab aliis admoneretur contra iudicii equitatem esse illis parcere qui alios a malis non studuerant retrahere, ab ipsis, quibus secundum quod prius fieri statuerat erat parcendum, ut inciperetur precepit. Videsne mutabilis error et insipiens iniquitas de irremutabili veritate et sapienti et clementi equitate
25 quam temerarie affert iudicium? A misericordibus admonitus, prius misericorditer agere disposuit sed tamquam oblitus esset iustitie, nisi ab immisericordibus admonitus esset spiritibus, a clementia et pietate ad districtam iudicii severitatem retractus est. Quod si verum est, immo quia verum non est, super nullius fron-
30 tem signum quod scribi iussum fuerat scriptum est, nec alicuius misertum est, sed universos una strages involvit. Sed nec hoc eorum insipiens impudentia fateretur. Cumque de mutabilitate voluntatis divine et memorie insufficientia, que monitoribus egeat, illis obicitur, non nichil respondere videntur. Sed cum de
35 ipsius prophete verbis, que statim subiunguntur, illis opponitur, quomodo vir vestitus lineis habens atramentarium scriptoris ad renes dicat: *feci quod precepisti mihi*, si super nullius frontem signum aliquod scripsit, cum hoc solum ut faceret illi preceptum sit, licet impudentissimi sint, obmutescunt. Quid opus erat huiusmodi
40 frivolis et exsufflandis et a procul neniis in sacris presertim scripturis intendere et in propheticis enigmatibus enodandis fabulas inducere? Dum errantium errorem insectamur aliquanto longius a proposito recessimus.

P. 164: COMMENT on Isa. li. 5; liii. 2-12

MS. *Pembroke 45*

Prope est iustus meus etc. Iustum et salvatorem suum i.e. quem fo. 70ᴸ
ipse daturus erat, vel Cyrum, vel secundum nos Dominum et
Salvatorem nostrum, vel secundum Hebreos suum messiam,
intellige.
Non est ei species, neque decor. Ad illud tempus propheta recurrit
quando hic idem populus gravi in Babylone captivitate preme- 5 fo. 71ᵇ
batur, quando revera nullus erat ei neque decor neque species;
et vidimus eum, ego et alii prophete, vel pluraliter propheta loquitur.
Et non erat aspectus: quod male est quasi non esse dicitur, unde:
Ne tradas sceptrum tuum his qui non sunt. *Et desideravimus eum* 10 fo. 71ᶜ
quasi *despectum et novissimum virorum*; suspiravimus et do|luimus
eum esse despectum et abiectissimum hominum. Quia suspiria
desiderium elicit, *desideravimus* et pro *suspiravimus* non absurde legi
potest. *Virum dolorum*: de populo agens tamquam de uno homine
loquitur, quem vocat *virum dolorum* i.e. tribulationibus et miseriis, 15
unde dolores, circumdatum et coopertum. *Scientem*, experientem
[*infirmitatem*], *absconditus*, qui [propter] obliquam feditatem ab-
scondi solet. *Unde nec reputavimus eum*: quia sic *absonditus* et despec-
tus *vultus eius*, nos etiam ipsi, pene desperantes de eo, numero
hominum *non reputavimus*, i.e. populus [propter] nimiam abiectio- 20
nem vix se inter homines reputavit. *Vere languores nostros ipse tulit*;
his verbis innuit propheta quod populus qui in captivitate Baby-
lonica affligendus erat, non solum sua sed et maiorum luiturus
erat peccata. Vere ille vir dolorum languores et dolores, quos ob
nostra ferre debuimus peccata, portabit. *Et nos putavimus eum* 25
quasi leprosum, etc.; propheta se illis connumerat, qui populum in
captivitatem iturum propter peccata sua captivandum et tanquam
leprosum a populo Domini separandum, exigentibus peccatis
suis, a Domino percutiendum et humiliandum fore putaverunt.[1]
Ipse autem vulneratus est propter iniquitates nostras: sic nos putavimus, 30
sed ipse *vulneratus est propter iniquitates nostras*, et *attritus est propter
scelera nostra*: ipse flagellatus est et lividus factus, ut nos pacem
haberemus et sanaremur; posteris, quibus castigatio illius pacem
peperit, se connumerat. *Quasi oves* qui sine pastores sunt; *viam
suam*, suam perversam; *posuit in eo*; peccata omnium nostrum in 35
eo punivit. *Oblatus est* quasi hostia *quia ipse voluit*; quia ipsi
Domino sic placuit. *Non aperuit os*, i.e. ad contradicendum.
Sicut ovis, non reclamans nec retinens. *De angustia et de iudicio
sublatus est*; tandem, miserante Domino, *de angustia* i.e. mentis
anxietate, et *iudicio* i.e. dampnatione sub Cyro, tolletur. *Genera- 40
tionem eius quis enarrabit*; etsi ita in captivitate et exilio et diminuto
futurus sit numero, | posteritatem eius quis enarrare poterit?

[1] MS. putavit.

l. 10. Esther xiv. 11.

fo. 71ᵈ *Quia* completiva est. *Abscissus est de terra viventium*; abscidetur et abstrahetur de terra, pro qua in scripturis *terra viventium* dicitur; *populi mei*, prioris; *et dabit impios pro sepultura sua et divitem pro morte sua*; percussus non interibit, sed impii et divites, Babylonii
5 viz. increduli et divitiis occupati, in sepulturam et mortem pro eo dabuntur. Quod est dicere: illi parcetur et illi interibunt. Ipsum dicit daturum, quia causa quare dabuntur erit. *Eo quod iniquitatem non fecerit*; hoc pro parte bonorum; *sicut etc.*: huiusmodi que nisi solis convenire electis possunt, electis dicuntur. *Et*
10 *Dominus voluit conterere eum in infirmitate*; etsi bonus, placuit Domino in infirmitatibus carnis et multis molestiis, quibus caro infirmatur, illum affligere. *Si posuit animam suam pro peccato*; si patienter et equo animo *pro peccato*, non modo suo sed etiam alieno, *animam suam* affligi sustinuerit, qui de eo seminati fuerint longevos videbit.
15 *Dirigetur*; directa erit et proficiet. *Videbit*; subaudi: quod videre desideravit. Possumus dicere quod de tenebris tribulationis et carceris eductus lumen *videbit* et intelliget, i.e. intelligentie dono donabitur; *saturabitur*; omnibus terre bonis usque ad satietatem reficietur. *In scientia*, quam meo percipiet dono. *Dispertiam ei*
20 *plurimos*; multos ditioni illius subiciam populos, et quasi in donativum illi dispertiam. *Tradidit*; hoc non potest nisi de illis dici qui voluntariam prophetarum consilio, unde ut Ieconias et qui cum eo Babyloniis se tradiderunt, transmigrationem subierunt; *in mortem*, angustiandum duris velut mortis angustiis. *Cum*
25 *sceleratis reputatus est*; pena sceleratorum in carceribus et ergastulis et duris operum laboribus promitti et dampnari. *Pro transgressoribus rogavit*; pro illis de populo suo, qui legem Domini transgrediebantur, pars electior, ut in melius commutarentur, Dominum simpliciter rogabat. Quidam etiam Hebreorum
30 totam hanc pericopem super Isaia interpretantur.

P. 166: COMMENT ON DAN. ix. 24-7

MS. *Pembroke 45*

fo. 131ᶜ 'Septuaginta septene indicte' vel 'imposite sunt super populum tuum, et super urbem sanctam tuam, ad finiendam falsitatem, et confiniendum peccatum, et delendam iniquitatem, et adducendam iustitiam in secula, et ad implendam visionem et pro-
35 phetiam, et ad unguendum sanctum sanctorum.'
Quoniam eam quam ab eruditissimis Hebreorum expositionem accepimus in hac operis parte ponere decrevimus, litteram etiam quam hic se habere dicunt ponere visum fuit. Quare potius per septenarium quam per alium quemlibet numerum de his annis,
40 quibus in captivitate Babilonica populus captivus tenebatur, agatur huiusmodi causam assignant: . . .
fo. 132ᵈ Et si cetera omnia in hac Iudeorum expositione huius tam profundi scripturarum loci, in quo explicando nostrorum non

minimum desudaverunt ingenia, licet inviti, probaremus, illud
tamen non video quemadmodum approbare valeamus: quod
Cyro regi Persarum post Babilonem subversam in regno vel nullos
vel paucos, cum et hystoriarum scriptores et philosophi, sicut
supradictum est, illi XXX attribuunt annos. Cambisis filii et 5
successoris Cyri, qui secundum nos annos VIII regnavit, et
Hesmeredes Magi successoris Cambisi, qui duos regnavit annos,
nec meminerunt.

At dicat aliquis: canonicarum auctoritas scripturarum, cui
nec possunt nec debent adversari, alios Cyri successores fuisse 10
dicere compellit. . . .

Ecce sacra scriptura statim post Cyrum Assuerum ponit, et fo. 133ᵃ
huic, nullo interveniente medio, Artaxerxen adiungit; in tertio
Darium loco collocat. An istis regibus tacitis quos et sue et
canonice nominant scripture, quarum scriptores eis contem- 15
poranei fuerunt, eorum quos nunquam legerunt recolent? Hoc
ab eis non exigimus ut suis presertim canonicis contraria loquan-
tur scripturis, quibus nos quoque nullatenus contraria loqui
volumus, vel ut eorum quos nunquam legerunt recolant, sed ut,
salva si fieri potest auctoritate, nostras suis traditionibus non 20
evacuent. Sic in hoc ancipite certamine congrediamur ut,
traditionem traditione non preiudicante, non victorie gratia
videamur contendere, sed investigande veritati invigilare.
Canonicis eque pro nostra et pro illarum parte stantibus scripturis, [utrum] nostris vel illi vel nos illis magis accedant et 25
rationabilius procedant videamus; ac de LXX desolationis
Ierusalem annis, nisi initium et finem habere debeant, quoniam
questionis hinc incipit exordium, primum agatur. . . .

Nobis videtur alios fuisse LXX annos quibus et Iudei et cetere fo. 133ᶜ
in circuitu gentes regi Babilonis et filio eius et filio filii eius 30
servierunt, et alios desolationis Ierusalem annos. . . .

Prudentia Danielis, primo Darii filii Assueri anno, cum iam
Baboniorum potestas finita esset, tempus relaxande captivitatis
quod propheta predixerat iam iam adesse videns, nec iam
relaxari conspiciens, ad orandum et deprecandum Dominum 35
faciem posuit: hoc sane est dicere quod Danielem, virum sanctum
et bonum et sapientissimum omnium qui in terra morabantur, in
Ieremie prophete verbis errasse, et quod non intellexerat se
intellexisse putasse. Ecce Daniel et Esdras, alter quo nemo
sapientior vel melior, alter quo nullus in lege scriba velocitior 40
in eo conveniunt quod in anno Cyri regis Persarum primo
relaxande captivitatis tempus quod Ieremias predixerat, ad-
venerat.

Nos vero idem asserentes, si forte a recto itineris tramite
declinamus, magnis auctoritatibus erramus, et nescio an non 45
laudabilius et tutius sit cum istis et nostris maioribus, viris
ingenio et industria magnis, istos sequentibus, ut illi dicunt

errare, quam cum istis temporis nostri Iudeis, multo maiore studio curantibus ut assis nimius coacervetur, quam ut diligenti scripturarum interpretationi invigiletur, rectam si illis credimus viam ambulare. . . .

fo. 134^b 5   His de LXX ebdomadibus breviter transcursis, ad huius operis sequentia pergamus, LXX annorum·septenas, quoniam secundum quod in nostra translatione habetur satis a nostris diligenter exposite sunt et assignate, [et] nos secundum quod apud Hebreos legitur, prout potuimus, eas exposuimus, iuxta translationem qua 10 nos utimur intactus relinquentes. Nemo miretur si diversorum sententias ponentes et eorum quibusdam in locis opinionem sequentes, nunc plures nunc pauciores quibusdam annis tribuimus.

ADDENDA

p. xiv.
The student is just acquiring his basic reference book in *Repertorium Biblicum Medii Aevi* collegit, disposuit, edidit F. Stegmüller (Madrid, 1950). Two volumes have appeared, i: *Initia Biblica, Apocrypha, Prologi*; ii: *Commentaria. Auctores A-G.*

p. 8, n. 1.
G. B. LADNER, 'The Symbolism of the Biblical Corner Stone in the Medieval West', *Medieval Studies of the Institute of Toronto*, iv (1942), 43-60; P. LUNDBERG, *La typologie baptismale dans l'ancienne Église* (Leipzig/Uppsala, 1942.)

p. 27, note to 2nd paragraph.
See J. BEUMER, 'Heiliger Schrift und kirchliche Autorität', *Scholastik*, xxv (1950), 40-72.

p. 84.
Godfrey of St. Victor must be added to the list of twelfth-century scholars at the abbey; *see* PH. DELHAYE, *Godefroy de Saint-Victor. Microcosmos*, i. *Texte*, ii. *Étude théologique* (Lille/Gembloux, 1951).

p. 194, note to 'the new Aristotle'.
See the forthcoming paper by L. MINIO-PALUELLO, 'Jacobus Veneticus Graecus', *Traditio* (1952).

p. 248, n.2.
But *see* R. W. HUNT, 'Notes on the Distinctiones monasticae et morales', *Liber floridus Paul Lehmann gewidmet*, ed. B. BISCHOFF & S. BRECHTER (St. Ottilien, 1950), 355-6. He suggests Louth Park as the house where the *Distinctiones* was written.

p. 254, n.5.
On the authorship of this sequence *see* R. W. HUNT, ibid., 360-1.

p. 270, n.2.
This etymology has been questioned by P. LEHMANN, 'Mittelalterliche Büchertitel', I Heft, *Sitzungsberichte der Bayerischen Akademie der Wissensch., philos.-hist. Klasse* (1948), Heft 4 (Munich, 1949), 42-7. Thomas Gascoigne suggests another,

which is interesting, even if it is a product of his own fancy: '... et ideo hoc idem quod sancti doctores in explanando scripturam intenderunt, hoc idem postillatores textum secundum ordinem textus exponentes fecerunt, veritatem manifestare querentes plano stilo. Unde dicuntur postillatores, id est textus post textum illatores ... Postillari est textum secundum ordinem textus inferre et exponere' (MS. Lincoln College, Oxford, 117, pp. 455, 457).

p. 275, n.3.
ROBERT HOLCOT quotes Albert's postill on St. Luke, however, *Com. in Sap.*, lectio 7 (Bâle, 1586), 24-5.

p. 307.
The secular master, Henry of Ghent, teaching at Paris 1276-92, restricts his commentary on the Hexaemeron to the literal sense; MS. Bibl. Nat. Lat. 15355, fo. 251a: 'In hoc ergo tractatu opus vi dierum cum requie diei septime supra, cap. 1a, interposita, secundum litteralem et hystoricum sensum expositum est, omni alia expositione spirituali omissa. Deo gratias. Amen.'

INDEX OF PERSONS

I. Persons Living Before 1800

Persons living before 1300 are indexed under their first names, those living after 1300 under their surnames.

INDEX OF MANUSCRIPTS